CHIBAYA MOYO 2

The Rhodesian African Rifles: An Anthology

Compiled and edited by

Captain Andrew Thomas Telfer SCR

& Captain Russell Haydon Fulton

Cover image: L Cpl Daniel Wushe served in 5 Platoon, B Company, 1RAR and was involved in a large number of fire force actions. He was an outstanding machine gunner and continued to carry the weapon as a Lance Corporal. The image was painted by Russell Fulton.

Chibaya Moyo 2

The Rhodesian African Rifles: An Anthology

Compiled and edited by Andrew Telfer and Russell Fulton
Illustrated by Russell Fulton
Published in 2019 by the RAR Regimental Association
Copyright © Andrew Telfer and Russell Fulton, 2019
Designed and typeset by the RAR Regimental Association
Cover design by Russell Fulton
ISBN:

Disclaimer

It is not the purpose of this book to present a researched history of the subject or the period, but instead to compile personal stories into an anthology.

Every effort has been made to make this book as complete and as accurate as possible. However, there may be mistakes, both typographical and in content. This book is an anthology of anecdotes provided by a large number of people and is sold with the understanding that the publisher and authors are reliant upon the authors of the anecdotes for the accuracy of their content. The views expressed are not necessarily ours and time has elapsed since the events of these stories took place, so we cannot therefore vouch for the authenticity thereof.

The authors and the publisher accept no liability or responsibility to any person or entity with respect to any loss or damage or offence caused, or alleged to have been caused, directly or indirectly, by the contents of this book. The authors have made every reasonable effort to trace the copyright holders of material appearing in this publication and to credit them accordingly. Any correspondence regarding this matter should be directed to the authors care of the publishers at the address herein.

DEDICATION

This book is dedicated to the men of the Rhodesian African Rifles.

After the Burma Campaign, Major Walter Walker (later General Sir Walter Walker KCB, CBE, DSO and two Bars), said of the RAR:

"The conduct of the askari, most of whom had never experienced enemy fire before, deserves a lasting tribute. Their energy and endurance on the march and on patrol through some of the worst country in the Arakan, their constancy and discipline under the stress of persistent mortar and artillery fire, and their cheerfulness throughout the appalling weather conditions, which developed in the latter stages of the operation, were beyond praise".

Further praise for the RAR came from a captured Japanese officer's diary, where he noted,

"The enemy soldiers are not from Britain but are from Africa. Because of their beliefs they are not afraid to die, so, even if their comrades have fallen, they keep on advancing as if nothing had happened. They have excellent physique and are very brave, so fighting against these soldiers is somewhat troublesome."

Of the RAR's performance during the Rhodesian Bush War, Combined Operations Commander Lieutenant General G. Peter Walls said:

"The men of this regiment are above faction or tribe or politics. They are an elite group of fighting men, both European and African, to whom the country owes an incalculable debt for their dedication and bravery. And their moral courage in the face of insidious assaults from those who would undermine their sense of purpose is nothing short of admirable... But not only are they brave and efficient soldiers. Their spirited approach to their task and their joie-de-vivre, their sheer love of serving is an example which many would do well to emulate".

Russell Fulton
Canberra, Australia

CONTENTS

ACKNOWLEDGEMENTS

We would like to place on record our grateful appreciation to Alan Doyle for his invaluable contributions to Chibaya Moyo and to our Regiment. In this volume, he has provided entertaining anecdotes and photos from his own service with the RAR; he has undertaken extensive research in support of the historical components of the work; he led the publication and is managing the sales and distribution of the book (a huge task undertaken with characteristic professionalism and good humour); and, on an ongoing basis, Alan has demonstrated his commitment to remembering our Fallen Soldiers through weekly memorials posted on the RAR Facebook page.

We thank all the writers who contributed to this book. Without your willingness to 'make an effort' there would have been no Chibaya Moyo (1 or 2) and your wonderful memories of our Regiment would have been lost. Brigadier John 'Digger' Essex-Clark DSM and Brigadier David Heppenstall MLM have contributed enormously. Both officers fought in Malaya in the 1950s, commanding RAR platoons, and are now of an age where lesser men might use advancing years as an excuse. Not them; they don't trade in excuses. Because of their commitment to our Regiment and especially our soldiers, they readily answered the call of this publication.

The guiding force behind Chibaya Moyo 2 has been Major General Michael Shute OLM and we thank him for his unflagging support and active assistance throughout. He actually initiated this second volume of *Chibaya Moyo*, in a conversation with Major Butch Zeederberg, who had served under Mike's command in two capacities - Platoon and Company Commander - during the Rhodesian Bush War. Mike is held in such high regard by those who served under him, that we asked Butch to describe him as a commander:

'When Andy and Russell first asked me to write a few words in recognition of General Shute's well known attributes as a Commander; I realised it would be difficult to find sufficient superlatives to do justice to him. I figured if I cheated a bit and plagiarised a few sentences from his OLM citation; that no one would be any the wiser. So I googled it only to find that all it says is 'For Distinguished Service'. Clearly the author(s) were as lost for words as I.

'Whilst General Shute was highly astute tactically and very strategically aware, he also had a keen ability to get the best out of all the arms, weapons and services available to him including the Air Force, Police and Internal Affairs – no mean feat in those early days. As a Company Commander, Battalion Commander and JOC Commander he was intuitive and decisive.

All parties under his command were absolutely sure of what was required of them and they deployed full of confidence and with clarity of purpose.

'However, probably his greatest asset lay in his man management. The welfare and morale of the troops under his command were always his highest priority and as a result he was highly respected, trusted and loved by his officers and men alike. He fought tirelessly throughout his distinguished career to improve the pay and conditions of all the troops, but particularly the African Soldier. His foresight and attention to detail of A and Q matters resulted in his men going on operations and fire force in high spirits and with confidence in the knowledge that they (as well as their families back in barracks or at home), were being properly supported and as well looked after as humanly possible.

'His diplomatic skills made him a natural to be involved at the highest levels in uniting the main protagonists after Independence and he was well respected by all sides for his fairness and consideration.'

The Editors' grateful thanks also go to eminent historian Professor Timothy J Stapleton of the University of Calgary for providing the material upon which many of the RNR and early-RAR articles are based; to Brigadier Patrick Lawless SCR for his chairmanship of the Rhodesian African Rifles Regimental Association and for writing the Foreword; and, most especially, to you the reader for your kind interest and support.

God bless you all.

FOREWORD

"… whoever said the pen is mightier than the sword obviously never encountered automatic weapons …"
General Douglas MacArthur

I am delighted to write this foreword, not only because I have been friends with Andy Telfer and Russell Fulton since we served together in the Rhodesian African Rifles, but also because I believe they have created something special with Chibaya Moyo 2 that will eclipse all that has gone before. They demonstrate they are truly master of the mighty pen, while each can testify to encounters with automatic weapons!

Building on the success of Chibaya Moyo 1, these two distinguished and former serving officers of the Rhodesian African Rifles have assembled a truly impressive array of reports, stories and anecdotes that span the history of this fine Regiment and in a sense, define it. The careful use of historical vignettes to introduce and link sections of the book might by itself form a valuable work of military history. The narrative is brought to life by rich and individual stories that reinforce the centrality of that which really matters in war – the qualities of the fighting soldier.

Little has changed about the nature of warfare over the generations. The qualities required to lead men in combat are enduring. However, to understand the Rhodesian African Rifles is to understand the nature of authentic leadership and the role of empathy: cultural empathy, patience, dignity and the basic tenets of respect and kindness. For those in search of insight, this book is littered with gems that bring this vividly to light. Contributions by Digger Essex Clark and David Heppenstall of service on operations in the jungles of Malaya; operations in the Rhodesian Bush War interspersed with Andy Telfer's and Russell Fulton's skilful weave of historical and technical narrative. Helen Dennison's story reminds us that battlefield scars are not always physical. The blend makes for a powerful layer that provides on the one hand a primer on warfare, while skilfully reminding us that warfare is a largely human endeavour.

There is a second important layer to this book. For those in search of tales of 'derring-do', adventure, heroism, humility, soldiering of the highest order under the most challenging circumstances, sacrifice, sadness and regimental banter – then there is plenty here for you. Mike Jones' modest mention of being based at 'Rear' for a while because of a 'bang on the head' masking what was his long and brutal gunfight with terrorists hidden in caves – and a serious wound. John Peirson's wonderful tale of joining 1 RAR by parachuting onto the battalion parade ground, during a parade, only weeks after the death of his identical twin Ken during OP NICKEL – and its impact on the soldiers on that parade convinced it was Ken re-joining from Heaven! And as for Andrew Krajewski….. such a delight to read, and testament to the officers and men of the Independent Companies, Rhodesian African Rifles, that unique combination of black, white, National Service and Regular Army officers and soldiers and very much part of the Rhodesian African Rifles family. ……. and such moving pieces by Carl Chabata, Tinarwo Ferrison Manema and Gift Munana.

I truly hope you enjoy reading this great book. It provides signposts to a quite unique country, to soldiering, combat, and a way of life that is quite unique – I know of no other book that achieves this blend so effectively.

Pat Lawless
Battle, nr Hastings, United Kingdom, March 2019

INTRODUCTION

We all have a story within us and some believe that is the best place for it. We, who had the privilege to serve with or alongside the Rhodesian African Rifles (RAR), cheerfully disagree and *Chibaya Moyo 2* is the second collection of our stories.

Within this volume, the reader will encounter tales from 1916 to 1980. The RAR's genesis lay in the barefoot soldiers of the Rhodesia Native Regiment (RNR), formed in 1916 to fight in the East Africa campaign of the First World War and disbanded in 1919. The RAR was its successor, raised in 1940 to fight the Japanese in Burma, serving in the 1950s in Egypt and Malaya before engaging in its longest conflict, the Rhodesian Bush War, through the 1960s and 1970s, until finally being absorbed into the Zimbabwe National Army in 1980.

Chibaya Moyo's approach honours the African tradition of an oral history, of stories and storytelling. This work makes an important contribution to the history of the RAR, not only because its anecdotes are authentic recollections by combatants and those affected by combat, but also because, through these stories, the reader will gain insight into the extraordinary spirit of brotherhood that existed between black and white soldiers in this Regiment, something that the world, even today, could learn from.

The aim of the *Chibaya Moyo* series is to create a published collection of RAR stories, told by those who were there. It has two objectives: firstly, to help preserve the memory of our Regiment for future generations and, secondly, to raise funds to assist our veterans.

We acknowledge its limitations. It is not an official history of the RAR; that role was fulfilled by *Masodja* (Binda 2007). Also, while we truly hope that you will enjoy *Chibaya Moyo,* we ask you to be patient and understanding. Although much of the writing is excellent, this is mostly the work of soldiers, with all our literary shortcomings, not a fault-free treatise by professional writers.

We have strived to improve on *Chibaya Moyo 1*. There are more images, including many more of Russell's entertaining cartoon sketches. We have researched material on the service of the RNR and the RAR in two World Wars, to better paint the picture of our heritage. Mindful that many readers will not be familiar with our tactics, or our time and place, we have added explanatory introductions to each chapter. Importantly, the bravery and tactical skills of our African soldiers are more fully described in this second volume.

You will travel through several landscapes in this book. We begin with the Rhodesian pioneers and settlers who personified the values that we fought to preserve. We then go to East Africa and stories from the RNR in WWI, onwards to Burma and Malaya with the RAR, arriving back in Rhodesia for the Bush War.

Our guides are the participants, telling their stories as they experienced them. Along the way, we will visit our Officer Cadet training and impressions formed on joining the RAR. Finally, we will immerse ourselves in the uniquely African nature of RAR Regimental life; give insight into the men behind the bravery awards; and recall fond memories of our *Masodja*. Enjoy!

Andrew Telfer
2 March 2019

THE RAR REGIMENTAL MARCH
"Sweet Banana"

"A, B, C, D, E, Head Quarters
Ndichakutengera Sweet Banana
A, B, C, D, Support, Head Quarters
Ndichakutengera Sweet Banana".

"Nhowo, Pfumo ne Tsvimbo,
Ndiyo RAR,
Muhondo ne Runyararo,
Ndichakutengera Sweet Banana".

"Burma, Egypt ne Malaya,
Takarwa Tikakunda,
Muhondo RAR,
Inorwa noKushinga".

"One, Two, Three, Depot RAR,
Ndidzo Dichapedza Hondo Dzvose,
One, Two, Three, Depot RAR,
Ndidzo Dichapedza Hondo Dzvose".

"A, B, C, D, Support, Head Quarters,
Ndichakutengera Sweet Banana,
A, B, C, D, Support, Head Quarters,
Ndichakutengera Sweet Banana".

GLOSSARY OF TERMS

2IC/2i/c	Second-in-Command	Bone (verb)	Polish (verb)
Acacia	Trees or shrubs with thorns or spines	Braai	Barbecue
AK/AK-47	Soviet/Chinese 7.62mm assault rifle	BSAP	British South Africa Police (Rhodesian police force)
Alouette III	French-built helicopter	Bundu	Bush
Alpha bomb	Anti-personnel bomb dropped from aircraft	Bunker	Part buried, hardened defensive shelter
AS/Askari	African Soldier		
AWOL	Absent Without Leave	Call-sign	Group of soldiers
		Canberra	Canberra bomber
B-10	Soviet 82mm smoothbore recoilless rifle	Casevac	Casualty Evacuation
Babalaas	Hangover	Catch Rays	Sunbathe
Balla Balla	Depot RAR	Chibaya Moyo	Strike to the Heart
Basha/basher	Grass shelter	Chibuli	Beer
Bde	Brigade	Chimbambaira	Landmine
BDF	Botswana Defence Force	Chimurenga	Liberation struggle

BEM	British Empire Medal	Chipili	Cheap
Bender	Drinking session, booze-up	chiShona	Language of the Mashona
Bent	Drunk	Claymore mine	Directional anti-personnel explosive device
Blue on Blue	Firefight between own forces	CO	Commanding Officer
BM	Brigade Major	Colcom	Cold Storage Commission - purveyor of cured meats
BMATT	British Military Advisory Training team	Comd	Commander
Bn	Battalion	ComOps	Combined Operations HQ
Bn Comd	Battalion Commander	Contact	Engage the enemy in battle
Boet	Brother	Coy	Company
Coy Comd	Company Commander	External	Operation outside the Rhodesian border
CPM	Colonial Police Medal	FAF	Forward Air Field
Crash	Sleep or rest	Fireforce	Airborne rapid reaction, vertical envelopment force
Crow	Girl	Flechette	Air-deployed explosive pod containing darts

Term	Definition	Term	Definition
CSM	Company Sergeant Major	Floppie	Terrorist
CT	Communist Terrorist	FLOT	Forward Line of Own Troops
Cull	Kill	FN	7.62mm Belgian assault rifle
		Four Five/4.5	4.5-ton Mercedes troop-carrying vehicle
Dak/Dakota	Douglas C-47 aircraft	Frantan	Napalm
DC	District Commissioner	FRELIMO	Front for the Liberation of Mozambique
DCD	Defence Cross for Distinguished Service	Fresh puss	Newbie
Debus	To get off a vehicle	Frot	Rotten
Donga	Gully	Frozen Area	Area restricted to Selous Scouts operations only
Doppie	Empty cartridge case		
Double tap	Two rounds fired in quick succession	Gap it/take the gap	To run away, to leave
DP	Soviet Degtyaryov light machine gun	G-car	Alouette carrying pilot, tech and four troops
Dragunov	Soviet sniper rifle	Golf bomb	Fragmentation bomb dropped by aircraft

Dwala	Bald flat expanse of rock	Gomo	Hill
DZ	Drop zone for paratroopers	Gonk	Sleep
		Gook	Terrorist
Ek sê	I say		
Embus	To board a vehicle	HDF	High Density Force Operation
Emplane	To board an aircraft	HE	High Explosive
HF	High frequency	LO	Liaison officer
Honoris Crux	South African decoration for gallantry	Lynx	Cessna air-to-ground strike aircraft
Hoot	Cheer, laugh	LZ	Landing zone for helicopters
Hooters	School of Infantry, Gwelo		
HQ	Headquarters	Mabinya	Terrorists
Hunter	Hawker Hunter jet	MAG	7.62mm Belgian general purpose machine gun
		Marie biscuit	A very thin round biscuit
Intaf	Department of Internal Affairs	Mary Jane	Marijuana
Internal	Operation inside the Rhodesian border	Masodja	Soldiers
IO	Intelligence Officer	Mbudzi	Goat
Ishe	Sir	Mellows	Music

IsiNdebele	Language of the Matabele	Mhondoro	Tribal or clan spirit, usually of an ancestor
		Mielie meal	Maize meal
JOC	Joint Operations Centre	Mombe	Cow
Jungle juice	Soft drink powder in rat packs	Mopane	Lowveld tree 4-18 metres tall
		Mopane fly	Tiny bee, annoyingly attracted to sweat and eyes
K-Car	Command helicopter	MPLA	Popular Movement for the Liberation of Angola
KIA	Killed in action	Mujiba	Young boy recruited by CTs to assist them
Kopje	Small hill		
Kraal	Rural African village	NGO	Non-Governmental Organisation
Kuk	Shit	No-Go Area	Area from which all civilians are excluded
Leg it	To run away	OAU	Organisation for African Unity
OC	Officer Commanding	R&R	Rest and Recuperation
OP	Observation Post	RAR	Rhodesian African Rifles
Ouen/oke	Bloke, chap, guy	Rat pack	Military issue ration pack

		Recce	Reconnaissance, reconnoitre
Paradak	Dakota carrying paratroopers	RhAEC	Rhodesian Army Education Corps
PKM	7.62mm Soviet general purpose machine gun	RhAF	Rhodesian Air Force
Pl	Platoon	RIC	Rhodesian Intelligence Corps
Pl Comd	Platoon Commander	RLI	Rhodesian Light Infantry
PO	Patrol Officer (BSAP)	RPD	7.62mm Soviet light machine gun
Pokey drill	PT with weapon to strengthen arms	RPG	Soviet rocket-propelled grenade launcher
Pookie	Mine-detecting vehicle	RPK	7.62mm Soviet light machine gun
Pozzie	Position	RR	Rhodesia Regiment
Povo	Rural people	RSM	Regimental Sergeant Major
PPSh	Soviet sub-machine gun	RV	Rendezvous
PRAW	Police Reserve Air Wing	RWS	Rhodesia Women's Service
PT	Physical Training		
Pulled	Shot	S Inf	School of Infantry, Gwelo

Puma	South African troop-carrying helicopter	SAAF	South Africa Air Force
Punch up	Contact with the enemy	SADF	South African Defence Force
Pungwe	Gathering/party, often lasting all night	Sadza	Mielie meal porridge
PV	Protected Village, defended by Intaf	SAM-7	Low-altitude surface-to-air missile (Strela)
PWO	Platoon Warrant Officer	SAS	Special Air Service
		SB	Special Branch (BSAP)
QM	Quartermaster	Seagull	Adjutant
QMG	Quartermaster General	Secra-phone	Secret phone
SF	Security Forces	Tokarev	Soviet 7.62mm x 25mm pistol
Sitrep	Situation Report	TTL	Tribal Trust Land
Skate	Man of dubious character	Two Five/2.5	2.5-ton Unimog troop carrier
SKS	Soviet semi-automatic carbine		
SNEB	Air-to-ground missile	UDI	Unilateral Declaration of Independence
Sparrow	Tracker	Unimog	Mercedes Benz military truck
Starlight	Medic or doctor		

Stick	4-man sub-section of soldiers	Vibe	Music
Stonk	Pound a position with mortars, artillery	Vlei	Wetland
Stop Group	Call-sign deployed in a blocking position		
Strela	See SAM-7	White Phos	White Phosphorous smoke and anti-personnel grenade
Subby/subbie	Subaltern		
Sunray	Commander	ZANLA	Zimbabwe African National Liberation Army
Svikiro	Spirit medium	ZANU (PF)	Zimbabwe African National Union (Patriotic Front)
Sweet Banana	RAR Regimental song	ZAPU	Zimbabwe African People's Union
		ZIPRA	Zimbabwe People's Revolutionary Army
Terr/s	Terrorists	Zoll	Marijuana cigarette

CHAPTER ONE

RHODESIAN HISTORY

A RHODESIAN PIONEER LOOKS BACK by Ronald Legge

Editors' Note: In *Chibaya Moyo 1*, we presented a brief history of Rhodesia, kindly contributed by Chris Cocks. In *Chibaya Moyo 2*, we present to you an article about the character of the kind of people who made that history. It describes a man who epitomised the unique blend of optimism, humour, tenacity and get-up-and-go that characterised the Rhodesian Pioneer and set the mark for the generations that followed. It is fair to say that the men and women who pioneered Rhodesia established the values that we fought to preserve, so a description of their nature belongs in this anthology.

The article was written by Ronald Legge in 1951 for *The Outspan* magazine. It is long by *Chibaya Moyo* standards but, in those pre-television days, one can imagine readers spending a quiet evening enjoying it, perhaps with a sundowner and a pipe. We invite you to do the same.

The Article:

If you ask Barnes Pope when he first started prospecting, he will tell you that it was a long time ago, when Southern Rhodesia was pioneer country – and his 'workings' were in the lounge of Meikle's Hotel, Salisbury.

In those days," recounts this veteran who for half a century has played a variety of roles in the drama of the Colony's growth, "men's habitual costume was khaki shirts and shorts. The shorts had very shallow pockets.

"I was sitting in the lounge on one occasion, when my hand accidentally slid down the space between the cushioned seat and the side of the chair. My fingers came in contact with some coins. I pulled them out and found I had retrieved seven shillings. I then went prospecting, sitting in various chairs. My total haul was £4 18s., a three-foot rule and an excellent pair of scissors!"

The wrinkles eroded by seventy summers in Barnes Pope's face deepen, and his eyes, set in a network of fine lines that bear witness to a bubbling sense of humour, take on an extra twinkle as he tells the yarn.

For Pope – pioneer, prospector and pre-historian – is quite irrepressible. Today, he is operating a tin mine on the Mtoko Road, twenty miles out of Salisbury, and doing very well out of it, but his favourite appellation for himself is still "the biggest ----- fool in Rhodesia," applied to him once by a friend who introduced him to a successful English brewer and explained that the youthful Pope was trained in Britain as a brewer with a big combine, but threw up his excellent prospects to farm in the Colony.

No one realises better than Barnes Pope himself that if he'd stuck to his vats he would probably have enjoyed a prosperous career. He confessed as much to his new acquaintance, but it is almost certain that his impish sense of humour asserted itself and that he told him of Rhodesia's latest industry – breeding frogs to extract the hops for locally-brewed beer! He is full of quips like that, and his enormous zest mocks at his occasional self-accusation.

For anyone who knows him will tell you that a prosaic occupation would never have satisfied this man with an inquiring mind and a love of open spaces, a man who was welcomed to the country he was to make his home by Rhodes himself, and who became the intimate friend of Leander Starr Jameson – the mercurial 'Doctor Jim', around whose name a legend has grown that will never be forgotten while there are those who enjoy tales of filibustering and carefree living in the spacious days when men began to carve civilisation out of the bush.

Rhodesia has always been a country that attracted the adventurous-minded, who saw vast sources of potential wealth in its soil and in the hard core that lies underneath it. Today the early 'gold fever' has been superseded by an equally restless urge to exploit the tempting deposits of other base metals, the prices of which have soared on the markets of a world preoccupied with the constructive and destructive uses of fissionable material and of steel and copper.

Barnes Pope was not a man to kick his heels idly while others were making quick fortunes by scratching at the surface of the land and extracting from it precious new ores with exotic names such as beryl and tantalum, corundum and scheelite.

Even before the last war he was dabbling in the production of corundum, which he discovered at Rusape and Marandellas, but he had no great luck. He exported a very large amount at a very low price - £7 10s. a ton. The current price is £25 a ton. A patch of tantalum that he found also failed to make him rich.

Then he became the first discoverer in the Salisbury are of beryl, the main ingredient in the production of beryllium, which is used as an insulator of uranium in the process of hardening copper. Other people, however, had richer claims. There was one farmer, for instance, who had earned a modest living for years tilling the soil, and who acquired a smart £15,000 by the simple expedient of carting away in lorries the stuff that had been turning over with his ploughs for as long as he could remember.

So now Mr Pope has turned to tin. He is convinced that there is a very large field of this metal to the east of Salisbury, where deposits were discovered in 1908 but remained unexploited because of the prevailing low prices. He has acquired five blocks of claims and opened a mine, where he sluices tin from the ore body and sends it to a refinery in Bulawayo.

Barnes Pope prospecting

Maybe he will at last reap the reward of his tenacity, but he will never open a deeper or richer mine than that of his own mind, in which is stored a wealth of knowledge of the history of Rhodesia. He brings it to the surface and separates it from the ore body of the commonplace with the tools of anecdote and reminiscence. To listen to Barnes Pope delving into the past is to hear the synopsis of a gripping adventure story. The opening chapters are written in 1901, when Lord Grey, one of the directors of the British South Africa Company, which formerly administered the territory, asked the 20-year old apprentice brewer to farm his 1,800-acre estate at Rusape. With his brother, Eric, and Mr H. Kay-Scoror, of Marandellas, Mr Pope undertook the project.

"Lord Grey," he recalls, "introduced me to Cecil Rhodes, who said 'My boy, you will love the country, but as a pioneer farmer never expect to make any money."

Rhodes's warning was justified. For 25 years Mr Pope farmed at Rusape, and, although he made a comfortable living there, it was left to others who followed his pioneering with Rhodesia's other crop of gold – tobacco – to draw the rich dividends it later earned.

Soon after Mr Pope's arrival, Lord Grey was appointed Governor General of Canada, and, in the words of his protégé, "forgot all about us".

"We and a few others built up the tobacco industry," he relates, I was a director of the first Tobacco Co-op for seven years. For the best crop I ever grew, however, I received an advance of twopence per pound from the Chartered Company and was asked for a halfpenny back"

Life for the young farmer in the lonely Rusape area was not without its excitements and its hazards. Three huge herds of sable roamed the bush, and lions were consequently plentiful, so that Barnes Pope had his shotgun as a constant companion.

But he makes no claim to fame as a big-game hunter. "I am always disappointing people in this respect," he says, "Sometimes when I have told perfectly straightforward but quite unexciting tales of encounters with lions, my audience has refused to believe me. So more than once I have related stories that would turn Baron Munchausen green with envy, and the wilder and more improbable they grew, the more spellbound the listeners became."

His most unpleasant experience he shared with his chestnut pony, 'Coffee', a cross between an Arab and a Basuto pony, who was by way of being an equine 'character'.

Coffee was known to and beloved by every European and Native in the district because of his predilection for alcoholic beverages. He would never pass a kraal until he was given a draught of beer, and on the occasions of his master's visits to the township of Rusape no one could induce him to turn his steps homeward until he had slaked his thirst with a bottle of stout.

On the occasion in question, man and beast were returning from the farm in Rusape. Coffee had shown signs of restlessness for some time, and eventually came to a halt with such a jerk that his rider was thrown over his head. If Mr Pope had not had the presence of mind to retain hold of the reins, the story might have had a different and unhappier ending for, not more than fifty yards away, he saw two lions devouring the carcass of a cow.

"I remounted very quickly, and we made an extremely wide detour, leaving the lions to finish their meal," he observes drily.

There are all the elements of a wild and woolly Western with some of the romance of Darkest Africa injected, in the story of a trip Barnes Pope undertook at the request of Colonel Raleigh-Grey, a cousin of Lord Grey's, in 1904. His mission was to go north to Sipolilo, pick up a herd of 1,000 head of cattle and bring them overland seventy miles to Mazoe.

From Rusape to Mazoe he travelled by the famous Zeederberg coach; the remainder of the journey was done on foot. Settlers he met on the way all had tales of hardship and danger to tell. One Englishman who had arrived in the new country full of hope only a short time before had lost one son through blackwater fever and another killed by a lion. It was a hazardous return trip. The leader of the expedition directed his Native gang to make kraals each night to avoid the cattle being snatched by the lion, which were prolific in that country.

A more dangerous foe, however, proved to be the tsetse fly, which claimed sixty beasts. They were left behind dying, and there is small doubt that they provided meals for the lions. It was with great joy that, at the end of four days, Mr Pope was able to turn over the slightly depleted herd to the Howick Ranch in Mazoe.

If the young Englishman at first found life strange in the wild country which he grew to love, imagine the effect it had on the delicately-nurtured girl who was to become his wife! She arrived at Rusape from East London in 1908, with her parents, who had come to farm in the district.

The last stages of the journey were through totally uninhabited grass and scrub land. No farms were visible, and the only signs of live were at the little trading stations at the railway sidings. Rusape itself appeared only slightly more civilised. Its 'hotel' consisted of half a dozen grass huts and a tin dining-room and bar. The stationmaster's cottage and the goods shed were in the open, no trees had been planted, while the little 'army' at the police camp, which constituted the first line of defence in case of Native trouble, was mostly accommodated in galvanised iron quarters. The most luxurious dwelling was the Native Commissioner's, a brick-built structure with an iron roof. The Commissioner's office, however, was built of poles and mud.

Fortunately, the future Mrs Pope shared certain qualities with the man who married her. Chief of these were an adaptable nature and a ready sense of humour. She rivals her husband as a raconteur, and one of her best stories is of her arrival in Rusape.

"The news had got around among the farmers of the district that a young girl of nineteen was due by a certain train," she says. "This was an event of such absorbing interest in the locality that I had a reception committee to inspect and greet me when I arrived. It consisted of about eighteen young bachelors, all togged up to the nines in their best Sunday clothes with shirts that had been starched until they shone and unaccustomed ties so constricting their necks that great beads of perspiration stood out on their pink, scrubbed faces. Every eligible young man from miles around was there, each one, of course, hoping that the newcomer would be a personable young lady who would help to relieve the monotony of life in the primitive conditions that then prevailed."

At this point in the narrative, a slight disagreement invariably occurs between husband and wife, for Barnes Pope stoutly maintains that he was one of the welcoming party. Mrs Pope as resolutely maintains that he was not, and that she did not meet him until later. "Of course I was there," he insists. "I still remember the dress you were wearing. It was a pink spotted frock." "It was not," Mrs Pope retorts, with mock indignation. "It was a blue dress."

Whoever's memory is at fault is a matter of small consequence, for the girl readily took to her new life, which was not all hard work. She was assiduously courted at the village dances, which took place in a concrete-floored mill with flour-bags for 'sitting out', but it did not take her long to choose as a mate the man with whom she has more than forty happy years. "I felt many qualms on my way to Rusape," she confesses, but ads with gentle irony that she never felt disposed to accept the offer of a companion on the train, a barmaid, who, noticing her apprehension, said: "Don't worry, darling. If you don't like it, I can always get you a job in Umtali."

For 25 years Mr Pope farmed on Lord Grey's estate, then he sold out and bought 3,000 adjoining acres at Cornucopia. In 1939 he left the land to do a war job in the Native Department. He became Director of Shabani and Mashaba Native Labour, and later returned to the Department to rehabilitate African soldiers.

Nowadays, in the 'tin age', Mr and Mrs Pope live in a spacious and elegant home on the outskirts of Salisbury, with their daughter, Mrs Thelma Hall, and her little daughter Jennifer. Their three sons are frequent visitors and much of the talk is inevitable of the old days. Barnes Pope himself is as hale and vigorous as ever and shows no signs of having twice contracted the deadly blackwater fever that killed so many empire builders.

He was still convalescent from one bout when he took part in an exploit that is part and parcel of Rhodesian pioneering history – the 1912 farmers' 'insurrection' against the payment of Labour Tax. One hundred and fifty farmers, Barnes Pope among them, trekked to Gwelo in protest, armed with rifles given to them by the British South Africa Company for the protection of their homes. There, they all has summonses served upon them. The magistrate, who is now dead, said to Mr Pope, "For heaven's sake, get out while the going is good." "I can't. I haven't got any money,' was the reply. "You can have £50 out of the till any time you like," the magistrate said. "Go off on a cattle-buying expedition."

Barnes Pope took himself off to the Chuduku Reserve, bought and sold cattle, netted a profit of £150, and returned to find that the summons against him had been withdrawn, while fines with the option of imprisonment had been inflicted upon those who had remained in Gwelo. Twenty or thirty refused to pay their fine and went to prison. Hadn't yet drawn the money I had made, so I gave the magistrate a post-dated cheque for the £50," Barnes Pope observes with satisfaction.

It was soon after this that he was told to return to England to recover from the effects of the fever. There Wilson Fox, one of the directors of the British South Africa Company, invited him to lunch with his co-directors at the company's head office in London Wall. Dr Jameson, who was vice-chairman, came onto the scene and demanded of Wilson Fox, in his picturesquely adjectival ay, "What the blue blazes are you doing with that -------- Barnes Pope? He was one of the Labour rebels. However, I have known him a long time. As long as you have searched him for arms, we will have him to lunch."

The directors did themselves very well, Mr Pope avers, and he found the company extremely entertaining, though he objected to a question by a visitor from Argentina, to whom 'Dr Jim' asked him to explain all he knew about ranching in Rhodesia. The Argentinian wanted to know whether grass had to be planted before it was possible to start farming. "I told Dr Jim that it was impossible for me, as a decent Rhodesian, to deal with people of that type," he asserts with emphasis.

This luncheon cost Barnes Pope £5, the result of a lost wager with Dr Jim. A decanter of whisky was brought by the Marquis of Winchester, one of the directors. The Marquis produced a key from his pocket and unlocked a padlock on the decanter. When his whisky had been poured, he locked it again and replaced the key in his pocket. Dr Jameson bet Mr Pope £5 that he would not get the Marquis of Winchester to give him a tot from the decanter. "I took him on," he says, "but with no success whatever with his lordship. It was a special brand of whisky he liked, and he would allow no one else to touch the bottle."

Barnes Pope was not only one of the founders of the new civilisation of Rhodesia; he has played an important role in uncovering the secrets of the ancient race that lived, mined and built fortified camps there, hundreds of years ago. Rock paintings, beads of gold, stone, glass and bronze, crucibles of gold, tin, copper and slag which he has unearthed at Rusape and Khami are preserved in a collection at Salisbury Museum. He also discovered a skull and bones while clearing out silted excavations at Rusape, which Professor Raymond Dart and other authorities established beyond doubt are of non-Negroid origin.

Mr Pope is in fact an ardent protagonist of the theory that the famous Zimbabwe Ruins and remains of other stone buildings in the Rusape and Inyanga districts belong to a period at least 1,000 years B.C. He believes that the mined and fortified areas were occupied at different periods by people from the Mediterranean seaboard who succeeded one another in the original buildings at Zimbabwe and the sister camps, and that the evidence is overwhelmingly against the suggestion that they were Native fortifications against the Matabele.

His contention is that the Phoenicians, who are known to have mined gold, copper and tin in Cornwall and Spain, also made their way south to the great fields of these metals in Central Africa and removed enormous quantities. The gold, he thinks, was to a large extent used in the building of Solomon's Temple, and he points to the fact that the same type of hammered gold foil which, according to the Bible, was attached to cedar pillars by gold tacks, has been found in the temple at Zimbabwe.

Rock paintings which have come to light in certain areas are so typical of ancient Egypt that he is convinced they were done by workers from the banks of the Nile or by a kindred folk. When, today, one finds Barnes Pope wresting tin from the ground for removal to overseas markets, it is a pleasant thought that a man who was among the first of the latest race of settlers may be following a precisely similar course as the ancients whose mysteries he has helped to probe.'

THE OLD MACQUE STRIKES AGAIN by Andrew (The Young Macaque) Krajewski

Editors' Note:
In the previous article, we met Barnes Pope, one of Rhodesia's Pioneers, a contemporary of Cecil John Rhodes and Leander Starr Jameson. As the 20th Century unfolded, the Pioneers were followed by the Settlers, young men and women of pluck and endeavour, hoping to make new lives in this land of opportunity. Two such people were Romana Wanda Krajewska (née Gradowicz) and Kazimierz Tadeusz Krajewski.

Readers of the first volume of *Chibaya Moyo*, became familiar with the wonderful stories of their son, Corporal Andrew ("I was only following orders") Krajewski, Sunray 22B (Known and Feared Throughout the Land). There are more of Andrew's tales of derring-do with the 'Braves' of 22B in *Chibaya Moyo 2*, displaying once again his unique sense of humour, his rapport with our masodja and his love of the Zambesi Valley.

In this article, Andrew writes about his parents with sensitivity and love, couching the story of their incredible hardships in wartime Europe with his gentle humour. The Krajewskis personify the indomitable spirit of the Rhodesian people that would prove impossible to subdue or defeat, even as the country slipped away. As in the case of Barnes Pope, they illustrate the values that we fought to preserve.

Andrew's Article:

One of the supreme talents shown by The Old Macaque* was his ability to find surface water. The only tools he needed for this divination were a golf-ball and a club.

This phenomenon was something openly discussed in our circle as well as by curious onlookers. It may have had something to do with his horrific experiences in Kazakhstan in 1940-1941, following Poland's 'partition' between two of the greatest Arch-Sphincters that history has ever known: Corporal Hitler and Comrade Stalin.

Ladies first: my late mother, Romana Wanda Krajewska (née Gradowicz) was a distractingly beautiful lady, tall and slender with blonde hair and blue eyes. She and her six sisters grew up on a large farm in the North of Poland, near the town of Sarny. By Polish standards they were wealthy, and Michal Gradowicz, my maternal grandfather, employed the heads of four households as farm hands. The family's life was idyllic. However, a son died in childbirth, after which the daughters were told by a grief-stricken father that he would have sacrificed them all for the life on his son. Strange thing, grief: makes people take leave of their senses. As it happens, things got much, much worse.

When war broke out, Roma's grandfather was living with them, and the entire family was given an hour to round up their belongings before, yes, you guessed it, being herded onto cattle trucks. This time going north and east. Anyone heard of Finland? Snow, huge pine forests and hordes of bears and wolves? Oh, and in a labour camp: you don't work, you don't eat. Welcome to Stalin's vision of the future.

The oldest daughter did not go with them. She disappeared soon after the war started, likely joined the Polish Resistance, or perhaps was raped and murdered by these standard-bearers of Teutonic and Soviet Culture. Their father Michal hid in the forests with Jadwiga, the youngest girl, literally for the duration of the war. They lost everything, but both survived, and I have two cousins from my Ciocia Jadwiga: Jurek and Theresa.

My maternal grandmother was a remarkable woman: my mother once told Shirley her story when we were visiting her in Bulawayo where she lived until her death in early 2002. Shirl had no idea that I'd never been told this story, so to this day details are sketchy, but my maternal grandmother managed somehow to keep the entire family together and had taken with them on the train a large churn full of home-made cottage cheese, which was doled out as rations to the children. In Siberia, Grandfather simply stopped eating and allowed himself to starve to death so that his granddaughters would have more to eat. To my knowledge at least two of Roma's sisters died in the labour camp.

Somehow, perhaps due to Churchill's ONE decent act, the family was allowed to enlist in the Russian Army, but soon went AWOL and made their way to (wait for it) Persia! Under the Red Cross the girls were sent to Bwana Mkubwa Camp and finished their education at Digglefold School in Marandellas. Roma secured a position as a governess working for O.B. Bennett, then head of Rhokana Corporation and took care of his two young children. They were very kind to her. Roma met Kaz in Kitwe and they were married in 1950. Mom died in Edith Duly Home in Bulawayo in early 2002. She had advanced Alzheimer's disease.

Dad's story was also sobering in the extreme. My paternal Grandfather, Jan Tadeusz Krajewski was a police commissioner in a relatively large, old and utterly beautiful town in the south of Poland, named Lwów (pronounced "Lvuf"). His only son, my father, Kazimierz Tadeusz ("Kaz") was in his second year of chemical engineering at the University there when war broke out. He saw a squad of stumpy, stinking Russki, led by some arsehole in a green cap (Stalin's NKVD) clutching a Tokarev. Jan was escorted out of their home, lead away and was never seen again. He was one of the Polish officers (a major in the Polish artillery reserve) who was murdered on Stalin's orders at a forest named Katyn. Their house and all its contents were seized. It is likely that their three hundred year-old oak furniture was burnt for firewood.

I know very little about Dad's life story, except that everyone was rounded up and shipped east on cattle trucks. Kaz and a Jewish friend of his escaped from the camp in eastern Kazakhstan, and hopped trains west; always west, on to Persia and so months later into the arms of the Red Cross. His sister, my late Ciocia (Aunt) Christine and their mother, my paternal grandmother Jadwiga, were together in a camp, where Kaz very nearly died of typhus. Christine read him passages from *The Arabian Nights*. He joined the Polish army, served in the Western Desert, was wounded (he hated the German 8.8cm high velocity antiaircraft guns) and invalided back to England; at that time a beautiful and welcoming place, as many parts most certainly still are. He tried to join the Polish air force, handsome fellow that he was. And trust me: he was. Alas that he was found to be red-on-green colour-blind. Given his aptitude, the selection panel asked him to stay behind and one gentleman with handlebar mustachios suggested to him that the RAF was very short of instrument technicians, which was the trade Kaz learned. When last I looked, L/AC Krajewski, K.T. was on the unit nominal role for 304 squadron.

After demobilization, he joined his sister who had met and married a Scottish ex-serviceman and had been given a grant of land to start a dairy at Kamfinsa in Northern Rhodesia. Together, they managed to locate their mother and were reunited at last. Dad took a job as instrument technician at Rhokana Corporation at Nkana near Kitwe, where he met and married my late mother. My late sister Suzanne was born there in 1952: and I in 1958. It was in 1968 that we moved from Zambia to Rhodesia. Dad joined the Rhodesian Iron and Steel Company (RISCO) and we moved as a family to Que Que.

My word: page 3 already?

Back to The Old Macaque. Now, several years' wandering about thousands of square kilometres of scorpions, saw-scaled vipers (?), and parched sand, infrequently punctuated by highly alkaline and camel-manure-strewn water-holes, is an excellent foundation for a lifelong fascination with water. Hence his skills at finding it.

With The Old Macaque, this preoccupation manifested itself most clearly on any golf course with so much as a single water hazard. So strong was this attraction that caddies placed dozens of small bets and some not inconsequential spondulicks changed hands on the outcome of "Meestah Kaiz's" shots on holes where water hazards came into play. Sometimes even on holes merely lying adjacent to these. Curiously enough, this extended to such impedimenta as irrigation sprinkler heads and those little circular steel covers that fitted over the top of greenside water reticulation systems. I recall several times when his approach shot to a green (itself quite a rare occasion, it must be said) had us watching in admiration as the ball fell ground-wards, only to rebound (with a slightly delayed "toink!") like an India- rubber ball in a fantastically energetic, skywards hop, before vanishing into the bundu behind the green. "Bloody macaque!!!" he'd say through clenched teeth.

I have vivid memories going as far back as to Northern Rhodesia and the Bancroft Golf Course in the mid-1960s. I remember snorting hippos, and sinister ripples from recently submerged crocodiles, and the "splosh!" of golf balls smacked into Watery Oblivion by my Scottish Uncle Donald (on occasion), but also by The Old Macaque. By the mid-1970s to early 1980s, these dunkings had come to routinely include the water hazards on Que Que Golf Club (hole numbers 10 and 18) as well as Alan Lowry's number 2 (a bloody great pool in front of the green), and the snaky stream that wound its way across the 9th, and close to, alongside- or across hole numbers 10, 11, 17 and 18.

It also technically included, for a brief period of ten days or so, a very narrow strip of the Indian Ocean athwart the golf course at St. Michaels-On-Sea on the Natal South Coast, when He and I holidayed there in late 1977 and stayed at the Golf Course Hotel.

Perhaps his most memorable interface with water was on one Saturday afternoon competition (there we go again!) at Que Que Golf Club. Now, on that day, he'd struck the ball with rare and exceptional purity and seemed overjoyed to watch it soar: whither being less of an issue than the marvellous distance the ball was propelled. His Best Effort, however, came on the last hole: QQGC's 18th; a 120 m, short par three. The two-tier green sloped back towards the tee box, and was surrounded on three sides by a horseshoe-shaped, concrete-bottomed pond. There was a narrow bit of fairway in-line with the pin, but short of the green, which featured thick kikuyu grass, mown short. Finning energetically in the pond were several hundred smallish tilapia fish, long the target of serious attention by bands of protein-starved caddies. This was the hole of which my golfing cousin David had always said: "This'll sort out the deep-sea divers from the frog-men!"

Club selection was an ongoing conundrum for The Old Macaque who on that day had miraculously - perhaps suspiciously - avoided the water hazards on the other holes. However, with the pin placed toward the back of the sloping green and with a freshening headwind breeze ahead of a summer rainstorm that had sprung up, he selected, after some deliberation, a six iron. He executed a number of unusually fluent practice swings. Just before he initiated Launch Sequence, he had been heard to mutter Words Of Omen to himself: "Now, don't be short!"

And so it was that the ball was struck "in the screws"; good and solid. Although somewhat misdirected, it soared to altitude like a V2 rocket. Those Present watched in silent admiration as it mounted in a sizzling parabola, seemingly almost wreathed in low cloud, but wide of the left hand edge of the green, wide even of the water hazard. The Hateful Sphere executed a high-altitude overpass of even the huge Prince of Wales' Feathers tree that stood some 15 m behind the back of the green. The ball seemed to hang, ominously now, above the caddy shack and surrounding compound. It then descended to land with a mighty "BANG!" on one of the roofs.

There came distant screams of "Waiweeeeh!" and a dozen or so young boys boiled out from behind the bougainvillea hedge and into the open, closely followed by the stubby, bow-legged figure of Benjamin, the caddy master. In one pudgy hand he clutched a sjambok. The ball lay several feet in front of him, still in play. For once, it seemed that the outsiders betting against The Old Macaque soaking his tee shot in the water hazard were vindicated.

However, vociferous arguments soon raged among the punters for he hit his second shot into the water short of the green. Having incurred a penalty stroke, with his caddy now standing with his trousers rolled up and spindly shanks dripping, Mister Kaz then whiffed his fourth shot over the green and into the water hazard behind. Another water-salvage operation by his now squelching caddy saw Meestah Kaiz playing six. He then stubbed the club-head into the thick kikuyu grass and summarily popped the ball back into the water, necessitating yet another Operation Noah, before nearly holing out for eight. A six inch tap-in putt then ensued for a score of nine!

What so impressed me was the dignified, even haughty, way with which he made his way back to the clubhouse, through the now thinning group of spectators:

caddies, the caddy-master Benjamin, and about a dozen players, all in hysterics over what they had just witnessed. A scuffle had broken out behind the caddy shack, as it will when fortunes are wagered and lost. Several spectators on the clubhouse's verandah, drinks in hand, were also roaring red-nosed encouragement and blowing raspberries.

The Old Macaque tilted his chin upwards: "I don't care about doze piss-cats and macaques!" He then brightened slightly and looked at me. "That was a good six-iron shot, eh?" Who doesn't love an optimist?

* My Old Dad became known as "The Old Macaque": a macaque being a member of the genus Macaca, including the Barbary macaque, the Rhesus macaque, and the like. Dad made use of this description often. He referred to most fools and morons as "That bladdy macaque!", and to me as "You're just a young macaque". For example, when his 5 handicap Son missed 12 inch-long putts for birdie on super long par four holes! He also used it after hitting his ball out of bounds, or into water hazards and after shanking an iron (the so-called "lateral" shot: the shot that Cannot Be Named: which MUST Not Be Named).

He was inordinately fond of using this highly descriptive term, and I believe he'd acquired it from conversations with the ex-Belgian Congo émigrés who'd fled the Civil war there in Katanga in 1960-1963. These Worthies had, during their tenure there, often referred to the Indigenous as "les macaques". Not polite, and after all, a sign of the times. Still, it's a good, satisfying word to use on a golf course, and I found it most useful. Especially in the Army…

"Major MacAque" had a nice ring to it.

CHAPTER TWO

WORLD WAR ONE

INTRODUCTION: THE RHODESIA NATIVE REGIMENT by Captain
Andrew Telfer

The Rhodesia Native Regiment (RNR), raised in 1916 to fight in the East Africa
campaign of the Great War, was the predecessor of the Rhodesian African Rifles.

At the outbreak of World War I, the commander of the German forces in
German East Africa (later Tanganyika now part of Tanzania) Colonel Paul Von
Lettow-Vorbeck recognised that he could best support the German war effort, not
by defending the colony, but by operating in such a way that the Allies were forced
to commit troops against him. Operating in highly mobile, commando-type units,
called *Schutztruppe*, his forces operated across East Africa and threatened both
Portuguese East Africa and Northern Rhodesia.

To help counter this threat, on 1 May 1916 the 1st Battalion of the RNR was
formed under the command of Lt Col A.J. Tomlinson, seconded from the BSAP.
Only about a third of RNR recruits came from Southern Rhodesia; they mostly
came from Nyasaland, Northern Rhodesia, Portuguese East Africa and a few from
other nearby territories. Some had previous military experience, while many of
them were migrant mine workers in search of a better job. On 16 July, after only
two-and-a-half months' training, the 450-strong battalion was sent to Zomba in
Nyasaland for further training. Their journey to Zomba is described in fascinating
detail by Lt Col Tomlinson in the article following this one, extracted from his
memoirs.

By the time they got there, the operational situation had changed and, instead
of further training, the battalion was deployed into an area north-east of Lake
Nyasa. At Songea, on 12 November 1916, the RNR (less one company that had
been detached to go to Buhora) were attacked by two German columns numbering
about 500 men, supported by Maxim machine guns.

The main attack lasted all day but was repulsed, and, over the following two
weeks, subsequent shorter attacks were driven back. Throughout, the RNR sent out
aggressive fighting patrols to take the initiative away from the attackers until, on

24 November, a relief force of South African infantry arrived. The holding of Songea had been sufficiently important for the commander of the Rhodesia-Nyasaland Field Force, General Northey, to write: 'The conduct of this newly raised regiment, put into the firing line earlier than was intended through force of circumstance, reflects the greatest credit on those responsible for their short training, and on all ranks of the regiment.' It's worth remembering that the RNR recruits had received just ten weeks' training before being sent into battle.

Meanwhile, the company that had been sent to Buhora, under the command of Major C.L. Carbutt, had also seen action. Encountering a German column, the Southern Rhodesia Column, commanded by Colonel R.E. Murray, deployed across its front and both flanks, while the RNR closed the rear perimeter, digging in 1,000 yards from the Germans. The RNR opened fire with their machine guns on the morning of 25 November, and the enemy responded with a 4.1-inch field gun. Lieutenant Simpson and a small group of RNR soldiers moved into a position to snipe at the gun crew, which re-directed its fire at the snipers, wounding three of them. That night, the RNR company moved closer to the German positions and totally boxed them in. By the afternoon, the German force had surrendered, and 57 European and 250 African soldiers were captured, as well as three machine guns and the field gun. They were taken to Njombe en route to captivity (along with 300 head of cattle, the fate of which is predictably unknown).

Historian Timothy Stapleton noted that the African NCOs did particularly well in these encounters, leading successful fighting patrols of 20 to 30 men against the enemy and doing most of the reconnaissance, thus disproving the racial stereotype of the time that African soldiers had to have European leadership. Consequently, African NCOs in the RNR began to gain more responsibility, and some, like Corporals Rita and Tanganyika, were promoted to Sergeant.

As 1916 ended, active patrolling out from Songea continued, aimed at locating and attacking enemy outposts and food stores. In January 1917, Lt Col Tomlinson was ordered to attack Kitanda, rumoured to contain about thirty enemy. They found it abandoned and began to return to Songea but were ordered to go back and occupy it, as General Northey had become aware of a German build-up in that area. The orders were to hold it "as long as ever possible".

Patrolling from Kitanda, RNR soldiers had frequent clashes with enemy patrols and then, on 16 January, a large *Schutztruppe* force of three Field Companies (about 300 men with ten Maxims and three 37mm field guns) attacked Kitanda, encircling it. The siege of Kitanda lasted until 4 February, with the RNR repulsing a number of deliberate attacks and deploying aggressive fighting patrols in retaliation, surprising the Germans who had expected "newly raised askaris who would be easily overcome".

By now, several NCOs had distinguished themselves. Sergeant Booth fought with distinction in several important encounters, frequently slipped through enemy lines to carry messages to and from Songea and helped lead the relieving force to Kitanda. He was awarded the Distinguished Conduct Medal. Among four Military Medals awarded was one to Sergeant Salima, the first black member of the RNR to be decorated. One month later, Sergeant Rita was awarded the Distinguished Conduct Medal 'for conspicuous gallantry in action on many occasions. His example and influence with his men is incalculable.' This was the highest award ever made to a black RNR soldier but regrettably his citation has not survived.

After six weeks at Kitanda, the RNR were returned to Songea for a spot of R&R. The day after arriving they were deployed along the road to Wiedhafen in response to German activity. In the ensuing actions, Sergeant Booth again distinguished himself, running forward under heavy German fire to rescue a badly wounded African soldier and rallying troops back into the attack. He was commissioned and, for this brave action, would be awarded the Victoria Cross, the only RNR recipient of this highest decoration.

In March 1917, again serving under command Colonel Murray and the Southern Rhodesia Column, Lt Col Tomlinson advanced towards a German force comprising five companies, fifteen Maxims and two field guns, under Captain Max Wintgens at St Moritz Mission. The attack on Wintgens' force went very badly for the RNR and, although there was blame and counter-blame between Murray and Tomlinson, some faults are clear. Tomlinson had sound intelligence that Wintgens had 450 men at St Moritz, supported by the field guns and machine guns, yet he attacked their prepared defensive position with only 300 men and six maxims. Failing in the attack, he withdrew to open ground where the *Schutztruppe* were easily able to surround his position and maul the RNR before slipping away.

Perhaps he had wanted to mount a surprise attack, but it would have been wiser to have waited for Murray's column to catch up and his subsequent retreat to open ground proved fatal. So, the decisions Tomlinson made were judged by his commander, Colonel Murray, to have enabled Wintgens' escape and to have cost the lives of many of his own men. Consequently, according to the records of the Southern Rhodesian Column, 'Tomlinson was relieved on the 27th March and taken to a place of safety'. On 30 March, when Colonel Murray called the RNR to join the pursuit of the Germans, he put Major Addison in command and left Tomlinson in charge of base camp defences. The same day, Tomlinson fell sick. He returned to Southern Rhodesia and the BSAP, where he rose to the rank of acting Commissioner (Tomlinson Depot in Salisbury was named after him).

Major Carbutt took over the battalion and, in the assault on a German force at Mpepo in August 1917, proved himself to be a more flexible field commander than his predecessor. By this stage of the East Africa Campaign, the German forces' tactics involved defending positions for only a few days before melting way in tactical withdrawals. This was wholly aligned with their strategy of tying up British forces in East Africa to prevent their deployment to the Western Front. The RNR had a significant success at Mpepo, when the combined RNR/NRP force inflicted over 100 casualties on the Germans.

Encounter battles with German forces continued through 1917 with the troops marching barefoot an average of 31 miles (50 kilometres) a day in the harshest bush conditions, displaying extraordinary physical endurance.

In September 1917 a newly-raised 2nd Battalion RNR entered the field and established a camp at Mbewa on the north-eastern shore of Lake Nyasa. On 28 January 1918, the two battalions, each of 500 men, were amalgamated into the 2nd Rhodesia Native Regiment under the command of Carbutt, now promoted to Lt Col, and deployed to follow Von Lettow's force, now reduced to 2,000 men, into Portuguese East Africa. On 22 May, they intercepted his supply column and captured it, and then continued the hide-and-seek pursuit of the *Schutztruppe*, marching an incredible 2,250 miles (3,600 kilometres).

The German force would eventually surrender at Abercorn, in Northern Rhodesia, on 25 November 1918, 14 days after the Armistice in Europe but the RNR were not there to see it. In October 1918, they had been ordered to return to Namwera on Lake Nyasa, where a smallpox epidemic broke out and they were placed in quarantine. When the quarantine was lifted, the regiment was ordered to Zomba to prepare for demobilisation. Then the 1918 influenza pandemic struck East Africa and the first eleven RNR soldiers contracted the illness and died.

The Southern Rhodesian administration directed that the RNR must remain at Zomba and not return home until the crisis had passed, to reduce the spread of the illness. This was a sensible precaution but, incredibly and inexcusably, Lt Col Carbutt and Major Wane, two of the most senior RNR officers, men who had been with their soldiers since the start of the campaign, were granted leave and returned to Salisbury. Lt Frank Hulley of the RNR, accurately summed this up with: "Col Carbutt and Major Wane left us to go to Salisbury much to everyone's disgust and condemnation."

Weakened by months of exertion and hunger and abandoned by their Commanding Officer and a senior Company Commander, a sense of panic and desperation gripped the RNR. Seventy-three RNR soldiers died of influenza, half of the total lost in the entire campaign.

In December 1918, having lost 159 soldiers killed in action or on active service, and 136 wounded, the RNR returned to Salisbury. The platforms were crowded and the RNR band played stirring martial music. Among those who welcomed them were the Administrator of the Colony, the Chief Native Commissioner, the Bishop of Southern Rhodesia and senior military officers. Their two Commanding Officers, Tomlinson and Carbutt, were absent.

Despite its humble beginnings as a hastily-trained collection of policemen, miners and farmworkers, the RNR rose up admirably to the extraordinary physical challenges of the East Africa Campaign. In doing so, it proved itself a very effective fighting force, especially in the use of 20-man fighting patrols and smaller reconnaissance patrols. These patrols were initially led by Europeans, most notably Sergeant (later Lieutenant) Booth VC DCM, until African NCOs, such as Sergeants Salima MM, Tanganyika and Rita DCM, demonstrated for the first time in Southern Rhodesia's short history, their outstanding potential in that role. This was something that we in the RAR would come to know very well.

After disbandment, selected members of the RNR formed the Askari Platoon of the British South Africa Police at Government House in Salisbury. Non-Commissioned Officers from this platoon provided instructors for the Rhodesian African Rifles when it was formed in 1940 to fight in World War II, thus connecting the two regiments. When the RAR was awarded its colours in 1953, it inherited the battle honours of the RNR: 'The Great War' and 'East Africa 1916-1918'.

References:
Binda, A 2007, *Masodja*, 30 Degrees South, Pinetown, South Africa.
McLaughlin, P 1980, *Ragtime Soldiers*, Books of Zimbabwe, Bulawayo, Zimbabwe.
Stapleton, T 2006, *No Insignificant Part: The Rhodesia Native Regiment and the East Africa Campaign of the First World War*, Wilfred Laurier University Press, Waterloo, Ontario, Canada.

REMINISCENCES by Lieutenant Colonel A.J. Tomlinson

Editors' Note: Lieutenant Colonel A.J. Tomlinson became the first Commanding Officer of the Rhodesia Native Regiment in 1916. This article is an edited extract from his memoirs, first transcribed by historian C. E. Rogers in 2003. It describes the period from the formation of the RNR to their arrival in German East Africa, providing a fascinating account of their deployment, as well as insight into the prevailing culture of the time.

Southern Rhodesia

The attesting and the training of the natives for the regiment began in the latter part of April 1916, my officers, the European N.C.O.'s and myself were engaged all day and every day with them until the eventful day, 18th July came, and the battalion entrained at Salisbury railway station for German East Africa.

We left at 9 a.m. being accorded a very hearty send off. Arriving at Beira next morning the regiment was soon being paddled out on lighters to the Ipu. When we were all aboard the steamer the Governor of Mozambique Territory, H.E. Mons. Pery de Lind and H.H. Sir Drummond Chaplin and Lady Chaplin came out to the Ipu to bid us farewell.

Portuguese East Africa

On the 20th July we anchored off Chinde, at the mouth of the Zambesi River, where arrangements had been made through H.B.M's Consul, Mr Hewitt Fletcher, for the regiment to be transferred into barges, and to be taken up the river by the steamers, Princess, Centipede and Panduma.

Sixteen acres of Chinde, stockaded by huge rough timber, except for that side abutting on the Zambesi, is British Chinde, and on this piece of the country our consul has his quarters, the postal officials and a few British merchants also residing there. The flotilla of steamers, with four barges each, (two on either side of the steamer and not towed behind as seen usually), filled with askaris moved slowly off in the afternoon, officers and European N.C.O.s being accommodated on the steamers. I, with Capt. New (adjutant) and Captain Forrester, (Medical Officer), was on the Princess, Major Addison being in command on the Centipede, and Major Carbutt in command on the Panduma.

The Zambesi was very low at this time of the year, and the water was intersected by many small islands. The skippers of our vessels, however, knew exactly the course to take, always tying up (anchoring) at dusk, and not starting again until the morning mist had cleared away.

The scenery on the river banks on the most part was not interesting, long grass everywhere, with a few trees now and again. Crocodiles were plentiful and engaged the attention of the sportsmen on board. Many a shout went up from the askaris when a hit was scored, as there was no mistaking when this occurred, the floundering and writhing of the reptiles plainly shewing when they were wounded.

At Marromau sugar estate, which we reached at 2.30.p.m on the 21st, it had been arranged we were to receive a ration of meat for the askaris, but the Portuguese Commandant would not allow this to take place, for the estate's cattle were said to be infected with trypanosomiasis or fly sickness. So, it was arranged the meat would be supplied the next day on reaching the Mopea estate.

On the 23rd we passed Chupanga Mission, which appeared deserted. This is where the wife of Livingstone died and where her remains are buried. A little beyond this place we stopped at Caia for fuel, and on the 24th reached the junction of the Shire River with the Zambesi, and soon after again tied up for the night. The Paduma, the skipper of which was a Portuguese, was considerably behind the Princess and the Centipede.

Nyasaland

On the 25th we reached Chindio at 11 a.m., the terminus of the Shire Highlands Railway, and where are river journey ended, the Panduma did not come up until late in the afternoon, and then not until a small steam vessel, the Scot, had been sent down to give her help. Mr Young, the General Manager for the railways, was down to meet us, and I arranged for the regiment to leave the following day.

Chindio is an uninteresting spot, composed of a few railway sheds and houses, with the Zambesi stretching away on either side, long grass with a few trees on the banks, occasional palms and native huts to be seen. During our stay some excitement was caused by a native being taken by a crocodile. The canoe in which he had been paddling was overturned by the croc when it was nearing a sandy spit, which then seized and made off under water with the man. The funeral party of his relatives that night was very noisy, drums going the whole time, with weird chants and moanings, sad to listen to in the otherwise stillness of the night.

On the 26th, at 5.30 a.m. entraining began, and the first train left at 6.05.a.m. the second following at a short interval. Lt. McGinnis with two N.C.O.'s was left to bring up certain baggage and equipment, which could not be with the two trains owing to the Panduma's late arrival at Chindio.

McGinnis's dog 'McIlwaine', looked upon as the regimental mascot, was sent up with our train. He was devoted to McGinnis and was never happy out of his sight. He caused some consternation when he bolted back on our first stop and arrival at Port Hereld. He made a bee line along the railway towards Chindio, now some 40 miles away. Natives were sent after him, and he was recovered after running many miles, McGinnis picking him up at Port Hereld on his arrival there a day or two afterwards.

Here some Nyasaland civil servants and Mrs Thorburn asked to join the troop trains, as they wished to get to Zomba. Permission was readily granted, and the officers were able to learn something of the country from our visitors.

Arriving at Limbe at 5.30 in the evening, Major Thorburn (Base Commandant, Zomba) met me. After detraining, the regiment was encamped about 1.5 miles along the Limbe – Zomba road, nearly all the officers being billeted at the hotel.

Rations, etc, had to be seen to, and we marched for Zomba at 9 a.m. on the 27th. Two motor lorries took our baggage and rations along, doing a double journey each march to bring them all up.

The weather was cool, the road good (metalled), and everyone was in the best of health and spirits. The country was bushy and at times hilly, with good bridges over the streams. There were Indian stores at each village as we passed, lining the road.

We reached Ntondwe on the evening of the 28th. This was Major Thorburn's estate, where a large amount of cotton is grown. Here there was a fine house, which he kindly told the officers to make themselves comfortable in.

Next morning Major Thorburn motored out from Zomba, and Captain New (Adjutant) and myself went in with him 14 miles to see our camping ground, the regiment in the meantime coming in with Major Addison. We motored out again and came into Zomba with them. Our band brought flocks of natives to see the regiment, and the whole population gave us greetings. Europeans and natives were much struck with the hats the R.N.R. askaris were wearing. They had never seen anything but the fez which is always worn by the natives of the K.A.R.

The arrangements made at our camp were most satisfactory. 'Bandas' had been put up for the askaris, while the officers and the European N.C.O.'s were placed under canvas, which was supplemented by grass and pole huts by each mess as they pleased. The site of the camp was on a rather steep slope, except in the centre, which was the Zomba Volunteer's rifle range. It was well out of town and the road to it was just broad enough to be used by motors, which brought our stores etc, out each day. Major Thorburn kindly placed a motor at my disposal, and in the afternoon after all had been settled in camp, I went to call, (Capt. New accompanying me) on Sir George Smith, K.C.M.G. Governor and Commander in Chief of Nyasaland.

During our stay in Zomba daily routine was carried out on the same lines as that done in Salisbury, training being got on with as actively as possible. On the 2nd August the R.N.R. attended at the K.A.R. parade ground, when H.E. the Governor presented to Sgt. Major Juma of the K.A.R. the D.C.M. Being senior officer present, I took charge of the parade, which, with the muster of all details of the Garrison, amounted to about 1,000. Our band headed the march past and did remarkably well. His Excellency was introduced to the officers of the R.N.R. and addressed the European N.C.O.'s of the regiment.

It was during our parade movements in the thick bush at Zomba that we first got to know of the fiendish buffalo bean. These beans have a coating of very fine hair, which if touched at all sticks into one, and creates a fearful smarting sensation. Natives suffered just as much as Europeans, and the more one rubs the places touched by the bean the more maddening sensation becomes, until it dies away gradually in about an hour's time.

On the 6th August Major Addison, with Lieuts. Williams, Bridges and Piggin, Sub. Inspector Long, 9 European N.C.O.'s and 105 askaris, moved out to go to Fort Johnston. This contingent was as much as could be taken at one time by the lake transport. They were to proceed from Fort Johnston, to Mwaya by lake steamer, and then march to New Langenburg.

On the 9th August a route march up the Zomba Mountain was made by the remainder of the regiment still in Zomba. The climb becomes very steep, and steeper still by a path that we took, and which cuts off some three miles of the road up.

The top of the mountain is broad with small hills, and there are many villas built up there by the residents, who live in them in the very hot season that occurs at Zomba. The streams on the top of the mountain have had trout bred in them, which are doing well. Forestry receives a good deal of attention on Zomba mountain, the wild cedar tree being cultivated. Roses and other English flowers are to be seen in abundance. The view from the edge of the mountain is one that is not easily forgotten.

Lt. Morgans, with Sgts. Moore and Cooke and 34 askaris arrived on the 10th August. These formed our Maxim gun detachment. Kaffir pox had broken out amongst these natives just before the regiment started from Salisbury, so they had to be left behind until their quarantine was over.

The following day the second contingent marched out for Fort Johnston. This consisted of Capt. Wane in command, Lieuts. Benzies, Poole and Morgans, with 10 European N.C.O.'s and 139 askaris. This left me with one company (Major Carbutt's) still at Zomba. I arranged with the O.C. Depot. K.A.R. to shew us an earthwork which General Northey recommended for 25 rifles; and we marched to the parade ground on the 16th and cut the trenches for this circular earthwork for instruction. We used this form of trench afterwards at Songea and elsewhere.

Here I would like to place on record the great kindness we all received from the residents of Zomba. Sir George and Lady Smith and others were most hospitable to us. Major Thorburn was constantly thinking of what he could do for the R.N.R.

On the 19th August the remainder of the regiment marched off from Zomba. The detachment comprised, beside myself, Capt. New (Adjutant), Surg. Capt.

Forrester, Major Carbutt, Capt. Burke, Lt. Simpson, R.S.M. Usher, 14 European N.C.O.'s and 204 askaris. Lt Rutherford and Sgt. Groves were suffering from lameness, so arrangements were made for them to proceed by motor.

We marched to camps Domasi, Nkula Hill, Liwonde, Ulongwe, Mpikajira, and Nsenga respectively reaching the bar, Fort Johnston, on Lake Nyasa on the 25th August. The section of the march from Zomba to Fort Johnston was very much harder than the previous march from Limbe (Blantyre) to Zomba, as the altitude was lower, and the heat very trying; the mosquitoes and midges were fearfully annoying. We found the small patrol nets useless, and I managed to get an issue of larger nets to all Europeans of the various detachments before the march was undertaken.

The march to Fort Johnston was uneventful. This was our first experience of the tenga tenga (porters), the only means in very many cases of getting our equipment, etc, along. All the boys try to get off with as lighter load as possible, and many and varied are the tricks they try on to get relieved of the load they are carrying. The camps were excellently laid out along the road, the officers and other Europeans having huts of a superior style to the askaris and the tenga tenga.

Commander Dennistoun, D.S.O. R.N. in charge of the transport arrangements on the lake, was able to send the contingent off by H.M.S. Gwendolen at 3 o'clock on the 26th August. On the following day we made Nkata Bay (on the west side of the lake) at noon, and we stopped here for fuel. The askaris were allowed ashore, and cooked and ate food after the fuel fatigue was finished. Lt. Tonge. R.N.R. (a brother of the Deeds Registrar at Bulawayo), commanded the Gwendolen, and with him was Lt. George. R.N.R. and several seamen. Commander Dennistoun accompanied us on the Gwendolen on this trip.

A very strong southerly wind came up at night, with rain for several hours, and in consequence in the morning when we arrived at Mwaya, it was found, owing to the rough night and heavy waves, the steam tug which was used for towing the barges for the purpose of landing troops had been sunk. We could see her funnel shewing out of the water. Our landing was carried out with much difficulty. From where we were beached the troops, equipment, etc, had to be got to a mission some two miles away. The mission buildings at Mwaya were all used for military purposes. The vegetation round about was rank and the ground very marshy in some places with streams intersecting, so it took some time to get all up to the camping ground.

German East Africa

General Northey's motor car was at Mwaya, so Commander Dennistoun and I proceeded to New Langenburg at once, leaving Major Carbutt to bring up his company, etc. The road from Mwaya to New Langenburg rises all the way, and the boma (a fortified enclosure containing offices, goal, quarters, etc) could be seen for some miles as we approached it, perched on the crest of a hill. I reported to the General and afterwards had lunch, meeting Major Knox Gore, C.S.O. Anderson and Honeywood, the General's A.D.C. Later, I went to where the officers of the R.N.R. were quartered in a large brick building which in German times had been a native hospital. Here I saw Addison who reported all going well with his company. Instruction with the magazine rifle was begun at once, as General Northey had told me that he thought he could arm the natives with the 0.303 rifle, in place of the Martini Henry we had brought from Salisbury.

On the 1st September we had a field day under General Northey I was set the task of attacking a position, and in the evening the General gave us a talk on trench fighting, and a few days after Major Knox-Gore instructed us in trench construction and earthworks.

Route marches, parades, musketry and other duties kept us all busy while we were at New Langenburg. A very interesting route march was the one to Massoko, twelve miles S.S.E. of New Langenburg. This was the German military station of the district, and the site had been well laid out, with buildings for officers and N.C.O.'s, and stores for equipment, etc. The askari lines were adjacent to the European quarters. There were picturesque grounds and vegetable gardens round about, with a circular lake formed from the crater of an extinct volcano. All the buildings had deteriorated at the time we visited the place – the effects of neglect from war. In all we covered about twenty-seven miles by the time we got back to quarters that day. When nearing New Langenburg, about three miles out, we attacked a 'flag force', representing an enemy, with the object of driving it out. We had undergone a considerable test of endurance by the time we had finished that evening.

The exchange of our Martini-Henry rifles for the 0.303 rifles was by this time nearly completed, and another four Maxim guns were handed over for the regiment. A few days later Lt. Honeywood gave a demonstration of the use of the rifle grenade.

Meantime General Northey informed me he intended to send a company of the R.N.R. to Songea, and on the 14th September No.1 Company, (Major Addison's) marched from New Langenburg for Mwaya. With this, Headquarters – myself, Capt. New and Capt. Forrester (M.O.) – also went. The officers of No.1

Company with Major Addison were Capt. Wane, Lieuts. Williams, Bridges, Rutherford and Piggin; there were also Warrant Officer Long (signalling), 15 European N.C.O.'s and 223 askaris. Capt. McCarthy of the N.R. Police was attached to me as Intelligence Officer, with Lt. Chas. Grey assisting him. Major Carbutt's company was for the present to remain at New Langenburg with our eight maxims.

Arriving at Mwaya at 12 noon on the 15th, our equipment and stores were transferred to H.M.S. Gwendolen. We ourselves with the troops embarked at 8.30 pm. We sighted Wiedhafen, on the eastern side of the lake, just after six o'clock on the following morning. Capt. Wane was landed with 100 askaris and the necessary complement of officers and European N.C.O.'s.

This party skirmished through the bush for some little distance and, it being clear of the enemy, the boma being found unoccupied, the disembarkation of the remainder of the column was proceeded with at 8.30.a.m. We knew afterwards from a captured German who had a patrol of ten askaris under him that he was watching our proceedings with considerable interest from one of the adjacent hills.

No time was waste. After landing us, the Gwendolen steamed away, and we bade goodbye to Dennistoun. I arranged that Lt. Rutherford and Sgt. Groves, with 12 askaris, were to garrison Wiedhafen, and Lt. Brown (afterwards Legislative Council. N.R.) was left to supervise the forwarding of stores, rations, etc, which would later be arriving for us at this base. Capt. McCarthy, Lt. Grey and 20 askaris who had been chosen for intelligence scouts, went off on the Songea road at 1.30.p.m. and the remainder of the force followed at 4.p.m. I had to leave a further 12 askaris under Sgt. Cooke, to escort some carriers with loads expected to arrive by the steamer Queen the next day; so that altogether the column now consisted of Capt. McCarthy's party in advance, and 165 askaris with officers and European NCOs with me.

I addressed the officers and N.C.O.'s before starting, impressing upon them the necessity for realising that we were indeed now in the enemy's country, and therefore we must be alert and make the most of our small force. Even as I was speaking we might be observed by the enemy…

References:
Tomlinson AJ, 1922, *1st Rhodesia Native Regiment, Some Reminiscences*, Rhodesia Defence Force Journal, Salisbury, Southern Rhodesia (transcribed by Rogers CE, 2003).

SHORT BIOGRAPHIES OF AFRICAN RNR SOLDIERS by Professor
Timothy Stapleton

Editors' note: the following biographies are transcribed from Professor Timothy J
Stapleton's book No Insignificant Part: the Rhodesia Native Regiment and the East
Africa Campaign of the First World War. They illustrate the incredibly diverse
origins of the men who joined the Regiment.

Private Aliki

Aliki was an Ngoni man from Nyasaland (Malawi) who was a mine worker in
Southern Rhodesia. Enlisting in June 1916, he was among the first five hundred
volunteers for the RNR. After completing two years' service in German East
Africa, Aliki, like most of those he had joined with, re-enlisted in the regiment and
went on to fight in Portuguese East Africa. In late October 1918, after just arriving
in Zomba, Nyasaland for demobilisation, he was one of the first RNR soldiers to
die of influenza.

Sergeant Brandy

Although his RNR officers believed he was an Ndebele, Brandy had been born to
a Malawian family living in the Inyati area of Matabeleland. He was the first
constable of the British South Africa Native Police (BSANP) in Fort Usher,
Matabeleland, to volunteer for the RNR and enlisted in May 1916. Brandy rose
steadily through the ranks, becoming corporal in November 1917 and sergeant in
July 1918. He was one of the few veteran NCOs left in the unit during the
Portuguese East Africa phase of the campaign. After two years and 260 days of
active duty, Brandy transferred back to the BSANP in Matabeleland in January
1919. In the early 1920s he was employed as a policeman in Bulawayo.

Private Chapotela

Chapotela was an Ngoni man from Nyasaland. He joined the BSANP in 1911 and
was a member of the Southern Rhodesia Mobile Column that was sent to the border
of Northern Rhodesia and German East Africa in 1915. Chapotela served in the
RNR from May 1916 to December 1918, fought in the East Africa campaign, and
was demobilised in Nyasaland. Despite his conviction for 'disobedience' in June
1918 which resulted in a five-shilling fine, his RNR officers rated his military
character as very 'good.' He soon returned to the BSANP and was based at the

Salisbury police camp until at least 1921. While the records are blank for his activities during most of the inter-war period, it seems Chapotela, as a middle-aged man with false teeth, joined the KAR in Zomba, Nyasaland in October 1939 but was medically discharged in April 1941 because one of his toes had to be amputated.

Corporal Chikoti

A Malawian of Chewa ancestry, Chikoti had spent three and a half years in the KAR. By early 1917, he was employed in a mine near Sinoia (Chinhoyi today) in Southern Rhodesia. In March 1917 he enlisted in the RNR and was quickly promoted to corporal because of his military experience. In April 1918, in Portuguese East Africa, Chikoti was convicted of being absent from his assigned sentry post during a march and was sentenced to be tied to a post for twenty-one days, the infamous Field Punishment Number One, and demoted to private. By the end of the war, however, he had regained his rank in the acting capacity.

Corporal Chitapangwe

Chitapangwe was one of the first BSANP constables to be transferred to the RNR in May 1916 and he remained with the regiment until he was demobilised in January 1919. With almost three years in the field, Chitapangwe was among the longest serving RNR soldiers. He was shot in the left arm during the fighting around St. Moritz in March 1916, was hospitalised in Fife, Northern Rhodesia, and then returned to the unit. Police experience, a 'very good' war record, and basic literacy gave Chitapangwe an advantage in establishing a postwar career within the colonial state. In the early 1920s, he was working as 'head warder' at the administrative centre (of boma) of Mkushi in Northern Rhodesia.

Corporal Kavote

At the beginning of the First World War, Kavote, a Chewa man from Malawi, was a member of the BSANP and sent to Northern Rhodesia as part of the ad hoc Southern Rhodesia Mobile Column meant to defend the border with German East Africa. He was part of a mixed force of Rhodesian police and Belgian Force Publique soldiers that defended an entrenched position at Saisi, twenty-eight miles west of Abercorn, from a German attack between 26 July and 3 August 1915.

For his part in the battle, Kavote was mentioned in despatches for gallantry in 'sponging out a gun (7 pounder) under heavy Maxim and rifle fire at night under no cover.' He was transferred to the RNR in May 1916, was promoted to corporal for 'good service,' and fought in German East Africa and Portuguese East Africa. Kavote was discharged in July 1918 because of 'long service in the field.' He then joined the Northern Rhodesia Police as a native constable and was in that position until at least 1924. Kavote was one of the few black soldiers in the RNR to receive the 1914-15 Star for his early service in the war. Like most RNR soldiers, he could not read or write.

Private Kurukuru

A member of the BSANP before joining the first contingent of the RNR in May 1916, Kurukuru, a Malawian, was described by his platoon commander as a man of 'exceedingly bad character.' Kurukuru deserted from the unit in November 1917 because he could not keep up with the advance – he had a sore on his leg caused by venereal disease. He asked another RNR soldier to take care of his wife who was with him. Several weeks later, he was arrested by a fellow black RNR soldier who saw him behind the lines masquerading as a sergeant. While being transported to serve his prison sentence, Kurukuru managed to escape from his guards who were distracted by their wives. After being recaptured, he was sentenced to a total of four months and fourteen days of imprisonment with hard labour as well as twelve lashes. He died in Zomba, Nyasaland, in December 1918 from 'pneumonia following influenza.' He could not read or write.

Private Lungombe

A Kalanga man from the Plumtree area, Lungombe was twenty-seven years old when he travelled to Salisbury in May 1916 to enlist as one of the first 500 RNR soldiers. His pre-enlist activities are not known but it is likely that he worked within the colonial economy. He was wounded at the Battle of Mpepo and then discharged from service as he was considered medically unfit. After the war, Lungombe worked as a messenger for the Native Affairs Department in Plumtree until 1929. He did not receive a disability pension until 1933 when his application was supported by a doctor.

Sergeant Mayega

In May 1916, Mayega was among the first group of BSANP constables transferred to the initial RNR contingent. He was most likely from the Matabeleland area. Promoted to corporal the day before the unit left for East Africa, Mayega remained in the field until the armistice. It seems that literacy helped his career in the RNR. Mayega was promoted to sergeant in early July 1917 just days before the Battle of Mpepo. He was mentioned in despatches, an honour just short of decoration, for rendering 'valuable service' during operations in Portuguese East Africa in 1918. Despite this, there is very little information on Mayega's personal actions during the campaign. He returned to Southern Rhodesia in January 1919 and after a month's leave, he returned to the BSAP and was posted to Bulawayo. His discharge record from the RNR described his military character as 'excellent'.

Private Mkulunyelwa Ndiweni

Enlisted simply as Private Mkulunyelwa, this man was the son of the famous Ndebele Chief Ndiweni who had fought against the British in the 1890s. Because chiefs were expected to provide recruits for the RNR, Mkulunyelwa's father sent him to join the first contingent to serve as an example to his other subjects. The young man's wife was pregnant at the time and she later gave birth to a son Kaisa (or Kaiser) Ndiweni. On 20 March 1917, just after the RNR had been mauled by the Germans near St Moritz, Mkulunyelwa Ndiweni raised his head slightly above his trench and was shot dead. His family collected the ten-pound death gratuity. Kaisa Ndiweni took over the chieftainship in 1942 and attended the Lancaster House talks in 1979 that led to Zimbabwe's independence.

Sergeant Rita (Lita)

Rita was part of the original RNR contingent. There are no detailed records on his personal background, but it is likely he was an Ndebele, since most of the first contingent came from Matabeleland and white officers sometimes spelled his name 'Lita' which is Ndebele. As one of the few literate black soldiers in the RNR, he was posted to the intelligence section and quickly promoted to corporal. Rita led countless small reconnaissance patrols and became an expert at collecting information on the enemy. Just after the siege of Songea, while on patrol, Rita shot a German askari sergeant and was pursued through the bush by forty enemy soldiers. Stealth, reliability, and narrow escapes from the enemy became his trademarks. Once he was promoted to sergeant, Rita was posted to a rifle platoon and entrusted with leading twenty-man fighting patrols that would locate and engage the Germans. Winning the Distinguished Conduct Medal, Rita was the most highly decorated African soldier in the RNR. He died of unknown natural causes in November 1917 and his family was paid a death gratuity.

Sergeant Salima

Judging from his name, Salima was probably from Nyasaland and likely came to Southern Rhodesia as a migrant mine worker. He was one of the first recruits to enlist in the RNR. Salima led important fighting patrols that harassed the enemy when the RNR was besieged at Kitanda in January and February 1917. For this, he received the Military Medal which was the first decoration awarded to a black RNR soldier. Along with dozens of others, he was discharged in June 1918 in Salisbury, having completed his two years' service. Nothing is known of his postwar life.

Private Stambuli

Stambuli was from Portuguese East Africa and had worked as a house servant in Southern Rhodesia. In April 1917, he was working in the Connemara Mine near Gwelo (Gweru today) when an RNR recruiting officer came looking for volunteers. Stambuli, along with six others, told the officer that they wanted to enlist in the regiment. As instructed, the next day these recruits went to the mine compound manager to collect their outstanding pay, so they could travel to Salisbury to join the RNR. Since the mine was short of workers, the manager refused to let them go and ordered them back to work. When Stambuli and another man refused, the manager called in the mine police who beat the would-be recruits and handcuffed them to a wagon wheel. The RNR recruiting officer discovered what had happened and had the mine manager charged with hampering recruiting and assault but he was convicted of only the latter offence. Stambuli joined the RNR in May 1917, went to East Africa, and was discharged at the end of the war. The exact details of his service and postwar life remain a mystery.

Sergeant Tanganyika

As a member of the first five hundred RNR recruits, there are no records of Tanganyika's background. His name would seem to indicate an East African origin and there was another Tanganyika, a private, in the RNR who was recorded as a Chewa from Nyasaland (Malawi). However, Tanganyika is also a phrase in the Shona language meaning 'to make the country.' Sergeant Tanganyika was either a Malawian of Chewa ethnicity or a Zimbabwean of Shona ethnicity. Since he was literate, he was promoted to corporal fairly quickly and became one of the most effective patrol leaders in the RNR. In October 1916, while leading a reconnaissance patrol near Songea, Tanganyika's six men fled but he still managed to single-handedly capture two enemy African soldiers. Strangely, he received no decorations. The only blemish on his record seems to have been leading the prisoner escort that was responsible for the escape of Private Kurukuru, a deserter. Tanganyika survived the war but there are no records of his postwar life.

References:

Stapleton, T 2006, *No Insignificant Part: The Rhodesia Native Regiment and the East Africa Campaign of the First World War*, Wilfred Laurier University Press, Waterloo, Ontario, Canada.

CROSS KOPJE by Captain Andrew Telfer

Just over two kilometres north of Zimbabwe's fourth largest city, Mutare (known as Umtali until 1983), the capital of Manicaland province, stands a huge stone cross. Constructed of granite and concrete, it weighs more than fifty tonnes, towers nearly ten metres high, is over a metre thick and has arms that spread five metres. It gives its name to Cross Kopje and the nature reserve that surrounds it. The cross used to be illuminated by huge floodlights, but they no longer shine. Instead it stands alone, a silent monument to the 269 African soldiers, including 184 of the Rhodesia Native Regiment, who died in East Africa in World War I.

It was erected in 1924 by Lieutenant Colonel James Allin Methuen DSO who overcame a wall of indifference by the colonial administration towards a memorial for African soldiers who had given their lives for Britain. There was already a war memorial in Umtali, an obelisk in the park off Main Street, but it made no mention of the askaris of the RNR or of any African soldiers who died in the Great War.

James Methuen arrived in Umtali in 1902 from Scotland and started an engineering business. He soon joined the Southern Rhodesia Volunteers, rising by 1910 to commandant of all Eastern District volunteers.

When World War I broke out, he immediately volunteered and was to serve with great distinction, first as second-in-command of the 1st Rhodesian Regiment in German South-West Africa, then as a Major in the 60th King's Royal Rifle Corps on the Western Front, where he was badly wounded and awarded the DSO for conspicuous gallantry. He ended the war as a Lieutenant Colonel, commanding the 18th Northumberland Fusiliers in France.

Methuen returned to Umtali at the end of 1919, by then married to Doris Airth, a nurse who had cared for him as he recovered from his wounds in hospital. He went back to his business, to his voluntary position of district military commandant and built a stone castle for a home, complete with turrets and field

Cross Kopje

guns. He was a man of deep Christian faith, helping people to learn to read and write in evening classes at the Anglican Church. He quietly funded and guided a mission in the bush and, despite recurrent pain from his wounds, walked there once a month, a distance of 18 miles. For such a man, the absence of a memorial for African soldiers was an injustice that he would not endure.

Methuen, with help from his brother Stuart, gained permission from a Mr Condy, a farmer, to erect a stone cross on the summit of a rocky outcrop that he owned near the town, then known as Baboon Kopje. The two brothers employed the workers, provided the materials and struggled up the steep-sided kopje for two months to build the monument. On completion, a grateful Council built a path to the top…

The Unveiling

On 19 August 1924, the first British Governor of Southern Rhodesia, Sir John Chancellor, passed through Umtali. Aware that the Governor would be returning on 30 August, Stuart Methuen asked him if he would preside over an unveiling ceremony on that day. The Governor committed that, "barring an act of God", he would.

Then the Civil Commissioner in Umtali, Norman Chataway, miffed that the Methuens had constructed the memorial without official sanction and uncomfortable with the concept of a memorial to African soldiers, intervened, seeking to dissuade the Governor from attending.

Not knowing this, Methuen forged ahead with his plans and, five days before the Unveiling, phoned Chataway to ask if he'd like to look over the programme before it was sent to the newspaper, The Rhodesia Advertiser. He'd arranged quite a show: a 17-gun salute, an askari guard of honour, a contingent of ex-RNR soldiers (now policemen in neighbouring Portuguese East Africa) and the commandants of the Portuguese garrisons at Villa Perry and Mascquece.

Chataway then told him that the Governor wanted to excuse himself from the Unveiling. He claimed that he'd never committed to attending, only that he'd try to; that he had other engagements such as Chataway's garden party; and that the kopje was too steep for a man of his age (53 years). Methuen was angry but undaunted and, fearing a direct approach to the Governor, Chataway telegrammed his ADC, Captain Lowther: "My opinion Governor should not be asked to make this very rough climb and unveiling ceremony unnecessary."

On 27 August, Chataway was instructed by the ADC to tell Methuen that the Governor would not be attending, there should be no formal announcement and "the ceremony should not take place."

It came too late. The newspaper had already published the announcement together with a fine story about the Bishop of Southern Rhodesia, Dr Frederic Beaven, cheerfully climbing the kopje and celebrating a dedication at the foot of the cross, clad in his scarlet vestments of office, despite his advanced age. He was 69 years old.

Methuen replied to the Governor's excuses by offering two, probably tongue-in-cheek, alternative proposals. The first was for the Governor's car to stop at the gate to Condy's farm and for the Governor to pull a half-mile long string to unveil the memorial, in a kind of drive-by unveiling. Alternatively, the Governor could perform the unveiling from Chataway's garden party, on a signal: "Man behind the house with a white handkerchief or flag. Man at Memorial to pull down the flag."

The Governor ignored Methuen's inventive proposals and the Unveiling went ahead without him, while he attended the garden party. The Mayor of Umtali, Councillor W. Stowe, undertook the task in his place. The inscription on the monument reads, 'To the Glory of God and in Memory of Africans Who Fell 1914 - 1918'.

Methuen then came under attack from the colonial Establishment. The chief of staff of the most senior military officer in the colony demanded to know: "Did you erect, or cause to be erected, a native war memorial in your capacity as District Commandant, or as a private citizen?" Methuen replied: "Neither", perhaps feeling that he alone couldn't take all the credit.

The Governor accused him of acting improperly in "publishing a programme of the unveiling ceremony without authority" and "inviting armed forces of a foreign country to enter S. Rhodesia, without authority, to be present at the unveiling." That would have been the two Portuguese commandants. Methuen replied by quoting a previous directive from the Governor and the military commander in Salisbury, who had "told me they wished to invite Portuguese officials on every occasion that anything of importance was taking place in Umtali."

For six weeks, the correspondence continued until the officials realised that they couldn't continue without further embarrassing the Governor and, so, finally let it rest.

Colonel Methuen had succeeded in his mission and the memorial stands to this day on Cross Kopje. It is fitting that, when the successor to the RNR, the 1st Battalion the Rhodesian African Rifles was finally granted a permanent home near Bulawayo in 1954, it was named Methuen Barracks.

Reference:
Lonsdale, C 2014, *The Colonel at Cross Purposes*, viewed 3 August 2018, https://www.churchtimes.co.uk/articles/2014/15-august/features/features/the-colonel-at-cross-purposes

CHAPTER THREE

WORLD WAR TWO

INTRODUCTION: THE RAR IN WORLD WAR TWO by Captain Andrew Telfer

Formation

In May 1940, the first Commanding Officer of the RAR, Lieutenant Colonel FJ Wane ISO, a former RNR officer, received the following orders in his call-up papers: 'There will be an African regiment; you will command it and the regiment will build its own camp on the Borrowdale road.

African NCOs from the British South Africa Police (BSAP), together with African NCOs from the Askari Platoon, were selected to transfer to the new regiment and begin the task of training the recruits. An advertisement was placed for recruits and, soon, two companies were formed and engaged in basic drill and weapons training in the mornings and building their camp in the afternoons.

On 19 July 1940, by government notice GN 374/1940, the regiment was charged 'with the defence of the colony, the maintenance of order and such duties as the minister may define' and, significantly, 'the regiment may be employed outside the colony'.

Submissions were invited for the design of a badge and the final selection, issued in August 1940, depicted a Matabele war shield, crossed by a Matabele stabbing spear or 'assegai' and a Shona digging spear or 'museve', upon which was laid a vertical knobkerrie. A scroll bearing the title 'Rhodesian African Rifles' was placed below the design.

On 20 September 1940, Regimental Sergeant Major Lechenda was appointed as the battalion's first RSM. RSM Lechenda had first seen service as a bugler, aged ten, in the KAR in Somaliland. During World War I, as a CSM, he had been awarded the Distinguished Conduct Medal for leading a platoon against a German force that had been harassing a British position and driving them off. He earned the Military Medal when, with a hastily gathered group of 12 men, he attacked a German force (including three machine guns) that was about to seize a rations dump. He captured one machine gun and, in a follow up, killed nine Germans.

Through 1940 to 1943, the battalion continued to recruit, train and expand to full strength. During 1942, troops were sent to the South African city of Durban to escort Italian prisoners of war. It was there that the Regimental song 'Sweet Banana' first began and, although it would evolve significantly, it would retain its chorus of 'I will buy you a sweet banana', influenced by the abundance of the fruit in Natal.

A, B, C, D, E, Headquarter,
Ndichakutengera Sweet Banana.

A, B, C, D, E, Headquarter,
Ndichakutengera Sweet Banana.
Banana, Banana, Banana,
Ndichakutengera Sweet Banana.

Nhowo, pfumo netsvimbo,
Ndiyo RAR.
Muhondo ne runyararo,
Ndichakutengera Sweet Banana.

Burma, Egypt ne Malaya,
Takarwa tika kunda.
Federation ne Rhodesia,
Takarwa tika kunda.
Muhondo, Muhondo, Muhondo,
Inorwa no kushinga.

One, Two, Three, Depot RAR,
Ndidzo ndichapedza hondo dzodze.
One, Two, Three, Depot RAR,
Ndidzo ndichapedza hondo dzodze.
Banana, Banana, Banana,
Ndichakutengera Sweet Banana.

A, B, C, D, E, Headquarter,
Ndichakutengera Sweet Banana.
A, B, C, D, E, Headquarter,

Ndichakutengera Sweet Banana.
Banana, Banana, Banana,
Ndichakutengera Sweet Banana.

Burma

On 17 November 1943, the RAR left Salisbury for Kenya to join the 26th East Africa Brigade. Training continued until 5 September 1944, when they entrained for Mombasa to board HMT Strathaven and set sail for Ceylon. After acclimatisation and orientation to living, moving and fighting in the jungle, on 2 December they boarded HMT Aronda for Chittagong, in the Arakan, Burma. There, as part of the 22nd East African Infantry Brigade, they came under command the 15th Indian Corps, part of Field Marshall William Slim's 14th Army, fighting the Japanese.

The RAR were to face a formidable enemy. Of the Japanese, Field Marshall Slim wrote: 'The strength of the Japanese Army lay... in the spirit of the individual Japanese soldier. He fought and marched till he died. If 500 Japanese were ordered to hold a position, we had to kill 495 before it was ours – and then the last five killed themselves. It was this combination of obedience and ferocity that made the Japanese army, whatever its condition, so formidable...'

At this stage of the War, the Japanese advance towards India had been halted and they were withdrawing through Burma. The RAR formed part of this pursuit, advancing through the jungle and making sporadic contact with the enemy.

In April 1945, the East Africa Brigade was serving under command the 82nd West African Division which had been tasked with clearing the Taungup area of Japanese. After the Brigade had occupied the town of Palawa, the RAR battalion was given the lead and, on 15 April, they advanced towards an enemy position on a hill beyond Dalet, following the south bank of the Tanlwe Chaung. They soon closed with the Japanese and, over the next ten days, fought them in series of encounter actions in the jungle, culminating on 26 April with a deliberate attack by A and D companies on two dug-in hill features code-named Bergner and Valerie. Both enemy positions were successfully taken, at a cost of seven Askari killed and one officer and twenty-two Askari wounded. On 27 April, C Company assisted 1KAR in an assault on another feature, code-named Abbott, occupied after the enemy withdrew that night.

The Brigade continued the advance, now following Taungup Chaung and the RAR battalion took the lead again on 2 May. Crossing Taungup Chaung, D Company came under effective enemy fire from a feature code-named Powell. On the morning of 4 May, B and C companies advanced on Powell, beginning an engagement that would last until 7 May, at a cost of six Askari killed, until the Brigade was ordered to bypass the feature and move to the Taungup-Prome road. Encounter actions with small groups of Japanese continued until the formal surrender by Japan on 17 July 1945. Afterwards, engagements continued sporadically against 'no-surrender' groups.

In March 1946, the battalion began its long journey homewards, returning to Salisbury on 10 May. The RAR was represented at the Victory Parade in London on 8 June 1946 and the band at the foot of the dais struck up Sweet Banana as the RAR contingent approached.

References:
Binda, A 2007, *Masodja*, 30 Degrees South, Pinetown, South Africa.
McLaughlin, P 1980, *Ragtime Soldiers*, Books of Zimbabwe, Bulawayo, Zimbabwe.

TANLWE CHAUNG by Brigadier John 'Digger' Essex-Clark

As a subbie in 1RAR, starting when I was commissioned in October 1954, I knew nothing about our Regimental Day on which we celebrated the Battle of Tanlwe Chaung on 26th April 1945. I didn't even know how to pronounce the words correctly. However, recently I spoke with a Burmese speaking military attaché at the Myanmar Embassy who, understandably, did not know that Rhodesians had fought with the British Forces in then Burma. He pronounced it as "Tunnelwear Chorng".

A chaung in that area of Burma is usually a steep-sided, tree root-tangled, vines and debris-obstructed, creek or large stream, and not a route for anything but very patient and determined persons; or mad monkeys, he added; though many chaungs in that part of Burma had roadways or donkey-cart pathways beside them.

My information and this potted story come from articles from the US Marine Corps Studies Center, in US Military Intelligence electronic format; bits of the archived '*History of the RNR and RAR*' by Lt Col Kim Rule; and the comprehensive '*Masodja*' compiled and written by David Heppenstall and Alexandre Binda. I have also been helped by some fine research by Gerry van Tonder and Alan Doyle.

Information about the battle is limited and confusing, probably because no one seems to have the Operation Order for the attack by 1RAR, or its Orbat, or the detail of the attack on the twin peaks, or decent maps. It seems to have been a series of heavy-fighting, rifle company skirmishes to force the Japanese off the twin peaks, nicknamed 'Valerie' and 'Bergner', (probably using the names of popular film stars Valerie Hobson and Ingrid Bergman with the latter miss-spelt, with shades of 'King Solomon's Mines' representing female breasts).

Descriptions provided by the written material pleasantly bombard one with a heartfelt fervour for the RAR, and two matters stand brilliantly in my mind.

Firstly, the courage, conviction and tactical nous of our RAR soldiers under fire in attack, plus, their steadfastness when on patrol. Also, we observe that the askari of 1RAR responded wilfully and enthusiastically to good leadership, especially that of Rhodesian officers.

Secondly, the exemplary leadership, initiative under pressure, common sense and tenacious courage under fire of Major Stanley Ernest Morris. This was Morris's first action in combat. He was a volunteer from the staff of the Rhodesian Native Affairs Department. He may have been a Rhodesian Territorial Force member, I do not know, but he was an 'Emergency Commission' during the war, so he may not have received effective military training before or during the war.

Although 1RAR had superbly slogged south through the jungle, along muddy roads and paths, with heavy loads of resupply stores to reach and join the East African 22nd Brigade, the battalion had yet to show its mettle in battle. Therefore, it was time to show our allies our 'battle-worthiness' and prove how thoroughbred Ma'Oto (warrior in chiShona), our Askari were. This they did with outstanding and continual bursts of bravery under fire on every attack or fighting patrol. Few individual Askari's names were mentioned though many European officers were so, in the available narratives.

Each rifle company had four rifle platoons, so 1 to 4 platoons were in A company and 13, 14, 15 and 16 platoons were in D Coy, and so back. Administration Coy also had the mule trains and Indian, militarily-untrained muleteers, and the battalion HQ was boosted by liaison officers and artillery FOOs, plus additional medical and veterinary attachments.

The Japanese may have been undernourished and despondent, but they still fought with fervour and tactical nous having already defeated the Brits in the Arakan. That's why they were defending the twin hills to prevent our brigade using the available routes on either side of the twins to stop us reaching Taungup to the south.

The Japanese troops were also scared of us because they thought African soldiers were 'fighters to the death' and cannibals also; and that they would rather be killed in action than eaten. Many Japanese died on the steep slopes of both hill objectives over the three days of the battle. The 24th and 25th were used to vigorously reconnoitre the Japanese positions on and around the twin peaks, irrespective of the jungle and impenetrable bamboo hiding the Japanese actual and dummy positions.

On the final day, the 26th started with the preparatory bombardment from 'Hurribombers' (Hurricane fighter aircraft stripped for bombing) and Spitfires in strafing tasks, and then by 57mm US M3 Mountain-gun bombardment from a Nigerian artillery battery. The fight started with 2 Platoon of A Company, under CSM van Heerden, taking *Bergner*. Finding the enemy foxholes on the forward slopes empty, with the Japanese rushing down to re-occupy them, the platoon charged forward and drove the Japanese back to the reverse slopes. This initiative carried 2 Platoon to the top of *Bergner* from where they watched the Japanese retreat into a chaung to the south.

2 Platoon was joined on *Bergner* by D Company led by the big booming-voiced and much respected, as would a Matabele induna, Major S.E. Morris.

Advancing on the track linking *Bergner* with *Valerie*, D Company, with 13 Platoon in the vanguard, came under heavy MMG, LMG and sniper fire, losing momentum when the platoon commander was wounded. Major Morris came forward to take personal command of the forward troops and, with a little flank support by the battalion armourer with a Bren, charged down the saddle linking *Bergner* and *Valerie* under heavy and raking Japanese MMG fire, mortars and hand-grenades. They successfully eliminated the Japanese and took *Valerie*. A few Japanese ran into an NRR stop group further down the spur from *Valerie*.

Morris's leadership, aggression and ultimate common sense seems to have won the day for 1RAR. Morris and his Askari, as were many other Askari on that cordite stanched, bullet crackling and shell crumped day, exemplars of the old adage: 'If you win without risk: you triumph without glory'. Major S.E. Morris was Mentioned in Despatches for his gallantry, leadership and aggression in that action.

From Tanlwe Chaung, 1RAR went on to assist in causing the Japs to withdraw from Taungup, another vital possession in the defeat of the Japanese in the Arakan area. The Japanese now, however, had virtually given up and, after the nuclear bombs on Hiroshima and Nagasaki, then surrendered. It took time to get the word to the forward Japanese troops in Burma and 1RAR was involved in tidying up the mess of uncontrolled Japanese units and well-armed gangs that were let loose after the war had officially ended.

1RAR returned home to Southern Rhodesia, having now earned its first battle honour 'Burma' for its future Colours.

LETTERS FROM BURMA by Captain Andrew Telfer

This article borrows its title and sources from the work of historian Timothy Stapleton who, quoting from letters written by RAR soldiers to the Bantu Mirror and to the regimental magazine, provides a fascinating insight of impressions formed on our men while fighting the Japanese in Burma.

The letter of an RAR schoolteacher, S.S.B Chekergwa, reflects a utopian view of the happy world he felt he lived in: 'We have a big congregation that will surprise you. Friendship in Christ is satisfying. We don't put each other down – we don't insult each other – it is smooth sailing my friend with no discrimination between big and small.' In a slightly more down-to-earth take on the situation, and perhaps a more recognisable one, Private Majora, in Burma for Christmas, wrote that he 'enjoyed the beer and meat and singing'. Whereas, for us in later years, every RAR pungwe would end with the singing of *Sweet Banana*, in Burma in 1944, *Ishe Komberera Afrika* closed the party.

The Burma terrain was tough going. Warrant Officer Peter, from Plumtree, described being driven along jungle roads: 'many of our journeys are rather bad and frightening, for the tracks are so slippery and the track slopes towards the valley. The trucks sway and swing all over the track and the valley is so far below that I was too frightened to look down.' Private Elias Mutambanengwe of Zimunya, near Umtali, wrote about the foot journeys: 'Our march seemed an endless walk up one hill, down another... We had full packs on, of course, and after a few miles the packs, rifles and ammunition seemed to weigh a ton. Sometimes we sang lively tunes on the march, but more often we sang sad tunes.'

The impressions made were deep, an eye-opening experience for men who had hardly travelled before. Private Augustu: 'if all the people saw what we saw while we were in this country of South East Asia they would not be people who have sleepy brains. We have seen a lot in this world... We are seeing a lot of things that are amazing, all things which I cannot talk about... We saw a country being destroyed and being built up.'

The kindness of our soldiers and their ability to get along well with rural people are qualities that are well-known to us. Stapleton notes them too, writing how Private Chiweshe described with sympathy how Burmese civilians' homes and fields had been destroyed in the fighting. Chiweshe also described how Burmese, many of whom had initially supported the Japanese, changed allegiance when they experienced how the RAR shared food with them and respected their women.

Private Mucateteyi told those at home, in characteristic RAR understatement, that 'the soldiers of this country of yours are doing an exceptional job here in the bush in Burma.' Having given himself an 'A', he referred to one of the myths that the Japanese had regarding black Africans: 'the Japanese think that we Africans eat people... When we are fighting, the Japanese will carry their dead and run away with them.' Stapleton writes that the RAR soldiers exploited this myth as psychological warfare, encouraging it by telling local people that they were indeed cannibals.

Sergeant Mbunyungu describes, when patrolling, how 'we had to be very careful where we walked, because the enemy had made all sorts of traps to catch us. They used the grenades to explode under our feet, and in some places, they laid mines – blocks of dynamite hidden under the soil – to destroy us.' He could have been speaking of any soldier in any war, when he wrote, 'do not think that we soldiers have fear; all soldiers, whether European, African or Indian become used to the sounds and sights of war, and the things a man knows do not frighten him.'

Sergeant James Ojesi Kachingwe was unimpressed with his enemy: 'The Japs looked such fearsome little rats; they squawked like goats. But when the fight developed away went my vertical breeze (fear), for the Japs cannot face an enemy, they rely on tricks; and we have now learnt their tricks... for we have killed them like flies in some fights.' His comments are reminiscent of the contempt in which the RAR soldiers of the 1970s held their enemies.

Private Kalaluka, described an ambush of a Japanese unit that was advancing to counter-attack near Tanlwe Chaung: 'We lay just off the track, I myself, lying just ahead of the remainder of the patrol forming the ambush. We had been lying there for half an hour when noises and rustling were heard. Then I saw several Jap soldiers crawling along, carrying machineguns. I let the first Jap get past me and then I heard the others of our patrol throwing the Bren gun into position. Unfortunately, the Bren gun jammed, and so I had to fire with my rifle, killing the second in line Jap at a range of five yards. I wounded a second Jap, for he screamed – how the Japs can scream! This man let go his machinegun and off he trotted. The machinegun we captured.'

Anyone who has been in action with the RAR can hear the words, even the accent, of Francis Mtirima, who wrote: 'My friends war is something which is amazing, if you hear the sounds of artillery you don't hear it as guns you hear it as thundering rain 'Huuv..., Guuu...' only. However, the soldiers are strong, they say 'here it comes, here it comes', this is for men only. Then you are determined to see the enemy, so that when you meet, only the guns will be talking like popcorn saying 'kwa-kwa-kwa, gu-gu-gu.' Guns will be saying 'gu-gu-gu.' Tanks will be saying 'gwa-gwa-gwa.' So I am happy for the end of the war because all these things are finished, water does not mix with blood.'

The final word should go to Regimental Sergeant Major Stephen Machado Banda BEM CPM, who wrote in 1945:

'I am proud to be in this battalion of brave men who fight, even as do the elephants, in this deep green jungle. We met the enemy who shelled us violently with his great guns, but they failed to make us turn away from the fight. We fought on until the enemy was outwitted and defeated, and through bravery and the help of God our losses were not big.

'Since the birth of the regiment I have known it. Since its formation I have done what I could to teach these men of the Rhodesian African Rifles. I have seen the glorious results of that teaching of mine and of the officers of the regiment.

'And today, we all smile together. For, have we not fought and risked our lives side by side to keep our land safe from the horrible things we have seen here? And the war being over, we feel that we may think of our fighting comrades and - having seen what the war can cause to people and lands - may humbly say, Ishe komberera Africa (God save Africa). We, who have known, sing these words with our thoughts resting on them, and our eyes seeing desolate lands, and the graves of the soldiers of the Rhodesian African Rifles.'

References

Stapleton, T 2010, *Letters from Burma: Views of Black Zimbabwean Soldiers during the Second World War*, in Falola, T & Njoku, R (eds.) 2010, *War and Peace in Africa*, Carolina Academic Press, Durham, N.C.

Stapleton, T 2010, *Extra-Territorial African Police and Soldiers in Southern Rhodesia (Zimbabwe) 1897–1965*, Scientia Militaria, South African Journal of Military Studies, Vol 38, Nr 1.

WHEN THEY'RE NOT FIGHTING... by Corporal Alan Doyle

...they're fighting: the story of soldiers everywhere, and no different for 1RAR in WWII. The Battalion's War Diaries tell not only of the patrolling and the battles, but also the ever growing list of conducts prejudicial: the booze, the women, and the brawling which are the stuff of every military life.

The battalion left Salisbury for East Africa on November 1943, in two drafts travelling by train up through the Copper Belt and cutting through the Belgian Congo and Tanganyika to Nairobi. It didn't take long for one soldier to decide there were better things in life than soldiering. Pte Kabuyi took off in Elizabethville and was never seen again.

Jungle training for the Far East took place along the Kenya/Tanganyika border, and in April 1944 the first crime-of-crimes - the accidental discharge – took place. Pte Davis pulled the trigger of his rifle in error, wounding three of his comrades, one of whom, Pte Malenge, later died of his injuries. Not long afterwards, local thieves entered the camp and made off with the personal effects of some of the officers. Nothing army-issue went missing. No change there, then.

When troops are kept busy, lapses in discipline subside. But after several months of manoeuvres and mock battles across the Kenyan/Tanganyikan savannah, the battalion took R&R at Yatta. Within hours, Pte Suwake was badly injured in a fracas in the nearby village of Liba Kasini. The regimental police soon reported that there were many RAR men at Liba Kasini, resulting in two officers and a picquet being dispatched to restore order. The after effects of the incident rattled on for several weeks, with the CO and two other officers summoned to a Court of Enquiry in Nairobi, where they no doubt had to plead in mitigation for their soldiers.

In September the battalion arrived in Ceylon, setting up camp at Horana, south of the capital, Colombo. Pretty soon, Pte Kukwesha and his truck failed to return from the bright lights. Four days later, two officers were sent to track him down. "No luck!" the War Diarist noted in the margin. It was almost two weeks before Kukwesha drove his truck back into camp one evening. There is no record of him being punished. Must have been one serious party in the fleshpots of Colombo.

In October, the first batch of RAR men were sentenced to imprisonment abroad. Ptes Zimanye, Bawa, Jeffery and Jim were joined in the Mahara Detention Barracks by Pte Kwemba (28 days for disobeying an order) and Ptes Chigodo and Fazwe, serving similar terms. Another man, Pte Mwinga, an ambulance driver attached to 1RAR, was sued in the civil court in Tangalle. Whatever the claim against him, it failed, and he returned to duty. Pte Chigodo took his own life after three weeks in prison.

In January, the saga of Pte Chidamba began. He was sentenced to 42 days hard labour and was escorted to Kamilla Detention Barracks in Ceylon on 3 January 1945. The weekly X-Lists (showing which members of the battalion were elsewhere) still showed him to be there on 14 April 1945, 14 weeks later. The X-lists aren't filed with the War Diaries after that date. For all we know, he may still be there in Kamilla. (Although, it may be that he was not actually imprisoned at that later date. 1RAR were by April engaged in heavy fighting in the Arakan, and sending him back to join his unit may not have been practical.) Later in January, two soldiers accused of sodomy appeared in front of the CO. They were acquitted.

Twenty-odd years after the RAR were in Ceylon, the term "fragging" gained currency amongst American soldiers in Vietnam. 1RAR had its own fragging incident in late February 1945, when a Type 36 grenade was thrown into a dug-out occupied by Maj Brown, one of the company commanders. Brown was injured and evacuated, and never returned to the battalion. No culprits were ever found. The last incident in Ceylon of any import was on 21 March, when Pte Bengesa accidentally discharged his rifle into his foot.

When the fighting in Burma ended in September 1945 the incidence of indiscipline resurged. So many soldiers were going AWOL that offenders were dealt with at Field General Courts Martial, rather than CO's orders. The mere possession of "local liquor" was punishable. Warning after warning appeared in Battalion Orders. One week, soldiers had to be told that ALL brothels were "Out of Bounds" even those which did not have a notice outside stating that they were "Out of Bounds". Punishments were harsh. Three months imprisonment was the standard tariff. In February and March 1946, more than a dozen FGCMs were held for this type of offence. Few were found not guilty. Such is the behaviour of an occupying army.

But there is one incident in particular which is tragic. It took place in March 1944, long before 1RAR ever got to the Far East. The battalion's first RSM was RSM Lechanda DCM MM. He dropped dead of a heart attack during a training route march in Salisbury. RSM Tekete DCM (MID) took over from him, and travelled to East Africa with the battalion. Some documents say he returned to Salisbury because a medical condition prevented him accompanying the troops to Ceylon. But the War Diary has a single entry for 30 March:

"12h00, RHO 548 RSM Tekete DCM sent to Transit Camp Nairobi for repatriation to S. Rhodesia on Bde Comd's instrs, in lieu of disciplinary action being taken against him for getting drunk and fighting with a Pte when he (the RSM) was on duty."

Tragic, because this is the citation for the DCM awarded to him during WWI:

"640 Clr Sjt. Tegete, N. Rhodn. Police. (EAST AFRICA) At Fusi Village, on 4th October, 1918. While under heavy machine-gun fire he set an outstanding example to all present, showing complete disregard of danger by walking up and down the line giving the men targets and controlling their fire. At Fife, 1st/2nd November, 1918, he showed conspicuous gallantry and devotion to duty."

As one former RAR officer said of this incident: "I think there might be a few defaulters who, like this man, are more 'character' than 'criminal'. There's a type of soldier who does well in battle but gets into trouble at other times. I honestly don't think I would have obeyed the Brigadier and sent him home if I'd been the CO. I would have squirrelled him away and taken him, quietly, as a CSM. Who leaves a guy like that behind when you're going to fight the Japanese?"

SOLDIERS FOR RHODESIA by Captain Andrew Telfer

It is not well-known that, during the First World War, between 60 and 70 percent of the askari in the Rhodesia Native Regiment (RNR) originated from countries other than Southern Rhodesia. Of the approximately 2,500 men who served in the RNR, about 1,000 came from Nyasaland (now Malawi), 250 from Northern Rhodesia (now Zambia), 200 from Mozambique and a smattering from other nearby territories. Some had previous military experience while many were migrant workers recruited from the mines of Southern Rhodesia.

Examining RNR records, historian Timothy Stapleton identifies examples of individual soldiers with prior military experience from outside Southern Rhodesia: Lance Corporal Chikoko had ten years' experience, six of them in the King's African Rifles (KAR) in Nyasaland and four in the BSAP; Private Sofora was a six-year veteran of the KAR and five in the Northern Rhodesia Police; Lance Corporal Lupenga, wounded in September 1918 while a signaller in the RNR, had previously held the same post for five years in the KAR; and Corporal Ndala, killed on active service in May 1918, had six years in the KAR before joining the RNR.

During the Second World War, about 45 percent of Rhodesian African Rifles soldiers originated from outside Southern Rhodesia. Among them were highly experienced African Warrant Officers and NCOs, many veterans of external conflicts, who played a vital early part in the RAR. The most notable of them were the battalion's first Regimental Sergeant Majors.

The RAR's first RSM, WO1 Lechanda DCM, MM was from Nyasaland. He had fought with the KAR in Somaliland in 1909 and in the East African campaign of the Great War, where he was decorated for several assaults on German positions. When he was demobilised in 1919, he moved to Southern Rhodesia and was on hand to join the RAR as it was formed in 1940. The old soldier regrettably died during a route march in Salisbury in October 1942.

His successor as RSM was WO1 Tekete DCM who had served in the Northern Rhodesia Police during the East Africa campaign, where he was awarded the DCM for conspicuous gallantry when, on 4 October 1918, 'while under heavy machine gun fire he set an outstanding example to all present, showing complete disregard of danger by walking up and down the line giving the men targets and controlling their fire'. He went with the RAR to East Africa in 1944 but did not continue to Burma for reasons described in the previous article.

The third RSM was WO1 Stephen Machado Banda. In 1927, he walked barefoot in search of work from Nyasaland to Southern Rhodesia where he enlisted in the BSAP Askari Platoon. How's that for great values? WO1 Machado was one of the instructors seconded to the RAR on formation in 1940. He was RSM during the Burma campaign, where he was known as a 'tough fighter' and, in 1946, was selected as part of Southern Rhodesia's contingent at the Victory Parade in London. A great man, whose famous letter written at the end of the war appears in the Dedication of *Chibaya Moyo 1* and, in this volume, in *Letters from Burma*.

Regional experience led to different skills, which were put to good use in Burma. An officer, who served there with the RAR, wrote that amphibious operations were challenging 'for Africans, many of whom came from Western Matabeleland where water is usually scarce and never navigable. At such times… each platoon marked down its men from the Zambezi and Lake Nyasa. Burmese boats are usually plain dugouts or a type of catamaran, but allow a Mulozwi or a Nyanja to make his own paddle and the craft was his… At one river crossing I remember, two Nyanjas from the lake ferried over a company of 150 men with kit, in two tiny craft holding no more than five men each.'

As sources of recruitment changed, so did the languages in use in the RAR. The Askari of the RNR during the First World War spoke isiNdebele, chiShona, chiNyanja and Yao (the latter two from Nyasaland) and some sub-units were grouped linguistically. By the Second World War, the predominant language of the RAR was chiNyanja. This persisted until the Malayan Emergency when Brigadier John 'Digger' Essex-Clark DSM, in 1956 a Second Lieutenant, recalls his frustration at being required to learn the language when 'the Nyasas were only a small element of the battalion and most of my askari spoke chiShona or isiNdebele.' Times had changed, and he was clearly observing the decreased representation of soldiers from other countries in the RAR.

External recruitment declined in the 1950s and 1960s as opportunities for military service improved in the recruits' home countries. Eventually, as neighbouring states came into conflict with post-UDI Rhodesia, the practice ceased. Recruitment of local people for the RAR expanded to take its place and the lingua franca of the RAR became chiShona. We should never forget, however, the tremendous contribution made to the RNR and the RAR by young men who came to Rhodesia in search of a better future and were prepared to fight for it.

References
Stapleton, T 2010, *Extra-Territorial African Police and Soldiers in Southern Rhodesia (Zimbabwe) 1897–1965*, Scientia Militaria, South African Journal of Military Studies, Vol 38, Nr 1.
Walker, W 1944, *1ˢᵗ Battalion the Rhodesian African Rifles, East Africa War Diary*

CHAPTER FOUR

MALAYA

INTRODUCTION: THE RAR IN MALAYA by Captain Andrew Telfer

During the war against Japan, the ethnic-Chinese in Malaya allied themselves to the British, who armed and trained them as members of the Malayan People's Anti-Japanese Army, an operation most famously chronicled by Lt Col Frederick Spencer Chapman in *The Jungle is Neutral*. After the WW II, armed with British resources recovered from jungle caches, the same ethnic-Chinese formed the Malayan Communist Party and began an insurgency against British colonial rule. No longer referred to as 'freedom fighters' but as Communist Terrorists (CTs), they began to attack soft targets, ambushing ex-patriate rubber planters and tin miners. Britain needed the tin and rubber for its post-War economy, so a state of emergency was declared in June 1948: the 'Malayan Emergency'.

Brigadier John Essex-Clark, who fought in Malaya as a subaltern, makes the interesting observation that it 'was titled an *emergency* so that the rubber and tin industries could claim against Lloyd's insurers, something they would not have been able to do if it had been declared a *war*' (van Tonder 2017, p. 124).

Whether it was a fight against Communism, or to protect British economic interests, or both, the usual call went out to the Commonwealth to come and fight for Britain, and once again Rhodesia loyally answered it. Rhodesian military involvement in the Malayan Emergency began in 1951 with a two-year deployment of a 100-man South East Asia Volunteer Unit (later C Squadron SAS) commanded by (then) Major G.P. Walls.

On 13 February 1956, an RAR advance party flew to Malaya to begin training and orientation with 1st Northern Rhodesia Regiment, who the RAR were to relieve, and 1 Fiji Infantry Regiment. While this took place, the battalion embarked on HMT Empire Clyde at Beira, arriving at Singapore on 26 April. From there they moved to the Far East Land Forces Training Centre in Johore where they came under command of 99 Gurkha Infantry Brigade and were orientated by the advance party including, for the first time, training with helicopters.

Deployed in June and operating from platoon 'jungle bases', sections sought to engage the elusive CTs in the thick jungle, employing fighting patrols, long- and short-term ambush operations, and gaining limited kills in fleeting contacts. It was the type of warfare that did not yield many kills for any unit operating in Malaya but, as the Americans were to learn in Vietnam, kill rates do not necessarily measure success. The intensive patrolling and presence among the civilian population maintained constant pressure on the enemy which, together with the granting of Malayan independence from British rule in August 1957, led to many CT surrenders and the eventual end of the Emergency.

Early in February 1958, the battalion completed its two-year tour of duty and moved to Nee Soon transit camp in Singapore. They returned via Beira and Umtali to Bulawayo, to find their barracks much improved in their absence and re-named Methuen Camp after their honorary colonel.

References:
Binda, A 2007, *Masodja*, 30 Degrees South, Pinetown, South Africa.
van Tonder, G 2017, *Malayan Emergency*, Pen and Sword Military, Barnsley, UK.

A SURPRISED SUBBIE by Brigadier John 'Digger' Essex-Clark

When I arrived in 1RAR in 1954, I had just been commissioned without any formal officer training whatsoever. I had been schooled in Australia, the UK and South Africa. I was, however, a trained drill and infantry weapons instructor and had just finished running the Drill Hall (B Coy, 1RRR) in Umtali.

My only experience with Africans was with my servants and my general factotum, Mr Dudzai, and his range staff in Umtali, so I could speak a little Fanagolo. Suddenly, I was a platoon commander with 35 raw African recruits straight from the Bundu and town reserves in Southern Rhodesia and Barotseland,

2 Lt John 'Digger' Essex-Clark, May 1956

49

plus two Nyasas who had had a tour in Malaya with 1 and 2 KAR.

We all had clear instructions that we were to learn chiNyanja, the language from Nyasaland's lake area which only the two Nyasas spoke. I was very fortunate to have three corporals: Tabuya, Jere and Taderera; one sergeant, Gondocondo, and one WO2, Pisayi Muzericho, as my platoon warrant officer, and all those five spoke good English and were my leadership and verbal conduit to my Askari. I thought that I was pretty flash on our infantry small arms but when I took our leader-group of six to our nearby 25-yard range I was shaken to find that their weapons handling and shooting accuracy was as good if not better than mine.

My Askari were intelligent but they were sadly uneducated, and our best English speakers had been snaffled by the Signals, Mortar, Headquarters, Int section and Administration platoons. I thought this was to our advantage as platoon commanders, because those we got sought improvement in their lives instead of being cocksure, over-confident and clerically-oriented. The challenge I faced with my platoon was to twist intelligence into knowledge and self-confidence so, teaching them to read and understand what they read was important to me. How to use weapons was hands-on and easy for my WO and NCOs, whereas my taking them and teaching them English and how to read would boost their self-confidence and morale, and our bonds, and make for better understanding in combat. I was sure, as were my Askari, that they wanted to learn English.

I got some slightly soiled but well used English primers from my Anglican friends in Umtali and elsewhere. I cut up plates of 3-ply and painted them with blackboard paint and made a slate for each of them plus white chalk and old nappies from the married quarters. So, each Askari had a slate-style writing implement and erasing material. We used the phonetic system of sounds related to the pictures, the alphabet and letters in capitals and script, personal pronouns, action verbs and simple items such as parts of the body.

We would hold up a slate on which was drawn a picture of equipment and its English military term, with the word in chiNyanja, chiShona, and isiNdebele. We concentrated on militarily useful words. I knew we were getting somewhere from the enthusiasm of the Askari, and not only from our own platoon. An Askari would often ask me to read him a word from his bible, from the bold characters in an African newspaper or a letter from a personal friend.

From there, we went on to simple mathematics such as plus and minus, then navigation using the protractor, compass and map (the magic stuff and the big leap forward). Then I gave them harmonica lessons and soon we had a band titled 'The Glee Club'.

This kept me both busy and satisfied beyond just training my platoon for operations in Malaya. We were also making more confident and better soldiers and ultimately worthy citizens, and I was learning sufficient chiNyanja, chiShona and isiNdebele to lead my platoon effectively in the language of my Askari.

THE LESONG SEARCH (THE DIARY) by Brigadier David Heppenstall

Introduction

This is the true account of an operation undertaken by 4 Platoon, B Company, 1RAR reinforced by a section of the Battalion's mortar platoon against Communist terrorists (CTs) of the South Malay Bureau in the deep jungle border area of South Pahang. Negri Sembilan and Johore over the period February to April 1957.

It was unusual for two reasons. In the first place there was a certain individuality about its inception, and secondly, although the losses inflicted on the enemy were negligible, the value of the intelligence gained was of great importance and filled in many gaps in the overall picture of the organisation, supply and habits of the South Malay Bureau. Within a year Hor Lung the leader of the South Malay Bureau would surrender with all his staff.

Events Leading up to the Operation

Over the latter weeks of 1956, Bill Curnow-Baker 2ic B Coy 1RAR and David Heppenstall OC 4 Platoon B Company 1RAR had many discussions on terrorists' habits and area of operations and were very keen to get into the area of the borders of South Pahang, Negri Sembilan and Johore.

The seed of the operation was sown one January day in 1957 at the B Company camp on the Dunlop Estate at Ladang Geddes in Negri Sembilan. The company had been moved up from Labis, 60 miles to the South, in order to have a better operational base for a crack at the South Malay Bureau chief, Hor Lung, with his bodyguard from 32 Independent Platoon, Malayan Races Liberation Army (MRLA) who were thought to frequent the area around and about the northern loop of the Palong river where the boundaries of Pahang, Negri Sembilan and Johore join.

The occasion was the visit of Brigadier Harris, Commander of 1 Federal Brigade, in which the battalion was operation at that time. The brigadier, Lt Col Jock Anderson (CO 1RAR) and Chief Superintendent John West (OC Police District Bahau) stayed to lunch and during coffee an interesting discussion on terrorist tactics developed. John West elaborated on his account of time spent on operations with C (Rhodesia) Squadron 22 SAS in South Pahang in 1951. These operations had been mounted to free the Aborigines in the Lesong Forest Reserve from CT domination to which they had been completely subservient at that time. The operation had been almost 100% successful and nearly all the Sakai were persuaded to leave the area and resettle where they could obtain protection from the Security Forces in the future.

The account of these operations had raised the interest of all those present, but none more so than Captain Bill Curnow-Baker the 2ic of B Company. He was convinced that an area as large as this, and one that had been neglected by the Security Forces for six years should provide good opportunities for those troops lucky enough to be chosen to mount an operation there. He explained all his theories to Brigadier Harris and Lt Col Anderson and expressed his willingness to go into the area for any length of time and with any troops that could be spared.

Both senior officers agreed that such a deployment was well overdue, but there would undoubtedly be a problem. The food denial operations of 'Cobble' in Segamat and 'Shoe' in the Labis/Yong Peng area were well under way, and it was obvious that the local District War Executive Committees (DWECs) would disagree with the syphoning off of any troops from their areas for use on operations which did not appear to be wholly in support of the efforts to make their own areas 'white' first. Only time would tell!

A Contact on the River Sekin

By the beginning of February 1957, the food denial operations around Labis, Chaah and Bekok were stepped up with increased patrol activity around the jungle and rubber edge in order to deny the CTs contact with their informers and food suppliers from the new villages. This necessitated the return of B Company from Ladang Geddes to their camp just South of Labis.

The first confirmed report of CT activity in South Pahang that the Battalion received was in the second week of February 1957, part of an intelligence summary given by the military intelligence officer (MIO) to the Segamat DWEC. The report indicated that, acting on information received from Aborigines living at Kampong Kedaik on the Rompin River, the Police Lieutenant from Kampong Aur had patrolled south from Kampong Kong King down the river Sekin to search for any sign of CTs.

At the junction of the Rivers Sekin and Seplap he had contacted and fired at a lone armed Chinaman who managed to escape, although possibly wounded. He returned to his base at Kampong Aur, and after submitting his report returned to the area of the contact with a Police Active Service Unit (ASU) to search the area thoroughly.

Although there could have been opposition from the DWEC to the use of troops normally at their disposal at a distance of some 50 to 60 miles North of Operation Cobble's usual operational area, it was pointed out that it was practical for the CTs to transport supplies from this far away down through the deep jungle to relieve the pressure on their hard-pressed branches further South.

The jungle bordering the River Rompin in South Pahang had been classified 'white' (terrorist free) some two years earlier. In practice this meant that Security Force activity in this area was restricted to a few small local police patrols which were completely inadequate to stop the flow of food to the CTs. The latter were also completely adept at deep jungle cultivation and these areas had not always been located by air recce.

Following the withdrawal of the Police ASU from the area it was decided that a reinforced platoon from 1RAR would be deployed into the area South of the Rompin River to search for CT sign and build up a picture of the area which had remained fallow since C (Rhodesia) Squadron 22 SAS had brought out the local Sakai some six years before.

As soon as this decision had been reached, Lt Col Jock Anderson told Bill Curnow-Baker that his operation was on, and OC B Company, Major John Salt, was to inform Battalion HQ which platoon from his company would be detailed for the operation. Lieutenant David Heppenstall (4 Platoon) and Lieutenant John Thompson (6 Platoon) tossed for the privilege and the former won, much to his delight and John Thompson's disappointment. The deployment into the area would

Members of 4 Pl, B Coy, 1RAR boarding a Pioneer aircraft,
Thurs 21 1957 at Segam

be in seven days' time by Pioneer light aircraft to the Kampong Aur airstrip and the hustle and bustle of preparations began in earnest.

Thursday 21 February 1957

Reveille in the base camp at Labis at 0530hrs. Early breakfast at 0600hrs. Leave for Segamat Airstrip at 0640hrs. The convoy transport consisted of six x 1-ton trucks and a Ferret scout car. All vehicles are Battalion transport! Arrived at Segamat at 0750hrs. The first of four Pioneer aircraft arrived at 0820hrs and the lift in to Kampong Aur began at 0830hrs. The whole platoon and Police Lieutenant Bob Graver ferried in by 1245hrs. Arrangements had been made for the platoon to sleep at the Police Post that night prior to the thirty-mile journey downstream by boat on the following day. The troops were given the rest of the day off to look around the kampong and beat the Police 3-1 at soccer that afternoon. This was the first game of soccer ever played at Kampong Aur!

Friday 22 February 1957

Police Lieutenant Bob Graver GC and Pte King - Batman to Bill Curnow-Baker (right rear), Friday 22 Feb 1957

Moved off from Kampong Aur at 0915hrs in four boats, two of which belonged to the Police at Kampong Aur, one large flat bottomed to a Chinese trader and the other one to the Police at Fort Gambier. The boats were driven and piloted by Police from Kampong Aur. The journey down the river was very interesting. Included in the sights were Sakai kampongs, multi-coloured birds of many species and a crocodile who scuttled off a sandbank into the river as soon as he heard us coming.

Police Lieutenant Bob Graver shot a jungle fowl cock on the river bank. This was a welcome addition to the pot that evening. We arrived at the point of disembarkation at 1530hrs. One boat was sent on downstream to pick up the second Sakai guide at Kampong Kedaik, a big Sakai settlement about five miles downstream. They arrived back at the disembarkation point, the old deserted Kampong Kong King at 1920hrs just as it was getting dark.

Saturday 23 February 1957

15,000 yards were to be covered today to an LZ constructed two weeks previously by the Police at GR 376 538. Police Lieutenant Graver led the way with a Sakai guide over some very rough country south down the Eastern bank of the River Sekin. We based up GR 376 535, just South of the LZ at 1545hrs. We had no communications with Battalion HQ that evening, as although we can hear them, they cannot hear us.

Sunday 24 February 1957

0700hrs, established contact with Battalion HQ and gave them our position. General security patrols were carried out up to 3,000 yds from the base camp, but nothing to report. Air drop demand prepared for passing tomorrow.

Monday 25 February 1957

Corporal Mundingi and Lance Corporal Obert consult their map, Saturday 23 Feb 1957

Air supply demand submitted on wireless schedule at 0730hrs. This morning I went on a patrol with Police Lieutenant Bob Graver, Captain Bill Curnow-Baker and 3 section to check out a known permanent CT camp at GR 959 843. On the way caught the scent of decaying flesh wafting through the trees at GR 376 524. It could have been the CT contacted by Bob Graver. The area was thoroughly searched but NTR. Corporal Zwidzayi and his section were detailed to continue the search but to no avail. That afternoon we based up at GR 355 495 and I proceeded with a small patrol to the CT camp. On the way we passed a small resting place at GR 968 851 which appeared that it might have been visited within the last three days. The main CT base did not appear to have been visited since Bob Graver had found it. On our return journey, a CT camp was found at GR 354 492 for three to four CTs about five months old.

Tuesday 26 February 1957

Returned to base near LZ. The smell of decaying flesh at GR 376 524 still apparent but the source cannot be located. CO suggests we use dogs to try and locate where it is coming from. Dogs due in the following day by helicopter. A work party is busy improving the LZ which is substandard. We have asked for Auster recce to our South, South East and South West to search for CT cultivations.

Wednesday 27 February 1957

Sergeant Chimba with one section sets off on a two-day patrol West and South West to look for sign in the river Seplap area. Two dogs and handlers arrive by helicopter at 1230hrs with the info that the airdrop is coming in one day early, today at 1500hrs. The patrol dog with six men search the area of the smell, but NTR. We shall try tomorrow with both dogs. The airdrop comes in two and a half hours late at 1730hrs amid gathering storm clouds. Eleven packs are dropped in all. All goes well until the ninth, but the guy-ropes get caught up in the tail-plane and the pack (eighty African ration tins) is severed from the parachute. The Valetta has received some damage but drops the remaining two packs onto the LZ before leaving. The severed pack has twenty-three tins unserviceable and most of the remaining fifty-seven badly damaged.

Airdrops this late in the evening are very unsatisfactory. It was dark before all the packs were collected and so unpacking and checking could not be done until the following day. We were informed by wireless that the helicopter would come in to fetch out the two dogs and their handlers from the South Wales Borderers (1SWB) the following afternoon.

Thursday 28 February 1957

All the rations and clothing issued. Both dogs go out on a last attempt to locate the smell, but once again this proves unsuccessful. Sergeant Chimba returns in the afternoon with his patrol and reports that there is no evidence of CT activity in the river SEPLAP area. The CO comes in by helicopter at about 1715hrs and the dogs and their handlers go out. The CO stays for about half an hour and goes out about 1800hrs by helicopter. He had brought some beer, much good cheer! I was able to celebrate my 25th birthday the next day with a can of Castle lager. This had been my second birthday running in the Ulu (jungle) as in 1956 I had been on Advance Party of 1RAR and had been in the jungle with Peter Clayton's platoon of 1NRR.

Friday 01 March 1957

On this day Captain Bill Curnow-Baker set off on a three-day patrol with 2 section to the Tahalai cultivation area. Police Lieutenant Bob Graver accompanied by Corporal Mundingi and Private William went back North to the Rompin River to collect a sampan to recover the parachutes. The remainder of the personnel stayed in the base.

Saturday 02 March 1957

Two patrols under Corporal Paupila and Lance Corporal Taruberakera search the river Marat area (GS 3850 and 3851). Out all day but report NTR on return. Police Lieutenant Bob Graver returns at 1615 hrs with escort and one additional Malay Special Constable in the sampan. They had a lot of hard work coming up the River Sekin owing to the number of sand bars.

Sunday 03 March 1957

Privates Mutambo and Sanangu on patrol capture two large tortoises. Fresh meat on the hoof! Apparently, this meat is most delicious! Sunday 03 Mar 1957

57

Police Lieutenant Bob Graver leaves us for the last time in the sampan with his Malay Special Constable taking all the supply drop parachutes with him. I hadn't mentioned previously that Bob Graver who comes from Portsmouth had been awarded the George Cross for conspicuous gallantry against CTs. He had been awarded the George Cross as armed and uniformed police were civilians rather than members of the Security Forces! Lance Corporal Obert patrolled the Mesnab river area (GS 3954) but reported NTR. However, the patrol brought back three live tortoises – Fresh Meat on the hoof!!

Monday 04 March 1957

One serviceable SF type groundsheet recovered by Private Paison at GR 375 533. Probably lost by Police Patrol from Kampong Aur. Captain Curnow Baker returns at 1700hrs with reports of CT activity to the South East as follows:

GR 000 838   Tracks for 3 to 4 CTs going South East about two days old.

GR 018 832   Very large very old CT camp.

GR 054 793   Tracks for 3 to 4 CTs going North East one to two days old. Followed to GR 064 801.

This was on Sunday 03 March at approx. 1700hrs. The patrol had by then virtually finished its rations. Monday returned to base. That evening Captain Curnow-Baker gave the following orders: 'Any sick personnel to be casevaced tomorrow. Whole callsign to proceed to GR 058 808 on Wednesday with all remaining rations'

Tuesday 05 March 1957

In general, packing up and burning boxes and unserviceable clothing etc. Private Sanangu (flu), Private Msikiswa (swollen legs) and Private William (back strain?) casevaced by helicopter. Called for additional troops but none apparently available.

Wednesday 06 March 1957

Moved off at 0820hrs. The terrain was very rough. We based up for the day at GR 011 834. Security patrol found marks where one or two CTs had scaled a cliff at GR 011 833 about two days previously.

Thursday 07 March 1957

Packed up and on the move again by 0800hrs. 1 Section under Sergeant Chimba was left to search the River Haha area. Based up at GR 059 804. The plan is to ambush the CT track facing west and track it to the east,

Friday 08 March 1957

Moved off East on CT tracks with 3 Section and JCLO Cheah. At GR 072 802 found the old cultivation of Tahalai. Here the CT tracks which were about five days old were lost. The tracks were again picked up at GR 083 795. The tracks were now following the old CT courier route (1950/51) on which we had received prior information from OCPD Bahau (Mr West). The patrol based up for the night at GR 083 796. The Security patrol found a CT base for four to five about one month old at GR 084 795

Saturday 09 March 1957

Moved off 0730hrs. Between GR 099 796 and 109 791 hockey boot prints were visible in numerous spots. Two different spoor were seen. Tracks were lost again at GR 110 790 but picked up after a search at GR 119 787. At GR 124 788 a large Kepong tree had been cut down within the last four months and stripped of bark.

Semi-permanent CT camp Lesong Forest Reserve, March 1957

There were three fires near the tree and a camp on the river bank which had been occupied by about six CTs two weeks before. The camp which was a temporary one had been used on two or three different occasions. About half the bark off the Kepong tree was in this camp but the remainder couldn't be found.

There may well be a cultivation and a permanent camp within two to three thousand yards of this place. I based up at GR 128 789 and then patrolled forward with Lance Corporal Obert and found the following:

GR 139 789 a camp for three or four CTs about one year old.

GR 142 790 a camp for five or six CTs about four months old, used three weeks and five days previously. We found a large fish trap in the river below the camp.

Sunday 10 March 1957

Sent Corporal Mundingi and Private Fred back to Captain Curnow-Baker with a detailed report of finds over the previous two days. Moved to GR 138 788 with remaining eight men and placed a two-man daylight ambush on the fish trap at the Kuku/Kinchin river junction.

Monday 11 March 1957

Fish trap ambush in position by 0630hrs. Patrolled South with Lance Corporal Obert to GR 156 782. Found one CT night stop for two men at GR 147 788 about six to eight weeks old. There were cuttings in various places on the West bank of the River Kinchin six weeks to six months old. No sign of any CT activity more recent than six weeks. Corporal Mundingi returns with four extra men at 1155hrs. Also brings in extra rations and other items. Sergeant Chimba had returned after finding a camp and cultivation on the River Haha.

Tuesday 12 March 1957

Fish trap ambush increased to three including an NCO. In position by 0645hrs. I patrolled North up the river Kinchin with Lance Corporal Obert starting at the CT camp close to the fish trap. Signs found indicated that the CT group who had vacated the camp about five days previously had headed north. Found a CT camp for fifteen to twenty men about eight months at GR 143 793. It seems apparent that there is considerable CT activity around this area.

Wednesday 13 March 1957

I sent two couriers with the latest info back to Captain Curnow-Baker at Tahalai cultivation. Fish trap ambush continues. Lance Corporal Obert on patrol to river running into the river Kuku at GR 132 788. NTR. Captain Curnow-Baker visits me at 1230hrs and it is decided that I shall go back to Tahalai on the following day for the airdrop with most of my group leaving a small ambush party at the fish trap. Captain Curnow-Baker leaves on his return journey to Tahalai at 1415hrs. This will take approximately two and a half hours. Welcome news that at last we were getting reinforced on Friday by about twenty men from the Mortar Platoon.

Thursday 14 March 1957

Left my base camp at 0745hrs to move back to Tahalai for the airdrop. Arrived there for the airdrop at 1020hrs. The drop was due in at 1100hrs, postponed to 1200hrs and finally arrived at 1530hrs.

    The lateness of the drop made it impossible to change over Lance Corporal Obert's party on the fish trap ambush until the following day. The Ordnance requirements turned out to be a complete shambles all round. The most glaring mistake being the sending of size 3, 4 and 5 jungle boots in lieu of trousers!! Packs 37 pattern were sent instead of packs 44 pattern. Due to the lateness of the para drop I had to spend the night at Tahalai.

Friday 15 March 1957

The troop lift started coming in at about 0900hrs. It included the RMO Captain Forbes Ainslie, six men of my own platoon as well as eighteen from the Mortar Platoon to give me another twenty-four men to cover the vast area we had to search. Mail, fresh fruit and newspapers come in and are much appreciated. The RMO went out on the last run. Lance Corporal Obert's ambush party at my advance base are relieved and arrive at the DZ at 1300hrs. They are re-equipped and re-rationed at Tahalai and I move back with them at 1400hrs to a new base further north up the River Kinchin.

    I now have 2 and 3 sections of my platoon and a wireless detachment whilst Captain Curnow-Baker stays at Tahalai to work west with 1 Section and the Mortar Platoon personnel. I reach my new base at GR 147 797 at 1745hrs. Security patrols have located a CT resting place for three about ten days old at GR 147 799. Sergeant Chimba took an ambush party to the cultivation at GR 413 839 for six days.

Saturday 16 March 1957

Four patrols out. Two north up towards the source of the Kinchin, two north-east up the river Puan. Footprints for one man going south-west found at GR 152 801 but lost immediately. A Nibong tree cut down about ten to fourteen days ago found just north of CT camp located the previous day, otherwise all patrols NTR.

Sunday 17 March 1957

Four patrols out again. My patrol found a large new vegetable basket near to previously reported CT camp. This had probably been made during the last visit to this camp. It seemed to point to there being a cultivation in the area, but none could be found. Corporal Zwidzayi who had been sent to patrol east, on reaching the river running north/south in squares 1678 and 1679 moved down it until reaching the Kinchin at GR 167 768 as he had been uncertain of his position. He returned north up the west bank of the Kinchin and found the following camps:
> GR 155780 for three CTs about six weeks old.
> GR 158 788 for six CTs about three months old.
> GR 167 767 for three CTs about seven days old.

Monday 18 March 1957

I moved off at 0900hrs to the South down the West bank of the river Kinchin to GR 169 764 where we based up. Corporal Mulize, Private Martin and Private Tsikayi sent back to Tahalai to guide a section of the mortar platoon down to our new location as these had been promised by Captain Curnow-Baker.

Tuesday 19 March 1957

A resting place for two to three CTs about one month old found near the water point. The following camps were found by patrols which were sent out today:
> GR 177 759 camp for four CTs six weeks old.
> GR 188 753 camp for three or four CTs five months old.
> GR 186 754 camp for two or three CTs four weeks old.

JCLO Cheah with Corporal Mulize, Private Tsikayi, thirteen members of the mortar Platoon and two Aborigine trackers/head hunters from Borneo arrived today. Private Martin had stayed behind to guide Captain Curnow-Baker if he wanted to come down later.

Wednesday 20 March 1957

I sent out three patrols this morning. WO2 Kenani (mortars) with Lance Corporal Dzingayi to Jiwang river with ten men, Corporal Mundingi with Corporal Chedi to Telang river to patrol and ambush river junction as a screen for the airdrop which was due on Friday. Lance Corporal Obert took a recce patrol to the area south and south-west. Remainder of personnel in camp occupied in digging rubbish pits and general clean up

KILL!!

CT killed by Corporal Mundingi's patrol Ho Yong (Endau Food Cultivator).
Corporal Mundingi, Lance Cpl Dzingayi and Pte Malinga (Bren gunner).
Wednesday 20 March 1957

Lance Corporal Obert returns at 1315hrs with one man from the mortar platoon carrying a CT pack and reports that Corporal Mundingi's patrol had killed one of three CTs they had contacted at GR 181 748. The immediate follow up had had negative results and the patrol were now returning, cutting a track and bringing the body back. I ordered the signaller, Lance Corporal Mbirikwazo to open radio communications at once and dispatched Corporal Mulize with four men to search the area west and south of the contact for two days. I took the remainder of the men across the river to where I had intended cutting the DZ and began cutting the LZ to fly the body out.

Corporal Mundingi arrived back with the body at 1530hrs after cutting and carrying for 3.500 yards. The dead CT was a male Chinese of about 30 years of age. Corporal Mundingi's report was as follows:

The time was 1030 hrs and I had reached GR 181 748 when the time came for the hourly break. The patrol spread out and sat down. Suddenly Private Muwayu (Mortar Platoon) saw a CT about fifteen to twenty yards away to his left front. Both he and the leading scout Private Fred (4 Platoon) opened fire with their Patchetts simultaneously. The CT was hit, dropped his pack and ran towards the river Kinchin. I shouted at the patrol to charge and saw another CT armed with a Sten gun running away. Private Malinga (4 Platoon), the Bren gunner, reached the river bank at the same time as the wounded CT and when the latter jumped in and attempted to swim across hit him again with several well directed bursts from the waist. The CT struggled back to the near bank and I shot him with my shotgun. Private Matambo then grabbed him by the hair and pulled him out just as he was sinking and shouted 'makan' (food) (during WW II in Burma African troops had the reputation of cannibals with the Japanese.) Corporal Chedi then said he had seen a third CT. We searched the area thoroughly but could find no trace of the other two CTs. We called off the search at 1200hrs and began to carry the body back to base. At about 1230hrs I met Lance Corporal Obert's patrol and sent him with one man and the CT pack back to report.'

Cpl Mundingi's patrol was given thirty minutes break and instructions to go and help cut the LZ at 1615hrs. At 1600hrs Lance Corporal Mberikwazo finally managed to contact Battalion Headquarters after trying for two and a half hours. The kill was reported and the LZ was ready to lift out the dead CT by 1730hrs. At 1715hrs Battalion Headquarters radioed that the helicopter could not come until the next morning, that the CO would come in and Captain Curnow-Baker would be lifted down to discuss future plans. The work on the LZ was finished by 1730hrs and the body of the dead CT was tied up in a tree near the LZ. News was received that the helicopter was due in tomorrow at 0830hrs.

Thursday 21 March 1957

First thing this morning the LZ was improved for the helicopter. Corporal Zwidzayi on patrol in general contact area for sign of CT survivors. Helicopter finally arrives about 1030hrs with the CO and then fetches Captain Curnow-Baker from Tahalai. The body is then flown out. The CO brings in mail, fruit and hand grenades and outline future plans. CO and Captain Curnow-Baker flown out by 1300hrs. Both the patrols of Corporal Zwidzayi and Mulize NTR. The dead CT identified as Ho Yong of the Endau Food Cultivation Unit.

Friday 22 March 1957

Patrol dog Rover with Handler from 1SWB arrive by helicopter, Thursday 21 March 1957

Airdrop day. Captain Curnow-Baker due to arrive tomorrow with 1 Section and remainder of Mortar Platoon personnel. Airdrop came in at 0930 hrs for a change. Rations arrived all correct, but clothing turned out to be the usual cock-up. Rest of the day spent in sorting out and issuing and make and mend. Sergeant Chimba returned today, NTR.

Saturday 23 March 1957

Four patrols out. Lance Corporal Obert to RV with Captain Curnow-Baker and guide him in. Corporal Mundingi to patrol tributaries north-west of base. Cpl Chedi and Lance Corporal Dzingayi South to junction Kinchin/Telang rivers. Captain Curnow-Baker arrived in with Lance Corporal Obert at 1220hrs. Corporal Mundingi's patrol NTR. Corporal Chedi sends two men back at 1330hrs to report the following:

GR 182 736 Lance Corporal Dzingayi's patrol found a camp for approx.
ten CTs evacuated that morning. Tracks for three to four CTs crossed to
the East bank of the river Kinchin at GR 183 739 and then proceeded north
up an old Sakai track. These tracks had been followed to GR 180 759 but
here the CT party found the track cut by Corporal Mundingi's party when
they carried back the dead CT three days previously and they had split up,
anti-tracking and the patrol lost the tracks. Wireless communications were
at once established with Battalion HQ and it was requested that tracker
dogs be flown in that evening if possible. Battalion HQ informed us at
1630hrs that the dogs could not be flown in that evening, but they could
come in the next day with the 2ic.

A typical jungle LZ. March 1957

Sunday 24 March 1957

Major Fitzgerald and one dog with handler arrive at 1030hrs and the helicopter
brings in the second dog with handler about 1115hrs. The 2ic concurs with all our
plans. One of the dogs is a patrol dog and the other a tracker. Length of stay six
days with possible extension if necessary. I leave with 3 Section, radio and patrol
dog at 1200hrs and make for CT camp, hoping to pick up a trace of the second
party from this base.

On the way South found sign that the CTs had crossed to the East bank of the river where the tracks had been lost on the previous day and had visited the area of the contact. From here all sign disappeared. No other tracks could be found near the CT camp although the area was searched thoroughly. I moved on to GR 187 729 and based up at 1800hrs. I contacted Captain Curnow-Baker on the radio, but he had not had any luck with the tracker dog.

Monday 25 March 1957

B and C Companies move into the jungle today with the object of linking up with us in the area of the Kinchin/Endau river junction. After talking with Captain Curnow-Baker on the morning wireless sched, it was decided that the whole callsign would move and search further south. I sent ten of my patrol back to collect surplus kit and rations. I left two in camp and patrolled south with Lance Corporal Obert and the South Wales Borderer dog handler and patrol dog. On this patrol I found the following:

GR 192 721 CT camp for approx. ten about ten months old.

GR 193 719 Tracks for two or three CT going south about two days old. Captain Curnow-Baker joined me with main party at about 1445hrs.

Tuesday 26 March 1957

I dispatched Sergeant Pwanyre with twelve Mortar Pl men to search the TELANG river area for two days. Three other local patrols sent out. At GR 193 728 a camp for three to four CTs about three days old found by patrol under Lance Corporal Dzingayi. This probably ties in with tracks found the previous day.

Wednesday 27 March 1957

I moved further south to GR 207 707. Mortar Pl catches up with us at 1330hrs. NTR on Telang river area. All security patrols NTR.

Thursday 28 March 1957

Four patrols out again today. Two patrols south down either bank of the Kinchin River to Kernam River junction. NTR. Corporal Paupila patrolled the Genut River area and found a CT camp for two about two days old at GR 197 704. Captain Curnow-Baker to investigate this area more thoroughly tomorrow.

Friday 29 March 1957

Captain Curnow-Baker takes a patrol back to the camp found on the Genut River. Returns just before the air re-supply at about 1030hrs. This camp had been used at least three times during the last three weeks by not more than four CTs at any one time. All occupation had been carefully concealed and tracks in and out had been carefully hidden in elephant footprints. The Valetta doing the airdrop circled for about twenty minutes before finally dropping owing to low cloud. This completely spoilt any security in the area.

Another typical jungle LZ. March 1957

The clothing requirements arrived reasonably correct for a change. Twenty-one X 2 Malay packs were sent in excess. These had to be either destroyed or eaten straight away due to the weight. It rained continuously from 1215hrs until after dark and it was impossible to issue any clothing today.

Saturday 30 March 1957

All clothing from the airdrop sorted and distributed. All parachutes cut up and destroyed but the cord retained for bridging the Endau if necessary. Corporal Chedi and Lance Corporal Taruberakera again take patrols to the river Genut area but again NTR. Moving tomorrow to the Kuala Kinchin. For the second day running Valetta aircraft spoiled any semblance of security in the area.

Sunday 31 March 1957

I moved off with two sections, the patrol dog and handler for Kuala Kinchin at 0800hrs. Reached our destination at 1300hrs. Captain Curnow-Baker came later with the second party after burning rubbish etc.

On the way Private Wunganayi had a fall and hurt his back necessitating a casevac. Captain Curnow-Baker stayed with the Mortar Platoon and sent on 3 Section with the tracker dog to me. LZ ready by 1300hrs. Helicopter takes out three casevacs about 1700hrs in rain and low cloud. The other two casualties were both from the Mortar Platoon, one hurt cutting the LZ and the other down with a fever. Based up on the Endau river at GR 236 644. Recced for crossing place to South bank but none found apart from swimming! Found a good site for an LZ on the junction of the Endau and Kinchin rivers with an horizontal approach for several hundred yards from the South.

Cutting the LZ at the junction of the rivers. Kinchin and Endau.
The Op is over! 23 April 1957

Monday 01 April 1957

Two patrols were sent out west along the Endau River to look for a crossing place to the South, returned about 0930hrs unsuccessful. Anyone crossing the

Endau would have to swim! We began cutting the LZ at 1000hrs on the junction of the two rivers. Captain Curnow-Baker arrives at 1130hrs with the Mortar Platoon.

News came through today that B and C Companies were calling off their part of the operation due to loss of security from the airdrop and lack of CT sign. Not now joining us at Kuala Kinchin. Length of para cord for mooring boats found tied to stump below the LZ at GR 238 643. This proves conclusively that CTs are working this part of the river in boats. This may even be the case farther west?

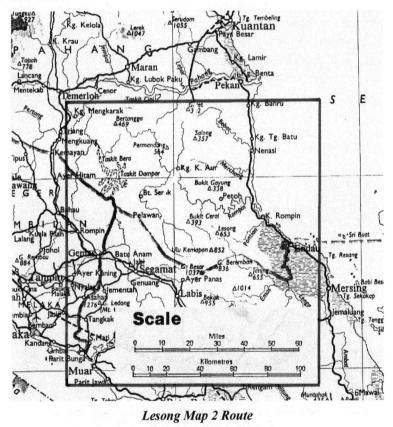

Lesong Map 2 Route

Tuesday 02 April 1957

All personnel worked on the LZ which was finished by 1045hrs. News on early wireless sched that we were to be lifted out on Thursday all being well. C Company required for food denial Op Cobble were to go out on Wednesday. Apart from sentries, platoon stood down after 1100hrs.

Wednesday 03 April 1957

Corporal Paupila takes out patrol on general search of the area North and West of our LZ/base camp. NTR. C Company cannot get helicopters for today. Everyone due out tomorrow. News that evening that we are not going out until Friday. The dogs are due out tomorrow, so Captain Curnow-Baker arranges for the footballers to go out with them so that they get one night in a decent bed before playing 1SWB.

Thursday 04 April 1957

Helicopter comes in at 1300hrs and takes our first lift out. Pilot says that the whole callsign may be lifted out after all as both LZs are very good. Second helicopter which comes in shortly afterwards is piloted by group leader who says all to be lifted out today. Whole callsign out by 1700hrs. A good job by the RAF.

Footnotes

1. Contents of pack carried by Ho Yong of the Endau Food Cultivation Unit killed on 20 March 1957 by 4 Platoon, B Company, 1RAR (Special Branch Wanted List WL 00385). Documents: various, in Chinese.
Food: twelve lbs of rice, six lbs of tapioca flour, five packets salt (Security Forces pattern). Equipment: one belt with pouches, one knife clasp (Security Forces pattern), one mug (44 pattern), one mess tin (Japanese Army), one aluminium plate, two pairs scissors, one dessert spoon, one Ever Ready torch, three pieces plastic, one fishing spear, large quantity of fish hooks (all sizes) and one cloth pack.
Clothing: one khaki drill shirt, three pairs underpants, two singlets, two face towels, one pair PT shoes, one piece of cloth and four cloth bags. Miscellaneous items: razor and blades, Lux toilet soap, various medicines including Tiger Balm, sharpening stone and various odds and ends. One glaring point was the amount of Security Forces kit in his possession including a large quantity of para cord presumably for use as fishing line! He was well fed and could obviously get little luxuries even though he was in deep jungle, such as Lux toilet soap.
2. Patrolling in the Malayan jungle was slow and difficult. The terrain was folded in knife-edge ridges, one after the other, so that men were constantly climbing or descending muddy, slippery slopes. Visibility was down to a

few yards and the vegetation was a tangle of vines and creepers to impede progress. Colonel F. Spencer Chapman DSO & Bar, who fought there in WW II described it thus:

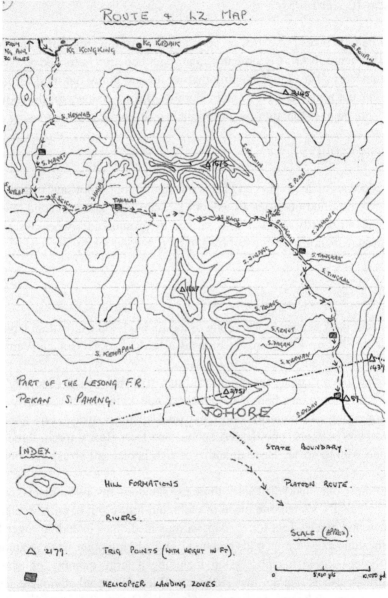

Lesong Map 1 Route

'Many of the boles of the trees were almost hidden by a network of creepers, occasionally breaking out into huge leaves but usually bare and often as thick as a man's thigh. In other places the vines and creepers hung straight down from the branches to the ground, where they had taken root again and looped themselves from tree to tree like the crazy rigging of a thousand wrecked ships... (We) found this jungle almost impenetrable.' (Chapman, 1949). 3. In this jungle, patrol distances were calculated in yards: 'In one hour of gruelling and exhausting work, we made only about a hundred yards.' (Chapman, 1949).

In addition, distances used in a map-time appreciation on a flat map did not consider the steepness of the ground or the deviations required to bypass obstacles; together, these added considerably to physical distance travelled. Add to this the vital importance of moving tactically, and one can understand why very few units in that conflict patrolled far. The RAR fighting patrols, in full kit under jungle conditions such as these, patrolled over 100,000 yards (just over 91 kilometres) during the Lesong Search, a testament to their strength, commitment and endurance.

References:
Chapman, F. Spencer 1949, *The Jungle is Neutral*, Chatto and Windus, London.
Binda, A 2007, *Masodja*, 30 Degrees South, Pinetown, South Africa.

A CHRISTIAN MOMENT by Brigadier John 'Digger' Essex-Clark

Saturday 5 November 1956. My brave and effective Platoon Warrant Officer Pisayi Muzericho was one of my shortest and almost smallest yet genuine Ma'Oto (warriors) in my platoon. We had been patrolling from a temporarily fixed platoon patrol base by a pleasant stream in the dense, overwhelmingly dominating Malayan primary jungle along the Sungei Palong and planning my next day's activities, when my Platoon Warrant Officer (2IC) returned from our water and washing point with the story that Private Chinemo had smelt a tobacco odour while he was bathing in the centre of the stream indicating that some CT might have been fairly close by upstream. Pisayi, always spoiling for a fight said he would take a recce patrol and sniff it out. I replied yes, but just a reconnaissance, we'd use the whole platoon when we knew what was going on. "Inde, Ishe, no Ma'Oto action. Eeyai!"

He then took two non-tobacco-smoking scouts from my Two Section and the non-smoking section commander Cpl Taderera and slipped quietly away into the ulu. While away they found a deserted CT camp-site in the next northern Grid square, which led to another central camp-site, then another, all with well-used paths between them. They finally found an armed CT using the wire-cage fishing-traps and carrying a Chicom AK47. Pisayi believed that he had too many fish for himself and the CT must have been expecting many others to join him in the camp area. It was spread out on a spur separating the junction of two streams, one of which we were based on, further downstream. Pisayi could see that the larger group was a preferable target to him shooting only one CT, so he and his recce patrol spirited away and reported his findings to me.

We considered our options. We had two sections deployed in ambush positions, with our main firepower (our Brens), on the west bank of the Sungei Palong (our primary task), leaving one section as my only manoeuvre patrol. Communications in Malaya consisted of only one Australian A510 HF radio for each rifle platoon back to Bn HQ, a far cry from the individual communications of the modern day.

2 Lt John Essex-Clark OC 8 Pl, C Coy, 1RAR

Attacking a widely dispersed camp with only a single section wasn't a practical option as the enemy would easily slip away into the thick jungle. We recognised that it would be best to call in an air strike. As it was possibly in the South Wales Borderers' area of operation, I reported to Bn HQ and requested that the Air Force bomb the CT site early morning in two days' time, after we, and any other friendly patrols, were well out of the way. RAF and RAAF bombing in Malaya using spotting Austers, Lincolns, Bristol Brigands, and even Sunderland flying boats, was notoriously inaccurate and was best well-avoided by many thousands of yards.

It was a remarkable bit of thoughtful tactical cunning. I then congratulated Warrant Officer Pisayi with the expression. "You're a clever little devil, aren't you?"

His querulous and distressed look surprised me, so I said: "What's wrong Sar'major?"

"You called me a Devil, bwana". I knew he was angry, switching from the chiShona, 'ishe' or 'nkosi' to the chiNyanja 'bwana', and not looking me in the eye. Then my English, chiNyanja, and chiShona failed me as I tried to explain that 'little devil' meant neither his stature (though he was small) nor a devil in the biblical sense. It took until that evening's stand-to and the return of our standing patrols before he relaxed and joked with me and said, "Do the CO and company commanders call you 'a little devil', ishe?"

"No, I'm too big for that, so they call me 'digger'."

Explaining the Australian relationship to the term would be too difficult, so I pretended that it was because they get angry with me and believe that I am only good enough for digging 'chimbudzis' (bush-trench, squat-toilets). Then we will call you 'Mopane' ishe, because it is the tree the elephant eats for 'chakudya' (food). It always recovers quickly for ndhlovu (elephant) to eat again.

I wondered how many other platoon commanders had been through the same embarrassing and double-demeaning language experience that I just had had. The lesson was that many of our Askari had strong Christian values, as well as their tribal customs, and all that we European officers essentially had with our Askari was that we were a 'band of brothers'. We respected each other's cultures but many of us shared a very different-cultured Christianity.

Not that all the Askari were strongly committed Christians but whenever I held bible readings from our miniature Malaya Command issue Bibles, at 0900 hrs on Sundays, in camp or in the ulu, I would always have a strong group, mainly from my own platoon. I didn't think that they were just being sycophants because they asked me questions, but I could answer them only in the field of morality, not philosophy.

PWO Pisayi Muzerecho MM after being invested with the Military Medal by the Duke of Gloucester

Further about that extraordinary Askari: Pisayi Muzericho. Apart from being awarded a Military Medal for exemplary leadership in action, plus tactical initiative, and bravery, he also made me aware and have empathy and show action towards the few who felt homesick, who worried about those trying to kill them, jaded about the overawing damp murkiness of the jungle and constant patrolling for little tangible success. It was a modern soldier's battle-fatigue which could lead to PTSD. Pisayi glimpsed that immediate action was required, and suggested to me: rest, friendship, discussion, light duties helpful to the whole platoon and the sufferer's friends, and counselling that Pisayi did naturally.

These were all lessons that helped my leadership in Malaya, Vietnam and elsewhere. Pisayi initiated my thoughts and future actions as I became responsible for leadership guidance in a battalion, the Directorate of Infantry, the Infantry Centre, Duntroon, and the Australian Command and Staff College. What a man he was then, and still is in Zimbabwe.

And the bombing? Bn HQ didn't take too kindly to my or Pisayi's suggestion and the bombing raid got no further than the stultifying but cool aroma of a sweaty, fan-smothering, Bn HQ Ops Room. It would have given the Bn HQ Officers' Mess a good chuckle, at my expense, that evening. We were not to be denied though; we got our battalion's first kill a few days later, but that's another story.

AT LAST by Brigadier John 'Digger' Essex-Clark

We are in Malaya in late October 1956, I am serving as a platoon commander in The Rhodesian African Rifles.

Comrade Hor Lung, commander of 32 Platoon of the MPLA (Malayan Peoples Liberation Army) has been up to his and their old tricks of rampaging through rubber-tapper kampongs (villages) killing any headmen, teachers, medics, and other communist-disliked citizens.

Comrade Hor lung with Sten submachine gun

Our battalion had recently been given a 'ripe plum' (high quality and accurate intelligence classification) report from Malay Police Intelligence through an SEP (Surrendered Enemy Person) that Hor Lung's group of about nine men and a woman, was making in a SW to NE direction the 1st Gurkha Division's area of responsibility. We were to prevent their crossing and eliminate the terrorist's lairs in the huge Rengam State Forest and they would soon have to cross the Sungei Palong (River Palong) to do so. We had been ordered to ambush likely crossing points on that river. My 8 Platoon was the forward element in the battalion's ambush effort.

We have been in Malaya for six months and this may be our first ability for seriously planned, rather than an off-chance action. Elements of our battalion had

had many 'incidents' of a firefight in which the enemy fired first, but no 'contacts' in which, through our initiative, a CT was killed.

On this day, everyone in our temporary patrol base is euphoric. Our patrols return. One, Corporal Munyameni's, with Private Pedzayi from my platoon, was on his mini-patrol's last leg at about 1150 hours when Pedzayi thought he could smell a CT odour of an unwashed, wood-smoked clothed, Chinese body. They were standing still, and he told Munyameni that he could smell '*Maliwongo*' ('enemy' in chiNyanja).

Munyameni's Ma'Oto took firing positions on the jungle floor that limited their forward vision. Munyameni stood up with his new user-trial 7.62mm FN and saw a CT about 10 yards in front of him. The CT raised his weapon and Munyameni fired an aimed shot as the CT ducked behind a buttress. Pedzayi was sure that Munyameni's shot had hit the CT somewhere because of how he ducked and fell behind the buttress. Munyameni shouted to his mini-patrol to "Look for others!"

Pedzayi and Mosi, also from 8 platoon, scooted forward past Corporal Munyameni but saw nothing. 'Munya' then closed on the buttress hiding the first CT, who must have been a forward scout, who then raised his head over the buttress and sprayed a burst from his weapon in the direction of the now standing mini-patrol. They fired back, and the CT ducked back again.

'Munya' walked closer and put two shots through the soft wood of the buttress in the area behind which the CT was hiding. There was no reply. Munyameni then trod forward and saw that the CT was dead. He had fallen forward, and his back was soaked in blood so Munyameni thought some-else had shot him. The mini-patrol left the body there and probed further forward to chase any other CT, there were none. We credited the 'kill' to Munyameni.

The CT scout had done his job well and bravely but should have known that the wood in a buttress is almost as soft as balsa-wood. Munyameni blew his whistle after the contact; and Pisayi and Yvo who were echeloned right behind Munya's men arrived on the scene followed by much whistle blowing for the other mini-patrols to RV with them and track spoor; and return to the patrol base.

Pisayi and Yvo arrived back at our patrol base at the same time as us with the CT body slung in the CT's plastic poncho between poles. Yvo had organised a patrol sweep through the action area and found no further sign. The rest had flown. The Senama had been, obviously, Hor Lung's alternative escape route to the Palong. We could have stayed at our patrol base and they might have walked straight into us, maybe? What was that? … 'The best laid plans of mice and men!'

We unwrapped the CT's gear and weapon, a shiny un-blued, oft-used Australian 9mm SMG Sten Gun. I hadn't seen a Sten since cadets at school in Australia. So, later, I took it out of the base and shot it into a tree about 15 yards away. It worked well, was accurate, and had been very well maintained. I reported this, inter alia, and as an aside, to Battalion Headquarters; I included that I guessed that the dead CT was probably only a scout from 32 platoon, and, therefore, not an important functionary.

It is the Battalion's first success, for which we'd trained and waited for nearly two years. I radio back to headquarters to tell them that we've had a successful contact.

ACTION IN THE TONG LEE ESTATE by Brigadier John 'Digger' Essex-Clark

This is the story of Corporal Tabuya's bravery, plus his shrewd tactics and leadership in a slurpy, leech-ridden, drainage ditch and his section's action in the huge rubber plantation of the Tong Lee Estate.

Imagine, you are on a small wooden bridge over a muddy drainage ditch looking westward down a shallow, flat, U-shaped, gloomy valley, filled with a scrubby, geometric rubber plantation surrounded by thick primary jungle on the north, west and south. Many flattish spurs run from the jungle's northern and southern edges to this straight-ish drainage ditch. A pump shed is faintly visible at the far western end, pumping water from the ditch over a flat, jungled rise into a far-off western swamp. All is threateningly quiet except for a faint 'tumpetty-tump' from the pump-shed. Got it? ... That's where this happened.

According to Malay Police Special Branch, the CT are supposed to be meeting a Min Yuen (clandestine local logistic supporter) in the distant pump-shed at mid-day to get supplies of ammunition, torch and radio batteries, and food. We were ridiculously forbidden to have our weapons loaded and cocked in the rubber plantations (the Fiji Regiment before us had accidentally shot too many furtive civilian rubber-tappers).

Corporal Tabuya and his 1 section were told to patrol west towards the pump shed, so he stealthily used that 3-foot wide and 3-foot deep, low-growth screened, drainage ditch. By the time he and his section, in prone single-bodied file, got near the pump shed, they realised that the jagged sound of cocking their weapons within 20 yards of the CT in the shed, with a CT sentry outside the near-side of the shed, would give their mucky ruse away. Tabuya's section had crawled and slithered about 300 yards to the shed and Tabuya had to whisper and demonstrate to his Askari to cock their weapons in synchronisation with the 'tumpetty-tump' of the pump engine in the shed.

Just then, a new small CT group was seen approaching casually along the rubber-tapper's foot-path from the north eastern jungle edge. Tabuya had the CT sentry, at the near edge of the shed, virtually in the sights of his FN when, suddenly, with their supplies packed, the CT started to leave the shed. The new group of CT continued to sneak down the jungle edge to join those in the shed, but they'd all gone, leaving no-one remaining in the pump shed with the Min Yuen supplier. Tabuya was in a quandary: shoot the CT sentry or wait until the larger target of CT was congregated in the shed? He couldn't see that the shed group were drifting away.

He had Corporal Taderera's 2 section patrolling 150 yards to his south, or his left flank, and Corporal Jere's 3 section with the platoon HQ on a flat spur above right and watching him. He decided, to use an English expression, 'That a bird in the hand is worth two in the bush!' So, he stood up and shot the sentry in the chest. The sentry fired his Sten-gun at the mud-slimed apparitions arising from the ditch, then another CT came around the edge of the shed to throw a 36 anti-personnel grenade at Tabuya who was now kneeling in the ditch. Tabuya believes that he shot him too.

Another CT sentry, along with other departing CTs, opened fire as the section rose mud-slimed from the ditch and returned fire. Private Tomisen's Bren was cocked but not loaded, he had only to slip open the magazine opening-slide of his Bren, insert a magazine, and press the trigger. However, he had opened the magazine opening-slide earlier to be ready for immediate action and allowed mud to get into the magazine-opening when in the ditch and rendered the weapon useless.

Corporal Tabuya received some tiny grenade fragments in his left shoulder but kept firing his FN at the CT scuttling uphill, and Private Fraser got the butt of his SMLE no 4 ·303" Jungle-Rifle smashed out of his hands by a 9mm round from a CT Sten.

Lance Corporal Simata then punched the remainder of the section (including Pte Tomisen, still scooping mud from his magazine-opening) charging forward under fire from the CTs on the jungle edge, who were giving the shed-escapees covering fire. Corporal Jere's Bren fired at the escapees who were trying to use the dead ground of a re-entrant to avoid our fire. Tabuya recognised the danger and got his Askari with Simata to fire at the weapons flashes coming from a third group of CT who were giving the fleeing CT covering fire from the edge of the jungle above them.

Sergeant Major Pisayi captured two of the less nimble CT who were scuttling-off up another shallow re-entrant, running transversely towards him. Simata continued the chase more circumspectly, using dead ground to cover his men's movement from our own and the CT fire while still firing at the flashes from the jungle. They then linked up with Pisayi, Sergeant Gondocondo and Jere's section who had also been firing and charging towards the CT group, on the same level of the northern jungle edge. The CTs soon skedaddled by scuttling into the northern jungle. The Askari chased them for about 60 yards and then came back to the platoon HQ Group, where Tomisen was still trying to clean his Bren with water from water bottles and his neck sweat-rag.

They radioed Bn HQ and were told to wait until the Police arrived. Tabuya wanted to keep chasing the CT but was calmed down by Pisayi, who was commanding the platoon and had done very well. Would I have done anything different if I had been there? No, I would not, Pisayi was not to know that there were two groups coming in for supplies, plus a CT covering group; nor that the CT porters were to be covered by another group of CT from high ground on the northern jungle edge. He'd used his resources well and was very brave himself, almost foolhardy. When my platoon got our next break, we practiced shooting at part-filled sand-bag targets swinging between trees, in some old, unused rubber plantation.

Afterwards, the Malay Police Special Branch arrived to collect and immediately interrogate the CT prisoners and follow the two obvious blood trails from the pump-shed CT. The police medic secured, quickly interrogated and then tranquillised the two very nervous and downcast CEP, as well as the quaking Min Yuen rubber tapper, who had crapped himself while lying flat against a wall in the pump shed and then had petrol poured on him to lessen the stench. The medic treated Tabuya and Fraser with mercurochrome and sticking plaster, and the platoon settled down in a patrol defensive position, less Taderera's 3 section who went with the police Sakai trackers. When the trackers got to the eastern swamp they gave-up. After Taderera returned, they were all transported back to our camp at the Tong Lee estate: task done!

Three CT and a Min Yuen virtual CT were eliminated, and two obviously wounded from the blood trails found. I was told that Corporal Tabuya's lads had spent 10 minutes after the contact was over, using insect repellent, salt, and cigarettes to remove the leeches sucking blood from their bodies. One Askari, the shamed Tomisen, removing a bulbous bull-leech from between his thighs after they got back to their lines in our camp adjacent to the Estate. His huge bull-leech bite needed more medical attention than insect repellent and mercurochrome or gentian-violet. Leech bites itch for ages and Tomisen scratched his for a month.

MAGIC by Brigadier John 'Digger' Essex-Clark

We arrived in Malaya without the Askari being aware of the capability and some even, any knowledge, of helicopters, let alone their existence. Most our Askari had seen piston engine and propeller-driven aircraft and heard the drone above them and hence the ChiShona onomatopoeic word of Ndegi: say it through the nose rhythmically: "Ndegi - Ndegi" and your throat rumbles "Ndegi".

On the Padang at JTC (Jungle Training Centre at Kota Tinggi) we had had a demonstration, but not training, in soldiers emplaning and deplaning from helicopters including men roping down from them. They were magical. Then, later, we had airdrops of weekly supplies, including one-day's fresh rations, replacement clothing and kit, extra cigarettes for the smokers, etc. Watching it tumble down and the parachute opening was magic.

More magical was the flat slab and tin of lithium hydride and the tiny bundle that, with water, would provide the hydrogen to inflate a six-foot in-diameter bright orange marker balloon that could force its way through the canopy of thick primary forest to be settled down on the canopy to enable Ndegi crew to eject the parachutes, one at a time, to deliver supplies to us, including the popular rum-ration. This, after cutting a Dropping Zone (DZ) using a magical coiled-up steel two-man, one each end, chain saw slicing through the enormous rain-forest tree trunks with ease to clear the DZ for the parachute drop.

Then to get on board a Westland Whirlwind helicopter, wide-eyed and nervous to take off from a log platform on a steep hill Landing Zone (LZ) first built by Gurkhas, who had cleared an area which then enabled CT to grow sweet-potato, that we retitled from 'Platform' to 'Sweet-Potato' and take us all, six at a time, back to the safe area of Kluang: Magic!

Then to rope-in on a thick knotted rope into a tiny clearing to ambush CT four miles away to save a twelve-mile jungle bash: Magic! Or evacuate sick and wounded using a special casevac set-up Sycamore helicopter with low whirling dangerous blades, from a sand-bank in a narrow thick-jungle-sided river: Magic! Inflatable boats to cross wide rivers: Magic! Further, back in Rhodesia, reading a flat map and its contours, and keys, plus using a prismatic compass and plastic protractor to determine a position on the map and ground; then the use of mortars and artillery for indirect fire: Magic! However, Malaya, to our Askari was more fabulous Magic.

'Second-one-In'

Trying to explain the principles of aerofoil and propeller-driven flight during training in Rhodesia, was an "Oooh and Aahh" exercise in explaining 'Magic'. That I had taken my PWO and NCOs to watch me pilot and fly an old Tiger Moth at

Kumalo airport with Sergeant Major Pisayi as my passenger gave me a sort of utterly ridiculous magician status, though I did no aerobatics whatsoever.

It was a bit bumpy and Pisayi felt a bit woozy during the flight and told me so, down the Gosport Comms tube; the flight ended very quickly. He was mesmerised and fascinated by the simple instrument panel, and huge threatening compass between his legs.

Preparing the Marker Balloon — Lithium Hydroxide is mixed with water in the generator (Sack at bottom of balloon) which fills the balloon with Hydrogen — tied up — and up she goes!

Preparing Balloons

CHAPTER FIVE

OFFICER CADET TRAINING

INTRODUCTION by Captain Andrew Telfer

In *Chibaya Moyo 1*, we featured articles on the selection and training of the African recruits who would become the fighting soldiers of the RAR. In this volume of *Chibaya Moyo*, we focus on the selection and training of the officer cadets who would, upon commissioning, lead them. We look first at the situation before UDI, when many Rhodesian cadets were trained at the Royal Military Academy at Sandhurst, in the UK. We then observe how the methodologies of Sandhurst were continued after UDI at the School of Infantry, Gwelo in the conduct of Officer Selection Boards and Cadet Courses. In the spirit of *Chibaya Moyo*, very little of this is taken any more seriously than it should be.

THE TRAINING OF RHODESIAN OFFICERS AT THE ROYAL MILITARY ACADEMY, SANDHURST by Lieutenant General K. R. Coster ICD, OBE

The forces of Southern Rhodesia in the years between the conclusion of the Second World War and the establishment of the Federation of the Rhodesias (Northern and Southern) and Nyasaland felt a strong affinity for the forces of the Crown. These bonds were reinforced by affiliations between regiments of the British Army and the Southern Rhodesia forces. For example, the Royal Rhodesia Regiment was affiliated to the Kings Royal Rifle Corps while the Rhodesian African Rifles was affiliated to the South Wales Borderers.

Officers of the Southern Rhodesian forces looked to the United Kingdom for training courses ranging from Drill Instructors to Staff Courses at Camberley and Bracknell. Until Southern Rhodesia became part of the Federation, however, there was no call for the training of subaltern officers for the then Southern Rhodesia Staff Corps. The reason was a simple one. When the Second World War ended, commissioned officers streamed back to Southern Rhodesia and many made their way into the armed forces of the colony. Most were expected to relinquish their commissions and revert to the ranks before being re-commissioned, once it was established that they met the high standards demanded by the Permanent Staff Corps.

This permanent corps was essentially a cadre of headquarter and instructional personnel whose function it was to train the territorial or part-time soldiers of the colony. Except for the Rhodesian African Rifles, there were no regular infantry battalions or equivalent units of other arms which required the services of very young subaltern officers for employment as platoon commanders for example. All new commissioned officers were therefore found from among the other ranks already serving in the Southern Rhodesia Staff Corps, most of them having previously been commissioned officers in the British Armed Forces or the forces of the Commonwealth during the war.

It was not until the two Rhodesias and Nyasaland were joined in Federation that regular infantry battalions became part of the order of battle and the need for young subaltern officers was felt. The Federation brought together four infantry battalions which formed the fighting core of the Federal Armed Forces. These were The Northern Rhodesia Regiment, the 1st and 2nd Battalions of the King's African Rifles and the 1st Battalion, The Rhodesian African Rifles. The latter unit was indigenous to Southern Rhodesia whilst the 1st and 2nd Battalions of the King's African Rifles were both found from Nyasaland.

Prior to the establishment of the Federation in 1953, The Northern Rhodesia Regiment and the two battalions of the King's African Rifles were part of East Africa Command with headquarters in Nairobi. East Africa Command (controlled by the British Army) was charged with providing a battalion for counter-insurgency operations against the communist terrorists in Malaya and this responsibility was carried over to the newly formed Central Africa Command which came into being on the establishment of the Federation. In the early days of the Federation the officer complement for the four regular infantry battalions was found by the British Army which seconded regular army officers to Central Africa Command for a tour of duty normally of three years.

Federal army

It was, however, always the intention that the Federal Army should eventually relieve the British Army of this task and provide its own officers for all the regular units of Central Africa Command. This, as a matter of interest, was accomplished by 1959, six years after the Federation came into being. The last British Army officer went back to Britain and the whole of the Federal Army was officered by men whose loyalty was no longer directly to the Crown but via a Governor-General appointed by the Queen. Many of the Federal Army officers were ex British Army who had resigned and re-joined the Federal forces. The balance was found from ex-officers of the Southern Rhodesia Staff Corps and a number of ex-officers from the Union Defence Force, virtually all of whom had seen service in the Second World War.

Training

It had become evident at the outset that the Federation would have to provide not only the more senior officers to replace returning British Army officers, but subalterns as well, and it was at that point in time that the idea of training Federal subalterns at the Royal Military Academy, Sandhurst, was conceived.

With the exception of the Rhodesian African Rifles, the other infantry battalions had been built on the traditions of the British Army and had (since before the turn of the century in the case of the King's African Rifles) been officered by British Army officers, most of whom had received their officer training at Sandhurst. It was only since the Second World War that Eaton Hall had begun to contribute subaltern officers as well.

The first small batch of Federal Army cadets selected in Rhodesia left for England in 1954 and returned some two years later having achieved the most extraordinary distinction of having won the Sword of Honour and the top Academic Prize. These great distinctions went to Cadet Crutchley and Cadet McKenzie respectively. On their return the newly commissioned officers were posted to regular infantry battalions as platoon commanders.

Regularly each year thereafter a small number of Federal Army cadets left for Sandhurst in order to keep up the flow of subalterns into the infantry battalions of Central Africa Command. In point of fact their numbers were inadequate to maintain the requisite total of young officers in these and other units of the Federal Army, and it became necessary, before the dissolution of the Federation, to commence officer training at the School of Infantry located in Southern Rhodesia.

The experience gained in training officers locally was to stand Southern Rhodesia in good stead when UDI was declared in 1965, and Great Britain pulled down the shutters as far as any further military training for Rhodesians in that country was concerned. The last Rhodesian cadets to be trained at Sandhurst returned to their own country in November 1965.

References: Coster, KR 1979, *The Training of Rhodesian Officers at the Royal Military Academy, Sandhurst*, Scientia Militaria, South African Journal of Military Studies, Volume 9, Number 3.

OFFICER SELECTION BOARD by Captain Andrew Telfer

School of Infantry Crest

The journey to becoming an officer in the RAR begins with the Officer Selection Board (OSB). Many senior officers in the Rhodesian Army were graduates of the Royal Military Academy at Sandhurst as, prior to Rhodesia's Unilateral Declaration of Independence in 1965, ties with the UK had been very strong.

Consequently, the OSB process was closely modelled on the Sandhurst version that these officers had undertaken in their youth. Officer Commanding Cadet Wing at the time that I attended the OSB, (then) Major Mick McKenna, had been one of the Rhodesian cadets sent to Sandhurst. He would be a future Commanding Officer of 1 RAR.

For my part, I had arrived at SAS Training Wing during the Christmas break at the end of 1975 and been placed in a barrack room to await the start of Intake 150 in January 1976. The return to work for Training Wing, and with it the start of my own recruit course, was only days away when the call came to go to the School of Infantry in Gwelo for the OSB convened to select cadets for the annual Regular Officer Cadet Course.

I had applied for this opportunity, so I was among five young men summoned to the Adjutant's office and told to pack our kit and board a Land Rover to take us to Army Headquarters to meet the Army bus to Gwelo. There was one SAS trooper, small and muscular, Graham Peake. Two were recruits from Intake 148 who had completed Selection just before Christmas: the superbly fit Bruce Thompson who had broken the Speed March record and Cyrille Fournier, a Frenchman who had finished right behind him. Tony Lynch, of Intake 149, and I made up the group. It was a beautiful morning as we drove through Salisbury, joking with each other, young and fit, full of high spirits, eyes left or right towards every pretty girl we passed. We didn't know it then but two out of the five would be killed in action before three years had passed.

Arriving at the School of Infantry, we found well over a hundred young guys gathered for the OSB. We all wore camouflage fatigues without insignia, to remove any advantage or disadvantage attached to existing rank or position, replaced by large cloth numbers worn front and back, by which we were addressed throughout a week-long process that aimed to assess officer qualities (OQs). To this day, I still don't know what those might be.

We were formed into 'syndicates' of eight and moved through a series of tests. On the rugby field, we each took a turn leading our team over an obstacle. Briefed by an officer, out of earshot of the group, I was told that my obstacle was a rapidly flowing, crocodile-infested river (marked by two ropes) with small rocks sticking out of it (partly-buried, wooden stumps). Our team of explorers, hotly pursued by head hunters, had to cross the river as quickly as possible. On hand were a few short planks, none of which would span the gaps between the stumps.

School of Infantry Main Gate

I walked back to my group, totally clueless about how to cross the river and, as a result, did exactly the right thing - I gave them the same briefing I'd received and asked for ideas. That was just what the Directing Staff (DS) wanted, albeit driven by a lack of imagination rather than a flash of OQs. One among my group was very bright and hit upon a perfect plan, which we began to execute, making the task look relatively straightforward, so the DS started to put the pressure on: "The head hunters are nearly here!" We carried on with the plan, carefully moving each person across and avoiding the more-haste-less-speed trap that the DS were trying to lead us into.

"The head hunters are here!" announced the hyper-active DS. This was directed at me as I balanced on a little stump, handling the final plank, myself the last one left on the stumps. All that remained was for me to get across and the task was finished. I hurled myself from a standing start towards the far 'bank', was seized in mid-air by two of my team and landed safely… just. So, I have one candidate's bright mind and two others' strong arms to thank for my 'successful' leadership test.

In the classroom, we were tasked with two lecturettes, one a prepared fifteen-minute talk and the other a spontaneous two-minute ad-lib. These were a test of the ability to put one's point of view across to a public audience, an obviously important capability for those who intend to lead others. I chose to talk about drugs and chalked up Morphine, Heroin, LSD and Cannabis in large block letters on the blackboard. Sweeping back the curtain to reveal the words, I told the audience a string of tales about them that I had, until that moment, thought to be part of my store of useless knowledge. They were great anecdotes and easy to tell.

OSB It's All About the Numbers!

The ad-lib was conducted by reaching into a bag and speaking for two minutes on the first word drawn out. Mine was 'cup' which, if you think about it, is a simple matter of logically tracing mankind's progress from cupped hands to fine porcelain.

There were also written exercises designed to test the candidate's powers of reasoning and logical thought. This was followed by yet another more complicated test in which the individual was required to absorb and analyse a body of information concerning a proposed mission and thereafter produce a workable plan of action.

Then there was a group discussion. The syndicate sat in a circle and the DS introduced a topic of current affairs. There was a moment of silence, so I said, "Who'd like to kick off?" Number 35 offered a bit of an opinion and then dried up, so I said "Thank you. What do you think, number 47?" and so it went on. The role of the facilitator can be an effective leadership position without the risk of opening one's mouth too much.

There was nowhere to hide in the Panel Interview though, but the officers who interviewed us were not there to grill us. I found myself speaking honestly and sincerely, drawing a nod of understanding and approval for my answer to the question: "Why do you want to become an officer?"

"Sir, because I'd sooner my life were in my hands than in someone else's."

It was a moment of clarity, not consciously considered before, an acknowledgement more to me than to them that this wasn't a game.

The evenings were filled with walking-about-in-the-dark exercises that we each had to lead. They were never far from the grounds of the School of Infantry, so they weren't particularly taxing. One evening, we had a Mess dinner with the DS, I think to see if we ate our peas with a knife or climbed into the free grog.

I never felt a sense of being in competition with the other candidates and that was probably accurate. The Army needed officers and, although they weren't going to lower the bar to get them, there was room enough for everyone who had, or appeared to have, what they were looking for.

At the end of the week, we were called before the Selection Board one by one and informed of the outcome. "Congratulations, you are accepted as an officer cadet and will begin Course Inf 25/19. Good luck." This was said with a smile by Lieutenant Colonel Tom Davidson, Commandant of the School of Infantry and Chairman of the Board. A handshake ended it and I was on my way.

I found that 28 candidates had passed the OSB, including all five from the SAS. On the bus back to Salisbury, Tony and I discussed our situation. At that time, we were both inspired by the notion of becoming SAS soldiers, more so than becoming officers. We weren't there for a career but for adventure, and the prospect of what would come with serving in that Regiment strongly appealed to us. So, on our return we went to the Adjutant, Captain Mike Curtin, and told him that we wanted to withdraw our candidacy. He offered no opinion or advice; we were, after all, simply recruits and I hadn't even started training, so our careers weren't big on his agenda. Instead, he sent us back to the Army Recruiting Officer, Lieutenant Alf Logan.

We stood in front of his desk and told him we wanted to withdraw from the cadet course and continue as recruits at Cranborne. He looked at us steadily and said, "Sit down and listen."

We sat down, and he leaned across his desk, pointing to the pips on his epaulettes, "It took me ten years to get these, coming through the ranks. You can have them in one. Do the cadet course. If you fail, come back and try for the SAS. Now go and think about it, separately. I don't want you talking to each other. I'll call you back in after I've had my tea."

I had listened, and I realised the logic of his words. When I returned to his office, I told him I'd decided to try for commissioning. So, in January 1976, I set off for Gwelo in the same green Army bus that had taken me to the OSB. To my original suitcase, I had now added a green canvas kit bag stuffed with a full issue of kit. I had the feeling then of commitment. It was like an embarkation, as into a fast-flowing river, a feeling of things coming that I could not prevent happening without turning back, something I didn't want to do.

Tony chose to withdraw from cadet course, returned to Cranborne and succeeded in becoming an SAS soldier. In 1978, Corporal Anthony William Lynch was killed in action in an ambush by Zambian troops while returning from an external operation. He was just 24 years old. Lieutenant Bruce Malcolm Thompson SCR was also killed in action in 1978, aged 27.

THE SCHOOL OF INFANTRY, FIRST PHASE by Captain Andrew Telfer

Passing the OSB was only the first hurdle. The next challenge on the journey to joining the RAR was earning a commission. For regular officers, this involved a thirteen-month cadet course at the School of Infantry. This article will describe the nature of first phase of the cadet course (the first sixteen weeks) and subsequent articles phases two to four.

Our suitcases containing all our civilian clothes were placed in a storeroom at the end of Alanbrooke barrack room and locked away from us. I was in military uniform for the first time in my life. It included items that were specific to officer cadets: peaked caps with white bands, white epaulette slip-ons, red lanyards and white belts to be worn with khaki drill shorts and shirts. We learned to tightly wind puttees around our ankles, long bandage-like cloth strips, just over the tops of our boots, tied off with an ingenious and neat knot.

Alanbrooke Barrack Room: Regular Cadets' 'home from home'

Shirts had to be tight and straight under the belt. The required tautness could never be achieved by tucking them in, only by pulling them down. And so it was that we helped each other by kneeling down, reaching up under the other's shorts and pulling the hems of the shirt downwards. Given that the shirt was already tucked into the underpants, an observer could be forgiven for misinterpreting this act of brotherly service.

Everything was to be aligned in one straight vertical plumb line from the centre of the cap badge, through the nose, mouth, chin, shirt buttons, belt buckle, fly, down to our boots on the ground.

During shine parades, Colour Sergeant Charlie Davies (Hotfoot) employed the cunning tactic of deploying one eye for checking alignment while the other roamed the barrack room to check for movement elsewhere. When apoplectic, which was often, this extraordinary independent eye movement gave him the appearance of complete insanity.

Shine parade conversations were amazing social discourses, conducted at the shout, inches from one another's faces. One day, he hovered in front of my face, deeply troubled by what his alignment eye was registering. In a voice that startled seagulls in Beira, he bellowed:

"Bitches!"

He called us bitches. Hotfoot's lyrics were way ahead of his time, enriching the English language in a way that would take thirty more years for Snoop Dawg and Fifty Cent to catch on to.

"Ah, bitches... and what is it this time? The cap badge, nose and mouth are not aligned. What is out of alignment Telfer? Tell me that!"

How to answer? If I said "badge", he might order me to move it on the cap and I really didn't want to poke new holes through the immaculate white band. Mouth?

"It's the nose, Colour. My nose is in the wrong place!" I shouted, desperately.

"Ah. Nose, bitches... nose! Where do they find these people?" Shaking his head at misaligned faces and the poor quality of the raw material he had to work with, he moved along to his next victim.

While Colour Sergeant Davies was our Drill Instructor, Sergeant Major Cocky Binks was our Course Instructor. Him, we called 'Sir'. He had a face like a human shark, a predator surveying its prey, was an archetype professional soldier and, like Hotfoot, a top-class instructor.

He would order us into a block formation: "Front rank sitting, second rank kneeling and rear rank standing!" and deliver a copy-book weapons training performance, straight out of the Manual, feet wide apart, arms folded, not missing a beat: "Now look this way for a complete demonstration..." Hands moving fluidly over equipment, synchronised with word-perfect explanatory instructions, he taught us each weapon with economy and precision. On the range and in the bush, he dropped the Parade Square manner and became a stern coach, carefully watching and relentlessly improving our individual performances.

There was a stage at which the shine parades were escalated to his inspection and he brought an uncanny level of understanding with him, seeming to know exactly what was going on in the barrack room: who was pulling his weight, who was positive and who was not. Years later, he told us that, after leaving us to our own devices in the barrack room between inspections, he'd quietly listen in at the window. Based on what he heard, he'd plot his next move: test, torment, tease or train, all the while driving us upwards.

His delivery was only affected by only one minor quirk, a tendency to reverse the order of words or even to create new ones. Words like 'immaculent', 'accreate' and 'aarghwakeupyooo' entered our vocabulary. We might be sent for a run up the kopje, arrive back and be told: "Too back, slow again!" or be ordered to "Front your face!" Desperate to understand him, we were at first worried as he baffled us but later, we came to look forward to his creations and mimic them in the barrack room (in his absence… we weren't suicidal).

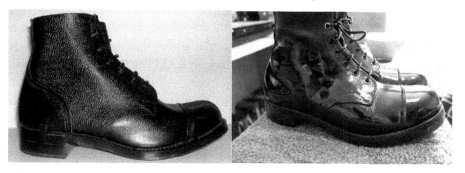

Boots Ammunition Initial Kit Issue   **Boots Ammunition Fit for Inspection!**

Most of the cadets fell into two groups: the soldiers and the school-leavers. Only a couple of us fell into neither group. The soldiers were young men who had already completed military training and, in many cases, full National Service. Those who had been through recruit courses in the SAS or the RLI were already very highly trained soldiers. Much of First Phase, although no less tough for them than for anyone else, was not new learning for them. The school-leavers included some very capable youngsters but, untrained and only 18 years old, they were up against it. The age range on the course was 18 to 26 and there is a great difference in maturity over an 8-year age span at that time of life. I was 21 years old, in the middle of the range, so I didn't face the same challenge that they did. We all had our own unique difficulties in the months ahead, but the youngsters had it toughest and only one school-leaver (the excellent future SAS officer, Mike Rich) would make it to the end.

Our Course Officer was Captain George Lambert-Porter. This man personified the image or picture of the officer that we all aspired to be: smart, confident, knowledgeable and authoritative. He looked like a leader, while we, at that stage, didn't even look like the led. George knew his business and presented matters-military in a style that was articulate and concise. His manner towards us was sardonic and aloof, disdainful and remote. His motive was pure: commission no-one who might be a threat to his good reputation. Secure in the knowledge that he did not have our individual interests at heart, we formed up daily to receive his disapproval. In truth though, in the lecture room, in the field and through his own personal example, he taught us what an officer should be, acting as a sort of high comparison between where we were and where we wanted to be.

Captain George Lambert-Porter

Years later, George would row a small boat, with his son, across the Atlantic Ocean, an extraordinary feat, but in 1976 he had the rather more difficult task of finding someone in Inf /25(19) suitable for commissioning. As young soldiers in training, we knew we were fortunate indeed. The best instructors in the Army were selected to train the annual regular officer cadet course and Captain Lambert-Porter, Sergeant Major Binks and Colour Sergeant Davies were superb. That, of course, did not make things easy.

Each day began with PT taken by the Course Officer. At 0555 we'd form up on the rugby field, watching the road for a semi-vintage blue car to chug through the gates, hoping it would not. It always did and out would step George L-P, immaculate as always and full of bright ideas to start our day. Sometimes it was a squad run which I liked. Running a body of men in step reduces the cadence and pace to that of the leading members, something not lost on Graham Peake, who'd run hundreds of kilometres in squad runs in his SAS training. Having noted that George invariably turned the squad to the right to set off for a run, Graham and I located ourselves at the right-hand end of the ranks, securing pole position and a degree of control over the pace.

From time to time, we ran the Assault Course, a series of rope, log and wall obstacles that, although tiring, did not take very long and, if our time beat our previous best, could earn us an early finish. Sometimes, however, we'd hear the dreaded:

"Pair off with a man your own size and weight and fetch the logs" The logs were 12-foot telegraph poles that should have been in the ground supporting national communications, not bouncing up and down upon cadet shoulders as we ran with them up the stony track to the top of the kopje. The kopje was one of our DS's favourite places for us to visit. It was a high rocky hill overlooking the School of Infantry, ideally positioned as an instrument of pain. Graham was very strong and I'm sure that on occasion he was pulling both me and the log along, anxious not to be among the last, who would have to repeat the exercise.

Having thus earned a leisurely breakfast and a good day's rest, we received neither. We doubled back to Alanbrooke, quickly showered (we'd already shaved before PT and woe betide the cadet who didn't) and bolted down whatever the Mess Hall had available (there was no time to wait for cooked food).

'Alanbrooke' Bed Layout

By 0755, we were on the side of the Parade Square, stick boots (highly polished black leather parade boots) gleaming, puttees strapped with the regulation three folds and shirts KD (khaki drill) tightly pulled down. The tallest among us, Cadet Soal, had the unenviable role of Right Marker. Hotfoot positioned himself in the centre of the square and bellowed, "Right... Marker!" and Soal would march out alone to selflessly face the singular attention of our Drill Instructor while we huddled on the side of the Square like sheep, safe in numbers.

When Hotfoot had finished berating Soal, he summoned the rest of us for two hours of "Shoot the left foot forward", or was it the right? Get that wrong at your peril as the kopje beckoned and it was even harder in stick boots. Hotfoot amazed with his ability to break a drill movement down into numbers, completing only part of the movement on each number, a feat that frequently required him to freeze his posture with one foot raised on the toe and the other suspended in a half step forward. Every time, he executed the movement perfectly, in spite of his legendary ventilated foot. Through endless repetition, hour after hour, day after day, we slowly came together and began to move in unison. George L-P then added his own inimitable touch: "Swagger. March with pride. March as if you own the place."

At 1000 there was tea, notionally. For us, tea involved doubling back to Alanbrooke, changing out of our drill kit and into camo clothing, beret, stable belt and weapon training boots, and doubling off to the Lecture Room to be there by 1025. This process of being five minutes early for everything became a habit that has stayed with me all my life. Captain L-P then took us for two hours of lectures, beginning with the organisation of the Army and developing over the year through each of the phases of war. It was fortunate that he lectured well as we were

'Alanbrooke' Bed layout Alignment

genuinely sleep-deprived by the late-night shine parades. We struggled to stay awake in class and I recall the hand writing in my notepad getting larger and rounder until it trailed off the page.

There were weekly Progress Tests but, as long as you could vaguely decipher your notes, they weren't hard as they were a test of rote-learning rather than understanding. The latter was examined more closely and relevantly in activities that came later in the course.

After lunch, which was about as leisurely as tea, we put on our webbing and ran to the range for weapon training or to the bush near the assault course for bush craft. In an early bush craft session, Cocky began a lesson on camouflage and concealment with what has to be the finest opening line ever: "To kill without being killed, you must know how to see without being seen". And, then he taught us. I truly believe that those of us who would later survive the war, did so because of the lessons learned on those afternoons.

If we had upset anyone during the day, which was often, we'd return to the assault course or to the top of the kopje to round off the day's festivities, and then go back to Alanbrooke to prepare for the start of our Course Instructors' evening entertainment, shine parades. Sleep for us, on the floor bedside our beds so as not to disturb our kit layouts, would come much, much later.

Finally, to ensure that First Phase wasn't one big, happy holiday, it ended with the fabled Endurance Exercise, described in *Chibaya Moyo 1*. When that was over, and after cleaning up, we formed up outside Captain Lambert-Porter's office and were called in one by one. Ten cadets did not re-join the squad, eighteen did. I was remarkably surprised to be one of them. First Phase had been sixteen weeks long, as long as a full course for a recruit. For us, there were forty more weeks to go.

THE SCHOOL OF INFANTRY, SECOND PHASE by Captain Andrew Telfer

Graduating from First Phase meant a move from Alanbrooke barrack room into the 'Hotel', a block of twin-rooms next to the Cadet Mess. It also meant reuniting with the civilian clothing taken from us at the start of the course. But, first an inspection to determine whether it was the kind of clothing 'that officers wear'.

Captain George Lambert-Porter and Sergeant Major Cocky Binks went from room to room, inspecting our wardrobe with the fearsome enthusiasm of Trinny and Susannah on a Fashion Fix. My best shirts, with fashionably large round collars (think Abba), made of 90% polyester, were hurled out of the window with the condemnation: "Officers don't wear plastic", to be seized upon by eager civilian batmen, never to be seen again.

"And what are these?'

"Sir, those would be my Oxford bags with the turn ups and the Prince of Wales check" said I hopefully. Out of the window... they went. "And these?" No point in explaining that the shoes he held so disdainfully were my very expensive, platform shoes in antique leather (think Slade). Hurled through the window, to batmen, delirious with delight.

Rick van Malsen suffered similarly. An ex-RLI troopie, his clothing would have been a great hit in Club Tomorrow, but it wasn't 'what officers wear' and so went the same way as mine. With little remaining, we were to endure the ultimate ignominy, the cruel injustice: we discovered that, after all our losses, Simon Willar's kipper ties and Vernon Prinsloo's chocolate brown suit had survived!

Whereas the objectives of First Phase were about the development of us as soldiers, Second Phase and beyond targeted our growth as future officers. This was the Classical War phase in which we were to learn and practice tactics associated with the phases of Advance, Attack, Defence and Withdrawal.

Our polite enquiry to French cadet, Cyrille Fournier, as to whether the French phases of war continued into the Retreat, the Rout, the Surrender and the Occupation was not met kindly, and we noted a similar reluctance to discuss Agincourt, Trafalgar, Waterloo and other pivotal moments in the history of his great nation.

We learned that under-pinning every phase, facilitating it, was a deceptively simple system called Battle Procedure which had as its aim: 'to ensure that every soldier arrives in the right place, at the right time, knowing exactly what part he is to play and what support is available to him.' It was fascinating to discover that this is how it's done; how tactical moves are connected into operations that deliver strategies. It wasn't lost on us that this was how the campaigns of history had been made possible. The groupings and the sequences made such sense and the recce/appreciation/plan process has been a tool that I have used to good effect in every field of business ever since. The structure of military orders is clever: it's easy to give simple explanations looking backward... orders provided simple explanations looking forward.

Learning a phase of war followed a pattern. It began with a lecture covering principles that governed that phase, to be learned and regurgitated in the weekly progress test. Next came an exercise around a model area of terrain constructed of a cloth surface, packed beneath to create topography and populated above with little features like buildings, streams, woods and roads. They were fascinating reconstructions, creating scenes onto which we were required to apply the principles: "Step forward Telfer and present your syndicate's solution to where you'd place the wire in this defensive position".

After the cloth model, the next stage of learning was the TEWT, a Tactical Exercise Without Troops. This was an extension of the current learning concept, taken out of the classroom and onto real terrain, and was where theory was grounded in practicality. It always began with a ground briefing, a description of the terrain in question, conducted in ground left, centre and right, near, middle and far. I was becoming fascinated by the structure of presentation evident in all things military. The vocabulary however could be a problem: George completed his briefing with the standard words, "Are there any questions?"

"Sir, what eez zis zing a 'donga'?" asked Cyrille. A gully or donga, however named, gradually began to mean something new to us; it became a route, covered from view and direct fire, and therefore important tactically. The ability to read ground was a capability that seemed to develop quickly, a natural skill among us that was at once interesting and revealing, like seeing with new eyes.

We learned about the characteristics and deployment of support weapons, including aircraft, filling our heads with ranges and fire control orders, our hands with new skills and our hearts with trepidation that we might drop something short or long and bomb each other. On one memorable occasion, I nearly did, but fortunately it was onto the DS. During an advance-to-contact exercise, I carried the 60mm commando mortar, a small but potent means of delivering mortar bombs to short range targets. Fired on by an 'enemy' from a tree line, the cadet commanding the patrol called for smoke.

Happily setting up the mortar and aiming the tube towards where I could see the fire coming from, I tilted it to an angle that I thought would provide the right range. George L-P, with characteristic irony, asked me if I was aiming at Bulawayo (a city in another part of the country) so I raised the angle, considerably shortening the range. He nodded confirmation that it would land between us and the enemy, placing smoke to cover our friendly forces flanking movement (the intent). In my wisdom, calling upon my many minutes of experience, I thought differently and eased it slightly forward again, just as I dropped a smoke bomb down the tube. Off it went and then down it went, a direct hit on the enemy position (not the intent).

The debrief was interesting: Cocky Binks (enemy for that exercise and the source of enemy fire), with eyes a little wider and speaking slightly more rapidly than usual, congratulated the mortar man on accuracy and handed over command of the enemy to Hotfoot...

The final phase of learning was the Classical War Exercise with troops. We advanced, attacked, defended and withdrew over half the Selukwe Hills in the middle of winter, digging trenches in ground selected not for tactical importance but for its impermeability to pick and shovel. While we scratched away, pitifully hoping to break through beyond waist-deep, cadet Thompson, as with all things physical, finished his work in record time, producing a perfect fire-trench of exact dimensions and angles. With nothing to do, he began to get cold and thought, quite logically if not tactically, "I'll make a fire", and so he did, in a little wooded copse to the rear of our position. Discovered by the DS, he was charged on our return to Gwelo and reprimanded. He was the only cadet to be charged on our course (I'd later make up for that).

We did lots of walking about in the dark during the exercises. One night, after I'd led the final leg of a patrol exercise onto an objective, I took position at the rear of the patrol while another cadet began to lead the first leg of the return to base. After we'd gone a very short distance, we stopped to cross a three-strand cattle fence and Major Mick McKenna, Officer Commanding Cadet Wing, came and stood next to me. "Oh, crap" thought I. This man's photo was in the first group on the wall in the Lecture Room, a preparatory course for Sandhurst back in the good old bad days; he had been George L-P's Course Officer; he commanded all cadet training at the School of Infantry... he was, in short, not someone I wanted to gain the attention of.

Pointing with his stick at a distant constellation, he quietly asked me: "What do those stars tell you?" Thankfully, I just refrained from answering, "That it's night time" and, instead, used the standard cadet fall-back position of denying everything: "I don't know, Sir." I should have said the 'night time' thing, as his face swivelled towards me and, even in the darkness, I felt the glare.

"That is the Southern Cross" said he and then went on to explain how it can be interpreted to indicate south.

I thought: "What a wonderful man, taking the time to explain such an interesting thing to a lowly cadet".

He thought: "When is this half-wit going to get the point?"

Eventually the half-witted cadet did get the point. If that was south, then we were heading west and we were supposed to be going east. I galloped off to the cadet patrol leader who had, it turned out, reversed his compass. The debrief for that exercise provided a perfect platform for McKenna to exercise the lowest form of wit as he recounted our conversation, milking every drop of irony out of "And what did Frederick Courtney Selous the Second reply to my question 'What do those stars tell you?'..."

THE SCHOOL OF INFANTRY, THIRD PHASE by Captain Andrew Telfer

We returned from a short leave to start Third Phase with the great news that we were going to Kariba. What could be better? Lake Kariba was the holiday resort of Rhodesia, with a picturesque town and a sandy beach on the lake shore, a casino, resort hotels, bars and discotheques. Full of the joys of spring and thinking this course wasn't too bad after all, off we went in the noble green bus.

Turning off the Great North Road at Makuti, we headed down into the wide Zambezi Valley. When the road was built, the engineer had the inspired idea of following the existing elephant trail, thereby finding the optimum route through the interlocking hills and tributary valleys. After about 50 km and still well short of Kariba and its cold beers, the bus inexplicably pulled over. It would not be accurate to say that we were in the middle of nowhere. 'Nowhere' doesn't have endless ranges of hills covered in dense mopani bush, nor does it have the Big Five or a host of other living, crawling, creeping or slithering creatures. And worst of all, 'Nowhere' doesn't have Selous Scouts.

"Off the bus, get off the bus!" ordered a huge, bearded Yeti who had lurched out of the undergrowth. "Now get your kit, you lazy, idle, useless bastards!"

Who or what was this guy? The brown beret, nesting in the thicket of hair, answered the question. This convivial, hail fellow well met greeting came from one of the bearded denizens of the deep bush, characters from the Brothers Grimm, Rhodesia's unique Special Forces, the Selous Scouts. Formed to meet the challenge of a war fought in the bush against an enemy at home in the bush, the Scouts were the bushmen, the trackers, the survival experts, the men who could pose as terrorists and infiltrate terrorist gangs. Their reputation was well-deserved and would have been greater if the true scale and nature of their operations had been fully known at the time. In August of that year, 72 Selous Scouts calmly drove into a ZANLA training camp in Mozambique and killed close to 1,200 terrorists at the cost of only five Scouts wounded.

I'd never seen one before and the Yeti cut a far from dashing figure, clad in ragged camo shirt, faded green PT shorts and stained vellies (tan leather desert boots) with no socks. Shouldn't he be off rustling yaks somewhere?

"Wafa Wafa is that way. Be there!" ordered the hairy hostile and then departed without another word, as did our DS with the bus, leaving us on the side of the road.

'Wafa Wafa, Wasara Wasara' was the name of their training camp on the shore of the lake. It translates: 'You Die You Die, You Stay You Stay', meaning they didn't really care either way. The Scouts ran their selection courses out of that camp and we now understood that it was to Wafa Wafa and not to the Caribbea Bay Casino that we were going... so off we went. "Be there", he'd said, and I certainly intended to be, and before last light; there was no way I wanted to be out there in the dark with creatures like him lurking about the shrubbery.

An afternoon run of several hours across stony ground and through the bush of the Zambezi Valley with nothing for company except the heat, the mopani flies and the occasional large bearded creature cursing by the trackside... is not fun, but we were fit and ran to the camp. Near the entrance, we saw a black soldier drenched in sweat, digging a huge hole in the ground. We were later told that he had killed a Fish Eagle and was being punished by having to dig its grave - he was still digging the next morning.

Sergeant Major Ant White, chief instructor, stood before us in the standard garb but surprisingly no beard (I had been thinking Scouts were born bearded), gave a minimal opening briefing and dismissed us. There was no food for us. "You are on a bush craft course. You'll have to learn to catch it for yourselves". We were shown to our rooms, as in an area of bush was indicated, "Sleep there", so we made little 'bashas', shelters of branches and leaves and went to sleep, dreaming of croupiers.

In the morning, we were introduced to the assault course. Unlike the School of Infantry with its poles, pipes and walls, this one was constructed mostly of ropes which, whether climbing or crossing, made short work of the skin of the hands. The route ended with a rope swing from a tree, off the bank and out into the waters of the lake itself, which was a great way to have a morning after-exercise swim if one ignored the potential to be joined by one of Kariba's many crocodiles. The Scouts kept them away, or so they said, by occasionally firing into the water. They used the same technique to discourage curious civilians in boats; it worked very well with them.

One of the obstacles, located near the end of the course, was a rope tied between two trees, spanning a thickly wooded gully. It was high enough to be daunting and long enough to make for a challenging crossing. The technique of the 'commando crawl' is the same the world over: lie on the rope, hang one leg for balance and use the other leg to lift and drive the body forward using the foot hooked over the rope. Well, that's the plan.

On the rope, one bright morning, I found a fellow cadet frozen halfway across. Nicknamed Wimpy, he was a good guy but a little overweight by cadet standards, not very agile and not destined to pass the cadet course. At that moment, he wasn't destined to cross the rope either. The Scout instructors noticed his discomfort and gently encouraged him: "Fall off, you fat bastard!"

I spoke to him: "Come on, you can do it. Just move a little bit at a time". The contrast in messages, between mine and the Scouts, continued until his top leg became unhooked and the poor fellow lay there, legs dangling painfully either side of the rope. If being prepared to put your balls on the line in situations of conflicting advice was a sought-after officer quality, he was surely demonstrating it. Unfortunately, this was overlooked by the DS, as Wimpy slowly rolled off the rope, hung by his hands for a few desperate moments and then fell into the jesse (thorn) bush far below.

Sergeant Peter Clemence presented the bush craft and tracking lessons. A quiet, introspective man, more attuned to the natural world than that of men, he had the physique of the very strong, gained from constant physical activity. He taught us how to set traps for food and, when our night-time traps caught nothing, he set his and every one of them was successful. He taught us how to read spoor, to look for sign, to "feel the passing of men". Under his tutelage, we replaced our laces with 'gusi-tambo' (string) made from threads of sisal woven by rubbing against our thighs; made fire from drilling thin sticks between our palms into a base of softer wood, blowing embers into a tinder of dry elephant dung. A fascinating instructor, he walked us through the bush, explaining the uses of plant and tree, cutting the depa vine to obtain water and demonstrating where to dig for water in sandy, dried-up river beds.

One day, our camp erupted. An impala had wandered into it by chance and, panicking, had run into the Lake. There was no thought except to kill it and so, in the evening, it was hung up in a tree for Ant White to demonstrate how to skin and butcher it. Explaining that people had died of thirst in areas of abundant game because they didn't understand how to take water from an animal, he showed us how to squeeze the stomach contents to draw plenty of water, giving each of us a drink. Then he took the raw liver and cut a piece for each of us, cadet Fournier first. I suspect, Cyrille being French, that White was hoping for a reaction of disgust, but Cyrille savoured it like a connoisseur, washed it down with a hearty swig of chateau stomach juice and pronounced the whole thing "delicieusement".

There was also 'Operation Egg' described in detail in *Chibaya Moyo 1*. The instruction we received at Wafa Wafa was of the highest standard and was fascinating. It was a tough place but what we learned was invaluable.

Our return to the School of Infantry saw our squad reduced from eighteen to ten. Once again, we were formed up outside Cadet Wing and called into the Course Officer's office one by one for a short interview, some returning while others disappeared to pack their kit. Their departure was felt keenly as we had been together for a long time and were close friends. And so, there were ten... and we began the most popular phase of all: Counter Insurgency, or COIN.

Patrols and patrol orders had been taught to us in Second Phase and these concepts were adapted for COIN. Immediate Action drills were practised for encountering the enemy.

COIN Exercise Debrief

Close-quarter encounters, with often simultaneous sighting between groups, were common in conditions of limited visibility in the bush. Consequently, we practised these as drills repeatedly over a range of possibilities: seeing the enemy first, being ambushed by the enemy, seeing each other at the same time, being ambushed in a vehicle, and so on. There was a clear connection with the section battle drills of earlier in the course and, as time would tell, we internalised these drills well.

Observation posts and Fireforce operations (described in detail elsewhere in this book) were taught during this phase, but it was the ambush that was my favourite tactic. The planning and execution had logic, creativity and cunning. I enjoyed preparing and giving ambush orders, setting out the groups, defining arcs of fire and eventually springing the ambush itself. The idea of acting on good intelligence to create a situation in which the odds were so heavily in favour of one's own forces made complete sense and there was true job satisfaction in getting it right. It was a satisfaction that was to carry forward into operations when I made use of this tactic as often as possible.

During our exam, my appreciation and plan were reviewed by OC Tactical Wing, Major Terry Hammond, in a one-on-one interview. I had the impression of a highly intelligent man who enjoyed taking the measure of the student, gradually raising the bar to see how deeply the subject was truly understood. He stood with his back to me, looking out of the window, casually testing and probing. I knew that I was a novice duelling with a master and, when he finally turned and nodded his approval, I felt that I had achieved something. One day, I would come to serve (and fight) directly under him and discover what an extraordinary officer he was.

Third Phase culminated in two operational attachments, one to the Rhodesian African Rifles Regimental Training Depot at Balla Balla and another to the Rhodesian Light Infantry, both described in *Chibaya Moyo 1*. Our counter insurgency phase at the School of Infantry was a critical stage in our development as officers. First Phase had trained us as soldiers, Second Phase had equipped us with the ability to think tactically in a conventional theatre of war and Third Phase in the unconventional sense, the kind of war we would be fighting.

THE SCHOOL OF INFANTRY, FOURTH PHASE by Captain Andrew Telfer

To enter the Fourth Phase of the Officer Cadet Course was to know that the process of selection was ending, and you were being prepared for a commission. Only ten cadets had made it this far.

Rick van Malsen and Simon Willar had both completed their National Service as troopers in the Rhodesian Light Infantry and were keen to return as officers to continue the mayhem. Vernon Prinsloo and Rich Blaylock were a little older and had both been sergeants during their National Service, Rich in the Corps of Engineers. Vernon had also been the Light Heavyweight boxing champion of Rhodesia and, of great interest, his sister was Miss Rhodesia. Pat Lawless had been an Air Force Cadet and nearly completed the eighteen-month course, failing a flying test near the end. The Blues place flying skills first and leadership second, which is fair enough, but their loss was the Army's gain.

Graham Peake had been an SAS Trooper and two other cadets had already passed SAS Selection: Cyrille Fournier, a graduate of the French Military

Academy at St Cyr, and Bruce Thompson, the oldest but fittest cadet on the course. The youngest cadet and the only school-leaver to make it was Mike Rich, son of the then Commanding Officer of the RLI. Mike had a ruler with the name 'Captain Rich SAS' on it. It must have been his father's and was a good example of beginning with the end in mind; Mike would one day fill that role with distinction. To my continued surprise, I was still there too.

I was taking my turn as President of the Mess Committee (PMC), a sort of OC Mess, when George L-P asked me how course spirit was going. Lulled by his unusually friendly manner into a false sense of security, I replied that it had gone off the boil a bit and we could perhaps do with something to pull us together. I should have known better. It was only a matter of days before we were summoned to the lecture room for a briefing. The next Miss Rhodesia Competition was to be held in the Bulawayo City Hall the following Saturday. Our mission was to kidnap whoever won and hold her to ransom for charity. As he walked out of a room stunned to silence, he looked at me: "Will that do, Telfer?"

The first to get his head together, Cadet Lawless walked to the front of the lecture room and, accepted by all of us, led the formulation of a plan. Simply put, we were to get ourselves accepted as a guard of honour through which the newly crowned girl would walk on her way to the car that was to take her to the reception after her 'coronation'. As she passed between us, we would whisk her away and hold her in one of our cars until the ransom was paid. So that we didn't frighten her, Vernon's sister Corinne, the outgoing Miss Rhodesia, would go in the car with her.

When Saturday evening came, dressed in our Greens (our number one dress) we waited outside the City Hall while the competition took place. We were just outside two huge doors, at the top of a wide flight of stone steps. When the word came that the new Miss Rhodesia, Jane Bird, was leaving the building, we formed up in two ranks, facing inwards and flanking her walk down the steps. I don't know who had waylaid the official limousine but, in its place, appeared cadet Peake in his battered Peugeot. Any hesitation that Jane might have felt at the sight of this banger was swept away, as was she, by the rapidly closed ranks of cadets who literally lifted her into the car. Graham, with two national beauty queens in the back seat of his jalopy, sped away to a nearby sanitary lane to lie doggo until the ransom was paid.

We entered the hall and announced that Miss Rhodesia was now in the hands of Inf /25(19) and would not be released until our peaked caps were generously filled with money for charity. Disconcerted but perhaps reassured by our uniforms, wide smiles and polite manners, the guests paid up and soon she was returned to them. For Jane, the experience cannot have been too traumatic as she would later accompany Vernon to the Cadet Commissioning Ball as his date.

Reports of this and other matters led Army HQ to become increasingly concerned at what was happening at the School of Infantry. Although the Generals fully acknowledged the sterling efforts of our instructors to make something of Inf/25(19), they resolved to recruit better raw material for future cadet courses.

And so it was we heard the news that a film crew was to be sent by the Rhodesia Broadcasting Service to make a cadet recruitment movie. The scope of the 30-minute programme covered the course from start to finish so, as we were close to the 13th and final month, we would be required to re-enact scenes from the earlier phases.

It began all over again with the Officer Selection Board. There we were, numbers on chests and backs, facing interview panels and crossing obstacles. Rich Blaylock was tasked with leading a team carrying a 'special piece of equipment' (a round concrete block) across a chasm spanned by a long pole. His confident voice-over was not quite in-synch with the 'special piece of equipment' slipping out of its rope harness to take an unscripted plummet to the ground below.

The famous big green bus made a guest appearance, bringing new cadets to the School of Infantry and depositing them outside Alanbrooke barrack room to be greeted by Hotfoot in time-honoured Blitzkrieg fashion. As our junior course, one year behind us, had already occupied Alanbrooke, Mike Rich and Vernon Prinsloo were salted in among their ranks and 'inspected' by Hotfoot, while Simon Willar played Duty Student, taking long, serious notes about fluff on caps and the length of sideburns. This curious combination of two courses confuses viewers to this day.

Gradually, roles in the movie started to emerge. Bruce Thompson featured strongly, literally so, in the physical training, muscles rippling as he demonstrated log PT and pokey drill (a strange ritual involving swinging and generally waving a rifle). His commentary about physical fitness reflects his passion for the subject and his very valid assertion that one couldn't function effectively as an infantry officer without it.

Oscar Wilde would have approved of 'life imitating art' as Simon played Chuck Norris, variously stripping and assembling an MAG, laying a mortar and firing a rifle on the range, with Cocky Binks standing behind him, arms folded and feet wide apart in his classic weapons-training posture.

A cinematic low point in our epic adventure was the 'Assault Course to Silly Music' scene. To the accompaniment of Monty Python sound effects, we crawled over, bumped into and fell off the same obstacles that we'd effortlessly jumped, swung and leapt over in First Phase. During one of the takes, which thankfully didn't make the cut, I tripped just before a concrete wall and ran head-first into it. There were similarly less-than-perfect performances by one or two of my comrades but, eventually, the better cuts were cobbled together into something resembling a commando assault on a Pre-School and there was much for the discerning viewer to admire.

The sequence of tactical training was explained by George L-P in a nice story about Classical War. Pat Lawless's role as a tactician of the von Clausewitz school was played to masterful effect, albeit on a cloth model in Gwelo against Anti-Rhods rather than the folding hills of Belgium against Napoleon. In an edge-of-the-seat lecture room scene, the script required George to ask a question and for two cadets to answer it, the first incorrectly and the second correctly (thrilling stuff). Rick van Malsen drew the short straw and was told to get it wrong. George asked, "What is ground of tactical importance?" a question Rick could have answered in his sleep. He is now immortalised in celluloid as his face reveals an inner struggle to find a wrong answer, let alone give it.

Ordered to be exhausted for scenes of the Endurance exercise, we took acting to a previously unplumbed low as we pretended to lug heavy things around the bush. At one point, acting in a coup scenario, we made an RV with an African partisan played by our mild-mannered, bespectacled, civilian batman dressed in immaculately pressed dungarees (just the image of a bush-dwelling, covert operative). Conscious of his day job, he had a cold Coke on hand and a sandwich for the DS, as you do in the bush, in a coup. Again, much for the discerning viewer to admire.

One bright Sunday, attracted by the prospect of an intro to Hollywood, Gwelo's prettiest young starlets were lured into the one place their mothers always warned them not to go (the Cadets' Mess) and joined us for the 'It's not all muck and bullets' barbecue-by-the-pool sequence. 'Le vie en rose' was dashingly over-acted by Frenchman Cyrille Fournier on tennis court and swimming pool, complete with Gallic wink at camera. His kind offer of boudoir scenes with one or more starlets was, surprisingly (to him), declined. Meanwhile, on the rugby field, a back line of cadets scored a try that would have been brilliant had there been an opposing team.

"This is a horse", explained a super cool-dude Grey's Scouts instructor standing next to one, hoping to establish himself as a master of the movie one-liner. Not exactly "Go ahead, make my day" or "They'll never take our freedom" but amusing to him at least. Our five-day attachment to Rhodesia's mounted infantry regiment, which had been very good, was reduced on screen to super-imposed, slow-motion scenes of shirtless young men displaying military tans (brown arms, white torsos), riding bareback through water, to weird music, in a sort of homo-erotic collage. Very dodgy combination: donkey-wallopers and movie-makers.

Back to muck and bullets, and an extraordinary scene of Graham Peake taking a round in the leg, falling and being set upon by Rick "I just wanna slay everyone" van Malsen (hardly Florence Nightingale) who promptly treated him for a neck wound.

Thrilling action of that standard abounded in this epic film. Rick appears again, getting his fix for mayhem by blowing up a (hopefully) disused railway line. A Land Rover wrapped in a tarp, slowly sinks below the waters of Gwenora dam, while my voice describes how to *float* a vehicle on a tarp, ending with the words, "Well, that's what's supposed to happen". An ambush is sprung on our long-suffering civilian batmen, this time scripted to play enemy and fall before our 'hail of lead', relishing their moment with over-extended and comically dramatic death throes worthy of an Oscar. And, frequently in voice-over, Pat Lawless pronouncing the whole thing "Helluva interesting", his favourite expression, a sentiment perhaps not shared by every movie-goer.

Between 'shoots' and 'takes' we fitted in Fourth Phase and somehow arrived at the moment we'd all been waiting for, our Commissioning Parade. This too was filmed, with ten cadets marching about and eventually off the Square… in Simon's words: "Often in step".

For anyone with time to spare and no interest in cinema as an art form, here are the various links:

https://youtu.be/qkUJeB0Gb2w
https://youtu.be/i27hOVni0IA
https://youtu.be/PW5SD_NYqBQ

The significance of the final step off the Square cannot be over-stated. With that single pace, each of us became an officer. I went from being 727410 Officer Cadet Telfer AT to becoming Second Lieutenant AT Telfer (781135). Each of us had entered a different way of being. As we fell out, the first person to salute each one of us and shake our hands was Sergeant Major Cocky Binks, our Course Instructor, following a tradition of old.

That evening at the Cadet Commissioning Ball, for the first time our uniforms bore the insignia of our new Regiments. Pat, Cyrille, Bruce and I were commissioned into the RAR; Simon, Rick, Mike and Vernon to the RLI; Graham to the Army Services Corps and Rich returned to his Corps of Engineers.

I still have a tin trunk with my name in tennis shoe-white smudged along the side. Bruce and I purchased one each from an Indian trader in Gwelo, packed our kit into them, marked our names on the outside and loaded them onto an open

Land-Rover. It rained, causing the tackie-white on both our trunks to run. And so, we were off to war...

INTERROGATION by Captain Russell Fulton

Regular Officer Cadet Courses were split in to 4 Phases:

1st Phase was of 16 weeks duration and a period that, historically, separated the proverbial 'sheep from the goats'. Alcohol was strictly forbidden and 'Passes' were neither issued nor entertained and "Visitors" were most certainly not part of the programme either. 1st Phase was specifically designed to summarily remove any vestiges of self-importance and/or worth, to completely break you down, and then mould you in to something that the establishment could work with and build upon in the ensuing three Phases, that is to say.... if you lasted that long! It was all a bit of a bugger being a cadet as you weren't worth a great deal in anyone's eyes except, perhaps, our Mamas' who were not seen or heard.

The 'First Phase' of a regular cadet course comprised the following:
Arrival, kit issuing, first photos taken (in PT kit), barrack room allocation.
Physical training – daily.... as in every day
Foot Drill
Weapon training (all platoon weapons)
Shooting – mainly on the 'Hooters' range.
Map Reading including three practical map reading exercises. In the main, these were conducted in the Selukwe area.
Voice procedure
Basic army organisations
Progress Tests
Endurance Exercise

The culmination of First Phase led up to the main event that was "Passing Off the Square". Three inspections and a drill performance followed by an assault course. First review was with the RSM, then OC Cadet Wing, followed finally by the Commandant (3 weeks to cover them all). In the case of my Course, the Cmdt (Lt Col Eric 'Sally' Sobey) was away on the date/day scheduled for that event, so the CI (Terry Hammond) took that in his stead. This was timed for Week 12 of the Course and when we passed it, we got our first pass (a one-week break).

The most challenging part of any regular cadet course was the endurance exercise that was headlined for three quarters of the way through, with an orchestrated 'capture' and comprehensive interrogation at the hands of highly skilled RIC members. The following provides an insight in to this challenging 24 hours.

Interrogation

And so, there we were, enslaved in the truest sense and standing with our genitalia exposed for all and sundry to laugh at as we were turned to face towards the sun. I would guess that the time was now roughly 1400B by the orange glow of the sun filtering through my hood and its position in the sky. We now wore over-sized and poor fitting trousers, hood, leg irons and handcuffs…no shirts. With the preceding fifteen weeks of limited exposure to the sun, when I tell you that we would have put 'Snow White' to shame you best believe it. What happened in the hours that followed was a combination of swelling of tongues (thirst has that untidy habit when denied moisture) and a hue that would make a banquet lobster proud. I think we changed from white to pink and then red and finally an angry claret; who's to know but we were sunburnt and there could be no denying that little fact.

After about three hours we heard the footfall of several troops and the sound of galvanized buckets being filled with water, presumably from one of the nearby water bowsers? From the sound, that you will come to understand in a little while, it sounded like 'Mugs, Aluminium' had been placed in each bucket so that we could hear them scraping gently against the bottom of the bucket with the motion of the water. These buckets were then carried up and down our lines with water deliberately being spilled on the ground and mugs full of that cool water poured on to the baking earth. It smelled like the first summer rain, but we were to be having none of it.

It was now the commencement of the game of 'PSYOPS' on which we had received some fairly detailed instruction (interrogation and counter interrogation techniques) about a fortnight prior and from members from "Tiri Tose" 1POU. "If you take anything away from this lecture, take this: 'If you are ever captured, give your interrogators nothing! These are skilled men and they will use whatever information you volunteer against you. From the moment you open your mouth they will have you by the 'short and curlies' and, over time, they will crucify you…be under no illusions about that! Say nothing!!"

Hmmm, Roger Copied Over!!

By late afternoon, circa 1700B, a few of the guys were really starting to take strain. Being hooded, in a state of physical and mental exhaustion, thirsty, hungry, completely disorientated and feeling alone…these things can get a swift grip on the least suspecting mind and soon there were plaintiff cries from a few: "What's going on? This is a F******* exercise isn't it!?!" followed by "F*** this, I've had enough…I've had enough!"

Having spent four months shitting-off together leading up to this little soiree you didn't exactly require a degree in audiology to figure out who it was that was surrendering. It was a mixture of emotions: sad, tragic but morbidly laughable in the case of some. I learnt many things during my time as a troopie in the RLI, on recruit course and whilst serving in my Commando and that it is folly to judge any book by its cover. There were many men who looked the part, talked the talk but most certainly never walked the walk. Many of these who gave up were those least expected to do so. You live and you learn don't you! These individuals were hauled off to a tent somewhere to be processed and removed from the course and RTU without further ado. Enough of that and back to the evening festivities if you don't mind.

We were then led in single file down a footpath littered with small, sharp gravel chips to give our broken, bleeding feet a taste of that 'loving army feeling' and ended up being placed in a small, disued mine working pit. It was roughly 30-40ft in diameter, about 6ft deep and completely exposed. Once we were all assembled in the pit, we were turned to face the setting sun and spaced far enough apart from one another to give you the impression that you were alone.

Orders were barked down at us in an unfamiliar and onerous tone advising us that we were to keep our mouths shut at all times or face punishment. All part of someone's sick mind whose 'tricks' had already started to resonate with many. The floor of the pit was covered with about a foot deep of sticky red mud that leant weight to our captivity. Once bedded-in it, it was difficult to withdraw your foot without exerting extraordinary effort. The sun dipped below the Great Dyke and the dusk took its dutiful place ushering in a new and altogether set of unpleasant experiences. We felt a lot colder than the actual air temperature suggested because, remember, we had all been quite badly sunburned. The true purpose behind our afternoon 'sunbathing' now became a whole lot clearer. As darkness replaced dusk the evening's revelry was about to commence in earnest.

Hooded and now in eventide darkness, we heard the chatter of our guards (RAR Demonstration Company troops) who had been placed around the pit at various intervals. They were preparing their evening meals and their blue gas cooker burners were discernible through our hoods. They fried up 'Fraybentos' bully-beef fried in butter and seasoned with curry powder and cooked sadza and feasted whilst we salivated like a pack of hydrophobic dogs.

No sooner had our senses been teased by these intoxicating culinary smells when our attention was drawn abruptly towards what was undoubtedly someone's entrance to the pit. It was the sound of scraping aluminium mugs and splashing water! Ahh, shower time no less...well, we did stink a bit. What happened then took us by surprise as water was generously ladled across our exposed and sunburnt shoulders so that the water ran like small rivers down our backs, under the waist band of our trousers and, perish the thought, between clenched buttocks.

Instinctively, we bent forward away from the cold water, but we were swiftly and roughly pulled upright by our hoods and the ladling was repeated to our fronts. For good measure, water was poured over our trousers sufficiently to saturate them. I don't mean to sound crass, but it was a good thing we weren't feeling amorous that night as 'Mr Wiggly' had 'left the building'! This went on for several hours at evenly spaced half hour intervals (guessing at that). As the hours passed the temperature in the Selukwe Hills dropped dramatically.

At the sound of the approaching water buckets we immediately started to shiver and almost uncontrollably. John Walters (RIP), at 26 years of age, was the oldest regular cadet and John was in considerable pain (kidney stones). John was a tough bugger and never one to cuff-it, but he called out for help; appealing to deaf ears for 'Starlight' (medic/doctor) to be summoned. It never happened, not for a while anyway. John's condition was regressing fast and despite receiving repeated slaps for breaking silence on his behalf, he was sensibly removed from the exercise and returned to "Hooters" for treatment.

Once John had been removed from the pit (guessing around 2200B), I was led from the pit and taken in to a tent that was filled with brightly glowing paraffin lamps. I was forced to kneel on some deliberately placed coarse gravel chips. That ominous voice we had heard earlier that evening was the one that greeted me now. "Give me your number, rank and name". I remained silent. The question was put to me again, this time it was not a request. I remained silent. "Listen here you little prick, if you want to play clever bugger with me…let's get on with it then shall we!" I received a vicious slap across the face that almost knocked me out and immediately had that metallic taste of blood in my mouth.

Now…I was very, very pissed-off! Whilst I was getting my head in order a bucket of cold water was thrown into my chest followed by a second that was poured over my hooded head and completely saturating it. My interrogator, let me refer to him as 'Satan', moved behind me and grabbed the back of my hood and forced my face upwards. He asked, "What is your mission?"

Again, I remained silent and expected another swot. In its stead came more water poured over my hooded face; I will tell you that wet twill fabric against a breathing mouth and inhaling nostrils is not a combination conducive to comfortable breathing. When saturated fabric is wrapped around someone's face, the natural process of breathing (inhaling more precisely) is significantly impeded. Satan released the tension on the hood before grabbing a bigger handful of fabric and forced my head upwards again as he poured more water over my face.

Within seconds I was in a state of near-drowning as water ran in to my mouth and down my flared nostrils. Satan laughed at my violent coughing and spluttering before putting the question to me again, "What's your f****** mission, you son of a bitch!" Well now, I couldn't suppress my temper any longer and told him to "F*** off!" I am of a generally sunny disposition, but I am no shrinking violet either; there are boundaries with me and one of these is to never paint my Mother as something that she is not, not even remotely.

Satan lifted me up from the floor by pulling on the short chain that linked the handcuffs together; pulling the chain as high up my back as he could without dislocating my shoulders. Now I was in excruciating pain and, like a very angry adder, I needed to 'bite' this person.

When I was standing, Satan lowered my arms and I swung my head back and caught him somewhere on the side of his head. Another bad idea and Satan repaid with a short sharp hit to my solar plexus. I was bundled out the tent and returned to the pit; bleeding from the nose and mouth, a bit of a 'shiner' and a little winded but, 'bastard', now I was cold! Throughout the night the interrogations became a Dr Jekyll and Mr Hyde role play with the 'good guy' trying to soften us up and then being replaced by 'Satan' himself.

My last visitation to the interrogation tent was the toughest. A female RIC operative was present who chortled infuriatingly about my 'diminished' manhood and then took pleasure in demeaning me with her sultry but seductive voice! It was followed by the return of 'Satan'. Another bucket of water was thrown over me and then I heard the humming of something that I was familiar with but couldn't immediately place. It was a cattle prodder. Again, I was asked what my mission was and when I remained silent, I received a touch from this item between my shoulder blades. I cannot tell a lie... it was an extraordinary but debilitating pain that only served to incense me. In my mind, I wasn't sure if this was still an exercise or just a bad dream. For me, I believe that my anger carried me through but who's to know. It's all beers and skittles you see!

When the hood, handcuffs and leg irons were removed at around 0100 hours, I was moved to a bonfire where I found my 'surviving' mates. We hardly discussed the goings-on from that night, who hadn't been broken, who had or anything else; we just sat silently, perhaps stupefied, wrapped in sleeping bags and sipping on hot, sweet coffee until we fell, thankfully, into a comatose deep sleep. Some things are better left unsaid. Time for reflection would come but for me it was a triumph of the spirit and not a measure of my endurance over any of my brothers; that would have been arrogant, self-serving and conduct quite unbecoming.

The exercise was far from over, we had the Escape and Evade section to negotiate. That's well covered by my brothers in the chapters that follow.

And so, for inquiring minds who might reasonably ask why this anecdote is in a book about the RAR? Fair enough too! It's not about me and it never was intended to be so. My record is a miniscule sweat stain on the armpits and heroics of those who preceded and followed me. The purpose, if I may be allowed the opportunity to expand, is what we officers endured and why. Regular cadets were required, in Fourth Phase and when commissioning was all but assured, required to list our three unit posting preferences. I selected the RAR in all three, got shat upon but ended up with the first prize, a commission and posting to 3Pl, A Coy, 1RAR.

Men of the highest standing and whose personal pride, dedication to duty and regiment were my reward. Without question, the greatest honour and privilege of my military career. Did I make a difference? That is for my good men to determine because that is all that matters to me.

DRILL PIGS AND BATTLE MARCHES by Major Tom Fulton
(Adapted by the author from *Into the Vortex*.)

The conduct of shine parades on a Regular Officer's Cadet Course, followed the pattern whereby everyone stood by their beds in the appointed dress form. On the arrival of the assigned Senior NCO the awaiting cadets were brought to attention and a detailed inspection, assisted by the Duty Student following the Instructor at an unobtrusive distance, writing down all of the comments. Quite what they ever wrote, I had never thought to ask.

It was impossible to predetermine who the instructors would be, who were detailed with the conduct of these shine parades. The only discernible common denominator was that none was below the rank of Sergeant; Sergeant Keith Bartlett boasted that sole distinction and they were all from the Regimental Wing of the School; where such grave matters as smart and soldier-like was the permanent flavour of the day.

To the man they were recognisable by the swagger in their step, and the way they held themselves – at all times. Sergeant Major Tom Van Rensburg, Colour Sergeants Louis Thackwray and Sandy Miller – you could tell them a mile-off. The swagger had nothing to do with arrogance per se`. No, it was the sheer pride that they took in their immaculate turnout, which they rightly believed should be displayed at its best; if it took an air of arrogance to round off that aura of splendour, that was what they did.

As my military mind started to slowly mature, I grew to understand the absolute necessity for this almost eccentric genre of quite-unique soldiers. Their immaculate representation of military pride, also echoed in the halls of the training institutions of the Police and the Air Force, whose instructors they trained. Their role was a vital part in the complexity of the intricate military juggernaut; and they were, in every way, a symbol of everything that it stood for.

Quite regardless of who took us for shine parades, or the occasional spin around the parade square, the Course felt a belonging to our own Course Instructor. Lou Hallamore, was a picture of everything in the other drill pigs and more. Beneath the veneer of the hard-arsed drill instructor, lay a personality of quite contrasting qualities. The softness of his eyes was the most obvious give-away to the latent intelligence, and experience. There lay within, an understanding, although it held a respectably professional distance from actual compassion. He gave the impression that you could talk to him. although in my wildest imaginings I couldn't even conjure up the picture of a situation of such gravity, that I would be required to do so. The rare interchanges that did take place at a personal level, were characterised by his obvious sincerity, and surprisingly close interest in each individual Cadet.

Another pastime peculiar to the Cadet first phase was the Battle March. This ordeal entailed first an inspection to ensure that everyone was carrying the prescribed set of kit. This was most important because the Battle March was not an activity to be taken lightly, and a set of rules had to be abided by.

The first leg saw squads of six doubling out of the side gate of the School, opposite to the northern kopje. The march from here followed a route that went out to the south and rounded in the area of Senka Township. It eventually married up with the rifle range road and came back into the establishment's grounds. This circuitous route was some six kilometres in length, and ended up at the start of the all-too familiar assault course. Each man carried a pack that was filled with the kit and equipment to carry out conventional operations, for a period of two days. The added complication of issuing rations was alleviated by the substitution of rations with two nine by four bricks which were carried in the kidney pouches.

To add further joy to what already bore the promise of a most thrilling excursion, an MAG light machine gun and its first line of battle ammunition were thrown into the mix. The final loving touch and reason for retaining the 'Classical Warfare' theme, was plainly to make sure that the entire exercise was endured under the comforting shelter of the matt olive-green steel helmet, which jostled and bounced heavily on the head of the wearer, and held in every iota of heat.

Because of its rigours, and the chances of a fall, our FN rifles were exchanged for what were termed 'DP Rifles'. These were obsolete .303 Enfield rifles that had been rendered unusable by the armourer. A few meaningless obstacles were passed before the most major hurdle, and this presented itself in getting the squad over the ten foot wall. The two first arrivals at the wall would face each other and together form a cup with their hands to launch the next approaching Cadet high and up, to catch onto the top of the wall. The first two such launched men would then avail themselves to assist those still to come. The spirit of the team was the lesson in this exercise and even the most athletically retarded were eventually dragged over.

It seemed to me that most of the other obstacles were actually a bit of a waste of time, although the added cumbersomeness of the rifle and helmet, made it a lot less comfortable than an hour at it in PT kit on Jannie Steyn's watch. There was a towering rope obstacle to climb, horizontal ladders to swing hand-by-hand from, and concrete pipes to crawl through, and when we reached the end, we reclaimed our real weapons and made off again.

At a brisk pace, we made our way to the south gate once more, and continued to the rifle range, via the scenic route. Finally, lying puffing and gasping and at our absolute physical limit, as soldiers we were, most reasonably, expected to engage and hit the targets. Scores were then taken, and compared to other squad's performances. It had apparently been carved on some sacrosanct stone somewhere that the current Regular Cadets had to be the holders of the current Battle March record. This was no mean feat, when one considered the number of Courses that had set and reset this precedent before us.

To be the reigning champions was a given, but to break the record took some brave attempts before that aim was eventually achieved. The finally selected conquering team was made up of those half dozen men who took some obscene masochistic pleasure out of such a torturous pastime, and I felt absolutely no personal slight at not being selected for the squad that would eventually break the record.

THREE LITTLE PIGGIES by Major Tom Fulton
(Adapted by the author from *Into the Vortex*)

Without question, quite the most trying physical and mental test of a Regular Officer's Course is the Endurance exercise. A week of forced day and night marches, carrying dizzying weights, without food and restrictions on our water in the middle of which we were captured, and subjected to twelve hours of physical interrogation. This involved a night semi-naked, in freezing temperatures, repeatedly doused with water and interrogators armed with cattle prodders and macabre, Transylvanian senses of humour.

We were liberated the day following the interrogation by Partisans, or so the narrative went. Then told by the DS that we had a day to recuperate, and regain our strength, there would also something for us to eat. A stores vehicle appeared, as if on cue, and started reversing into the area we had chosen for our base for the day, as it straddled the bubbling Ferny Creek in Shurugwi. As the tailgate dropped, there was mayhem. The air was filled with the plaintive screams of the three piglets that were unceremoniously thrown out to the still-bemused looking cadets.

One piglet never made ground fall, as Mac MacIntosh snatched it out of the air athletically, and tucked it under his arm. Acting as nonchalant as the squirming porker would allow, he turned to his syndicate with his lop-sided grin and said, Shall we dine, Gentlemen?

My syndicate was almost as lucky. Our little porker ran straight into Spider Webber's waiting arms, and I took the chance to start sharpening my army clasp knife on a nearby rock, while the others collected some wood.

The third syndicate was making rather heavy weather of capturing their determined porcine morsel. Our piglet was secured at front and back, and although the knife was by no means sharp, I was able to cut the throat without too much bother.

I was busy, and kneeling to the task of eviscerating our meal, when I looked up to see Tonks Jones break into view, with their hapless piglet under his arm. I put down the knife and rinsed my hands in the small stream that ran through our temporary camp. I never took my eyes off them.

The other fellows in my syndicate, had clearly become spectators, as Tonks stepped purposefully into the water, the squealing piglet, held fast. He uttered an instruction back to Chris McLennan that wasn't quite audible, but it still wouldn't have prepared me adequately, for what I was about to see.

By now, Tonks had reached a point in mid-stream, and was up to his calves in the cold, bubbling water. He glanced over at me, and there were still some remnants of blood around my upper arms, face and chest, and he seemed to be saying to himself, Bugger that. This way I don't get covered in blood.

This is starting to get interesting, I thought to myself…as behind Tonks stood McLennan and he was bent over the two-handed weight of a large flat boulder. At a given signal Tonks, holding the little pig's front legs to its sides, thrust it under the water and looked up at Chris in signal.

Chris lowered the obelisk gently and placed it as inoffensively as he could on top of the writhing piglet. There was a sustained flurry of semi-submerged splashes at first, as the piglet vainly sought to wrestle from its weighty bondage, and the two brutal murderers stood there for a full minute, or presumably until the bubbles had stopped, and then jumped to the task of collecting their wood.

I returned to the business of butchering our carcass, while my syndicate brought in enough wood for an opulent Hindu funeral. The idea was that once the carcass was gutted and washed, the meat would be impaled and held over the flames to remove the hair.

I looked up to see what was happening in the Jones and McLennan camp, and saw that the next act of the pantomime was sure to start soon. I was still shaking my head at their method of execution…it was bizarre.

The cadaver of the drowned piglet had been recovered from the stream, and was lying in state on a small grassy bank, not far from where the remainder of the syndicate were industriously making a fire. I watched as McLennan morbidly strolled over to the prostrate form on the bank, a dejected hands-in-pocket walk, perhaps feeling a trace of remorse at his active part in the piglet's heartless demise.

Supposing that its lungs full of water might in some way taint the meat, he put the sole of his boot on the ribs of their lunch. Exerting as much pressure as he dared, without breaking the little ribs, he forced every drop of water that he was able, out of the small chest. The springy young bones of the piglet's thorax, returned to their original posture, and the surface tension created by the sudden change of shape, filled the little pig's lungs with air.

The first sign of life was the flickering of a little pink eye, and giving off an outraged, indignant squeak, it bulleted off into the undergrowth. The chase was on – again.

The piglet never survived the follow up. I never bothered to ask…

(The Regular Cadet's Endurance Exercise would always be the yardstick by which Officers who had completed it, measured those who hadn't. Rightly or wrongly, that remains an indisputable fact, to this day.)

NYAMA, NYAMA EVERYWHERE BUT NOT A GRAIN OF SALT by
Major Tom Fulton
(Adapted by the author from *Into the Vortex*)

Enjoying a day of rest on our Endurance Exercise as Officer Cadets, we had been given a piglet per syndicate. We had not eaten in nearly three days, and had spent the previous night under interrogation. It went something like this, that day…

There certainly is a suggestion of a salty taste when meat is cooked to a frazzle, but it didn't seem enough for our bodily needs. We struggled to deal with the questionable flavour of the unsalted meat, and our bodies were crying out for the replacement of the electrolytes that had been lost in the process of getting us where we were. Perhaps not surprisingly, very little was actually eaten, and by now everyone was looking for somewhere to sleep. There was plenty to share out later, and it would keep us going for a while.

If only we could get our hands on some salt.

I cut out a section of the ribs that remained. Wrapping it in a piece of sandbag inner, I stashed it in my shirt before looking around to see that no DS were lurking, and I stole out of the sleeping camp.

My first intention was to get to high ground, to better survey the terrain, and to hopefully see some sign of habitation. The nearest that was plain to the eye, was situated on top of the next rise and I was genuinely bemused at how out of breath I was, once I had arrived at the gate of the kraal. So, this was what the first signs of malnutrition felt like?

The kraal itself was devoid of any tribal identification that I could tell, the hut surrounds, neatly swept and a few chickens free ranged about. Seated with his back to a tree was a man of indeterminate age. Closer scrutiny brought my attention to the muscles of his back and the head was shaven like a bullet. I hazarded first a greeting in chiShona, which also begged permission to enter.

The man rose and turned, and I saw at once that he was aged about 40 and immediately his unbuttoned shirt revealing his tribal scars, and made me adeptly change tack, Zakubona Malume. Lichonenjani. (I see you Uncle. Good afternoon; in siNdebele.)

The man smiled and replied in English, Come in Baas. Good God! Where are you coming from? He asked with a look of concern. He hurried into the hut and collected a stool for me, before seating me comfortably in the shade of the eaves of his hut. I had barely started the story when my host, urging me to continue my explanation, put a container of water on his fire. Still listening attentively, he drew up his stool and sat opposite me, and confirmed his still undivided attention. I apologetically offered him the piece of meat, and explained that I was willing to trade it, for whatever might be on offer.

Sorry Baas, I'm finding it hard to understand. He said, accepting the meagre offering. Why are these people, who are supposed to be your 'teachers' treating you like this? He asked in shocked disbelief. I was pleased not to have to explain something that I found difficult to answer myself, so it was with some relief that the host put a cup of hot sweet tea in my hand, following the ritual washing of hands. The cup itself was pale blue and it sported many black chips in its enamel, from years of use.

Try as I did repeatedly, the rim of the cup was too hot for me to sip from, but it was the peripheral sighting of the bread, that drove the tea right from my mind. The bread was sliced neatly by the slow sawing action of an almost complete hacksaw blade. By wrapping one end neatly with electrical tape, the discarded blade had found a less rigorous life; the softness of the loaves would never wear it out. The slice of bread itself was a good three inches thick, and the Sun Mixed

Fruit Jam that had been liberally smeared across one surface, had never tasted so welcome. Downing's doughnuts… I thought absently.

Although I knew that to 'hombera' or to gently clap ones hands in gratitude, was essentially a Shona custom, I knew that my host would accept the not-so alien gesture as one offered with sincerity.

"Ngiyabonga kakulu Malume wame" (Thank you very much, my Uncle) was the easy part. It was trying to swallow the bread that was difficult. There was nothing wrong with the saliva glands beneath my tongue, but they simply weren't working fast enough! Before long the rim of the cup had cooled enough for me to take the first sip and I marvelled at how I could trace the passage of the hot liquid as it made its way into my inner body.

The effect of the energy in the sugar was almost instantaneous, and even as I was thinking this, my blood stream was racing to gather up all the nutrients suddenly on hand. It was the instant reaction to the energy-filled sugar that so encouraged me but try as I did, I simply could not finish the slice of bread. Fearing my manners might come into question, I explained to my host that the forced deprivation had led to my stomach shrinking. The man waved the explanation aside and gave me a piece of newspaper into which I could wrap the precious morsel.

I had been too shy to ask, but my new friend saved me the effort, as he dug in his breast pocket and removed a small green and white cellophane packet. I smiled to myself when I had sight of the tobacco – 'Shamrock' that my Oupa used to hand out gratis to his labour. I remembered how I had coughed when the Security Guard had given me my first 'pull', but that hadn't entered my mind yet. After admitting that I'd never been trained in the art of rolling a cigarette, I watched in fascination as the process before me was enacted.

First, my miner host explained to me that every paper had a grain, and he demonstrated this by lifting up an old copy of the Bulawayo Chronicle. He slowly tore the paper in the direction of the print, and explained as the paper tore raggedly, that this evidently was against the grain. He repeated the action tearing across the print and down the page and I acknowledged that I saw the difference. My mentor then tore a strip about three inches wide and about the length of a normal cigarette. The paper was made more malleable, by rolling it between the fingers and thumb, and what was left was a rectangular curved receptacle of paper in his hand, into which he poured a measured amount of the shredded tobacco.

It was with a sure, practiced dexterity, that the tobacco within was now physically rolled into a cylindrical shape, before one edge of the paper was tucked in and rolled, while the loose end was licked and stuck down with saliva. A matchstick was used to tamp the tobacco at both ends, and he finally tore the excess paper from those ends.

The finished product was then presented with a smiling, proud flourish and an offered, lighted brand from the fire added the ignition required as I gingerly took the first pull. It was coarse. It was harsh, but God it was good. I felt the immediate wave of dizziness that naturally follows a period of abstinence. It was the relaxation it produced that must have led to eventual addiction I thought idly to himself, and it was with a physical effort I floated back to Earth, when I realised I had better get back to the remainder of the crew. I felt quite drunk by the time I handed back our communal smoke.

The proud but pitiful contents of the hut told me that my new acquaintance was struggling to make ends meet. I also knew that my newfound friend would have given me anything I asked for, and it was for this reason that I asked only for a small amount of salt. At least I could take this back to my companions and make the rest of the exercise a bit more tolerable for us too. I bade the man farewell, with all the customary promises and good wishes, and covertly returned to our makeshift temporary camp.

ONE STORMY KARIBA NIGHT by Major Bruce Sand

In 1973 just before Christmas, the Rhodesian Bush war commenced in earnest. The North Eastern part of the country saw farms attacked and landmine warfare became the norm. The intensity took the Rhodesian army by surprise, as the previous insurgent tactics of confronting the small, highly skilled and thoroughly determined professional security forces head on had changed dramatically. Ambush of civilians (mostly white farmers) and hit and run with active mining of bush roads while avoiding any contact with Rhodesian soldiers became the norm. The insurgents were truly as fishes in the sea, a well-found principle of Chairman Mao's doctrine. Regular army units were fully committed, and Reserve units were slowly coming on line. Op Hurricane was in full swing.

Yours truly was still an officer cadet in training at the School of Infantry and me and my cohorts were preparing for our final major Counterinsurgency (COIN) Exercise prior to being commissioned as shiny new Second Lieutenants. It was not to be.

With mixed emotions we were told no troops were available and the exercise was off. Our Course Officer and the School Staff had to develop, from scratch and at very short notice, something to replace the defunct exercise. They rose to the occasion and came up with a two-part scenario. A two-week local COIN exercise on a much-reduced scale followed by a two-week operational attachment with B Coy 1 RAR, who were offensively and aggressively patrolling the shores of the

Western end of Lake Kariba to prevent a suspected insurgent incursion in the North West, much like the active and ongoing bush war in the North East.

Phase 1, the local COIN Ex went well but was somewhat anti-climactic after the much anticipated but now cancelled final Ex. Phase 2 was very much an unknown quantity. We were to deploy and join a fully operational RAR company engaged in active border control. Anything could happen. The reality really set in for the Cadets who had joined straight from civvy street when live ammo at full scale was issued prior to the long drive to Binga on the shores of Lake Kariba. The former soldiers who had successfully competed for Cadet training were far more stoic. All of us had seen active border Control as

Bruce Sand as an MAG gunner in the RLI

Private soldiers and a couple, me included, had seen action in Mozambique during Op Lobster 2 in 1971.

The trip to Binga and B Coy's base was a very long and boring 16 hour run in four Landrovers. Tired, very dusty and short of humour, we settled in for a night's sleep as soon as we arrived. Our Course Officer Capt Nick Fawcett was safely ensconced with the B Coy Commander to plan our deployment with his fighting patrols. The next morning after a simple but filling meal, Capt Fawcett called for an Orders Group so we could be tasked with our various jobs over the next couple of days. We were split into three groups: the two larger teams were to deploy on joint foot patrols whilst the last team of two, me and OCdt Dave Marais, were warned off for a night Recce patrol by boat that evening.

Dave and I linked up with our infantry team of a Cpl, rifleman/Radio Operator and Machine Gunner plus the two RhE Sapper boatmen who would be our transport. The plan was simple. We would leave Binga by boat at 1630 that afternoon and head east along the lake shore to a small island close to Chete Island (in Zambia) and overwatch the international border between Chete Island and Rhodesia. At 0600 the next day we would return to Binga for de-briefing and a day of rest. It was only 1100hrs, so Dave and I checked our kit, cleaned our weapons and drew our rations. With nothing else to do we hit our beds and went to sleep while we could.

The run to Chete was entirely uneventful and we crept into our designated observation point just after last light. All we had to do now was watch and listen for the enemy. You should note that Lake Kariba is really an inland sea. It is hundreds of km long and over 50 km wide at its widest. With such size comes the risk of big waves in bad weather. The lake is large enough that it influences local weather. What we didn't know was it is very prone to sudden and violent storms in the late evening with high local winds and very nasty wave action depending on the fetch and strength of the wind. Nyaminyami, the local tribes' fabled snake god of Kariba gorge, must have been in a serious snit that night, and we, in a small, open 18ft aluminium assault would later bear the brunt of his wrath.

When Lake Kariba was built, it flooded a massive area of forest and bush. Almost all the shoreline was very liberally studded with dead standing trees that had almost petrified in position. They were a serious obstacle to navigation and very easy to run into at night in blackout conditions. We were tied up to one of these trees, about 15 metres from the shore of our designated island location. The night was very black with no moon and we soon realised, at about 2100hrs, that we were going to be in a storm. Within minutes the weather was atrocious.

Rapidly increasing nasty short fetch swells and increasing winds convinced the Sapper Boat operator it was time to withdraw. No argument from us or the Cpl patrol commander. Then disaster struck: as the boatmen were starting the twin 40hp outboards a very large wave completely swamped the boat from the stern. We were instantly shipwrecked, and in crocodile infested waters.

Crocodylus niloticus or the Nile crocodile is second only to the Australian Salt water crocodile for size, aggression and appetite. They are very active at night! A snack of tender young soldier would be very welcome to any resident croc. The speed which we left the capsized boat and made for shore was, I'm sure, something to behold. Once ashore on a shallow rocky beach, a quick check revealed only Dave and I had kept all our webbing, and weapons, and even worse, we were one person short! The machine gunner was missing. Dave and I were also the only ones to wear our bulky military life jackets, so it was imperative we search quickly for our missing gunner.

We did what we had just spent the last year in training to do. Dave and I took command. The Infantry Cpl and the senior sapper were tasked to watch for crocs with our rifles and Dave and I swam back to the capsized and partially sunk boat which was still tied to the tree at the bow.

To our great relief, who did we find perched on the very top of the bow and dressed only in his underwear: our missing Machine gunner. With a great deal of cajoling, perhaps even some threatening, we managed to convince him we could tow him to shore safely. African solders rarely are swimmers of any description so it's not surprising he was rigid with fear of drowning or being supper for a crocodile. We finally got him into the water by me giving him my life jacket and two of the outboard motor portable fuel tanks to put under each arm. We paddled him ashore safely.

Then, just as we were starting to take stock of our serious circumstances, wouldn't you know it, Nyaminyami was appeased and the squall literally died in a minute. It did not stop raining however 'til well after 2:00pm the next day. We must have had a least 4 inches of rain over the next twenty hours. We were wet, cold and thoroughly miserable. No radio comms, no food, no shelter and no dry smokes and far too much fresh water. To add insult to injury, the Cpl's map was mush and we had only two rifles with 300 rounds of ammo between seven soldiers. I clearly remember thinking that we would be in deep Kimchee if we were discovered by either insurgents, or a Zambian army patrol before we were rescued by our own guys. It was a very long and sleepless night.

With the dawn came the realization that perhaps things were not so bad. By 0800hrs we would have been overdue by 2 hours and a search would quickly get underway. The weather remained very unpleasant, with continuous rain, at times very heavy, so helicopter extraction was unlikely. We decided we needed to take more careful stock of our resources, and make sure we were the only island inhabitants. A quick sweep by the RAR team of two with our rifles and webbing (the gunner still had only his underpants) revealed our island was about 200 metres by 50 metres and deserted. Dave and I decided to salvage what may have been washed ashore and we quickly discovered the Gunners missing shirt and trousers snagged on a small tree on the shore. We also saw that the boat was still barely afloat at the bow and that the water beneath was clear, about 10 ft deep and a white sandy bottom. Perhaps we could recover the missing weapons, radio and webbing with ammo.

As soon as we were together again, and the Cpl had confirmed we were alone, Dave and I decided a salvage op was on. The crocodile question was solved by the expedient use of my HE grenade into the water not too close to the boat. After a muffled thump and small bubble cloud of a successful detonation, we felt safe enough to swim out to the boat. It took us about 45 min to recover everything lost: weapons, webbing, radio and sundry boat stuff. The only things we could not find was one boot (the gunner's) and a machete. The boat was just too much weight for us to recover, so it would have to wait until we were rescued.

Still very wet and very hungry we regained semblance of being soldiers. We could defend ourselves if necessary. By noon the rain was easing somewhat, and I tried to get my water-logged cigarette lighter working. After two hours of trying, I finally managed to start a very small and feeble fire that needed constant care to maintain. Then, at about 1400 we heard the most welcome sound of an aircraft. The fire was quickly made to smoke and in no time a civilian Cessna 172 flew over us and waggled his wings. We had been seen. A second pass and a streamer dropped within a couple of meters of us. The note attached said: Locstat (location) noted. Call Sign 2 (B Coy) advised. Boat en route. LUV PRAW (Police Reserve Air Wing). A great collective sigh of relief ensued. We would be rescued.

About an hour later, the Binga Police launch arrived, and we finally recovered the capsized assault boat. A quick check to make sure nothing was forgotten, and we were on our way to a hot shower, food, a cold beer and a well-deserved night of sleep in a dry bunk. The look of relief on Capt Nick Fawcett's face was something to behold. I'm sure he had spent hours trying to figure out how he was going to report the loss of two officer cadets to Army HQ. The trip home was uneventful and a week later we were preparing for our graduation parade. I later took command of the RhE national service field troop and was responsible for a short while to provide sapper boatmen to man the Binga boats. Little did I know I would be seconded to B Coy 1RAR for two years from 1974-76 and do two tours based in Binga. No shipwreck then!

SCHOOL OF INFANTRY: ALTERNATIVE DRILL MOVEMENTS by 118794 O/Cadet Krajewski A.J. Sah!

Now then: I thought to share with thee three infamous and one hilarious moment on the Hallowed Ground of the Parade Square at School of Inf. These involved four worthies, all casualties of the Winter Cull, and all RTU: perhaps not a moment too soon!

Do you remember a man named Graham Behan (RTU)? A dark-haired, scruffy lad, with black hair and beady blue eyes? And when I say "scruffy", think of what this must mean from one who can spend three minutes in a suit tailor-made and fitted by the best of Saville Row, yet present the appearance of having spent three weeks in the same suit, living in a bus shelter on Boar's Pond Road....

I have a wonderful memory involving Graham of one of our earlier sessions of drill: more-or-less at the "By the right, quick MARCH!!" stage. At this word of command, given in a spray of saliva by Sergeant Hendrikus Janse van Vuuren (known to us all as "Yes SERGEANT!!"), the squad took off in a reasonable facsimile of marching; left leg and right arm in phase, right leg and left arm and so on. Not so O/Cadet Behan, who made off in manky fashion, left leg and left arm and right arm and right leg conjoined in a terrible parody of this dignified and martial movement.

Sgt Van's eyes bulged with horror and he spake thusly: "Bee-Han! What are you doink! Get in step, man! BEEE-HAAANNN!" All the while Brian tried and tried again to disconnect his left arm (thumb pointed smartly forward, and parallel with the ground) from his left leg and vice versa. Alas, he failed utterly in this attempt and the squad was left in tatters. We were called to a halt ("Halt, check, one-two!") and without delay doubled away at speed up the Kopje. Another perfect morning in sunny Gwelo.

I'm sure you all remember one Arthur de Sweeten, a pale, shivering youth of some 18 summers, with pale blue eyes, a curious avocado-shaped body, featuring shoulders about 50% the diameter of his hips, knock knees, the very flattest of feet (size 12), sun-scorched elephantine ears (mind you, who's talking?), and a cucumber-like nose (again...) on which several high-velocity projectiles and (alas!) several "Adult toys" may well have been modelled?

On the "Day of Infamy", we were practicing the marching salute past the saluting dais, on which was perched our beloved Sgt. Van, seeing without being seen, killing without being killed. On the march, with eyes fixed firmly to the right, we were commanded to salute. However, to the collective Horror of All Present, as all our arms flashed up beret-wards, O/Cadet de Sweeten also smartly saluted, but, alas, with his LEFT arm!!

Again, Van's eyes bulged out of his crew-cut cranium, looking remarkably like two peeled litchis in his sun-bronzed visage, his jaw sagged, and his lower lip quivered. Before he could recover, O/Cadet de Sweeten made good, saluting with his RIGHT arm. For five or six paces, this curious-looking youth marched along, knock-kneed and jug-eared, with both arms held up to his temples, palms forward, and fingers rigid with military dignity. Never before had we seen the Double Salute. Apparently, neither had Van.

"De SZZSweeetenn!!!!" Roared Sgt. Van in a froth of blown spray "What the faaaaack are you doink!?! Are you on drucks (i.e. drugs)?"

Predictably, we were called to a halt, and were soon enjoying yet another splendid view of the peaceful town of Gwelo: as usual, from the top of the Kopje. We could clearly see Van on the parade square far below. He appeared to be holding his head in both hands. The other squads drilled away at all times and everywhere. They all looked like ants.

How about O/Cadet Dick Darter? Dick was just one of those fellows who was destined to spend at least some time in some army, somewhere, yet spend 90% of the duration of his National Service on the back of a Land-Rover being

School of Infamy: Alternative Drill Movements

'transferred' somewhere else. I saw him about a year after I left Hooters, myself having been sent 2 (Indep) Coy, RAR at Kariba. Within SIXTY seconds of Dick's walking into the NCO's canteen, one fellow from the mortar section and two fellows from the 'Mahammad Cars' (that is Armoured cars) were lining up to punch him in the ears, nose and throat. Just that kind of lad was Dick!

Whilst still at School of Inf., Dick was eventually 'outed' as the Perpetrator of an Outrage performed during bayonet drill. On the day in question, we were marched off the square and were on 'Dad's Yacht' resting under the line of trees bordering the road that flanked the far side of the square when, with a bull-like bellow, Sgt. Van assembled us all and at the very mightiest of the Double. His face was white with rage as he demanded to know which of us has pegged his rifle, bayonet fixed, into the ground as we relaxed on our smoke break. This was apparently a class A Military transgression, punishable by thirty lashes, walking the plank and death by firing squad ("in your own time, carry on") but, perhaps curiously, no-one owned up. Van let us know in no uncertain terms what was going to happen to us; the DREADED change parades!!

I have dim recollections of many trips up the kopje, but perhaps you gentlemen have a better memory of the sordid details than do I. All I do remember was that we shat! I do remember several O-Groups being held in the barrack rooms, during which this was all discussed. We had no proof, but certain person or persons claimed to have seen O/Cadet Darter, Dick, for the use of, commit this infraction. Van of course knew this all along, but this was the whole point of the episode. I cannot recall the outcome beyond it leading directly to the downfall of the aforementioned Dick Darter, knob-nose extraordinaire and first man to go three weeks without stopping. As I recall we all went without stopping in the days immediately following this Atrocity! Truly a case of "keep your mouth shut and your bowels open"!

Finally, do you perhaps remember towards the end of the School of Inf. Experience, I guess sometime around June 1978, when we were instructed in Riot Drill? Now THIS was more like it: a bunch of herberts marching about the local Compounds, bayonets fixed, making jabbing motions in the air, and shouting various anti-nimarangie slogans. This drill featured the display of banners ordering the mob to disperse (the reading of the riot act, literally), anti-communistic and morale-sapping blasts on the bugle (by lips untutored), volleys of 7.62 x 51 mm NATO fired (typically) at "the man in the red shirt". And finally, the pressing forward of the squad to retrieve the limp and tattered mortal remains of the recipient of the most recent volley, the same being scraped up and dropped onto one stretcher, canvas, for the use of. This promised to be enormously fun stuff for one and all.

Except of course for the wearer of the red shirt. But then again, that's life.

Well, practising this drill was a joy, but it reached a climax when a certain Captain Mick "Get a grip" Hardy OLM, made a startling discovery. One of our comrades at arms, one O/Cadet Dobson, was a slightly built, blond, curly-haired fellow with a slightly effeminate way of speaking, and a weak and strangulated voice.

So, Quite Naturally, he was singled out to shout out at the very top of his voice, commands many and various, and again and again. Both Mick Hardy and Van leant on supporting structures, weeping with laughter and in convulsions of mirth at O/Cadet Dobson yelling out in a curiously feminine register the Commands "Bannn-nneeeer!" [banner unfurled]; "Bewww-gullll!!" [terrible raspberries on the dented and mangled bugle blown by whoever was operating this Satanic instrument] and Others.

It was actually very funny indeed, but poor Dobson!! He was gentle and docile fellow, and in consequence was RTU! But not before he had 'bannered' and 'Byeeewgled' his way into immortality of a sort, and we had all just about peed our trousers with mirth, and Mick Hardy most of all. Mick Hardy laughing until he cried is one of my most enduring memories of this ferocious and quite unforgettable man.

THE CURIOUS BOKNAAI AFFAIR by 118794 O/Cadet Krajewski A.J. Sah!

"I have enough decency, Sir, not to move when I am naked!"
-Major Dennis Bloodnok in The Goon Show: '*The Case of the Missing CD plates*' (18 October 1955, series 6, episode 5).

It was winter and dawn's pale light poked impudent, marmalade fingers through the trees that ringed the sports field. There, steaming and gasping, a group of white-legged and hapless officer cadets scuttled hither and yon, bent double with their exertions, driven by the clipped military tones of Lt Marcus ('Down for Thirty') Adams. Eventually the PT session ended. However, those assembled were not yet out of harm's way, for with a cheery "Last one in the pool's a cunt!" the steaming, panting masses were directed to partake of some healthful thrashing in freezing water.

Alas! that from behind the bougainvillea hedge that ringed the pool, Gash's invitation was answered, somewhat churlishly, by a Voice Anonymous (i.e. the late O/Cadet Brian Baker).

"Fuck you!" it said.

You could have heard a pin drop. However, no word was uttered until the assorted herberts, buck-naked, goose-fleshed and dripping freezing water from their aquatic exertions were commanded to form up pool-side in a squad before a smirking Lt. Adams.

"Right! Don't think that some gash fucker can say "Fuck you!" to his course officer without consequences! Therefore, what I want you all to do is assume the star jump position, and on my command (wait for it!), leap upwards in the star-jump position. When you reach your maximum height, I want you all to shout out the word "Boknaai! Right? Begin!"

ALL: "Boknaai! Boknaai! Boknaai! 'BOKnaai!! BOKNAAAIIII!!"

What a sight this must have been!

As a participant, I confess that for many years I was taunted and troubled by strange and surreal visions of hairy-arsed, naked bodies leaping upwards in unison, roaring "Boknaai!" It was, after all, a fearsome war cry whose origins remain uncertain. Certain military historians maintain that its origins hail back to the Battle of Culloden Field (1746). Others, however, take the view that its origins are more recent: namely the Second Anglo-Boer War, and specifically, the 217-day siege of Mafeking (17 October 1899 to 17 May, 1900), where the encircling Boer Commandos taunted the British Army with many cruel and hurtful jibes.

But I digress. Whatever the origin, this was, for us all, a new experience, I am relieved to be able to say. Thinking back on this though, the indignity and the exertion of this fearsome and morale-sapping boknaai-ing were tempered by the curious, and dare I suggest slightly pleasurable, sensation of one's wedding tackle remaining fractionally out of synch with the rest of one's body.

This was manifest by a strange sensation of weightlessness at the height of one's leap, where not all portions of One's Self paused in mid-air, before succumbing to the pull of gravity.

Upon One's descent also there existed a curious and somewhat compelling feeling in One's loins. This sensation was somewhat ostentatiously called whiplash by the fortunate few so gifted as to be a length more obviously masculine, and was manifest at the bottom of One's leap, a quintessential instant before springing skywards again.

Not that I've given this much thought, you understand.

Still, just how much more of this sort of punishment could the Communist Inspired Forces of Evil endure? "Boknaai" for Rhodesia, indeed.

"Right? Begin!"

"Boknaaai! BOKNAAAIII! BokNAAII!"

GRADUATION by Captain Russell Fulton

There were fewer greater moments and wanton ruffling of one's own proud-as-a-peacock hackles than receiving the news in your final interview with your course officer that, and within a month or two, you would be receiving your long-sought commission. To attend and pass a thirteen-month regular cadet course was no small matter; it required peak physical, emotional and mental stamina, the likes of which most of us hadn't even begun to comprehend before we entered those hallowed, feared but respected portals that were the (Rhodesian) School of Infantry.

Credit, in the fullest measure, goes to the many cadet course officers and instructors, hand-picked by the Commandant of the School of Infantry from the regular army nominal roll, who played a pivotal role in training, mentoring and moulding a ramshackle bunch of unlikely officer cadets in to a body of men deemed 'fit for purpose' following thirteen gruelling months.

We loathed and feared them all for at least half of the course but, as with all things, came a maturity, a clearer sense of purposeful understanding and a desire for personal success. Long before our commissioning, we understood what it was all about and why we had been treated as we had, and it became the topic of general banter and much jest amongst us. Many cadets went on to become outstanding officers and that is due to the direct and professional commitment of good, unsung 'heroes.'

We who were commissioned, owe those that we left behind, a debt of enormous gratitude. For my part, and that I survived our conflict, is a credit to my mentors; then my course officer Capt Martin 'Wakkers' Wake (RIP) and regular cadet course WSM WO2 David 'Sandy' Miller and CSgt 'Barney' Rumble. These were true 'men of men', as were their predecessors and those who filled their boots.

Commissioning was a personal highlight and a moment of self-indulgent pride, but our truest test and our worthiness awaited us all. When we reported for duty at our respective units, that short-lived arrogant pride would rapidly dissipate, and, in its stead, a period of awakening to the very harsh reality that was war was ushered in; no more cloth models, TEWTS and artificial practical exams, it was a true baptism by fire for many.

We were now in 'the real world' and our very actions would mould our futures and the very welfare of those under our command. To the many who underwent regular cadet, NS cadet and P.O.C. courses, they will find common ground in this paragraph:

"Here we will stand and fight; there will be no further withdrawal. I have ordered that all plans and instructions dealing with further withdrawal are to be burned, and at once. We will stand and fight here. If we can't stay here alive, then let us stay here dead."

Field Marshal Sir Bernard Law Montgomery, 1st Viscount Montgomery of Alamein, KG, GCB, DSO, PC, DL

That just about sums it all up for us, we veterans of the Rhodesian bush war.

CHAPTER SIX

JOINING THE RAR

MY GRAND PARENT RAR by WO2 Tinarwo Ferrison Manema SCZ

Born 17 /12/51, at Impilo Hospital, Bulawayo, Rhodesia now Zimbabwe. Went to school in Bikita distinct lower primary level. My upper primary at DRRR in school at Llewellin Barracks standard 4 to 6, 1964 to 1967. Went to Bikita for my secondary education after my father had died in 1967.

As it was difficult to find school fees, I decided to go back to Llewellin Barracks to join the army. It didn't take long when I saw a convoy of RAR vehicles Landrover and RL Bedford troop carrier vehicles going past, as I was walking some direction to Bikita District commissioner place.

Heard from the RL a voice shouting, "Hey Ferrison come at the DCs office we are looking for you guys". It was Edward Solani who was one class ahead me and was in the RAR already, in the Mortar Platoon. In thirty minutes, I was there when I saw C/Sgt Tsvetai HQ Coy and Major Harvey OC HQ Coy and a Sgt from the Education Corps. Already other guys were writing exams as an entrance to join RAR.

I did not write the exam as Maj Harvey had remembered me from Llewellin Barracks Golf Club as his caddy, "I know him he can read and write." Straight away I was now an RAR applicant under Maj Harvey's batman who I helped with laundry cleaning.

Arriving at Methuen Barracks we surrendered all our civvies to HQ Coy or at a relative's place. And we're now applicants. The following week we were taken to Llewellin Barracks Ordinance supply depot where we were issued with military uniforms. Everything had just started to go military style when the Cpls told us walk back to Methuen Barracks with your 'katundu' rolled in blankets.

On arrival we were issued with number, rank and name as 644683R Rct Tinarwo. During our training our training officer was Lt Tourle, Sgt Shamhu, Cpl Zangai and Cpl Ngenge. Our training took six months which was not all that hard since I had grown up in the military place as well as Coleen who I had been to school with during our school days. Preparing our laundry was simple because we had done that during our school days for soldiers.

After our six months training, we were posted to different Coys. I was posted to B Coy where I was put in 4 Platoon, number 1 Section. My platoon commander was Lt Bryan McDermott, CSM WO2 Ngulube Jonas, Platoon Sgt Gibson Mugadza. My sec commander was Cpl Mangarai. B Coy commander was Maj Eric Sobey, also Maj Langdell, 2i/C was Capt J. Duncan (Manyangamanyanga) (big Horns).

Lt J Hill was my last Platoon Commander. WO2 Jonas acted platoon commander many times since Lt B McDermott went to act Coy 2i/c all the time. B Coy commanders changed all the time. In three years, I was in B Coy we had Majors Langdell, Eric Sobey, Maj Englis. So, Lt McDermott was 2i/C many times in B Coy and WO2 Jonas was 4 Platoon commander many times too.

My first contact with the enemy Op Hurricane was in Mozambique at Makombe airstrip along Zambezi River. We were patrolling north of the Zambezi when the whole Platoon was moving with two up one down as that ground favoured. The left section was fired at and I as a signaller had my TR28 aerials out reported contact, contact, contact to our Coy HQ C/s 2 it was the first platoon battle drill I had experienced. We had several contacts in ten days' time when Lt J Hill took over the platoon.

I went to 6 Platoon temporarily as pronto there under Lt K Adams on OP Hurricane when we followed terrs and had a contact. Nobody noticed that Lt K Adams himself had been shot in the back only to find out when we prepared our evening meals. I had already sent a sitrep when Lt K Adams opened a bully beef which had an AK47 bullet in it and we had to send in another situation report. Coy commander that time was Maj Burford (Chibayangwena) who was good at Fireforce.

Returning to Methuen Barracks we had heard of the recruitment of Selous Scouts where Martin Chikondo went on the first selection course. In 1974 I went to Selous Scouts Selection course. I passed the course of with several ES and AS from RAR, RLI, SAS and other units. The RAR and RLI that had passed selection course were enough to make 2 troop after the dark phase.

I was made LCpl in one years' time after a few successful operations, posted to Training Troop Selous Scouts with WO2 Ant White who later on was Lt. at Training Troop, we ran Selous Scouts Selection courses where I saw many young men from different units. A lot did not make it because it was a hard course.

From Training Troop, I went back to operational troop, 3 Troop as Troop Sgt. I was with the Selous Scouts all the way to Zimbabwe Independence when we went back to our RAR colours. Then with Lt Col L Dyck we formed the Zimbabwe

Parachute regiment. Then I was the first troop commander SAS as Sgt under command of Lt Col E W D Coventry in 1982 (A Troop).

When SAS grew bigger, I became a WO2 and Troop commander C Troop. We had a few operations in the Matabele land when a few ZAPU cadres went back to bush and in 1983 Mozambican operations started with MNR disturbing Zimbabwe borders and fuel pipe line.

During Mozambican operations I was decorated with a Silver Cross of Zimbabwe (SCZ).

I retired, in 1997. It was a sour retirement after I had not been in good relations with the then commander SAS Lt Col R F Matonhodze who was a tamed Terr. Currently now in RSA.

Kind regards TF Manema SCZ

SWEET BANANA by Colour Sergeant Carl Chabata BCR

In 1972 I was working for PTC on a casual basis. My duties involved digging trenches to lay telephone cables on pavements in Bulawayo.

As a result, there came a time when I was working from Grey Street prison going up in town that I used to see various soldiers from 1 Brigade smartly dressed and seated in orderly manner with their rifles at fixed bayonet pointed upwards passing my position in RL trucks.

The people I used to work with were talking in hushed tones saying those soldiers are going to the Zambezi valley and they all going to die because they won't be able to see the terrorists since they vanish mysteriously but to me it was a different story all together and I had made up my mind that I wanted to be a soldier.

CSgt Carl Chabata BCR

At 1RAR Methuen barracks my sister was married to Sgt Kasirayi Dzinemurumbi and he was in C Coy. So, one weekend I decided to pay them a visit. On arrival in the company of my elder brother, we were told that there was a recruitment taking place and I and my brother said chance given. I was nineteen years old. Come Monday sometime in April 1973 with my brother we joined a group of about three hundred applicants where the recruiting was taking place.

We registered our name and, in the afternoon, we were taken to Llewellin Barracks at a ground which was situated near an assault course. Myself I had a big hangover due to the fact that my brother in law had supplied us with considerable amount of Indlovu that came from the canteen.

We were then told to run and the first few meters I was a bullet but eventually faded because of the effects of beer however I pushed at a very slow pace whilst at the same time surrendered to myself. I was second from last but as I approached the finishing line I could hear the instructors encouraging me to run faster but I was completely finished my legs could no longer carry me but I made it. We were given a couple of minutes to rest and we were off to the assault course. There I made wonders and became number two.

The selection was for two weeks and on 1 May 1973 we started training. We were the first recruits to train carrying 10 kg sand bags on our shoulders from point A to point B on the double shouting left right leffffft.

My training officer was Lt. Getliffe. He was a very nice man but the instructors were tough in that sometimes they made us to uproot a tree and to plant it at a different spot during the whole night just as a punishment of which I still feel was good for us so as to take out the babalaas which was in our heads.

During training we embarked on a two-week trip to the following areas, Melsetter where we did some swimming in pools which were in the mountains. From there we went to Mozambique by buses. In Mozambique we stayed at Dondo a military camp and we enjoyed quite a lot.

On 10 October 1973 that was my pass out parade and subsequently posted to C Coy which was based at Inkomo Barracks. On arrival at Inkomo barracks, we didn't stay long at the barracks since the Company was on deployment at Msengezi Mission therefore we were on the wanted list dead or alive. Soon we were on our way to join the others by road. I really enjoyed the trip but as we approached enemy territory, the situation changed but with no incidents.

On arrival at Msengezi mission we found the helicopters waiting for us. We were given rations chop chop and were told be ready for deployment, myself I was not ready for that and as a new recruit I didn't know what rations to pack and for how many days but we were given enough rations. Myself I only packed a few rations I think for about three days and we were in the helicopters in route to Mozambique but can't remember which area we were going to.

We arrived to our platoon which was commanded by PWO Mavhengere deep in Mozambique. The situation had dramatically changed from beautiful looking places to mopani flies and there was no water in the area. Luckily, I was assigned to a lance corporal who became a mother and my commander he truly looked after me. His name was Jameson who ended up being a Col.

The deployment in Mozambique was tough just because of one thing, there was no water to drink in the area life became tough and some of my fellow recruits fainted since we were clearing the area towards Mukumbura River. There are times when we camped for the night and you happen to sleep one would dream drinking nice cold water only to wake up with nothing. We were unable to eat especially with the tinned beef or anything because the body needed water. We did not encounter any enemies except their spoor. We eventually arrived at Mukumbura River and it was like arriving in bright lights.

From Msengezi mission we were deployed to Stacey farm and I was attached to TFs who were based at St Albert mission. Our duties were to lay ambushes at night and to carry out some patrols. We went back to barracks for R&R and after R&R we were deployed to Chombira in Chiweshe but still nothing came of it in the form of gun battle. Again, we went back for R&R after rest and recreation the Scouts recruiting team arrived.

The RAR beret, and blazer I loved them more than anything and also any story about RAR makes my heart to jump.

Conclusion.

Sometime in February 1974 I left 1RAR for selection in Makuti and that's another long story somewhere.

Thank you.
Sweet Banana.

MY INTRODUCTION TO THE RAR by Major Colin Hendrie

Maj Colin Hendrie AKA
"Nyengure"

After being commissioned in February 1970 I was posted to D Company 1 RAR who at the time were based at Inkomo Barracks outside Salisbury. On arrival at Inkomo Barracks I was told that a land rover had been arranged for me the following day in order to get to the company HQ which was located at Kanyemba. I would have an opportunity to meet my platoon briefly since they were at Mashumbi Pools which was en route to the Company HQ, but I would be staying at Kanyemba for a few days to be introduced to the Company and briefed accordingly.

Following the HQ visit I returned to my platoon and went about introducing myself to the men. I was well received by all except my Platoon Warrant Officer, one Siyakeya Makokera. He appeared a little aloof but did the pleasantries as best he could. A few days later the weekly ration resupply was to take place at Kanyemba and oddly WO2 Siyakeya insisted on going. This seemed a bit odd to me but I went along with it. (Months later my OC Major Vic Walker advised that Siyakeya had voiced his concern that a schoolboy had been posted in as platoon commander and that I was too young for the role and he disapproved of my appointment.

I concede that at that time my youthful appearance belied my age.) I imagine Vic Walker suggested he give me a chance to prove myself which was the only option really.

Months later during another border control deployment along the border near Mukumbura, my platoon was tasked with locating and destroying a possible terrorist camp a few kilometre to the North inside Mozambique. Special Branch had information that there were several armed people at a village there.

I decided we needed to locate and attack this base at night since any movement by day would have been noticed by the locals. I briefed my platoon and that night after dark I led the platoon across the river and after a reconnaissance located the target. I then carried out a closer look at the camp with two other men and then briefed the platoon on the plan which was to surround the camp shortly before first light with myself leading an attack group to storm the target.

There was no resistance as we skirmished through the village and no sign of any armed individuals. However we then noticed a lot of meat hanging in trees adjoining the village and it transpired that the locals had shot a kudu for themselves using one of the four muzzle loaders that they possessed. We negotiated the release of two of their muzzle loaders as evidence and headed back to our base. WO 2 Siyakeya seemed pleased with the sortie and adopted a much friendlier disposition towards me.

At the end of the deployment the company regrouped at Company HQ in preparation for the move home the next day. While the officers were together at the officers mess tent, the CSM Wurarayi requested that I accompany him to where the troops had been gathered. When OC Vic Walker asked what it was about the CSM politely suggested it was business for OC 10 Platoon only. The CSM addressed the men in Shona which I could not fully comprehend, followed by loud applause and handshaking. I then realised that I had been formally given my Shona nickname "Nyengure" which has stuck with me ever since. Clearly my PWO Siyakeya had instigated the affair and thereafter we had a very close working relationship and a very good friendship. He would frequently invite me to the WO's and Sergeants Mess followed by dinner with his family at home.

THE BOND by Sergeant Jo Amos

In the face of adversity and war, the bonds among soldiers are as strong as kinship. There is a mutual respect and a Bond that can only be experienced by those that have been there, done that and, for some, still carry the scars.

I had the honour of serving with a fine Regiment – the Rhodesian African Rifles. I was not a regular soldier and to be honest my attestment into the RAR was unexpected. After being called up for National Service, I was selected to attend officer training at 'Hooters'. During my training, I took part in a boxing tournament and my 'Second' was an RLI corporal who was on a Drill Instructors' course. As we progressed through the fights against various potential Ruperts, he was in his own words surprised that I could actually throw a decent punch. Afterwards, he lavished heaps of praise on me by putting his arm around me and saying: "You're an old skate, hey". A Bond had formed.

Whilst we were still undertaking our basics, we were informed that the Rhodesia Regiment Independent Companies would be rebadged to the RAR, and that we would now serve with African soldiers. As most of us had never encountered African soldiers before, we were to say the least a little apprehensive. On completion of our training we were sent back to Llewellin to pick up our platoons and undertake a battle camp to get us used to operating in our individual units.

You can only imagine the faces of some of the African soldiers when these boys, some barely shaving, myself having only just turned 18 years and 3 months, arrived to take them forward into the operational areas. However, someone higher up the food chain had a wise idea that we should undertake a battle camp to get to know our troops. After a week of intense training, we got to know, respect and understand each other a lot better. That Bond had been formed.

In November 1977, before we left for our various units, we marched with our African soldiers, around 600 strong, through the streets of Bulawayo to the distinctive sounds of 'Sweet Banana'. Without a doubt, and to this day, one of the proudest moments of my life.

Our platoon was deployed to 2 (Indep) Coy in Kariba. Our area of responsibility, the Zambezi valley and escarpment, with a forward base in Chirundu. We, like so many other operational units, worked in four-man sticks, just in case someone actually granted us the use of an RLI taxi. These sticks usually comprised of one European and three African soldiers. During those long hot days and nights on patrol, we got to depend on and trust each other. That Bond was growing.

Within my first couple of weeks of arriving in Chirundu, whilst on patrol with two sticks near Ca Camp, we received notification of a possible crossing over the rover by CTs gapping it back to Zambia. We immediately humped it to the potential crossing point and proceeded to set up our ambush position. Whilst in position and waiting for the CTS to come towards us, six dugouts were noticed leaving the bank a little further down and, on confirming they were in fact carrying gooks, we opened fire on them. The next thing, all hell broke loose, and we were soon taking heavy fire from the opposite bank. This included mortar fire and RPG7s.

After a brief exchange, I thought that to minimise the chance of taking unnecessary casualties, the best course of action would be to disengage and await further orders. As the guys pulled back I, as I'm sure any officer or NCO would do, remained offering covering fire. The next thing there was a large thump and a cloud of dust next to me. I turned, half expecting to see a crater next to me, and was instead greeted with a large ebony face, covered in dust with a huge smile, and the large frame of my MAG gunner, the aptly named Nyathi P. He looked at me and said, "I'll stay with you Sarge", and promptly opened up on the opposite bank. That Bond was growing.

I never had the pleasure of operating alongside the RLI Fireforce but certainly experienced them on a personal level. One night I was out on the town at the Lake View Hotel, with a young lady from Kariba. My biggest worry at that stage was that her fiancé who was in the Selous Scouts might suddenly appear. During the evening and many beers later, I proceeded to get into a compromising situation with a number of local guys. A firefight soon broke out and I was soon taking heavy flak, and in serious danger of being overwhelmed by enemy forces. The next thing a number of RLI lads, who were based at FAF2, waded in and evened the odds. It turns out that the young lady's brother was in the RLI and had summoned the Fireforce to bale me out. That Bond was there… and I shall be eternally grateful.

There has of course always been inter-unit rivalry, and it was that rivalry and the resultant determination to perform at your best, that made the Rhodesian Armed Forces one of the most potent fighting forces in the world. In boxing terms – 'The best pound for pound fighter around'. That rivalry has however, never undermined the respect or weakened that common Bond between us.

There is no finer example of this than those famous words uttered in March 1968. Platoon Warrant Officer Herod, of the RAR, was recovering in hospital from wounds received in an earlier contact and, whilst talking to a visiting RLI officer, said of the RLI troopies: "They have the faces of boys but fight like lions". The respect and that common Bond was there.

As time goes by, and as our numbers dwindle, as we gather, and we remember those no longer with us, the respect and the Bond between our band of brothers grows ever stronger. I have the utmost respect for all who served and feel privileged to be part of that band of brothers.

JOINING SUPPORT COMPANY 1RAR AND MEETING PWO ABIAS MASHONA BCR by Captain Mike Jones

Joining the RAR was a big breakthrough in my life. If someone had told me during my NS (Intake 134) that I would be in the regular army within a few years, I would have thought they were out of their mind.

I had the good fortune to be selected to go to School of Infantry and my course officer was Major Simon Harrof. How this man did not RTU me I have no idea, but he persevered and I came out as a grossly over ranked T/Sgt. I was posted to 1 Indep Company and came into contact with a man whom I came to admire and respect, Captain Bruce Snelgar.

After NS I was attached to B Company 2nd Bn RR. I came in as a private, but over the years and continuous service, I came up through the ranks and became a subbie. After continuous service was discontinued, I resigned from Liebigs Ranches and stayed on with 2RR as a supposedly regular officer. Sadly, I was still paid as a TF, and as I had resigned, I had no make-up pay from Liebigs. My Colonel at the time, Cedric French, told me to stop whingeing.

As I was desperately short of cash, I went to Salisbury to go before the regular army selection board and be transferred to a regular unit. I was accepted and, to my shock, was told I was not going to RLI, but, with my background, I was going to RAR. I asked if I could change units and they replied that I would have to wait another 6 weeks and apply again. I accepted my posting.

I arrived at Methuen Barracks and was told I was now the anti-tank platoon commander and that I was to travel to Wankie and join Support Company under Major Butch Zeederberg, the OC Support. It was with trepidation that I set off. These were true and professional soldiers, while I was a farmer who had come up through the ranks.

I was made very welcome by Butch Zeederberg and the other subbies, Pat Lawless, Tom Fulton, Jim Hardy and Ron Revel, I think. I was then introduced to my Platoon Warrant Officer, WO2 Abias Mashona BCR. Abias was a slight man and turned out immaculately. He was very formal and took me to introduce me to my platoon. They all had to fall in and again were all immaculately dressed. (I am not a snappy dresser at the best of times, and was once told, by the late RSM

Kirrane, while on parade, that I looked like a bag of horse shit. Nothing more needs to be said).

The introduction to the platoon was formal and quite stiff. I did not realise it at the time, but the previous platoon commander of the anti-tank platoon had recently been killed in a vehicle accident, when the vehicle he was travelling in had a front wheel blow out. They also noticed that when I looked at the 106 mm recoilless, I had no bloody idea of what it was or how to use it.

Abias then introduced me to my batman. I had no idea what a batman was, but vaguely recalled something from a classical war exercise that, this was the man who crawled back through lines when all comms were lost and passed messages backwards and forwards. I thought it a bit strange, but did not want to show my ignorance, so I said nothing and asked no one.

My first deployment, with the whole platoon, was to set up OPs above Devil's Gorge on the Zambezi River. We were duly dropped off on the Deka road and started the long walk to the river. We stopped for lunch and a smoke break and I got out my one man cooker, and started to prepare lunch. Little did I know, but I was about to get my first lesson in RAR etiquette. As the water was beginning to boil, I noticed Abias had spotted me so I gave him a friendly wave. He did not acknowledge it and disappeared. The next thing I knew, I was shoved off my back pack and a distressed figure took over my tea making. I recognized him as the batman I had been allocated. Abias appeared and said to me, "Sah I wood like to have a werd with you".

Abias took me aside and away from the platoon and proceeded to lecture me. If you can imagine a slim, immaculately turned out shortish man with a wagging single finger, politely dressing down his platoon commander, under the shade of a Mopani tree, surrounded by Mopani flies, in the heat of the day, you would get the picture. The conversation went as follows.

"Sah you r an officer in the RAR. In the RAR officers do not cook. Your job is to lead us ande kommunicate lokstats ande takitiks, ande to give orders bute not to cook."

I realised I had a lot to learn, but I also realised that Abias was used to taking on fresh subalterns, taking them under his wing until they had gained confidence and found their feet. I needed to assert my authority and make it pretty clear that I was no green horn and that, while I was not familiar with the regular army and it's protocols, I knew the bush and had been in a number of successful contacts before.

The first subtle changes in Abias's attitude, and subsequently mine, came when I was speaking to one of the IsiNdebele in Ndebele and then communicating with one of the Karanga in Karanga. My Ndebele was much better than my Karanga. The troops' attitude started changing. I also noticed that a few of the platoon had Catties and presumed correctly that these were for the odd guinea fowl, pheasant, rabbit or hare that we might come across. On one of the smoke breaks, we were sitting around a Baobab tree, heavy with fruit so I issued a challenge on who could bring the first and most fruit down with the Catties. The challenge was on, and while we posted our sentries, the marksmen and ammunition were selected. Abias was one of the marksmen.

Without going into great detail, I held my own, and the ice, with the platoon and Abias, was starting to show signs of cracking. The deployment was uneventful apart from a false crossing report from one of the OPs which lead to a Lynx dropping a night flare. I was most impressed. It was the first one I had ever seen and it lit up the Gorge beautifully.

Our next deployment was a reaction to a homestead CT attack in the Deka Halt railway area. One gook had been killed and we did the follow up, but lost tracks going into the closest TTL, as cattle had been driven over them, but it was noticed that the "sah" could track and suddenly I became "Ishe". The cracks in the ice were getting bigger.

After going back to company HQ for resupply, a fresh meal and refreshing sleep, the platoon was deployed by train, to go back into the TTL, in the area where we had lost tracks, and set up OPs. The intention was to find the gang that had carried out the homestead attack. The train was late and we disembarked late. We were still in the National Park by early morning, so I decided to base up for the day and continue the walk in that night. Abias was thawing, so that evening I asked him how he had got his BCR.

He explained that he had gone home on R&R and one night the Ters came into his kraal line, calling out his name. He got away by climbing through the roof of his house and escaping in the darkness. Unfortunately, the gooks slaughtered his family. He reported what had happened and went back into the area with a 9mm and radio and spent some days working out where the CTs were. He then called in FF and the group was taken out. I could see that he had one mission in life and that was to kill as many CTs as he could. I could live with that.

We did a successful night walk in and deployed. From my previous experience in OPs in TF, I knew that if you had not spotted any enemy after the first 3 days, you could assume the walk in had been compromised by the local Mujiba network and it was better to call it a day, move out and redeploy to another area.

During the first few days I was introduced to a delicacy that my guys had trapped and cooked, mice and rats! After building up courage I tried a couple, more to save face than from any form of gastric excitement. They were not too bad, however, I decided sticking to Bully Beef and Sadza was better suited to my gastric inclinations and gastric fulfilment. Having grown up in the bush, I loved the RAR ration packs.

Day three came and went and in the early hours of Day four we captured a young Mujiba who was exploring our position. He, of course, was looking for a lost goat!!! By midday I radioed JOC Wankie that I would be pulling out of the TTL and informed Abias of our pick up RV. Little did I know, but I was about to get a lesson in just how good the RAR were when it came to operating in populated areas and how dedicated Abias was to killing CTs.

Abias responded to my radio message. "Ishe let us remane here as soma thing is not correket. Do you see the girls karring the washing?"

I replied that I did.

"Du u see the chilen?"

I said I did.

"The wumen shud notie be washing cloths butie cookin for the chilen and the cloes r too many. Let usie wait Ishe".

We waited and I informed JOC that my sunray minor had spotted unusual activity and that we would remain another day. Our Mujiba was still with us, so he went through a thorough RAR interrogation and admitted CTs had been there, but were not around anymore!

The ladies returned and started cooking. Abias radioed me and pointed out that they were cooking far too much for the number of people in the village. Another hour or two went by and low and behold, three armed gooks appeared at the edge of the village. I called for FF, but Abias was having none of it. He said FF would take too long to get to us. I made a quick plan. He would have a go at the CTs he had visual as he was the closest call sign to them. One OP was to remain to be our eyes, and the remaining OPs were to set up stops on likely escape routes. Each stick was given its position and arcs fire and we set off, keeping to dead ground. My intention was to link up with Abias, but as in most cases, things did not go quite to plan.

Abias made contact first and one of the stops came under fire while moving into position. It was all over fairly quickly and when FF arrived the light was fading fast and the gooks had fled.

The following morning, we swept through the contact area and apart from the odd live round and grenade and some blood, nothing of interest was found. Due to cattle movement, no substantial tracks were located either. We left the site to SB and the BSAP and returned to Wankie. We had had our first contact together. I often wonder if we should have waited for FF.

That night, sitting with the platoon, sharing a few beers, I asked if they knew a few of the Karanga and Ndebele traditional songs. They did. The ice was broken.

The following morning, much to my horror, I was told by Col Mike Shute that I was being sent to School of Infantry to go on a 106mm Instructor's course. Somehow I scraped through.

B GUARD AND MY CLASH WITH RSM ERASMUS by Sergeant Roy Amm

My journey to 2 (Indep) Coy RAR began as recruit, a member of Intake 159. We attested July 13th 1977 at Llewellin Barracks.

After nine weeks of 1st Phase training we advanced into 2nd phase and our platoon numbers dwindled as individuals started specialising in different fields. During this 2nd phase the 'additional' duties were piled onto those of us that had selected training that took place within the bounds of Llewellin Barracks itself.

I had opted to attend the Service Training School (STS) course as a platoon driver and was one of about 20 learner drivers. On one occasion we were allotted a Sunday night 'B' Guard duty. 'B' Guard was assigned to look after the barracks ammo dump.

As memory serves, there were five patrols allotted to the duty, Alpha through Echo. Alpha through Delta were tower duties, while Echo performed a roving patrol around the perimeter fence of the facility, each patrol was assigned a field radio for communications.

On this particular cold Sunday night I was standing on Delta tower trying to stay awake and warm, it was early morning, perhaps 4am and I noticed in the pre-dawn light that there was an old radio set, the type that had a hand crank on the side of the unit, lying in the corner of the tower. It was old and covered in dust and cobwebs. In the headset the two speakers were still in apparently good shape so unscrewed the covers and used my pocket knife to cut the wires. My plan was to set the speakers into my motorcycle helmet and connect these to a portable tape recorder that I would strap the tank. I could then listen to music while riding down the road. Easy, no issues….or so I thought.

The following Wednesday afternoon after our driving duties were completed for the day, our platoon was told to report to the Guard house located at the main gate. We duly arrived and formed up in front of the building. After a few minutes we were joined by various members of the MP's who were accompanied by none other than the RSM Erasmus (Moose, as we called him). Moose had a reputation that was legendary… many of the readers of this book will agree - you didn't mess with this man!

RSM Erasmus instructed us to form up into the groups to which we were assigned the previous Sunday evening and after a few moments we were lined up into 5 rows each representing Alpha through Echo. At this point the RSM asked

Delta to move to one side and the balance of the men to form up in a single group. Up to this point RSM Erasmus had been nothing but polite and extremely professional.

He approached Delta group, we were formed up in two ranks of two, I was standing front right. Holy Crap! All politeness flew out of the window he pressed his face up to us standing in the front row and let us have a tirade of abuse which included questions as to whether we were in fact members of the human race! In short he was not at all happy about the "misuse of government property" located in Delta Tower. At the end of the tirade he stood to attention in front of our little shivering squad and stated:

"I'll go easy on the man that owns up within 10 seconds!" I believe that I perhaps took two of those seconds before I responded... "Sir, I am responsible Sir!"

RSM Erasmus then proceeded to show the entire platoon his interpretation of 'going easy' – I was bombarded with a verbal tongue lashing amidst a flood of spittle, while he went ruby red and I shat myself! MP's whistled me into the guard house so quickly I don't remember my feet touching the ground. In what seemed like seconds I was processed, my belt, bootlaces and dog tags were confiscated (so I couldn't hang myself) and I was thrown into a cell which measured perhaps 4' x 8' – there was a small window which let in some light, it was covered with an expanded metal grid/mesh which would hinder escape. My bed was a mat about an inch thick with one blanket. The door was solid wood with two slots in it, one to allow communication and the other permitted food to be passed into the cell. Fortunately I was allowed to mix with the general population during meal times and for exercises each day.

I spent four days in that cell during this time I contemplated being sent to DB at Brady Barracks and the real threat of having to redo my National Service training. I do not know of anyone who would willingly agree to go through that 1st Phase training a second time. I determined that I would do anything to avoid that happening.

On the Monday morning I was escorted to my barracks where I was allowed to shower, clean up and dress appropriately for my 'Orders' set for later that morning.

I went on orders before the A Company Commander who at that time was a Capt. Robinson. As I was double stepped into Capt. Robinson's office I noticed that RSM Erasmus was seated to the right of where I stood. We went through what I believed was the standard process, of questions and answers, and at the end of it all Capt. Robinson asked me if I would accept his judgement or if I wanted the matter to go before a higher authority? I accepted his judgement which was time served (4 days) plus a $30 fine. RSM Erasmus was clearly not happy with this result but he said nothing and I was marched out and re-joined my platoon.

$30 fine might sound small right now, but in those days our pay was $45 per month so I had lost two thirds of my pay – that was not easy and it took me some time to recover from the loss. On pay day that month I lined up to receive my dues and at the first table I was paid the $45 – next table was the Coy Adj who promptly removed the $30 fine then to the QM who took $12 for a new pair of boots and a few dollars for some barrack room damages, then there was the set fee for the cinema entertainment, (you paid whether you went to the cinema or not). Bottom line, I walked away from that pay parade with a total of 26c – in those days this was exactly what was needed to buy a pack of Maddison 20's and a box of matches.

Ironically one of the ways I earned some additional cash was to cover off 'B' guard duties for others who were willing to pay a fee for someone to do the duty for them. The going rate was $5 at the time. Needless to say, I did not mess with any government property for the duration of my time at Llewellin.

WINNING THE LOTTERY by Lieutenant Michael Matthews

Having arrived at Llewellin Barracks at the beginning of January 1977 along with a great many other young men conscripted into the Rhodesian Army with Intake 156 for what had by then become a two-year National Service stint, it didn't take long for many of us to conclude that any fate would be preferable to spending any more time than necessary at that God forsaken place. It was for this reason that when an entourage from the School of Infantry in Gwelo arrived to put hopefuls through their paces in the hope of becoming officer cadets and striving for a commission, I and a number of my school mates took the opportunity with both hands.

Fast forward to the classical war phase of our training where I conspired to completely blow my opportunity in a simulated situation by having my platoon annihilated and having to take the slow coach back to Llewellin. Shortly after my return to Llewellin I decided to go on a drill and weapons course at the School of Infantry and before long found myself once again at the hallowed 'College of Knowledge'.

Shortly after my arrival and to my great surprise, I was called for by my previous course officer, (then) Captain Martin Wake, who told me that he had been disappointed that I had been culled from the officer's course, and that he still felt that I was officer material. He asked me if I would be prepared to give the course another go, not starting from scratch but commencing at the final counter-insurgency (or COIN) phase.

I agreed without hesitation and I comfortably completed the course. When the time arrived for our passing out parade, I felt fairly confident that I would receive my commission, and it was normal for newly commissioned national service officers to be drafted into the so-called Independent Companies, which comprised mainly soldiers, including officers and NCO's who were not so-called 'regulars'.

When I went into Captain Wake's office, I was hugely surprised when he advised me that I had been commissioned into a regular Battalion, the 1st Battalion, Rhodesian African Rifles (1 RAR). I knew very little about the RAR at that stage, other than that it was a predominantly black and very proud regiment which had served with distinction in World War II in Burma, and later in Egypt and Malaya. In fact, a great number of RAR Regulars were the direct descendants of soldiers who had fought in World War II.

I was immensely proud that I had been selected to serve with such an elite unit and I knew that, since these were regular soldiers, their knowledge of matters 'on the ground' would be immensely superior to mine. I determined then that, in the face of such experience, I would serve early notice on my platoon NCO's that I was prepared to learn from them, and not simply attempt to take control.

It wasn't long before I was taken by Landrover to Methuen Barracks, the Headquarters of 1RAR, not one kilometre from Llewellin Barracks. If I had thought that I would have an opportunity to settle down before joining my appointed company, I had another think coming. Some three weeks prior to my arrival, Charles Bickle, an old Plumtree school mate of mine who had also been commissioned into 1RAR and who joined A Company was tragically killed in a vehicle accident when the 2.5 Unimog he was driving overturned just outside Bulawayo.

Charles had been 3 platoon's commander in A Company, and the gap which his death had left needed to be filled quickly. I had just enough time to settle myself down in Officers' quarters, kit myself out at the Quartermaster's store and visit the magazine to equip myself with a rifle and ammunition when I was in a Land Rover en route to Wankie to join 'A' Company.

On arrival at the Company's bush camp, I met my Company Commander, Major Barry Getliffe, and his second-in-command, Captain Craig Beachell. Again, any thoughts I had of settling in and acquainting myself with my new surroundings were quickly dashed when Major Barry, as I came to call him (other than when I was addressing him personally, in which case it was simply 'Sir'), advised me that my platoon had already been deployed on a five day patrol, and that he wanted me to join them immediately.

In view of the fact that my platoon had been deployed clandestinely into an area under cover of darkness, arrangements were made for me to be taken to them by helicopter summonsed from Wankie airfield. My first meeting with my second-in-command was a moment I will never forget. The Alouette III landed just long enough to enable me to deplane, and I remember wondering why I had apparently been dropped off in the middle of nowhere.

The chopper was a distant speck when seemingly out of nowhere emerged PWO Collins Munyika. He was not a particularly tall man, but he was built like a pocket battleship, and he had a ready smile. PWO Munyika introduced me to my Platoon Sergeant, Sergeant George Mleya, a man with whom I ultimately forged a very strong relationship. It was immediately apparent to me that both of these wonderful men enjoyed the respect and loyalty of 3 Platoon.

I was introduced to the remainder of my platoon and, since it was late afternoon, we began looking for an appropriate place to make our camp, since the sun was going down. I began discussing various matters with my NCO's in an effort to get to know more about my new platoon and the personalities in it and I was assigned a batman by the name of Rwanqa, a quiet unassuming young man for whom nothing was too much trouble. Rwanqa's job was to see to all my needs both at camp and in the bush. He was always extremely devoted to me, and never disappointed me when it came to ensure that my kit was always clean, and my personal belongings in good shape.

We returned to camp by foot about two days later for a two-day rest prior to leaving for our next patrol, and this afforded me an opportunity to get to know my fellow officers. Major Barry was a friendly, approachable Company Commander to whom it was easy for me to relate. He always insisted on having meals with his subordinate officers whilst we were in camp, and it was clear that his easy-going, yet firm manner had earned him the respect of all of his troops.

Captain Craig Beachell, A Company's Second-in-Command, was an American and a veteran of the Vietnam War. He was a strong, sturdily-built individual, who had earned two Purple Hearts, and had witnessed the virtual annihilation of two Companies by the Viet Kong whilst involved in the Vietnam military conflict. I confess, I didn't really get to know him very well and occasionally found his methods somewhat unorthodox.

Of the Platoon Commanders, of which we were three, John Aird was approaching the end of his conscription period, and 'Pee-Wee' Holmes (as he was known) had joined A Company some three months prior to me. Since we invariably patrolled independently of one another, the only time any of us got to talk was when we were at base camp. It was clear to me, however, that I had become part of a united and cohesive team with a strong chain of command and I looked forward with great confidence and anticipation to engaging the enemy with all of them.

MY BROTHER by Lieutenant Colonel John Peirson

My identical twin brother Ken was unique in that he attended three cadet courses to get his commission. To undergo two was not unusual, but three was unheard of.

On his first course in 1961 the course officer caught the two of us wrestling on the lawn out of sheer high spirits. We were both RTU'd (Returned-To-Unit) for displaying "NCO tendencies". The fact that we were both sergeants appeared to have escaped that individual's attention.

On his second course, on an exercise as a company commander with RAR troops, he sent a four-man recce patrol to ensure a small knoll in front of the objective was clear, a perfectly normal operational procedure. Two days later back in barracks, he was dumbfounded when the same course officer RTU'd him. He was told he "showed a lack of moral fibre" and should have commanded the patrol himself. The term LMF was actually written on his course report, which he had to sign. Honour was restored when Gen Coster ordered the acronym "LMF" be expunged from the report a few months later as it was not possible to judge on a peacetime exercise, but by that time the damage had been done.

2 Lt Ken Peirson

In retrospect it is interesting to know that fifteen years later, the same course officer, by then a senior JOC commander, his first ever operational post, asked Army HQ to relieve him as he could not take the stress, a fine example of LMF. He was side-lined permanently to an obscure desk job.

Ken sailed through his third course with a different course officer in 1962 and was posted to 1KAR in Nyasaland. On the break-up of the Federation he was posted to his beloved 1RAR as a Lieutenant. By then 1 was a Captain in 1RLI, and he told me after a few months he had never been so content in his service.

Ken sailed through his third course with a different course officer in 1962 and was posted to 1KAR in Nyasaland. On the break-up of the Federation he was posted to his beloved 1RAR as a Lieutenant. By then 1 was a Captain in 1RLI, and he told me after a few months he had never been so content in his service.

The early years were in the piping days of peace and platoons were undertaking Border Control independently. It was the ideal way for subalterns to practice their trade under the watchful eye of the very experienced and wise Platoon Warrant Officer. Having been an NCO himself Ken was never afraid to seek advice as he found the approach to leading askari was very different to instructing white national servicemen. Most if his deployments were to the area where the Deka River joins the Zambezi, a game hunter and fisherman's paradise. Ken developed a good knowledge of bush-craft and a deep love of the Deka area.

In those days the area was totally unspoiled, a fisherman's paradise with a rough track leading to it. The only building was a rough trading store which also served as accommodation for the owner, Bob Inngs, a real wild man and a character of note. The store served mainly the local African trade but also tinned food and basic fishing equipment. What it did stock was crates of beer and a copious fridge of cold ones one could consume at any time of the day, provided you bought Bob one.

Ken had always been good with his hands and set about improving the living conditions for the single members. The single quarters had recently been vacated by the Teacher's Training College. The 12 rooms were in a straight line with a covered verandah. In front of the rooms was a 50-yard wide belt of packed earth where cars were parked haphazardly. At the time new modern barrack blocks were being constructed at Llewellin and the old wartime corrugated iron blocks were being dismantled.

Ken organised a raiding party at night to 'liberate' a huge stack of corrugated sheets and a lot of building timber. Using freely available convict labour he constructed a line of twelve very well-built car ports in front of the accommodation. As the packed earth became a quagmire in the rainy season, he organised through official channels for a twenty-yard wide strip of granite chips to be laid down for the vehicles. His final act was to have the thirty yards between the verandah and the chips planted with Kikuyu lawn. When 1 first saw it months later the lawn had been cut and the area looked immaculate. I was very proud that Ken as a fairly junior subbie had the gumption to improve their lot, while his seniors had been happy to put up with alternate dust or mud.

Ken was known for his sense of humour. The Officers Mess had a well-kept, neatly written foolscap book, known as the 'Lines book', in which Subbies could post amusing factual happenings. The only proviso was the writer had to enter his name to ensure authenticity. It was sacrosanct that field officers and above were forbidden to read it, so horrendous illegal happenings could be entered.

One in particular amused me: "Guess who stuffed up Major Howden's bed roll with heavy stitches, so he had to bend his legs severely all night to fit in." Mike Ainslie. Below that was the line: "Guess who will get stuffed up if Major Howden reads this." Ken Peirson.

He was a good shot and was a member of the battalion shooting team. At one memorable Army Weapons Meeting, I was a member of the HQ 2 Bde team against his RAR team. At his suggestion we ducked behind a tent and changed shirts and headgear and shot for each other's team at falling plates. We were so identical no one caught on. At this stage 2Bde was leading, but to my surprise the RAR won. Afterwards he told me with a smile "Of course RAR won .... we were both firing at MY plates!"

A month prior to his death, my parents visited Rhodesia. Ken took a few days leave and took us to Deka. Bob Inngs lent us his personal boat, making a point of telling my parents that Ken was the only person ever allowed to use his boat. We went some thirty miles downstream and had a marvellous lunch including chilled wine on a shady riverbank. My parents marvelled at the various moods of the Zambezi which Ken knew so well by then.

Ken and I were extremely telepathic, but I had no inkling, and was shattered to learn that he had been killed on Op Nickle. Ironically it was a few hours after his closest friend Nick Smith's death. They were the first officers killed on operations since WW II and the effect on Rhodesians was profound, as no one had foreseen it could ever happen on anti-terrorist operations.

A month later Bob Inngs lent me his boat and I scattered Ken's ashes in the Zambezi in rapids opposite his beloved Deka River. That was 50 years ago almost to the day, and I will always miss my other half, having been blessed to know him for 27 wonderful years. He is in my thoughts constantly.

AIRBORNE DOUBLE by Lieutenant Colonel John Peirson

I believe I am the only person to have set foot in Methuen Barracks, for the first time, on posting, under a parachute.

In 1968, a few months after my identical twin brother Ken's death, I was posted to 1RAR from HQ 2 Brigade.

The posting was officially from a Monday, so I arrived on the Friday to settle into single quarters, and to ensure I was ready for a full day's work on Monday.

That evening in the bar, the 2 I/C Maj 'Buttons' Wells-West asked me what I was doing over the weekend. I told him I had organised an aircraft at Ntabazinduna Airfield, four miles from Methuen and would be skydiving on my own as I was training for a forthcoming championship. He thought for a while and said the Battalion was having a parade rehearsal the next morning, and it would be interesting for the soldiers if I dropped in. The CO, Col Bill Godwin, said it was a great idea, provided I did not interfere with the rehearsals and I should jump during the smoke break at 1000 hrs.

The next day conditions were ideal, and at 1000 hrs I was 8,000 ft above the grass parade ground when a white cross, was put out.

Lt John Peirson with friend

I dived out, pulling a smoke flare attached to my ankle to make my progress visible. At 2,000 I opened my trusty Para Commander. Sound travels upwards and even through my helmet I could hear a muted roar like a thousand bumble bees. The breeze was perfect, enabling me to do a stand-up landing right on target in front of the Battalion.

As I removed my helmet the muted roar became a stunned silence. We had not thought the effect through, but of course to the soldiers, who had not been briefed about the jump, it was as if Ken had descended from the heavens. It normally takes time for a new officer to be accepted by the Battalion. In my case that had already occurred.

CHAPTER SEVEN

THE RHODESIAN BUSH

INTRODUCTION TO THE BUSH by Andrew Telfer and Grant Telfer

The effect of warfare on the environment is well-researched and documented, but the effect of the environment on warfare much less so. We fought our war in the Rhodesian bush, sharing that pristine environment with the African wildlife that roamed free around us.

The effect of the African bush is both physical and spiritual. Grant Telfer describes it thus:

'What makes the bush special is the unique experience and self-discovery that each individual finds within themselves. This can be triggered by horizon to horizon sunsets and sunrises, the distant sound of lions roaring late in the evening or the booming call of southern ground hornbill advertising their territories pre-sunrise when the wind is still and sound travels.

'It may be the smell of the earth, fresh vegetation and damp elephant dung after a night of rain or the heat and dust kicked up by a swirling dust-devil that originates in the open areas and then sweeps through the dense jesse-bush and around the smooth boughs of the baobab trees rooted into the drier soils on the top of the crest of the hills.

'Moments spent along the deep, chocolate swirling rivers - whether you are resting in the shade on a rock to avoid the biting ants and needle like white thorns of the acacias (vachellia) or you have snuck out of camp armed with a fishing rod, ball of sadza, fatty offcuts of bacon or the famous Kariba red wriggler worms – are times when the "real" world disappears and is replaced with a feeling of now, a feeling of being alive in the moment, listening and reacting to movement around you and very much aware that this is a good place to be. You know then that you are in the right place – in the African Bush.

'When one has the opportunity to spend weeks that lead into months, then years, in the bush, there is an awareness that develops within you of your surroundings but also a keen realisation that the bush and all the individual mammals, birds, insects, amphibians and reptiles communicate in various, subtle ways when the presence of danger is sensed or seen.

'Often what first betrays the predator is their scent blowing downwind, swirling under bushes and through deep dry river beds, advertising their presence. On more still evenings and under the cover of darkness, it might be the crack of a small leaf or twig that draws the prey's attention towards the danger stalking forward. Seeing the predator is the most ideal situation as it leaves no doubt to the presence, location and intentions of the enemy.

'The senses of animals are far superior to ours and we can use them to our advantage to learn what or who is moving about our surroundings. Animals are governed by the physiological reaction of the fight-or-flight response. Initially, at the detection of danger, an animal may freeze its behaviour – a zebra's tail stops swishing from side-to-side, a warthog stands upright and raises its head to try see above the grass, an elephant stops feeding and the trunk searches for the scent to confirm the presence of something it suspects is there. Frogs at a pond may suddenly stop calling, indicating the presence of something approaching the water. Crocodiles or hippos suddenly race into the deeper water, disturbed from their slumber in the warm sand and sun. When a chirping cricket at night or the crescendo of a cicada on a hot summer day suddenly stops their call, that would certainly make one direct their attention in that direction.

'Clear and obvious danger is communicated with an assortment of loud grunts from buffalo, nasal snorts from impala, short sharp alarm calls from oribi and steenbok. Similarly, vervet monkeys begin chattering high in the Natal mahogany or baboons start booming their loud, alarm barks from overlooking cliffs. Mouse birds will let out a shrill, single pitch call, while red billed oxpeckers make a gregarious racket as they fly up off the back of a rhino, where they had been feeding on ticks and other ecto-parasites.

'A predator on the move can be tracked by listening out for guinea fowl, spur fowl, franklin or buttonquails that explode out of the long grass and guarrie thickets at the last second. A bird of prey such as a crowned eagle in the area might be indicated by the vervet monkeys descending below the top canopy of the trees to try and avoid being in the aerial strike zone or a smaller sparrow-hawk may result in all the doves, fire finches and canaries making a bee-line towards a dense thicket. A slender mongoose hunting in the leaf litter or a boomslang snaking its way through grey branches could most certainly find a green backed camaroptera and an assortment of sunbirds, dark capped bulbuls and shrikes accompanying it from above and alarming at the enemy below.

'These varieties of alarm calls, barks, trumpets, squawks, screeches, snorts, sneezes and moments of sudden silence are the prey's way of telling the predator that its presence has been detected. The alarm calls and signals vary hugely between species but they are always directed intently at the predator to signal that it no longer has the element of surprise and, by default, alert all the other animals and species in the area to the presence of an enemy. These signals can do the same for us humans and therefore become our ally. 'The presence of danger in the bush is real and it comes quick and fast. This doesn't mean that we as humans have no place in the bush; in fact it's quite the opposite. We are meant to be part of the bush, to live in it, live off it and move freely around in it. What keeps you alive and well is learning those skills and recognising those signs that the animals share to advertise the presence of predators and then make sure you keep your chin up and eyes ahead.'

What Grant understands and describes is how the bush can become our ally, how it can speak to us, warning of danger that 'comes quick and fast'. This was a two-way phenomenon: just as the bush could warn us of others, we had to learn to conceal signs of our own presence. In the stories that follow, you will see how that became intuitive to us.

We were young men turned loose and free into this wonderland, living in it, drinking from its rivers and sleeping under the stars, thriving on its spirit and beauty. While there were some who were uncomfortable in the bush, our African soldiers were completely at home there and most of us adapted to it happily, revelling in the sheer physical joy of being alive within it.

In summary, the effect of the African environment on our war was so profound that it even became known as *The Bush War*.

BRANCH MANAGERS I HAVE KNOWN by Corporal Andrew Krajewski

I love those magnificent, tall vegetables we call trees. They were so much a part of our lives in the military. Apart from their utilitarian nature in providing cover, concealment, communication and even points of reference (Ground: "Two two Bravo: roger! Now then: do you see that huge green tree next to that squiggle in the river? Well, five hundred metres south..." Cyclone call-sign: "Sonny, all we can see from up here are huge green trees. Can you give us a clue?").

155

Trees are also objects of real beauty. They more than pay their way by producing oxygen and purifying water and giving us shade and sometimes even fruit. Some of them also provide an unrivalled platform by which to evade rampaging nyamazaans Hell-bent on flattening anything on two legs that appeared before their eyes. And that meant tree climbing.

Some were better to climb than others. The African mahogany trees at Mana Pools, for example, were gentle, considerate and calm trees, inviting an easy and gentle climb, whether for recreational or other purposes, up conveniently angled branches into a dense, shady, blissfully cool, evergreen canopy.

Branch managers I have known

Other trees were, however, far less tractable. Some are thorny or spiny (the difference being the depth of penetration and the nature of the injury sustained through contact); others produce their lowest branches several inconvenient metres from the ground surface; and yet others sport rough, palm-, knee- and bollock-shredding bark of cheese-grater texture. Such trees are clearly less easy to climb, and some even possessed several of these characteristics. However, all and any "deficiencies" were swiftly overlooked providing the tree(s) in question provided sufficient separation of One's Standard Six Body (thank you, Wrex Tarr) from some enraged, snorting, puffing, bellowing, roaring and/or trumpeting beast.

Somewhere between these two extremes lay a number of commonly encountered trees which sufficed for climbing, depending upon circumstance.

Depending on what circumstance? Perhaps I might use another example from Our American Allies to explain what I mean by this. Take the design of so-called "tactical" or "fighting" knives. This is a hotly-debated issue, vigorously contested in print, practical demonstrations (mostly on You Tube), and in instructional video tapes and DVDs. The protagonists are in the main academics, rather than actual practitioners of The Way.

Now, as is usually the case, bringing an American into this kind of debate seems to multiply the complexities: sabre-or reverse grip; hollow- versus convex blade grind; D2 or ATS 34 steel, drop-point, clipped point, or double edged; smooth or serrated blade, and which of a baffling array of natural and synthetic materials affords a firm grip upon a weapon perhaps slick with blood. You name it: some suitably steely-eyed Knobnose has produced a video or DVD of it (available for $39.95 excluding postage).

But to cut to the chase (if I may), when all is said and done, THE most pragmatic view is this: the best fighting knife is that knife you have with you when you urgently need to defend yourself.

And so it is with trees. I have participated in many discussions, usually at rest clutching a large, steaming mug of strong sweet tea, seated in the shade of a tree. Various views were put forward on the best sort of tree to climb when put to flight by a large, ill-tempered or perhaps insatiably curious nyamazaan. The point being that when you HAVE to take to the trees to get out of the path of a very angry rhino or buffalo, one seldom has a choice: the best tree to climb is the one nearest to hand.

In this account, I shall limit my remarks to the situation where all members of a call-sign have taken refuge in one tree, and usually from buffalo or rhino, for such has been my experience as leader of the callsign 22 Bravo, Known and Feared Throughout The Land; for just over a year the Scourge of the middle Zambezi Valley.

Up there, surprisingly many night pozzies were chosen because of the presence of a large, climbable tree; one affording suitable perches to each member of the call-sign(s) in question. Tall and easily climbable was good, with multiple limbs allowing a number of personnel to become, in perhaps the most literal sense, branch managers. Alas! That this was an exalted state that precious few went on to occupy after The Struggle.

The ideal climbing tree comprised of a strong, substantial trunk; resistant to being horned and tusked and rent by claws or teeth. Bark should be rough enough to afford good purchase to highly adrenalized soldiers carrying 80 lb packs and full webbing, ascending in squirrel-like fashion. Excessively rough bark, such as that of the commonly encountered mopane tree, usually shredded the palms, shins, inner thighs and trousers of upwardly mobile soldiers forced to take refuge in the crown of such trees.

Regarding choice of convenient branches, there was always a balance between branches low enough to occupy, yet high enough to put one out of Harm's Way. Mind you, this was not usually a problem when climbing UP a tree, which was a process rendered effortless due to the high-octane effects of adrenaline. Rather an ideal tree was one from which one could get DOWN once whatever nyamazaan that catalysed the Ascent had wandered off to continue its day's business.

Personally speaking, there were several occasions when it took me nearly an hour to get down from a tree I had swarmed up in nanoseconds.

Multiple, nicely spaced branches always added a democratic touch to the proceedings, and such branches made unnecessary the frenzied, undignified scrabbling over the top of those comrades already firmly attached to their own branches, in trees where side branches were at a premium. This was, after all, no time for rank or other privilege. "One man, one branch" was the rule. Still, there were frequent infractions, and I have witnessed acts of the basest poltroonery whereby wild-eyed nimarangies have scrambled over the top of one of their comrades and actually kicked him lower down the tree and closer to the marauding creature below.

Truly, behaviour reflects personality, and these same dastards were also suspected of peeing on toilet seats and covert flatulence in confined spaces. Alas that life seldom deals out just retribution to those of such low moral fibre. But I digress.

One of the perks of being a horticulturist is that one gets to use, on a daily basis, some splendid terminology. Take some of the technical terms relevant to tree growth patterns. "Crotch angle" is a favourite of mine and describes the angle that the main axis of a branch assumes from its point of attachment to the main trunk. A nice wide angle affords a relatively comfortable perch on which a climber may sit. This is a not insignificant aspect, because no account of tree climbing would be complete without discussion of one other critical detail: namely, when it is safe to descend.

I have spent up to four very long hours up a tree with a fractious buffalo beneath: four hours spent clinging to some rather willowy branches, with only the sight of Pte Ngwenya, clinging to a branch on the opposite side of the same tree waving his hat at the buffalo, hissing the word "Voetsek!!" at the rolling eyed, frothing-at-the-mouth beast. And these four hours were as nothing compared to one evening spent up another tree on another occasion, with what sounded like several dozen snapping, whooping and giggling hyenas beneath us. Their hellish chorus was punctuated by the Jew's harp sproingings of our steel braai grid (recently used to braai a whole tiger fish over some mopane heartwood coals) being re-purposed as dental floss by these powerful and ravenous beasts.

And the term "crotch angle" was to assume a more baleful aspect to one occupying a low branch and looking upwards at any colleagues above. This was never a wise move, especially where Those Above sported a pair of those minimalist camouflage shorts many of us wore, nor indeed normal battledress long trousers, but recently rent and shattered by furious contact with the rough bark of a mopane tree. And all without underpants!

Which naturally brings us to the final and inviolable "rule" of tree climbing: Never look up.

This was not just a precaution to avoid getting shards of bark in one's eyes. It was in no small part to avoid the adverse "shock and awe" effects of inadvertently catching sight (above one and danger close) of Things Best Left Unseen.

High on the list of things I hope never to see again is the gruesome vista on display to anyone sharing a tree with, say, the rest of his call-sign. Looking up at the soles of the feet of those above afforded a seldom-seen view of that mini-constellation of five stars, part of the distinctive pattern of the standard issue army boot sole. To take this "celestial" theme further, on display also were the assorted "moons" of naked buttocks, exposed by the shredding of shorts and trousers by spiteful bark.

But it got even worse: There too for all to see was the traditional "braai pack" (chop and wors) of the Climber(s) above. The psychological effect on the onlooker of this unspeakable assemblage is difficult to overestimate. After all, everyone knows what a totem pole looks like.

But a Scrotem Pole?

It has been over 35 years since I last saw this dreadful sight, for above me were Spunky in a pair of shattered shorts, and privates Dube and Ngwenya; both in exploded trousers.

Of even a pair of underpants there was no sign.

That day I broke the inviolable rule.

AiiiieeeEEEeeEE! Will the psychological scars ever heal?

WHO WERE WE MOST CONCERNED ABOUT: THE TERRORISTS OR THE LOCAL INHABITANTS? by Colonel John Pritchard

The Rats of Sebungwe Narrows

The Sebungwe Narrows are located SE of Binga and at some point, may have been or was suspected to be a crossing point for terrorists into the Binga operational area. As a result, the company deployed to Binga was always responsible for ambushing the crossing and the reserve platoon invariably had the task of mounting a seven day/night long term ambush. All supplies were carried in on our backs.

In true School of Infantry procedures, a rear base would be established and every night the ambush party would move forward in to position overlooking the Narrows. At first light the next day the party would withdraw to base, and an OP deployed to keep watch. So, rotation continued day and night until the end of our 'tour' of duty.

In the handover between commanders' emphasis was always on the operational aspects of the task. No mention was ever made of the local inhabitants in whose territory we were. Well after the first night (for those too slow to work out the danger, maybe two nights) we discovered virtually every soldier's pack had been 'attacked' with the packets of sugar, mealie meal, biscuits and powered milk eaten into and left with pieces of plastic strewn around like a mini tornado site.

On closer inspection of the damage we realised we had provided the raiding party with food for weeks!!!They did not care about the evidence they left in their wake – that was for us to clean up. Overnight our seven-day powdered rations had been reduced to four or five days!!!

While a few AS were upset at losing their supplies, most saw the funny side of the situation and in true RAR fashion decided to fight back. The next night packs were fastened securely and placed up every available tree and traps (a flat rock supported by a stick with left over mealie meal, sugar or the like as bait on the ground below) were set for the next raiding party.

Throughout the night one constantly heard scampering of tiny feet and falling rocks as one by one the raiding party was accounted for. The next day and every day thereafter body counts took place and the rats were later cooked to supplement what food they had previously stolen.

As for the real enemy they never crossed in the years I was deployed in the area.

The Elephants of Chete

Chete Island down the lake from Binga but in Zambia, was always considered a likely crossing point into Rhodesia. Thus, a platoon was permanently based opposite Chete and tasked with patrols and ambushes up and down the lake for the duration of its tour of four to eight weeks.

Being in a national park the area was teeming with game and patrols were always a tourist's dream, if one forgot about the war.

During my tours I would often deploy a section to ambush likely landing points. On one occasion it was my turn and with a stick from platoon HQ we set up ambush on the beach. At some time during the night I was awakened to find the entire stick alert. Now was our chance, I thought, to make regimental history. I searched the area in front for the suspected landing party but alas no boats, no enemy.

However, following my soldiers' line of sight I spotted in the moonlight four elephants meandering straight towards us, maybe 75 metres away. As they approached, I thought of what to do; gather up our kit, abandon the ambush position or wait. I decided to wait. Fortunately, we were downwind from the locals and they did not smell us and certainly in the poor light could not see us. They got closer and closer and just when I was to give the order to withdraw (more likely run), they changed direction and went up into the vegetation not to be seen again that night. Whew!!

Elephants are huge animals but can blend into the bush extremely well. On one of my patrols we walked into a herd of elephants before any of us had spotted them. Again, we were fortunate and must have been down wind and they were too busy grazing to notice us slowly back peddling until we were out of danger. They caused a wide detour to our patrol route.

Hippos of the Zambezi

During my time with 1RAR we patrolled (on different deployments) from Kazungula in the west to the Sengwe River about mid-way down the lake and from A Camp below the gorge, almost all the way through Mana Pools to Kanyemba in the north.

The RAR soldier, being African, has an inherent knowledge of the bush, the local habits and village life. He is often a one-man OP, wonderful to work and fight with and blessed with a wonderful sense of humour.

On one of my patrols from Vic Falls to Kazungula we stopped for the day, to eat before setting up an ambush overlooking the river. The vegetation was very thick so any paths along or down to the river were used. I dispatched a water patrol of two down to the river and waited for their return before moving off. A short while later running up the path shouting or screaming came my two ashen faced soldiers. When they had composed themselves, I asked what had happened.

After collecting the water, they began their short journey up the hill but came between a hippo cow and her calf. Little did they or us know we were on a hippo path. Mamma hippo gave chase, but the AS quickly out ran Mamma, who, sensing danger was over, returned to her calf. The reader can only imagine the remainder of the patrol collapsing in fits of laughter.

On patrols between A Camp and Chirundu these locals often came between us and the perfect ambush position. Like elephants in the bush, hippos in the water are often hard to spot until they show themselves. We were always kept alert by either the hippo calls or their foraging on land during the nights. In hindsight why would terrorists chose to cross a fast-flowing river teeming with hippos to disembark into a perfect killing ground, but we did as we were ordered!

Cattle of Chibi

During my time as OC B Coy 2RAR 'hot int' was received one day to the effect that a group of 20 – 30 terrs were to RV at a location the next night. At the time I was under command a TF JOC who decided it was a two-company ambush operation. B Coy was to ambush the road leading into the RV as the ters were expected to use the road as the route into the RV and the second company, a TF company was to ambush the RV.

The next afternoon we walked in arriving in time to set up our positions and settle in for the night. Radio silence was ordered, and it was to be my stick who initiated the ambush if all went to plan. Sometime in the early hours of the morning we were alerted to the sound of footsteps on the gravel road approaching the killing ground. We waited and waited...... not wanting to open fire too soon. With impending danger always comes a degree of nerves, however well trained one is.

As the footsteps became louder the enemy came into view and there they were, at least a dozen cattle slowly walking into our killing ground. One of my AS whispered in my ear "mombies Ishe". On this occasion we watched as they continued down the road and off into the surrounding bush.

There was no sign of the suspected ters that night and the next day the int was 'revised' and we returned to base.

ELECTRIC STORM IN 'THE VALLEY' by Lieutenant Noel Smith

It was one of those unbelievably hot and humid days during the month of November in the Zambezi Valley and all normal life sensibly sought relief in any available half decent shade and then remained motionless in the lifeless air for the rest of the day.

As was so often the case, we continued with our standard orders which were to cover as much ground as possible with our reconnaissance foot patrols even if it meant slogging through the heat of the day. I was now beginning to understand why the RAR had such a respected and unsurpassed reputation for undertaking lengthy patrol work, covering huge areas of the bush veld in all conditions and in good time too. This type of work was second nature to the hardened and experienced African RAR soldiers, but it was heavy going for an urban raised European kid like me! I tried hard not to think of those ice cold cokes in the shady confines of the Officers Mess back at Base Camp.

However, as the heat continued to relentlessly increase, I wisely decided that enough was enough and finding a patch of higher ground, chose to hide in the sparse shade of the mopane bush scrub. By late afternoon enormous thunder clouds came rolling in over the escarpment, darkening the sky and the atmosphere became burdened with expectation. The lightning and thunder began to crack and thump around us and then almost incredibly the air started to crackle with the build-up of static electricity. In the rapidly dimming light our rifle barrels took on a faint eerie bluish glow as if the demons from hell had been set loose. I hurriedly collapsed my radio antenna and realizing that a tropical storm was about to break with a vengeance, we scurried under our hastily erected bivvies for cover.

The storm broke with unbelievable ferocity and instantly rendered our fragile shelter totally inadequate as we became drenched with the unrelenting wall of water. The power of nature unleashed was truly awesome. I subsequently spent a cold, wet and exhausting night huddled up in my waterproof poncho against a protective tree trunk, as I vainly tried to shelter from the streaming downpour of rain. It was a hopeless task.

BEELZEBUB'S BUZZERS by Corporal Andrew Krajewski

Spending extended periods of time in the bundu was rather like the Allied bomber onslaught against the Third Reich, with raids carried out both night and day. In our case, these raids were conducted by "biteys" many and various. During summer months and especially with the seasonal rains, these attacks actually intensified. Oh, what misery!

The raiding parties were a diverse group of flying insects and included the following:

So-called "house flies". First off, this is NOT what we called these dreadful, inquisitive, persistent insects with no sense of personal space nor personal hygiene.

Now, much has been written about flies, and perhaps most of all those dreadful representatives living in Australia's outback in vast, buzzing clouds. An entry in "Brewer the dictionary of phrase and fable" (1993) states that Beelzebub (a demon allegedly second in command to Satan) was the god of flies, supposed to ward off flies from his votaries. If only we'd known...

In his book "The Devil's Dictionary" the American writer Ambrose Bierce wrote the following:

Sunray 22B Cpl Andrew Krajewski & Shirley

"Fly (n): A monster of the air owing allegiance to Beelzebub. The common fly (Musca maledicta) is the most widely distributed of the species. It is really that creature that...with comprehensive view...surveys mankind from China to Peru. He is everywhere and always the same. He roosts impartially upon the summit of Olympus and the bald head of a sleepy deacon. By his illustrious line we are connected with the past and future: he wantoned in the eyebrows of our fathers; he will skate upon the bald pates of our sons."

Such high densities of over-familiar insects often hampered free and full communication. Our AS, to a man very voluble and eloquent, were given to long and impassioned discourses at all times and everywhere, and often in quite spectacular settings. I first saw "fly-strike" in the Chewore area of the middle Zambezi Valley, when Pvt Nyika in the full flow of mellifluous dialogue, surrounded by a haze of buzzing flies, suddenly choked, gagged, and eye bulging like peeled lychees, clutched his throat in apparent distress. The hapless fellow hacked and spluttered and before long spat out a saliva-drenched fly, after which he spent several uncomfortable minutes gulping from his water bottle, gargling and spitting. Around him, his audience, hysterical with mirth. For it is written "Into a closed mouth no fly enters".

Other, more baleful flies existed and added to the misery. These were mostly variations on the basic design of the abovementioned house fly, and the most notorious of which were the weaponised versions with either armour-piercing capability or chemical weaponry.

Of the former, Tsetse flies (known to one and all as "tsotsi flies") were the commonest, and these spiteful and malevolent creatures were the bane of our existence, and never more so than on marches through wooded bush with mopane trees. Our movement drew their attention, and amongst the hundreds that were drawn to us was a minority seemingly happy to perch on our packs and cadge a lift to other destinations. Infinitely worse were those which sought out a variety of tender spots on our bodies, settling without making their presence felt, and then biting with the savagery of having a hot soldering iron applied to the soft spot on the back edge of one's armpit (where the sweat-soaked denim was pulled tight across the skin, and right up against the strapping of chest webbing and backpack), or immediately under one's chin.

There were others of this sort too: so-called "horse flies" and even "hippo flies" also put in lightning fast sorties and were certainly capable of drilling though the canvas of a pair of Superpro tekkies to inflict a searing bite on the ankle beneath, where the fabric pulled tight. This was a nasty surprise, and all affected sought out suitable small branches with tough springy branchlets and flailed wildly at these dreadful insects. Those creatures swatted to the ground or caught between the fingers were traditionally impaled on long thorns and left in misery, or fed to columns of voracious ants, usually with a gleeful chuckle, alas!

The second group of buzzers comprised creatures weaponised by virtue of their venom. Of these bees and hornets were the commonest, and even out there in the unpopulated bundu, honeybees were often quite irascible. A special mention is made here of hornets, of which Bierce had the following to say:

"Hornet. (n). A red-hot meteor of many tons weight, which sometimes hits a fellow unexpectedly between the eyes and knocks him silly. It is represented symbolically as an insect with a bald head and an influential tail, but the man who has incurred a hornet shot out of a clear sky is not satisfied with that kind of representation and avers with feeling that an instantaneous photograph of a hornet in flight would tell a different story".

I recall one incident when we were travelling along the main Makuti-Kariba drag on a 4.5. One of the fellows was standing up behind the cab, looking forward at the road and enjoying the rush of cooling wind on his face. Suddenly, "Whammo!", as he pitched backwards with a yell and sat down with a thump, before rigorously rubbing his forehead. There, neatly centred between his eyes, was a visibly growing, angry looking lump. My immediate thoughts were that he'd been shot, but there'd been no "crack" of a bullet.

He was consoled and comforted by his comrades in the traditional manner; namely, amid roars of laughter and impromptu pantomiming, and with much finger-pointing he was mocked and ridiculed for the entire duration of the trip back to Kariba Heights, as with many an "Ah, but-i shoowa!!" he dismounted and, with eyes swollen virtually shut, groped his way to the medic's sickbay for antihistamine treatment.

Of course, no account of satanic flying insects would be complete without mention of mopane flies and mosquitoes. Mopane "flies" are not flies at all, rather they are tiny, stingless bees (Pleniena hildebrandti) associated with mopane woodland. They are drawn in sometimes staggering numbers to moisture around and in the eyes, nose, mouth and ears, and believe me, they can become very irritating when hovering around one's face and getting into eyes, nostrils, ears and mouth.

That they also produce a thick, very dark and sweet honey is little consolation to exhausted and heat-stressed herberts trudging through thick bush carrying their worldly belongings on their backs and trying to steer clear of cantankerous old buffalo bulls and elephants, whilst swatting frenziedly at house- and tsetse flies. The standard defence against these creatures was to wrap the issue camo veil around one's head, covering nose and mouth, and swishing a suitable leafy branch in front of one's face to keep the little devils out of one's eyes.

To get one or so of these little insects in one's mouth was not pleasant: they exuded a strong, musky, rather unpleasant smell, with a flavour to match. Oh, how they used to drive us crazy!

And mosquitoes? Well, in all the time I spent Up There (late July 1978 to early November 1979) I never had malaria, so choking down those anti-malarials obviously worked, or else without human habitation in the area, there was no active pool of malarial parasite to be spread by skeeters biting a carrier and then flying on to pester someone else. Still, skeeters up there had other attributes. Again, to borrow from Bierce:

"Mosquito. (n): The spore of insomnia, as distinguished from conscience, the bacillus of the same disease. "I am master of all things!" Men cried. "Then what, pray, am I?" the mosquito replied.

My first "bush-trip" up at Kariba was a four week patrol up to the confluence of the Chewore and Zambezi Rivers, in August 1978. During this time, I was driven insane by the sleep deprivation, followed by the dreadful itching and scratching of hundreds of mosquito bites, each and every night. That hateful trumpeting squealing buzz of cubic metres-full of those little bastards and the frenzy of hand-flapping and swatting that accompanied it was something we all experienced. I'm not sure about the other lads, but I've never quite regained my sanity since then.

Finally, there were areas and times of year when yet another insect plague descended to smite us. For all the biblical scholars out there, please consider Deuteronomy 28:27: "The Lord will smite thee with the botch of Egypt, and with the emerods and with the scab, and with the itch, whereof thou canst not be healed".

And that itch whereof we couldst not be healed was due to the onslaught by swarms of near-invisible blackflies (technically members of the Simuliidae). These tiny, dreadful creatures produced huge red welts and wheals that itched in the worst possible way for days. This itching was so severe that we commonly applied either an antihistamine cream, or more commonly, that ghastly pale pink calamine lotion.

As before, the sight of one of our AS troops with his face dabbed with copious pale pink spots always reduced onlookers to hilarious mirth, and the sufferer was left with little recourse but to petulantly pout.

Pte 'Rapala' Dube

Speaking of which, and in conclusion, there was the never to be forgotten incident when Pte Dube, having opened a tiny rat-pack issue tin of sweetened condensed milk the night before, awoke in the grey hours of dawn. Reaching for the tin in the dark, he put it to his lips and sucked vigorously, anticipating a sweet, delicious flow of sustaining condensed milk. Alas! That some creature of the night, perhaps a bee, had discovered this windfall in the dark and perched on the rim of the can to feed or perhaps just to sleep off the aftermath of a good feed. Dube's bottom lip had more or less enveloped the creature in a clammy embrace; perhaps like a "Kreepy

Krawlie" swimming pool cleaner. Having found itself thus enveloped, it had retaliated with a savage sting.

There was a scrabbling commotion in the dark, with many sibilant whispers and barely suppressed snorting and puffing. With dawn the cause became evident, for there was Pvt. Dube, sitting upright in his sleeping bag, displaying a spectacularly swollen bottom lip. Already one possessed of rather thick and sensual lips, Pte Dube now presented a remarkable likeness to one of those deep-dive, lipped artificial minnows so popular for bass fishing: the "Deep-Dive" Rapala.

Such were the dimensions of his "remodelled" bottom lip that his speech was impaired and a pronounced lisp developed. He sat in angry and wounded silence as the other members of the two call-signs that had based up together for the night made fun of him. His every protest was greeted with much sniggering and suppressed howls of mirth, whilst every few moments, someone would look at his bottom lip and burst out laughing again.

I can assure the reader that one would have to hear his final word on the subject to fully appreciate just how funny this was.

"Phaack deesth sheet!" he lisped, savagely.

Around and opposite him, his comrades wept with laughter.

BUSHWACKED BY BUFFALO by Corporal Rob ('Buffalo Bill') Delaney

It was late autumn in May 1979 while I was doing my National Service at 2 (Indep) Coy RAR, which was situated at Kariba on the northern border between Rhodesia and Zambia. Our area which we patrolled was from Kariba to Chirundu, from Chirundu through the old Sugar Estates up to the Mana Pools National park area and occasionally from the western boundary of Mana Pools into the Chewore Safari Area, as well as inland along the escarpment and in the gorge below the Kariba Dam wall.

At this particular time our tour of duty was drawing to an end as we were due to de-mob in August of that year. As a young Rhodesian, National Service was compulsory, and one had to make the best of a bad situation. It all came down to individual choices of what you wanted to do and where you wanted to go for the duration of your N.S.

I opted to stay in the infantry and after basics I was offered a few places where I could do my border duty and I chose Kariba as one of them and that was where I was posted. 2 (Indep) Coy was a great place and the areas where we patrolled were mostly in National Park or Safari areas. The animals and land scape were something you would never experience as a normal civilian. Not to mention the Mighty Zambezi River.

Having the rank of a two liner, I was made a stick leader in 2 Platoon and being fresh out of basic training one had to rely a lot on the knowledge of the permanent members of the RAR to guide us on the bush conditions and animal behaviour, with most of them having served a few years in that area already.

Anyway, on this particular patrol I was accompanied by Privates Nyathi F, Ngwenya and if my memory serves me correctly Sibanda F. My orders were to be deployed along the main road to Makuti and walk to a trail at the end of the gorge that led from the Zambezi River up the escarpment to the inland areas. This was to be a two day walk to get to our Locstat and once there we were to set up an observation post and monitor this particular trail. When we arrived at our OP position, we set up on the gorge side of a tributary in an elevated position amongst huge boulders.

The trail we were watching was on the far side of the tributary about thirty meters from us in a position where the trail narrowed and was flanked by a rock face directly opposite us. An ideal ambush place, I set up two claymore mines facing down the trail towards the Zambezi aiming directly into the bottle neck. The rest of the platoon were spread out along the Zambezi River and they had to conduct cross grain patrols in the hope of picking up spoor and relaying info to me. After about eight days nothing materialised from the info we were given about a possible crossing and our rations were running low. I was given new orders to vacate the OP and head down to the flat lands near the old Nyamumba airstrip for a re-ration drop in two days' time from a fixed wing.

It was the 9th May 1979 when we packed up our OP and headed down towards the old airstrip. It was about a 10km hike through rough terrain and thick bush, the going was to be tough. At approximately 14:30 while following an elephant trail through thick Jesse bush I got the biggest shock of my life. I was leading the stick with my gunner behind me followed by the other two riflemen when I entered a clearing in the Jesse bush, about 6 meters in diameter. Before I could react or do anything to avoid it, it hit me with the force of a locomotive. Prior to this encounter there were no signs or sightings of any game in the area.

A lone buffalo charged me and before I could get a shot off or take evasive action the buffalo was on top of me. My rifle was knocked out of my hands with the initial impact. All I could think of was to turn my back towards the animal, so my back pack could take the brunt of the impact. I remember being butted, picked up and tossed around. At one point one of my arm straps broke and I fell to the ground with my pack stuck on the buffalo's horns. It continued mauling my pack and this was when I crawled under some dense Jesse bush and held my breath for what seemed like eternity. After a while the buffalo left the pack and wandered off into the thick Jesse bush.

I suppose because there was no more screaming and movement from the pack the buffalo must have thought this invader of its territory must be dead. I cannot recall as to how long this ordeal lasted but once it was over I was gasping for breath again after holding my breath while I was cowering under the Jesse bush. At that stage I was not aware of how serious my wounds were except that I could not walk. After another eternity I called out to my braves who had gapped it to safety somewhere out of sight. My gunner replied to my calls and asked if "IT" was still there. I don't know if they saw the buffalo or not. When I told him "IT" was gone, he let off a belt of 7.62mm rounds into the surrounding area before entering the clearing to come to my aid. Luckily I was not hit in the spray of rounds.

Eventually all three braves entered the clearing and helped me retrieve my rifle and back pack, which contained my radio. They then assisted me to another much larger open area where I assessed my injuries. I had been gored in the right groin area and in the back in the area of my right shoulder blade. My right leg was immobile but as far as I could make out it was not broken. As it turned out I received a massive blow to my right leg just above the knee and had the mother of all muscle spasms rendering my leg immobile.

My first priority once in a safe area was to attend to my wounds with the help of one of my braves namely Fanwell Nyathi. He helped with the bandaging of my groin and back, but none of them were willing to put my drip in. This I had to do myself as well as administer Sosogon, the pain killer we were issued with. Morphine was not issued due to it being abused in certain circles. The next step was to call into HQ in Kariba and get casevaced.

My radio had been in a side pouch on my back pack, so I was worried as to what condition it would be in. On inspecting the radio, it appeared to be in on piece except the hand set was broken in two. Luckily Pvt Nyathi F had done a signallers' course so he repaired it as best he could by twisting the broken wires together and taping everything together with plaster and there we had a working radio. Now I had to work out our Locstat and the call in to HQ. This I managed to do and within about an hour and a half a chopper arrived, loaded me and set off for Kariba Hospital. My braves were left behind, and they were to join up with another stick for the duration of the deployment.

On our arrival at Kariba hospital the doctor and nurses were waiting for us. I was removed from the chopper placed on a gurney and pushed into the emergency room. Here the doctor, if I remember correctly, he was a Greek guy but can't remember his name assessed my injuries and gave me a shot of morphine. What a wonderful drug, no wonder it was abused. It felt as if a sheet was slowly being pulled off me from my head towards my feet as the morphine took effect and a feelings of pain disappeared. Next, they cut off my clothing, which I still have in my possession, removed my boots and sent me for x-rays. Luckily there were no broken bones or damage to internal organs. The theatre was prepared, and I was wheeled into the theatre.

As I was going into theatre one of the nurses said my mom was on the phone asking how I was, and I called out "I am okay don't worry". Once in theatre the anaesthetist gave me the anaesthetic and I can remember telling him this reminded me of MASH and everyone started laughing. He then told me to start counting to see if I could join the over thirty club. This was to see how long it took the anaesthetic to take effect. I remember counting to forty five and the next thing waking up in the recovery room.

Because my wounds where the buffalo horns pierced my flesh were basically tears, the doctor had to cut away the rough edges of the wounds and then stretch the edges of the wounds together to stich me up in order to get as neat a scar as possible. I was kept in hospital for about ten days then the stiches were removed and after that I was sent home to recuperate. I was flown to Salisbury, had a connecting flight to Bulawayo and was met at the airport by army medical staff who took me to Brady Barracks where I saw another doctor who gave me a check-up, arranged for physio and rehab at a centre in Bulawayo then sent me home in an army ambulance.

This physio and rehab lasted for two and a half months after which I was sent back to Kariba just prior to our intake being de-mobbed. I met up with all my intake buddies who were back in Kariba and who had arranged, in my absence, among themselves a farewell outing on an island in the lake. One of the guys brought a boat and we spent the day braaing and drinking on an island just off the town shore. A few days later we all left for home as civilians again. There were a couple of guys who stayed on at 2 (Indep). To carry on serving instead of having to do camps at a later stage as the rest of us would have to do.

Despite my ordeal I would not change that period of my life for anything, having had good experiences, sights and having made lifelong friendships. Thanks to a very special army buddy and friend for getting me motivated to write this story. AK you beauty.

HOW DO YOU AVOID A RHINO CHARGE? by Major Colin Hendrie

In December 1970 my platoon, 10 platoon 1RAR was deployed on an OP /Ambush on the Zambezi River upstream from Kanyemba where information suggested a terrorist crossing by boat. We manned the OP by day and moved into the ambush position after last light and returned to the OP before fist light.

The first couple of days were without incident, however on about the third night while in ambush position we were harassed by what appeared to be three rhino. We remained in position in ambush despite a few close calls during the night and as usual started our relocation to the OP just before first light. In order to get back to the OP we had to cross a wide open area which was very uneven due to animal prints during the wet season. When we were approximately 200 metres into the open area the three rhinos started trotting towards us clearly heading for us. I gave the order to run and after a short distance it was evident the rhino were determined to attack us.

We continued to run when it was clear myself and the signaller were the selected target when I noticed my signaller trip due to the weight of his radio. I helped him up and noticed the one rhino was only a few metres from us. As I prepared to fire a shot to dissuade the rhino from coming any closer one of the soldiers realised we were feet away from being gored and fired a warning shot and then one to stop the animals attack. Fortuitously the shot found its mark and the rhino was halted in its tracks. The remaining two animals stood their distance and then reluctantly left the area.

Not surprisingly my OC had many questions and little sympathy. A second conversation from the OC informed me that a Parks and Wildlife team was being helicoptered in to assess the situation. On arrival the two rangers went straight to the animal to examine it and then started what felt like an interrogation as to why we had to resort to killing the animal. Despite the clearly impossible situation we were in, they felt we could have avoided using our firearms. They offered no details on what else we could have done and left muttering that this would not be the end of the incident. Nothing further was ever communicated to me however I would still like to know how we should have reacted in the circumstances.

FULL MOON, EMPTY HEAD by Corporal Andrew Krajewski

I've long held a fascination for the moon, and what with the recent celestial events of Blue Moon; Supermoon and even a blood moon, these have been special times indeed. Makes me grateful I'm still here to see this. Which got me thinking...

Sometime in 1979, the callsign 22 Bravo, Known and Feared Throughout The Land, had been deployed to the so-called "Flat Lands": those regions of the Zambezi Valley floor downstream of Kariba Gorge, towards and past Chirundu and the then defunct Sugar Estates, and more or less to the confluence of the Rukomeche River with the Great River itself. The area around Mana Pools wasn't really considered part of this. The lands to the east of Mana were a sort of Terra Incognita: "Here be dragons", and all that sort of stuff, but in many ways, a hot contender for God's Own Country. Or so I'd say.

We were not far from 'A" Camp and settled into a cosy and secure location beneath dense hardwood trees and sparse-leafed shrubby things. We had a good view of the river and the opposite bank, which below the towering escarpment to its east, had an abandoned fishing village comprising about a dozen grass huts. Probably a case of these Poor Ones being harassed and molested until they just decided to up stakes and bugger off. Thinking back on those times, we surely were shitty neighbours, what with the constant jitter-firing, exhibition of morale-sapping brown eyes and exaggerated cod-piece clutching. And all on a several-times-per-day basis.

So, there we sat, sipping tea. My 2 i/c had left us for a well-deserved week or so's leave, and so we'd been joined by another character, the MAG gunner Pvt Makore. He sat with Privates Dube and Ngwenya, talking in whispers under the deep shade. It was more or less then that Sunray, 22 Bravo had one of his infrequent but usually ill-fated ideas; apparently the product of the kind of addled reasoning that marked much of his brief but "interesting" military career. By then, he ought to have known better.

The Idea was to stow their packs and katundu amongst the baboon-haunted ruins of what in Oldentime was the Game Ranger's House about 500 m inland of where they were based. The Lads were then to set off at dark and more or less at moonrise, clad in their webbing and set off north on a night patrol. The plan was for them to walk a bit, find some likely place to draw into an impromptu ambush position, and lie there and look and listen for an hour or two, before setting off again. The objective was to reach Old B Camp more or less at Dawn, then to sit down, brew tea and then hit out south again for a riverbank cross-grain patrol back to our pozzie at the neck of the gorge. To at least one person, it was a sound, simple and elegant plan, but various nervous looks were exchanged amongst the Braves. Private Dube cleared his throat and spoke.

"Ah, but-i Corporal! We have never done this night patrol here before! There are too many nyamazaans!" The others nodded vigorously and added their assent.

"Those blarrfacken lions will eat us, shoowa!" added Ngwenya.

But I insisted, and so we set about repacking our bergens, moving them off to the ruins of the old house, and heaped them in a shaded corner of one of the rooms. By and by, we set off, and at the head of the stick, I stepped confidently out into the short grass, with a huge and luminous moon rising above the treeline. The intention was to more or less follow the river, which was about one to two kilometres away, north and east of us. Simple. What could possibly go wrong?

Within a very short time, however, the mission got 'derailed'. On display, again, was Sunray 22 Bravo's uncanny knack of wandering off course, even when marching on a compass bearing. Within an hour or two, spent thrashing through increasingly dense and spiky bush, and nowhere near the well-worn elephant path so effortlessly followed by day, we had deviated considerably further inland than planned. So we paused to take stock, beneath a brilliant silvery moon and black-blue sky, thickly peppered with glittering stars.

Of specific concern was the crucial aspect of location, put succinctly by Sunray, 22 Bravo Himself:

"Okay, guys! I just want to ask you this: Where the fuck are we?"

A demoralising silence and lack of response immediately followed.

By midnight we were plunging through thick, thorny vegetation the like of which none of us could remember traversing in the year or so we'd been patrolling the area. Perhaps these bushes only sprouted during the full moon? I asked myself.

It was strangely disquieting to walk around the bundu, totally lost, amongst sinister and threatening shadows cast by the moon. In the distance, lions roared (unusual, since they usually saved their roaring for black and moonless nights), hyenas gave their traditional insane giggling and grab-ass whooping, jackals yelped and there were other voluble contributions from the hippos in the distant river; snorts, barks and snufflings from various antelopes, and the odd "Bogôm!" from the thick trees that bulked blackly in front of us.

Two hours later we drew to a halt: sweat-spangled, panting and pickled onion-eyed, at the squelching edge of what appeared to be a vlei, over which a tall mass of so-called adrenaline grass was growing. None of us knew of any vlei in the area. Funny thing, that....

Full Moon, Empty Head...

Bugger! Now what? Four forlorn shapes stood stalled on a moonlight-drenched landscape. Clueless. A breeze sprang up and set the saw-grass rustling. A strong smell of cattle filled our nostrils, and we sniffed in trepidation. Double bugger: buffalo!

Sure enough, within seconds we heard crunching, loud rustling in the thick grass and soon, muffled lowing and belching, all the time drawing ever nearer. We happened to be standing on a section of stony or pebbled ground. I stooped and fumbled around until I found a stone about the size and shape of a large egg. By now there seemed to be a continuous rustling, punctuated by the odd loud grunt or snort, and sounds of heavy chewing. We could clearly hear the muffled thud and splash of huge, cloven hooves. They were heading straight for us.

I nudged Ngwenya, who had a rocket-like throwing arm, and handed him the stone. Handing me his rifle, he turned, drew his arm back and let fly into the dark patch to our front. The stone whirred off. There was a second or two's pause, and then a startling, loud "WHOCK!!" followed immediately by a very loud sniff and what sounded like a large number of very big, powerful creatures taking flight. In our direction. With wild, bovine bellowing and steam-train snorting and puffings, they pounded in our direction and we felt the ground shake beneath our feet. To a man, we spun around and bomb-shelled, each adopting the traditional "Swastika Position" of Experienced Runners From Big Game. As Ngwenya passed me, I handed him his rifle: "Here! You'll need this!" he later told me I said to him.

The sounds behind me did not diminish as I rushed through the moonlit bundu, bug-eyed and panting. Already, I could see no sign of my comrades, so I stuck to the tried-and-tested "keep running until you can't run any more" method of evading The Big Five, long the mainstay of our relatively peaceful co-existence with these large, powerful and sometimes truculent creatures.

However, when doing so, it is important to work out, beforehand, a few details.

Heading this list was the location of so-called "crash RVs": easy to locate positions either pre-designated on the map, or else pointed out along the way. These were positions at which the call-sign was to reassemble in the event of a bomb-shelling of its personnel. Alas that there was but one map, and it was in my webbing, and no crash RV had been designated in our meanderings through the thick bushes when we'd been routed by the buffalo. Also important was the recognition signals to be used to initiate contact; what with the obvious limitations of the dated and long discredited "Halt, who goes there? Friend or foe?" challenge. So, is was another detail which had escaped notice by Sunray 22 Bravo during his somewhat off-the-cuff "O Group" briefing.

I now draw a veil of silence over the events of the rest of that ill-fated patrol save this: Dawn saw the eventual reunification of 22 Bravo's members, with the appearance, at long last, of Private Dube, clutching Private Makore's MAG, its muzzle plugged with mud. This wraith-like apparition materialised, guerrillas-in-the-mist-like, whistling loudly in the grey light of predawn.

By some remarkable miracle, we'd all assembled, by degrees, at Old B Camp. This reunification involved a continuous cacophony of loud whistling; chirps and beeps from a dog whistle; clapping; tapping together of rifle magazines; and periodic and very unmilitary shouts of "I-wé!!!" and "Where are you, Corporal?". This sophisticated strategy had also involved a certain amount of tree climbing, with frequent pauses to listen hard, which set the baboons a-bogôming again.

Our walk back to "A" Camp was rapid and direct. The final insult of a highly eventful night of adrenalising, solo orienteering was discovered upon retrieval of our chattels. The baboons had but recently infested the ruinous buildings in which we'd stored our packs. They'd diligently and conscientiously shat on every single one. It took weeks to get rid of the fearsome reek.

It was also the last time the phrase "night patrol" was ever used by the callsign 22 Bravo, and the furthest we ever moved again at night was to climb a tree beyond the reach of an over-familiar elephant or to pee on the bushes. After all, everyone knew there were some dangerous nyamazaans out there at night, and you don't want to meet them...

AN RAR OFFICER'S REMEMBRANCES by Lieutenant Colonel Bryan McDermott

Lt Col Bryan McDermott

I was commissioned off Officers' Course Inf/ 25(11) in February 1969, it also happened to be my 21st Birthday that day. I, along with freshly commissioned Officers John McDonald and Errol Mann, were posted to 1RAR at Methuen Barracks. Also seconded to 1RAR off the same course was Barry Getliffe who had been commissioned into RhASC. If I recall correctly Barry went to E Company. I was posted to B Company, Errol to C Company and John Mc Donald to A Company.

My Company Commander was Major Nigel Langdale a former British Army Officer and was an interesting character to say the least. I had many experienced soldiers, some with the Malayan Campaign in 4 Platoon, one of whom was Mufanebadza Taruwona as Platoon Sergeant He would later become the CSM of D Company 2RAR, which I commanded, and subsequently RSM of 2RAR.

During this period the majority of our deployments were on Border Control, Also known as the 'Hunting, Shooting and Fishing Days'. As the Battalion had five Rifle Companies there was a Company always deployed to Mashonaland, based at Inkomo Barracks on a year's rotational basis. Deployments were for four weeks and in Matabeleland under 1 Brigade. One Company deployed to Binga on Lake Kariba. The Platoons were sent to the following areas: Deka Fishing Camp, the Msuna River Mouth, Chete Island and Chizarira Game Reserve. All of these locations were on either on Lake Kariba or the Zambezi River with large quantities of Game and obviously fishing, hence the 'Hunting Fishing and

Shooting Days'. In between, we also patrolled looking for incursions by the 'Bad Guys'. As 4 Platoon, we had a single Contact with three gooks who were all captured. They were remnants from Op Nickel and other incursions. I remember seeing them in Court during their trial. They were not recognisable having been fed proper food in their stay in Prison. They were all found Guilty and sentenced to death. Not sure if this was actually carried out though.

During that year we moved to Inkomo Barracks to do our year's rotation under the command of 2 Brigade. Here we got to do Border Control in Mashonaland at places such as Chirundu, Mana Pools, the Chewore wildlife area, Mukumbura, Rukomeche Mission, the Angwa River Bridge, Hunyani and Rushinga. Same Border Control patrols just different areas, teeming with Game and fishing along the Zambezi. We shared this space with tsetse fly, mopani flies and other interesting 'goggas'. I remember listening to Neil Armstrong's moon landing on a TR48 whilst based on the Angwa River Bridge. The Masodja refused to believe it was possible to get radio comms that far. The radio operator put it into perspective. Radio is line of sight and we could see the moon so there was no problem!! Sorted!

Border Control Days were great, interesting and we covered and got to know huge areas of the country which stood us in great stead in later years. After Op Cauldron in 1970, things were quiet for the next two years before Op Hurricane started. In 1971, I did my Platoon Commanders' course and on completion of that got posted to the School of Infantry (Hooters) where I became part of Tac Wing in early 1972. During my stay at Hooters I became adjutant to the Commandant, Tom Davidson. In 1976 I was posted to 2RAR as adjutant of the Battalion. During this time, the formation of 2RAR took place a Company at a time. Not long after D Company was formed, I was promoted to Major and posted to D Company as OC.

The Company spent the next few years on Operational Duties of six weeks out with ten days R and R in-between. Most of our deployments were in the Op Repulse and Thrasher areas with rotational Fire Force duties. The soldiers were all parachute trained and we became a very efficient Fire Force. To me, what made an efficient fire Force Unit hinged on the following:

* A good rapport with the K Car commander. We had some great K Car pilots, some who come to mind are Pete Briscoe, Chaz Goatley, Ian Harvey, Mark McLean to name but a few. In general, we were lucky and always got great K Car pilots. This rapport was essential to a successful Fire Force.

* Good stick commanders and ground commanders. D Company was blessed with a plethora of great ground commanders. Andy Telfer being the epitome of a great ground commander. There were many great stick commanders who became extremely efficient as their experience grew.

* Creating a good rapport with the OP who called out the Fire Force. This in my view was essential to a successful Fire Force call out.

* Good Fire Force commanders who controlled the situation. The Battalion was blessed with great commanders: Andre Dennison and Colin Hendrie, to name but a few, who were calm and determined to wrap up a callout, making the Battalion very successful in Fire Force operations.

* Good logistics by the ground forces for resupply etc.

During this period, we were also involved with the Jumbo Fire Force with the SANDF. This involved two K Cars, one with 20mm cannon (Rhodesian) and one with 4x50mm Brownings (South African). The troop carriers were Puma Helicopters which allowed you to get a great number of troops onto the ground very quickly. The sticks were integrated half 2RAR and half SANDF. The majority of these Fire Force ops took place in the very south of the country. It also served as training for the SANDF on Fire Force operations.

My time with D Company was the greatest and most enjoyable of my military career. I was then posted back to Hooters as Chief Instructor to Trevor Desfountain and then took over as Commandant when he was promoted to Colonel, Commander Midlands District. During this period, we were involved in the amalgamation of the three different forces, former Rhodesian soldiers, ZANLA and ZIPRA in conjunction with the BMATT (British) training teams. There was a huge amount of political interference and I was not sad when I was posted out of Hooters to Defence HQ where I spent the remainder of my army career.

CHAPTER EIGHT

THE BUSH WAR

THE CONTEXT by Captain Andrew Telfer

In the Rhodesian History chapter, both articles referred to 'the values that we fought to preserve'. We presented Barnes Pope and Romana and Kazimierz Krajewski as examples of people who personified those values. Their generations of pioneers and settlers had instilled them into the Rhodesian way of life, but why did we have to *fight* to preserve them? Because, by the 1960s and 70s, that very way of life was being threatened by the 'wind of change' blowing through Africa (Macmillan 1960).

Most intelligent, thinking people recognise that history should be read *in context*. For the modern reader, who may not have a clear picture of Africa in the 1960s and 70s, the following edited extract from the biography of Rhodesian Prime Minister, Ian Smith, (Joyce 1974) explains what the Rhodesian government was trying to achieve in the context of post-colonial Africa.

'Smith has dedicated himself to the task of keeping power in 'responsible hands' — and that, in the Rhodesian idiom, means European hands for decades to come.

'Majority rule, he is utterly convinced, would be disastrous for the country. He himself could not live under a black government but, on the other hand, he is one of very many white settlers who would find it difficult to move if the black man did take over. They are settlers in the best sense of the word: they own farms, houses, factories in Rhodesia; their savings are tied up in the country; their children are educated there, married there and, in turn, put roots down as second, third, fourth generation Rhodesians.

'Liberal advocates of majority rule will suggest that the white man in Africa is politically expendable.

'Smith disagrees. The longer whites retain political control, he believes, the better for the people of Rhodesia, *all* the people. His mission is to delay the inevitable moment when power has to be transferred. He is a realist and he knows that moment must eventually come, but he wants *time*: time for African society to evolve, to learn, to develop the capacity to govern intelligently.

'His profound hope is that, when the black man is finally in the saddle, the fabric of good government will have been woven and there will be enough educated, wealthy and experienced Africans in the country to keep it from being ripped apart.

'Rhodesia, says Smith, is nowhere near ready for transition. Nor has the rest of Africa been well enough prepared. Bitterly, and with some justice, he cites recent history. In the mid-sixties, at the time when he was pleading self-governing Rhodesia's case before the sceptics of Whitehall, most of the continent had just been freed of its colonial ties and there was anarchy everywhere. By 1964 the Congo had lapsed into primeval barbarism; there was genocide in Zanzibar; Ghana, in that year, declared itself a one-party democracy — the megalomaniac Nkrumah was busy squandering £250-million of his country's desperately needed foreign reserves and £570-million worth of aid on prestige projects; rule by decree had replaced rule by law.

'Nigeria, the great black hope of the post-imperialists, had been granted her independence in 1960 and, in fact, enjoyed a relatively trouble free first six years. But in January 1966 the scene changed dramatically: Major General Ironsi staged a military coup; the aristocratic Sir Abubaka Tafawa Balewa and a number of his Cabinet were murdered. Six months later Ironsi himself was liquidated and replaced by Major General Gowan. There followed Biafran secession, and civil war, and two million civilian deaths.

'Sierra Leone underwent a military coup and five changes of government occurred in a single week in 1967. Tanzania declared herself a one-party state in 1966 — two years earlier an army mutiny had been quashed by hurriedly-summoned British troops. In Uganda, Milton Obote personally assumed governmental powers in 1966, persecuted the Kabaka's followers and, in 1972, lost his job to the highly original Idi Amin, who unceremoniously expelled the large Asian minority.

'Kenya has been one of the most stable of Britain's ex-colonies but even there the official Opposition went into 'voluntary' liquidation in 1964. Malawi has a one-man government. In Zambia, Kenneth Kaunda savagely repressed the Lumpas in 1964, went on to nationalise the major industries, dispossess many non-African businessmen and declare his country a one-party state. Sudan has had a succession of Arab military governments who have systematically butchered the Africans of the southern region. Ethiopia is a medieval monarchy.

'The Central African Republic is ruled by the insane Bokassa, who personally beats state prisoners to death. Somewhat surprisingly, there are still some people left in Rwanda and Burundi; the Hutu and Tutsi tribes, however, continue to slaughter each other in their tens of thousands. Liberia is under the personal control of the President. Chad, Congo (Brazzaville), Sekou Toure's xenophobic Guinea, the Ivory Coast, Senegal Cameroon, Gabon, Mauretania and Niger have single-party systems, and Mali, Dahomey, Somalia and Malagasy are ruled by military juntas.

'There have been 26 successful coups in independent Black Africa and 16 unsuccessful ones; tribal conflict is endemic throughout the continent; mismanagement of the land is creating millions of square miles of desert; elections are rigged; criminals are publically executed; there is graft and nepotism and, in most countries, standards of public administration have plunged to abysmal levels.'

In conclusion, faced with overwhelming evidence from post-colonial Africa to their north, the Rhodesian people had every reason to believe that theirs was a fight for the survival of a civilised way of life *for everyone* in Rhodesia. At the time of writing Smith's biography, back in 1974, Joyce had no way of knowing that a future black majority government would tragically confirm that Ian Smith was absolutely right in wanting more time before handing over power.

From 1980 onwards, the government of Robert Mugabe would bring genocide and economic ruin to this once-fair and prosperous land. All Joyce and the Rhodesian people could know then, was that they stood alone, besieged by terrorists armed and trained by Russia, China and their proxies, and increasingly strangled by economic sanctions led by Britain and America.

This was the context in which the Rhodesian Bush War was fought.

References:
Joyce, Peter 1974, *Anatomy of a Rebel*, pp. 29-31, Graham Publishing, Salisbury, Rhodesia.
Macmillan, Harold 1960, *Speech to South African Parliament*, 3 February 1960, Cape Town.

INTRODUCTION: THE RHODESIAN BUSH WAR by Captain Andrew Telfer

For the RAR, returning from Malaya to Southern Rhodesia in 1958 meant a return to training and to 'duties in aid of the civil power'. At the end of 1963, the Central

African Federation broke up to be replaced by the separate nations of Rhodesia, Zambia and Malawi. The RAR came under sole command of the Rhodesian Army and its deployments were mostly made along its Zambezi Valley border with Zambia in response to the first Nationalist rumblings emanating the north.

By the time of the Unilateral Declaration of Independence by Rhodesia from Britain, on 11 November 1965, the Nationalist movement as it affected Rhodesia had split into two groups.

The Zimbabwe African National Union (ZANU) was mainly Shona, led initially by Ndabaningi Sithole but ultimately by Robert Mugabe, supported by China and with a military wing known later as the Zimbabwe African Liberation Army (ZANLA).

The Zimbabwe African People's Union (ZAPU) was mainly Ndebele, led by Joshua Nkomo, supported by Russia and its military wing was the Zimbabwe People's Revolutionary Army (ZIPRA).

Beginning in 1966, members of these military wings, known (as in Malaya) as CTs, began an escalating series of incursions into Rhodesia with the aim of subverting the local population and overthrowing the government. This was known as Chimurenga (Liberation War).

The Rhodesian Security Forces' response was to establish a Joint Operational Command (JOC) system incorporating elements of the Army, BSAP, Air Force, Internal Affairs and other relevant services and to define each separate incursion as an *Operation*, ending when the terrorists in the group were all accounted for. Later, the country was divided into geographical *Operational Areas* each with its own JOC and sub-JOCs. The RAR was deployed under this system throughout what came to be known as the *Bush War* until the Commonwealth-brokered *Ceasefire* of February 1980.

During this time, the regiment expanded from one to three battalions, with 1RAR remaining near Bulawayo, 2RAR established near Fort Victoria in 1975 and 3RAR near Umtali in 1979. Shaw Barracks, a regimental training depot, was established at Balla Balla and the Independent Companies of the Rhodesia Regiment were incorporated into the RAR.

This was a Counter Insurgency (COIN) war, to be fought with the people, not against them. As members of the African community, the all-volunteer African Soldiers (AS) (the term Askari was dropped during the 1960s) were very adept at interacting with the local people, both in direct contact with them on patrol and by observing villages from covert Observation Posts (OPs).

Frequently, RAR soldiers could 'sense' the presence of terrorists, by reading the signs of their effect on village life, even before they were physically visible.

The RAR, as an infantry regiment, employed infantry COIN tactics against its enemy: patrols, ambushing, OPs, cordon and search of habitation, attacks on located terrorist camps or hides, tracking and follow up. These tactics were used both internally in Rhodesia and externally in Zambia and Mozambique. As with all professional units, and in collaboration with other Rhodesian Security Force services, these were refined and evolved. The evolution of the Fireforce concept was the most significant example of that.

Covert OPs of tribal areas were an effective tactic for sighting CT groups, but the challenge lay in concentrating force onto the sighting sufficiently rapidly to destroy them. In conjunction with the Air Force, the Army had, by 1974, developed Fireforce as a response to this. Fireforce involved the vertical envelopment of an enemy group by troops deployed from helicopters and (from 1977 onwards) by parachute, supported by air-to-ground fire from helicopters and fixed wing aircraft.

Combined with OPs, who located and talked the Fireforce onto targets, they would prove the most effective tactic of the Bush War. The Rhodesian Light Infantry (RLI) and the RAR provided most of the Fireforce troops. Within an RAR battalion, of the five companies, the pattern was very frequently for one company to be on Fireforce, three on OPs/ambushes looking for targets and one on R&R at any one time.

Many hundreds of CTs were killed or captured by the RAR during the Bush War in Rhodesia but not without loss. Between 1967 and 1980 the regiment lost nearly 200 soldiers killed in action, killed on active service or murdered in their homes by terrorists. The following stories were written by those who experienced that war.

References:
Binda, A 2007, *Masodja*, 30 Degrees South, Pinetown, South Africa.

WEAPONS USED BY THE RAR DURING THE 1965-1980 BUSH WAR by Captain Russell Fulton

This section of the book will introduce the reader to a few of the more commonly used weapons by the RAR Regular Battalions and Independent Companies. As you will soon establish in the chapters that follow, frequent reference will be made by many contributors to these and it is for this reason that this section has been included to familiarise those who have little or no knowledge about them.

An important distinction to be made between standard issue Rhodesian weapons and those of our enemy, ZANLA and ZIPRA, was that ours were of NATO origin whereas our enemies were principally of Chinese or Warsaw Pact origin.

FAL-FN: 7.62 x 51mm Infantry Assault Rifle (FN)

The FAL-FN is a Belgian designed and manufactured battle rifle that became a popular standard for NATO aligned countries during the Cold War. It was first manufactured in 1953 by FN Herstal in Belgium and was later manufactured under licence in dozens of countries.

The rifle is chambered for the 7.62 x 51mm NATO cartridge (originally designed for the .280 British intermediate cartridge.) Various conversion and redesigns of the FAL were implemented and British imperial units integrated in to the redesign and produced as the L1A1 Self-loading rifle (SLR).

More importantly, from a Rhodesian perspective, was that it was manufactured under licence by Lyttleton Engineering Works in South Africa where it was known as the R1. This made procurement simple and lead-times from order date very efficient.

FAN-FAL: 7.62 x 51mm (NATO) Infantry Assault Rifle

Technical Specifications:
Cartridge: 7.62 x 51mm NATO
Weight: 4.30 Kg's (9.48 Lbs)
Action: Gas operated, tilting breechblock
Rate of Fire: 700 rounds/minute (fully automatic). Variable semi-automatic selector.
Muzzle Velocity: 840 meters/second (2,756 feet/second)
Effective Firing Range: 200 meters – 600 meters sight adjustments
Feed System: 20 or 30 round detachable box magazine
Sights: Aperture rear sight, post front sight, sight radius.

This weapon was favoured by the Rhodesian Security Forces because of its reliability, simple assembly, hitting-power and deadly accuracy in the hands of a skilled operator. Once hit by a round from this weapon, the beneficiary would either be dead or completely incapacitated. Whilst capable of fully automatic fire our troops were trained to 'double tap' and did so with a clinical efficiency. A neat entry wound would usually be followed by a heinous exit wound. A truly outstanding infantry assault weapon with few peers and perfectly suited to the Rhodesian conflict.

FN MAG 58: 7.62 x 51mm General Purpose Machine Gun (MAG)

The MAG 58 is, like its little brother the FAL-FN assault rifle, the creation of Ernest Vervier and was first manufactured by Fabrique Nationale in Belgium in

1958. It has also been licensed for manufacture around the world and has been used in over 80 countries and in 23 conflicts/wars since inception.

This machine gun is extremely versatile and can be used as a light infantry support weapon fired from its bipod or from a tripod in an extended range/sustained fire role. During the Rhodesian bush war, the MAG was carried by some with a leather shoulder strap attached to a swivelling clip on the right-hand side close to the gas regulator and the sling point at the rear top-side of the butt. Most MAG gunners in our conflict carried the weapon without a sling as it encumbered swift deployment in heavy bush or if the operator need to adopt the prone position promptly in contact.

Our gunners either fired the gun from the hip, with the butt tucked into the armpit and, in some cases, from the shoulder whilst in the standing position. Not many had the strength to manage the latter but there were a few who could and did!

It is a fully automatic, belt-fed, air-cooled, gas-operated weapon, firing from the open bolt position, and is capable of a sustained high volume of fire. Stoppages can be easily and quickly remedied.

Our ammunition belts were continuous linked belts but there were, occasionally, belts made up of disintegrating links. For operations, belts were routinely loaded in a ratio of four ball rounds to one tracer round. The maximum effective range of the MAG 58 in the sustained fire role is 800 metres.

FN-MAG 58: 7.62 x 51mm (NATO) General Purpose Machine Gun

Technical Specifications:

Cartridge: 7.62 x 51mm NATO

Weight: 11.79 Kg's (25.99 Lbs)

Action: Gas operated, open bolt

Rate of Fire: 650 – 1,000 rounds per minute.

Muzzle Velocity: 840 meters/second (2,756 feet/second)

Effective Firing Range: 800 meters

Feed System: Non-disintegrating 50 round segmented belt

Sights: Folding leaf sight with folding aperture and notch, front blade.

Barrel: Rifled and chromed internally to reduce wear.

Gunners would, generally, join two belts of 50 rounds for operational deployment and load in to the feed tray ready for immediate use. Apart from its obvious advantages during contact with the enemy it was also used to cut down small trees when there was a need for rapid clearance of helicopter landing zones (LZ's). Rhodesian gunners were very attached to their weapons and they would nurse them as a mother would an infant. Many was the time when fists would be deployed swiftly when 'nuisance' riflemen kicked dust on their gun or touched them without permission. It was an idiosyncratic behaviour unique to machine gunners who, for the most part, went as far as to affectionately name their gun.

Despite its weight and the first line ammunition (200-300 rounds) most gunners would carry on operations, the author neither witnessed nor heard of a gunner requesting a change over to a FN. The role of a machine gunner on operations was viewed by their peers with great respect; oftentimes putting themselves in positions of extreme peril whilst providing covering fire for their call sign and they were, together with their commander, routinely, the first to be fired upon by a disciplined enemy.

STAR BM: 9mm Parabellum Pistol

The STAR 9mm pistol is a single-action, semi-automatic pistol that fires a 9mm parabellum pistol cartridge. It is Spanish designed and manufactured by Star Bonifacio Echeverria SA and is known to have been used in the Libyan and Rhodesian conflicts. Its introduction in to the Rhodesian conflict was as a means of secondary fire support for paratroopers deployed in to 'hot' drop zones (DZ's). Whilst the hitting power of this, or any other 9mm weapon for that matter, is limited to close quarter battle given its limited effective firing range it was, and nonetheless, an important part of our Fireforce arsenal.

STAR BM: 9mm Parabellum Pistol

Technical Specifications:

Cartridge: 9mm Parabellum.

Weight: 0.99 Kg's (2.14 Lbs)

Action: Single action with locked breech.

Rate of Fire: Single shot.

Effective Firing Range: 100 meters maximum. General use for close quarters: 10-20 meters

Feed System: 8-round box magazine + 1 in the breech.

Sights: Fixed, notched rear blade and serrated front ramp.

The Star (and Browning 9mm) were introduced in the mid-1970's as a means of immediate close support for Fireforce deployed paratroopers who would, oftentimes, deploy in to hostile drop zones. The main weapon of a paratrooper would be securely attached to the paratrooper's body by means of the body-band of the parachute harness rendering the individual a 'sitting duck' when he hit the DZ. A holstered 9mm pistol afforded some security during the moments that a paratrooper was completely 'impotent' in the face of the enemy.

To illustrate, I draw from an anecdote in *Chibaya Moyo* written by Captain Andy Telfer SCR [MFC (Ops)] about one of his NCO's, Corporal Ananias Ali SCR: "On 16 July 1978, Corporal Ali approached what he thought was a dead terrorist. The terrorist sprang to life and gripped the barrel of Corporal Ali's rifle, trying to wrest it from him. Although Corporal Ali could have pulled the trigger and killed the terrorist, instead he calmly drew his pistol and ordered the terrorist to surrender, which he did. The captured terrorist proved to be a section commander and much valuable information was gleaned from him, leading to several other contacts."

This was not the only time that he did this. One day, landing on a hot DZ, he was confronted by a terrorist who, seeing that the fallen paratrooper was momentarily helpless, smiled and raised his rifle. Corporal Ali, his own rifle restrained by the body band of his parachute harness, lying on his back on the ground, smiled back and said, in chiShona, "I've got another one", and shot the terrorist with a pistol". For this and several other repeated gallant acts, Cpl Ali was awarded the Silver Cross of Rhodesia.

On 28 September 1977, in a joint RAR/RLI operation, a Support Commando junior NCO (LCpl Russell Phillips) entered a cave in Op Hurricane to rescue Lt Lionel Jeremy Fisher of A Company, 1RAR who had been grievously injured. Phillips, with complete disregard for his own safety, entered the cave to assist Lt Fisher and, armed with a 9mm STAR pistol, accounted for two ZANLA terrorists before recovering Jerry Fisher to safety (shortly thereafter he succumbed to his wounds). For his quite outstanding conspicuous gallantry, Phillips was cited for the Grand Cross of Valour but was awarded the Silver Cross of Rhodesia. Those who speak lightly of a 9mm pistol might wish to reconsider their position.

AK-47: 7.62 x 39mm Assault Rifle

The acronym for this weapon is Avtomat (Automatic) Kalashnikov (after the designer Mikhail Timofeyevich Kalashnikov) 1947 (the year of design). It is, arguably, the most widely used and recognisable shoulder held assault rifle the world has ever seen. It was introduced in to the Soviet Army in 1949 following recognition of its simple assembly, rugged reliability under extreme conditions and amenable to mass production. It was to become the forebear of many future and much improved AK versions. The first version was the AK-47 with a wooden butt and was followed by the AKS, a folding metal stock version and, in 1959, the AKM. The AK-47 was not without its own unique set of problems with accuracy caused by the high velocity generated by the 7.62mm cartridge.

AK-47: 7.62 x 39mm Assault Rifle

Technical Specifications:
Cartridge: 7.62 x 39mm (standard Ball, tracer and armour piercing were common place)
Weight: 3.47 Kg's (7.70 Lbs) unloaded
Action: Gas operated, rotating bolt
Rate of Fire: 600 rounds/minute (fully automatic). Variable semi-automatic selector.
Muzzle Velocity: 715 meters/second (2,350 feet/second)
Effective Firing Range: 350 meters (380 yards)
Feed System: 30 round detachable box magazine
Sights: 100-800 metre adjustable iron sights. Sight radius 378mm (14.9 inch)
They have long been the weapon of choice for many nationalist and guerrilla movements around the world. The symbolic value of the AK-47 to such movements is borne out by the inclusion of the weapon on various coats of arms (Angola, Mozambique, Zimbabwe, Burkina Faso, and national flag (Angola). It is estimated that over 100 million AK-47's have been produced, half of these outside the Soviet Union. The AK-47, the most ubiquitous firearm of the modern era.

Because of the lower hitting power of the AK-47, compared to the FAL-FN, a wound from this weapon could, and did, cause challenges for many medical teams. If a round struck bone, it would often deflect from its intended flight path and rip through other organs ending up some distance from the entry wound. There are records of men receiving head shots who survived as the bullet head traversed between the skull and skin and exited innocuously to the rear! It was a dangerous weapon by all accounts.

RPD: 7.62 x 39mm Light Machine Gun

The RPD (aka Ruchnoy Pulemet Degtyarova – Degtyarov Light Machine Gun), designed between 1943-44 by Vasily Degtyarov, was one of the first weapons designed to fire a new, intermediate cartridge 7.62x39mm. It entered manufacture in 1944 and became the standard squad automatic weapon of the Soviet army in the early 1950s until 1960s, when it was generally replaced by the Kalashnikov designed PK and RPK light machine guns, which, in many quarters, was a poorly regarded decision. The RPD is still found in Russian army reserve stocks, and these are widely exported to many pro-Soviet countries and regimes around the world. It was also manufactured in other countries, such as China, where it was known as Type 56 LMG.

RPD: 7.62 x 39mm Machine Gun

Technical Specifications:
Cartridge: 7.62 x 39mm (standard Ball, tracer and armour piercing were common place)
Weight: 7.40 Kg's (16.31 Lbs) unloaded
Action: Gas operated, long-stroke piston system
Rate of Fire: 650-750 rounds/minute
Muzzle Velocity: 735 meters/second (2,411 feet/second)
Effective Firing Range: 100 meters – 1,000 meters with sight adjustment
Feed System: Non-disintegrating 100 round segmented belt stored in a drum magazine

Sights: Open-type sights with rear sliding notch and semi-hooded front post, 596.60mm (23,50 inch) sight radius.

Those who encountered the RPD in action will be all too familiar with its dangerous report and will recall that it was responsible for the death of many good Rhodesians, civilian and military alike. Its merits have long been argued when compared to the MAG; each to their own.

The author of this write-up carried the MAG58 on operations and would never consider exchanging it for the RPD despite the benefits of lesser weight and the capacity to carry far more front-line ammunition. There are pros and cons attributable to both machine guns and, ultimately, it was simply a matter of personal choice. Whilst the RPD was held in the regular RAR battalion company-controlled stores, it was never used on internal or external operations. It was however used quite extensively for internal operations by 1 (Independent) Company RAR in COIN and pseudo operations. By all accounts, it was a much-respected weapon and those who carried it aggressively against our own would be singled-out for special attention.

RPG-7: Shoulder-Launched Rocket Propelled Anti-Tank Grenade Launcher

The RPG-7, designed by Bazalt and manufactured by Bazalt and Degtyarev in Russia, is the acronym for the Russian "Ruchnoy Protivotankovy Granatomyot" or hand-held anti-tank grenade launcher (although it is more frequently referred to as a "Rocket Propelled Grenade" or "RPG"). It is an advanced development over its predecessor, the 1949 RPG-2, based on the World War II German Panzerfaust and US Bazooka. Improvements over the RPG-2 evidenced increased range and increased armour penetration capabilities.

The RPG-7 is undoubtedly the most (in)famous anti-tank rocket launcher ever invented since its introduction in the Soviet Union in 1961. It remains in production to this day with far in excess of 9 million units produced to date. The RPG-7 continues to be employed in over 40 countries, including increasing numbers of irregular militant groups.

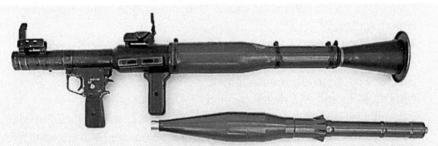

RPG-7: Shoulder-Launched Rocket Propelled Anti-Tank Grenade Launcher

Technical Specifications:

Weight: 7kgs (15 pounds)

Length of Tube: 950mm (37.40 inches)

Calibre: 40mm

Muzzle Velocity: 115 meters/second (boost) with 300 meters/second flight

Effective Firing Range: 200 meters (Maximum 500 meters). Self-detonation at 920 meters

Sights: PGO-7 (2.7x), UP-7V Telescopic sight and 1PN51/1PN58 night vision sights. Red dot reflex sight

The RPG-7 is a reusable, single-shot, smooth-bore steel tube with a diameter of 40 millimetres. This recoilless, shoulder-fired, muzzle-loaded launcher can shoot a wide variety of rockets. Optical and iron sights generally come standard, although night vision sights can be used. The barrel is covered in wood to protect the operator from heat and the two handles are located close together in the centre of the weapon.

Another advantage of this versatile weapon is that it can be fired inside buildings due to its relatively small back-blast. Nonetheless, this weapon gives off a highly noticeable flash, noise, and smoke. After 10 meters, the rocket's internal rocket motor ignites, and four stabilization fins fold out, giving the weapon a maximum muzzle velocity of 300 meters per second. The RPG-7 is operated by a gunner and an assistant who holds extra rounds and defends the gunner from attack.

During its 55-year service life, the RPG-7 has been used to knock out tanks, destroy armoured personnel carriers, buildings, fortifications, attack infantry, and shoot down low-flying helicopters. Furthermore, the simple RPG-7 has brought down more helicopters than most man-portable air-defence missile systems.

During the Rhodesian bush war, it was carried by various elements of the Rhodesian Army on external operations for use against fortified enemy bunkers, mortar and both anti-aircraft and anti-personnel gun emplacements. It was used extensively by ZIPRA and ZANLA forces within Rhodesia and most notably, on the Fort Victoria to Beit Bridge road where vehicle convoys were attacked frequently by gangs operating out of the Nyajena TTL. A notorious RPG-7 ZANLA operator who plied his trade under the pseudonym 'Rocket Man' was eliminated by elements of 2RAR in 1979. His body, and those of several of his comrades were displayed for all to see at the Ngundu Halt Business Centre.

Closing

How we got our hands on them:

Since the beginning of time, mankind has sought out, manufactured, stolen or otherwise contrived to possess weapons as a means of defence and/or, for offensive purposes. Following Rhodesia's 'Unilateral Declaration of Independence' from her colonial master, Great Britain, on 11 November 1965, Rhodesia was placed on a world economic sanctions blacklist that included an international arms embargo. What Great Britain and, for that matter, the rest of the world did not realise was the resilience and ingenuity of the Rhodesian pioneer spirit. If we never had something, we simply made it ourselves or made-a-plan.

Rhodesia was rich in natural resources, the most significant of these being her incredible mineral wealth. Rhodesia developed creative pathways around these sanctions via her southern neighbour South Africa who, it can be argued, understood the implications for their nation state if Rhodesia fell to communist backed insurgents as South Africa would certainly be the next to fall!

Through an assortment of global third-party weapons dealers, and funded through the sale of gold, emeralds, chromium, bauxite and other highly sought-after minerals, Rhodesia was able to import her defence needs through the backdoor, the strategic South African port of Durban. "Money talks!"

During the mid-1970's our conflict escalated exponentially. A strategic decision was made to hit our enemy where they least expected it; in their conventional defensive positions and insurgent training and staging camps, much to the sympathetic uproar of a left-leaning world.

Rhodesia remained undeterred and impervious to such criticism and our defence force conducted frequent covert attacks on communist camps in neighbouring Mozambique (ZANLA) and Zambia (ZIPRA). During these, and of which there were many, weapons caches were generally recovered back to Rhodesia and used by our own forces, principally for training and pseudo operations.

"You never look at a gift horse in the mouth" certainly rang true.

CHAPTER NINE

THE BEGINNING

OPERATION GRAMPUS: PART ONE by Brigadier David Heppenstall

Introduction

Operation Grampus concerns events which took place in the Binga District of Matabeleland over the period 10 to 17 August 1966. During this time 11 of 12 ZAPU terrorists who crossed by boat from Kariba to the Rhodesian shoreline near Chete on the night of 31 July 1966 were captured by Security Forces.

Army sub-units which took part in this operation were as follows:

a. Coy HQ D Coy 1RAR.
b. 12 Platoon D Coy 1RAR.
c. Three members of 10 Platoon D Coy 1RAR.
d. 8 Platoon C Coy 1RAR.
e. Coy HQ C Coy 1RAR.
f. 15 Platoon E Coy 1RAR.

This report has been divided into two parts. Part 1 concerns events over the first 24 hours from 1300hrs on 10 August 1966 when the first gang of six well-armed terrorists were captured by a patrol of five RAR soldiers led by PWO Wurayayi. Part 2 concerns events over the next six days during which time five of the six terrorists who comprised the second gang were also rounded up.

Wednesday 10 August 1966.

At about 1300hrs two prospectors from Anglo American arrived at the Binga Police Station and one of them, Mr A Taylor, reported having seen three Africans washing in a pool in the Nagapande River between 0900hrs and 1015hrs that morning.

These Africans had almost new clothing. Two were in possession of khaki bush jackets and trousers whilst the third was in similar attire but in olive green.

For footwear they had fawn veldt schoens and their toilet requisites included such items as new bars of lifebuoy soap and toothbrushes etc. At least one of them had a packet of 20 Life cigarettes.

Their answers to questions were most evasive. They stated that they were travelling from the Siabuwa road where they had been working with a road gang and were heading for Lupane. They had walked across the Chizarira Range in getting to their present position. On being asked where their registration certificates were, they vaguely pointed up onto the north ridge above the river and stated that these documents were up there with the rest of their possessions.

Mr Taylor offered them a lift as far as Ciwali, the next morning and suggested that they come into the Anglo American camp that afternoon or evening and spend the night there.

On receipt of the above information, a combined military/police party was hurriedly assembled to go to the scene to investigate. This party consisted of eight policemen including the SB officer from Wankie, DSO L Wilder who was visiting Binga at the time, the member in charge Binga, SO Jack Parker and a member of the quartermaster's staff from Bulawayo, Inspector Reay. Maj Heppenstall, OC D Coy 1RAR, and six RAR soldiers formed the army contingent. This party left Binga shortly after 1400hrs and arrived at the Anglo American camp on the Nagapande River by 1630hrs.

It was quickly established that the three suspects had not arrived at the camp, and so the whole party, guided by Mr Taylor and the African who had accompanied him that morning set off to the Nagapande River to the place where the suspects had washed. The soldiers led the way with the police following.

The pool in question was reached shortly after 1730hrs and a search of the surrounding area was mounted. At the washing point itself certain items were recovered including the wrapping of a lifebuoy soap bar made in Zambia and an empty Life cigarette packet. Tracks in the immediate vicinity were of plain treads normally associated with veldtschoens. Despite an energetic search which lasted until dark no route out was found.

The party made their way back in small groups to the Anglo American camp and except for one policeman they were there by 2015hrs. This policeman was picked up later that evening on a road near the camp.

It was considered that with the evidence available, it was almost certain that there was a terrorist gang in the area as:

a. The description of their clothing tallied with information already received.

b. One packet of Lifebuoy soap was made in Zambia.

    c. They had not reported in to the Anglo American camp for the promised lift to Ciwali on   the next morning.

With the information available and after studying the map OC D Coy deduced the following:

    a. This gang appeared to have crossed recently into Rhodesia from Zambia in view of their little worn clothing and new toilet requisites.

    b. As those members of the gang washing had no possessions with them, it was possible that there were others looking after their kit some short distance away.

    c. As part of the gang had been spotted that morning washing, they were likely to move on as soon as possible unless they had established a base for operations in that area.

    d. The most likely route for them to take would be south towards Lupane or east towards Kana. In both these areas they would be able to expect some support from the local population. To their north and west were Batonka who would be less likely to help them.

    e.. The washing place on the Nagapande River was in an area which was surrounded by a circular route which ran south from the Anglo American camp to the Gongo fly gate, then north east to the Chipongo Pan near Lusulu, then north west and west south west back to the Anglo American camp. The distance of this route was about 50 miles.

As a result of these deductions OC D Coy decided to return with the police to Binga as soon as possible and request troop reinforcements to be moved into the area with the least possible delay. The ideal would be three platoons situated at Lubimbi, Ciwali and Lusulu.

In the meantime, arrangements were made with Anglo American to use one of their Landrovers from first light on Thursday morning for PWO Wurayayi and the four RAR soldiers with him. Their task was to search the circular route for any tracks and to question every man they saw on this route for signs of the suspected terrorists. PWO Wurayayi and his party were fully self-contained and had two days' rations. They were ordered to stay on any trail they might pick up and track it to its logical conclusion. It would also be arranged for as many of 12 Platoon who might be available at Siabuwa to be in the area as soon as possible the next morning.

The police, in their Landrover, departed from the Anglo American camp at about 2045hrs to return to Binga after checking on the store at Kariyangwe Mission. OC D Coy left about the same time, proceeding direct to Binga.

On arrival at Binga at about 2300hrs, the OC's Landrover was at once dispatched with two fresh drivers to Siabuwa to bring back all of 12 Platoon who might be available. As there were two patrols of five men each, this would mean that the platoon strength would be about sixteen RAR soldiers.

At approximately 2330hrs the Police party returned from Kariyangwe Mission store with the information that two Africans fitting the description given by the Anglo American prospector had bought six tins of corn beef the previous weekend. The African tailor at the store had given the most exact description of the two men who had posed as grader drivers going home on leave from the Siabuwa road gang.

Communications with Wankie were immediately opened on the police SSB, but atmospheric conditions were bad. In fact, it took nearly an hour and a half to get the facts across to Mr Wright, OC Police Wankie District. This included switching from SSB to VHF and back on several occasions. Mr Wright was requested to phone the information through to HQ 1 Brigade in Bulawayo and recommend the IS Company 1RAR be deployed at Lubimbi, Cewali and Lusulu with the least possible delay. The time was then about 0100hrs on Thursday 11 August.

Thursday 11 August 1966.

The OC's Landrover reached 12 Platoon's base near Siabuwa at about 0145hrs and gave the PWO, WO2 Turgwe Mushingi, commanding the platoon instructions to withdraw his standing patrol on the Chunga Escarpment (PL165935) about eighteen miles away and get to the Siabuwa turn-off on the main Kamativi / Binga Road with the least possible delay. The message having been delivered, the Landrover broke a half-shaft and limped back to Binga in four-wheel drive, arriving back at base at 0640hrs.

Voice communications were possible with 1RAR by about 0630hrs when Major Heppenstall spoke to the Adjutant, and also received a slidex message that 8 Platoon, C Coy were proceeding direct to Binga via the Kamativi road. All the information available at that time was also sent to 1RAR in slidex although all communications on the police net had been in clear.

A radio message was sent to BSA Police, Lupane, to re-route 8 Platoon via Lubimbi to the Siambolo fly gate where they would be met and re-deployed depending on the information available at the time of their arrival.

Meanwhile PWO Wurayayi and his four men had set off at 0600hrs that morning and about two miles south of the Anglo American camp had picked up tracks leading south on the road. Two Europeans from Anglo American accompanied the RAR soldiers. They were Mr Alan Taylor who had originally found the suspects washing the day before, and John Tolmoy a young man of about 22 or 23. John Tolmoy sat on the bonnet of the Landrover and the tracks were followed south to the warning sign just before the Gongo fly gate where they led off into the bush. After searching the area, the tracks were found to have appeared again going south a short distance past the fly gate and they were again followed in the Landrover with Tolmoy on the bonnet. The same procedure was followed at the Siambolo fly gate where the tracks were again picked up going south east.

Within a mile of the Siambolo Fly gate the tracks led off into the bush going north and it was here that the Anglo American Landrover and the two Europeans left PWO Wurayayi to continue the pursuit with his patrol. The distance that they had covered by Landrover from the Anglo American camp was about twenty miles. The time was then shortly after 0800hrs.

A police party reinforced by one or two patrol officers from Wankie who had arrived shortly before, left for the area of Kariyangwe Mission about 0815hrs. Their task was to see what information they could pick up from the surrounding kraals.

The company commander's Landrover was fitted with a new half-shaft and returned by 0830hrs, but the CMED mechanic, Mr Wilson, reported that two bolts holding the front axle had also sheared and mechanically it required considerable attention. Once the front axle had been repaired it should manage a return trip to the Kariyangwe area. The front axle was secured by 0915hrs.

12 Platoon had arrived at the Siabuwa turn-off on the main road Kamativi/Binga by 0830hrs and by 0900hrs they were re-routed to Kariyangwe. The platoon strength was 18 AORs. Their RL TCV was giving trouble and had three stoppages due to fuel blockages.

Major Heppenstall left Binga at 0930hrs in his Landrover FFR (fitted for radio) which was still far from mechanically sound, and by the time Kariyangwe was reached it was obvious that the Landrover could go little further. 12 Platoon was waiting here with the information that PWO Wurayayi and his patrol had picked up tracks and were in hot pursuit. The police had gone ahead and had named the Siambolo fly gate as the next RV.

Major Heppenstall transferred to the 12 Platoon F250 truck and continued to the new RV as quickly as possible after calling in at the Anglo American camp for the latest information. The F250 reached the Siambolo fly gate at 1235hrs but the RL with the majority of 12 Platoon on board had again broken down with fuel trouble. The Tsetse gate attendants had instructions to direct all military and police vehicles on down the Ciwali road. Major Heppenstall also instructed the Tsetse attendants to direct the troops arriving from Lubimbi (8 Platoon, C Company) in the same direction.

Two police Landrovers were found parked on the side of the road guarded by a patrol officer with a Sterling. He stated that 'apparently' some soldiers had captured some terrorists and that they were being searched a short way off in the bush by the other police from the Landrovers. On arrival at the scene, about 300 yds to the east of the road with the PWO of 12 Platoon, WO2 Turgwe Mushingwe, Major Heppenstall found PWO Wurayayi and his patrol guarding six uniformed terrorists whom the police had just started to search. The police party had apparently arrived ten minutes earlier and had been stopped on the road by one of PWO Wurayayi's patrol. The time was now 1250hrs.

The captured terrorists had first class arms and equipment. Five of the six were armed with sub machine guns and the other had a SKS self-loading rifle with bayonet attached. In addition to his SMG the leader had an automatic pistol. Four of the SMGs had circular drums underneath (PPSH – Burp guns) and the fifth was an AKS.

PWO Wurayayi reported as follows:

'After leaving the Anglo American Landrover shortly after 0800hrs he and his patrol had tracked the terrorists north for about 800 yards until they reached the Tsetse fly fence. From here the tracks led east south east down the track which ran alongside the game fence for about three miles. Then the tracks led off north into the vleis at the headwaters of the Nkotakota River. The spoor then led back in a south easterly direction until it hit the same game fence and track that it had been on before. After another mile on the fence track the spoor again branched off north east down a vlei which formed the beginning of the Nagapande river.

'PWO Wurayayi and his patrol moved continuously up the vlei which was thickly wooded with mopani trees in extended order. On the left were C Sgt Mavengano (Coy Admin NCO) and Pte Tichawona (Coy 2IC's batman). In the centre were PWO Wurayayi and L Cpl Mabasa (both 10 Platoon) and on the right flank was Pte Sorry (10 Platoon).

'After moving up the vlei a little over a mile PWO Wurayayi suddenly saw the terrorists resting about 50 yards to his front. L Cpl Mabasa saw them almost at the same time. Pte Sorry was well over to the right of the vlei and still moving slowly forward. Neither C Sgt Mavengano nor Pte Tichawona on the left flank had seen the terrorists, and they were still moving slowly forward. The terrorists had no sentry and were sitting, resting in a group. They had walked over 25 miles in the last 24 hours.

'PWO Wurayayi and L Cpl Mabasa closed in to about 30 yards when the SM challenged the gang. By this time Pte Sorry, on the right flank was out of sight in some thick mopani, but C Sgt Mavengano and Pte Tichawona were well placed on the right flank. On being challenged all six terrorists jumped up and it was only then that PWO Wurayayi saw how well armed they were. All of them raised their SMGs and two of them cocked their weapons.

'At that moment C Sgt Mavengano and Pte Tichawona ran in from the terrorists' right flank with their rifles at the ready, and PWO Wurayayi shouted at the terrorists that they were to drop their weapons, or he would kill them. Seeing that they were covered in a cross fire, the terrorists dropped their weapons. They were ordered to walk forward five paces with their hands up and then lie down while they were searched. A pistol was found in the pocket of the one who subsequently turned out to be the leader. On checking the weapons which the terrorists had dropped, all were found to be loaded and cocked.'

The capture of the six terrorists took place at 1030hrs. After a brief check through the terrorists' belongings, the patrol started back on their five-mile march to the Siambolo /Ciwali road at about 1100hrs. They heard the police Landrovers when they were about 400 yards from the road shortly before 1230hrs and Pte Sorry was sent to the road to guide the police in.

By 1330hrs both Lt Cameron-Davies with 8 Platoon C Coy and the remainder of 12 Platoon had arrived at the scene of the capture. Shortly afterwards Supt Wright, Officer Commanding Wankie District drove in from Binga where he had arrived that morning. Information of the capture was passed back over the police SSB shortly before 1400hrs, and Maj Heppenstall gave the details to the CO 1RAR shortly after 1400hrs on the company 62 set.

A directive came from Police Bulawayo that all six prisoners were to be dispatched to the city with the least possible delay. This was vigorously opposed by Maj Heppenstall on the grounds that it was essential to gain as much operational intelligence as possible, since it had already been learnt that there was another gang in the area. Eventually it was agreed that one prisoner could be retained in the Binga District. All troops and police with the prisoners then moved to the Siambolo fly gate where a brief interrogation of all the prisoners took place. A considerable amount of useful information was gained on the possible movement of the second gang.

At about 1530hrs five members of the gang were taken out under escort to the Gwaai River Hotel whilst the leader, one Lancelot Ncube, an ex-school teacher, accompanied the Security Forces to Binga. This brought to a successful conclusion the first part of Operation Grampus as it was soon to be called.

OPERATION GRAMPUS: PART TWO by Brigadier David Heppenstall

At their initial interrogation on Thursday 11th August the six captured terrorists divulged the following information:

    a.   They had crossed into Rhodesia from Zambia on the night 31 July/01 August by boat. They had left Zambia somewhere in the area of Sinazongwe and had landed on the Rhodesian shoreline somewhere near Chete.

    b.   When they crossed, there were two gangs of six Africans each.

    c.   The destination of the two gangs were as follows:

        i.   The gang already captured were to operate in the Nkai area.

        ii   The gang still at large were heading for the general area of Que Que/Gwelo.

    d.   One of the second gang had pleaded sickness and had not landed in Rhodesia. He had gone back to Lusaka with this group's map in his pocket. This group were marching on a direct bearing from Chete to Que Que. This bearing had been worked out off the map belonging to the captured gang.

From the above information it was possible to work out a rough line of march for the second gang. It was thought that this group might already be south of the Chizarira Range.

Friday 12th August 1966.

All troops, Police and the captured terrorist leader had spent the night at Binga. At a conference held at the Binga Police Station at 0800hrs between Maj Heppenstall and Supt Wright the priority of tasks was agreed as follows:

    a.   All stores and kraals on the Siabuwa road were to be visited by a police patrol with one African Constable (AC) dressed as a terrorist.

    b.   Troops were to be moved into the area of Lusulu and to search the area between there and the Busi/Sengwe river junction.

    c.   A combined Military/Police patrol were to be moved by boat to the Chete area to search for the exact spot at which the terrorists had landed.

    d.   An Army patrol would search the area of the Sengwe River from the Siabuwa road bridge down to the Busi/Sengwe junction.

A police Landrover with one AC dressed as a terrorist left for the Siabuwa road at 1130hrs accompanied by L Cpl Parinovengwa and one other RAR soldier.

    At 1230hrs the DC's launch, the Sir Patrick Fletcher, returned to Binga after having picked up the two outstanding patrols of 12 Platoon. The first patrol had been picked up from the Sinamwenda Research Station and had nothing to report. The second patrol which had been picked up at the Chete Game Camp reported spoor for three to five persons on the tracks in that area. This spoor appeared to be at least two weeks old. The spoor was definitely made by veldtschoens. It was later realised that these tracks were made by an RRAF survival course and not by terrorists.

It was decided that Lt Cameron-Davies with 8 Platoon C Coy would move into the Lusulu area and would base up initially at Tivuli Spring. He moved out at 1330hrs accompanied by one Patrol Officer and one African Constable who knew the area. Clearance was obtained from HQ 1 Brigade for them to cross the District boundary into Gokwe if necessary.

The patrol to search the Sengwe River from the Siabuwa road bridge to the Sengwe/Busi river junction consisted of L Cpl Sesa and six RAR soldiers with an A10 radio. They left Binga by vehicle at 1415hrs after BSAP Gokwe had been warned of their patrol route, as it was the boundary between the two districts.

The party to search for the place at which the terrorists landed consisted of 12 RAR soldiers under PWO Wurayayi and PWO Nguluwe with 2 European policemen and one African Sergeant. They also had one A10 radio. They left Binga in the Sir Patrick Fletcher at 1545hrs and reached the Chete shoreline at 1800hrs. The prisoner was brought out in the police launch, Admiral Tait, which arrived in the area as it got dark. Although he was kept in the area all night, he denied being able to recognise where he had landed. The Admiral Tait with the prisoner on board returned to Binga in the early hours of Saturday morning.

Saturday 13th August 1966.

8 Platoon C Coy had arrived at Tivuli Spring the previous evening and commenced their patrolling soon after first light both on foot and in vehicles.

Following suggestions from OC D Coy the police sent a further Landrover up the Siabuwa Road with a CID section officer and the prisoner to try and locate the spot where the gang had crossed the road. They were accompanied by CSM Jairos Mutepfa BEM of D Coy and one RAR soldier. Shortly before reaching Siabuwa at 1200hrs this Landrover was stopped by an African on a bicycle who told the CID officer that Chief Siabuwa's messengers had detained two suspects in the Siabuwa store at 1030hrs that morning.

When the Landrover arrived at the store the chief's messengers, one of whom was armed with a shotgun, were found guarding two Africans dressed in the normal terrorist clothing except that one of them had a navy blue blazer on top. The prisoner, on seeing these two greeted them as long lost friends and at once volunteered the information that these were two of the other gang who had crossed the lake with him.

After a brief period of interrogation these two agreed to lead the Security Forces back to the spot where the other three of their gang were hiding in the foothills of the Chizarira Range.

SSB and VHF communications were not possible from Siabuwa in the police Landrover, and it was not until 1435hrs that the information was received at the Binga Police Station. There was an immediate scramble and by 1450hrs eighteen RAR soldiers, under Maj Heppenstall, all with two days rations were ready to leave for Siabuwa. They were accompanied by about twelve policemen under Supt Wright.

This party met up with the police Landrover, complete with prisoners and escort at the Chete road junction at 1615hrs. From here the convoy proceeded to a debussing point 1.5 miles west of Siabuwa, and the prisoners pointed out the position of their camp below a prominent hill in the Chizarira. This was about seven miles from the road.

The patrol moved off from the debussing point at 1625hrs in the following formation:

a. Three RAR soldiers as scouts in extended line, 30 to 50 yards in front.

b. One of the two prisoners with CID escort and two RAR soldiers on each side in extended line.

c. Command element of Maj Heppenstall accompanied by Supt Wright and one RAR soldier immediately behind.

d. Six RAR soldiers commanded by platoon Sgt 12 Platoon in extended line about 15 yards behind.

e. Miscellaneous police personnel under the Member in Charge Binga and the second prisoner.

f. CQMS D Coy with five RAR soldiers.

The hill at the base of which the terrorist camp was situated could be seen for almost the whole march so that there was no difficulty in navigation and no guiding was required from the prisoner

The going was rough and by 1815hrs it was apparent that the patrol could not reach the terrorist camp before last light. At 1830hrs Maj Heppenstall ordered a halt for the night on the reverse slope of a rocky ridge. All the troops were in patrol order and were carrying combat jackets and enough food and water to last them until lunch the next day. Packs had been left in the vehicles. The police had not even any water, and some were only wearing thin shirts and shorts making it a night to remember!

After the halt the prisoners were questioned further, and both were adamant that they were now close to their camp. A distance of half a mile was mentioned. The camp was in the river bed below the hill and it could be recognised by a large mopani tree growing on the bank at that spot. Maj Heppenstall's plan was to move forward at first light on Sunday morning, and once the lie of the land could be seen, to send twelve soldiers and some police around as stops, and attack with four or five soldiers.

One patrol officer and one soldier as his guide were sent back to the transport to report the position and intentions of the patrol. They were also to bring the vehicles up at 0730hrs the next morning.

Sunday 14 August 1966.

The patrol moved off cautiously at 0550hrs, but very soon ran into some very thick scrub and jesse bush which was almost impenetrable. The result was that the patrol was divided into three groups. Maj Heppenstall was in a small group which arrived in the vicinity of the camp at about 0845hrs, but the prisoners, with a larger group, had not yet arrived. The third group was now under the command of CSM Mutepfa BEM, and it was that group that located the camp first, only to find that it had been vacated some time before. (It later transpired that the three terrorists in the camp had left before first light after they had got worried about the failure of their comrades to return with food.)

An immediate search of the surrounding area was mounted and, within ten minutes, four packs were recovered about 150 yards north of the camp. These contained mainly clothing and medical supplies. The only arms and ammunition consisted of one Russian hand grenade and five rounds 7.62mm (short). No tracks could be found out of the area although it was suspected that the terrorists had moved off either to the west or the south as no spoor had been seen by the various parts of the patrol approaching from the north and east.

After the search of the immediate area had been completer with no other results, the whole patrol moved back to the transport which had now moved up to within four miles of the camp at a borehole, arriving there at 1145hrs.

A short conference then ensued in order to plan a wider search. A radius of fifteen miles was drawn on the map and it was agreed to try and cover the circumference of this circle as well as work out from the centre.

At this time information was also received that a helicopter with police dog and handler had been standing by at Gokwe and that it was moving to Siabuwa now.

A redeployment of Military and police was agreed as follows:

a.   Sgt Simbi and six RAR soldiers with the Member in Charge Binga would remain at the borehole and continue to search the immediate area. The Helicopter and dog would remain with them.

b. Lt Cameron-Davies with 8 Platoon C Coy would be flown onto the top of the Chizarira and would work north to the front of the escarpment searching for any sign of the three remaining terrorists going south or south east.

c. BSAP Gokwe were to continue to be responsible for the district boundary, the Sengwe River, but they were to be reminded that L Cpl Sesa and his patrol were in the area until midday Monday.

d. To the west CQMS D Coy (C Sgt Girison) and ten soldiers were to patrol the area of the Mawuli River to the south east into the Chizarira Range up which there is a road to the top. This party would be reinforced as soon as more men could be found.

e. The police would be responsible for the Siabuwa Road on the north side of the area and would be responsible for visiting all kraals near the road for information.

f. 15 Platoon E Coy was somewhere in the Gokwe area and it was hoped to get them to Sinasenkwe with the least possible delay to fan patrol in the Ruziruhuru River area.

The helicopter piloted by Flt Lt Nettleton landed on the LZ which had been hastily prepared at the borehole by 1245hrs just as Maj Heppenstall was leaving. The former was briefed on the operation to date, and later that afternoon flew a sortie over the immediate area of the terrorist camp with a stick of the Member in Charge, Binga, SO Jack Parker, and four soldiers.

Maj Heppenstall returned to Binga later that afternoon after the troop deployment had taken place to find that two Provost aircraft had also arrived. As it was an Army responsibility to supply rations for aircrews this created a problem, as there was little more than two days rations for two Europeans at the Company base.

Full details of what had happened were passed back to 1RAR over the radio and a further helicopter was called for to lift 8 Platoon on to the top of the Chizarira Range at first light the next morning.

The DC's launch, Sir Patrick Fletcher, was also sent out at about 1500hrs that afternoon to bring back the troops and police searching for the landing site near Chete, as they were also required to join the search.

Sunday evening came with troops and police regrouping to begin the wider search.

Monday 15th August 1966

At 0545hrs the second helicopter on its way to Binga radioed in that it would land at the BSAP LZ at 0555hrs, and that it was short of fuel. When it had not arrived by 0615hrs the Provost crews were warned to take off and locate it in case it had come down somewhere in the Valley out of fuel. Before the Provosts were ready to take off, a radio message was received from Victoria Falls saying that the second helicopter had lost its way and had landed there. It would fly back to Binga as soon as it had refuelled.

Meanwhile the DC's launch had failed to locate the patrol it was due to pick up at Chete, and so the Provosts were sent to the area to find them and re-route them back to the Chete harbour where the launch would wait. By 0730hrs the Provosts had located the patrol three miles down the Chete road and had dropped a message telling them to return to the Chete harbour.

Due to the non-arrival of the second helicopter, the lift of 8 Platoon C Company was carried out by Flt Lt Nettleton with one helicopter and was completed by 0930hrs. The lift was from an LZ just north of the Busi/Sengwe river junction on to the Chizarira Range. At 0900hrs a Dakota flew into Binga carrying fuel for the Provosts and helicopters and one hundred European ration packs, less biscuits, for the aircrews.

At Siabuwa that morning Sgt Simbi and his men patrolled the foothills of the Chizarira in the vicinity of the terrorist camp but without success.

During the day the Provosts carried out two recces over the general area and plotted out all the water in the area on to their maps. There was no shortage of water in the area. They also gave Lt Cameron-Davies a good idea of the terrain to his north on the Chizarira where water was scarce.

The DC's launch with the patrol from Chete arrived back at Binga at 1215hrs. PWO Nguluwe and five soldiers immediately routed to the area of the Mawuli River where the former took over the CQMS D Company, C Sgt Girison, who was required back at Binga. PWO Wurayayi and a further four soldiers were dispatched to Siabuwa to cover the stores in case any of the other three terrorists came in for food.

At 1325hrs Maj Heppenstall and Supt Wright left for the Sengwe river bridge in the second helicopter for a meeting with Chief Supt Berry to coordinate operations on the Binga/Gokwe District boundary. This helicopter which had arrived at Binga before 1000hrs was now piloted by Flt Lt Becks who had been flown in from New Sarum.

At this meeting it transpired that Mr Berry had deployed 15 Platoon E Coy 1RAR into the eastern gorges of the Chizarira Range to the west of the Sengwe river, and they were now in a superfluous position behind 8 Platoon C Coy. In addition to this he had pushed police patrols across the Sengwe River and these were now five miles inside the Binga District. Although Mr Berry was most emphatic that the information regarding these moves had been passed to Binga, neither Supt Wright nor Maj Heppenstall had any idea that it had taken place. Information from Mr Berry was apparently passed back through three radio relay stations and this might have accounted for Binga not receiving full particulars of these moves. The outcome was that 15 Platoon E Coy would not be available for two days for any tasks for which Maj Heppenstall wanted to use them.

L Cpl Sesa's patrol of seven men were waiting at the Sengwe river bridge, and they were moved back to Siabuwa by police Landrovers to reinforce Sgt Simbi's party. The Tac HQ for the Siabuwa area was moved back from the borehole near the terrorist camp to the DC's camp at Siabuwa.

Supt Wright and Maj Heppenstall accompanied by Supt Bannister who was in charge of the police patrolling the Siabuwa/Binga road, returned to Binga at 1630hrs by helicopter.

Maj Stokes, OC C Coy 1RAR, had in the meantime, arrived at Binga from Bulawayo and was briefed on the current situation. It was agreed that HQ D Coy would remain at Binga and that HQ C Coy would move to Siabuwa the next day to control the military side of the present operations. Discussions were also held between Maj Heppenstall, Maj Stokes and the DC Binga, Ian Findlay and it was agreed that there was a requirement for boat patrols to check all the fishing villages in case the three remaining terrorists tried to escape the country to Zambia. Internal Affairs boats would cover all the fishing villages up to Chete and the BSAP would be asked to cover those to the east of this location as the Admiral Tait was the fastest boat at Binga. After consultation the police agreed to this arrangement.

Another Dakota with Provost ground crew, radios, an RRAF guard dog with handler and other miscellaneous equipment arrived later in the afternoon.

At 1930hrs CSM Mutepfa BEM left Binga for Siabuwa with a three ton vehicle loaded with helicopter fuel, police walkie talkie radios and rations. They reached the DC's camp at Siabuwa by 2200hrs.

Tuesday 16th August 1966.

In the morning further patrols were mounted from Siabuwa into the area of the terrorist camp and HQ C Coy prepared to move to Siabuwa.

On the arrival of Maj Heppenstall and Maj Stokes at Siabuwa, they were informed that the patrol commanded by L Cpl Sesa had recovered all the arms and ammunition cached about three hundred yards south west of the terrorist camp. A helicopter had flown in to bring them out. The helicopter returned from the site of the arms cache with the weapons and ammunition at about 1230hrs.

The Officer Commanding BSAP Matabeleland Province, Mr Sherren, accompanied by the PCIO and one other officer flew into Siabuwa by helicopter from Binga about lunchtime for a briefing on the progress of the operation.

Shortly after their arrival a radio message was received from Binga to the effect that the fisheries officer, Peter Banks, on checking the fishing villages, had been informed at Siatili that three strangers, alleged to be fish buyers, had slept there the previous night. That evening they had been taken to an island where an African fisherman named Diamond lived and had had discussions with him. Diamond had an outboard motor for his boat. The three strangers had been dressed in khaki and their footwear was veldtschoens. They alleged that they had left their truck at the end of the road one mile inland from Siatili. Before first light on Tuesday they had left the fishing village and their present whereabouts was not known.

The District Officer (DO), Jim Latham, accompanied by Lt Jones, the Education Officer 1RAR who was temporarily attached to D Coy, had left Binga as soon as possible after receiving this information in a small fast boat belonging to Internal Affairs. The Provosts took off and soon confirmed that there was no vehicle parked on the Siatili road. A helicopter took three European policemen from Siabuwa to Siatili but, due to a misunderstanding, only dropped off two of them before flying on to Binga.

The DO in his launch picked up the two policemen from Siatili and they proceeded to Diamond's island where they arrested the latter. He was surly and refused to answer any questions.

As a result of these developments, Maj Heppenstall, together with C Coy HQ, returned from Siabuwa to Binga. En route they met the CO, the Adjt 1RAR and the BM 1 Brigade who were proceeding towards Siabuwa. The CO's Landrover was having fuel pump problems. Maj Stokes had flown in to 8 Platoon on the Chizarira in helicopter with three days rations and had then returned to Binga by the same means. The road convoy reached Binga at 1815hrs.

The latest information available over the lake safety radio was to the effect that it was still not known whether the three suspects were in Rhodesian territory or had got over to a Zambian island in the early hours of Tuesday morning.

There had apparently been some disagreement on the DCs launch and the DO asked Maj Heppenstall for direction as to who should be in charge until such time as more troops and police were moved into the area. As the DO, Jim Latham, was in charge and responsible for the boat and also knew the fishing villages he was told to take charge until Maj Stokes and reinforcements arrived on the scene.

This took place at 1900hrs and it was estimated that Maj Stokes and eighteen to twenty RAR soldiers would be in the area on the launch Malvern by 2200hrs. The senior police officer in Binga at that time was Mr Allen, an Assistant Commissioner from Bulawayo, and he was informed of Maj Heppenstall's decision. r Allen stated that he could not accept this decision, but he was told that this arrangement would have to stand until Maj Stokes arrived on the scene. It would be for no more than two hours.

Maj Stokes left Binga on the Malvern at 1945hrs and dropped off small parties of soldiers at Diamonds Island and Siatili. Before reaching Sengwe they made contact with the police launch, the Admiral Tait, and proceeded to Sengwe together. On arrival at that fishing village the Admiral Tait ran aground, and the local villagers were roused to help push her off. This happened sometime after midnight.

Whilst this was going on, one of the villager casually mentioned to African police Sgt Gideon that the three people who they were looking for were asleep in a hut in the village. Maj Stokes quickly ordered SM Wurayayi and a cut off group to the back of the village, and accompanied by the police and some AORs was taken to the hut. On entry the three terrorists were found inside asleep fully clothed in their uniforms. They had been so exhausted that they had not heard the commotion when the Admiral Tait was re-floated.

Wednesday 17th   August 1966.

Information of the capture was passed back over the Lake Safety Radio at about 0200hrs. One prisoner was brought back by the police on the Admiral Tait and the other two on the Sir Patrick Fletcher with the troops. Both launches had returned to Binga by 0415hrs.

It transpired that the second gang had also been six strong, but that one member had deserted his comrades some days before near the Siabuwa road. He had left his weapon and pack behind but had absconded with about £50 of party funds.

The automatic pistol belonging to this gang was in the possession of one of the two captured at the Siabuwa store. After he had been apprehended by the chief's messengers, he made an excuse to go to the African toilet and alleged that he had dropped the pistol down the hole. The police intend to attempt to recover the pistol if possible!!!

This brought to an end 'Operation Grampus'.

WITH THE RAR AT BINGA, by Ian Findlay

One of my most enjoyable periods of service as a District Commissioner in the Ministry of Internal Affairs, formerly the Native Affairs Department, was in the Binga District from February 1963 to February 1969. My close association, during this period, with the Rhodesian African Rifles served me well when in later years I served with JOC Hurricane in Centenary and Bindura and the Command JOC in Salisbury.

An early visitor to the area was Brig Bob Prentice, commanding the Rhodesian African Rifles in Bulawayo and together we patrolled the shores of the Lake from Mlibizi in the West to the Chete gorge, halfway to Kariba in the east. It was the beginning of a long, delightful and fruitful relationship with the Rhodesian African Rifles who, after a few months attending to our needs from Bulawayo, stationed a company of troops with us, who were ever available, at a moment's notice, to ensure our wellbeing whenever terrorists entered the country through the district. David Heppenstall and Mike Shute were early Company Commanders who served with distinction, bringing their Companies of highly trained troops to Binga on many occasions. They became good friends and were well known to us all.

The terrorists, who initially were Ndebele, trained in Russia and Northern Rhodesia, generally entered my District by either crossing the Zambezi river in the area of the Gwaai river where it became Lake Kariba or by crossing well to the east of Binga in the area of the Chete gorge in Lake Kariba, directly into the Chete National Parks and Wild Life Land, adjacent to the Chizarira Forest Area - both areas being uninhabited but well stocked with elephant, buffalo and most other forms of wild life. On the lake shore, there were a couple of small fishing camps in the game reserve area but they were only occasionally occupied by fishermen from Chief Siabuwa's area.

When I first arrived in Binga I used to take Air Force trainee pilots on a survival training course exercise which required them to walk across the Chizarira Game Area with the Game Ranger and me and then from Chete back to Binga in pairs, after my having taken them there on my official launch, the Sir Patrick Fletcher. It was always a difficult task as the thick bush was teaming with large game and, apart from a number of tracks, had few roads of any value to help them find an easy way home. Sadly, this enjoyable exercise had to be discontinued when it was appreciated that footprints in unoccupied areas could be excellent evidence of terrorist infiltration.

Within a year of my appointment as District Commissioner, my loyal Tonga tribesmen reported the presence of a small group of Sindebele speaking young men, very heavily laden with landmines, grenades and firearms who had entered the country by crossing the Gwaai River where it flowed into the rising Lake Kariba, moving through Chief Binga's area towards the Kamativi Tin mine and the Lupani District in the Province of Matabeleland, the home of many Ndebele Chiefs, Headmen and tribesmen.

The Binga Member in Charge of the British South Africa Police was Insp Jack Parker and he, having alerted the Army Headquarters in Bulawayo, under command of the Rhodesian African Rifles, accompanied them on a follow up. The troops were good at their work and on every occasion, except one, captured the insurgents almost as soon as they picked up their tracks.

Initially the terrorists were very poorly trained and surrendered as soon as they were challenged. Only on one occasion during my service in Binga did insurgents fire back, and this contact ended with the death of most of them.

In later years they were better trained, killing innocent civilians from ambush positions and, although they were always killed or captured as soon as they were spotted, they invariably fired back causing security force casualties. The group that was not discovered, passed through the district because two groups had entered the area a day apart by crossing the Lake in the Chete area and when they moved into the inhabited area, the Tonga, in informing the troops of the terrorist movement, mixed up the days of the week on which they had seen them, giving the impression that only one group was involved. The RAR did however contact them soon after they moved into the Lupane District and neutralised them before they could do any harm.

My launch, the Sir Patrick Fletcher, with a large flat deck, could comfortably carry some twenty-odd, fully armed troops and I well remember checking out crossing points after troops had back-tracked a group following a successful contact. We would approach land with all troops alert and ready to open fire or to carry out an assault the moment we touched the shoreline and saw any signs of a terrorist presence - interesting as we had massive fire power and only disciplined well trained terrorists with a well sited machine gun would have had us at a disadvantage when we had nowhere to take cover. Fortunately, they were neither disciplined nor well trained and, if they had been about, we would have had a ball. In the event, if we ever alerted terrorists, they elected to remain well hidden, no doubt with happy thoughts of the joys of meddling with the RAR in the days ahead.

OPERATION BREEZE by Major G. A. Lloyd

Editors' note: this report was originally written by Major G. A. Lloyd for the Joint Planning Staff in January 1969. It was selected for Chibaya Moyo by Brigadier

David Heppenstall and kindly transcribed from the original by Mrs Ruth von Stranz.

Operation Breeze coincided with Operation Bonfire to deal with another ZANU crossing in the Deka River area of Matabeleland. The nine terrorists involved in this operation had been trained in Tanzania with the Bonfire group and the two groups were together until they left their holding camps to infiltrate Rhodesia. Thus they attended the rite outside Lusaka and were initially briefed with the Bonfire gang. The Breeze terrorists were formed into two gangs, the Ngomanyarira group of five and Dubula group of four.

The Ngomanyarira group was destined to operate in the Fort Victoria area. They were told to travel there on foot, to proceed with caution and not to hurry to their operational area. The Dubula group was instructed to move on foot to the Wankie area, thence to Salisbury. Should they fail to reach Salisbury, there were to make for the Gwelo and Que Que area.

The groups were briefed by Noel Mukono and Felix Rice to avoid contact with Security Forces until reaching their operational areas. Attacks were to be carried out against European farms in the rural areas and terrorist incidents were to be created against European civilians in urban areas. The latter were to include indiscriminate shooting and throwing grenades into cinemas and clubs.

Like the Bonfire group the two groups were given £50 a head and were issued with nicknames and code numbers. They were also given ZANU flags, pamphlets, training notes and copies of Mao Tse Tung's quotations.

On 27th December, 1967, the gangs, together with all their equipment, were taken from Lusaka in a Land Rover and two Toyota Vanettes, one of which carried a blue dinghy and two unknown Africans whose task was specifically to paddle the terrorists across the Zambesi. The two gangs travelled separately from Lusaka and met up again on the road South of Kafue. From there they were driven to Choma and then took the Nkandabwe road for 30 miles before turning right on to a track which led, after several hours' journey, to the river. A mile north of the river the party debussed. They were accompanied on the journey by members of the ZANU Hierarchy in Lusaka.

The crossing point selected for both gangs was almost opposite the Deka River mouth and about a mile East of Mapeta Island at grid reference. Using the boat that they had brought with them, the two groups, with their equipment, were ferried across the river to the Rhodesian bank. The dinghy made several trips before they were all carried across. The Ngomanyarira group was the first to cross and immediately upon landing moved off into the bush without waiting for the Dubula group to cross.

The Ngomanyarira group had no map. Although they had been given a compass the terrorists claimed they had no training in the use of it. Making their way slowly they reached the vicinity of the Flourspar Mine at Tinde, which is North-East of Kamativi Mine, on 3rd January, 1968.

The Dubula group of four appeared to have made better progress, reaching the Kamativi area on 1st January, 1968. On 2nd January, two members were sent to Kamativi to buy food but on their arrival went straight to the beerhall. The two terrorists aroused the suspicions of a Compound Policeman as although they alleged they were schoolboys they had offered £4 for someone to give them a lift by motor vehicle to Dett. The Compound Policeman challenged these two but allowed one to go and fetch their identification papers allegedly left in the Compound.

The Compound Policeman then made a report to Constable Mathew (on patrol from Dett) and the remaining terrorist was searched revealing he carried a pistol and ammunition. Under initial interrogation the captured terrorist, Nelson Mtinkulu, said he was one of a group of six terrorists whose destination was Salisbury. He added that the six were part of a group of 44 ZANU who were to operate in the Que Que, Fort Victoria and Salisbury areas. He also claimed that 56 SAANC terrorists had crossed at the same time and were heading for South Africa via Plumtree. This was regarded with great suspicion as it was known there was no affiliation between ZANU and the SAANC.

Following Mtinkulu's capture, a JOC was established at Dahlia at 1000 hours on 3rd January and E Coy 1 RAR moved by road from Methuen Barracks to Dahlia. The FASOC normally based at Wankie airfield moved to Dahlia and an RRAF Sector HQ was established at Brady Barracks alongside HQ 1 Bde. Aircraft allocated for the operation were two helicopters, one Cessna and one Trojan with two armed Provosts and jet strike aircraft on standby at Thornhill.

On 3rd January a Police patrol went to a camp indicated to them by Mtinkulu where the two remaining terrorists were hiding. The camp was near one of Rabison Sialinda's kraals where it is believed the two terrorists had been hiding. These two travelled to Dett by bus, bluffing their way through an Army road block by saying they had lost their registration certificates and were on their way to Bulawayo to attend a funeral. From Dett they boarded a train for Bulawayo on 6th January.

One was arrested by Police at Nyamandhlovu on 7th January but the other escaped detection as he was travelling in a separate compartment. He was eventually arrested by Det. Constable Mqanjelha on 12th January at the Valley Hotel, Mzilikazi Township, Bulawayo, on indications made by his brother-in-law. The last member of the Dubula group, who had escaped from the beerhall when Mtinkulu was captured, was arrested unarmed at a kraal in the Narira Reserve,

Enkeldoorn, on 18th January by Detective Section Officer Wray, acting on information. He travelled to his kraal on foot as far as Kana Mission, thence by bicycle via Que Que, Central Estates and Umvuma, arriving at his kraal on 10th January.

Meanwhile the Ngomanyarira group was being sought by the Security Forces following the capture of two of their number on 4th January. These two were sent into Kamativi to buy food, their comrades at this time being hidden up in the Tinde Hills. On the way they met Constable Banda who was on leave from BSAP Dett. After talking to them for a while, Banda became suspicious and thought they may be terrorists. Showing great initiative he arranged to meet them later at the beerhall and immediately left for Kamativi Mine Compound, where he arranged for mine police to assist him to arrest the two men on their arrival. As soon as the terrorists came into the beerhall they were arrested.

Under interrogation they admitted belonging to a group of five terrorists and said the other three were in the Tinde Hills. It was now apparent to JOC members that there were two terrorist groups involved in the operation, one of four and one of five.

On 4th January, at 2300 hours, a terrorist stopped a prospector named D'Oliveira who was driving on the Kamativi-Binga road. The terrorist asked to be taken to Binga, which D'Oliveira refused to do. D'Oliveira reported the incident to the Police at Kamativi and added that other terrorists were believed to be hiding in a prospector's trench near Tinde Mine. A report from Special Branch, Wankie, that the two terrorists captured earlier that day had admitted that their colleagues were hiding in the hills near Tinde, confirmed this report. It was decided to take no action on the report until the following morning when a platoon of E Coy, 1 RAR, and two Police mobile units would move into the area and search it, supported by an armed helicopter. Two Hunters were placed on 15 minute standby for rocket and cannon attacks should the terrorists be located and pinned in a suitable target area.

The following morning 15 Platoon, E Coy, 1 RAR and a party of Police, along with the two captured terrorists from Wankie as guides, set off to locate the camp and attack it. About two miles from the area of the camp the platoon was stopped by Mr. D'Oliveira and another prospector named Raimondo who said that the three terrorists, dressed in civilian clothes, had come to the mine for food and medical attention. With considerable risks to their own safety these two men entertained the terrorists and shortly afterwards left for Kamativi to report developments. They said the terrorists were now sitting in their mind compound waiting for them to return before being given a lift to Binga. It is presumed their motive in going to Binga was to attempt to get a boat to take them back to Zambia.

The platoon commander, 2 Lt. J.W. Pritchard, decided that speed and surprise were the best means of dealing with the terrorists. He borrowed the prospectors' Land Rover and driver (who could identify the terrorists) and loaded nine members of his platoon into the vehicle. The African civilian driver drove back to the mine compound and pointed out the terrorists to 2 Lt. Pritchard.

The vehicle stopped about three yards from where the terrorists were sitting, the patrol debussed and formed a half circle around them. The two terrorists who were nearest the patrol were taken completely by surprise and had no time to react before they were captured. The third terrorist made a bolt for it but, on being called upon to halt he looked around, saw the soldiers' weapons in the aim position and surrendered. On being searched, one of the terrorists was found to be in possession of a primed hand grenade. Their weapons and equipment were hidden nearby. With their capture the whole of the Ngomanyarira gang had been rounded up.

While this was going on, 13 Platoon, E Coy, 1 RAR and four Police patrols were searching for a camp for 20 terrorists in the area of a kopje which had been reported to the Police by an African civilian. It was in this area that the four terrorists' packs belonging to the Dubula gang had been found earlier. An airstrike was requested on the strength of this information while the platoon patrolled the area to ensure that a target did exist. Despite a thorough search, no signs of a camp were found. The airstrike was aborted and the two Hunters which had been hopefully orbiting the area returned to Thornhill. The report was later proved to be false.

At this time there were still three members of the Dubula group outstanding. Although the members of the Ngomanyarira group stated under interrogation that only the two groups of four and five terrorists has crossed, Nelson Mtinkulu still maintained that 44 ZANU and 56 SAANC had crossed at the same time. While the search for the three terrorists continued, two of the captured terrorists were taken to the area of the crossing in an attempt to find evidence of the alleged larger gangs having crossed. None was found and Mtinkulu's story was finally discounted – he eventually admitted that it was based on hearsay.

On 8th January, E Coy 1 RAR was relieved by D Coy 1 RAR. The terrorist had been captured on the train the previous day and it was now apparent that there was only one terrorist possibly still in the Kamativi area. On the recommendation of the JOC the operation became solely a police operation and the Army and Air Force returned to their bases at 1200 hours on 10th January. As stated earlier the two outstanding terrorists were subsequently arrested outside the operational area.

During Operation Breeze, the value of using aircraft to relay messages to and from ground forces was again apparent. Although an expensive method of ensuring communications, its use greatly facilitated the interchange of orders and information and was found to be particularly useful when ground forces were in close contact with terrorists, when there was no time to erect orthodox antennae. The Police Reserve Air Wing provided this facility on most of the operation and performed a very valuable service.

Weapons Recovered:

SKS	4
AK	2
MAT	2
M.25 pistol	1
Tokarev	3
Assorted Ammunition	2939
Grenades	22
Grenade primers	19
TNT	21 x 200 gms 7 x 400 gms
Mines	6
Igniters	15
Detonators	30
Switches	8
Bazooka rockets	3
Bazooka	1
Safety Fuse	22 x 1' lengths
Haversacks	9

Plus an assortment of safety fuse, clothing, uniforms and boots.

OPERATION LONG WALK by Sergeant Colin Prain, SAS

About a week after Sergeant Andre Rabie, SAS was killed in September 1973; I was instructed to proceed to the Bindura JOC to be briefed on a special project involving the tracking wing. The Commanding Officer of the SAS, Major Brian Robinson told me that Troopers Clive Cripps, John Graham, Dennis Boyd and Chris Robins, all SAS, were to be going with me. Early on Monday 25th September, the five of us were collected by Aaron 'Baron' Rukavina, SAS and taken to Mount Darwin. On arrival we were met by Captain Mick Graham, SAS and Lieutenant Pat Armstrong RLI.

Mick Graham had been posted to 2 Brigade as G3 Ops and his boss was Brigadier Hickman who gave the go-ahead for the Experimental Teams. Graham had heard all Major 'Spike' Powell's stories from Kenya about pseudo-gangs and it struck him that the same scene could work in Rhodesia. He had thus been able to get Rabie and Franklin on loan from the Tracking Wing.

We were told that we would be joining members from other units and told to remove all SAS insignia, later we were collected by Alan 'Stretch' Franklin, SAS and taken to the Trojan Mine buildings. We were now to wear civilian clothing and were under Special Branch control.

Standing, (Middle): Prain, Cripps, Robins
One week before being transferred to the experimental teams

At the house on the mine we were introduced to Basil Moss from the Air Force, Robin Hughes from National Parks and Sergeant Rabson Maposa from the RAR. Maposa had six other RAR soldiers with him. We also saw six more black men, which Franklin told us were tame terrorists. We were to form pseudo teams, to impersonate the terrorists and be redeployed as such back into the field. These along with Rabie's team, were later referred to as the Experimental Teams.

For the next three days we stayed at the mine house, played volley ball and cleaned weapons. On the fourth day we were all picked up by two Bedford RLs and taken to an area near to Sipolilo, there we set up camp (Palm Towers).

For four days we were made to run up the highest gomo in the area, when down, only to be told to go back to the top again. Daily Mick Graham came to the camp with water and rations.

Moss and Hughes left with Mick Graham one morning and I was told by Franklin that they were going to work in another area. By the fifth day, not having washed or shaved or changed our clothes, we all looked like hobos. Finally, the

RLs returned and we were all taken to a farm house near Centenary where we were given better food but told not to wash or shave.

Two days later the five of us and Maposa were briefed by Franklin; he told us we would be getting dropped off about twenty kilometres south of Sipolilo at the Shinje River. We would follow the river towards the Zambezi River and where the Shinje met the Angwa River, we would turn east along the Mozambique border following the Mkumvura River to the Ruya River then turn west towards Centenary (distance of about 320 kilometres). We would carry water but would get food from the villagers along the way. Our task was to locate terrorist groups in the area, we would move by night and rest during the day.

Later the same day boxes of terrorist equipment, webbing, uniforms, packs etc were dropped off at the farm, by sundown we were all looking like terrorists, being white we were blackened up, face, neck, arms and feet, as we would have to take off our shoes to avoid leaving tracks when entering villages, we had to wear long sleeved shirts and long trousers. Cripps, Robins and I were in one of the farm rooms getting ready when John Graham and Boyd walked in, and on seeing Graham, Cripps shouted 'Hey, Chunkie'.

The Chunkie character, a detective, was from a South African Photo Story Magazine; that is real photos with what they were saying printed in little boxes coming out of the mouths printed in Durban by Republican Press. The black actor who played Chunkie was a little over weight and as Graham was also a bit over weight and now black, he looked like the actor in the comic, and from that night on John became known as 'Chunkie'.

The RLs arrived at around midnight and we were taken out to the drop off point. We walked following the river until day break where we hid and waited for the sun to go down.

For the next ten days we walked, resting by day and moving by night, we entered numerous villages and were well received by the locals. Maposa and the RAR men did all the talking and arranging for the locals to make food for us, the food was left at pre-arranged places, the RAR men ate first then the tame terrorists, Franklin and the five of us ate last, it was brought to our attention by a RAR lance corporal that the 'black is beautiful' that we had on was staining the plates, so we ate last and empty plates were wiped clean.

Maposa and some of the RAR men had gone out early one morning to fetch water and returned as the sun was rising. Maposa informed Franklin that the locals had told him that a large terrorist group was in the area. Franklin told Maposa to return to the village and arrange a meeting for that night. Maposa came back approximately four hours later and told Franklin that the terrorists were hiding about five kilometres from our location and wanted to meet with us now.

Franklin briefed us; there was a local who would take us to them, so we moved out at around midday, the guide leading, followed by Maposa and two RAR men, then Franklin and I, Cripps, Boyd, Graham and Robins, then the six tame terrorists, and at the rear the remaining RAR men.

When the guide told Maposa that the terrorists were about five hundred metres from our position, Franklin gave the order to drop all non-essential gear, packs, radios etc, and we then proceeded to the RV. When we saw the terrorists, we were in a Mopani forest, it was just after 3.00 p.m., there were about twenty of them, the nearest group to us numbered five, then the rest, and behind them I saw five females carrying baskets on their heads.

Maposa and a RAR lance corporal went forward and exchanged greetings with a coloured terrorist who was wearing a blue T-shirt, Rhodesian camo cap, brown trousers which were tucked into his boots, and carrying an AKM. As Maposa and the RAR lance corporal were talking, Franklin moved towards a big Mopani tree, and we moved to his right in an extended line facing the group. The tame terrorists moved to Franklin's left and sat down, the RAR men at the back also sat down facing the direction we had come from.

Maposa was standing on the left side of the terrorist leader, facing us, and was trying to pull him away from the group, the rest of the terrorists were dancing, clapping and waving for us to move closer, Franklin whispered to me to stop, as I stopped the four SAS men to my right stopped, by this time the terrorist leader had noticed Franklin, as Franklin was well over six foot two he was taller than the average ter.

Maposa was still pulling the terrorist's left arm but the terr was pulling away and making his way towards Franklin, at a distance of about five to six metres Franklin lifted his head and looked at the terrorist. Maposa let go of the terr's arm and put both hands onto his AK. The terr leader on seeing Franklin's face grunted and went wide eyed, starting to lift his AK. Maposa put his AK against the terr's left ear and fired; the leader dropped, and as he fell we all opened fire, and as we were firing there was a loud explosion. A minute of two later we advanced, changing magazines and still firing, while to the best of my knowledge the other terrorists never fired a shot in our direction.

We advanced passed the remaining terrorists and the five females, all of whom were lying on the ground, then we then heard shooting to our left in the distance, as we reloaded. Franklin made his way over to where the RAR men at the rear of our group had stopped and the tame ters were now nowhere to be seen. We checked the females, and then the ters, all were dead. The RAR lance corporal who was with Maposa started shouting that Maposa had been shot.

I sent Cripps and Robins to go and collect our kit, which included the medics pack and radio, and on their return, Franklin radioed the contact through to the Centenary JOC via a relay, while Cripps and I treated Maposa, who had been shot through his right thigh although fortunately the bullet had missed the bone. I think one of us might have accidently shot him.

On checking the terrorist leader, we found that his right arm had been blown off by the explosion; there must have been a grenade in his webbing which had been hit by a bullet.

The tame ters returned approximately ten minutes later and told Franklin that they had chased the remaining real ters, this was lies as all the group had been killed.

Franklin told us that a chopper was on its way to our location to pick up Maposa and that we must move out of the area as an RLI stick was also being choppered in to do a follow up. The first chopper arrived and Maposa was casevaced while we collected our packs and left the area.

We continued walking for the next six days and the info we gathered was used in future operations carried out by the RLI. Apart from a brief encounter with a Rhodesia Regiment patrol who were way out of their area, we made it to the prearranged RV, where were collected by Mick Graham with the RLs and taken back to the farm. After cleaning up, I went with Franklin to the Centenary JOC for debriefing and the rest of the men were taken back to the Trojan Mine.

I was given Rabie's pale blue Land Rover to use. I collected Cripps, Robins, Boyd and John 'Chunkie' Graham and we returned to Salisbury for R & R. For the next two months we were split up. Cripps and I joined Moss, while Graham, Robins and Boyd went out with Franklin.

By this time there were a number of rumours that the experimental pseudo teams were going to be incorporated into a unit, although this was only confirmed later in mid-December.

In early December, while we were returning to the mine after days off, before leaving Cranborne Barracks, I received orders to pick up an officer and take him to the Mount Darwin JOC. We proceeded to a double storey house in Avondale and picked up Lieutenant Dale Collett from the RAR. Over the next few weeks we were joined by men from other units, the next to arrive was Charlie Krause. I remember him arriving as he had malaria and had to be treated.

By mid-December the mine house was crowded and the outside house I had been using to sleep in was converted into an armoury, new showers and toilets were built. One morning we were visited by Armstrong who informed us that the group was to be attached to a new unit, to be called the Selous Scouts, which would be based at Kariba or at Inkomo Barracks outside Salisbury, and that we must now decide which unit we wanted to stay with. Cripps and I decided to return to the SAS as we did not trust the 'tame terrs'. Robins, Boyd and Graham stayed and joined the Selous Scouts.

By January 1974, Cripps and I were re-deployed with the SAS to Macombe and it was during this deployment that Trooper Mickey Morris, SAS, was tragically killed. Out of the original twelve members of the Selous Scouts, eight were SAS.

Editors' Note. This article is SAS-focused, and rightly so as it is written by an SAS soldier, but it is also historically important to the RAR as it provides a credible first-hand account of the often-overlooked involvement of RAR soldiers in the formation of the Selous Scouts. We are grateful to Colin for his permission to include it and to Darrell Watt and Hannes Wessels for their help in making that possible. For further reading, from a credible author who researches his work thoroughly and presents it in an engaging and fascinating way, we recommend Hannes' two books about the Rhodesian SAS titled 'A Handful of Hard Men' (with Darrell Watt) and 'We Dared to Win' (with Andre Scheepers). Refer: exmontibusmedia

THE FORMATION OF 2RAR by Colonel Ian Pullar

I was recently asked by Mike Shute if I would write something about the 2nd Battalion, the Rhodesian African Rifles, having been both the second in command and the CO during the period 1975-1979.

When the Battalion was formed as a response to a growing political and insurgent threat, it had no troops, no barracks and no home. All we did have was an identity and that was enough to get us going. The 1st Battalion provided enough soldiers and officers for a Rifle Company and a skeleton Headquarter Company. Officers were plucked from various positions throughout the army, but primarily their parent Regiment was RAR. Peter Hosking was the first Commanding Officer with me as his Deputy and I had come from the Artillery via a very, and thankfully, short period at D Mil Studies.

Army Headquarters had either leased or commandeered the Fort Victoria Showgrounds, because Fort Victoria was where the Unit was going to be based. Bryan McDermott was the Adjutant, John Cameron-Davies was OC Headquarter Company, John Irvine was the Medical Officer, Alf Logan the Administrative Officer, and Tony Hine the Transport Officer.

The idea was that we would recruit from the South-East of the country and start our own training. We were supported with new recruits and training by the 1st Battalion, without whose assistance and significant sacrifice we would never have got off the ground. The Showgrounds had very little by way of infrastructure. The Show Ring was a large oval area which had been used for parading cattle and horses and such like in more agrarian times. This became the Parade Ground. It did not have much grass on it, as I recall, mostly dust. There were a number of wooden structures, cattle pens and stables. Quite how anybody was supposed to form a battalion with this as an infrastructure, was something of a head-scratching exercise. We got financial and material assistance from the Army, but had to build our own accommodation and office blocks.

Fortuitously, John Cameron-Davies was quite handy with a survey level and had obviously had some sort of building experience because he put down concrete slabs and built huts all over the Showgrounds. This allowed us to at least house our embryonic Unit and its logistical support. The whole thing was like a massive initiative test that one might encounter in a particularly vivid nightmare.

The Officers' Mess was a rented house in the suburbs, the entrance hall to which was swiftly converted into a bar. It only had three bedrooms and sleeping in the passageway was standard as we expanded. It was very difficult to rent housing and most Officers, initially anyway, were living as single. Before long we had managed to build up two Companies from our own training. Still relying very heavily on the expertise of NCOs and Warrant Officers from the 1st Battalion, we had managed, after a relatively short time, to produce our own trained soldiers from recruits.

We were soon joined by two Company Commanders, former British Army Officers. One, whose name escapes me, was going by a different identity to his actual identity and although a number of possible reasons could be drawn from this, he was not with us long enough for us ever to unravel it. The other, was Andre Dennison, who served brilliantly until his untimely death four years later in a contact at the Zimbabwe Ruins Hotel. In addition, several Platoon Commanders from various backgrounds also arrived. There was considerable rumour in some quarters that, because of the general circumstances in the country and the appearance of officers from other backgrounds, that these, or some of them anyway, were in fact British spies. I was convinced that Major two-names was not actually a spy, but a rather nervous British Officer who was worried he might lose his pension if the Brits ever found out he was in Rhodesia. I never gave the spy theory any credibility. We likely had enough of our own entrenched at much more senior levels for anyone in Whitehall to bother with placing any more amongst our Battalion Officers.

Army Headquarters had budgeted for a proper Barracks to be built with accommodation and this would be sited near the airfield some three or four kilometres from the town itself. The site chosen was former farmland and woodland savannah. Surveying started pretty soon after we had established ourselves. Quite how a barracks of this size was going to be built before we outgrew the Showgrounds was an unknown. It required accommodation for four Rifle Companies, Headquarter Company, Support Company and a Battalion Headquarters, as well as the various messes. In addition, every soldier of the rank of Corporal and above was going to have married accommodation in blocks of flats three stories high within the Company lines.

I understand that the government budget for the Barracks was in the order of $5 million dollars which was to include internal tar roads, fully fenced perimeter, armouries, magazine, vehicle parks, workshops as well as Company and Battalion office blocks The whole was bigger and more modern than the RLI Barracks, but it wasn't going to have an Officers' Mess, nor a Chapel. Nonetheless occupation was still quite a way into the future.

Housing for married Officers and senior white NCO's also had to be built, as did housing, and I mean proper housing, for all the Platoon Warrant Officers and CSMs. The first requirement was to get water to the site, and that had to come from the pump-house at Kyle Dam which was a considerable distance from where the Barracks were to be built.

Fort Victoria Town Council managed to get political influence, not to help the contractors build the pipeline, but to demand that the water supply to the new Barracks must also be diverted to provide a new supply source to the town itself. This meant a much bigger diameter water-pipe because the Barracks was like a small town. Interestingly, this pipeline, which had to be buried, was made of asbestos the thought of which would cause serious health concerns today, but presumably because it was always wet, the fibres never got to have serious consequences. As far as I know, that pipeline still serves that Barracks and the town, Masvingo, which was formerly Fort Victoria.

After about six or eight months we were still in the Showgrounds, but starting to show something of the very fine Unit that 2RAR would eventually become. Just when we were beginning to feel a little more relaxed about the way things were going, we were told to form and deploy a JOC to Chiredzi for operations in the South-East which, since the inception of the Frelimo Government, had become a new Front Line.

We were also required to deploy a Rifle Company from our limited resources, but not to Chiredzi, to another JOC. We established the JOC at Chiredzi itself. The Engineers built a small ablution block but everything else was under canvas. The Air Force component was at Buffalo Range which had a long tar runway, but for the time being, the Police and Army components remained at Chiredzi itself. The CO, Peter Hosking, spent four to six weeks at a time at the JOC, while I looked after the Fort Victoria end. We would switch over, I would then spend about two weeks at the JOC and Peter Hosking would return. At JOC Chiredzi, apart from one of our own Sub-Units, we had mostly territorial, mostly understrength, companies, a small air-force contingent and a Police PATU.

The South-East at this stage was not a particularly serious operational area, but it was developing into one. All the indications at that stage were that it was going to become a major front, which it subsequently did.

So we had now moved from the development of a new Battalion to four separate but related issues. Firstly, the further development of temporary accommodation at the showgrounds and the training of new recruits to build up the company strengths. Secondly, the command of the JOC at Chiredzi and operations in the South-East. Thirdly, the Administration and Logistics of the various Sub Units under the command of the JOC. Fourthly, our involvement in the planning of the new barracks at Fort Victoria. This last required more attention than one might imagine because civilian contractors, some staff officers and government financial people had very different views as to what the Infantry Battalion Barracks should look like and be able to accommodate.

Before long, we were required to move the JOC from Chiredzi to Buffalo Range because we needed to be close to an airfield for future Fire Force deployments. Buffalo Range was a new metalled airfield, the cost of which had been covered by Government and the Anglo-American Corporation (AAC) to service the sugar industry. The Rhodesian arm of the AAC was called the Chartered Company. The region was an important agricultural centre. The Chartered Company was Cecil Rhodes' creation and was the de facto and subsequently de jure entity that ruled the embryonic country of Rhodesia in the 1890s. The Charter being the British Governments authority for Rhodes' company to become a government.

The Chiredzi farming region was divided into a very large number of small, irrigated, one to two hundred hectare lots. These were fully irrigated to the equivalent of eighty inches of rain a year, which meant that sugar cane grown there was enormous and of high yield. Because of the climate and the irrigation, the farmers were also rotating wheat and cotton. The soil was incredibly fertile and although the farms were small, their owners were mostly wealthy, and lived a very up-market lifestyle.

The Buffalo Range Camp was a properly laid-out, engineer-constructed, Battalion Tactical HQ. It was built primarily of asbestos, walls as well as roofing. It was about midway up the airfield. It did not have a proper sewage water disposal system but I had seen a sewage waste water treatment plant in the Fort Victoria area and managed to get army engineers to build, with a front-end loader, a series of evaporation ponds to handle our effluent. I hadn't the remotest idea how this worked except that fairly grubby water entered the top pond, descended into a second and then a third by overflow, and amazingly enough it did not smell. The first pond took water directly from the septic-tank system and showers, kitchens etc. and by the time it arrived at the third pond it was quite clear. This made a big difference to our camp hygiene. One Officer suggested that we farm fish in the bottom pond. This was declined.

The army camp at Buffalo Range was quite a big one, set amongst mopani trees and completely fenced. We ran operations from here for at least a year as the Battalion grew to pretty much its intended size. The Selous Scouts had also established a base in Chiredzi and mini cross-border operations were planned from there. But I must emphasise that even when the Unit was pretty much up to full-strength, our Sub-Units were mostly deployed to other operational areas, although in the later stages we usually had a company of our own together with territorial Units.

We never had enough troops to fight that war and while we were still at Chiredzi, I can remember the Prime Minister visiting with General Walls. While General Walls always looked concerned whenever operational matters were discussed, I can't say that Ian Smith ever did. Either he was not in possession of the true facts or he did not believe them, probably the latter.

In Fort Victoria itself, the old Meikles Hotel on the main street had closed. I don't know when it had opened originally, but it must have been around the twenties or thirties. It was procured by Army with the intention of using it as the 2RAR Officers' Mess. I think this would have been around late 1975 and it was probably the reason that an Officers Mess was not built on the site of the new barracks.

It had a bar, a big kitchen, about thirty rooms with the original furniture, which looked as though it could have come up with the Pioneer Column. About half of the rooms had more recently been converted to en suite and it was actually a pretty good mess. Apart from my occasional periods of R and R to Salisbury where my family remained, I lived there until the married quarters were built in the new barracks. The European Sergeants' mess shared the hotel, but did not have a bar. The RSM, Lou Hallamore, got one built, pretty quickly, as I recall.

The JOC at Buffalo Range was working extremely well and by now Headquarters 4 Brigade had become well established at Fort Victoria. The Battalion was moving up to full strength and we needed to get into the new barracks. We had also started taking casualties in the field and our soldiers were proving themselves to be a formidable force. We had some fine Officers and I have to say that those who graduated from our School of Infantry were very high quality.

Eventually the new barracks was ready for occupation, but regrettably Peter Hosking had been transferred before this happened. He went on promotion to Army Headquarters and was replaced by John McVey. It was around about this time that we were told to move the JOC Headquarters from Buffalo Range to Grand Reef in Umtali. This was an airfield serving that town and was some 20 km west, just off the main road to Salisbury.

Just before we moved the JOC to Grand Reef, there had been a cyclone which followed the Sabi-Lundi River line into the Chiredzi area. It was a pretty rare occurrence by all accounts. It was a category 2 or 3 by the time it reached us.

There was exceptionally heavy rain in the late afternoon which continued into the evening, accompanied by very strong winds. The topsoil at Buffalo Range was very deep and fine and it very quickly turned to mud in wet weather. The rain intensified and, by nightfall, it became obvious that we had a serious problem. I had never experienced a storm of this nature. The rain was practically horizontal. The asbestos roofs and walls of just about all the buildings were torn loose, became airborne and smashed into pieces. A sheet of corrugated iron which must have been blown off the ablution block landed right next to the Mess where we were sheltering and embedded itself like a spear right in the mud.

Everybody else had vacated their buildings and sought refuge in the somewhat waterlogged trenches situated around and in the camp area. Mopani trees were bending over at 45 degree angles and I saw one ripped right out of the ground, roots and all, and it wasn't a small tree either. The storm took maybe another hour to ease, but the rain continued through most of the night. The camp, being of flimsy construction, was all but destroyed and needed engineers support to rebuild it, which took several weeks.

The Air Force at the other end of the airfield fared no better, but they had moved their aircraft to Fort Victoria earlier in the afternoon. We had no physical casualties and, apart from the buildings, it was mostly antennae masts that were damaged and it took us a while to re-establish communications. Didn't do a lot of good to the effluent ponds, still minus fish, but they did not breach.

The transfer of Peter Hosking broke up a team which was very successful and I was very sorry to see him go. I have to say that I have been very fortunate in my military and civilian existences to have had mostly high quality superiors. But of all those for whom I worked, the one that stood out was Peter Hosking. He was given a very difficult task, to start a Battalion from virtually nothing, with limited resources and assets, and turn it into a useful fighting force. I know it was a team effort from the bottom to the top, but it was under his leadership that the 2nd Battalion became a Unit that would be difficult to better anywhere, not just within Rhodesia.

It would have been around this time when our Sub-Units started converting to an Airborne role to enable us to become part of the Fire Force system and we eventually became Fire Force Charlie in the South-East, but that was a considerable time later. Our Sub Units were on constant deployment with other Fire Forces and were becoming very experienced in Airborne operations.

When John McVey was the CO and I was still the 2IC, he spent a lot of time in Salisbury planning the future Special Forces Headquarters, and as a result I spent more time at Grand Reef than I would have done under Peter Hosking's system. A lot of time and effort was spent on building up the defences of the JOC and building protective embankments around the camp. This would have been in 1977. We had a really good JOC and I thought we did pretty well during that period. We were eventually recalled to Fort Victoria and handed over a very efficient and well-defended base to the 4th Battalion Rhodesia Regiment. Shortly after we left, Grand Reef was attacked. Thanks to our defences and the ability of 4RR, there were no own forces casualties.

John McVey was not with us for very long, before he too went to Army Headquarters on promotion and I was appointed to be the CO. This more or less coincided with us moving into our new barracks, which was an interesting exercise.

There was one very unfortunate and ugly incident before we left the Showgrounds. As I said earlier, we had started to take casualties soon after we commenced deployments and we were in the process of conducting a funeral for one of the soldiers. This would have been around about 1976 as far as I can recall. We had a company on R&R who were drawn up on the temporary parade ground expecting a proper hearse to arrive. The 2nd Battalion did not have its own band, although we did later get some buglers, again courtesy of the 1st Battalion. The days of a military funeral with a gun-carriage and a full band, especially being as far from Salisbury and Bulawayo as we were, were long in the past. Nonetheless, the funerals we did were conducted with dignity and respect, and with proper funeral administrative back-up. But not this one.

First of all we waited, and waited. Eventually the Admin Officer made a phone call, and he said the hearse was on its way. What arrived was an old and dirty grey Volkswagen Kombi which stopped where the Guard was waiting. The doors were opened and they proceeded to remove the coffin. Relatives who were present also wanted a last look at the deceased before the final trip to the cemetery. In this case there was no coffin. The body was wrapped in a blood-stained plastic sheet tied up with cords.

I immediately told the so-called undertaker to take the deceased back to his premises, which were a supposedly reputable undertaking business in Fort Victoria, and he was left in no doubt as to my feelings on this issue. I immediately got onto Army Headquarters. 4 Brigade had not been established at that stage and I expressed my serious concern and wanted to know what was going to be done about this. I spoke to all the Warrant Officers and Senior NCO's who were available at that time and subsequently to others who came in until I had covered just about everyone. I expressed my sincere regrets and disgust. To say they were unhappy is an understatement.

The following day, a proper hearse with two attendants, a Chaplain and all the necessary equipment arrived and we conducted the funeral and others which followed, in a proper way. The original contractor was taken off the tender list. I would have liked to have seen something rather more drastic happen to him. I was extremely angry and depressed over this incident. This was quite clearly a case of racial abuse, made worse by the fact that the undertaker couldn't understand what he had done wrong. After all this was how Black people were buried. In different graveyards too.

We expected the African Soldiers to fight, and sacrifice themselves in many cases, for a cause which at that stage favoured the white government and its policies. These men were our comrades in arms and while racism was not an issue in the military, it most certainly was in some elements of Government as well as the general population. I think at this point I realised that for us to prevail in this war there had to be a massive change of culture and I was not sure that was going to happen.

We had a huge problem with soldiers' families whose lives could be measured in days once the insurgents learnt of the connection, and it was not just wives and immediate children but parents as well.

We had accommodation in two and three bedroom flats, in three storey blocks for every Corporal and above. And it was quite an adjustment for families who had never experienced this type of living, and it required guidance and monitoring to transition them from grass roof huts in the tribal lands to modern flats. There were of course the inevitable critics who scoffed at the disaster such sudden modernisation would cause but as usual they were proven utterly wrong.

This still left us with the problem of parents, some of whom who could be accommodated in the flats, but without overcrowding, which we were not going to do, we needed an alternative.

We got some grants to buy materials and, practically by ourselves as a Unit, we built a village on government land just outside the main gate to the Barracks. Again, I think it was John Cameron-Davies and his Dumpy level who came to the rescue. The buildings were brick and cement on a concrete base and all were circular. They were a far better quality with proper water reticulation and sewage than anything that was to be found in the tribal lands, and we moved hundreds of older people into them.

When it came to giving a name to our new barracks, Army Headquarters said we could choose between Shaw and Parker. None of the Officers nor Warrant Officers believed this to be appropriate. This was a Black African Battalion living in an historically important region in African culture and it needed a name that reflected that.

We decided to have a referendum where the soldiers could put down their choices for the Barracks name. One must also remember that the majority of our soldiers were recruited from Mashona background and a lot from the local clans who were Rozwi, traditional residents of this region. The majority wanted the barracks to be called "Masvingo" because this was the traditional name of the Fort Victoria area. Loosely translated this means "place of stone" or "stone buildings". "Place of ruins" was another interpretation. We never got a definitive answer about the precision of translation. The meaning was, nonetheless, clear.

So we went back to Army Headquarters and pointed out our concerns and our results, and although it probably did not go down too well, we mentioned that a name was required that would not be changed in the future. And indeed Fort Victoria itself is now known as Masvingo. This was finally accepted by Army Headquarters and Masvingo Barracks it became, and as far as I know, remains so.

After John McVey left on promotion to take up position as OC Special Forces and we had left Grand Reef, we formed, under HQ 4 Brigade, Fire Force Charlie. We had three fully airborne companies and we conducted operations in the South-East until I was transferred to Army Headquarters in early 1979.

Our operations in the South-East were based on selecting a suitable Battalion Tactical Headquarters site near an Airfield with the Fire Force and at least two companies under command. Suitable areas were infiltrated and Observation Posts were established close to the tribal lands where terrorist activity was identified. The troops would move in on foot by night, targeting likely areas according to Special Branch Intelligence and establish observation posts for up to four days, by which time they had usually been compromised or successful, and we were very often successful. Some of the troops would be in bare feet carrying their boots. They over-walked the booted spoor and kept our infiltration secret for long enough to be effective. We would remain in a region for perhaps two weeks and then move to another district and repeat the process. The tactic of calling in the Fire Force following observations from ground troops, had long been proven and worked extremely well.

One of the problems we encountered though, was the continual declaration of "Frozen Areas". Quite often after we had deployed, an area would become off limits because the Selous Scouts wanted to operate there. Sometimes our Fire Force did deploy on information from a Scouts OP and we often worked well with them. Unfortunately not always and some serious difference of opinions sometimes arose.

The Tactical HQ was always properly defended and trenches, as opposed to shell scrapes, were the norm. We had B80 encrypted communications and teleprinters as well. The South African Staff Course visited us on one deployment when we were close to the main Fort Victoria/Beit Bridge road. Subsequently, in later years, I was told that they had been impressed with our system, morale and efforts and had learned from them.

By now the Battalion was at full strength with no shortage of willing recruits. We were completely equipped with Mercedes Troop Carriers and Unimogs. Apart from a couple of staff cars, I don't think there was a single non 4X4 in the Unit. Initially our greatest threat was from Land Mines and we lost a lot of vehicles as well as soldiers until our counter measures became more effective. We had 106mm Recoilless Rifles and a proper 81mm Mortar Platoon; we had highly competent officers and a wonderful morale.

I think the importance of this region was not fully appreciated. There were stone walls everywhere and evidence almost wherever you went of iron-smelting and gold production. It wasn't just iron that was being produced, steel too was a product and it is likely that in antiquity it had been a major centre in central Africa. This part of Africa had entered the Iron Age at least as early as the Middle Ages and probably before that.

The routes from Great Zimbabwe to the sea to export slaves and gold and copper from probably the same period and were the same trails in many cases that the terrorists used. The superstition which surrounded the area and the awe in which it was held by local people was significant. It is also of interest to note that if you look at the origins of many people who held and still hold, high political office in Zimbabwe, many have their roots in the Masvingo region.

In summary, the history of the 2nd Battalion covered formation and development, the construction and occupation of an impressive Barracks complex, probably the best in Africa at that time, the JOCs at Chiredzi and Buffalo Range and Grand Reef. The gradual build-up of equipment and men to full strength and a high degree of training and efficiency, Airborne training and probably the ultimate of having a battalion under almost independent deployment with its own headquarters and Sub-Units in the field as well as top class equipment and weapons. It was a privilege to have served with them, and an even greater one to have commanded such a Unit.

CHAPTER TEN

PATROLS

INTRODUCTION: PATROLLING by Captain Andrew Telfer

'Victory usually goes to the army who has better trained officers and men'
Sun Tzu
'Discipline is the soul of an Army. It makes small numbers formidable'
George Washington

RAR Masodja on Patrol

When I was first commissioned, I joined D Company, 2 RAR at Bikita. The company was then commanded by Major Noel Morgan-Davies, prior to him moving to Support Company.

He introduced me to my PWO, WO2 Gwatirera, and we set off on our first patrol.

We were carrying out a typical RAR patrol task of that time, moving by day through a Tribal Trust Land with the aim of gathering information and encountering the enemy. At night, we ambushed paths (see 'Ambushing' elsewhere in *Chibaya Moyo 2*).

I sensed WO2 Gwatirera quietly watching his new young Platoon Commander and I felt him gradually relax as he saw me follow the simple tactical rules taught at the School of Infantry. He would have seen the correct use of hand signals to change patrol formations, watched sticks sent to clear potential ambush sites, observed the careful selection of stopping places and the all-round defence signal as we arrived at them. He approved and relaxed because he was accustomed to officers trained on Rhodesian Army cadet courses and had confidence in us.

Fast forward to Christmas 1979, after I'd left D Company for Support Company and 10 Platoon is being commanded by an officer trained overseas. Lance Corporal Canaan Moyo has been killed and several soldiers wounded in a contact during a follow-up on 22 December. I am in Fort Victoria hospital with Major Bryan McDermott at the bedside of Private Mugwagwa, one of the wounded men, listening to his anger that their officer, on spoor of terrorists, had led them across open ground against their urging. The terrorists had caught them in the open and taken full advantage of the officer's mistake. That officer was removed from his post but the lesson was clear: on patrol, if you lacked either training or self-discipline, someone could pay with his life.

Yet, most of the time, patrolling seemed *so* innocuous. It didn't seem as hard as moving at night into an OP, when it was vital to be covert; in contrast, the daytime patrol was visible to anyone, completely overt. It wasn't tense, like sweeping through thick bush on Fireforce operations, as the presence of the enemy was so much less certain. And yet, it was a dangerous situation and so easy to get wrong. Patrolling was not simply walking; it was tactical movement across ground, manoeuvring for advantage over an enemy who just might, suddenly, be there.

Patrolling was not a journey from A to B; it was like chess. A Platoon Commander often had six or seven four-man sticks to work with, each connected to him by VHF radio comms. So, he had to move those sticks like chess pieces: out to the flanks to clear high ground; hooking around to the far side of villages or hills to act as cut-offs; around the covered edges of open ground; onto high features to observe ahead; along thickly wooded river lines to search them; into villages to talk to locals. Never revealing or exposing the whole force, always ready to contact the enemy.

If enemy tracks were found, one stick formed a combat tracker team. The tracker followed the spoor. His commander moved behind him, looking ahead so that the tracker could look down. Diagonally forward and on each side, flankers patrolled, checking the bush in front and on their side. If spoor was lost, the tracker gave the hand signal and the stick commander signalled for a 360, a wide rotation by the flankers, around the tracker, until one of them cut the spoor again.

If *contact* was made with the enemy, the contacting soldiers would pour fire into them to win the firefight, forcing them down, while others sprinted around to attack from a flank. Once, patrolling in Mozambique, my stick of four men from 10 Pl, D Coy, 2RAR bumped into ten terrorists in very long grass in broad daylight. The MAG gunner fired to supress them, while the remainder of us hooked around to the right flank. The RAR soldiers moved so quickly that all ten terrorists were killed.

That incident occurred very early in my career (just six months after commissioning) and taught me a valuable lesson. On that hot and sultry day, around noon, we were tired but we were not 'thumb up bum and brain in neutral'. We were moving tactically, and we were alert, so we saw the enemy when they came into sight. Had they seen us first, all they had to do was crouch down in the long grass and we'd have walked right into an ambush. We lived and they died, because we were patrolling in a trained and disciplined manner, not simply walking.

COMMENTS ON PATROLLING by Captain Russell Fulton

Patrols were a part of the RAR's D.N.A. and there was no room for error. It's what we did and, largely, we did it effectively. For a RAR patrol call sign of four (elements of 10Pl, D Coy, 2RAR) to kill a group of ten CT's whilst on patrol on foreign soil illustrates, with crystal clarity, what adherence to basic tactical operational protocols could, and did achieve. Andy Telfer commanded that very call-sign and it is a clear testament to his sound leadership and tactical savvy that a 100% kill rate was achieved under such extreme circumstances.

There will be very few, if any, four-man call-signs from any unit in the Rhodesian army who achieved such success on patrol! I stand corrected of course but I have never heard of anything close to this and without 'top-cover'. How/why did it pan out as it did? Because the patrol was not conducted as a walk-in-the-park. Andy learned and applied in practise every single aspect of what he was taught on his officer cadet course.

Shortcuts in the preparation and execution of patrols resulted in a number of things:

1. In the late 1970's, patrol deployments were never conducted to pass the time of day. Troop deployments were made on the strength of Special Branch, Selous Scouts or Ground Coverage and/or other intelligence sources; there was always the potential for contact.

2. Success or failure was contingent upon the quality of intelligence received, the source, the detail of that intelligence, how 'fresh' it was and operational orders from the top down. A breakdown at any point in that chain would result in failure. Compromise and/or casualties would be your unwanted 'reward'. Sound battle procedure was the cornerstone to success.

3. The men of the RAR were completely at home in the bush and their natural and inherent awareness of their surrounds separated them from their white counterparts. There can be no doubt about that. Andy references being under the watchful eye of his PWO, WO2 Gwatirera, as a newly joined subaltern. That is exactly as I recall my time in the 1st Battalion. To command in the RAR effectively one had to undergo microscopic scrutiny by the senior and junior NCO's. As I said in *Chibaya Moyo*, one was always

under scrutiny and everything you did was a constant 'litmus test'. That was the RAR way.

My first operational deployment with A Company, 1RAR was also a patrol in the Urungwe TTL of Op Hurricane, an area infested with ZIPRA, and I too was accompanied by our CSM, WO2 Yangama Kupara BCR. He was almost skeletal in stature but as sinewy and tough as they came.

A man of very few words but possessed with a commanding presence. He had asked our OC, Maj Craig Beachell, if he could deploy with me. I know why he did. During that seven-day deployment with overt patrols by day and ambushes by night, we were successful and had a 'simultaneous sighting' contact with five ZIPRA cadres and accounted for four.

When we returned to our TAC HQ in the Magonde TTL, he came to see me in my tent when I was preparing to attend debrief with Craig Beachell. He stretched out his hand and firmly shook mine, his left hand wrapped around the outside of my right and, devoid of any emotion, looked me in my eyes and said "Makorokoto Ishe. You have proven yourself to 'Simanjemanje' (my Platoon's nickname': Young Ones)", saluted me and left as swiftly as he had arrived. Of all my personal experiences, that is a lasting memory as it demonstrated that I had done something right and it was seen by those who counted the most, my men. There was no greater compliment paid to me.

Oftentimes, it was not about personality, personal heroics nor joie de vivre but, more importantly, earning the trust and respect of those under your command. One was constantly under scrutiny by our men but what they truly sought (and expected), was a commander who cared for their welfare, a man who led them and one who would not recklessly endanger them. How one went about fulfilling that was, indeed, a very personal thing.

A SAD DAY by Lieutenant Noel Smith

On another occasion we were patrolling in the Kachuta TTL, in the Sipolilo area. An unfamiliar sound or different smell, a flicker of movement, a wrong splash of colour and we would be instantly alert. However, sometimes it was your sixth sense that kicked in too and it gave you that sensitive sub conscious warning well before any other indication of danger. On this particular patrol the hairs on the back of my neck were now definitely tingling.

There was something odd about this place. The villages were sparsely populated, and the hills surrounded us with their brooding presence. The local inhabitants made furtive glances as we passed by. It was those eyes, eyes that could not look you in the face and instead were focused on their shuffling feet. The eyes that could not hide the truth, the terrs were here.

We had with us a young African male who we had earlier apprehended when we noticed him carefully following our tracks. He was no doubt a terrorist scout or mujiba, but he was not telling us anything at the moment and instead I was relying on his actions to warn me of any impending danger.

I had him walking up front with me, and as we left the village, he suddenly broke free and bolted away and ignoring our shouted commands to stop, sprinted for the cover of the surrounding bush. One of my African soldiers instantly opened fire and a spray of red mist marked his strike on the fleeing figure. I ran in pursuit of the mujiba, all my senses on high alert being very aware that I could be running into a terrorist ambush and I followed the blood spattered trail before finding the boy lying spread-eagled on the ground. He had been hit in the left arm pit and the FN round had blown a large exit hole in his chest.

I tried desperately to stop the bleeding and revive the kid, but it was in vain and in seconds the boy had leaked his life away into the African dust. At times like this, the futility and waste of war is so apparent and heart wrenching. He was only a youngster and he should have been innocently herding the village cattle with his friends, not caught up in an ugly war. Like all wars, it is the local people, who caught between a rock and a hard place, suffer the most. I will always remember that day and it haunts me still.

The surrounding bush went ominously quiet and not a sound could be heard, nor any movement observed. I closed his eyes and as we recovered the body, I called up HQ to report the incident. A mobile armoured escort was soon on its way and carrying his body, we made off in the direction of the nearest road to wait for the pickup vehicles. In the meantime, we remained alert and for the rest of the day I could not rid that feeling of being watched nor shake off the menacing aura of danger and evil which hung in the atmosphere. After the body had been collected, we made our way into the cover of the wooded hills and eventually based up for the evening under the security of a dark, starless night, each of us left quietly alone with our thoughts.

A FLEETING CONTACT by Major Jim Hill

In mid-1973, as a very new Platoon Commander in 1 RAR I was deployed at somewhat short notice to take over a follow up in the Valley near Sipolilo. We RV'd with an SAS call sign commanded by Darryl Watt and which included the late Andy Chait who I'd started my Officers' course with at SInf.

The tracks were of a large, heavily laden group of terrs who the SAS guys had tracked from Mozambique. Even though the tracks were now very fresh, the SAS team had requested changeover as they were whacked, had been out of food for two days and had no water.

I took over the tracks and started the follow up whilst the SAS guys took over my transport and headed home. 20 minutes later, my lead tracker and I simultaneously sighted a baboon near a tree and quickly realised our mistake as the 'baboon' started shooting at us.

We immediately came under heavy fire from an excellent extended tactical position in a dry donga, which whittled out very quickly and we assaulted the position. A Provost, which had been loitering nearby to provide air support, attacked a group of about 12 gooks running away but his frantan failed and his front guns couldn't provide effective fire on a bomb-shelling bunch.

Two choppers that came in to move troops also sighted terrs and engaged them but, with Murphy's Law ruling the day, they both had weapons' malfunctions as well and were only partially successful, hitting one gook in the backside.

Running to the edge of the donga my batman, as my 'buddie, and I saw nothing but shaking bushes and the huge volume of dust from our rounds hitting the ground where the gooks had been based up. There was a further big eruption of dust from behind a large bush and another, almost simultaneously, a few metres to our left so, with training automatically kicking in, we both double tapped left, right and centre which stopped any further movement. Then, in the manner of such contacts, it was all over.

Returning to the point where the eruptions of dust had taken place, my batman noticed something lying partially embedded in the soil, on the side of the donga where we had been. Stupidly, I bumbled down to it and went to pick it up only to have my hand burnt by the heat of the object – that gave me pause for thought and then I realised that it was an RPG 7 projectile, probably fired at us as we came to the edge of the donga and presented a perfect target. The projectile, fortunately for me, had not been armed before firing (thank God for Murphy and his law).

There were no bodies although there were several blood stains and some of the discarded kit was blood stained as well. With tracks going in all directions I was directed to secure the scene and all the equipment, sweep the surrounds and try to put together a picture of the most likely direction to continue follow up ops.

I later discovered from SB and Ground Coverage that info from several villages in the area indicated that several gooks had been wounded, some seriously. Most had abandoned their weapons and kit and 10 who passed through one village had sticky gunge all over them from the frantan. We recovered a large amount of kit and weaponry including several mines, and there is no doubt that the documentation recovered from one rucksack came from a very senior commander on a major operation.

Of interest is that, in those early days of the war, many villagers were not necessarily on the side of the gooks. In this particular case, according to my Ground Coverage contacts, one village used their grain threshing baskets to cover the gooks' tracks to prevent their erosion by the elements, so that SF trackers could pick up quality spoor and follow the terrs up.

When I shared this story in a Facebook post in November 2018, historian Richard Wood commented with the following account of the contact and its aftermath, much of which was unknown to me at the time:

'Jim, what I have written on 22 June 1973 in my current book might fit your experience: 'A contact at 1245hrs with Callsign 21 (4 Platoon, B Company 1RAR) split up the ZANLA group who had crossed the border from Mozambique in May into the Mazarabani TTL. It had been 33-strong but five men had deserted. The contact took place just west of a minor north-flowing tributary of the Dande River in the foothills of the Rukowakuona Mountains (part of the Zambezi Escarpment), three kilometres north of the Mzarabani-Bakasa TTL boundary. During the contact an RPG rocket was fired but failed to explode and a grenade thrown without injuring anyone.

'Callsign 21 called in Flight Lieutenant Ian Harvey and Flight Sergeant A.J. Pawson, in Alouette 5087, and Air Lieutenant Trevor L. Baynham and Flight Sergeant B. Thomson, flying Alouette 7501, to collect two sticks (ten men) from 5 Platoon in the Bakasa TTL and to drop them north-west of his position in stop positions to block any northward movement. Having delivered his stick, Baynham climbed out southwards. As he did, at 1305hrs, he saw five to ten armed men dressed in a mixture of blue overalls and civilian clothes running westwards away from Callsign 21 and 730 metres south of Callsign 22's stop position.

'Because Air Lieutenant A.W. Wild and Senior Aircraftsman Bartlett in Provost 6300, flying top cover, did not spot the men, Harvey ordered Baynham to have Thomson fire at them with his MAG machine-gun as they crossed a grassy clearing. The fire was ineffective because the MAG was misfiring due to fouling of its gas ports. Thomson turned the gas regulator to maximum but could only fire single rounds. He managed to fire 50 rounds in all. Harvey's gunner, Pawson, had a stoppage but changed barrels and fired 200 rounds into the trees. While the two helicopters orbited the target, Wild attacked but his 17-gallon Frantan bomb did not ignite on impact. It bounced over the ZANLA men and set fire to the clearing, killing one man. His other Frantan failed to release.

'The fleeing insurgents swerved north-eastwards into dense riverine vegetation and were hidden from the Provost. Baynham flew over the trees with Thomson firing at them but without result amid fresh stoppages. Wild then strafed the trees five times with his twin Browning .303 machine-guns on direction from the helicopter pilots before they flew away to collect further sticks from 3 Platoon, Callsign 23, who were near the Hunyani River in the Kachuta TTL. After placing them 500 metres to the west of the clearing, Harvey left to refuel at B Company's position in the Bakasa.

'Baynham flew to assist Callsign 22 and spotted the insurgents 250 metres north-east of Callsign 22's position. The group dispersed, running north-eastwards through open woodland as Thomson fired 300 rounds knocking down one but the others disappeared into more dense woods followed by the bullets fired by Wild who strafed the trees four times from different directions. He fired a total of 1,200 .303 rounds and drew some return fire, with a bullet hitting his rudder. The wounded man was seen to limp away, hit in a leg and buttock.

'Baynham left to refuel as Harvey returned. Replaced by a second Provost, Wild flew back to his base at Musengedzi Mission to re-arm and refuel. As he was rolling to a stop on landing, his second Frantan fell off but fortunately did not ignite. Harvey landed at Callsign 21's position to load up with 26 packs dropped by the insurgents and an RAR soldier who had twisted his ankle. The packs contained a considerable amount of ammunition and explosives. The troops were left to sweep the area, finding two dead insurgents, and capturing four burned by Frantan and the 18-year old hit by Thomson.

'In the follow-up and the days to come four more of the gang were caught bringing the number of the captured to nine, eight of whom had been abducted. Three were 29 years old. The first had joined ZANLA in December 1972. The second was found with an unfired rifle and was carrying a landmine. The third was wounded and captured in a subsequent ambush, he was found with a cocked rifle. He was the veteran of two incursions into Rhodesian and six contacts with the Rhodesian Security Forces after having been press-ganged by ZANLA in early 1972.

'There were three 18-year olds: Thomson had wounded the first; a farmer caught another and a third who was found asleep in the bush had been abducted from a kraal in the north-east in December 1972. On a promise of financial assistance for his education, a 19-year old had been lured into

Botswana and onto to Zambia where he was pressganged into ZANLA. Finally, a 49-year old from the north-east had worked as a cook in a Rhodesian town.

'The final haul of war materiel comprised eleven AK assault rifles, two SKS rifles, 8,807 rounds of medium 7.62mm ammunition, 47 AK magazines, one RPD machine-gun magazine, two Tokarev pistol magazines, 15 RPG projectiles and three RPG propellants, 15 stick grenades, 13 60mm mortar bombs, seven TMH landmines, four landmine igniters, 15 200-gramme slabs of TNT, two reels of detonating cord and one of safety fuse.' (Wood, 2018)

Editors' comments: Jim's honest article vividly recollects the nature of Bush warfare: an explosion of sight and sound, lasting just a few seconds... and then, nothing. The terrorists knew if they stayed to fight, they would be killed, so they almost always broke and ran as soon as they could.

Richard's Facebook comment adds an air-perspective and illustrates that this patrol did particularly well in those brief seconds. Wounded terrorists often died. War materiel, that had been man-carried into the country at great effort, was captured before it could be used by the terrorists to cause harm. That, too, is the nature of Bush warfare, with outcomes often greater than the patrol commander knew at the time.

Reference:
Wood, R 2018, Facebook comment November, viewed 1 February 2019, https://www.facebook.com/groups/myrhodesianwateringhole/.

"IT'S JUST A JUMP ... TO THE LEFT!" by Captain Russell Fulton

It was early March 1979 and A Company, 1RAR was deployed on framework operations in Op Hurricane under the command of Temporary Major Craig Beachell. Craig was a former US Special Forces officer on a short service commission with the RAR. He had seen service in Vietnam and was as hungry for a joust as we all were and that made an interesting start to my early commissioned life.

This was a man who was as unorthodox as they came, who had a dislike for regimental life and all the protocols it involved but he wanted, and expected, results. He had been 2ic to Maj Barry Getliffe and now commanded the same Company and he was intent in setting about doing so with his own brand of leadership. He was an interesting character and, perhaps, his greatest asset as a commander was his flexibility. Once you had gained his trust, 'flexibility' was one of the 'perks' you could expect as your reward. He was not suffocating like some; he was results focussed.

Our Company TAC HQ was based in the Magondi TTL adjacent to Zvimba TTL, the birth place of one Robert Gabriel Mugabe. As a consequence, this general area was a hotbed of ZANLA activity and I, a newly commissioned subbie of the lone pip variety, was in the mood to 'introduce' myself and my Platoon to these motley fellows. Craig Beachell was similarly disposed, and no sooner had we off-loaded the vehicles and struck camp when I was summoned to attend an 'O' (Orders) Group and seated myself opposite him in the Ops Vehicle.

This was a Bedford RL stores vehicle that had been converted in to his command centre with one full side of the vehicle filled from floor to ceiling and from the tailgate to the drivers cab with a map board. On said board was an impressive display of 1:50,000 map sheets that covered an enormous part of Op Hurricane and was overlaid with a heavy transparent plastic sheet. Craig had already plotted our position with a 'Chinagraph' pencil including all 'Frozen Areas' within 100km's of our LOCSTAT. As an aside, 'Frozen Areas' were those occupied by C Sqn or Selous Scouts operatives and other unit troop movements in these areas was strictly forbidden.

Maj Beachell provided his subbies, 2Lt Ian 'Putties' Macdonald: OC 1Pl and who was on the same regular cadet course as me, Lt Willard 'Chompkin' Fleetwood: OC 2Pl, a former US Ranger and yours truly: OC 3Pl with an INT briefing and orders for deployment that evening. 1 & 2 Platoons were to deploy, in to the Zvimba TTL and eastern Magondi TTL's respectively.

SB Sinoia had advised that a local GC (Ground Coverage) team had received intelligence from one of their informers about the presence of a small group of 'magandanga' in a camp located in a thickly wooded area in the Umfuli TTL where the Umfuli and Chipani Rivers met. My Platoon orders were to establish OP's and stop group positions around the target area with a call sign, led by me, to be in position by 0430B. At first light we were to sweep the area where these two rivers joined and eliminate any CT presence.

My orders provided for two O.P.'s; one positioned to the north-west and one to the west of the target. In addition, I wanted three stop groups to cover the north-west and one to the south east of the Umfuli River line and one covering the Chipani River to the west. At first light, we crossed our start line and were advancing towards the target when our presence was compromised by barking 'KD's' (dogs) that had been tethered to trees and bushes within 75 meters of the camp. This was a first for me; I had never heard of this tactic being employed elsewhere in Rhodesia!

Almost immediately there was a withering hail of incoming small arms and light machine gun fire being hosed in our general direction. We returned the compliment as we skirmished forward before we were abruptly halted by a thick blanket of mist rising like some ghoulish spectre from the two rivers that now shrouded the objective making matters a touch dangerous.

We couldn't see more than 10ft in front of us and our ZANLA 'connections' were similarly handicapped. It was an 'atmospheric' disaster! I halted the advance until the mist lifted, which it did fairly quickly but, the element of surprise had been lost because of those bloody dogs! I thought about 'stiffening them' when this business was over and made good on that thought.

We moved forward, firing into likely cover, and saw some 'bashas' in the tree-line immediately to our front and my machine gunners gave them a good raking; their 1:5 tracer setting the bashas alight. Fire was coming from areas that appeared to be in the riverine bush beyond the camp and then we saw what appeared to be an AFA. (African Female Adult). The bitch was sitting in the open with hands in the air no less; no doubt she had been seconded from a nearby village for matters 'domestic' and whose functions would have included washing, cooking, ironing and you can guess what else!

I shouted at her to lie flat on the ground with her arms outstretched in front of her or she would be shot without further warning. Very wisely, she obeyed the command. As we entered the camp I saw what appeared to be a dead gook lying beside one of the bashas and we moved forward cautiously; there was no weapon beside him, but he wore the usual CHICOM chest webbing that irrefutably confirmed what he had been a few brief minutes before!

As we moved past him I heard a metallic click to my half right and knew instinctively what it was…it was the sound of an AK47 assault rifle safety catch being disengaged! I jumped to my left performing a 'Rocky Horror' dance move that may, or may not, have impressed Dr Frankenfurter and double-tapped in the direction of the sound.

Simultaneously the air around me was whipped-up by the cracking of a short burst of incoming 7.62 x 39mm. I felt something hit me in the side but, to my surprise, there was no pain…well not yet anyway. To my front, at less than a dozen paces, a young boy lay slumped beside a basher cradling an AK47! He would have been no more than 15 years old, but he was now history and I felt no remorse. This 'hondo' business had a way of tempering one's conscience to the point of indifference. Some may view this as a callous act and, frankly, I don't give a damn. This youngster had evidently received instruction in how to use an AK and was, therefore, a combatant was he not? You be the judge.

There was a wetness on my side and down my leg and I thought that I had taken a round, but we still had work to do. I gingerly felt my side expecting to find a nasty mess but was relieved to find that the whack I had felt was a round that had hit one of my water bottles and it was leaking all over me. Just as well, and as I recalled from circa one year prior, I really didn't feel in the mood for jousting with another oil-leak.

We advanced towards the river and whilst clearing it, whacked another gook who was hiding in some long grass against the nearside river bank and found another nearby who had been clinically dispatched but there was nothing else going on. The other gooks must have gapped it in to the mist and had, miraculously, escaped detection by my other call-signs. A few packs, a PPsH and one SKS were recovered together with the AK that had recently ruined my hitherto perfectly serviceable water bottle. My 'Sparrow' determined that this camp had housed six; a 50% kill rate just wasn't good enough but there would be more to follow in the days ahead.

I ordered my stop groups to follow-up along the Umfuli and in both directions with the third to sweep the Chipani. My call-sign gathered the three stiffs and ordered the 'bitch' to assist in removing the body of the youngster to a road about 15 clicks to our rear where we handed them over, together with the recovered weapons and packs, to an SB team escorted by elements from our Coy HQ.

Yes, yes…I know, very callous behaviour but when you have been on the receiving end of hostility one very swiftly dispensed with matters of decorum. What I will say, with a crystal-clear conscience, is that I never personally mutilated nor did I disrespect a corpse; it's not in my D.N.A. That said, I would never countenance behaviour contrary to my own by any man under my command. We were soldiers after all, not savages.

The truth of the matter was that this was a war and I had far more important things to occupy my mind…. like keeping my men and 'yours truly' in one piece.

There could be no doubting that the intensity of our hondo was about to increase exponentially and we would be kept very busy indeed. In the very near future we, 3Pl, would be 'woken-up' by a larger, cockier group in the neighbouring Piriwiri TTL. Another tale for another time.

"Muhondo RAR, Inorwa noKushinga"

CLUNKING NIGHT PATROL by Major Tom Fulton

My platoon (5 "Tinourayaese" Pl) and I were in reserve at the time, and the Company 2ic drew my attention to the fact that our sub unit had recently been in receipt of an exciting new piece of materiel. Ed Fouche and I reverently opened the expensive-looking, inner-cushioned case containing a new-fangled Starlight

Intensifying Telescopic Sight. My first thought went to how cumbersome the entire ensemble seemed. My misgivings were only partially appeased by the fact that the sophisticated instrument was snugly mounted on what was obviously an FN rifle dust cover. This essential addition gave it a far more utilitarian air, and I was immediately determined to try it out.

I spent a wise hour studying the comprehensive, but user-friendly manual and was a little shaken at its many idiosyncrasies, the dos and don'ts, and concluded that it was a very fragile, but extremely useful piece of kit. The thought of seeing, and not being seen, catered for the very essence of my most scintillating childhood fantasies. The thrill of perhaps being able to use that faculty in a combat situation totally enthralled me – the adage regarding ducks in a bucket came to mind...

A rifle range close to the camp provided a chance to zero the mounted scope. A curious eerily green, glowing picture presented itself. (Yes, exactly like the movies!) The manual stated that the glowing post, central to the picture, was roughly the same height of a man at 100 metres? (As a serious competition shottist, regularly in the Battalion Shooting Team, this methodology didn't sound like a very exact science to me, but I left the range happy that I could hit a man centrally at anything under 50 metres – no mean feat, I supposed, in the dead of night?)

Intelligence reports seemed to indicate that the gooks were feeding from a certain CV (Collective Village) in the area and we were to be deployed to investigate. I would deploy with the whole platoon, in case we had the good fortune to locate a sizeable target. It would be a one night covert deployment, as the chances of our remaining in the area undetected were nil. It would also enable me to put the new toy to some practical use.

We conducted a debussing on the move manoeuvre, and walked about 10 clicks through the bush before we stopped on a rise overlooking the CV. Since the concept of the CVs was still relatively new, they weren't even featured on our maps yet. So, a preliminary reconnaissance at a distance was clearly indicated.

I was already a blooded Platoon Commander with months of night operational and Fire Force experience with the same body of men. Lengthy and numerous rehearsals of night movement had ensured that each man was completely conversant with 5 Platoon's nocturnal modus operandi.

Surveying the CV through the scope, almost half of it was surrounded by cultivated land. The other half was Msasa woodland, which, whilst providing us with cover from view, was disquieting from the point of view that it was the most obvious. If the gooks were around, and they weren't in the village, this is where we would find them. Although our operation was regarded to be one of reconnaissance, no infantryman would leave up the chance of closing with, and killing the enemy. (I was also dying to put the new-age scope to the test.)

Deciding that stealth overrode every other factor, I selected a team of three men to accompany me, my Platoon Warrant Officer inclusive. The remainder of the men would move with my Sergeant to a point of cover, and a vantage from whence I could deploy them as the situated demanded.

As the recce group left the main body, I stopped after a short distance, in order to scan the bush ahead. Before continuing, I glanced around and privately swelled with pride, to see the diligent way in which my men had automatically taken up postures in defence of the flanks and the rear. What a pleasure it was to work with these professionals…

The night sight was cumbersome to say the least, and it became necessary, where possible, to sit down and provide a more stable platform from which to scan the areas of interest. Each time I stopped to get myself comfortable, I could sense the concentration and hear the muffled movements of my men, as they went about providing the essential security I needed. Admittedly, my Platoon Sergeant Major was amongst their number, but I was confident that each man would have behaved as instinctively in that great man's absence.

Taking heed that we avoided any obvious cover, we made our way to a slightly thicker area of the wooded belt, and I was able to position myself on an almost perfect, but partially vegetated roll in the ground.

Clunking Night Patrol

Now, there is nothing quite so distinct, as the smell of human excrement. A permeating, nauseating attack on the olfactory factory. I was seated cross-legged and automatically checked the soles of my shoes. Although the wind at ground level was minimal, a brisk breeze blew aloft, and the puffy cumulous clouds

243

scudded across a sulky half-moon. The result was a contrast of dark and light that was playing havoc with the inaugural outing of the night scope, and making the conservation of night vision impossible.

It was only after some minutes of intermittent light and dark, and frantic scraping with a stick, that I finally gave my clandestine tackies a clean bill of health. I also sensed a disturbing and increasing dampness in the seat of my pants…I felt the bile rise in my throat.

It was obvious that I had sat myself in some tribesman's quite revoltingly substantial faecal deposit. I slowly stood. In the dark, I could hear pieces of the abominable matter being detached by gravity, and landing on the leafy cushion below. But the weight of the stubborn residual mess, caused the seat of my trousers to hang in a sad droop, and I was certain that my uncomfortable efforts to keep the amorphous mass from touching my living skin, must have had an hilarious effect on the state of my gait?

Uncomfortably, yet surprisingly undaunted, I sallied forth – knowing very well that I, and my intrepid band were fast approaching one of the four main thoroughfares in and out of the CV.

Out of the varying gloom, the pathway became evident – almost white in the darkness. Holding my rifle in the crook of my right arm (to protect the precious telescopic sight), I sat with my feet ahead of me. Using my left hand and feet, I proceeded to laboriously drag myself across the 10 metres of pathway. In retrospect, my movements must have been comical, as I tried my utmost to expose the greatest surface area of my soiled trousers to the semi cleansing effect of the abrasion provided by path's surface.

I reached the other side feeling completely foolish, before getting up and moving smartly into cover. I stood pensively alone for a moment gathering my humiliating thoughts, before I became aware of a loud and distinctive scraping sound.

I turned and watched in dumbfounded amazement, as my entire stick took their rifles into the crooks of their right arms, and got down and mimicked my embarrassing movements of a few moments before. I stood in momentary mesmerised fascination, as I witnessed this confusing behaviour.

It took a few minutes, as he brought up the rear, but when the Platoon Warrant Officer repeated the other men's actions, I thought, noooo, these ouens must definitely be pulling my piss!

The Sergeant Major could detect the quizzical look on my face as he strode up, and said brightly, "Anti tracking Sir!"

(For those of you who don't get this. The men following me were so completely baffled by my bizarre behaviour, they (bless them) were at a complete loss as to how to behave, or, for that matter, exactly what to do next? Thinking that the safest course to take, would be to imitate their Platoon Commander; they followed suit. The wizened PWO had picked up what had happened and had also aped the boss, in an endeavour to save him face (bless him too). We all had a great laugh about it later, and, as far as I know, the story never left the platoon.)

AN UNUSUAL EXPERIENCE by Captain Joe Columbus Smith

On a night patrol we heard chatter noise coming from a kraal well into the night. By some miracle, the kraal dogs had not reacted to us. I got my men in very close while the low-key chatter continued… but I could not quite figure it out. It was not the loud stump speech type of rally. I had got very close and my machine gunner whispered, "Give me a tap on the shoulder, Ishe, and I shall give them a burst of 50!"

But something made me hold off and I am so glad I did!

Finally, I made a decision in the pitch black of the kraal. In line, in the dark I walked our guys into the crowd. Of all things in the world, it was a marriage ceremony between a geriatric couple. In fact, no-one appeared to be under 65 in the whole crowd. Unbelievable. We simply swept through and disappeared. Wedding crashers in the boldest sense. No-one said a word.

OF BUFFALO BEANS AND BERE (HYENA) by Captain Russell Fulton

During the summer of 1979, A Coy 1RAR deployed in to the Chiswiti TTL immediately following a ten-day 1RAR CFL (Concentrated Force Level) operation in the neighbouring Dande, Gutsa and Mazarabani TTLs, all within the infamous 'Zambezi Valley'; home to strict scorpions, angry snakes, assorted and intemperate horned beasts, 'sabre-toothed' kitties and the very unfortunate looking 'bere' (hyena).

It would be to completely understate the fact to describe summer in this vast piece of real estate as simply being "hot" because it was, in-point-of-fact, unreasonably so! What never ceased to amaze me with the good *Masodja* of the RAR was their apparent indifference to heat; most of whom, and almost to a man, wore standard issue combat trousers, combat shirts and their combat jacket regardless of the season. Most wore the standard issue Caps, Combat with the woven 1RAR label or, in some cases, face veils tied around the forehead with the two ends knotted either side of each ear that hung like a Spaniel's ears.

Regardless of their attire, these were not men to trifle with and they had proven that time and time again; they were always happy but their outwardly, sunny disposition belied a fierce pride and a dangerous, instantaneous aggression. Disrespectful civvies would, routinely, be issued corrective 'kleps' as was the wont of the RAR soldier but our Charlie Tango (Communist Trained) 'mates' suffered an altogether different fate where oil leaks; various, liberal and deliberate, were their fare. It's what our men did best and they did it with consummate ease.

And so, just to pass the time of day and earn our daily keep, we deployed by vehicle out of our camp late afternoon and headed in the direction of "Mukumbura-By-the-Sea", a quite delightful place where Mopani Fly and Anopheles Mosquito abounded but there was, sadly, no beach to write home about. We debussed on the move and the vehicles, with their escort, continued up to Mukumbura.

I regrouped my platoon and we moved off in a north-easterly direction setting up our camp close to the Mkumvura River shortly after midnight. This river formed part of the border between Rhodesia and Mozambique and both ZIPRA and ZANLA were known to 'play' here. Of interest to us was the fact that a week earlier when we were on our CFL op, C Coy under the command of Maj Lionel Dyke, reported a sighting of what looked very much like a 'murungu' (a white man) in one of the groups that they had engaged. This aroused an enormous amount of interest and it was presumed that he could be any number of things; Cuban, Russian, East German or, possibly, an incantation of Daniel Carney's 'Whispering Death', a 'musope' (albino).

Apparently, this 'fellow' held some authority as he was seen directing troop movements, so it is more likely that he was one of the former? We hoped above hope that we would meet up with this chap again as he would be invaluable as a capture or, second prize, if we were able to ''stiffen" him. Sadly, he wasn't seen again, and his origin remains a complete mystery. Perhaps he was simply a "mudzimu" (a 'ghost') vanished in one of those plentiful 'Valley' mirages!

I split up my platoon in to our three sections under command of my Platoon Warrant Officer, Platoon Sergeant and yours truly. We deployed within our defined area of operation conducting overt patrols by day, cross-graining for spoor and laying ambushes by night. The area was flat as a saucer and the bush thick but festooned with ridiculous and impregnable belts of the much reviled 'Huriri' ("Mucuna pruriens" to those intrepid botanists in our midst) or, more commonly to the arbitrary and majority of us, the "African Buffalo Bean".

To enter areas where these nasty trailing or climbing vines grew was to play games with a 'botanical devil incarnate'! To brush against these day or night would render you 'Sleepless in Seattle' and in the most incredible discomfort. Even if the pods were avoided, their fine hairs would fall on to leaves and in the grass and you ran just as much risk of being 'fixed-up'. There are few of my brethren who didn't happen to find them.

And so it was. 3 Section, under the command of my platoon sergeant, fell afoul of them in the very early hours and it was all over for them bar their suppressed grumbling and vigorous gnashing of teeth. It would have been funny had it not been for the reality that they were now in pretty serious trouble. There were several ways of removing the irritating hairs from one's body that extended to using plasters to extricate them, packing mud on the area of affected skin and peeling it off when dry but the latter wasn't an option in this arid and inhospitable neck of the woods. Once it got inside your clothing you were up 'shit creek' and that's all there was to it. Never mind, "cowboys don't cry!"

After a couple of days I took my section and patrolled in a south-easterly direction and parallel to the Mkumvura River. On the third night, I recced an excellent ambush site where we had come across a considerable amount of spoor indicating an obvious infiltration/exfiltration route. I contacted my other call signs and ordered them to make their way towards my LOCSTAT and "ikozvino" (immediately) because I didn't want any watery eyes if a large group of ZANLA decided to tramp their way on our side of the fence.

I needed to ensure that my 'customs & immigration' welcoming party was ready to receive them. I sited a killer group covering the approach in/out and brim-full with MAG's and a killing ground that was peppered with Claymores. Stop groups were positioned on either side of the killer group to stop anyone wanting to evade the arrival/departure formalities I had set in place. That night we watched and waited with adrenalin charged expectation.

Early that morning the silence was broken by the sound of something approaching from our rear. I was about to change position when the spine-chilling cackle of hyena livened things up just as unexpectedly; there was a clan of several spotted hyena within 15 meters of where we lay and the matriarch, a big 'androgynous' bitch, flared her nostrils and showed her set of filthy canines in a decidedly unfriendly grimace. They appeared

Bere (Hyena)…

intent on having breakfast early as they spread out and moved in towards us with a deliberate purpose.

Well now, I hadn't ever thought of myself as being particularly appetising but I sure as hell wasn't about to allow myself to be dragged off by one of these necrophagous creatures as an early morning snack. Our *Masodja* hated them because, and according to African folklore, hyenas belonged to witches and our men were as superstitious as all hell. We were in a tenuous position and so I sighted down my barrel and dropped the matriarch where it stood. The remainder of the clan bolted and we fixed them too. It wasn't the contact I had been hoping for and our position was now well and truly compromised by the gunfire!

I sent the morning 'Stop Press' to my OC who ordered our withdrawal informing me we were being redeployed elsewhere. Before we left the area, I decided to do a little 'housekeeping' and positioned my platoon in all round defence whilst I dragged the stinking carcasses of this 'clan' and placed them all around the entry area where we had found the inward/outbound gook spoor. Being an old RLI skate, I set up a shit-load of trip wires attached to a brace of M962 fragmentation grenade. Why? If our motley 'comrades' decided to use this area to famba in or out of God's Own Country, they would have a welcoming or departure party of a different sort and a little more than "Eyes right with Eyegene' would be required to clear their eyes. Yes indeed, it was a tad unsporting wasn't it!

Welcome to the 'Nyamapanda Philharmonic Orchestra'

When we returned to our Company TAC HQ we received orders for redeployment to Mudzi. Mudzi!!!!

I often wondered why A Company was always deployed to the very bowels of the earth but ours was not to reason why, and so forth.

After my earlier royal 'lemon' in the greater Mudzi metro area, we were ordered to head up the main road to Nyamapanda where a TF company was to be temporarily relieved pending the arrival of their replacement.

The area was being revved from the 'Pork' (Mozambican) side of the fence and so we debussed about five clicks out and walked in. It was like watching a firework display as the still night sky was lit-up by red and green tracer and exploding 82mm mortar shells that were being thrown down tubes hand-over-fist.

Stalin's Organ

Fortunately, the mortar teams were either poorly trained or shitting themselves in anticipation of inbound retaliatory fire (which, of course, we gave them) but their munitions were, for the time being, dropping short or falling behind the TF camp. We relieved our brave TF brothers and 'stood to' in our assigned trenches and not sure whether Frelimo and/or ZANLA wanted to 'make a go of it' and try crossing the border.

Furthermore, and because they were proving to be so kuk with their mortar fire, we considered the obvious and that they would have sited forward observation officer's (FOO's) on the ridge to eyeball their fall of shot and give corrections. We took delight in firing Icarus illuminating flares over their position and revving any and all likely forward observation post positions.

After a cessation in fire we were about to 'stand down' when we heard the rumbling sound of vehicles deploying beyond the ridge line on the Pork side. This was followed almost immediately by the repeated roar and an unholy screeching in the air. I had never heard this before but soon realised that it was the 16-rail release of 132mm rockets being fired from 'Stalin Organs'!

I cannot tell a lie, I nearly shat myself when said ordinance screamed over our position and detonated to our rear. Thank God they never had their act together with their ranging!

Interspersed with this came more accurate 82mm mortar fire that was now landing in and about the camp. One mortar bomb went through the roof 'turret' opening of a 4.5 stores vehicle and exploded inside the cab. Personally, I could handle a one-on-one joust but this business of being mortared and rocketed was never a favourite pastime with me.

In the morning, we took stock and it was evident that the mortar fire had caused damage but, and very surprisingly, there were no reports of any casualties. The next day the incoming TF relief Company arrived, we handed over and shook hands and returned to Methuen for some much-anticipated R&R. It was to be cut-short, again of course, but there you have it, 'If you can't take a joke, you shouldn't have joined the army'.

Our lives were filled with all manner of excitement, but this particular bush trip remains clear in my mind and for all the wrong reasons too.

"There's none so fair that can compare with the fighting infantry!"

PSEUDO OPERATIONS by Colour Sergeant Carl Chabata BCR

After joining the Selous Scouts from 1RAR, most of our troop commanders were given nicknames depending on their characters resembling animals or how they acted. For example our troop commander's name was *Mudahondo* meaning someone who liked war too much. Others were, *Chidembo* a squirrel, *Nengure* a bird and so forth. These nicknames were given to our white troop commanders in order to protect them once in the operation area because one cannot call them by their real name which could have resulted in big trouble and we also had our nicknames.

In late November or early December 1974 the road from Mt. Darwin to Rushinga had become a problematic area with almost daily landmine blasts especially in the Chesa purchase area. However before this deployment, I can still remember a fire force call out, prior to the operation I'm going to talk about, which took place at Bob Garandi in Chiweshe TTL. The fire force was from RAR and they performed brilliantly whereby a large number of gooks were killed.

This was after we approached the locals for information early in the morning. They indicated to us where the gooks were positioned thus fire force was called in. Oh the K-Car 20mm cannon was fantastic combined with the G-Cars and the Lynx unleashing its bombs. Also not to be outdone was RLI and SAS Sqn, they were a marvel to watch. With RLI there was a corporal who was always called by the K Car commander and his name was Shoko or Chalky, most of the time you could hear the K Car commander mentioning his name and he will answer "one or two down" thereon meaning kills.

After some various deployments, it was then decided for us to be deployed in Chesa purchase area and the concept was for us to be deployed at the Mozambican border so that we act as new recruits from training in Mozambique. After moving through the bush for a whole day we came to a kraal at sunset and waited for it to get dark so as to approach the locals to get information on the whereabouts of gooks but the locals were a bit sceptical about us and no information was obtained. Whilst on our way to the others, we suddenly heard the gooks making a big noise talking to the locals behind us.

We rushed to the platoon commander and informed him and he without wasting time ordered us all to go and attack the gooks. As we advanced to the gooks area the noise stopped abruptly. By so doing I don't know what the gooks were up to and we abandoned the mission since it was now dark with no moon.

The following day we continued with our patrol towards our destination Chesa. We arrived in Chesa in the morning after a gruelling move from the border and selected a suitable mountain for our platoon commander which also acted as a relay for us. But truly speaking I don't remember how I climbed that mountain but what I still remember is when we left, the troop commander and his protection team descending the mountain. The HQ or relay station had also its ups and downs because of drinking water, guys had to climb down to fetch water from the river which was hazardous.

We got down the gomo and selected a kraal to approach. Due to the fact that we had one captured gook who once operated in this area, we were well received and took our positions at a relatively covered area but not suitable in case of a contact as there was only tall grass which made one not to see even a meter in front of you.

At approximately 0900hrs, one of the locals brought a letter from the gooks asking us that we meet. This was one of the most difficult parts of the operation because all the men in the troop had to make a split decision and to be in agreement at the same time to reply to that letter telling the gooks that let's meet. The other thing was whether to trust the captured gook, otherwise by the time you meet he might compromise you. During Selection, the concept was to operate at night with the platoon commander present whilst his face was painted with black camouflage. We were supposed to meet up with the gooks and then open fire without talking to them. But tactics changed on that particular day.

When going to the villagers we would make sure each of us had his rucksack similar to those of the gooks where our commander had a radio A63 switched off while the rest of us were carrying emergency rations because most of our food was supplied by the locals. On approaching a village we made sure our rucksacks are well hidden far from our positions.

The reasons for doing this was, if something crops up, the commander or one of us will sneak and go to the radio and tell the platoon commander of whatever is required be, be it fire force or support. So on this particular day one of us sneaked out to warn the platoon commander of the impending danger.

We gave the local a reply informing them that we agree to meet at a certain place but the area was only covered in tall grass. We had no option so we advanced on the ready for any action.

We were challenged and the way they challenged us was, "Hey who are you???" We replied plus we had this captured gook so it wasn't difficult to link up with them.

It was very simple but inside a lot of questions cropped up thinking how are we going to disarm and capture them. They were four and we were six.

Myself, I was allocated one so we were two at my post talking crap lies about where I was trained and the like. The only thing I was worried about was if more gooks came to join us and I will be posted to another area within the gooks ranks it gave me goose bumps otherwise that silly thinking I was relaxed.

At around 1700hrs, just before last light, we informed the other two gooks that we had ammunition we wanted to collect from a certain mountain so their help is required. They left at last light going straight to our platoon commander's position where they were disarmed and captured whilst I and one of our own remained with two gooks. While I was with this other gook, I was thinking of shooting him from behind then saw that I was going to put my colleague's life in danger and I decided against it. I just don't know why this stupid idea came from because everything was in order.

My commander was with the other gook while I was with the other one and we slept for the night each of us being a guard of his own. Early in the morning the others arrived with the other two and without wasting time captured the ones that were left with us. After capturing them we would remove the firing pins from their weapons and carry on with operations.

With us there was no such thing as when a gook is captured SB will take him for interrogation, by so doing that could have caused a lot of time wasting. Also this was not to arouse suspicious with the locals of the area they operated in.

That day the Army Commander Lt General Walls and our CO Major Reid Daily were on their feet and not to mention our troop commander. The fire force was on standby at Mt Darwin. Following the capture of these gooks, the landmines menace did not stop on the road we could hear the blast from our area which was very close by. So one day while on the move, I said to one of our guys, "Hey this area is quiet, at least we can relax for a while". Soon after saying these words and while approaching a kraal without any warning we were challenged by six gooks.

"Heyeee who are you????" We were all shocked and we were sitting ducks because we were on the open with no cover while the gooks were in a better position and their weapons trained on us. To try to take cover was going to make them more suspicious so we just froze and waited for their move. Questions were fired and we let the recently captured gooks to do the talking of which they let us in.

The newly captured gooks were now our commander. This was one of the most difficult times in my life and I could see the danger I was in at the same time one came to me asking me where I was trained and other crap questions. He was carrying a LMG and myself I was also carrying one but now mine was on a relaxed position while his was pointing right at my chest. This gook was really on me asking me questions. I finally told him that it was too much and he was making me angry because of the continuous pointing of his gun on me. That's when he left me but the situation was tense. This time there was no time to sneak around to go and report to our troop commander but we had our rucksacks and if they had wanted to search us I really don't know what was going to happen because the situation was so tense.

The job was of mind games reading a person's mind and deducing whether they accepted the lies we were telling them. That night nobody slept we were all thinking of how to capture the gooks. Early in the morning at first light without any warning we ordered them to surrender by shouting "Surrender surrender" and we all jumped into action but one tried to resist and we shot him but it was a chaos since no prior planning was done as to how we were supposed to capture them.

At that particular time we informed our troop commander and requested for a chopper to uplift this one gook who was still groaning because we didn't want the locals to know what had happened otherwise he was going to compromise us but I don't think he survived. The chopper picked him early and everything was back to normal. We tried to find out from other locals whether we were compromised and we were told no.

With the capture of these gooks the mine incidents were a thing of the past and we recovered 17 landmines and various arms of war. We captured a further 16 gooks since we were now moving with the district commander. We ordered the district commander to write them a letter and they came without any problems.

After meeting up with the sixteen we were given positions in the base so the problem of capturing them were as follows. All of us were to go and relieve themselves but while doing this we had to pretend that our weapons had no bayonets. We would borrow one of the new gook's rifle and say "please I want to go for a shit can I have your rifle mine does not have a bayonet?"

The flimsy reason for wanting a rifle with a bayonet was to use the bayonet to dig a hole to relieve oneself but in actual fact we were stripping those rifles and removing the firing pins. As a result all rifles had their firing pins removed and the task of telling them that they were under our command and had been captured was so easy.

At around 1140hrs there was a large number of locals in the base providing us with food and the normal thing that was required of them like just telling them war stories most of it lies. We told them that they should leave the base because we want to organise ourselves and they left. The commander who was now the captured district commander ordered us to fall in and we did that. Whilst on fall-in, the sixteen gooks were informed of their capture and were also told that any funny tricks they would be killed since their weapons were now useless. Since our number had increased, we distributed the other gooks to other troops.

Our days for R&R were due, thus we went back to camp. On arrival we were told not to change our operating gear since the Army Commander wanted to see us dressed in those clothes and to greet us. I was so happy to meet with the Army Commander and he promised us that for our actions we would get something.

Conclusion.

Meeting with gooks was dangerous in that you don't know whether you are already compromised or not. So it was just a risk and it required team work because one slight mistake from one of our members was costly. Even the captured district commander wanted to wipe us out but he didn't know that his rifle had no firing pin. He actually took a position whilst we were at the arms cache and tried to shoot us but to no avail. We didn't give a damn about this incident, since we had a mission to carry out with him he was not yet expendable, otherwise we could have finished him off.

I would like to thank the following members who I operated with:
CSgt Fitzimmons. Troop Comd (late).
Sgt Head Wuranda. Troop Sgt (late).
Sgt Rangarirayi Hungwe (late).
Cpl Mugandani Felix (late).
LCpl Chigudu Fanuel.
The above mentioned A.S. members we were together from 1RAR to selection course and formed 3 troop.

Current Position : I'm working in Durban as a carwash manager. I love my job but I'm thinking of looking for another one in any country except the Middle East. Driving is my passion so if I get that type of job it will come in handy. My family is in Zimbabwe and things are not favourable. Thank you.

HI, WHERE YOU BIN? by Major Tom Fulton
(Adapted by the author from *Into the Vortex*)

B Company 1RAR was operating out of the permanent army base camp in Rushinga. We had been detached to operate under the command of the 1RLI JOC at Mount Darwin. Deployed in a major ZANLA 'corridor', we were doing aggressive patrolling and trying to dominate by our persistent presence.

One morning, after being ordered to regroup my platoon, I was told to proceed to a kraal line, at a certain grid reference, where we would find a LIVE, and armed, communist terrorist hiding! I knew to be a fact, that it wasn't the 1st of April, but I obviously did as instructed. The young SB Officer was a bloke called Hans Sittig. Evidently German in origin, he was as Rhodesian as a box of Madison cigarettes, and from the way the Boss (Major Wayne Thompson) was talking, was in the Ops Room at that time. He was completely adamant that the gook was there; and he was there right NOW!

We had no trouble locating the kraal and, because it was deserted, assumed that the occupants had been picked-up by the Special Branch for questioning? Knowing exactly what the operational situation was, Sar'major Africa almost ordered me to sit aside, and brew myself the cup of tea I had missed that morning. I found a perfect vantage point, a short way up a large ant-heap, from where I could witness the search as it took place. I watched as a stick of four men was deployed at the double, to cover any attempts at escape out of the back of the kraal.

With the remaining sticks, the Platoon Warrant Officer and Sergeant were easily able to coordinate and conduct a comprehensive search of a line of a dozen, or so huts. Respectful of the meagre belongings of the absentee occupants, the men probed the thatch with bayonets, looked under mattresses, and indeed, looked carefully anywhere it was physically possible for a man to hide. Sar'major Africa and Sergeant Saul reported back that nothing untoward had been located – certainly not a living, breathing, gun toting gandanga.

The two NCOs stood by as I reported as much to the OC. After a moment's silence, the Boss came back with such vehemence, that I was annoyed at the inference that the job hadn't been done properly. With Corporal Gumbo Owen accompanying me, I went and looked at the interior of each hut in turn, merely to be able to say that I'd done so. I'd inadvertently been forced to question the veracity of the report from my own NCOs.

The remainder of the platoon was 'brewing up' in case we were unable to cook a proper breakfast. I sauntered listlessly back to my spot on the ant-heap. Not looking forward to reporting to the OC again. I sat cross-legged, and got a second brew going, rummaging through my webbing pouches for something to snack on, and putting off calling the OC, for the time being.

A short distance away, the remainder of my stick were in the arc of responsibility allocated to them. Pte Khanye Mazenzo, my batman, picked up his

MAG and went over to the senior NCOs to indicate his intention to leave the precincts of the platoon defences, to evacuate his bowels. He slung his MAG with a familiar ease, the swinging belt loosely slung over the feed tray. He informed the men on the perimeter of his intentions and sauntered off into the privacy of the tree line, some 30 metres away.

I ate some left over rice from the night before, with some pilchards and tomato sauce, when I noticed Mazenzo's return from his ablutions. Noticing that there was a Mashona type grain bin, slightly away from the kraal, Mazenzo decided absently, to have a peek inside.

PTE MAZENZO, KHANYE
5 Pl, B COY, 1RAR

The bin itself was perhaps one and a half metres high. Manufactured with a combination of natural fibres, bark and stripped saplings, and sealed from the elements with clay, these grain bins are similar in outward appearance to an oversized laundry basket, and are mounted on a crude wooden plinth.

Approaching the bin with a detached nonchalance, he unslung his MAG, the better to climb onto the plinth, and peer inside. The design of the bin had a slightly narrowed top, so that the influx of sunlight was restricted. Mazenzo fumbled in the pockets of his denims for a match, struck one and threw it in. The match had gone out, before he had the chance to crane his neck, and get a look inside. Positioning himself to get a more immediate look, he repeated the action of throwing in the lighted match.

I watched in incredulous amusement, as Private Khanye Mazenzo launched himself backwards, like a cat suddenly discovering a snake. He landed flat on his backside, dignity out the window, some feet from the machine gun he carried. By the expression on his face, one would have sworn he had looked Satan himself in the eye, and it was enough to get me and other observers armed, and moving quickly towards the bin.

As I approached the young machine gunner, his eyes never left the clay storage bin, his machine gun levelled and looking deadly. It took him a few moments before he was able to speak, but by the time he did, Sar'major Africa had arrived, and he simply took the situation out of my hands.

In the native chiShona, he ordered the man to rise up, showing his weapon first. At this time, the entire platoon had surrounded the site of the bin, and slowly an AK appeared above the mouth of the receptacle. The grip was around the stock.

Benevolent and far from the trigger – I dispelled any fears of a kamikaze-style exit by this gook. He slowly rose to his full height, dropping the assault rifle harmlessly on the ground. He struggled to get his frame from the clay storage vessel.

The greatest irony of the day was that the gook and I actually recognised each other! Two weeks previously, I had led my platoon on a successful follow up, which culminated in a contact not far from where we were today. During the firefight, I had been kneeling, when this same man had burst out of the bush on my right. He had been beyond the limits of the arc in which I could swing to bring my rifle to effectively bear, and I had lost balance, and fallen inelegantly, on my backside. I had emptied a magazine into the likely cover, but this man was able to somehow evade my unsociable efforts to end his life – but not before throwing me a stick grenade!

I reminded Sergeant Saul, who had been next to me during the attack on that day. Surprisingly, neither Saul, nor I felt the slightest bit of enmity towards him? We were professionals. In all battles, someone won, and someone lost – it had always been that way.

JANUARY MOYO by Captain Andy Barrett

March 1979. While our call-sign (Sgt Theo Nel, Cpl Phil O'Donnell, Cpl Norman Hulley and Capt Andy Barrett) were very wearily walking out from the Siyoka TTL towards the main Bulawayo to Beit Bridge road, a blue Zephyr approached from our rear.

Stopping the vehicle, Theo asked the lone driver his name, only to be told: "January Moyo, Sir."

"I see that you are going in the same direction as we are, so may the four of us please have a lift?" Theo asked. We were heading to Robin and Paxie Watson's Makado Ranch homestead which was immediately to the west of this junction; in fact, it formed part of it.

"Sure," January responded, where after Theo and I jumped into the vehicles cabin while Phil and Mark sat in the boot area. Phil was our RPD gunner so to make thing comfortable he removed his chest webbing which he placed beside him in the boot.

On arriving at the road junction, we all bailed out, thanked January for the lift and with smiles all around waved him on his way as he was heading towards Beit Bridge town. No sooner had January departed when Phil realized that he had forgotten his chest webbing which contained two full RPD drum magazines in the boot of Moyo's vehicle.

We frantically bolted towards the Watson's farmhouse to inform them of this debacle so that they could get on their Agric-Alert radio to inform the police at the roadblock just prior to entering town. By the time this was accomplished,

January had been stopped, his vehicle searched, the booty discovered, and he pulled from the vehicle for questioning.

Finally, on receiving the message, the police released January and we collected the webbing on our return to base the same day. Approximately 3 months later while passing through the very same police checkpoint we yet again saw January amongst loud cheers, big smiles and frantic waving.

CRACK 'N THUMP ANGLING by Corporal Andrew Krajewski

Recent photos from an ex-army pal now living in Canada showed his lovely wife holding aloft a magnificent salmon, artfully captured, with no less than the greatest skill and finesse, I doubt not. They also show a not-so-lovely fellow (yes, Himself) also holding aloft a stubby salmon of stupendous size. This I found somewhat suspicious, and I uncharitably thought that this fish of his was "captured" using a

Zambezi River 1978.

Red Breasted Bream-A Camp Left to Right: Pte Tembo, Cpl Andrew J "Sunray 22B" Krajewski and Pte Vincent Ngwenya.

hand grenade. But it is written: let him without sin cast the first stone. I confess: I've been a bounder and a cad (it's the only way you can have any fun these days!).

These photos set me scrabbling in the cesspit of my bedside credenza, in search of evidence of some of the less conventional fishing episodes we enjoyed during our sojourn on "The Eastern Front", downstream from Kariba in the "A" Camp Area. It is an area of the Zambezi Valley no doubt well known to some. I have a confession: I, Sunray of the notorious callsign 22 Bravo enjoyed halcyon days with FN rifle, war-surplus hand grenades and, on one spectacular occasion, a critically injured mini-claymore mine, with a cracked exoskeleton through which could be seen its innards. Specifically, what was visible was about 200 g of PE and several hoops of 10 mm steel round bar, half-filed through by some incarcerated nimarangie in Chikurubi Prison, so as to induce the so-called "Cadbury's Effect" ("Everyone gets a square!"). And damaged ordnance is very dangerous, yes?

There is some skill in shooting fish with a service rifle. The hapless creature has to be sufficiently shallow to absorb the massive concussion of a 148-grain, metal-jacketed round slamming into all but incompressible water at close to 2700 feet per second. However, rarely was the fish actually punctured by the projectile. Sometimes, though, due to "over exuberance" by Certain Blackguardly Types (who so far forgot themselves as to place their FN on automatic and loose off three to four rounds sommer quick), the fish came out almost completely scaled.

In most cases, I must say this reprehensible habit of shooting fish was done rarely and mostly to procure bait (small tigerfish or bream) that would then be scooped from the water, belly up, by several pant-hooting hominids clad in their Army Underpants. These unfortunate baitfish would then be skewered on huge and rusty hooks, either whole or in part, and lobbed water-wards attached to 70 lb handlines in order to drum up some serious business. Which they soon did!

Sometimes, however, hunger would overtake us, and a Gollum-like feral gleam ("Yessss, famisssshed we are! Niccce Fisssshhh, my Prrrecioussss!") would enter the eyes of the assembled Parishioners. If no bait-fish were forthcoming, the method of capture would escalate somewhat and a "liberated" RGD- 5 hand grenade would be lobbed water-wards into the limpid depths of water "salted" an hour or so before with stale lumps of cooked sadza. As they say in the Classics: Sic transit gloria mundi! [literal translation "Gloria was sick in transit on Monday"]. How the Mighty Had Fallen; what with Izaak Walton spinning in his grave like a top. Gone to the dogs, all!

And all to procure fresh fish for The Masses, who were frequently on the verge of mutiny, cannibalism and ovo-lacto-scroto-veganism at the sight of just one more tin of bully beef! Still, the Wounded Claymore Mine Episode was an act of eco-terror that was hard to top, even for feckless herberts crazed by heat, flies, vermin and trillions of bloodsucking insects, and at a time when a cheery greeting would elicit an unexpected reply, thus:

Auctor: "Ah, Good Morrow, good fisherman! Are they biting today?"

Lector: "Yes!! And I scratched them all last night as well!"

But our real introduction to crack 'n' thump fishing came one day when my good friend "Buffalo Bill" and I wandered down to the river more or less opposite Chief Chiawa's Village in Zambia. For some reason, our overt patrolling ("we were only following orders") of this entire area of The Zambezi usually went more or less unchallenged, except in this one area.

If there was so much as a glimpse of anything on two legs on the South bank of The River opposite Chiawa's, the sky used to light up and everything from B10, 82 mm recoilless rifle rounds, 61 mm mortars and copious RPD and Degtyarev DP (7,62 x 54R, long, rimmed round) would crack and thump merrily, and we would tactically withdraw from the bank into the thick jesse and mopane scrub. This coitus interruptus militarius was always carried out in text-book fashion, and at all times and everywhere in a disciplined, decent, military fashion. I recall to this day shouting in a strong and manly voice the following commands and hearing in answer a number of morale- boosting slogans from my comrades in arms:

Corporal Krajewski: "RUN AWAY! RUN AWAY!!"

Private Dube: "MAAAAIIIIIWEEEHH!!!"

Private Ngwenya: "SHITI - AKO, GOMBINGO!".

And so we learned to steer clear of Chiawa's area, at least when it came to getting some quality fishing time!

Imagine then our shock and outrage when on one calm and balmy afternoon in October 1978 the Rules of Engagement were violated in most unsporting fashion by some chaps on the Zambian side. It was obviously a case of mistaken identity for when BB and I settled down at the waterside, nowhere near Chiawa's Village, with baited handline in one hand and bottle of Jungle Juice in the other, as was our wont of an evening, a curious thing happened.

We become aware of a great deal of distant jabbering. To our front and across the 900 m or so width of apple-green, clear and inviting water (were it not for the crocodiles) voices were raised to (high) heaven in hallowed African fashion. Behind us was the steep riverbank upon which, about 200 m way, were perched our Braves: Privates Dube, Ngwenya and Sibanda, S.

They were pointing their rifles at the gibbering Villagers across the water and making jabbing motions in the air with them. Ngwenya, however, was not content with this, so he added some exaggerated cod-piece clutching; Elvis Presley-like knee gyrations; and several quite explicit pelvic thrusts. To each his own.

Anyway, BB and I took the discourse opposite to be of an alcohol-inflamed, domestic nature. It was, after all, a Sunday afternoon, so we paid it no further heed.

Within several minutes, though, the volume of the noise had appreciably increased and we discerned, in the gathering gloom of sunset at water's edge on the Zambian Side, a knot of chattering reekies gesturing in what we assumed was our direction. "How rude!" I thought. Still, there are Certain Standards that One Must Uphold, so I gave them a cheery wave.

Almost at once we heard the unmistakable crack and thump of a high volume of automatic small- arms fire punctuated by a sequence of four deep "THUNKs" of mortars. Rob and I looked at one another. Our exchange may have gone something like this:

BB: (fishing line held in one hand) "What the fuck is that?"

AK: (knee-deep in cool, clear water) "Nah: bugger me if I know! Who are they shooting at anyway?"

Within a few seconds, a single geyser of water exploded about 200 m in front of us. Seconds later a second explosion shook the ground about 25 m in front of our braves who without a backward glance fucked off at the high port into the jesse-bushes. They appeared to be running south-east towards a large clump of trees visible about 100 metres from their last location. But something was wrong:

AK: (still knee-deep in water) "Hey, where's the third bomb?"

BB was just about to answer when an explosion rent the clump of large trees towards which our braves were last seen running, limbs in variations of the traditional "Swastika" position, scrambling over each other to place the maximum distance between themselves and the still-airborne munitions. This was the last we were to see of them for a considerable while. There was no fourth explosion.

In the meantime, the crack and thump of small arms continued. The fire sounded as if it was passing about 400 metres ABOVE our heads. So, we just stood there, handlines limply trailing off into the water, with bottles of JJ at the trail, and rifles propped against a mopane log just behind us. We both looked upwards in bafflement. Every now and again I saw a flicker of a tracer, but way up high and above us. After perhaps 200 rounds had passed overhead, the firing ceased. With the sun setting slowly in the west, we wound in our handlines and at last gave some contemplation to the awful truth. Bully beef again!?

We trudged disconsolately off up the bank to where we had last seen our braves. Five packs lay where we had put them. Of our comrades there was no sign. What now? we wondered. After all, if we went off into the gangen tracking their deviant migration across the bush, the very real prospect existed of us walking straight into an ambush, sprung by three hyper-adrenalised fellows fully capable of shooting first.

BB spoke first: "Let's go find them." he said. "I'm getting hungry and it's almost dark."

So off we went, tapping our FN magazines lustily like we used to do to warn off elephant and rhino and buffalo and lion and hippo, and cane-rats at night. We had gone about 100 metres and I was about to suggest to BB that he and I start to sing "Sweet Banana", the RAR regimental song, when we came upon two of our braves, Ngwenya and Sibanda S. They confirmed more or less what we surmised had happened. They had seen the first mortar bomb explode in front of us and heard the machine gun fire go way high above their heads. They had just stopped laughing and were about to lay down withering covering fire on the other bank when a huge explosion rent the "adrenaline grass" about 20 m in front of them: the air howled and whirred with jags of shrapnel, and blazes of bark were blown off the trees around them.

"So, it has come to this?" they all apparently asked themselves, and without further ado, very sensibly took to their heels. During the nine or so seconds it took them to traverse the 120 metres to the copse of large trees for which they were making, the lead reportedly changed several times, with first Sibanda, then Ngwenya and finally Dube taking pole position.

They were about 15 paces from the trees when the third mortar bomb exploded in the middle of the copse, and right in front of Dube. After this, we found further details hard to glean, as with still-shaking hands and with many an "Ah, but-i shoowa!" they lit cigarettes and sat in brooding silence. People get like that when they run right through the middle of jesse bushes.

It was then that we found Dube. He emerged, wraith-like, from what appeared to be a shallow grave scraped into a low earth bank. His entire face was thickly white-grey with clay dust. He appeared to have dug the shallow shell-scrape using, by the look of him, an ingenious reciprocating action of his lower lip and his eyebrows. Even his ears were plugged with dry soil.

He was a man of few words, but these were well-chosen:

"FAAACK DEEES SHEEET!" he said.

FROM 1 TO 3 WITH BANGS IN BETWEEN, by Captain Russell Fulton

During the latter part of 1980 I found myself posted from A Company, 1RAR to the newly formed 3rd Battalion whose Headquarters were based in Addams Barracks in Umtali. My initial posting order indicated that I was being posted in as the Adjutant, an appointment that came very early on in my commissioned life. I was a young Lieutenant and a mere twenty years old. On arrival at 3RAR, I reported to the acting Adjutant, one Captain Trevor Leeshon Hughes (formerly Admin. Officer of 1RAR) who took me to meet the Commanding Officer, Lt Col T.D.E. (Terry) Leaver. Hughes was dismissed, and I was left alone with Col Leaver who struck me as being an impressive and highly professional officer and I liked him immediately.

Not only was he immaculately turned-out but he had a personable, engaging and welcoming manner. Col Leaver asked me how I felt about taking up the Adjutant's appointment to which I offered a sincere and candid response. I indicated that I was extremely proud but that I was, and nonetheless, a little saddened that my time as an operational platoon commander was being cut-short. I think this was what he had hoped would be my response as he smiled and said, "Russell, I am in need of a young and disciplined Adjutant, but I have a proposal for you that you may find to your liking and I will accept whatever your decision. I have a rock-solid OC in Chipinga, Major Marius Meiring who was 2ic to Major Andre Dennison of A Company, 2RAR and who really could do with a 2ic. I would like to offer that to you given that you're keen to remain in one of the rifle company's?" Postings were not the subject of negotiation and I (sensibly) regarded this as an opportunity that best suited me, and I very readily and gratefully accepted the offer and, at that, escaped the clutches of premature regimental life.

I departed Umtali in a Rhodef 2.5 and drove the 188km south to Chipinga considering this windfall and I knew, most certainly, that good fortune had smiled very kindly upon me. B Company, 3RAR was located adjacent to the Chipinga aerodrome and a couple of kilometres to the east of that pedestrian, dimly lit rural metropolis that was to become my new stamping ground and home-from-home. A far cry from Methuen Barracks and Bulawayo and, dare I say it, a far cry from anywhere but I quickly fell in love with the place and the great community who gave it such depth and strength of good old Rhodesian character. My OC, Marius Meiring, was a first-class man who I 'clicked' with immediately; a truly wonderful guy who was switched-on but as laid-back as they came. Tough and demanding but far from what I would regard as brusque; a thoroughly decent bloke by every measure and, once again, I realised how truly blessed I was as I knew that I would thoroughly enjoy this posting. As time would prove, I wouldn't be disappointed.

To all intents and purposes this was a 'peace time' posting as the integration of the former Rhodesian Army, ZIPRA and ZANLA was steadily taking place throughout the country. Being based where we were in the southern reaches of what we all knew as Op Tangent, this was a district surrounded by commercial tea estates and wattle plantations and to the southern and eastern reaches were APA's and TTL's. Chipinga was within reasonable proximity of the Mozambique border and rogue elements of the MNR were becoming a nuisance crossing the border and robbing rural stores and generally behaving in a manner that required us 'Crusader' types to 'put some stick about'.

After a short while in B Company I was selected from the army nominal roll to travel to the UK as an exchange officer and did attachments with The Green Howards in Catterick Garrison, North Yorkshire and 3 Parachute Battalion who were based in Colchester. Within a fortnight of my return, and late one Friday afternoon, I was busy reviewing some CQ store reports when Marius walked in to my A-Frame prefabricated 'office' and requested that I join him in his.

Ominous I thought but this was my Ishe so I jumped up and presented myself in front of him. He told me to take a seat and then gave me one of his endearing, kindly smiles. "Sunray Minor, I have some concern about you being my 2ic and that you are incorrectly dressed." I was astonished at the notion that I was "manky" and hastily looked myself over; I had always prided myself in being 'squared away' and I was certain that there was nothing in my turnout that would, fairly, draw the attention and criticism of my 'Sunray'. I responded, "I apologise if I have disappointed you Sir but, frankly, I can't see anything wrong?"

Marius opened his desk drawer and withdrew a signal that had come off our telex machine and pushed it across the table. I read it, and then re-read it to make sure that I was reading it correctly. It was a signal from Army HQ providing notification of my (and other) promotions. In my case from Lieutenant to substantive Captain and effective immediately! I looked up at Marius who was smiling broadly at me; he tossed a pair of well-worn RAR Captain rank slides to me and said, "These were mine 'Sunray Minor', slip them on and join me in the bar... correctly dressed".

I was dumbfounded; I was 20 years and 10 months old and had been commissioned for a mere seventeen months. I was now senior to everyone from my cadet course including the good men who had graduated ahead of me on course! That night, in buoyant mood, I drank a tad more than I should have. What can I tell you!

The next morning, a Saturday, I was woken at 0530B by my dutiful Batman who was armed with the ubiquitous tray of tea. He took one look at me, frowned a touch and disappeared only to return a few minutes later with the Company 'Starlight' (Medic) in tow. Without prompting, 'Starlight' placed a small oxygen cylinder beside my bed and handed me a mask to place over my face. He turned the oxygen on and I inhaled it greedily. There was a cup hook in the wall above my head where a saline drip was hung, and he went about preparing and administering a cannula. Opening the tap full he departed with a smart brace-up and returned an hour later to 'tidy-up'. What was, hitherto, the hangover to beat them all, was now a figment of my imagination... I was cured...miraculously! No headache and no 'babalaas' whatsoever! No matter and whatever. This was one of the many privileges of serving in the RAR; these 'things' were simply accepted by our men and there was never a word uttered. It was what it was and that's all there was to it.

We had two newly commissioned subalterns join us from 'Hooters' who came in the form of a regular cadet off Course Inf/25(23), 2Lt John Garland, and a NS subbie in 2Lt Brett Nielson; two splendid young subbies whose roles as platoon commanders I would have traded for my own and in a snap. I don't recall where they were at that time and that's unimportant right now.

Save the last 'dance' for me:

With all that was going on in the Eastern border area there was a need for sleeves to be rolled-up and to get-down-and-dirty once again and I was very much available and hungry to 'get in there' one last time. I gladly put my hand up and took on the command of a team that was to deploy in to the area of Mount Selinda, some 10 clicks west of the "Pork" border. The MNR were becoming a security risk, were too full of bravado and they were in desperate need of a generous dose of 'Sanatogen' (a hiding in other words). Working off INT that was less than reliable compared with what we had become accustomed in the recent past, we still needed to act on it. This neck of the woods, and as many will recall, was less than hospitable and if you wanted a description of what 'broken ground' truly meant, you needn't have ventured too far from this general LOCSTAT.

Our INT, as crap as it was, told us that there was an active group of MNR (Mozambique National Resistance), circa 9 strong, operating with some impunity in the area of Mount Selinda, robbing stores, raping rural womenfolk and harassing locals but that posed little concern to me. These were no more than undisciplined rogues whose power came through the barrels of their uncleaned weapons, 'bully-boys' if you will and whose bravado would eventually be their undoing and we, the men of the RAR, were about to teach them a lesson or two about soldiery in general and aggression in particular.

We followed tracks that eventually split in several directions indicating that they had bomb-shelled in very broken ground and we followed a group of three in to an area that was wall-to-wall with granite boulders and, what else, cave country! I had had a great deal of experience 'playing' in caves during my time in the RLI and as a young subaltern in 1RAR but, and despite my 'experience', it never made the task ahead any more agreeable. Frankly, the mere thought of jousting in caves filled me with dread but hey-ho, "ours was not to reason why, nor make reply...."

Caves were, by their very nature, dark and inhospitable places that, ordinarily, contained an assortment of 'toothed' creatures that were inclined to nip you without warning. As it turned out, the group we were following knew we were on to them and they had decided to ensconce themselves in one of said caves. I don't mind sharing with you that I was a bit nervous of these dark and foreboding places, knowing full-well that you could very swiftly 'die without being sick' if you didn't have your shit completely together. What I had learned, as a young RLI troopie, was that it was wise to remember those methods of instruction that were imparted by young but very experienced and battle-hardened NCO's.

In matters of fieldcraft, it always reverted to the basics; 'Why/How things are seen?' The answer, as we knew, was as a compromise of any one, or more, of 'Shape', 'Shine', Shadow', 'Silhouette', 'Sound' and 'Movement'. If you ignored these six basic principles, as surely as light would follow day, a 'third-eye' would most certainly be opened for you.

Entering a cave, with the outside naturally light behind you, silhouetted you perfectly for a kill shot. These gooks had taken refuge in a cave some 100 meters up an incline from where we were positioned, and it was now my job to extricate them; by whatever means and whatever tactic. Today, there would be no air support and it was simply a case of 'suck it up Princesses' and 'In your own time, carry on!' I deployed half of my call sign above the cave in case there was an exit point and my men could sting anyone attempting to take the gap. I retained a call sign of two for the cave entry (me and one other) with four in reserve. I fired a few 32Z rifles grenades in to the cave and these detonated as I had expected they would; loudly and accompanied by the instantaneous shrill of angry, hot shrapnel. A few M962 HE (shrapnel) grenades were hurled in for good measure, just to show that there was 'no hard feelings' but, and inevitably, we 'Grunts' on the ground still had to do our job and go in.

The big problem with grenades tossed in to caves was that they could, and oftentimes were, completely ineffectual because you didn't know where the enemy was nor what cover they might have. If anything, they would have an impact on morale and in these confined spaces, would certainly blow the wax out of their ears. The entrance to this cave was not much more than three meters at its widest point which was at the floor of the cave but it opened-up, almost cavernously, a few feet in. Not knowing the lay of the land, I entered first and was followed by one of my trusted Corporals, an ex-A Coy, 2RAR man that Marius had convinced into requesting a posting to 3RAR. He was on my right as we cautiously entered.

I carried a pump-action shotgun loaded with SSG grape shot as my preferred weapon for this 'activity' and Corporal Bhere carried his issue FN. Our eyes quickly adjusted to the dim, dust-filled light and we arrived at a dog leg to the right; Bhere and I, momentarily exposed when we turned the corner, we were disturbed by the loud chatter of a short volley of fire. Cpl Bhere took a round in his side and fell, partially protected by a small boulder but he was now the focal point of some special attention from the gooks as the floor around him was whipped-up.

Given the confines of the cave and high velocity rifle fire, there were ricochets and tracer all over the place and the general timbre of this little encounter suddenly took on a new and entirely unpleasant flavour. I tossed a grenade to where the fire was coming from and, as it detonated, I scrambled to where Bhere lay and dragged him by his webbing yolk around the corner and out of harm's way. This generated some excitement amongst the gooks who opened-up and sprayed the area where Bhere had fallen. I called for my reserve team to extricate Bhere and attend to him as I went back in to the cave.

I had a single bunker bomb that I now intended to use. I now had a good idea where the bad boys were and edged my way along the right-side cave wall and pulled the pin. I needed to create a diversion to break the status quo and this 'mother' would create that opportunity. By now I had been joined by a private soldier who was directly behind me. I turned around and looked at him, squeezed his arm and smiled before I lobbed the bomb and waited for it to detonate. On the count of five, just like the manual said, it did just that. There was an almost deafening bang and the cave was filled with the acrid smell of high explosive and dust. I ran forward towards the gook position and fired repeatedly pumping the stock as I went. By the time I had emptied the 1+5 SSG load in my shotgun everything was still.

When the proverbial dust had settled the three MNR chaps lay in an unseemly heap. One was 'history' and the other two were moaning annoyingly and bleeding about the place as a result of considerable oil leaks but pleading with me not dispatch them to the 'land of free sadza'. The private soldier behind me swore at them in colourful language that I'm not sure I should repeat here, and I had my doubts these 'maSatan' understood the profanity either. I did, and I loved it! He gathered their discarded weapons and made them safe as I called to my back-up call sign to fall-in and ordered them to recover the 'stiff' and the two profusely 'leaking' prisoners. We delivered this untidy heap in to the eager clutches of the local constabulary and that was the end of that.

For me, this action brought down the curtain on my military involvement in matters where our general behaviour required participation in the close proximity to hostile bangs and where the gnashing of teeth was the order of the day. Would I change any of it? Well now......................!

Bhere was not grievously injured, thank God, and he soon returned to active duty and I salute the man and his gallantry.

"Muhondo RAR, Inorwa noKushinga."

DR LIVINGSTONE I PRESUME? by Captain Russell Fulton

During our time on operations, and in conformance with the basic norms of humanity foremost, there were occasional "civvie" annoyances that required one to partake in matters that fell beyond the scope of 'general duties'. Be they as they were, these were simply things that needed to be done; preferably in private and well out of earshot of humanity.

Enough said? I'm afraid not…

This is an anecdote that is as unsavoury in subject as it was in 'execution' but I share it with you simply because I can. Will there be lessons learnt? Perhaps not but you can read and decide for yourselves. Some may well be able to relate.

It was during my time as 2ic of B Company, 3RAR when, to all intents and purposes, we were in post-hondo (war) mode… well, at least for the time being. My Company Commander, a wonderful man and much loved and respected commander, Major Marius Meiring (RIP), had summoned me to his office, by means of a hand written "Warning Order", to advise that we (he and I and a recce party comprising a signaller, medic, cook and two sections from our company strength) had been cleared by 4 Brigade (Op Repulse) to conduct a recce in the general area of the Sabi-Lundi junction to prepare for a company battle camp and border control operations that would follow shortly thereafter.

We departed Chipinga and made our way deep in to the south-east of the country passing various locations that remained vivid in my memory from my time with A Company, 1RAR when I was deployed in several of these very 'places'. It was a magnificent part of the country and Marius and I revelled in its raw and majestic beauty…the deja vu of it all was a little unnerving, but it was inevitable. We found a magnificent site dominating GTI (ground of tactical importance) overlooking the Lundi and opposite the Chitove Falls. We unloaded the vehicles, struck camp and so began the pleasure of peacetime soldiery. That night, over a bottle of rare single malt Whiskey, my 'Sunray' and I sat in the comfort of his tent on 'Chairs, Camp Folding' in the light of a hissing Hurricane Lamp and sipped, chatted, bonded and made final our plans for the coming week.

A couple of days later, I took a stick with me and we made our way down to the Sabi-Lundi confluence. At a little after midday we stopped for a brew and a bite and that was when, as nature would have it, and in its own time carry on, I received the call of nature. I ordered my call-sign to adopt an all-round defensive position to my rear and I eased my way down towards the river where there was plenty of natural cover. Personally, I require peace and quiet during this time. It is a time for quiet contemplation, reflection and doing what should have come naturally. On this day, it would be far from it…

There I was, a picture of camouflage and concealment, betwixt and between the bulrushes and lantanas, with trousers-combat drawn to half-mast and in a perfectly poised squatting position a good 50 meters (or so) from my men. I lit a Madison cigarette, suitably crumpled, and tugged on it deeply savouring its pungent taste, as "nicotine addicts" did. The 'hondo', now recently in our past, I thought nothing of this as I had a 'hornet's nest' perched on GTI above me who were ready, willing and prepared to issue oil leaks. Never mind that; this is not about one's tactical prowess or lack thereof.

In this perfectly regal pose, I was about to do what was required when I heard the unfamiliar wailing of what sounded very much like a woman in distress? I cannot tell a lie, I stopped "deployment" seconds before the (proverbial) 'bomb bays' could open, hauled up my breeches quick-smart and listened intently to these quite unnatural sounds emanating from no more than 50 meters distant! My initial, and natural-instinct, was to presume that the noise I was hearing was either emanating from the dry and possibly bloodied mouth of a poacher fallen foul of one of his own devilish traps or, and mores the like, it was a grievously injured dissident in trouble. It was none of the above!

Through hand signals I ordered my call sign forward to join me and we swept forward toward the river bed that was in slow-flow and offering several crossing points. Tactical prowess was never ignored, and we crossed the 'obstacle' as we had been trained. The riverine bush was incredibly thick and, in places, impregnable and we negotiated slowly but steadily towards the desperate wailing.

We rounded a riverine copse at the water's edge and soon found what we were looking for and it shocked us all!

Here, in 'no man's land', was a heavily pregnant AFA (African Female Adult) who was lying on the bank of the river with water gourds strewn about her, her dreadfully thin legs agape and in the throes of childbirth! What does one do in situations such as this? I was not Rhodesian Army "MA3" trained. Show me a fracture of any description, a gunshot wound wherever, and I'd be able to stabilize you, but I had never received any medical training in the delivery of a human being! Forgive the profanity that is included only in the interests of accuracy, but I responded thus (or words to this general effect): "F*** me! What the hell am I supposed to do with this lot?"

I cast a fleetingly and inquiring glance about my troops 'hoping' that someone might be able to give me a steer, but this was 'greeted' with that unfortunate 'thousand-yard stare'. There were no CASEVAC aircraft to think of, this poor woman was on the other side of the river to the road and I was basically in Shit Street. As my late regular cadet course officer, Martin 'Wakkers' Wake (and later my very dear friend) had said during a 'non-instructive' bull-shit session when asked about how to handle something that we hadn't received formal training on. His response was the classical: "Tup, tup, tup!! An officer must always make a plan; that's what you're paid to do".

Dr Livingstone, I presume?

And so, armed with 'Wakkers' pearls of wisdom, there I was in no-man's-land, enveloped by this almost deafening cry for help and all my *Masodja* eyes focussed on yours truly! I was a very young Captain, less than one month shy of my 21st birthday, now preordained with the unwanted title of "UDokotera Ishe" (Doctor Sir); a veritable 'Dr Livingstone I presume'! One thing that the Rhodesian Army did well was it taught you how to grow up quickly and assume responsibilities that were, oftentimes, beyond the pale. As I surveyed what lay pitifully and quite helpless before me, with growing apprehension and a suppressed terror, I accepted my 'calling' and positioned myself between this poor woman's legs. I ordered everyone to light their gas cookers and to boil water and called for all 'First Field Dressings'. I lifted the woman's skirt to see what was going on and I could see the crown of an infant's head. The woman had long since broken her water and was now in distress and the unborn infant was now a likely 'still-birth' candidate and I didn't want to be the principle subject of any Boards of Inquiry in to something like this!

269

As soon as I had sufficient hot water and dressings, I withdrew my personal Gerber boot knife (a gift from a former A Company, 1RAR fellow platoon commander, Lt Willard Fleetwood, ex-US Ranger) placed the razor-edged blade in one of the containers of boiled water brought by the Company Medic, Cpl Moyo, Julius a splendid 'Starlight' who was both very knowledgeable and keen to assist. The blade was as sharp as I could hone it and it would just have to do. I told the woman to 'bare-down', more because I had watched way too much TV and thought that this may be of some use……. contraire!

I knew nothing about childbirth but knew from the ashen-pallor of this distressed woman, things were critical. I inserted a cannula in to a vein in her foot as I couldn't find a vein anywhere else and opened the drip fully. I withdrew the clasp knife from the freshly boiled water and placed the blade point close to the baby's head and literally touched the taught flesh and it split. I was sprayed with blood but reached down and gently assisted in withdrawing the infant from its mother. Before I could give the infant a smack on its bum, it wailed ever-so-softly and my heart all but broke with relief. It was a 'musikana' (girl) and I wrapped her in one of our first aid issue 'shoulders, sling' (it's all I had) and passed the little thing to her mother. She had tears streaming down her cheeks and so did I. For her part, perhaps relief that she had been helped and her child had been delivered. Every one of my men were similarly afflicted because they were all fathers in their own special right. For me, well that really doesn't matter at all, does it?

I injected a 30mg phial of Sosogon in to her and went about "suturing" the tear using a sanitised (boiled) needle and thread from my 'Kits, Housewife'. The stitches were crude, but they did what was required for the immediate and short term. I ordered my men to chop two saplings for poles and for two pairs of combat trouser to be brought for the 'cradle'. We lay the woman in this with her infant and we carried her to her kraal several kilometres distant. I had ordered my men to fill our water bottles and all the woman's gourds and we carried them too. On our arrival, we were greeted by a group of inquisitive youngsters and then the village elders who seemed to appear, ghost-like, out of nowhere.

I sought out and greeted the headman in customary fashion (hombera and general greeting in the vernacular) and explained what had happened whilst the new mother was assisted to her hut. With gratitude expressed we bade these good, peace loving rural folk farewell and resumed with the execution of our original orders. What became of this 'musikana' and the life she has lived since, are all questions that I cannot answer. I facilitated one life and I truly hope that it has been one well lived?

It was an interesting episode in my life. It was also one that has been compartmentalised in the deepest recesses of my mind for nigh on four decades; I'm not sure why... Dr Livingstone I presume?

There are many things in life that will catch your eye, but only a few that will catch your heart. Pursue those...

A MEMORY OF A GROUND COVERAGE OPERATOR by Senior Patrol Officer Dave Ward

2nd Lt. Graham Watson Smith, stick leader of a Crusader call sign, came to see me on the 7th February 1979. He was with two African Soldiers of 1 (Indep) Coy RAR and two European national service soldiers of the 1 (Indep), based out of Beitbridge.

I can recall to this day how very keen he was as his first sentence contained the words "no lemons". I was sure he thought me mad as I had to explain between laughter and smiles that the Ground Coverage base was new and that hardly any worthwhile intelligence had filtered back. However, I had a hunch about a kraal in an area that was tough to get to.

Less than 48 hours later:

On the 9th February 1979 at 1250, I got a call on the Bailiff radio that a Crusader call sign had just had a contact in my area. There was only one such call sign near me as others were south west of the area. It took quite a while to get to the call sign as there were no roads or even paths and a lot of dongas. On arrival I was met by Graham who then gave me the report.

The contact had been initiated by Graham who had crept into a kraal to check it out with the call sign in a position to support and defend. He sighted a CT walking towards the kraal and so climbed into a small livestock pen and watched as the CT just kept coming towards the kraal.

At a point where he was sure he would been seen, Graham just 'dropped' him. As this happened, a full contact with a further 9 or 10 CTs started at the callsign's position. The CTs had been using little dongas and river beds as a way of moving around the area, as if they were trenches, but had come up to the callsign without seeing them. The MAG gunner that day showed just how lethal the MAG was and just how good Rhodesian Army training was. By all accounts it was the MAG that did most of the damage that day. 7 of 9 CTs were killed outright in the contact and one in a personal joust between Graham and an unknown ZIPRA CT. These ZIPRA CTs were better trained then the ZANLA lot and had better weapons and all in good condition. At the time, taking out 8 ZIPRA in a contact was not normal and I believe this was the most enemy killed in one contact by that time in the Tangent Operational Area.

Many years later, I corresponded with Tony (Anthony Barlow) who was the MAG gunner and I asked him if he would like to comment on the contact or the others that followed. His reply to me is as follows:

'It would be an honour to be in the book. But rather than talk of contacts, it's something we did and something we did with our hearts. We didn't have to go in, although we were called up. We could have got out of it but the blokes who went did so with passion. I think. I know we believed we were doing the right thing. I just feel for the families of those who never made it or came out lost, and some are still lost within themselves, and us who left and moved all around the world living in different countries have left all our good and bad memories behind. Although we have taken some with us and when we meet up we sit and chat about the times. But leaving there I think we left something behind. I give All Honour to those that lost their lives. Amen'.

On a personal note, up to September 1977, I served 18 months of Ground Coverage work and so came to know many of the 1 (Indep) Coy RAR soldiers. When I transferred to GC Manicaland in Sept 1979, I did not just leave some of my good friends in the BSAP but many in 1 (Indep) and I am privileged today to remain friends with many. The fact that the community and leaders of Beitbridge presented 1 (Indep) with the Freedom of the City is a testament to the leadership and courage of all that served. I salute them.

MY FINAL JOUST WITH 'SIMANJEMANJE' (3 PLATOON, A COMPANY, 1RAR) by Captain Russell Fulton

"Op Agila": 1Km from AP Juliet: Late February 1980

In this, my final anecdote about my service in 1RAR, the intensity of the Rhodesian bush war had escalated exponentially and proverbial 'Lemons' were now a thing of the past. Contacts with ZIPRA and ZANLA became more frequent and casualties on all sides were an inevitable consequence. That's what 'hondo' was all about, we accepted it as our bit and we simply got on with the business professionally and stoically.

Background:

An official ceasefire by the three warring sides was agreed upon and implemented at 2359 hours on 28 December 1979, at which point the war effectively ended. A British Governor, in the form of Lord Christopher Soames, an altogether unfortunate looking toad-like man, with a permanently sweaty brow, bloated midriff and an overzealous proclivity towards distilled alcohol, arrived in Rhodesia to complete the circle of British rule in the colony; restoring symbolic 'legality' to the rebel republic and, ostensibly, to oversee elections, which, in practical terms, Soames enjoyed neither the physical power nor the political support to moderate or control. This ceasefire ended on 4 January 1980, at 2359 + 1 and, with that knell of the clock, the ceasefire ended. And with that my dear friends, our hondo was 'history', or was it?

A Company, 1RAR was already deployed on framework operations in south-eastern Matabeleland during this time and had two CMF personnel attached. One was a Captain from the New Zealand Army and one a Sergeant from the Australian Army and whose names, very sadly, I simply do not recall, and I apologise to them for that failure of memory. I can see both as clearly in my minds-eye this day as I would have forty odd years ago. Bugger!

Both men were agreeable types and, as infantry men themselves, there was something of a 'veiled' appreciation and respect for what we were doing and why we had fought the good fight. Both were serving in peace-time armies and the conventions of warfare were distorted by the overly clinical doctrine prescribed by the Geneva Convention and their CMF superior officers under Major-General John Ackland (British Army and Commander of CMF in Rhodesia). Their orders did not translate well on the ground with Rhodesian troops and their interpretation of the same tended to blur the harsh reality of what was going-on on the ground rendering them questionably opaque at best.

Ours was a counter-insurgency war where we had been fighting in the country of our birth, for our very survival and way of life and not on foreign soil; it wasn't even remotely similar to the last conflict the Aussie and Kiwi Diggers had been involved in in Vietnam. Their attachment as monitors in ours, a majority black regiment, worked in our favour and 'blind-eyes' were (apparently) 'proffered' in our direction. Perhaps it was involuntary leniency on their part, I really don't know suffice it is to say that we interacted with the expected decorum expected of us and in which we prided ourselves.

That is my personal and honest assessment and, to be fair, the CMF had an unenviable task fraught with 360° aggro. Clearly, there was a great measure of suspicion on the part of our *Masodja* surrounding the CMF attachment to our company, but we too had been briefed on the protocols that had to be observed. They had a job to do and we did too; it was merely a question of managing those conflicting mind-sets and emotions and integrating them into a common purpose (not dissimilar to the Principles of Battle Procedure). A tough ask but we managed the process well enough. Like everything, time took care of these matters and our relationship improved and was founded upon goodwill between soldiers. Nevertheless, we never took direction from the CMF. Ever.

By the end of the ceasefire it was estimated that some 22,000 ZIPRA and ZANLA forces had converged on some twenty odd Assembly Points dotted strategically around the country. A Company, 1RAR was deployed within close proximity of a ZIPRA Assembly Point, "AP Juliet", which was based at Zezani Mission within the Dendele TTL and sandwiched between the Siyoka and Dibilishaba TTLs; this is my story.

Contact:

3 Platoon, A Company, 1RAR were deployed on overt patrol, O.P. and ambush operations in the Dibilishaba TTL, south-west of AP Juliet, and we covered that TTL comprehensively knowing that there would be large numbers of guerrillas who had either not heard about the ceasefire or had deliberately ignored orders from ZIPRA High Command to lay down their arms. Our orders were, when we happened upon them, to recognise them for what they were and to engage and eliminate them without deference to higher authority. In late February 1980, twelve months after my commissioning, I took command of number 1 section from my platoon and moved in towards the 1Km 'buffer zone' clearly marked on our 1:50,000 map sheets in a red hash format clearly delineating the area in 'Chino-graph' pencil as being a "no-go-area" for any/all forces.

It would have been late afternoon, circa 1700hrs, as we were approaching the buffer zone when the still of that hot summer evening was disturbed by the unnatural sound of cloven hooves clapping the hard, dusty access road we were flanking. What caught our attention around the bend through very thick 'Jesse-bush' must have been as bewildering to us as it was those who confronted us; a group of well-armed and recently well bathed ZIPRA gooks whose kit and bodies smelt like a Lever Brothers 'Lifebuoy Soap' factory. It was a 'simultaneous sighting' in Rhodesian army parlance, but with a difference as we brought our weapons to bear and rained all manner of hail and pestilence upon them. It was not what an infantry soldier expected nor a situation we enjoyed but they were armed, and we were ready, willing and very capable.

Standing atop a scotch-cart drawn by four tethered and less-than lethargic donkeys, stood a ZIPRA cadre with AK47 slung over his back and looking every bit like one of those western cartoons of a stagecoach driver whipping the 'bejesus' out of his stallions. They were off for a bit of leg-over or whatever it was they did, but they met us instead and we put paid to their scheduled frivolous and dangerous nocturnal activities. A 'buffer zone' was what the name implied, and they had crossed-over in to hostile territory.

As we opened fire a few of their own engaged us with assorted RPD, SKS and AKM's and the immediate beating of alarmed wings and startled shrieks of Crested Francolin added to the raucous cacophony of the moment. We held fast momentarily before skirmishing toward and past the 'cart' and secured the area. There was neither defensive nor offensive return fire. I returned to the scotch cart with four men and found three dead donkeys and one in extremis that I was obliged to dispatch, and, with compassion, I did. There and thereabouts lay three ZIPRA cadres and the rest, however many there might have been, were gone like a streak of duck-shit in to the dwindling sunset never to be seen again.

I radioed the contact to Sunray 19 and withdrew a safe tactical distance from the contact area, fully expecting an angry response from those several hundred ZIPRA within AP Juliet who would have heard the contact in the still evening air but there was nothing of the sort. The next morning, we cautiously returned to the contact site with orders to recover bodies, weapons and the like which we did. My platoon vehicles arrived around midday, much to my chagrin, as the three fallen ZIPRA cadres had not responded well to the near 40-degree Celsius heat. It was to be the last offensive engagement for me in 1RAR before my posting-out to 3RAR and, who knows, one of the last in our regiment before Entumbane 1 and 2 but that's entirely irrelevant now.

Our CMF mates at Gwanda airfield, our Company TAC HQ base, were falling over themselves crying foul and demanding to interview me. I was directed by my OC to oblige and attended the same with the Corporal (Maumburidzo, Chipo) whose section I had commanded. Our recall of the circumstances was consistent, and I never heard another peep about it. Whatever.

Am I proud? Let me simply say that I served with extreme pride and with an uncompromising loyalty with truly outstanding men, by every conceivable measure, and we executed as we had been trained to do; with instinct, a common purpose, aggression and with extreme prejudice against those who sought to do us and ours harm. That was the RAR way, men of honour and distinction and history should judge us fairly and respectfully. Four decades after the fact, I stand tall knowing that we were professional soldiers in the strictest sense and no one under my command may be accused, even remotely, of conduct unbecoming. Barbarity was never what the RAR was about, and our enemy knew it too. We were aggressive, and we responded in kind when threatened. Those from ZIPRA and ZANLA might well agree after the fact? Frankly my dear, I don't give a damn.

Me? I was a merely a privileged subaltern who rotated through the exalted portals of our regiment, having had the high distinction and honour of being an operational platoon commander in a regiment steeped in history, but surrounded by exceptional men who were far the measure of me. Those whom I once commanded will be my judge and no one else matters to me.

A closing, heartfelt tribute to my men:

To have known you, was to love you as my own. I will remember you always and honour your memory. That is my solemn promise to you all.

"Kuti azive kuti iwe unofanira kukuda iwe sega. Ndichakuyeuka iwe nguva dzose uye kukudza pfungwa yako. Icho ndicho chivimbiso changu chese kwamuri mose".

CHAPTER ELEVEN

LANDMINES

LANDMINE by Major Bruce Sand

Since the turn of the 20th century landmines have been synonymous with fear, pain, and suffering for soldiers and civilians alike. They are the most insidious lethal weapon in conflicts world-wide. They have no conscience and an active longevity in the ground that defies imagination. Little did I know as a young Combat Engineer Officer (at the start of my long military career) how intimately I would be involved with these highly effective, very dangerous lethal weapons.

By the middle of 1973, the Rhodesian Bush War (modern day Zimbabwe) was in full swing. Rural farms were being attacked, black and white families were being murdered. Large vehicle landmines were a weapon of fear and destruction employed to kill, injure and restrict security forces movements. The fledgling Rhodesian Corps of Engineers was hurriedly thrust to the forefront of action clearing roads of easily camouflaged, buried mines. The sappers were stretched to the limit. Laboriously clearing roads by hand and on foot became the norm. We quickly excelled at this difficult and dangerous job! Mine clearing dogs were trained and deployed to great effect (the dogs never failed to find any mines along the routes they cleared).

Mine protected armoured troop-carrying vehicles were developed. They reduced casualties when a mine strike occurred. Clearing and movement standard operating procedures were implemented to combat these mines. Mechanized detection systems were invented and deployed against mines as the conflict progressed. These first generation of modern counter mine techniques were the direct forbearers of the sophisticated modern anti-mine and improvised explosive devices vehicles and equipment. They are used by the western world today in places like the Middle East and Afghanistan.

In spite of the technology, mines must still be laid by a person and cleared by another person. It is a deadly dance between the "layer" and the "lifter". The advantage is always with the layer. The clearer always has to respond to the surprise in the ground!

I have laid many mines in my military career. Dangerous certainly, but much less so than lifting a well-hidden buried mine. I have lifted many of these deadly surprises. Thankfully without physical injury. The mental strain and stress never leaves you, and it is not often you find humour in this difficult, very dangerous military task. Therein lies the only funny mine clearing incident of my career. Black humour at the time, but funny after the fact.

The tale of a champagne cork mine:

Landmine

In 1974 I was seconded as an infantry Platoon Commander to 4 platoon, B Company the 1st Battalion Rhodesian African Rifles (1RAR). Half way through this two-year attachment, the whole Company was tasked with conducting an overt sweep on foot through a remote area south of Fort Victoria. Our aim was to attempt to flush armed insurgents into locations where they could be detected by covert observation patrols and engaged in vertical envelopment combat by Heli-born assault. It was the height of the rains! We had been on the ground for a week, cold, wet, hungry and generally miserable. The sweeping task was tedious, thankless, with little prospect of any combat for our efforts. We were the beaters to drive the enemy to the hunters in ambush.

The company was stretched out in line over about 8 km of frontage. Each of the three platoons was responsible for about 3 km of the frontage. My platoon left, 2Lt Tom Fulton's 5 platoon centre and Lt Bill Liversidge's 6 Pl on the right flank. Rations had run out, no one had any smokes and we had way too much water! At about 3:00pm in fairly heavy but intermittent rain, Tom called me on the radio to ask me if I could help him with a mine one of his soldier trackers had located by accident.

It was buried in a gravel road they were crossing. Our Heli-born Company Commander Major Charlie Piers had been forced to return to base for fuel. Bad weather added to the problem. We were on our own! There was nothing for it, but for me to join Tom and deal with the mine. I was the only sapper for miles, and we had to get on with our primary mission. To this day I can never be sure if this was just Tom's way of gaining access to my carefully hoarded small stock of dry cigarettes and tea fixing's (I was well known to always have a few spares of each, whatever the circumstances)! He was notorious for always running out before the end of a patrol.

About an hour later, wet, muddy and short fused I reached the mine site. I found Tom and some of his platoon waiting under the nearest tree. They were soaked, and just as short fused. He had carefully exposed the top of the mine to confirm it was indeed a "nasty" or chimbumbira in Shona. After a short discussion we started the slow process of further exposing the mine enough to be able to remotely and safely pull it from the hard, wet gravel roadway. Imagine my surprise when the mine turned out to be a vintage WWII British Mark 5 tank mine. This one was probably recovered from the still active WWII minefields in Libya and here now courtesy of Libya's Col Gaddafi; a gift to Zimbabwe "Freedom Fighters". I had only ever seen one previously on display in the Engineers museum. I had no idea of its intricacies. I also did not have a mine clearance kit with me. I was acting as an infantryman, not a Sapper. I had no mine pulling grapnel and line, or explosives to destroy it in place. We could not leave it in the road for an unsuspecting military or civilian vehicle. Improvisation became the name of the game that day.

While Tom continued to carefully chip away the concrete-like gravel from around the long-buried mine, I looked for something to remotely pull it free. It took another hour to expose the mine enough to pull it out of its hole in the road. I had joined a number of cords from our one-man shelter tarps to pull the potentially booby trapped mine clear of the ground safely. Just as we were ready to attach the cord to the mine and pull it, Tom's soldier batman cheerfully appeared with one big steaming mug of tea for us to share. It had been made with my last teabag! It was too hot to drink so we carried it with us to the spot we deemed safe enough to protect us if the mine detonated when we pulled it free from the road. We started pulling, to discover the cord we were using was parachute cord with a great deal of inherent elasticity! Hooks Law of springs was about to apply! As we pulled, we took up the elasticity and loaded the cord and mine with elastic kinetic energy. Tom's digging had not been great, so resistance to movement from the clutches of the compacted gravel prevailed. More force was needed. We went from just me pulling to both of us slowly increasing the already taut, steady tension. A final bit of extra effort rewarded us! The mine suddenly popped free of the gravel's clutches!

Imagine the next microcosm of slow motion time. Our lives flashed before us. The energy loaded cord yanked the mine out of the ground straight towards two dumbfounded young officers. It was just like a champagne cork. How we did not kill each other in our collective haste to avoid this potentially explosive missile I don't know. Laurel and Hardy had nothing on us. It took some effort to compose ourselves in the face of a near run thing. Hysterical laughter from about a dozen on looking *Masodja* made us realize: the mine had literally come to rest about 10ft from us; it had broken up without exploding; and in escaping our folly we had spilled our much coveted last mug of hot tea we were to see for three more days.

All is well that ends well. I made the mine safe by removing the partially sheared fuse from the mine body, and we cached the mine safely for follow on pick up by the sappers. We bivouacked that night, cold, wet, miserable with no food or tea! Just soggy hard to light smokes which I had crushed during my escape efforts. Our sweep mission continued uneventfully the next day, for three more days. When we got back to base tired and grumpy, we discovered everybody knew about "champagne cork mines" – jungle drums had preceded us. The final indignity was a substantially increased mess bill as our peers demanded we buy the drinks in homage to our "dumb and dumber" mine clearing techniques.

I never went anywhere again during that war without a proper mine clearing kit in my webbing!

BLOODY RUSHINGA CONVOY by Major Tom Fulton
(Adapted by the author from Into the Vortex)

After handing over Fire Force duties in Mtoko to D Company 1RAR, B Company was temporarily detached to Operation Hurricane, firstly to take part in an HDF (High Density Force) Operation in tandem with a Commando of 1RLI, in the Mavuradonha Mountains. About two weeks later, we were regrouped and redeployed, after taking part as the Third Wave in the 3 Commando contact, five minutes flying, out of Mount Darwin.

After the chance contact, we were briefed by the 1RLI Intelligence Officer, Captain Andy Samuels; and the Battalion 2ic, Major Pat Hill. We were to be deployed to a village called Rushinga, which was about 40 kilometres out, on the road to Marymount Mission and the Mozambique border. The village and fortified, permanent army camp lay astride one of ZANLA's infiltration corridors, into the hinterland of Tribal Trust Lands and white commercial farms in the region. Straddling the road between Mt Darwin and our new home to be, lay the black owned commercial farms of the Chesa African Purchase Area (APA).

Normally, this route is continually plagued by mines, said Andy Samuels, in the process of concluding his intelligence briefing. But the Chesa farmers are in the middle of reaping the annual maize crop, and the farmers are all bringing in their maize. The caveat, we haven't had a mine on that road for weeks, did little to comfort any of the attendant B Company officers.

5 Platoon regarded it as a privilege to be asked to lead the convoy, with Major Wayne Thompson, bringing up the rear of the Order of March, in his 'unmine-proofed' Landrover. He was travelling in our vehicle tracks. We pulled out of the hamlet at mid-morning. It was a clear sunny day, and the wind was minimal. I was very pleasantly surprised at the excellent surface of the unpaved road – no doubt paid some attention to by the council, to facilitate the exodus of the harvest. It was hard for the mood not to be affected by the twisted detritus of military and civilian vehicles that were mine victims, along the side of the road.

I was strapped in, in the forward part of the passenger bench, closest to the front, and on the left, where I had to crane my neck to observe the road ahead. Trying to generally assess and reassess tactical situations, as they changed. As I was gazing ahead, my peripheral vision picked up a bright flash. This flash was almost immediately followed by the incredible bang, and soon after, the gentle but discernible slap of the shock wave. I hadn't been looking at the approaching civilian truck at the exact moment of detonation, but was cognisant of its presence, and quickly diverted my eyes back to it.

The truck seemed to be momentarily travelling with its wheel-less front, some four feet off the ground. Perhaps not able to travel any faster because it was so over-loaded, the momentum was enough to create a gory tragedy. Weighted to the gun-whales with 100kg bags of maize, the entire macabre scenario was topped, like a birthday cake, by a mass of helpers and hangers-on. In what seemed like slow motion, the ensemble of weighty bags and humanity was airborne for a moment. Then the front of the truck dug into the surface of the road, creating a lever-like, catapult effect in the lifting of the box at the rear, throwing the high-riding passengers and lethal bags of maize, onto the concrete-like surface of the road, in front of the devastated vehicle.

DEBUS! I screamed. Our vehicle slid to a halt, and all my men poured out of the two leading vehicles, favouring the left side of the road, for its better cover. Although the peripheries of the road never lent themselves to ambush, we still approached tactically – because that was the way the RAR always moved.

A pall of grey-black smoke hung in apocalyptic accusation, over the catastrophic scene. The force of the blast had blown the entire engine assembly through the air, and it lay forlorn, on its side, still leaking oil onto the hard road surface, a good 20 metres ahead of the stricken truck.

Some of the survivors were still whimpering, and while the platoon secured the area, the Platoon medic, Corporal Tarsisious and I, walked through the scene of carnage together. I stood and viewed the scene that surrounded me. Bodies and body parts were everywhere. Two people who had probably been in the cab, were completely without lower halves. A baby in a dusty soiled nappy had probably just regained consciousness, as its heart wrenching cries for its nearby dismembered mother, forced the tears down its dusty, chubby cheeks. A kneeling soldier, setting his rifle within reach, picked it up and comforted it.

A grey-haired old man was recovered from under the fallen maize sacks. Expectedly, he carried the evidence of the impact with the road, but his face was strangely peaceful and serene. More asleep, than dead…content with this, his lot. Others had evidently not had it at as easily as the old man, but all had died in a moment of surprised shock, and momentary terror, and it showed on some of the post mortem expressions.

I requested and had Bill and his platoon up to assist with the immediate care of the critically injured. The helicopters from Mount Darwin were only minutes away and I stood and watched how the medics were working. They were professional at every turn, but the underlying empathy was there, in plain sight. I tried to imagine myself dealing with white people in the same way. Innocents caught in an evil, politically driven web.

I shook my head to clear it and lit another cigarette.

HIGH STEAKS IN MURAMBINDA by Corporal Alan Doyle

An army marches on its stomach. Or not: think Delhi-Belly or the Rangoon Runs. The Cairo Two-Step. Nothing like that in the sweet waters of home, of course. Of course not.

Mid- April 1979 and a mass mobilisation was underway to protect rural polling stations in the first one-man-one-vote general election. 5 (Indep) Coy RAR, for its part, formed up in a long convoy at Addams Barracks, snaked its way through the suburbs of Umtali at the speed of a particularly zolled-up puff adder, and began its journey south-westwards through Derowa Mine to St Richards Mission, near Murambinda in Buhera District. "No Pookie", the 2 i/c Capt Jim Hill warned before we left. "It's broken down near Odzi." No-one took a blind bit of notice, of course. You're still a teenager (just), the sun is shining, and sitting on the back of a 4.5 is way better than walking.

Pit-stop just outside Derowa. (Piss-stop actually – the verge-side grass has probably still not fully recovered.) Remount the vehicles and off we set into the rural areas proper, on dirt roads that hadn't seen a grader for years. Convoy discipline looked good: drivers keeping in the same tyre tracks, decent slow-ish forward speed (Don't Go Too Fast – You Won't Miss the Blast), and views all round of the bucolic countryside: small kopjes bursting up amongst the villages and maize fields.

Talk about the "B" of the Bang. We were unbuckled and off the back of that 4.5, laying down prophylactic fire, before the truck had settled down into the vast hole which had appeared beneath it. There was no killing zone, thank goodness, so ceasefire was immediately yelled by the stick leaders on both sides of the road. Stock was taken.

Our 4.5 was new. Armour plate had only been fitted under the cab the day before, so the driver, a strange shade of white and unsteady on his feet, was thankfully unhurt, although his hearing probably didn't survive for very long. Mine didn't and I was further away than he was. The right front wheel was missing. I'm not sure where it went. The gearbox had been blown in its entirety, from front to back under the truck, emerging to bounce into the air and demolish the trailer which the 4.5 had been towing – and with it the platoon kit and sundry rations packed into it. And, I forgot to mention, our 1Pl 4.5 was second in the convoy.

Sticks were broken up and reassigned to other vehicles. It's amazing how a bit of bad luck hangs around like a bad smell: no-one wants a mine-magnet sitting next to them. I eventually found a berth on the MT 2.5, second last in the convoy, 11th from the front and statistically safe from further incident. One might even have laid money on it.

The next to last vehicle in the convoy was towing a mobile surgical unit – a large caravan filled with medical equipment, and lucky 13th in the convoy. I suppose it probably had different width axles than the vehicle towing it. Whatever. It disappeared into ten thousand bits: scalpels, syringes, and small shards of steel and aluminium flying around like shrapnel. How no-one was hit, I haven't the foggiest. But whatever small chance my hearing still had of surviving into my dotage disappeared in that second blast.

By now nerves were, you might say, a little on edge. The convoy was halted near a fork in the road, one branch of which bent away behind one of the now less-than-bucolic-looking kopjes. Pickets were sent out fore and aft and the sides of the road were scanned with unusual intensity by those left near the vehicles. Until some sudden movement to the front attracted the attention of everyone.

From around the hidden bend, in single file, came a group dressed in blue jeans and a variety of rakish and not-so-rakish headgear, and all carrying, in various casual attitudes, the familiar curved-magazine AK47. They were only saved from their immediate demise by their brown T-shirts which came fully into focus as they came closer. Phumo re Vanhu (the state-sanctioned militia of the soon-to-be government of Zimbabwe-Rhodesia), come to investigate the noisy neighbours.

...led by a Pookie, like the chief undertaker in a funeral cortege

We managed to find our assigned camp site, an abandoned former district office, but only after a second 4.5 hit a third mine. It was another 1Pl vehicle, who were in high dudgeon at being used as mine detectors. Sleeping pits were dug, with coverings of tree trunks to protect from mortar bombs that anyone might wish to lob in our direction. Signals were set up in the ruined district office, and a detachment was sent to the nearest business centre to buy a large consignment of steak, to restore morale and replace some of the lost rations.

There were no further incidents during that deployment. One splendid day was spent on the banks of the Sabi, bathing and establishing, by scientific method, that the purple ink used to identify those who had already voted was easily removed by the vigorous application of river sand. No-one stonked our camp: the local hoods must have been satisfied with the destruction they had already wrought.

And one-man-one-vote? Most of the men had been persuaded to boycott the poll, but for some reason their persuaders thought the new suffrage didn't extend to women.

And vote they did, in their thousands. Five days of polling returned a victory in that district for Muzorewa's UANC.

We did see our ruined 4.5 again. On the road back to Umtali, its wrecked remains were spotted being towed by a RhASC reco-truck. With both vehicles being led by a Pookie, like the chief undertaker in a funeral cortege.

But back to that steak. A braai hadn't been part of the plan, so the camouflaged-coloured woven-mesh radiator shields from the fronts of a couple of the MAPs were unscrewed to serve as grills. Wood was gathered, a fire was started, and the steak was delicious, even if it did have rather strange green and brown squares burnt into it when it came off the coals. And off we went to crash that first night.

Until just after midnight, when an urgent and severe stomach pain woke me up. After creeping over and around my companions and their curses in the sleeping pit, I reached the entrance and staggered out, to find a queue was rapidly forming at the door-less outhouse that stood in the middle of the district office compound. It wasn't the last visit I and many others made to that outhouse that night. So a new variant was added to the list of travellers' ailments: the Murambinda Shuffle.

(Many thanks to Major Jim Hill for filling in the land-mine-sized gaps in my memory.)

CHIMBAMBAIRA by Major Tom Fulton
(Adapted by the author from *Into the Vortex*)

Chimbambaira (Shona) n; sweet potato. (Or, a rather quaint nickname for an anti-tank landmine.)

It all started in November of 1976 in Mtoko. B Company 1RAR was redeployed to the northern parts of Inyanga in a follow up deployment to a massive kill in the Honde Valley by 3 Commando, 1RLI. After about ten days on framework operations, we were redeployed (again) to JOC Repulse in Fort Victoria, where we took part in Barnard's Circus.

Barnard's Circus was a High Density Force Operation in which the company started patrolling south from the Bikita area, and the large-scale sweep culminated on the banks of Bangala Dam, in the lowveld. Due to spend Christmas with our families, our R & R was suddenly cancelled – no explanations. If you can't take a joke...

From there we were sent down the famous Boli Road (known as Harper's Alley – the Minister of Mines at the time), in the extreme south east of Rhodesia. In spite of the massive convoy's being equipped with a mine-detecting Pookie, the 23rd vehicle in the convoy detonated a mine with no casualties. The vehicle belonged to a Territorial company. The brief was to cross the Mozambique border in a Fighting Patrol posture, and dominate, harass and kill.

After less than a week, we were regrouped and told that, from the extreme south east, we were to be moving to Binga – the opposite side of the country, on the shores of Kariba. The consolation was that we would at least overnight in Bulawayo – on New Year's Eve.

Moved from pillar to post, like some cumbersome chess piece, by the time we got to Binga, Bill Liversidge and I calculated that we had covered some 3 000kms since we had been deployed, two months before. Circus was an apt word for it, with little regard for the morale of the soldiers. (The orders came from high up; there was nothing that could be done about it.)

Arriving in Binga after a gruelling 600 km drive, my platoon was deployed with an almost indecent haste, to the ransacked National Parks camp at Chizarira; only to be recalled to Binga, before I was even able to deploy my patrols!

It seemed that when ZIPRA had sacked the Chizarira camp, they had abducted 3 National Parks game scouts, and one of them had walked into the Binga Police station. He was able to confirm intelligence that the ZIPRA commander had injured himself badly in a fall, when negotiating the downward step of the escarpment. The game scout could accurately indicate the camp. As usual, 5 Platoon was tasked with the dawn attack on the camp.

Planning the route in, it seemed that an old road would give us access to the area of the camp – we would drop off in the silent hours, some 10kms from the target and walk in. We would attack the camp at dawn. Piece of piss.

After giving very detailed orders – as detailed as was possible, considering that we still had to locate the camp positively, we enjoyed a hot meal and were on the road by 21h00. We retraced our steps towards Chizarira, passing the turn off and into the realm of Chief Siabuwa. The road I was looking for was little more than a track, and a light rain made its exact locality difficult to pinpoint. This was further exacerbated by the fact that the Roads Department had graded a swathe of soil from both sides of the road, in their endeavours to maintain the road surface. After over-shooting twice, I espied what looked like a gap in the trees and called a halt. Jumping off the vehicle, I carried out a detailed reconnaissance on foot. Locating the disused road that I sought, I beckoned to the vehicles to turn onto it.

From my close inspection, I reckoned that the road hadn't been used in months, if not years. It was now raining with a new purpose, far more than the weak drizzle we had been subjected to. As the truck drew level, I opened the door, and stepped up on the metal footplate, and sat down on the passenger seat of the cab. I realised that this was contrary to Standard Operating Procedures, but the rain and my cellophane covered map, coupled with the imperative necessity of having a drop off point that would mask the sounds of the vehicles, I chucked the rulebook out of the window. Nobody would lay a mine on this shit excuse for a road...

I placed my rifle across my lap, as I busied myself trying to locate the lap-straps of the safety belt. I believe I had both straps in my hands when we detonated the mine, with the wheel, over which I sat. To me, the bang was so loud as to be inaudible – beyond the capabilities of human hearing. I remember well, the blinding orange flash, and screaming at the top of my voice, DEBUS!

All around there was thick black smoke and dust, and I fumbled with the handle of a door that wasn't there.

Trying to get out of the vehicle was a priority as the dread of a simultaneous ambush crossed my mind.

Trying to take my weight on my left leg, I fell from the cab, into the massive crater left by the explosion. How I never landed on the dangerously jagged, mangled rim, which lay contorted in the smoking, gaping abyss, I will never know.

The engine was still running and racing. The accelerator cable had somehow become snarled, and I waited for long seconds as the ruptured fuel line spent what diesel was left in it. I tried to stand, and my left leg simply gave way under my weight. When I looked down and saw the impossible angle of my lower leg, I screamed, MEDIC!

I could hear the sounds of the voices of my senior NCOs. Quick to take hold of the situation, they were hastily organising the men into all round defence, and I was approached shortly by Corporal Peter Barclay Tarsisious – the Platoon medic – never have I been so happy to see him.

I asked after other casualties, and he reassured me that neither of the other two injured men were serious, and that they were being attended to. I unwound the tape from the morphine on my dog-tags and gave myself the injection out of the utile little toothpaste tube-like ampoule. The effect was instantaneous.

Out of the darkness loomed six and a half feet of Corporal Gumbo. He knelt down beside me and put his hand comfortingly on my shoulder. Corporal Tarsisious could be heard hewing a splint from a mopane sapling nearby – no mean feat, given the darkness that night. As mine had evidently succumbed, Gumbo's radio provided me with an insight into how my senior NCOs were consolidating the men, and arranging for casualty evacuation. They both joined us shortly.

2 Lt Tom Fulton

Tarsisious returned a few minutes later with the splint. He spent some time trimming and padding the crude pole with articles of clothing and said to me, I'm going to have to set that leg before I splint you Sir. It's going to hurt like hell, that's a promise, but I have to do it. Are you ready, Sir?

Soliciting the assistance of Gumbo and Sergeant Saul, Gumbo took a firm hold under my arms, and Saul held my left foot. At Tarsisious' command, Gumbo's Herculean strength forced the air from my lungs, as Saul pulled at my foot. The morphine completely deadened the pain, but the sound of the scraping, broken bone ends, was unnerving, to say the very least. Working quickly, the end of the splint was placed into my armpit, and my leg was secured top and bottom.

The medic then started bandaging my supposedly good leg, to the injured limb and splint ensemble. Thankfully, my arms escaped mummification, and I retained an infantryman's dignity, by holding onto my rifle!

As luck would have it, the Company Medic had left his stretcher on the back of one of my platoon vehicles – the result of being shipped all around the country at short notice. I was gently lifted onto it, and the litter was lofted to shoulder height, and I was transported to the undamaged vehicle.

My Shona was good enough to understand what the men were saying, and I was deeply touched. Overjoyed that I was alive, it seemed that they were more concerned about me leaving with the juju that had stopped anybody from 5 Platoon from ever being killed in action? They actually believed that I carried some form of witchdoctor-blessed talisman, and that without me, dismal times, apparently, lay ahead for them. It was true, that we had seen a lot of action together, as a Platoon, and to date had never buried one of our number.

I arrived at the Binga camp as the sun was paling the eastern sky. I could faintly hear the Islander aircraft circling the airfield and waiting for the light to improve enough to land. I realised that it would be a long time before I was able to lead these wonderful men again. We had grown into so much of a family, and we all loathed the thought of separation. I learned later that both of my legs had been broken, and by the Engineer's assessment of the crater, two mines had been laid on top of one another.

Many weeks passed in the Wankie Colliery and Bulawayo hospitals, before I was reunited with the fine men of 5 Platoon. In a halcyon storm, I hit the beerhalls and illegal shebeens of Luveve township with my NCOs…but that's another story.

OF PULL-SWITCHES, "SHATO NE VAVANDIRI ZVAKAWANDA" (OF PULL-SWITCHES, PYTHON AND AMBUSHES APLENTY) by Captain Russell Fulton

During our days 'touring' in the not-so-lush Rhodesian summer 'gangen' and keeping a beady eye out for Charlie Tango, there were many interesting things that we experienced and happened upon.

During one deployment in mid-1979, deep in the bowels of the Urungwe TTL, 3 Platoon, 1RAR was patrolling close to the eastern side of the Sanyati River whilst advancing in a north-westerly direction.

As one did, I called a halt around midday for a short rest and a brew. I chose a position on an elevated piece of ground, 'ground of tactical importance' in Rhodie army parlance, close to the river affording 360° observation and positioned my platoon in all-round-defence with sentries posted NE, E and SW with the Sanyati providing a natural obstacle to our west. I removed my pack and rested it against the base of a large 'Sausage Tree'.

I seated myself next to my para-bergen and as I lay my rifle next to me, my right forearm pressed against something taught. I knew, instinctively, what it was and cautiously looked sideways and saw a thin trip wire and followed its direction. Half obscured by a large tuft of grass was the unmistakable sight of an olive-green 'pineapple' of a POMZ-2. This was a Russian-made, stake-mounted, anti-personnel fragmentation mine.

There will be few who did not know about this 'bugger' and that would do far more than make your eyes water; weighing in at around 5lbs, with a fragmentation radius of +-50 yards, you would be lucky to escape a body bag if detonated! It was super sensitive with a pull switch that could be set from 0.5 – 6kg pressure. The Good Lord was looking out for me on this day and there is no doubt about that; the safety pin was almost free of its housing! Instead of trying to be 'too-clever-by-half' and pretend I was a 'Sapper' (Engineer) and safely rearm the thing, I became very shy of my surrounds and signalled to my men to move out with extreme caution.

As my men adopted patrol formation I looked about with different eyes and noticed several of them positioned haphazardly around the general area and noticed that one was tied to a branch at around waist height; the trip wire almost invisible to the untrained eye! Such were the "joys of life" as a 'Brown Job'; what we had to go through just to have a sip of "Tanganda, Tanganda…it's just your cup of tea!" without having a brand-new arsehole torn for you that is! In all my service I never came across another POMZ and that was a great comfort to me. Whoever had sighted these devices on this piece of ground were very 'switched-on' to Rhodesian forces modus operandi and it was an ominous sign.

POMZ-2 and "Shato"

A few days later, now eight days into the deployment, something quite unexpected happened. A local was spotted walking down a path so we hid and waited for him to come close to where we were concealed. One of my Section Commanders, Corporal Maumburidze Chipo, jumped up and grabbed him and tossed him unceremoniously to the ground, forced a face-veil in to his mouth and tied it securely behind his head with the veil forced between his teeth like a horse's bit. We took him some distance from the path and interrogated him. He told us what he knew about ZIPRA movements, their strengths, weapons and general dispositions in the area and where some weapons had recently been cached near our current position.

Suddenly, things were looking-up! We laid low for a couple of hours to make sure that he wasn't being followed or looked for and then told him to take us to the cache site. It must have been around 1600B when we arrived at the site and he pointed to what looked like a hole that a warthog would take up residence in. There was old spoor that indicated that that supposition was probable. Not wanting to upset my good Mother by returning home prematurely with assorted 'wart-pig' punctures, I ordered our captured 'comrade' to get his hand in the hole and to retrieve whatever had been pushed in. He was lying on the ground with his arm in the hole up to his shoulder and retrieved a few cases of 7.62mm short ammo, several RPG7 rockets and their boosters, a TM-46 anti-tank mine and was about to retrieve the next whatever it was when he screeched through his 'muzzle' (the face veil) like a terrified girl. I knocked him out with the butt of my rifle and by means of a swift blow to the temple because compromising us here wasn't part of the plan. I told two of my soldiers to pull him out thinking that the poor bugger had been stung by a centipede or scorpion. They struggled to pull him back by both ankles and then we saw what had caused him to squeal!

Attached to his forearm was a "Python sebae", more commonly known as a bloody big snake…it was, of course, a 'Shato' in the vernacular and to us arbitrary types, an African Rock Python! It had bitten him around his upper forearm near the elbow and had started wrapping itself around his arm to prevent him from getting away. When our 'comrade' was free of the hole, a whole lot of Shato still lay within, several meters of it in fact! It was a 'sekuru' but I wasn't about to allow this leviathan to crush and devour our hapless prisoner was I? The fangs had taken purchase of his forearm and were deeply embedded, and I wasn't about to do a 'Steve Irwin' trick and try to unravel it with my own fair hands (pardon the pun won't you).

Out came Rhodesian army standard kit issue, "Knives, Clasp for the use of" and I simply cut head from body. Whilst this headless 'thing' was twisting and writhing about the place in its death roll, I looked like I had been shot in the face with a shotgun at point-blank range from all the blood that had squirted all over me. I gingerly removed the severed head from his forearm and tossed it aside; much to the complete horror and revulsion of my *Masodja*. My medic gave him a shot of penicillin to stave-off infection, wrapped his arm in a bandage and then I woke him from his slumber with a splash of water over his face and a few slaps about the cheeks. He awoke and promptly fainted when he saw the remains of Shato's msoro (head). Tup, tup, tup!

I chuckled at the collective expressions of my good men; a mixture of fascination, horror and complete disbelief. My faithful and trusty batman, Private Emanuel Thomas Mukonweshuro, later shared with me privately that the men in my platoon had given me another nickname, 'VaShato' (Mr Python). I sent my OC a SITREP and he ordered me to withdraw to the nearest road for uplift with the prisoner and items recovered from the cache. Before we left, I tossed an M962 HE fragmentation grenade in to the hole to collapse it and render unstable anything that remained. Last-light was upon us and we moved off in the direction of the grid reference I had been given for our uplift, a good 20+ clicks away.

Before first light we stood-to and, when I gave the signal to 'stand down', we started cooking the remains of our rat packs for breakfast and in relays. I was certain I could smell 'nyama' cooking and my batman chuckled at my expression and asked me, "Waizoda kudya zvimwe Shato mangwanani Ishe?" (Would you like to eat some python for breakfast Sir?). Aiwa! Handidi! (No! I don't want!) I replied and we both laughed quietly. It seems my good men, despite being mortified by the goings-on of the previous evening, they remained carnivorous and well inclined towards eating 'fresh rations'; what good buggers they were.

A few hours later, at 'hurry-up-and-wait' time, my platoon vehicles arrived, and we had to take a circuitous route back to our Company TAC HQ. About an hour in to the journey we entered a section of road that was flanked by broken, elevated ground on either side and I was suddenly filled with a sense of foreboding and, instinctively, I knew something was about to happen. That 'little voice', my guardian angel or whatever one wishes to call it, 'spoke to me' and I had grown accustomed to hearing and implicitly trusting its 'messages'. This time it was cautioning me to be alert to a clear and present danger. I told my driver to slow down whilst I contacted my PWO in the vehicle to my rear on the small means telling him to 'stand by' for a joust.

Roughly 300 meters down the road the shit hit the fan…. BIG time! (I wrote about this in a missive in *Chibaya Moyo 1* so I won't bore you with it again) As we were negotiating a bend in the road, we got a fierce rev from a tactically well sighted ambush position. I shouted to my driver to put his foot down and to get us out of the killing ground. The armour plating of our MAP 7.5 was taking strikes from incoming fire. I shouted for the driver to halt so that we could debus and execute a vehicle anti-ambush drill; the vehicle halted abruptly as the radiator took a direct hit from an RPG7 from a second 'killing ground' about 30m away. This was a first for me being 'revved' in one killing ground and then being hit again in a second! These gooks had obviously gained experience and fully understood our vehicle anti-ambush "I.A." (Immediate Action) drills and had prepared thoroughly for them. (Read my earlier scribble for the details of this action).

I had the dubious misfortune of being ambushed several times during my service, but this was, by far, the most intense. How we never suffered injuries or a fatality remains a complete mystery to me to this today, such was the weight of fire directed at my two vehicles and its concentration. I put our survival down to the outstanding training that our *Masodja* had all received during their intensive recruit training at Depot RAR, the detailed and repeatedly rehearsed anti-ambush drills I put my men through and their repeated exposure to hostile fire. Above all these things was their preparedness, aggression and determination to close with and kill the enemy. That was the fighting spirit of the men of the RAR.

One of my life's greatest privileges was to have served with these men, to have earned their trust and their respect and to have fought shoulder-to-shoulder with them in battle. They placed their own unique measure on what boxes they required you to tick as their Ishe. If you did, they would do anything for you. I wasn't decorated, and I wasn't gung-ho either, but I think I qualified in their eyes. That's my medal. From a humble platoon commander's perspective, I can best sum-up my experience serving with these wonderful men with the title from a hugely popular song by James Taylor from way back in the day, "How sweet it is to be loved by you".

CHAPTER TWELVE

OBSERVATION POSTS

INTRODUCTION: OBSERVATION POSTS by Captain Andrew Telfer

'The essence of life is the smile of round female bottoms, under the shadow of cosmic boredom.'
Guy de Maupassant

What on Earth does that mean? Well you might ask. That and other questions of grave import occupied my befuddled mind as I sat on hills, many and various, counting mopane flies, during the better part of my early adult life.

When describing the Rhodesian Army tactic of Observation Posts (OPs), those two elements are omnipresent: cosmic boredom and mopane flies. Boredom came from spending days keeping still, not easy for fit young men, but let's talk first about *plebeina hildebrandti*, the mopane fly, a tiny stingless bee, native to Africa and, hardly surprising given its nuisance value, the only member of its genus. It loves moisture and yet chooses to live in dry savannah.

The stupid creature would die out through natural selection were it not for the moistness of the eyes, nose and mouth of soldiers on hills. It hovers in front of eyeballs and nostrils during the day and departs at night, when it hands over the field to mosquitoes. Don't swat it, as its dead scent attracts battalions of its brethren. *Plebeina h*'s constant presence, just in front of the eyes, produces a kind of madness in subalterns that often emerged during the next R&R in strange, sometimes inexplicable ways.

Leaving further discussion of *plebeina h.* to enliven the tea breaks of entomological conferences, and 'the smile of round female bottoms' to Maupassant's imagination, we can now focus on Observation Posts. Rhodesian soldiers of every regiment, with nothing in common except a profound desire to be somewhere else, spent large tracts of time on OP.

Their purpose was simply to get a sighting of terrorists, in order to introduce them to the Fireforce, kind of like match-making. We took turns in each role, OPs and Fireforce, and there was no doubt the latter was more popular. But, if ever the saying were true: 'If a job's worth doing, it's worth doing well' then it is especially true as applied to OPs. The terrorists knew of the tactic, knew that men in hills meant helicopters, the 'gun that speaks twice' (the K Car's 20 mm cannon), frantan (napalm) and lots of nasty soldiers. Unsurprisingly, they did everything they could to see and not be seen.

Successful OPs begin with good intelligence, not about the presence of terrorists as they were potentially everywhere and anywhere, but about their *transit routes*. If deployed across transit routes, a platoon commander can do a map appreciation to identify natural features that might funnel the enemy, villages to attract them and open ground to repel them. Then he could look for water on the map, for them and for us, and select positions for OPs, ideally only about 150 metres up a hillside and one to two kilometres from the target village.

To get there, requires a bit of a walk in the dark. There are golden rules for approaching an OP and they all come from understanding that it's a process of infiltration, not of getting from A to B. The ultimate success of the OP depends upon infiltrating covertly.

First, if it involves a vehicle drop-off, which must happen after dark and a long way from the target village; sound travels by night and word travels by day. Second, you must memorise the route before departure; if you need to use a torch to look at a map, you might as well stay at home. Third, no walking on paths, through fields or near villages; if you do, well… stay at home. Fourth, not a single sound or the village dogs will hear you and… you know. You must plot a route through the bush, where locals don't naturally go about their lives and you must be covert.

The thing about OPs is that you'll never know when you've compromised your presence; no-one will tell you, you just won't get a sighting.

Night navigation is like bowling in cricket; it's all about line and length. The total walk-in is broken into manageable legs. Each leg has a bearing (the 'line'), memorised and set on the compass so that the navigator can align and follow tiny fluorescent markers on the compass.

'Length' comes from counting paces. Walking carefully at night averages 130 steps per 100 metres. Carry ten beads on a loop of string, like worry beads, and move one each time you've counted 130 paces (or 65 right-foot steps if, like most junior officers, you can't count into triple figures) and, by the time you've flicked ten along the string, you've travelled one kilometre. Line and length: dead reckoning.

Other lines help too. A natural feature running parallel to the direction of travel, like the slope of a ridgeline, serves as a guideline, a kind of handrail.

Another feature, such as a river line, running across the direction of travel, offers a linear waypoint that supplements and verifies your measurement of distance travelled. Moving carefully like that at night is slow. The effective covert speed is less than two kilometres an hour so, if the walk-in is longer than 18 kilometres, it should sensibly be split over two nights. Long walk-ins are fine for other purposes but not for infiltrating onto OPs.

Once you've trod on enough gnarly roots, collected sufficient spider webs with your face to put on an arachnid display, and found every thorn bush in the district, you arrive at your hill feature. Now you must get up it. By then, first light may be only a short while away and, because so much depends on leaving no sign, you need every minute of available time. Softly, gently, quietly ascending, one foot at a time, pausing often to listen, unable to see the way, feeling for it until you're there.

While three soldiers crouch in all-round-defence, the commander selects two locations. The first is the exact position of the OP, the place where the village will be watched from. To avoid silhouette, it must be on the side of the hill, not the top. To prevent sunlight reflecting off binocular lenses, it needs thick bush above to create deep shade, but thin bush in front to see through. It needs covered access, rearwards to the second location, the laying-up-place. That must be in 'dead ground', ground that cannot be seen from the target village below. A laying-up-place is somewhere for those not in the OP to sleep, eat and rest.

Now, as the sun starts to rise, one soldier with binos is already concealed in the OP, while the other three are settled in the laying-up-place. In hourly cycles, from now until after last light, and all day the next day and the next, the men will covertly rotate in the OP. At night, the stick ambushes the route up to the OP in case someone comes calling.

What are they looking for? Terrorists may show themselves, they may move along the edge of the bush below, but that's unlikely. It's more likely that the OP will notice a slight change in the pattern of life in the village. So, they watch the village and allow themselves to be drawn into its rhythms. With RAR soldiers, children of this environment, it doesn't take long to get a feel for things. Usually, however... nothing happens, nothing changes, and the only companions are, you guessed it, cosmic boredom and mopane flies.

Then, an almost imperceptible change occurs: the OP sees food being cooked at an unusual time or perhaps in greater quantities. Why are they doing that? Why are they taking it into the bush? Where are the young women today? That rocky kopje behind the village...

Then the OP commander speaks softly into his radio to Company HQ: "Fetch Sunray". Shortly thereafter, the Fireforce lifts off.

COMMENTS ON OBSERVATION POSTS by Captain Russell Fulton

My experience in the art of OP deployments was not without repeated early failure. Everything that Andy's erudite articulation conveys to the reader may be regarded as a mirror of every other man's experiences in our army who was ordered to take up temporary residence on gomos various. This tactic was an extension of the RAR soldiers' being and the more we did it, the more proficient and adept we became.

Within a very short time, I realised that my NCO's and men were my best teachers as they had an inherent quality in them, that we 'snow white' types lacked, and that was a comprehensive intuition of what constituted typical day-to-day rural village routine. Without this one would flounder where others excelled. There was occasionally a sprinkling of luck but, and more often, success was measured by tactical awareness, thorough preparation and execution of one's orders.

Many was the call-sign that humped-off in to the dark without thorough preparation, cuffed orders and, with that, a flagrant disregard for security. To be compromised was a blight on one's record and, more importantly, a reckless neglect for the very welfare of the men under one's command. Everything we did, everything we said and every action we took was always under scrutiny by our men, it was a continuous litmus test of our worth as their Ishe.

In mid-1979 I was withdrawn from operations in Op Hurricane to attend the first O.P. Specialist Course held at the School of Infantry. This was an excellent initiative and the course was led by two outstanding Selous Scouts operators, WO2 Pete McNeilage SCR (the first member of the RLI to receive this award) and Sgt Rangarirayi 'Ringo' Hungwe SCR, BCR.

Fortuitously, I was grouped with the latter when we went NO DUFF and deployed on intelligence from SB about the presence of a group of CT's in the Chironde Range west of the Selukwe TTL. Everything that Andy has shared about battle procedure, preparation and leading to the deployment and operation of the OP was executed precisely as he has narrated it.

Whilst sharing watch with Sgt Hungwe I noticed an almost imperceptible shift in his demeanour, it was akin to a Puff Adder about to strike at an unsuspecting rodent. I followed the line of his binoculars and, with my own, surveyed the ground ahead. A lone woman was emerging from some heavily vegetated bush with several pots. There was no river line anywhere nearby that would suggest she had been washing. There were gooks in that thicket who had recently been fed.

He contacted McNeilage and we moved to the rear of our position and dog-legged around towards the sighting. McNeilage moved in the opposite direction to deploy his call-sign as a stop group. We approached the camp and sure enough, there were gooks. We engaged and killed three of the five who had been there. No Fireforce support and no 'top cover'; it was basic soldiering at its best.

Every deployment required comprehensive analysis and detailed planning and this course demonstrated the full benefit of that. Rehearsals of every conceivable sort were conducted, and every man knew precisely what role he was expected to play. Short-cuts were folly and dangerous and I learnt from the best in the business. Do it right first time, every time and leave nothing to chance.

RAR OBSERVATION AND INTERPRETATION by Major Michael P Stewart

RAR soldiers proved themselves capable of every task they were ever asked to do. They participated in Fireforce, limited external operations, extended patrols in the bush, and airborne operations. They earned respect for their loyalty, spirit and discipline. But they truly found their strength patrolling the bush, working with the local population, and manning Observation Posts (OPs) for extended periods.

They were much more patient and attuned to local customs than their RLI counterparts. In one example, an RAR soldier on an OP with an officer observed three women walking down a path towards a village, one of whom was carrying a suitcase. The white officer thought nothing of it, but the black soldier said, "Ishe, the one with the suitcase is a terrorist."

"How could you possibly know?" asked the officer.

"She is carrying the suitcase in her hand. Our women carry things on their heads."

A patrol caught up to the 'women,' who were in fact insurgents dressed as women walking into a village. This was the strength of the RAR as a counterinsurgent force. They knew the tribes and customs and could instantly spot what was out of place.

On another occasion, a group of male civilians, walking along, was spotted from a distance. The RAR OP pointed out one of them as an insurgent, even though at first glance nothing distinguished him from the rest of the men. He was picked up, however, and found to be carrying an AK concealed beneath his coat. When quizzed, the RAR soldiers said that they knew he was an insurgent as he swung only one arm when walking (the other held the weapon against his body).

The ability of RAR soldiers to notice and blend into the culture around them, obviously, came from the fact that they grew up in the same culture they were observing. This fact, however, was not always to their advantage, especially when their identity as RAR soldiers was revealed to insurgents operating near their family homes.

Source:
Stewart, Michael P 1998, '*The Rhodesian African Rifles, The Growth and Adaptation of a Multicultural Regiment through the Rhodesian Bush War, 1965–1980*', US Army Command and General Staff College, p. 75.

MY FIRST CONTACT by Private T Chitapo, Sp Coy, 1RAR

It was in October 1977 when we went to operate in the Victoria Province, based at Fort Victoria airstrip. We spent two days there before the whole platoon was deployed into a certain Tribal Trust Land. That same night we went into OPs waiting for the following day's movement in the area. My stick, under the command of Corporal Mukanga, went to a high feature near a mission where we expected to see the enemy after first light.

Butch Zeederberg

As we expected, early the next morning, we saw a terrorist running from the mission school to a nearby hill. Before our commander had a chance to report the sighting, call sign 53C, under Corporal Chesango, reported that they had seen five more in the area that the first terrorist was see running to. The incident was reported, and we were told that the Fireforce would be overhead in 30 minutes. Our call sign prepared everything, adjusting our pouches, packing our rations;

ready for anything since we knew we were going to be called upon first as we were the nearest call sign to the scene.

Soon we were ordered to descend from our hill and prepare a landing zone. Without wasting time cutting down trees, we ran to some nearby fields. Corporal Mukanga talked the helicopter onto our position, we emplaned and were taken to the other side of a thick hill feature where the terrorists were. We were the fourth stop group.

Later, more support arrived, and SAS troopers were dropped. The contact continued, and we were ordered to sweep the area. We moved through the thick hillside and I was a little afraid as I had never seen a terrorist before.

When we finished sweeping, we found that we had killed four terrorists and captured two. All their weapons were recovered. Our OC, Major Zeederberg, was very pleased to hear of our success and he prepared a merry party for us. Much experience was gained from the scene, and I discovered that these people can die easily and without hesitation.

Source: *Nhowo*, April 1978.

THE CROCODILE 'GARWE' by Lieutenant Noel Smith

Below our position, the glistening waters of the river beckoned invitingly. It was late October and two sticks of RAR soldiers were sharing OP duties on a hill feature in the Masoso TTL in NE Rhodesia overlooking the Ruya River, a renowned route for terrorist gangs as they entered Rhodesia from their bases in neighbouring Mozambique.

The heat at this time of year was unrelenting and we anxiously awaited the arrival of the rainy season. The storm clouds would slowly build up during the day and then frustratingly disappear before dusk. We were hot and getting low on water supplies and the ever present mopani flies did little to ease our discomfort.

It was now time to move our position further downstream closer to the border with Mozambique and this meant crossing over the river to the northern side. We could thankfully replenish our water supplies as we made the journey and I looked forward to having my fill.

We made our way down to a suitable river crossing point and as I cautiously broke cover near the river's edge, I was startled by a sudden movement, followed by a large splash as I spied a fairly large crocodile launch itself from a nearby sandbank and into the water.

Trying to calm my racing heart I turned to see my Platoon Warrant Officer with a large grin on his face as he chuckled at my sudden fright. I do not like crocodiles at the best of times. It's their prehistoric malevolent grin with their explosive attack and primeval killing methods that send a cold shiver down my spine. Such is their fear of the crocodile that the African tribesman would also refer to a lightning bolt from a thunderstorm as the 'garwe' in the sky. Death from a lightning strike can be as swift and as unexpected as an attack by a crocodile.

As the soldiers took their turn to fill their water bottles, I conferred with my Warrant Officer on how we could best cross the river especially as there was now a very unwelcome presence in the water. We chose a point where the water was relatively shallow and as I took my first tentative steps, my Warrant Officer who was wading right behind me, cheerily remarked that he now had nothing to fear from the crocodile for it was a well-known fact that the 'garwe', when given the choice, always preferred European meat!

AS THE SUN SETS IN THE WEST by Captain Andrew Telfer

In early 1978, Bruce Thompson and I were sent from 2RAR to attend an Anti-Tank course at the School of Infantry in Gwelo. Apart from anti-tank tactics and armour recognition, the course centred around training to instruct in the 106mm recoilless rifle, Rhodesia's anti-tank weapon. Each battalion of infantry included an Anti-Tank Platoon in its Support Company, equipped with that weapon.

"Scratch the paint and you'll see they're sand-coloured underneath", remarked an instructor, enigmatically hinting at their Middle East origin. Out of necessity, sanctions-hit Rhodesia purchased its weapons from many strange and dubious sources.

The following year, when the position was next vacated, I was posted out of D Company and into Support Company. I was so attached to the members of 10 Platoon that I was sad and reluctant to be leaving them. My callsign changed from 41 to 73 and, with it, my comrades.

Generally speaking, the Support Company soldiers were slightly better-educated than those in the rifle companies, selected as such because of the extra learning associated with support weapons. However, in 2RAR, they were less-experienced in combat, as Support Company hadn't done Fireforce, greatly reducing their exposure to contacts.

My own exposure didn't stop as I continued to be detached to other companies when they were on Fireforce, especially to D and B, and to Lieutenant Colonel Hammond when he commanded a combined Fireforce. It was unfortunate that I couldn't take members of my new platoon with me as it would have been good development for them.

In the few months that we were together, I enjoyed the men of the Anti-Tank Platoon and was interested in using the added operational capability provided by the 106s. For example, on one occasion we were deployed as a platoon for six weeks into an area that had a very strong terrorist presence, so much so that Police and Internal Affairs vehicles were almost certain to be ambushed if they entered it. The terrorist commander in this area was the very famous Fastmover (his

Chimurenga name, like a nom de guerre) who I'd often heard of but never, to my knowledge, fought.

I asked my Company Commander, Major Noel Morgan-Davies for permission to take the 106s with us and he approved it. As a platoon, we walked into the area, clearing and dominating the road, along which followed a land-tail of our Unimog 2.5s with the 106s mounted. Once in the centre of the general area, we selected a dome-shaped, grassy feature as our platoon base. That day, we sited and dug in the recoilless rifles and picked a target.

About a kilometre away, and slightly below us, we could see quite a large village, behind which stood a rocky kopje. Fairly typical of Zimbabwe, erosion had removed the soil around stacks of boulders, leaving them with the appearance of balancing rocks. We selected a huge rock, perhaps half-a-car in size, 'balancing' on top of another.

In the late evening, Private Shunje, acknowledged as the best 'Number One' in the platoon, aimed and fired the 12.7mm spotting rifle at that boulder. The spotting rifle is coaxially-mounted with the 106, enabling the gunner to aim, fire and make adjustments with the smaller weapon, before firing the main armament. In this case, he hit dead centre so we left it as ready.

Much later that night, after the inhabitants of the village were long asleep, we fired a 106mm High Explosive Anti-Tank (HEAT) round, knowing that it would fly straight at the boulder, unseen in the darkness. We heard a huge bang and, the next morning, the boulder was gone, shattered and toppled from its perch. Why did we do this? Rocks like that have spiritual significance to African people. That one would have stood like a sentinel over that village since the beginning of human memory. We were announcing our presence and our challenge to those who thought the area was under control of others.

For the next six weeks, we patrolled the area, moving tactically on foot from village to village, helping the civil authorities re-establish normality through things like organising the dipping of cattle or getting kids to go to school. We searched the kopjes and found plenty of evidence of terrorist camps, all empty, and I left lots of notes to the ZANLA commanders, especially Fastmover, translated into chiShona by my soldiers, challenging them to come out and fight. For example, on a dip tank: "We are going to be dipping cattle on Thursday. If you want to stop it, be here." Often, we added our insults and abuse but there was never any response.

Fastmover wasn't stupid, he knew he was fighting a guerrilla war, in which you avoid hard conflict and pick soft targets, but I worked in the hope that I could get under his skin and provoke a reaction. This was a strange operation, very different from the kind of action experienced at D Company but nevertheless relevant and useful in that it restored authority over the land in a classic 'military support to the civil power' scenario. Realistically, though, after we departed, I'm quite sure the terrorists returned.

Some months later, Support Company was based at Shabani (modern-day Zvishavane). Evenings with Major Morgan-Davies always included a few beers and he would use each round to toast the departing day: "As the sun sets in the west, we say farewell to yet another day in God's own country". Gradually, as the rounds progressed, he'd become a little disorientated and, when he declared "As the sun sets in the south..." we knew it was time for bed. He was a very amiable and sociable man, nicknamed '*Cokes*' by his fellow subalterns at 1RAR for his habit of rehydrating with Coca Cola the mornings after the night before and '*Tamba wa Guta*' by the African soldiers, '*Plays When Full*'.

He was a very good sportsman, having played high-level rugby, cricket and even basketball, which had to be seen to be believed as he was only about 1.7 metres tall. A heavy-smoker, he would dribble the basketball with blinding speed and dexterity, set up a score and then collapse on a side-line chair to get his breath back. A kind man and a very knowledgeable support weapons officer, he was a pleasure to serve under.

Among the BSAP contingent at Shabani was an Inspector with an ancient porn movie. One evening, while our OC's sun was still setting fairly close to the west, he brought it to show us, using an equally ancient, flickering projector and several spools of film. It took a while and several beers to set up, by which time the sunset was north-west and Major Colin Hendrie, OC B Company, based then at Belingwe, was on the radio. Someone had told him about the 'training movie' and he was offering beers and a braai if we brought it there. So we did, about an hour's drive through the operational area, in a police vehicle driven by our policeman/projectionist.

The following day, the good Inspector visited us again, this time to say that there was a terrorist group, including a senior commander, currently active in the villages between Shabani and Mashaba (now, Mashava). After consideration, the OC decided that my platoon was to be dropped at a road/river junction north-east of Shabani, infiltrate the area and establish Observation Posts (OPs).

The only problem with that was the ground appeared to be almost featureless: extensive cultivated fields, many villages, but hardly any hills for OPs to hide and observe. We discussed it and agreed that I'd take only seven men with me, two sticks of four, as a full platoon would almost certainly compromise itself.

That night, we set off. It was moonless, overcast and, as Major Morgan-Davies said: "Black as a witch's tit". Without any topographical features to assist, it was necessary to follow compass bearings only and calculate distance-travelled by counting paces. The process of following bearing and distance is called 'dead reckoning'. It's easy without obstacles but is made progressively more complicated if something forces you off course. Then, you have to box around the obstacle to regain your line on the other side of it. If you don't exactly regain the line, you end up walking on the correct bearing but side-stepped to one side or other of where you should be.

That night, there were cultivated fields and villages everywhere, each one an obstacle to be bypassed. Those villagers lived all their lives in that habitat, a home range that was completely familiar to them. If we left any sign of our passing, they would see it in the morning. We worked patiently and carefully, me plotting bearings around the habitation using the tiny fluorescent markers on the compass and my soldiers finding places for our feet that would not leave spoor.

After midnight, as my pacing was telling me that we'd gone too far, I began to sense a glow in the sky far ahead, indicating habitation with electric lighting. In modern suburban areas, street lighting is everywhere and the night sky glows in every direction. In rural Rhodesia in the 1970s, a glow indicated a small town and it could only be Mashaba. I realised with a sigh that I had side-stepped my line and walked past the OP. We considered what to do and agreed that we were confident we hadn't been compromised: no dogs disturbed, no tracks left by crossing fields or paths, no locals encountered. We were in a rare patch of thick bush, so we decided to hide there for the day, figure out where we were and return to our OP the following night.

The day passed uneventfully, just lying doggo, maintaining radio silence, not cooking or smoking but watching the world around us. The only people that we saw were women working in a field, quite far from us and they didn't see us. I worked out where we were, only a short distance from the OP and, that night, we set off again. We arrived after only about an hour and crept up a small hill, slowly and carefully, listening and waiting, before separating into two sticks near the top, each to observe in a different direction. There wasn't much vegetation on that hill so it took quite a while to find a suitably covered site for my OP but, by the time first light came, we were well-hidden and observing the awakening world.

Around mid-morning, Corporal Nkomo, commanding our other stick, whispered into his radio that he had a sighting of terrorists. He wasn't sure how many but confirmed that he had seen weapons. I reported the sighting to Major Morgan-Davies at Company HQ and was told to stand by. While I waited, I tried to move towards Nkomo's position so that I could see the terrorists and do the Fireforce talk-on, but the bush was much too sparse. It was all on him.

I spoke softly to him on the radio, revising his voice procedure and helping him find the right words to describe what he was seeing. Then the K Car pilot called us. They had been very quick and were on their way in. The Fireforce troops were from 2RAR and their commander was Captain Jean Vos. I was glad of that because I'd called him out before and knew him to be patient and clear with African NCOs who are, after all, speaking a second language in a high pressure situation.

Corporal Nkomo's talk-on was accurate and effective, and soon the Fireforce was engaged. I could still see very little, only the occasional orbiting chopper or the passing Lynx, listening instead to the contact develop as the sticks were dropped and moved about on the ground. We prepared ourselves to be ready if called but we weren't required. I regret that I cannot remember how many terrorists were taken out that day but they included a capture: the senior commander that we'd been sent to find. Afterwards, the choppers uplifted our two sticks and flew us back to Shabani.

There, I went to report to Major Morgan-Davies who was very happy. He asked me what had happened the previous day when nothing had been heard from us. I explained about my navigation error and how I'd missed my target OP, laid up for the day and come in through the back door this morning. Just then, Captain Ed Fouche BCR, 2i/c Support Company, came into the Ops tent.

Ed Fouche was a very good soldier, a former RLI NCO who was one of the earliest recipients of the BCR in the Rhodesian Army. He was a hard man, very tough and difficult to get along with. This morning though, he was very friendly, shaking my hand and complimenting me on "taking two nights to infiltrate... so many people get it wrong and think it's a rush to get in... they're missing the point... the way you did is right... well done Andy". I opened my mouth to explain but saw Major Morgan-Davies wink and shake his head.

That evening, as the sun set in the west, our kind and sociable Company Commander, who enjoyed his sundowners with his subbies, quietly explained: "Take the good breaks when they happen, Andy". As a Lieutenant Colonel, he would one day become the last Commanding Officer of 2RAR.

INCURSION by Corporal Tony Faulkner

Wading the Limpopo River at night is not many people's idea of fun, and it was certainly not mine, nor the other NCOs and the RAR soldiers that we had in our sticks, as most of them could not swim. This we found out when we first joined with the RAR troops at Llewellin Barracks in November 1977. The Company all went to the Llewellin pool for a swim one afternoon, and as all the RAR troops jumped into the water, a couple of them started flailing around and we realised that they could not swim. They were quickly helped out, much to the amusement of their comrades.

We were with 1 (Indep) Coy RAR, initially based in Victoria Falls then, in the mid to latter part of 1978, we moved to Beit Bridge, which had to be the armpit of Rhodesia. Apart from operating in Fireforce, most of our 'work' involved patrolling and OPs, two-week stints (resupply after one week).

On one operation, our orders were to move into a 'no go area' under the cover of darkness by travelling in closed SADF trucks into South Africa, then being dropped off and crossing the Limpopo River at a certain point, then walking to our designated OP positions on gomos 20 to 25 kms away.

We collected our rat packs, ammo, maps etc., jumped on the SADF trucks and were taken into South Africa, over the bridge. We drove for several hours sneaking the occasional peak at 'civilisation' through a gap in the canvas covers. We were eventually dropped off close to the river on the South African side, at a supposed crossing point. By now it was dark - this was to be an *incursion into our own country*.

I and the other stick leader stripped to our shorts, leaving our rifles and kit with our men (in case we ended up swimming) and proceeded to wade into the river, to check that we could cross safely. There was no moon; however, the stars provided enough light so that we could see where we were heading. Initially the water was up to our knees but as we got closer to the opposite bank it started to get deeper and we ended up in chest deep water. As it was getting deeper there was a large splash, we nearly jumped into each other's arms, and thoughts of crocodiles were now very prevalent in our minds!

The crossing point turned out to be okay, so we returned to our sticks, still waiting on the South African bank. After some gentle persuasion that the crossing was OK, the RAR guys came up with a cunning plan to get across without getting our kit wet, and without being weighed down. They joined several bivvies together, wrapping our packs inside them, and turning them into two rather clumsy rafts. Dressed in just shorts, rifles held high and dragging the floating cargo behind us, we carefully crossed the river. It worked, nothing wet apart from our shorts, and the journey across the river went without mishap.

Once on the bank, we got dressed, sorted our kit and headed off north, walking together, in file, initially within touching distance as it was dark under the big trees near the river. As we moved from the riverside vegetation into shrub land, we were able to space out a bit more. We stopped every hour for a break and to check the map and compass, which was done in a donga.

The first OP gomo was reached at midnight, and the one stick peeled off to climb it, whilst we continued towards our gomo. Although it was now getting late and we were starting to tire, we kept moving quietly, at a slow steady pace.

A VOICE FROM THE GRAVE by Captain Joe Columbus Smith

Was it God's hand that led an RAR patrol to a miracle, or just a one in a million lucky discovery by this subbie when he tried to muddle his way out of a bungled mission? Either way.... what began as a mundane patrol ended in a 'needle in a haystack' discovery that warmed our hearts and made us proud to be in the Rhodesian African Rifles.

Scenario: Captain Lionel Dyck, Company Commander C Company 1RAR, orders me to deploy that night into an adjoining Tribal Trust Land (TTL) with my soldiers, and be in position at first light to observe the TTL from a perch high atop a small mountain. He, very specifically, marked that 'gomo' on my map. From there we were to look with our binoculars for armed terrorists... come off the mountain and engage them of course. Seems easy enough. Find the mountain and be atop it at first light.

It is so long ago - 41 years - I cannot remember the name of the TTL or even the names of any of about a dozen fine RAR soldiers that I was lucky enough to command that night. But I do remember a number of unusual things about this particular mission, perhaps because I screwed it up! For one thing the night march in was about twice as long as it normally is. The terrain was pocked with a large number of hills called gomos.

They were cone shaped structures, but only the ones that were 50 feet or taller were actually shown on the topo maps we used. So, there were a lot of 49 footers that simply did not appear on the map.

CSM Jonah Chitereka and Capt Joe Columbus Smith

Just after dark I launched the patrol, and we were quickly engulfed in a misty soup, called 'guti' in Southern Africa. It is finer than rain but a little courser than a fog.... but just as blinding. I could barely see twenty feet. We slogged on, but we never found my gomo, of course bypassed it in the guti. I finally halted the exhausted patrol for the night and next morning awoke very early in just a bit of panic. It was a very clear bright day, and there we were, exposed! And the clock was ticking. But I was not about to call Capt Dyck and tell him that I had lost the Observation Post (OP) in the guti. Not yet!

I called over my very able platoon sergeant Wilson (Willie for short), and together we scoured the map and figured out where we were. "Hey sergeant, do you remember any old terrorist base camps around here?" This sergeant had a sensational memory and, on an earlier patrol in a different TTL, he recalled a water source he had not been to in five years. It seemed as though every step he had ever taken was engrained on his memory. "Yes, Ishe, I do!"

Well off we went, but with a plan. I picked out 'stop group positions on the back side of the terror camp, and then led the remaining troops in an assault line right over the top. We assaulted through the old camp but found no-one. I then sent out a patrol to do a complete 360 around the old camp. Within a minute I heard a crackle on my radio. "Sunray 2. I hear voices from the ground!'

He was very excited, and I quickly joined him. The soldiers had formed a circle near the base of a giant ant hill. There was a large bed of rocks through which a very distressed voice was calling for help in a voice ever so faint. It was a very spooky moment and for a moment we all stepped back. I then gave the order to start pulling the rocks out of the hole. The rocks were as large as grapefruits and, after three feet of digging, we found a very old man very much alive. He was slightly bloodied but otherwise okay. He was overjoyed to have been rescued.

The Communist terrorists, trained by the red Chinese had captured him, accused him of being a 'sell-out' (anyone assisting the Government), dug a hole and threw him in it. They threw the large stones on top of him and, by some miracle, the rocks were just big enough to let air reach him.

Immediately I called Sunray 1 – Capt Dyck and told him the good news. He was thrilled and quickly sent the BSA Police to pick up the old man and give him safety. Capt Dyck graciously NEVER asked me how this all happened, and I didn't fill him in. He was a very proud RAR company commander that day and the rest of us were chuffed as well.

And, YES, I have often wondered if God's hand swept that guti blackout over my long night patrol, preventing me from seeing the OP gomo. Did he make me ask the platoon sergeant about old terror camps? God only knows! This subbie and that unearthed old man were the two luckiest guys in Rhodesia that day.

ABIAS MASHONA, SUPPORT COMPANY 1RAR AND THE MAVURADONHA by Captain Mike Jones

I am not sure if this took place in late 78 or 79 but as it was dry, I would presume it was mid-79.

Captain Kevin Johnson was OC of Support, and the whole company had been deployed to Mt Darwin. We were tasked with setting up OPs in the Mavuradonha mountain range overlooking the TTL, facing north toward Mukumbura and Mozambique. The TTL was classified as liberated by the CTs and our task was to identify and engage with whatever means available. We had, in direct support, a Lynx, we presumed Fire Force, and later artillery.

The company did the normal 20 to 25 km night walk in, after being dropped off by vehicle and by mid-morning my platoon, the 106mm anti-tank platoon and the rest of the company were in position. Kevin Johnson had set his command centre on a prominent mountain and the whole of Support Company had broken up into 4 man sticks and were deployed across the whole range of the Mavuradonha mountains. My platoon, as well as other platoons, had a number of new recruits from Balla Balla.

The first few days were quiet with no activity apart from the odd stray cattle ambling about, but things rapidly changed on day three. I was sitting having a cup of tea, dog biscuits, and bully beef, when I noticed one of the new recruits, leopard crawling towards me. As he got close to me, he suddenly stood up, came to attention, and gave me an immaculate salute, and bellowed, "Ah have therty Ters visual Sah."

I nearly put a dot on my underpants. After explaining to him that there was no need for formal procedure while on ops, I went to take a look for myself. Sure enough there were a group of CTs in the fringe line of trees, just before the start of the abandoned cultivated lands. I reported the sighting and Abias Mashona BCR, my platoon Warrant Officer, confirmed the sighting from his position. We sat back, observing the Ters, and waited and waited for FF to appear. Nothing. Fire Force was not available and had been deployed elsewhere and the light was fading fast.

The next morning, lo and behold, the gooks were still in the vicinity and, again, no FF was available. Abias had a better view of the group, and he had a long distance tripod telescope. He explained that the gooks had some recruits with them and were giving them weapons training on the PPSH, a small machinegun similar to the Sten gun, but of Soviet make. This was too much to bear and, as FF was still not available, I requested and was granted permission to collect together two sticks and go down and see if we could make contact with them. Abias was to be my eyes and talk me onto their position.

I collected my stick and two others and we set off down towards the gooks' position. The bush was pretty thick and we walked carefully and slowly to where we thought the position was. I radioed Abias and gave my locstat and he confirmed I was right at the gooks' position, but that he did not have me visual. There were cattle around and there was a lot of noise towards my east, which I presumed was animal. We moved towards it only to be told by Abias that the gooks had broken out from the tree line and were heading north toward Mozambique. We came across the gooks' position where they had rested. We had been less than 50 metres apart, and what I had presumed was animal noise was the gooks moving out.

Abias confirmed that there were 40 plus in the group. He then told me he had us visual and that we should remain in the tree line, as the group was being joined by another group of similar size. This happened again, as two more groups had joined on what, I now presumed, to be a re-supply run into Mozambique. With that number of gooks, I was suddenly not so keen to catch up.

Sunray instructed me to follow at a safe distance and, with Abias as my eyes, we managed to stay about half a kilometre behind, and then the radio crackled. It was Abias. "Sah they heve spotted you and are settin up an ambush." We stopped, retreated a kilometre and found a prominent anthill for cover and set up our three MAGs in the direction of the gooks, knowing Abias had us covered visually. Again no FF.

After some time, Abias let me know that the gooks were on the move, still heading north and getting close to the Mozambique border. Abias had sent me the locstat of the ambush position, which had been on a dry river bed with some tree cover. We gave this position a wide berth and were soon back on tracks. Abias estimated the group, with recruits, was over 200 in number and they had increased their pace and were moving rapidly north towards Mozambique. Sunray, in the meantime, was desperately trying to get FF or some form of air support. It was a golden opportunity that was soon to go to waste.

Well the inevitable happened and we walked into the back of the group, and all hell broke loose. We took cover and started returning fire. Fortunately for us the gook fire was very high and not effective. As with most contacts with ZANLA, we did not have to win the fire fight, but the noise fight, and with this in mind, we opened up with all three MAGs and fired all our rifle grenades.

I was onto my last magazine when I noticed the recruit lying next to me, the saluter, had eyes like dustbin lids and had not fired one round. I shouted at him to throw me his magazines and continued to return fire. Finally, a Lynx appeared and once we had marked our position, did a bomb and machine gun run. Abias continued to direct the Lynx onto various targets and all went quiet.

We swept through the contact area, and apart from one dead Terr, shot by his own people by the looks of the bullet wounds, some equipment and blood spore, we could find no other casualties.

Once we had swept through and secured the area, I called for the new recruit and asked him, very sternly, why he had not opened fire. His reply was a classic and a reflection on his strict, disciplined training at Balla Balla. "Aye was waiting for u to give the order to open fire Sah." What could I say, the fault was mine!!

The rest of the deployment was similar, many sightings but no air support, as FF was deployed and engaged elsewhere. In the end we had to call on artillery for support and once again Abias was involved in spotting and calling in the artillery support. A frustrating bush trip!

A TALE OF TWO SUBALTERNS by Captain Andrew Telfer

This story blends two accounts of the same incident to illustrate the interdependence of OPs and Fireforce, and the difficulties faced by OPs.

During October 1979, two former soldiers, employed as farm guards to prevent cattle rustling, walked into a group of more than a hundred terrorists on Wanezi Ranch, Section 7. In the brief firefight that took place before the two guards could get away, one of them, Andy Davies, earned the unique distinction of being wounded four times by one round (it passed across his buttocks: left buttock entry wound and exit wound, right buttock entry wound and exit wound). He received much ribbing and little sympathy for his troubles, but an incursion of this size got the attention of Comops. This was big cattle country and the vast herd across the Wanezi-Nuanetsi area was of Forex-earning, strategic importance to Rhodesia.

As a result, B Coy of 2RAR, under command Maj Colin Hendrie, was sent to base up on the airstrip adjacent to the home of Wanezi ranch manager Bob Gawler. Bob was an interesting man, fearless in his commitment to lead a normal life and run his ranch properly. Although he knew that the RAR presence was temporary and that he and his family would in time be left without our protection, he unhesitatingly used his local knowledge and fluency in isiNdebele to help us interrogate captives.

The RAR soldiers liked and respected him. From this company HQ, B Coy was ordered to deploy OPs into the adjacent Maranda TTL, believed to be the home of a resident terrorist group and a major transit route for terrorists targeting the ranching areas. One of the Platoon Commanders was 2Lt Terence Hewitt, only commissioned in February of that year.

On the day that Hewitt arrived at Wanezi to receive his orders, another 2RAR officer, Lt Andy Telfer was across the South African border, just completing a week with B Coy, 1 Para Bn (the 'Parabats') with Lt Col Terry Hammond and RSM Lou Hallamore.

South Africa had extended its support to the provision of Parabats and Lt Col Hammond had been tasked with orientating this Coy to Fireforce tactics. He worked with the Parabat Coy Comd, Capt Johann Blauw, briefing him on how an OP would call out a Fireforce; talk it onto a target; how to deploy the sticks and control them; how to make use of the air weapons; and how to uplift and re-deploy.

Telfer worked with the stick commanders, including the NCOs and the three subalterns, 2Lts Loffie Eloff, Steinkie Stein (imaginative nicknames) and Richard Breytenbach, son of the legendary Colonel Jan Breytenbach. He taught them what to expect in a Fireforce operation and what to do. This training was extended by RSM Hallamore to all the members of the Coy. Except for the OC and the most senior NCOs, they were all National Servicemen, very fit and very proud.

As Hewitt prepared to deploy, Lt Col Hammond gave orders for the entry of the Parabats into Rhodesia at dawn the following day. A land-tail had already departed, vehicles carrying extra troops, and towing stores trailers and fuel bowsers. In the air, there would be two K Cars; he would fly in one and Capt Blauw in the other. Telfer and Hallamore would take off slightly later in the much faster Pumas, three of them, each carrying 12 soldiers, while a further 16 men would fly in the Dakota. All flights were timed to land at the Gawler airstrip at the same time.

Darkness fell and, while Hammond, Hallamore and Telfer wound up the Parabat orientation with South African steaks and beers at a campfire somewhere in Venda, Hewitt set out with his platoon. He was deployed by vehicle to within 3 kilometres of the boundary between the ranching area and the Maranda TTL, then quietly debussed. His objective, a hill selected for his OP, was about 10 kilometres from the drop off (7 kilometres inside the TTL). His plan was to move in file formation, following a farm dirt road with his Platoon until they reached the edge of the TTL, and then disperse towards their various OPs.

While still on the farm road, they encountered a group of four men coming towards them. The RAR soldiers heard the men first, crouched and, thinking they were terrorists, some soldiers opened fire. They turned out to have been cattle rustlers, armed with axes and knives for cutting up meat, and Hewitt continued on his way, worried that the noise of the firing may have compromised his presence.

Hewitt and his men were well-trained and entered the TTL with great care, taking almost the whole night to cover the 7 kilometres to the objective. They approached it from the east, just an hour before first light, climbed the gently sloping eastern side and looked down almost vertically into a dry stream bed below them on the western side.

They established a good OP below the summit amongst broken boulders and vegetation, mindful and watchful of mujibas who they expected to start their sweep at first light. Mujibas was young boys used by the terrorists to search hill features for soldiers.

Meanwhile, in South Africa, the Parabats were separating their kit. They had been told to kit out for Fireforce and pack into their rucksacks all non-Fireforce equipment. As the sun rose and daylight came, the aircraft began to take off. Telfer was enjoying himself, sitting in the open door of a

2 Lt Terence Hewitt (l) with Cpl Peter Smith, RhSigs

Puma, legs hanging over the side, flying much faster than he ever had in an Alouette, just above tree-top level, with an armada around him.

Hewitt was enjoying himself too. His diligent approach and hard work during the night was paying off and they had a sighting. His OP was looking down onto a group of about ten CTs emerging from morning mist, walking along the streamline in single file, only about 150 metres away. They were so close that he turned the radio down very low, in case another callsign spoke on it. Then it all started to happen at once. Behind them, they saw two mujibas about a kilometre away, moving towards them, slowly and warily. Then, the OP saw another group of nine or ten CTs moving towards the first group. Softly, softly, Hewitt radioed B Coy HQ and reported the sighting.

Meanwhile, the Fireforce was arriving at the airstrip on the Gawler Ranch. On board a Puma, Telfer looked ahead to see an officer with a piece of paper in his hand, running across the airstrip towards Lt Col Hammond in the K Car. The urgency was obvious, so Telfer walked to each Puma and told the Parabats to throw off their rucksacks, switch on their radios and stay on board. Immediately, Lt Col Hammond ordered the Fireforce airborne and off it went. The young Parabats had less than five minutes on Rhodesian soil before they were airborne and into action.

Still sitting in the door of a Puma, Telfer craned forward, unable to hear anything on the radio because of the noise of the rotors but watching for the tell-tale sight of the K Car pulling up.

As Telfer watched, Hewitt waited. He could see that it was a race against time. The mujibas had been slowly sneaking closer to his OP, moving warily and watching carefully, their suspicion obvious. Now, about 20 minutes after the first sighting, the two groups of CTs had met up and were sitting in a treed and grassy area about one kilometre north of his OP. Suddenly one mujiba ran off, leaving the other behind. This was an ominous development.

Just at that moment, he heard Lt Col Hammond's calm voice in the K Car, calling him. It was a fantastic feeling for the young Second Lieutenant to hear his Colonel speaking to him, just in time, as he had been very worried that the mujiba was surely about to alert the terrorists.

Approaching at tree-top level, the K Car suddenly pulled up over the OP, and Hewitt talked it onto the target. In his Puma, Telfer saw the climb of the K Car and signalled to the Parabats inside. They responded with slight smiles and quick, confident nods. The K Car flew straight to the enemy location, Hewitt called it out, and the chopper dropped orange smoke. From the smoke, Hewitt gave a correction to the target, but it wasn't needed. The K Car had seen the terrorists and the 20mm cannon was already speaking to them.

For Telfer, Hallamore and the Parabats, it was now 'game on'. The Pumas off-loaded them in a storm of leaves, sticks and dust, and then went back to the airstrip for three more loads, this time of RAR soldiers and more Parabats. The Dakota dropped its paratroopers, and, within 15 or 20 minutes, there were nearly 90 soldiers on the ground, deployed as stop groups and sweep lines, controlled from the air by Lt Col Hammond in the K Car.

While the contact played out, Hewitt relaxed with tea and biscuits, and enjoyed the show. His men captured the remaining mujiba, so he got to watch it too. Hewitt noticed how the Parabats used first names on the radio, not call signs, and spoke in Afrikaans. Every time they shot a terrorist, they said "Ek het hom", as in "I got him". Hewitt recalls it as 'a splendid show... with brisk fighting and skirmishing for most of the morning... plenty of coming and going of aircraft all the time'.

They had more tea and biscuits, which they shared with their mujiba as they downloaded plenty of good information from him. He cheerfully identified most of his mates who were in the process of being sorted out below the OP. There were 19 terrorists killed that day, believed to be all of them, with no own forces' casualties.

Later the same day, Hewitt and his Platoon walked out of the Maranda and were uplifted by vehicle at the Wanezi boundary. The vehicles dropped them at the end of the runway and they walked along it, amazed at the South African aircraft and equipment that had arrived since they'd left the previous evening. As they passed, the Parabats crowded against a fence and gave them a rousing cheer. At the far end of the runway, the first RAR officer to welcome Hewitt was Telfer, both their jobs now finished for the day.

References:
Hewitt, T 2015, *Calling Out the Pumas*, *Chibaya Moyo*, 30° South, Pinetown, South Africa.
Telfer, A 2015, *Masodja and MaParabat*, *Chibaya Moyo*, 30° South, Pinetown, South Africa.

CHAPTER THIRTEEN

AMBUSHES

INTRODUCTION: AMBUSHING by Captain Andrew Telfer

Ambushes cut both ways: we ambushed, and we were ambushed. If we were ambushed by the enemy, we carried out immediate action drills designed to escape the killing ground and turn the tables by attacking his position. This was a situation to be avoided. In the type of counter-insurgency (COIN) warfare fought in Rhodesia by the RAR, there were three forms of ambush initiated by us: I'll call them the immediate, overnight and long-term. I've no doubt that our brothers in the SAS and Selous Scouts had other forms of ambushes but this article will describe those most common to the RAR.

First, the Immediate Ambush. Imagine walking through the Rhodesian bush. Picture belts of acacia and mahogany woodland, areas of mopane and jesse-bush, tall termite mounds eroded by rain. In the warm afternoon, with heavy clouds building for a late afternoon thunderstorm, in hot sultry air, it's easy to switch off, to let attention drift into neutral. In Rhodesia in the 1970s, that could be fatal.

Terrorist groups and Army patrols were moving through the same bush at the same time and, from time to time, walked into each other. Usually, they saw each other simultaneously but, sometimes, soldiers saw terrorists first. On those occasions, the prescribed tactic was an immediate ambush.

It was supposed to be initiated by three hand signals from the patrol commander: thumbs down for enemy, hand over eyes for ambush and a pointed finger for ambush location. In practice, there was no need for hand signals. It was enough for the lead soldier to aim and crouch; everyone understood. Since there was never time to find effective cover, the tactic simply bought time for the enemy to get nearer, closing the range until the soldiers opened fire as the terrorists saw them. After the firefight, the contact area was swept by the soldiers. This had to be done very cautiously in case an apparently dead terrorist was bluffing.

For that reason, it was usual for the MAG gunner to stand on the flank while other soldiers swept past. He would be able to put down heavy fire to supress any Lazarus who rose up from the long grass.

Second, the Overnight Ambush. This was like 'sleeping with intent' or 'sleeping aggressively'. When deployed, soldiers should never be passive, they should always be on the offensive, and sleeping was just as good a time as any to kill terrorists. In endless cycles of six-week bush trips separated by ten days' R&R, the RAR soldier spent about 42 weeks a year on operations. During bush trips, roughly 80 percent of nights were spent deployed. Therefore, just over 230 nights were spent in the bush and, in the mind of an aggressive patrol commander, every one of those nights was an opportunity for an overnight ambush.

On Observation Posts, a patrol commander would consider the question, 'If the enemy has spotted my OP, and if he wanted to attack it by night, which route would he take up this hill?' Then he'd ambush that route every night.

On daytime Patrols, the commander would adopt the view that he had been seen, was being watched. Just before last light, he'd stop his men and appear to settle for the night in a location with only one natural access route. Well after dark, he'd move his patrol covertly to ambush that route. Soldiers would lay next to the route, rifles laid at the shoulder, aimed at the path. In rain, there would be no use of lightweight shelters as the noise and shine would give them away. One man would be on watch at a time, passing on the wristwatch each hour.

If the enemy came, the soldier on watch would wake the men next to him by silently pressing down on them with his hand. They would wake others, hand by hand along the line. Hands closed around the pistol grips of rifles and, when the figures were alongside, a wave of firing was poured into them. This contact area would also be swept but not until first light. In the meantime, the soldiers moved away from it to distance themselves from any grenades that might be thrown by a wounded terrorist.

Third, the Long-Term Ambush. If intelligence was good, and there was a very high likelihood of terrorists visiting an exact location or passing along a specific path, a long-term ambush may be established, remaining in place for many days and nights. Officers were taught and practised in this tactic as cadets and knew that it required perfect security, detailed planning and rehearsal, and very careful execution. Troops were organised into groups and quietly rotated through them at intervals of several hours: a killer group covered the killing ground; stop/early warning groups covered entry and exit routes; and a reserve resting away from the killing ground in dead ground (ground that couldn't be seen from the target area). The only place to sleep or eat was in the reserve group; all other soldiers remained alert and very well-concealed.

When terrorists arrived, the closest stop/early warning group would let them pass by, quietly pressing the switch on their radio twice, alerting everyone. The killing ground was an area rigged with claymore mines (curved explosive blocks, plastered with shrapnel) and covered by the platoon's MAGs in interlocking arcs of fire. Flares weren't used as they were a distraction that added no destructive value. When the terrorists entered the killing ground, the patrol commander pressed an electrical claymore initiator and the MAGs opened fire. If anyone survived that, the stop groups shot them as they tried to escape. After the contact, the soldiers moved away from the killing ground to wait for morning before sweeping it.

Finally, whatever the circumstances, the critical element of ambushing is surprise.

> 'Surprise is a most effective and powerful influence in war, and its moral effect is very great. Every endeavour must be made to surprise the enemy, and to guard against being surprised. Using surprise, results out of all proportion to the effort expended can be obtained, and in some operations, when other factors are unfavourable, surprise may be essential to success. Surprise can be achieved strategically, tactically or by exploiting new material. The elements of surprise are secrecy, concealment, deception, originality, audacity and rapidity.'

Sir Francis Young-Husband (1863-1942)

COMMENTS ON AMBUSHING by Captain Russell Fulton

Once again, the absolute need for comprehensive orders and rehearsals (followed by more rehearsals) were critically important leading up to the reconnaissance, siting and execution of night ambushes. During our conflict there were cases of officers neglecting to observe the very orders that they communicated to their men. Orders were issued for good reason and they were expected to be acted upon without deviation, including the very officers who issued them. In the RAR, night ambushes were frequently established by PWOs, NCOs and officers alike and when there was a failure to tick every box during the siting and occupation of these tactically sited death-traps, there were inevitable and fatal outcomes. One mistake that was made following the siting and occupation of the ambush position was as follows:

Once troops had been positioned in their respective 'Killer' and 'Stop' group positions, the officer in command of the ambush site knew full well never to return to his position via the killing ground, so named because this was the channel selected by the commander to exact maximum collateral damage to the enemy when the ambush was sprung. Anecdotal evidence in the form of Boards of Inquiry, established that several officers were killed by their own forces for neglecting to observe this critically important point. Returning to one's position, usually in the Killer group, was always conducted from the rear of each position for this very reason and would have/should have been communicated without ambiguity to everyone involved in the ambush party. Lessons should have been learnt but, as history has shown us, some cuffed-it and paid the supreme price.

War was a dangerous pastime where errors of judgement, lapses in concentration and laissez-faire mindsets yielded unsatisfactory outcomes. That is the nature of the human psyche and, in the words of Sir Isaac Newton: "For every action, there is an equal and opposite reaction!" That was the penalty for sloth.

THE BEST CHRISTMAS I HAD by Corporal Mkanga, Sp Coy, 1RAR

All c/s 53 had been deployed in the area two days before Christmas Day. Information had come from police that terrorists would break into a store and rob it. Callsign 53A under Sergeant Major Abias and c/s 53D under Corporal Fanson were sent in the area to ambush the store. The two c/s did the ambush at the store and nothing good came of it. The third day we thought of doing day observation and listening patrol. We did that east of the store. While doing that we met a boy who told us there were three terrorists in the area. He told us the route they were using when they were in the area. We searched all over but found nothing.

We returned to our OP where we stayed for at least one hour. After that hour we thought that we had not done our patrol thoroughly. We went back again, did the patrol along the river, and came to the kraal, listened but still found nothing. We were now very weary, and we returned to our OP. On our OP we stayed there for half an hour. At half-past seven we heard some shots southwest of our OP. They were shots of terrorists and they were firing at the DC's camp. The DC's people returned the fire. During the firing we left our OP and went down. We had gone down to the ambush route that we had been told by the boy that terrorists always use when they are in the area. Call sign 53D took the first ambush position. Call sign 53A moved further south of c/s 53D's position. Before they found their position to lay their ambush, they heard a noise. Sergeant Major Abias ordered his men to take positions quickly. This they did. They stayed there for 15 minutes but nothing happened.

Immediately after we had taken positions, the man on my left heard some movement. He told the man next to him and the first man that he had the terrorists visual. He counted and found there were five. The man on my right also saw the terrorists. I ordered the two men who had seen the terrorists to spring the ambush.

They fired at the same time. Other people who had not seen the terrorists also fired. We were very successful and eliminated this entire group. This gave us much to celebrate over Christmas.

Source: *Nhowo*, April 1978.

A TRIBUTE TO AN EX-RAR SOLDIER, SERGEANT AARON MAFU by Daniel J Scholtz

When the war intensified it was decided to create a specialised infantry unit within Internal Affairs (INTAF). The unit was to primarily go into areas where the gooks were 'ruling the roost' and to re-establish civil administration, as well as assist INTAF in 'hot' areas to maintain civil administration. Each province was allocated one Administration Reinforcement Unit (ARU) made up of volunteers from INTAF districts as well as other units within security forces. Many of the District Administrators (DAs) who volunteered were ex-RAR who had served their time and then joined INTAF. The ARU's were self-contained, well equipped, well trained and could react offensively as well as defensively. I was the Unit Commander for ARU in Matabeleland South. The ARU Mat South had a Sgt who was ex-RAR and his name was Sgt Aaron Mafu. This is the story of Sgt Aaron Mafu.

On Sunday 18th December 1978 I decided that we should do a diesel and rations run. On our route we had to cross a bad dogleg weir and the river was in flood. No person could cross the weir by foot, so the drill was that I would cross the weir with the Kudu (with 5 men), park on the other side, then sweep the area on the opposite river bank as well as the road leading away from the river. Once we had the area safe the two Crocodiles could safely cross the weir.

On our return journey we followed the normal drill and all seemed well. We swept up the road and when we got about 300 metres of the 500 up the road, my side of the road got fired on from a rocky outcrop. We took cover and returned fire. Sgt Mafu and another DA who were on the other side of the road joined us on our side of the road and joined the fire fight.

I ascertained that there were a maximum of 4 gooks as we were drawing sporadic fire from 4 very well covered positions. Suddenly I heard heavy automatic fire from another rocky outcrop to my left and identified it as RPD fire. I indicated the target to Sgt Mafu and shouted for him to give me cover fire so that I could get myself in a position to have a clear shot at the target - as the firing was getting very aggressive. Sgt Mafu gave me thumbs up, I changed mags and as I got onto my knee to get into a running position, Sgt Mafu pushed me with a massive force to the ground, jumped up and advanced towards the RPD gunner, double tapping as he was running.

Sgt Mafu placed himself between myself and the RPD gunner, so I could not take a clear shot at the RPD gunner. As I opened up fire at one of the other gooks, I saw how Sgt Mafu took shots to his upper body. He went down on one knee, got up and advanced towards the RPD gunner double tapping as he advanced, and I saw him taking more shots. Sgt Mafu went down on both knees and I could see he was in big trouble. When he fell forward on his chest (still firing) I had a clear target and silenced the RPD gunner.

When the RPD fell silent there was a roaring silence. We managed to eliminate two enemy (RPD gunner inclusive) - but we paid an expensive price for it. Sgt Mafu was dying. When I got to him all I heard him say was "Ishe Jesu" and he died. Sgt Mafu saved my life that day, for if he had not forced me to the ground, I probably would have run straight into the RPD gunner's line of fire. It only dawned on me afterwards that I am sure Sgt Mafu had taken a shot to his upper body before I asked him to give me covering fire - as I had blood on me that I did not know where it came from. Sgt Mafu took 16 shots to his upper body that day.

Sgt Aaron Mafu was an ex-RAR soldier, a man that I owe my life to. Sgt Mafu was an important player in the ARU Matabeleland South team. The experience, knowledge and discipline Sgt Mafu brought from the RAR was of great value to us and made ARU Mat. South the good unit it was.

That evening my men (as was I) were in a very sombre and sad mood. Every now and then someone would softly sing praises to a man and friend we could never replace. Plenty of silent tears were shed that night. The RAR surely produced a soldier and hero of note in Aaron Mafu. From the time the first shots were fired up to when there was silence, took a few seconds – however, it felt like hours – long hours in seeing a friend of yours being shot to pieces in front of you.

Due to administrative bungling, Sgt Aaron Mafu never got the recognition for his act of tremendous bravery. Every period roundabout the 18th of December - onwards from that fateful day - I have given my friend and Sgt a salute. Sgt Aaron Mafu did the RAR proud and the RAR made him a proud soldier and hero.

Salute Sgt Aaron Mafu. We will remember you. May your brave soul rest in eternal peace.

OF CATHERINE WHEELS, BUFFALO BEANS AND AMBUSHES by
Captain Russell Fulton

A 1RAR subaltern's journey down memory lane...

During the summer of 1979, 'A' Company, 1RAR was deployed on framework
operations in the Chesa, Madziwa and Pfungwe TTL's within Op Hurricane; areas
that one could reasonably refer to as being 'Gook Central' given their proximity to
known ZIPRA and ZANLA infiltration routes. After several days of dancing to the
crack and thump of incoming lead neatly wrapped in their soiled copper jackets,
we received orders to move to various grid references (the nearest roads) for
immediate uplift.

Going 'overt' in the middle of a deployment was not a common occurrence
particularly after having walked in to our respective target areas under cover of
darkness and frequently over extreme distances and remaining clandestine for
days; these new orders had a bit of an ominous ring; we'd soon find out why.

Back at our Company HQ we received convoy orders for immediate
deployment to Doma, the arse-end of the world for anyone interested, and within
proximity to the infamous 'Zambezi Escarpment'. 3 Platoon (mine) was lead
platoon in the convoy (we always were) and this was becoming the source of some
chagrin within the ranks. My men (reasonably) opined that 3Pl was considered
'expendable' by the OC as we were always "on point". As their platoon
commander I can assure you that this never worried me, but it tested my leadership
time and again. What do you tell your men when they ask you why it is that their
platoon was the lead platoon and, without exception on gravel (dirt) roads? The
roads were frequently mined, and 3 Platoon had hit its fair share of these. Never
mind, just something that was an increasingly compromising morale and becoming
an annoying command & control nuisance for me.

When we arrived at Doma early evening we were allocated our platoon areas
where we subbies, in turn, allocated firing positions, arcs of fire and so on to our
men pending receipt of full operational orders from our OC. We were deploying
in to the Zambezi Valley and the 1:50,000 map sheets highlighted the fact that this
little walk was going to be quite interesting. The 'vertical interval' (distance
between contour lines) on a 1:50,000 map is 20m and when I looked at the FUP
(Forming Up Place), the colouration of the map sheet to our North and the general
direction of march was almost completely brown. Contour lines were brown in
colour and when they were almost touching it indicated that the terrain of the
Mavuradonha Mountains was mountainous............a slight understatement of the
fact! Alas…

"Let's Go Walkies"

The next morning after a quick brew and a few fried dog biscuits coated in Sun Jam we were ordered to embus at 04:00 and we were taken to our drop off-point. Our 'hike' now commenced and for once, I wished that 3 Platoon was 'point platoon'. We were positioned at the rear with 2 and 1 platoons to our front. The OC and his Company HQ echelon were at the front. For the benefit of those who have never been in uniform, hiked in the 'gomos' or are otherwise witless to these things, allow me to respectfully explain what happens.

Somewhere over the Mountain

Perhaps the best analogy is what happens when one of those awful accordions is played; it opens (when one marches up hill) and it compresses (when one goes downhill). Over distance, when marching in single file as we were, those to the rear would be concertinaed because of the length of the file to the extent that when those ahead were scaling the next incline, we, bringing up-the-rear, would be hundreds of yards apart and would be forced to speed up our march and sometimes jog to catch up with those to our front.

Over some 40+ kilometres in the blistering October 'sunshine', in an almost barren landscape sans mvura (no water), you require little imagination in understanding that we 3 Platoon types were on what was akin to a regimental 'battle march' (marching and running) throughout the day. It was a tedious and tiresome affair and, unbelievably, there was no rotation of platoons. To make matters a tad more discomforting we were soon accompanied by a plague of Mopani Flies whose sole purpose in life was to seek out moisture and they found it on our profusely sweating hands, faces and necks. It seemed as though the more you swotted the more that replaced them! It was enough to make a grown man scream but they were, after all, only thirsty mites were they not!!!

At around 1600B hours we were cresting a lone version of 'Mt Kilimanjaro' when I stood on a loose rock, rolled my ankle under the weight of a 60kg Bergen and took a rapid, unguided tour of the landscape as I did the proverbial "Bollemakiesie" spinning like a Guy Fawkes Catherine Wheel 'arse-over-tit' down a decidedly steep re-entrant. Alright…I confess, it wasn't quite what I had in mind and I didn't see much of the landscape anyway. It was all rather annoying as I fleetingly and pointlessly pondered how this might all turn-out. These were immediately dispelled when my skull decided to flirt with a quite impressive but unfriendly 'dombo' (boulder). Aye, it 'deadened' things momentarily as I drifted into 'Noddy-Land'.

When I came around, groggy and blurry-eyed, blood streaming from an impressive gash above my right eyebrow and looked in to the concerned eyes of my PWO. I got to my feet, collected my Bergen that lay some 30m away and swayed my way up this ridiculous incline. There were a few expletives flying about in that dazed compartment I call my head and they motivated me to show my platoon that I wasn't one of those 'It's all beers and skittles' subbies. Never mind…

About three hours later we arrived on the 'valley floor' and made our way to the TAC HQ position identified in the Orders Group the previous evening. On arrival we were directed to our respective platoon areas and I was summoned to the OC's tent. I received orders to draw five days rations, issue orders and to deploy with my platoon to an ambush site some 15 'clicks' NE of Coy TAC HQ that same evening! We had marched (and run) all day over comfortably 40km's+ as the crow flies but remember that the march in was over seriously broken ground so the distance must have been closer to 50km in real terms and in suicide month (October)!

Ambush & Contact!

We had a light meal, rested and departed camp on foot at 22:00B deploying in a north-westerly direction to the target area, a much longer route but this was unknown ground and security was paramount. Compromise wasn't an option, so it was better to walk half a dozen extra kilometres to achieve that aim. I halted my platoon about 2 clicks from our proposed ambush site, an elevated piece of ground in thick riverine bush that overlooked the Angwa River with excellent observation of the North bank with excellent fields of fire. This was a known ZANLA crossing point who would cross the river by dugout canoe from a village on the northern bank. I went forward to recce the area before returning to give final orders and take my sections to their respective positions. By the time I had positioned my own call sign, the Killer Group, and my Stop Groups it was nigh-on 04:00B, nigh on 24 hours since we had commenced our deployment! No rest for the foolish it seemed, and I smiled wryly to myself as I recalled that ridiculous cliché "If you can't take a joke you should never have joined the army". It now had a peculiar resonance with me.

At around midday, directly to our front, a group of three motely 'magandanga' (terrorists) approached the river with AK's shoulder slung! These 'binya' must have thought that they were still in Tanzania; so slack was their security! My orders for initiating fire were clear; this would be by me followed immediately by my MAG team (4 gunners). I was so very tempted to drop one of the buggers in my sights, but I held back believing that there were more gooks where these had come from. We maintained strict radio silence all the while and remained absolutely still. My heart sank as the three of them walked back under cover of twelve-foot tall reed banks back to the village and from whence they had come. There was a bit of a commotion on the other side and it continued for about half an hour before things became interesting. One of the villagers, a grey-haired AMA (African Male Adult), hopped in his dugout and paddled crossed the river, climbed out and walked right past my killer group completely oblivious to our presence. It was a tense moment for us all. I directed one of my sodja who was covering our rear to be on the lookout for this civvie who might return later. He never did.

At around 15:00B a group of five gooks made their way down to the river and started shouting, presumably for that old 'madala' who had taken the dugout. I couldn't wait longer as these gooks appeared restless and may have decided to look for a crossing point up or downstream from their current position and the initiative would be lost. I double tapped and dropped the most vocal amongst them and who seemed the most likely to be in command who carried an RPD. There was a roar as the four MAG's (two either side of me) opened fire. It was lekker! Those magandanga were tripping over themselves in mid-stride trying to gap it; three lay where they fell and there were cries from the reed banks of another who had fallen foul of our nyere (bullets). We raked the reed banks in the direction that we believed the path followed. The challenge now lay in knowing we would be crossing the river to follow-up and sooner rather than later. The Angwa was a deep river so fording it was out of the question unless you thought you were a Barble. I radioed Sunray 19 and gave him the run down and was ordered to cross immediately. With only one dugout I left two call signs who had been Stop Groups roughly to the east and west of my position who were to cover our crossing and left my PWO, Munyika Collins, in command.

I crossed the river in the dugout with three sodja (my MAG gunner Pte Sibanda, Earnest, my faithful batman Pte Mukonoweshuro, Emanuel and Cpl Makhulumo, Victor who was a brilliant tracker). When we reached the opposite bank, I lead my men up the embankment and through the reed bank expecting to hear the unfriendly chatter of a Kalashnikov but, in its stead, was the soft moaning of a mortally wounded gook. He tried to raise his weapon, but my gunner 'stilled' him with a stunning blow rendering him unconscious. His hands were bound behind his back and secured to his bound ankles by means of a length of para cord. We moved forward to the outer fringes of a small village and saw the spoor of the fifth gook and it indicated that he was gone like a streak of duck-shit with great strides in to the middle distance. We followed at the jog and found his pack and an SKS that he had decided to dump to make good his escape. We followed the spoor for about two clicks at which point we lost it over a sheet of granite.

We cast for spoor for the best part of an hour and I decided to return to the village to question the locals; our 'escapee' would probably be sprinting in 'Swastika' mode through the outer suburbs of Blantyre by now. When we returned to the village, we found the village deserted except for an elderly AFA (African Female Adult) who was the spouse of the wandering 'sekuru' who had passed by our ambush position earlier. We gathered as much INT as we could from the old woman who was visibly shaken by the firing. We asked where her husband had gone' and she said that he was sent by the comrades to go to the next village a good distance away to get some mbanje. I doubted he would be returning in a hurry after we had disturbed the peace and the sound of gunfire would have carried a reasonable distance.

We recovered the gook weapons, made them safe, removed webbing, documents and anything else that might prove useful from an intelligence perspective.

After Action, Satisfaction, Man Relax with a "Lexington!"

Whilst all of this was going on, I noticed a lone tobacco plant on the edge of the field that looked decidedly unwell but bore a few dried leaves. I told my batman to collect one and to roll us a fodya (cigarette) which he did within a piece of paper from a signals pad and that looked more like a Fidel Castro cigar! I lit it and inhaled deeply before changing hue to something more akin to a Jamaican Rasta man! Gasping, coughing and spluttering (and perhaps farting) I hastily passed it back to him. My lungs were on fire and my mouth tasted like a shebeen ashtray....it was the poorest excuse for a 'skyf' (cigarette) I had ever tasted! Not quite a Lexington but hey-ho, you live and learn.

We loaded up the gook weapons, webbing and documents and climbed back in to the dugout and returned to the south bank. I briefed my Ishe by small means and received orders to ambush the area overnight which made complete sense. As one did, we left the area overtly moving in a westerly direction for about eight clicks and then stopped before last light for evening chow. We loaded up at around 23:00B and dog legged back towards the general area of the earlier ambush site. As for those hapless and quite deceased gooks, who had started to bloat in the stifling heat, we left them for the crocs. What!? Grave digging wasn't part of our job description!

It was a moonless and oppressively hot night as we marched through the 'Rutsitu' (African cocoa tree) woodlands endemic in this part of the country and then we happened across a soldier's worst nightmare in the 'gangen'; a thick belt of 'Buffalo Beans' in nefarious subterfuge under a moonless night sky. There are few, if any Rhodesian servicemen,

After Action Satisfaction …

who hadn't heard reference to or experienced them first hand. The Latin name is "Mucuna irritans" and the chiShona name is "Huriri"; it is a bastard of a plant that usually grows like vines but can also grow to a height of two meters. Brushing against the fruit or flowers will leave you covered in fine hairs that will inevitably gift you a severe burning rash. The best way of removing the fine hairs is to apply mud to the affected area, allow it to dry and then peel the dried mud and 'bonded' hairs away. Once afflicted, and if left untreated, forget about sleeping because it sure as hell wouldn't be happening! A handful of my men fell afoul of the dreaded 'bean', but they all demonstrated admirable professionalism in dealing with their discomfort. I was extremely proud of them as they suppressed their acute discomfort and treated one another quietly.

The ambush was a lemon and we withdrew two days later and returned to Coy HQ after which we were deployed as part of a 1RAR CFL (Concentrated Force Level) operation involving three of our five companies. C Company, under command of Major Lionel Dyke, had a couple of kills but that was about the strength of it. A few days later humping around this enormous, inhospitable piece of real estate, we heard that there was a 'murungu' (white man) terrorist in the area. My immediate thoughts were of a 'musope' (albino) but it was later established that it was an accurate account and the white oke was either of Cuban or Eastern bloc origin. I think that a call-sign from C Sqn or 'Scouts accounted for him later, but I don't rightly recall.

We did the business back in the day and walked hundreds of kilometres over all sorts of terrain, in wind, rain and sunshine. Was it all worth it? Hell yes, I was serving in the RAR!

SELOUS SCOUTS TRAGEDY by Lieutenant Michael Matthews

During January 1978 A Company 1RAR was based at Shabani, some one hundred kilometres or so West of Fort Victoria, the largest town in the Repulse area. Unusually, we had been spared two precious Alouette helicopters for our operations, mainly O.P.'s and patrols, and there was therefore a small air force presence at camp with us.

We had been deployed by chopper in O.P.'s and on clandestine patrols for about a week, and my platoon had just returned to camp for resupply, when a call came in from the JOC at Fort Victoria on 5th February 1978 that a small group of Selous Scouts had been ambushed by what appeared to be a large group of gooks in the infamous Nyajena TTL, near Fort Vic, and that they had suffered casualties and required urgent casevac and assistance.

My O.C., Major Barry Getliffe, instructed me to assemble two sticks for deployment by chopper to the ambush scene, and we quickly prepared ourselves to depart. It was about 16h00 when we left, and I anticipated that we would simply be assisting in a casevac and returning to camp before dark. On arrival, however, it quickly became clear that the situation was far worse, and more complicated than I had thought or anticipated. I saw a handful of Selous Scouts in a huddle next to two of their column vehicles and the dead bodies of four of their comrades. One of their number (Keith Moss as I recall) was critically wounded, and we immediately set about loading the fatalities and the wounded soldier onto the choppers.

It was getting dark and one of the chopper pilots passed on to me orders from JOC that we were to stay with the remaining Scouts, seven as I recall, and accompany them by vehicle to Renco gold mine, some twenty kilometres away, at first light the next day. The survivors were all badly shaken and shocked, and in no condition to commence our journey in the remaining light anyway. I arranged for us to move a short distance away into better cover, whilst the choppers disappeared, presumably straight to Fort Victoria.

I spoke to the Scouts' leader, and as the shadows grew longer, he told me what had happened. It transpired that his group had been dispatched by their Commanding Officer Lt. Colonel Ron Reid Daly by vehicle to recover from a village in the Nyajena TTL, the wife of a Scout's NCO who had apparently been with the Regiment since its inception. Although the NCO had been kidnapped by terrorists during 1976, and was presumed dead, it was the policy of the Selous Scouts to look after their own, including their families, and it had apparently become known in the village that this woman was indeed the wife of a Rhodesian soldier, the equal of a death sentence in a community heavily under the control of and sympathetic to ZANLA.

Having fetched the NCO's wife from her village, the group were compelled to use the same route back to Renco Mine, since this was the only road access. Their movements had been monitored by a very large group of ZANLA insurgents who, knowing full well that the Scouts would have to use the same jeep track to exit the TTL, established a highly effective ambush position in anticipation of the Scouts' return.

He told me that they had been taken completely by surprise, that both column vehicles had been caught square in the ambush 'kill zone' and that the fire fight had lasted no more than a few seconds. He was adamant, however, that the ZANLA group was extremely large, and that the Scouts simply hadn't stood a chance. This didn't surprise me, since Nyajena TTL had for some time been a 'no go' area, simply because the locals had become so subverted that their loyalty lay firmly with the enemy. As a result, they couldn't be relied upon to supply intelligence, unless under duress, and such areas were generally avoided both for this reason, and because their strategic importance was by and large not that great. What was clear, however, was that we were heavily outnumbered, and that the gooks well knew that there was only one way out of the TTL by road.

I must admit that I have never seen such a dispirited and demoralised group of soldiers but, given the intensity and ferocity of the fire fight that they had just been involved in, it was hardly surprising. We all settled down and spread ourselves out defensively in anticipation of a possible night attack, and endured a long, cold and anxious night without sleeping bags or food and took turns to keep guard.

At first light, a brief recce revealed that we weren't under any immediate threat, and we prepared ourselves for the journey to Renco Mine. What followed was the longest twenty kilometres I have ever travelled. The two Scouts column vehicles we would be traveling in were modified open Land Rovers, one of which was fitted with a fifty calibre Browning, and the other twin 7.62 medium automatic guns, and both of which were otherwise troop carriers.

I split us up into two groups and travelled in the front vehicle, which was equipped with the twin 7.62's, and took with me our most experienced 'sparrow', or tracker. We were all extremely tense since there emerged early signs, demonstrated by fresh spoor that many insurgents had recently been walking on either side of the track. Every three hundred metres or so, trees had been felled or other obstacles placed across the road to hinder our progress. On each occasion, we would all exit the vehicles, save for the drivers, and commence a slow sweep through likely ambush positions. There was a very keen sense that we were in 'enemy territory' with large pro-ZANLA slogans painted on the walls of most of the kraals and small buildings which we passed.

The air was palpably thick with the anticipation of a contact, and it was now obvious from the spoor that our Sparrow was picking up, that the terrorist group was about fifty in number, and close to us. There was no doubt that the insurgents were planning a further ambush along the road somewhere, and every bend in the track revealed a potential ambush position for them. The bush was very thick.

I gave orders for the gunners on both column vehicles to fire into likely cover, since this would obviously dampen the Gooks' enthusiasm to lay a static ambush, and the Scouts had with them more than enough ammunition to allow us the luxury to do so. I also made radio contact with the JOC at Fort Vic and asked whether they could afford us any air cover. Happily, they were aware of our precarious position, and informed me that they would be making a 'Lynx' (Cessna with two push/pull engines and some armament) available to assist us and, of course, to act as an additional deterrent to the ZANLA group.

I decided to stay put until the Lynx arrived, and it was overhead us within about half an hour. I cannot describe our collective relief when we heard the familiar drone of its engines, and somehow, for as long as the aircraft was with us, we felt that we held the psychological upper hand, despite our small numbers. I contacted the Lynx pilot, and his voice was reassuring. He would be flying slow orbits ahead of us and would warn us when we were approaching spots which, aerially, looked like potential ambush positions.

Keith Moss' brother, who was on my vehicle, asked me to enquire with the Lynx pilot as to Keith's condition. The news, however, was not good, and it fell to me to inform Keith's brother that Keith had succumbed to his injuries during the previous night. The tragic news added to our anxiety as we approached a copse of dense bush. For the umpteenth time, we commenced a sweep, whilst the Lynx took a few strafing runs at the likely ambush spot.

As we moved through the dense bush, our Sparrow came upon the first of what turned out to be in excess of fifty recently abandoned and well-prepared individual ambush positions where foliage had been freshly cut to provide added cover. There was no question that the gooks had gone to a great deal of time and effort to lay their ambush, and I am certain that the presence of the Lynx, and our ploy of firing into likely cover had made them skittish and caused them to abandon their plan.

The relief amongst us was tangible, since we were now probably no more than seven or eight kilometres from Renco, and it was most unlikely that the insurgents would be going to the effort, and risk, of laying a further ambush. The Lynx had been with us for several hours now and needed to return to Fort Vic to refuel. In discussion with the Lynx pilot, he and I mutually agreed that the worst was probably over, and that he wouldn't need to return after refuelling. He assured me, in any event, that there was little in the way of dense vegetation alongside the jeep track for the remainder of our journey.

Although still slow, the rest of our journey was nonetheless uneventful, and we arrived at Renco Mine at about 15h00 that day. It had taken us about nine hours to cover some twenty kilometres! The news of our arrival during the day had obviously been communicated somehow to the Renco Mine staff since we were treated to an already prepared slap-up meal by them. Separate arrangements had been made for the Scouts to be taken back to their headquarters at Inkomo Barracks, just outside Salisbury, and since the Alouettes which had deployed us were otherwise engaged at the time, Major Getliffe had made arrangements for one of our Company vehicles to uplift us and transport us back to Shabani.

We bade farewell to an extremely grateful and relieved group of Selous Scouts and arrived at camp shortly after dark after what had been probably the most harrowing and nerve-wracking experience, I had ever had to that point in my brief military career. Even today, I find it uncanny to think that, whilst we were operating well within the borders of our own country, we may as well have been involved in an external in Zambia or Mozambique.

A BIRD IN THE HAND IS BETTER THAN TWO IN THE BUSH? by Sergeant Jo Amos

I'm sure we can all remember those days, when you were due to go out on patrol and ordered to draw rations to last you a certain amount of days. Easier said than done! If you were scheduled to go out for a 7-10 day hump, there was no way you were going to draw 7-10 'Rat Packs' and shove them straight into your pack. Add to those the radio, radio batteries, drip, grenades, extra ammunition, water bottles, binoculars, FN, or MAG, and sleeping bag, and you were going nowhere fast. You needed to streamline the food you were going to take as much as possible.

Next stop the QMS. In our case, it was a visit the ever smiling Colour Stevenson. Ration packs were drawn and then it was off to the two 44 gallon drums sitting outside the stores. Everyone sorted through their packs, to decide what they would need to take, the rest went into the drums. Best part was always rummaging through the drums, looking for a decent 'throw away', and waiting for our African Soldiers to draw their rations. Then the trading started, chopped ham for corned beef, creamed chicken for Sardines in Tomato Sauce and so on. Worst part about cutting back the rations was getting the potato smash and milk powder mixed up. Nothing more demoralising than that mug of that dreaded lumpy tea at the end of a long day's hump!

On this particular occasion, whilst in charge of two sticks, and we were out on patrol north of Mana Pools. Our orders were simple enough, locate crossing points that the CTs were currently using when gapping it back to Zambia. Unfortunately, we had not had much success and already been out on patrol for 9 days, 2 days longer than expected. Needless to say, as we were starting to work our way back to Chirundu, the boys were starting to scrape the proverbial barrel in terms of sustenance. Thoughts drifted from juicy cheese and tomato sandwiches, to freshly grilled steaks and a cold beer. As we took a well-deserved break and topped up water bottles etc, a couple of the guys noticed a number of Guinea Fowl close by. Immediately the banter started, followed by the pleading. Please "Sarge" just two. After discussing it with my corporal, I made a decision to allow them to shoot 2 birds, and thankfully a couple of "Double Taps" later we had two fine looking birds in hand.

As the guys began to pluck and prepare the birds for cooking, fully aware that they would be as tough as a pair of old Bata takkies, there was what sounded like a distant "Double Tap". We looked at each other, firstly for confirmation, and secondly to make sure that we weren't imagining it. I then made another decision. I ordered one of the guys to let off two rounds. Then we waited. We couldn't believe our ears when we heard another "Double Tap", much closer this time. Immediately we set up an ambush position with our backs to the river, leaving a small area for us to withdraw if the need arose, and when settled, proceeded to let off another two rounds. True to form, there was a response virtually immediately. We lay and waited, and it wasn't long before a CT peered from behind a bush on the other side of the clearing I had chosen as the contact area. Shortly thereafter, he emerged followed by a number of his fellow CTs and the ambush was initiated.

I couldn't believe what had happened. After 9 days of having no luck locating any signs of recent crossing points, we had, by chance, stumbled across an active one.

Maybe a bird in the hand is not always worth two in the bush after all!

A BRAVE MAN by Aircraftsman Rory Williams

I was asked by the RAR Association if I had any stories of note to share for the second edition of *Chibaya Moyo*. I had the privilege of working with the RAR and I remember a day when one RAR soldier showed amazing courage. To set the scene I will firstly give a little background to the story to give it context. It will help to place the events involving the RAR.

I was in the Air Force Regiment and was permanently based at Mtoko forward airfield in the region known as Op Hurricane. Most of the time I was the only person from the RhAF in camp. Fire Force would come and go but they were based in Mount Darwin so rarely stayed very long. A contingent of RhAF personnel would come and go in support of the flight crews operating with Fire force. They were sporadically around. The other permanent man was Corporal Mike Lawrence an Engineer and Pookie driver. There was, for quite long periods, a medic by the name of Pete Mitchell, a Kiwi who also got me at times to exceed my brief as a simple Airman. Mike Lawrence was later KIA in April 1979 in the Mount Darwin area. He received the Bronze Cross posthumously for his outstanding bravery.

There was a Support Unit section which was almost always busy. It was positioned a short distance across from the Air Force section. I got on very well with the CO and the small group of men based there. As I had no command structure whatsoever, I pretty much did whatever I liked. This lack of command structure was probably not great in the long run but that's another story. I chose to carry an MAG and, very often, units passing through would invite me along for the ride. I even managed to hop on for a free ride over the border with several hundred men in a very large convoy in late 1978. I had never seen so many men or trucks lined up. It looked like a full-scale invasion.

This story begins with a Support Unit stick of 5 men who stumbled upon sixty terrorists on parade in an open area outside a large cave. The Mtoko region is full of caves and it made it very difficult to flush terrorists out or spot them from the air. The stick had come over a rise whilst on patrol and had come across a large group of terrorists. The Support Unit stick had positioned themselves in an elevated position directly above the cave entrance.

Approximately 40 meters away were 60 terrorists all lined up in rows on parade. The terrorists were sitting ducks. However, it's surprising how fast people can move when under fire. The stick leader made it clear all weapons to be on single fire only. Any man using automatic was to be charged. As one can imagine there was pandemonium on contact and my memory is vague but at least 8 terrorists died and several more injured in this initial contact. The information of this initial contact is from the original brief and subsequent debrief.

The first I knew about this initial contact was when the Support Unit CO came running over the compound to inform me. I was no doubt doing very little of any consequence and listened intently as he briefed me. He said he needed an MAG gunner for the follow up and he knew I would jump at any opportunity to volunteer. He was right. There were 5 of us 4 Support Unit and I in a Hyena and I positioned myself at the rear of the vehicle, so I was first out in case of any trouble.

There isn't much space in a Hyena for an MAG. The plan was to meet up on route with two trucks of heavily armed RAR. We arranged ourselves in a small convoy consisting of the Hyena leading the way and one armoured two five with an MAG mounted in the back and an RL bringing up the rear. The crew compartment of the two five was heavily armoured but the MAG was very exposed.

The route to the contact site in front of the cave was down a very narrow gorge several kilometres long, very slow going on a rough track. The Hyena had got ahead slightly, and a gap had appeared between us and the RAR trucks. The contact which took place was in a narrow part of the gorge.

What remained of the gang of some 40 plus gooks allowed the Hyena through and they opened up on the Gunner in the armoured truck and RL behind us. The RAR *Masodja* immediately bailed out and took cover outside the vehicles and returned fire whilst the MAG gunner continued to fire from the mounted gun position within the truck. The terrain was too slow and narrow for either truck to clear the kill zone. We had cleared the kill zone in the Hyena by a few minutes. The RAR were in a very exposed position especially in the narrow confines of the steep gorge taking fire from an elevated position.

Undeterred the MAG gunner kept firing under heavy fire until he ran out of ammunition. We would later find out how intense the fire had been on his position by examining the hits on the side of the armoured vehicle. The next thing the gunner did was exceptional. He climbed out of the armoured vehicle under heavy fire and ran to the RL some distance away. In the rear of the RL were extra boxes off ammunition. He dragged a box back under heavy fire reloaded the MAG and continued the fire fight. An exceptionally brave soldier.

Several more gooks were killed and injured during that contact and the RAR trackers followed them for several hours. No casualties on our side which is amazing considering the position the ambush took place. The other Support unit guys and I continued to the cave to recover information and documents for Special Branch whilst the RAR continued the follow up.

We were able to recover all kinds of documents, ammunition, mortars. The site was clearly left in a hurry and, although the security forces response had been anticipated and the ambush set up, they had not returned to recover the valuable documentation. My memory is not what it was, but I seem to recall the group of terrorists were in fact more heavily armed than the average gang and there was talk of a Cuban being involved.

Later that day back at Mtoko we were looking at the armoured truck. It was covered in dents. However, it was also peppered with huge holes which were large enough for a 7.62 NATO round to pass through with ease. The rounds had gone through the steel plate like it was butter. Had any *Masodja* remained in the armoured vehicle there is no doubt there would have been many causalities. On the inside of the opposite wall there were dents the size of half an orange and some rounds had passed through both sides.

An incredibly brave man was spared any injury that day and almost certainly the gooks were shocked at the ferocity of the RAR counter attack. I have told the story to the best of my memory. My apologies if it's not 100 percent accurate. These things happened a long time ago. I will never forget the bravery of that RAR gunner it is still clear in my mind.

BACK ON TERRA FIRMA by Lieutenant Michael Matthews

For the two months or so through to August 1978, A Company 1RAR was given some welcome relief from Fireforce duties, and we resumed our usual three to four-day patrols in the Matabeleland (or 'Tangent') area.

My recollection of the events of these few months is rather vague (in the absence of a log book to guide me), but there was always something happening to keep us on our toes. One event that I will always remember, began innocuously enough whilst my platoon was en route to a camp in the vicinity of the Inyathi Mission, some one hundred or so kilometres north east of Bulawayo in two Bedford four-fives, with trailers since, rather unusually, the Company had split up into its three platoons, and Headquarters.

I was driving the front Bedford through what seemed to be a rather tame looking area, when I heard and felt a huge explosion which lifted and detached the back of the troop-laden Bedford from its trailer – we had hit a landmine! Instinctively, we all peeled out of and off the Bedford, as did the rest of my platoon in the Bedford behind us. We were all anticipating an ambush, and we all opened fire. As it transpired, there was no ambush, just a huge hole in the earth underneath our rear right axle about one and a half metres deep which we discovered had been home to not one, but two TM46 anti-tank mines.

Of all the close shaves I had during my time in the army, this was arguably one of the closest. Since we were on a straight dirt road in a vehicle which had no mine-proofing, the front right wheel (which was situated almost directly beneath me) had clearly first passed over the mines and failed to detonate them, yet the rear wheel caused the detonation. Again, thankfully, there were no injuries sustained at all, and the Bedford was repaired without too much ado.

Some weeks later and whilst on patrol in roughly the same area, I and my platoon came upon a deserted Mission at dusk. Although nothing traumatic or eventful was to transpire at the Mission, it sticks in my mind simply because of its eerie and haunting presence. The Mission, no doubt abandoned because of the War, had obviously in time past been home to a number of rural children and, no doubt, a few nuns/nursing sisters, and perhaps even a few doctors, who had devoted themselves to the children's welfare. Given the proven propensity of our enemy to pick on small and defenceless civilian targets such as Missions if the opportunity presented itself, I didn't blame them at all.

Strangely, the Mission had not been ransacked, and it housed a well-equipped medical clinic. There were large quantities of assorted medicines and syringes in cabinets and drawers, and at least thirty or so new looking beds, all sprung and with neat mattresses on them. So cosy did this look against the prospect of a night out under a cold sky that I decided we would 'pozzie' there for the night. After a short while, however, I began to feel uneasy about the decision, since we seemed so exposed and susceptible to attack, and I moved my rather disgruntled *Masodja* back into the surrounding bush – this was all too comfortable.

During about August 1978 we relocated to Shamva (in the 'Hurricane' operational area) for a month or so and conducted patrols in the area. It was not the first time we had been in this part of the world, and we were well-liked by the local farming community. In fact, A Company 1RAR was privileged to be given the Freedom of Shamva, and we held a parade through the town. It was unforgettable, and a tangible indication of how our work was appreciated by a lot of wonderful people.

CORPORAL CHIDIDI'S AMBUSH by Captain Andrew Telfer

I recently obtained a copy of *The War Diaries of Andre Dennison* and discovered that I had made a mistake in *Chibaya Moyo 1*. In an article entitled *God Bless Tiny Tim*, my half-baked memory led me to wrongly attribute an OP/Ambush/Fireforce operation to Christmas Eve 1978 when, in fact, it was New Year's Eve, of the same year. Six days is no big deal, I agree, but the discovery led me to realise a more important omission in the 14 lines I used to describe that incident.

Enamoured by the Christmas metaphor, I failed to adequately describe the work of one of my Section Commanders, Corporal Chididi. His tactical skill led directly to the deaths of three terrorists and, indirectly, to five more, and the aim of this article is to put that omission right.

Firstly, the entry by Major Dennison in his A Company war diary (Wood 1989, p. 295), which read:

> 'At about 1730hrs on 31 December the Fire Force deployed to a 'D' Company sighting of 18 CTs. Before the Fire Force arrived on the scene the CTs walked into a 'D' Company deliberate ambush, and three were killed. When the K-Car was five minutes out, call-sign *Four One* spotted five of the survivors hiding in a stream bed. These gooks engaged the K-Car and stops were dropped to east and west. Charlie One killed two CTs, and the other three broke and were killed by the K-Car.'

I was call-sign *Four One* and this is as accurate a description of the contact as I can recall, writing in December 2018, forty years after the event.

At the end of December 1978, D Company 2RAR, commanded by Major Bryan McDermott, received intelligence about transit routes into the Chibi Tribal Trust Land from the south. A map appreciation sought to identify natural features that would lend themselves to the establishment of OPs in support of the 2RAR Fireforce, based then at Rutenga. Our attention was drawn to an area of large hills that spread westward from the main Rutenga-Fort Victoria road, south of the Chibi. We knew these hills had thickly wooded sides, bare-rock, dome-shaped summits, and were divided by stream beds that might funnel anyone moving from south to north. Major McDermott divided the hills into three platoon areas of responsibility and gave his orders for deployment that night.

Together with my PWO, Sergeant Major Gwatirera, I studied the map and selected OP sites within our area. Our operating procedure was to select the site from the map but obviously allow the stick commanders the latitude to find the best location once they arrived in position. I am not sure how many four-man sticks I had available for that operation but, usually, there would be from six to eight. In an RAR battalion, D Company's call-sign is 4, within which 10 Platoon's call-sign is 41 (used by the platoon commander), 41A is the PWO, 41B the platoon sergeant, 41C, 41D, 41E the corporals and any additional call-signs were commanded by the lance-corporals.

During my orders group, Corporal Chididi studied the map closely, smiled and raised his hand. He told us that he had grown up in the area, had looked after cattle there and roamed around its hillsides as a boy. This was a game-changer, his local knowledge was a huge asset that we could now benefit from. In the discussion that followed, he was able to select a low-lying section of the main road for our vehicle drop-off, an infiltration route that would avoid habitation, improved OP sites, advice on water sources, and one more very important thing. He recommended laying an ambush in a specific defile between two features that he felt would be the most likely transit route through our area. He said that he knew it well and could cover it with his stick. We still needed to undertake our OP tasks, so I allocated the ambush to him and he went off to the CQMS to draw his claymores. Claymore mines are laid just above the ground on spikes, facing the enemy. They are fired by electrical remote-control and spray metal fragments into the killing ground like a shotgun.

After dark, we embussed onto our two platoon troop-carrying vehicles (4.5 tonne Unimogs) and departed from our company base camp. The drop-off point on the main road was just as Chididi had described it, a low stretch between high banks, where we quickly slipped off into the darkness, leaving the vehicles to continue along the road. Much later, out of sight and sound, they would turn around and return to base. We waited, in all round defence, listening and watching for 15 or 20 minutes before we moved off on foot.

Infiltrating an area was always a difficult time as everything depended upon doing it accurately and covertly. I confess to having been obsessed about getting it right, usually walked first in line, completely focussed, concentrating on many things at once: direction, distance, speed… sound, shapes, smells… all in the ominous darkness of unfamiliar terrain and the potential for a hostile presence. This time, however, it was a whole lot easier. The enemy threat was still there but Corporal Chididi led the way with the sure-footed certainty of moving on home turf. He still moved very slowly, still paused to listen and sense, but the navigation aspect was in the bag.

I'd memorised the route before departure and could, as he led us through the bush, recognise the natural features that I'd seen on the map, mentally marking them off as waypoints along our journey. Moving carefully at night is slow, less than two kilometres an hour, but our walk-in was only about ten kilometres, so we were in our area of responsibility by about 0100hrs. Gradually, progressively, at pre-determined locations along the foot of the hills, we dropped off the other call-signs. Each one waited to allow us to depart and then waited longer still, to watch and listen before turning to climb their hill and select an OP on the other side, facing northward.

Finally, there were just two call-signs remaining, Corporal Chididi's and mine. In the darkness, I could just see the slope of the ground beginning to curve to my right. We didn't need to talk as we both understood that this was the entrance to his defile and he would leave me here. He would go on to find the exact place to set up his ambush while I would turn right and head up the side of the feature to establish my OP. He set off slowly with his stick and I waited with mine, until I was sure I could hear nothing unusual. We quietly and carefully ascended, so slowly, placing one foot down gently, then the other, pausing often to listen, feeling for the route. When we reached the beginning of the rock dome, we traversed around to the left, remaining in the bush so that we didn't present a silhouette, even at night. We passed fully around the hill, high above where Chididi was laying his ambush, until we were on the northern side.

Again, we waited, listening, crouched in all-round-defence. Then I selected the site of the OP in thick, shade-giving bush to hide the soldier and keep the sun from reflecting off the binoculars. The bush dropped away below it and I knew I was looking out over the sleeping villages of the Tribal Trust Land below. Rearwards from the OP, I could see where we would be able to crawl under the bushes to a laying-up place in dead ground. It was a good OP and I was happy. We sat together in the laying-up place, silently listening and trying to sense if anything was wrong. There was nothing, no voice, or scrape or rolling stone, just silence. Before first light, I moved into the OP and was watching as the sun rose over the villages. Every hour thereafter, we would rotate OP duty until after last light.

Meanwhile, Corporal Chididi had been moving into his ambush location. What I relate now is what he told me straight afterwards, so I believe it to be as factually accurate as my memory allows. After leaving me, he didn't walk straight along the defile, he skirted along the edge of it, in the bush to avoid leaving any tracks. When he arrived at his objective, he paused to listen and then carried out a close reconnaissance of the ground, looking at every boulder, tree and bush, studying how the path threaded between them, imaging people following this route by day and by night. His three men crouched in all round defence, protecting him.

After a while, he had seen enough and had decided exactly where to place his claymores and his men. They grouped together, and he briefed them. It is important that the reader understands the challenge facing these four infantry soldiers. They would be occupying a position adjacent to a pathway that Chididi knew would be well-used by locals every day. They must be positioned close enough to the path to ambush any terrorists who came, but completely concealed from any passer-by. They would have to maintain this standard of concealment for several days. At night, they would be able to eat (no cooking), drink and relieve themselves but, by day, they would have to remain motionless. To their eternal credit, they did it.

I cannot say with certainty how many days Corporal Chididi's ambush remained covertly in position because I don't know the date of our deployment but, in the late afternoon of 31 December, the OPs in the hills had a sighting. I had thought it was of 12 terrorists, but Major Dennison's diary was written shortly after the event and he recorded it as 18 CTs, so I'll defer to his record. The CTs were first spotted by the OPs in the hills to my east, moving from right to left across our front. Speaking softly on the radio, I called in the sighting report to Captain Kay Choruma, now acting in command of D Company while the OC was in Fort Victoria.

The Fireforce was manned by A Company 2RAR, commanded on that day by the 2ic, Captain Jean Vos. It lifted off from Rutenga and began to fly towards us. I was told by Kay that it was on its way at about the same time as the CTs came into sight from my OP. As they passed across my front, far below us, I could see that they were walking along a dirt path that would later turn into the defile to the west of my OP. That was Corporal Chididi's ambush position. I radioed Chididi, warned him of their approach and told him to turn off his radio until the Fireforce was overhead. Still watching the CTs, who were moving in small groups, I heard my radio come to life and call-sign 19 (Jean Vos in the K-Car) asking me for a sitrep. While I was speaking to him, I heard a 'boom' from the defile.

Corporal Chididi described the ambush as follows. Lying in position, motionless and straining to sense the enemy, he heard the sound of approaching voices, male voices in good spirits. Then he saw a small group enter his killing ground. Others were further behind. Then he heard the far distant beat of helicopters. The CTs heard them too and stopped suddenly, their faces raised and their mouths open, gradually crouching down. He waited no longer but pressed the electrical initiator of his claymores. The first group of CTs were only a few feet from the claymores, caught the full force of the blast of steel fragments and would have been killed, he was sure, even without the firing that he and his men poured into the killing ground. When the dust cleared, there were three lying dead and he switched on his radio.

On my OP, I reported the sound of the explosion and the Fireforce continued towards us. It was approaching from the south and would pass overhead my OP. My soldiers began pointing to a thickly wooded stream to the north of my position and I saw what they were indicating (African soldiers have much better eyesight than Europeans). I reported on the radio that we had CTs visual and gave the K-Car a target indication. The rest is very much as the A Company war diary described it. When the K-Car passed overhead my OP, it flew straight to the stream-bed and opened fire on the CTs, who fired back. Two G-Cars put down stop groups at either end of the stream. One was ordered to remain static while call-sign Charlie One closed in. That call-sign encountered the CTs and killed two. The others broke cover and were shot by the K-Car as they tried to 'bombshell' across open ground. So, ended the last day of 1978.

Now here is the thing. If Corporal Chididi hadn't suggested siting an ambush in that defile, the CTs would have passed through it *before* the Fireforce arrived on the scene. I wouldn't have been able to get down quickly enough from that high OP to intercept them, and all I would have been able to tell the Fireforce would have been where I had last seen them, not where they were. Also, if Corporal Chididi and his three men hadn't been able to maintain concealment for all that time, in spite of the extremely close proximity to passers-by, the terrorists would have got word of our presence and there would have been no sighting. Corporal Chididi, section commander of 10 Platoon, D Company 2RAR was an excellent young soldier and I truly hope that this account will serve to place that on permanent record.

Reference: Wood, JRT 1989, *The War Diaries of Andre Dennison*, Ashanti Publishing Ltd., Gibraltar.

CHAPTER FOURTEEN

FIREFORCE

INTRODUCTION: FIREFORCE by Captain Andrew Telfer

'I had forgotten that, while Thor hurls his Hammer from storm-clouds, Odin prefers his strike to come out of a calm sky'
Robert Low, The White Raven

Fireforce was the Rhodesian Security Force's most effective tactic, if one measures effectiveness by body count. However, if it were evaluated strategically, in relation to the core reason why a nation has Security Forces - to protect the civilian population - it was the opposite.

Fireforce was a paradox. On the one hand, the role of the Infantry is to 'close with and destroy the enemy' and Fireforce was a means to do exactly that. However, it turned the villages of black civilian Rhodesians into killing grounds, contrary to a fundamental counter-insurgency lesson: there is no stronger incentive for joining an insurgency than having your home burned and your family terrified, hurt or killed by your own Security Forces.

Nevertheless, the death toll on the enemy was huge and asymmetrical, and it was a very popular tactic. The RLI and the RAR provided most of the Fireforce troops and, as young men, we preferred Fireforce bush trips to any other, frequently finding ways to join other Companies on their rotation, a practice known fondly as 'snivelling onto Fireforce'. Young men, if impelled into warfare, want to fight and will fight well. Fireforce was pure fighting.

For the enemy, it must have truly felt like Odin's strike out of a calm sky. The terrorist was terrorised and there was great satisfaction in knowing that. For the civilian population, however, it must have been a nightmare of death from the sky, panic, burning homes, cross-fire, chaos and carnage. And then we left, gone in the helicopters in which we came, leaving the traumatised civilians to the influence of the omnipresent insurgents.

This article seeks to briefly explain how Fireforce operations were conducted and, together with the article *We Searched* that follows later, an insight into how they felt.

When an RAR Company was deployed on Fireforce, they co-located themselves at a Forward Air Field (FAF) with the Air Force. Examples of FAFs were Rutenga, Buffalo Range, Fort Victoria, Grand Reef, Mtoko, Mount Darwin, Wankie... places with air strips long enough for the fixed wing aircraft, a unit of often-stoned Rhodesia Defence Regiment ouens to 'guard' it, resources and facilities to maintain and refuel aircraft, and beds with clean sheets for the pilots.

RAR Fireforce-Early Days

On arrival at the FAF, the first thing that the soldiers of the incoming Company did was to lay out their kit in readiness to take over from the outgoing Company. From that moment, the next call-out was theirs. Each day, a blackboard was updated to assign individual soldiers, in sticks, to helicopters and to the Dakota. Each stick included a commander (from junior NCO to junior officer), a rifleman and two MAG gunners.

The air compliment of the standard Fireforce comprised very few aircraft, reflecting sanctions-driven shortages of military hardware. There were usually three Alouette III G Cars, each armed with twin .50 Brownings, carrying a pilot, a helicopter technician (chopper tech) and one RAR four-man stick. The command Alouette, or K Car, had a 20mm cannon firing HE rounds and carried the senior pilot, the Officer Commanding (OC) the RAR Company and a chopper tech. Air to ground strike capability was enhanced by a small fixed-wing Cessna aircraft (Lynx), which dropped all manner of unpleasant material on terrorists. An ancient Dakota completed the armada, carrying 18 paratroopers (four sticks and two soldiers who remained on the Drop Zone to pack parachutes during the contact). The latter were given the callsign Wanker since, for that deployment at least, they were not doing any fighting.

Call outs were usually initiated by men on an OP sighting terrorist activity (see *Observation Posts* elsewhere in *Chibaya Moyo*). The OP gave basic information about the sighting, including the location, number, description, weapons and activities of the terrorists, their own location and that of other friendly forces and, often, a recommended approach route. As soon as the sighting report was received, a siren would sound across the FAF, officers would go to the Operations Room for a briefing, and soldiers would move to their kit, light up cigarettes and have nervous pees. Briefings were very 'brief' and almost irrelevant; we knew what we were doing and what to expect. We knew that, whatever the overall scene, our experience would be confined to a few metres of bush.

The best approach route was over the OP towards the target as that gave the pilots the same perspective as the OP during the talk-on and, as the OP was usually on a hill, shielded the noise of the incoming choppers. As the K Car approached the area, the pilot called the OP for an update on the terrorists and a target description. The OP described the target from his perspective, referencing features that would quickly catch the eye of the pilot, like tin-roofed buildings. The choppers flew as low as possible until the K Car pulled up over the OP and flew rapidly towards the target, seeking to sight the enemy from the OP's description. It may drop smoke, calling on the OP to direct it from the smoke to the target. Meanwhile, the G Cars flew in a wide orbit around the target area.

The terrorists, at this time, would be manoeuvring out of their skin, trying to evade the notice of the K Car and escape out of the target area. The high-explosive rounds fired by the 20mm cannon gave it the nickname 'the gun that speaks twice': each round was heard once as it was fired and again as it detonated on the ground. It was understandably unpopular among ZANLA and ZIPRA cadres.

As soon as the terrorists were sighted from the K Car, the tech engaged them with the 20mm cannon and the K Car flew in tight orbits around them. The OC made a rapid appreciation of likely escape routes and sited his stop groups (or confirmed a pre-selection made on a map back in the Ops Room) and the K Car pilot instructed the G Cars to place their sticks in those locations.

For a stop group, the tension of being carried in the air disappeared in a cloud of rotor-driven dust and sticks as the chopper touched down and four soldiers sprinted from it, deploying in all-round defence as it took off again. The sound of the departing helicopter was soon replaced with that of the OC's voice on the radio, directing the stop group to either sweep towards the K Car or remain static to prevent a break out. In both cases, the soldiers knew to move into ground that offered overhead cover from view as that would be where the enemy sought to make their escape from the aircraft.

3 Sqn RhAF C47 Para Daks

There would come a time when the contact 'went to ground', meaning that the terrorists were no longer moving. At that stage, the OC and the K Car pilot determined a DZ for the paratroopers and they were dropped. For those in the Dakota, this was a welcome relief from the heat of the aircraft and the constriction of the harness. A lot of fuss has been made about the low altitude of the drops (500 feet AGL) but it was fine, as it minimised the time in the air, sometimes under fire. More should be made of the DZs, chosen for tactical advantage rather than quality. Rhodesian paratroopers were dropped among trees, rocks, stumps and holes. It was the arrival that was the problem, not the overall altitude.

On landing, soldiers struggled out of harnesses, cocked weapons and crouched facing the K Car. The OC directed the young officer among them to sweep towards the K Car and the sweep line would advance. Thereafter, the OC moved the sweep line and the stop groups around like pieces on a board, sometimes for hours. The terrorists sought to evade us and fought when we found them.

In those fights, the young soldiers of the RAR and the RLI were extraordinarily successful. Fireforce success rates gave Comops wonderfully encouraging statistics to feed the media and reassure the nation: 'People sleep peaceably in their beds at night only because rough men stand ready to do violence on their behalf.' (George Orwell)

Except, we weren't rough men. We were boys, enthusiastic, inexperienced, wholly committed to doing well, but wanting to enjoy the vibrancy of young life…

not die. And here is the second Fireforce paradox: we wanted to do it and volunteered for it… but it took a massive toll on those of us who did it repeatedly.

COMMENTS ON FIREFORCE by Captain Russell Fulton

Andy has touched many a raw nerve with is brilliant, graphic and incredibly accurate introductory article to this quite incredible Rhodesian Army tactic. I cannot, in all sincerity, think of anyone else better qualified to write about such a complex subject.

For those who don't know, Fireforce was, in very simplistic layman terms, the concept of vertical envelopment. All good military commanders worthy of their rank and appointment would, and did in Rhodesia's case, research past conflicts and dissect and analyse them in minute detail to glean as much information as possible with a view to establishing what lessons could be learnt. The all-powerful United States military machine during their war in Vietnam decided, in their infinite wisdom, that troop saturation of target areas with Bell 205 "Huey" heli-borne troops was the way to stop advancing conventionally trained NVA and a belligerent but determined Viet Cong guerrilla enemy.

Colonel David Gladwell Parker aka 'The King'

With Fireforce in mind, there are indeed parallels, but our concept was vastly superior and dangerously effective.

Where the USA believed that their air superiority was their primary asset in terms of troop deployment by Bell 205 helicopters and an effective means of stopping their enemy, it was far from effective. As history attests, the tactic was a dismal failure and by any strategic measure. Good men were lost through an ideology borne of ignorant and arrogant commanders who wrongly perceived troop saturation as a means to an end.

They either did not understand the tenacity of their foe or, perhaps, ignored the fighting spirit of those they were pitted against. One would have reasonably thought that a few lessons would have been learnt from the Battle of Dien Bien Phu when the French were comprehensively routed by an unconventional but disciplined guerrilla force.

Colonel David Gladwell Parker (AKA 'The King'), former and much revered and respected CO of the RLI and later Deputy Commander of 3 Brigade, may be credited, together with elements of the Rhodesian Air Force, in developing and refining the Rhodesian Fireforce concept, a derivative of the U.S. heli-borne troop deployment concept. Colonel Parker was tragically killed in a helicopter accident on 23 December 1975 whilst visiting troops in the Cashel area before Christmas. This was an officer of enormous standing who was undoubtedly heading for higher rank appointment and he was widely and, justifiably in my opinion, regarded as a future commander of the Rhodesian Army.

The operational effectiveness of the Rhodesian Fireforce concept as both a tactical and strategic deterrent, both internally and externally, can never be challenged. Our former ZIPRA and ZANLA foe will agree as much.

WE SEARCHED by Captain Andrew Telfer

We searched from the air,
Flying into combat,
Tight with anticipation.

Flying into a Fireforce contact felt like being swept over a waterfall. Years later, when I took up white-water kayaking, I recognised that feeling again: going beyond the point of no return, when forces stronger than you impel you over the edge, when you must bring your top game or suffer potentially fatal consequences

We searched the bush,
For foreign cloth,
Denim blue or camouflage.

As we swept slowly forward, our eyes searched for the tiny piece of cloth that would give our enemy away. Mostly, they wore blue denim, sometimes flecked camouflage, occasionally something else. We knew to look through the bush, not at it, and that little piece of clothing was what we sought. Our African soldiers, natural hunters, always saw it first.

We searched the air,
For sound that warned,
Scrape, scuff, sudden nothing.

The advantage is with the combatant who is not moving. Able to see very little in thick bush, a key sense was hearing, and we developed it as our close friend, able to separate out the chopper noise. If something alien was heard, our reactions were almost ethereal: a simultaneous silent crouch, heads cocked, ears and eyes seeking, weapons aimed. The silhouette of an African soldier in that posture is of a pure predator.

We searched huts,
Silent people watching,
Waiting, knowing.

I respect and feel sorry for civilian people in war, and I believe soldiers should protect civilians. That's why I hated searching villages... but, we had to do it, our enemy moved amongst them. He sought food, women and the opportunity for intimidation and indoctrination. Sometimes, he cached weapons or hid himself there, and so we searched. RAR soldiers were not brutal; they were gentle and polite, but the villagers volunteered nothing. They were too afraid of the terrorists to speak to us or to help us. They just wanted us gone and, if we had a firefight in a village, it was a tragedy.

We searched our hearts,
For strength to advance,
Lift, move, tread, and repeat.

There were times when we knew the enemy was hiding in front of us but could not see him. We had to sweep forward in extended line, sometimes in bush so thick that we couldn't see more than a few metres in front of us. That takes willpower: lift the foot, move it forward – no, not into a hover, forward – place it down, move weight onto it, repeat with the next foot... All the while, waiting for the explosion of sight and sound that you knew was coming.

We searched for advantage,
When the air exploded,
Feet flying, eyes aiming.

Contacts were like an explosion of senses, perhaps like being hit by a swarm of bees. We were so well-trained, and our self-belief so strong, that we always reacted by attacking. This was no place for trepidation, only a scramble for tactical advantage.

We searched for movement,
And struck at it,
Willed ourselves onto it.

Sometimes, we didn't see anything at all, even after the firing started. Then it was simply a case of rushing forward to cause movement, to flush the enemy out. The RAR soldier in that mode is a sight to behold: darting, hunting, aiming; seeking out the enemy.

We searched for the killing shot,
The end of the fear,
The coup de grâce.

It was only over when the enemy was dead. Wounded, he could be a nightmare. So, we closed in, aiming to get the shot that killed him before he got the one that killed us. When we got it, all I ever felt was relief, simple relief. He dies, we live, relief.

We searched the bodies,
Taking weapons,
Leaving death.

The weapons we used, especially the MAG, caused a lot of damage to human tissue. Searching bodies for weapons and documents was messy but not disturbing. We were completely detached from the humanity of who we had killed, had no sense of a person.

We searched the eyes,
Of our friends,
Seeing all, saying nothing.

Sitting with another Second Lieutenant, on the edge of a field, grass burned out, bodies of terrorists in bags being loaded into helicopters…nothing to say, even when he started to silently cry. Nothing to offer except a cigarette, understanding completely but unable to put anything into words.

'One more dance along the razor's edge finished. Almost dead yesterday, maybe dead tomorrow, but alive, gloriously alive, today.' (Robert Jordan, Lord of Chaos)

We searched our weapons,
For grime, sand, grit,
Fearful of the nightmare stoppage.

I had, and occasionally still have, a dream: a terrorist raises his rifle, I raise mine, I squeeze the trigger, my rifle does not fire, his does. Perhaps you may say, as nightmares go, that's a nursery rhyme, but it was my most real dread. I cleaned my rifle obsessively and made sure my men did too. Every evening and early the next morning, I slipped away with a little cup of aviation fuel and cleaned every part of my rifle, carefully oiled and assembled it, cleaned my rounds and magazines, checked my grenades, sat quietly and disappeared into myself.

We searched for meaning,
Searched for meaning,
For Meaning.

We did find it: farms run by determined and brave mothers while husbands were on call-up; the wonderful ladies of the Women's Institute freely giving tea and sticky buns to our soldiers at makeshift roadside cafes; anxious families formed up in convoys to travel between towns; a tiny baby impaled on a terrorist bayonet (stop… think about that); civilian passenger planes shot down and survivors murdered... and we found it in the brotherhood that was the Rhodesian African Rifles.

NOW YOU SEE THEM, NOW YOU DON'T by Lieutenant Michael Matthews

A Company 1RAR spent a considerable amount of time on Fireforce duty in the Hurricane area during early 1978, and based mainly at Bindura, Mtoko and Mount Darwin.

On 3rd May 1978, whilst based at Mtoko airfield we received a callout from an O.P. in the nearby Mtoko TTL. My 3 Platoon were in the Dak this time performing the para role, and we spent several minutes waiting on the runway whilst our O.C., Major Barry Getliffe, proceeded ahead in the K-Car followed shortly thereafter by Peter (Peewee) Holme's platoon, spread amongst four G-Cars. Our destination was no more than about fifteen minutes away, so it wasn't long before the Dak commenced a tight orbit whilst the stop groups were being put down at likely escape routes to set up ambushes.

Within a few minutes, we received orders from the air force jump master to "stand up and hook up". As usual, I was first out of the door with Sergeant Mleya positioned in the middle of the group and PWO Munyika taking up the rear when we commenced our run in at the standard drop altitude of five hundred feet. I had made the conscious decision to invariably exit the aircraft first after my platoon had completed its para training earlier in the year because I considered that it would set a good example to them and somehow reduce the risk that any one of them might 'freeze' in the door. In retrospect, however, I'm entirely convinced that I need never have concerned myself on this score. We all believed fiercely in our cause, apart from which we would have parachuted into the fires of hell for each other – of that I am sure.

Whilst descending, I could see the K-Car in orbit over what was obviously the point at which the insurgents had been sighted, and the fact that the twenty-millimetre cannon was putting down a lot of fire was a sure sign that they had been seen and were probably trying to make their escape from the scene already. The G-Cars having deployed their sticks, had obviously also made independent sightings, and there was a large volume of fire coming from all of the choppers.

Having organized my *Masodja* into a long sweep line, we commenced our sweep towards the stop groups under Major Getliffe's instruction. A small, largely granite kopje lay between us and our stop groups, and our OC informed me that three or four gooks had taken refuge amongst the rocks and bushes at its summit, since no movement had been detected since they were last seen by both the O.P., which was still in place, and the K-Car.

By the time we had reached the base of the kopje, things had become uncannily quiet. The K-Car, being low on avtur, had to return to Mtoko for refuelling, as had the G-Cars. The O.P. assured me, however, that they were able to pick up any movement from the group of gooks at the summit, and that they would let me know immediately they detected any movement.

This was one of several occasions where the disappearance of our aircraft into the distance and the onset of an eerie silence became particularly unnerving. Somehow, for me, when the Blue Jobs were involved in the contact, I always felt that we had the upper hand. The aircraft were a source of great comfort and I often felt a great deal of 'aloneness' and anxiety when they weren't at hand.

Our sweep line had reached the kopje and we cautiously commenced our ascent. It seemed to me that my own heartbeat was audible, and a giveaway to the terrs who were ensconced in the rocks at its summit. We gradually crept up the small granite outcrop with low bush scattered around it, and near the top it became evident that the insurgents were indeed huddled together at the top of the kopje from the lie of the land. I had to climb up a large boulder in order to obtain a sufficiently good purchase to enable me to get a first-hand look at their position. Having successfully negotiated the boulder I knew that, once standing, I would be able to get a good look at what lay beyond, since I was almost at the top of the outcrop. I slowly raised myself up, only to find four AK 47's trained on my head, and no more than two feet away from me.

I instinctively ducked at the precise moment the gooks opened fire on me and remember feeling granite chips flying through my hair as my head disappeared rapidly behind the rock which separated us. It was almost as if all of this had taken place in slow motion. I quickly gathered my wits (no heroics like storming their position alone for me!) and made radio contact with the O.P. who again assured me that they would be able to see any movement, and that they had me visual.

Since it seemed the enemy were well and truly cornered, I decided to lob a few grenades onto their position. I communicated my intention to Corporal Maxwell, who was closest to me, and he gave me his two grenades to add to my own. In all I tossed four grenades into the rocks above me, two HE and two white phosphorous and the platoon immediately mounted an assault on their position. The result was unexpected, and with the pungent smell of the remnants of the white phos grenades still thick in our nostrils, we were shocked to find their position deserted, with no apparent sign of casualties. I made contact with the O.P. once again, and they again assured me that they had not detected any movement after I had thrown the grenades.

I noticed, however, a small gap between the granite boulders through which, in my view, no human being larger than a six or seven-year-old could have passed. We threw two more H.E. grenades into the small gap for good measure and I maintain now, as I did then, that so desperate was their plight that the Gooks had all contrived to squeeze themselves through this tiny gap. As most who had been in contact situations with terrorists would vouch, they had an ability to be extremely elusive, particularly when their lives depended on it, and I am sure that the one hundred metres world sprint record was probably unofficially broken by a number of them in such circumstances.

We continued our sweep, and no further contact was made with the enemy by the time we had passed through our stop groups. Our sortie resulted in eight confirmed kills, all of which had been achieved by the K-Car and the G-Cars initially. The feeling was that the four insurgents who had 'vaporised' on the kopje represented the balance of the terrorist group so, all in all, our Fireforce mission was successful.

THE ENCOUNTER by Corporal Peter Fuyane, 1RAR

Mtoko, North Eastern Rhodesia, March 1976.

At 0400 the sentry woke me from inside my basher. I got up and rolled up my sleeping bag and fastened it to my webbing. I then took my towel and washed my face with cold water before taking my rucksack and kit bag to the stores for safekeeping. It was still dark, but it was one of those nights when the moon decides not to set before the sun comes up and as a result it was still hanging up there in the western sky. So, by the light of the moon I checked my area and satisfied myself that the CSM would have nothing to discuss with me when I came back – you see he does not normally like to see bits and papers lying around.

By the time I finished checking my section area the east was red, the time was 0445 and I took my mug and went to the kitchen. The cook was in a good mood despite the early hour and I got a full mug of tea. The whole platoon was there in the kitchen this morning and they were talking in low tones, joking and laughing quietly. We had been briefed the previous evening and everyone knew what he was going to do today but it seemed that no-one was worried at all.

At 0500 hours we were summoned to the Ops tent for more orders (the NCOs that is) and were briefed for 10 minutes. Helicopters were allocated to the various sticks and soon after we poured out of the tent to brief our sticks. As the sun peeped over the horizon we were sitting in our helicopters. The pilot in our helicopter switched on his engine and after a whining noise the huge rotors started to turn, as if they really did not intend to, then gathered momentum until they were a blur.

All five choppers were now roaring and slowly, one by one, they lifted off from the side of the bush airstrip. Soon we were up and circling the base camp waiting for the rest of the choppers to lift off. I looked down below me and saw amid the reddish brown dust the last of the helicopters lifting off. Before long, the choppers were off to the north of our base camp. Up there the wind was cold and crisp, and it blew on my face from the open side of the chopper. Down below the trees were green and some turning grey, but they all seemed to be of identical height, so that looking down one was reminded of those advertisements for carpets.

I have enjoyed riding in a helicopter ever since I was a recruit and, right now, I was enjoying myself looking out there below as the world slid past. Then I got to thinking. I thought of the first day I came to Methuen Barracks, six years previously and of the jumble of years between; it was hard at times. There were moments of happiness and sorrow, and I thought of people, faces of soldiers that had come and gone, faces of men who are and were a family that is one of the greatest and happiest of all families, the RAR.

I was brought back to reality by the bank of the chopper; we were now in an area with a lot of small gomos and we were flying at tree-top level along a small river with water and a lot of reeds. There were quite a lot of rocks on the river bed itself, but the sand showed here and there. The suspected base camp was down near a waterfall next to a big rock and I saw the leading helicopter circling around the rock. All around the area were very thick bushes and tall trees and, slightly right and away from the river, was a field. Already, one of the choppers had landed there while we were circling.

The pilot indicated a clearing in the field and gave the sign that he was going to land and went down. As soon as the chopper touched down, we spilled out, took up defensive arc and cocked our weapons. I was ordered via the radio to join the other stick and move down the river on both sides. I took the left bank and the other stick commander the right, and we moved forward. Behind us could be heard the deep bark of the FN and the clatter of the AK.

Occasionally a stray bullet went cracking above us. I thought any moment now a bullet would find its way into me, but the sound of the crack indicated that the bullets were well to the left. Then, without warning, automatic fire broke out about 75 metres in front of us.

The bullets hit the rock in the river bank and the ricochets made an ugly sound. We opened fire from both sides of the bank – aimed fire was impossible, because we could not see anyone, but only hear the firing. A grenade exploded, though I was not sure who threw it, our people or the terrorists. Ahead of us someone shouted an order, and I guessed the direction of the voice. Already we were moving from cover to cover in bounds towards the firing. The fire from the terrorists was not very effective because it was not aimed either. As we neared the place where the firing came from it stopped. We carried on firing and this time we were running as fast as we could.

Reaching the place, we spread out, then as I was passing a large tree, I saw a man lying face down. I stopped to take a look, he was dead, his AK carbine lying by his side. Here and there in the thick bush were well-concealed hideouts and it seemed they were empty. We went quickly through the area, then fanned out into all round defence. By that time, I was sweating a lot. I reported on my radio and sent a searching party into the camp, then I checked for any casualties in my stick – there were none. Ammunition state was satisfactory. When the searching party arrived, they reported two dead ters and about seven packs in the base camp. There were four hides of three men each. I reported that and was told to carry on sweeping until I met a stick that had been deployed 400 metres further on. There was a stick and I was informed it was making its way into the area of my contact.

Then, as we prepared to advance, firing broke out about 300 metres ahead of us and we were told to lay an ambush on the river bank and we quickly did that and waited. It was getting very hot now as the sun was halfway up and sweat kept blinding me. I used my face veil to wipe my face. Then as the firing stopped ahead of us, one of my men kicked me and showed a thumbs down sign and pointed, and sure enough, moving along the river bed were two terrorists.

One had an RPD and the other an SKS, and they were walking in the shallow water to lose tracks. We waited until they were parallel to us and let go. They never had a chance. Leaving two men covering me, I took the other man and we went to pull the bodies from the water and recover the weapons. The helicopters came to take away the bodies. By that time the day was high, and the sun was very hot now.

We were told to rest as trackers were looking for tracks. Other sticks arrived and a follow-up was initiated. After a thorough search of the contact area, we were told to go to the clearing and the helicopters arrived. We ran to them, keeping our heads down, because you see, every soldiers who is in love with his head bends down in order to keep it where it belongs. As the chopper lifted off, I looked down in the contact area, now so peaceful.

We climbed high and sped back to base, the wind blew on my face and, I thought, that was the life, never a dull moment. Then I got to thinking of that cold beer waiting for me and I settled back. Today is good and gone, and tomorrow out of sight.

Source: *The Lion & Tusk*, 2011, volume 17, number 2.

OF OIL LEAKS AND OTHER AFFLICTIONS by Captain Russell Fulton

Gunshot wounds (oil leaks) in the line of duty were all part of the infantry job description and, as unwanted as they might have been, they were bound to happen at some point in time. That was an inevitable consequence of our war and as it progressed, exponentially in the late 1970's, there was an increasing number of communist trained insurgents who were willing and, quite agreeable to, issuing them without invitation.

This is not at all about glamorising my own experiences, of which there were several, but is intended to answer the questions from many good and genuinely interested civilians and non-infantry friends who have put them to me. This write-up is to briefly explain my personal experiences but, and more importantly, the emotion and all that that entailed witnessing the injuries of my fellow brothers-in-arms.

I have been asked, more times than I really care to recount, what it felt like being shot. There is no short, stereotypical answer to this as it is a very subjective matter and we are all made differently in the eyes of our respective God. Everyone has a different pain threshold, control over their mind and emotions but the mere act of being wounded is, initially, one of surprise, shock and, dare I say it, an element of fear. The human body, comprising some 60% water, does not respond well to military munitions in general and high velocity projectiles (bullets) in particular.

Oftentimes, there would be a neat entry wound the diameter of the offending projectile that made the wound appear quite innocuous. Depending upon the velocity and range from which the weapon was fired, if its trajectory was altered by a twig or hit bone, there were often no exit wound. 7.62 x 39mm cartridges used by our enemy were notorious for deflecting off bone and causing tremendous internal tissue and organ damage. The 7.62 x 51mm cartridge used by the RAR (FN & MAG 58) would punch through bone leaving a massive exit wound, often fatal.

The earlier reference to 'surprise' as one of the likely responses on being wounded, is one of the most important paragraphs in the 'Principles of War' simply because, 'Surprise', in all its guises, can result in a breakdown in morale, discipline and expose those weaknesses to a determined and disciplined enemy. In our military teaching, it is defined thus: "Surprise is the consequence of shock and confusion induced by the deliberate or incidental introduction of the unexpected". Sustaining wounds during action proved to be a challenging test of leadership as it could compromise the other nine principles, no question about it.

Whilst serving in A-Tk Tp, Sp Cdo, 1RLI in late 1977 on fire force deployment, our callsign, under the command of Lt Simon 'Crispy' Willar, was fired upon by K-Car 20mm HE incendiary canon whilst tactically crossing a sheet of exposed granite rock atop a small hill feature whilst advancing toward the contact area (see *Chibaya Moyo* anecdote on this). Simon Willar sustained similar, but more grievous injuries to his calf muscle than mine and, it is fair to say, both were 'decommissioning' oil leaks. Simon, for his pleasure, had lost around a third of one his once muscular calf muscles (I could have pushed my fist in to his wound, that is how severe it was) and me, about one quarter.

I knew that I had been hit because I simply fell mid-stride as my right leg decided it was no longer available for locomotion. My initial thoughts were for those in our call sign and if they were all safe. I never realised at that time that friendly forces were behind this. I looked back down the incline of granite to where Troopers Ivan Farmer and Dougie Miller lay, covering Simon's and my advance, and they were, thankfully, unscathed. Down that sloping granite rock was a steady stream of ruby-red blood, mine. I decided best to not look at my leg as I did not want to see the extent of my injury.

For my part, my right calf felt like, for the sake of poor analogy and because I had never felt something like this before, it was akin to how a red-hot branding-iron might feel being pushed in to one's calf. Because we were still effectively in contact, I knew that it was all a bit of a nonsense until I looked towards Simon crouched behind a large boulder shouting "Stop, Stop, Stop!" over his A76 radio.

Simon was, in RLI parlance, 'in seriously shit-order' but he was the consummate professional and a man cut from the right jib, be in no doubt about that. He accepted his bit and seemed completely impervious to the true gravitas of his injury. An extraordinarily tough bugger and from whom I drew much personal inspiration. I never saw him wince and never heard him complain. That is as fine an example of leadership and self-control for you.

Sometime later, as a newly commissioned subbie in 1RAR, I would see things from an entirely different perspective. Now, as a commander of men, they (my men) rightly looked to me for inspiration but, more importantly, for decisive leadership. These recalls will, no doubt, be recorded in various SITREPS, Contact Reports, CASEVAC and NOTICAS signals from that time.

Thank God, I never lost one of my own as a platoon commander because that would be the subject of an entirely different and emotionally charged discussion. For my part, I would like to think that it was because I had been comprehensively trained on cadet course but, and as life has shown us, some things were simply 'meant to be'. Fate is what you make of it and, as we well know, you can be the orchestrator of that fate by personal and wanton desire, or, as evidenced during our war, because 'fate' was the ultimate arbitrator and the dice would fall as they were destined to fall.

Apart from the loss of a member of your own family, there can be fewer, more emotionally challenging times than losing a brother in arms. I saw it on several occasions, outside of my platoon, whilst attending military funerals and each one had the same raw and heart-rending emotional resonance with me. Military funerals, in which many of us were involved, were deeply respectful, sombre and emotionally charged events and, with indigenous customs acknowledged, a manifestly trying time for all. With some of our A.S., injury brought with that fate, a sense of foreboding. I cannot begin to explain cultural divergences and will leave that, respectfully, as I should. It was almost idiosyncratic with our A.S. where the passing of a loved one, breadwinner and head of the family spelt the demise of those left behind. The RAR can pride itself for always looking after her own and, we did and still do.

As I reflect upon those difficult, dangerous and challenging times as a young subbie, like countless hundreds of my peers, predecessors, superiors and, despite our respective unit pride, we always stood together, united in a common cause, and grieved the loss of all good and gallant men.

The British people, during WW II and the London blitz, are rightly referred to as a 'stoic people'. Rhodesians may lay claim to that same mantra and, without equivocation too. For fifteen years, as a politically and economically marginalised people, we did the business and we did it militarily because we could, and as history accurately attests, never losing a single military operation. We trained hard, we fought hard, we grieved hard, but we never yielded, not ever. That is the most fitting tribute we place at the graves of our beloved fallen comrades, those brave men who were taken too soon.

'Tis better to have fought and lost than never to have fought at all'.

Alfred, Lord Tennyson

Tinorwira kukunda! Zororayi murugare, tichazo sangana.

HOPPING ABOUT IN A HURRICANE: CORPORAL BONANZA AND CHOPPER DOWN by Lieutenant Michael Matthews

On about 14th May 1978 A Coy 1RAR relocated to Bindura on Fireforce duty, since it was unwise to base Fireforce at any one place for any appreciable period for the obvious reason that terrorist groups quickly became aware of the presence of Fireforce bases, and thereafter generally conducted their activities outside Fireforce's area of influence. They had also, from time to time, mounted mortar attacks on Fireforce bases, infamously at Mount Darwin on more than one occasion.

It wasn't long before we received our first call out, a sighting which an O.P. had made in the Chinamora TTL. We were in a contact on 15th May which accounted for three terrorists, and where I achieved a rare 'stand up landing', rather than landing on my butt! Our second call out into Chinamora came two days later, when we responded to a sighting near Mermaid's Pool, a place at which we had in days gone by had a great deal of fun as a family, sliding down rapids on tractor tubes and always thoroughly enjoying ourselves.

We received the callout at about 16h30 in the afternoon, so there wasn't much daylight left within which to complete our operation. In the result, we killed one terr, but there simply wasn't enough time to get back to Bindura before dark, given the after-dark limitations of the Alouettes. Major Barry (as we rather personably called our OC, Major Barry Getliffe) therefore determined that we should make for New Sarum, not fifteen minutes flying time from Mermaid's Pool.

The prospect of a night in Salisbury was enticing, even more so because our choppers passed at fairly low level over my dad's house in Helensvale, an outlying suburb of Salisbury, on the fringe of the rural area known as Domboshawa. I made an impassioned, but ultimately vain request to Major Barry by radio to drop me and my Platoon off at my dad's house, but as much as he would have liked to assist me, his hands were tied by Air Force protocol, and we proceeded to New Sarum.

Happily, however, I was able to persuade Major Barry to allow me to take those of my Platoon who were with us, about twelve in number, back to my dad's place for the night, and to procure transport at New Sarum. I phoned my dad and broke the news to him that he was about to be descended upon, and he was all too happy to accommodate my 'guests' who, in turn, were all too happy to accept the benefit of a wonderful meal, and a restful night under cover in secure surroundings. We returned to New Sarum at about 05h00 the next morning to meet up with the remainder of the Fireforce contingent and were on our way back to Bindura at first light.

Between the 19th and the 23rd May 1978 we were particularly active and were called out on at least half a dozen occasions. We achieved a number of kills during the period, the most significant of which was nine kills in a callout we received on 23rd May from an O.P. position in the Weya TTL which had reported a sighting of a large group of gooks. Unfortunately, the day was also significant for the fact that one of our number, Corporal Bonanza, was shot.

The Weya contact sticks in my mind more clearly than any other. It was 12h00 when we received the callout, and I and my Platoon were assigned to Dak duty that day. We were deployed into a good DZ whilst the K-Car was maintaining its usual tight orbit over the sighting and the G-Cars were laying down their stop groups. So began what was left of what would be a very long and harrowing day.

I had a sense of foreboding about this operation, not least because we knew that we were up against a significant body of insurgents, but also because the area through which we were moving comprised dense pockets of bush which provided ideal cover to the enemy. I honestly felt that in some places we might literally need to stand on them to know that they were there!

The sweep area which we had to cover was flat and extensive, and the likely routes of escape at which our stop groups had been deployed were some two kilometres distant. Matters were also complicated by the fact that large canopies of tree cover made the K-Car relatively ineffective as an offensive weapon, and markedly reduced the K-Car Commander's effectiveness in conducting operations.

I had organized my sweep line and, as usual, was in the centre and slightly ahead of the shallow, inverted 'V' formation which was required. Thus, each of us were about ten meters apart from each other stretching out on either side of me and Corporal Bonanza, seconded to us from C Company as I recall and one of the most deft and accomplished 'Sparrows' (trackers) I ever had the privilege to know, was slightly behind me and to my left.

'Alouette Down'

We had come under fire from small isolated pockets of gooks periodically for about two hours and had ourselves accounted for two gooks whom we had flushed from positions of cover when, having just passed a small copse of dense bush on our left a shot rang out, and Bonanza dropped to the ground like a lead weight. It was obvious from whence the shot had come, and we all pasted the bush with rounds. We established that we had (not unexpectedly) killed the single insurgent who had shot Bonanza, and I went to Bonanza's assistance. He was unconscious, but alive, and blood was streaming profusely from his left temple. The bullet had struck him just behind the left ear, and there was no sign of an exit wound.

Head wounds are notoriously 'bloody', and I applied a bandage to stem the flow of blood, radioed Major Barry to inform him of Bonanza's plight and called for a casevac for him. Since we were in a densely treed area, we had to carry

Bonanza a few hundred metres to a break in the tree canopy where I let off an orange smoke grenade to alert the casevac chopper pilot to our whereabouts. It was testimony to the pilot's skill that he was able to land and extract Bonanza with no more than a few centimetres of rotor clearance around his chopper.

Happily, we soon learnt that Bonanza's condition was critical, but stable, although it was not yet clear whether he had sustained any permanent brain impairment. I went to see Bonanza in hospital in Salisbury during a subsequent R&R and am relieved to say that he recovered fully.

This wasn't the last we were to see of Weya TTL, a hive of activity for insurgents, and we responded to a call out the very next day. This time around I was in a chopper stick, and our pilot was a Gifford Old Boy and old water polo mate of mine, Jeff Oborne. The bush in the sighting area was particularly dense, and Jeff had a lot of difficulty finding a DZ where he could safely deploy us. Jeff eventually saw a small clearing and had commenced his descent to below tree level, when all hell broke loose. A small group of terrs opened up on us, including an RPD gunner, and Jeff was forced to abort the deployment. He swung the chopper around and started to climb, but in doing so, our tail rotor got minced in a tree. At the same time, the chopper lost power and dropped out of the air like a brick.

Ignoring the threat of being decapitated by the main rotor blades in favour of the seemingly more imminent danger of being cut down by an RPD, we all scrambled out of the chopper and sprinted for the nearest cover. Fortunately, there was a shallow dry river bed nearby which we all thankfully tumbled into. We were all shaken but alright, except for the air force gunner, Charlie Norris. As is usual, Charlie had been wearing a flak jacket, and when the chopper hit the deck the jacket was driven up and into his nose, turning it into one hell of a bloody mess.

Fortunately, Major Barry was alert to our plight and, preferring to pull us out of the contact, he deployed a spare G-Car to extract us and take us back to camp. My coccyx ached for about six weeks after the event, and happily the duty didn't fall on us to spend the night guarding the grounded but for the time being at least, useless Alouette, a precious commodity our severely hamstrung and stretched armed forces couldn't afford to lose.

Unfortunately, the remainder of "A" Company was unsuccessful in accounting for any gooks that day, and the Fireforce operation was called off when visibility became too poor. Little did we know, but Weya TTL was going to give us more scope for activity the very next day.

So confident was this group of insurgents that, unlike their comrades, they chose to stay in the area, perhaps because they were aware that a chopper was down, and they were again spotted by the same O.P. which had compromised them the previous day. This time, we achieved spectacular success, and accounted for nine gooks that day. During our sweep, I came across the body of their RPG gunner whom we disarmed. Since insurgent RPG gunners didn't have the benefit of a conventional weapon like an AK to defend themselves, they were generally equipped with an automatic handgun like a Soviet Tokarev pistol, and this gook was no exception. Keen to keep some memorabilia for myself, and certain that I had not been seen by anyone, I relieved the gook of his Tokarev and took it home with me on my next R&R, even taking it and a few rounds to the Cleveland shooting range in Salisbury to try it out.

I heard nothing further about the issue and had become comfortable that this trophy would remain mine when, during our following Fireforce deployment Major Barry called me over to his tent and asked me whether I had removed the weapon from the previous contact scene. It was a mystery to me how Major Barry had fingered me, and I immediately disclosed to him that I was the culprit. To this day I still don't know how he found out, other than if Special Branch had informed him that some inventory was missing and that he took a stab at me being the culprit.

Between us, he ordered me to 'lose' the Tokarev at our next contact and, thankful that no sanction would apparently follow, I dutifully obeyed his order and my indiscretion was thereafter consigned to history. Phew!

MORVAN NDLOVU by Captain Andy Barrett

Beit Bridge, November 1978. Morvan Ndlovu was an extremely prominent ZIPRA information officer residing to the west of Beit Bridge, his house being situated close to the Umzingwane River. We (Capt Andy Barrett and Cpl Phil O'Donnell) were thoroughly briefed by SB with regards his appearance, stature and very large frame, and were so tasked to snatch him for interrogation purposes. This never materialized as he was not present at his residence at the time, we went to undertake the task.

While doing Fire Force we were tipped off that he was visiting a village on Bishopstone Ranch to the west of Beit Bridge. Summer was approaching, the rains had not yet come, and the land was barren and dry, first light was early, and the cicadas had already started their ear piercing tinnitic scratch. After being dropped near the village, our call-sign commenced sweeping through the maze of huts; past partially feathered chickens, malnourished mangy dogs, smouldering fires and African folk as they started their day. Lo and behold, Phil easily and rapidly identified the man in question as he sat rather majestically on a small mound of earth with his large frame surveying the goings on. We hastily bundled him at rifle point into a chopper, flew him to Beit Bridge to be handed over the SB. He was released as being declared clean after a three-day interrogation process.

After independence as the new State President Robert Mugabe was establishing his government, none other than Morvan Ndlovu was appointed as one of his state senators. To this day the entire tasking and interrogation process remains a mystery. Was he a double agent? An unknown gunman assassinated him in Beit Bridge in 1987.

THE DANCE OF THE FLAMING ARSEHOLES by Captain Mike Jones

Having taken a bang on the head, I was on light duties and was on sick leave. The boredom was driving me crazy. With a little skulduggery, I managed to end up with Support Company 1 RAR 81mm and 60mm mortar platoons and we were attached to RLI Support Commando, under Major Henson. The whole regiment was going on an external into Zambia. Col Charlie Aust was the CO.

What I knew about mortars was dangerous, but I had two very competent PWOs in charge of both platoons, who knew what they were doing. We convoyed to Mana Pools on the Zambezi and were briefed on the external. The op was a long way into Zambia and the RAR platoons were to secure the refuelling and ammo replenishment zones, half way to the target. Well, to cut a long story short, the politicos were talking and the op was postponed and the battle group, choppers and all, were moved back to Karoi. I ended up with the Support Commando, Fireforce, and we dug in around the Enterprise Golf Course. It did not take long for me and Maj Henson to clash.

The first clash came when he invited me to join him and his NCOs in their Officers' and NCO's mess for meals. I asked if my senior NCOs were invited as well. He said no, so I remained with the two platoons and ate with them. The second clash came when I was invited to join them for drinks in the Enterprise Club house. Again I asked if my senior NCOs were invited and again the answer was no. So again I politely turned down the invitation. In no time at all we were told to pack up and that we would join 3 Commando, under Major Bruce Snelgar. I was delighted to leave and I think he was relieved when we left.

Major Snelgar made us most welcome and the platoons settled in. Food was served from a common mess and the troops were getting on well. It was great to run into the late Chappy Rosenfels and other friends and to catch up with Major Snelgar on what had happened since the 1 Independent Company days.

The Int coming in from SB was very good as ZIPRA were operating in a Shona-speaking TTL. RLI were not being successful and it was very frustrating for all. Maj Snelgar called me in and, being the soldier he was, asked me what I thought they were doing wrong. I gave my opinion that I thought the walk-ins were too short and the gooks would be alerted to the troops' presence and move on. I offered, if he wanted, for RAR to do the next walk-in for him. He was happy to let us do this.

SB brought in an informer who said he had a large group of CTs feeding in his village and forcibly having sex with the young girls. We kitted him out in uniform and boots and plotted his village on the map. When I pointed out our drop-off point and the 15 to 20 km walk-in, there was disbelief.

We were dropped off and, at first light, we were in position. Major Snelgar had contacted FF and the choppers were in the air. Quite by chance, in the early morning dawn, I spotted the choppers on the horizon many k's away. I radioed the pilot to turn left and when to roll out. After a couple more corrections, FF was on track to our position. I let Major Henson know that we would mark our position with orange smoke and we would indicate the target direction with a pencil mini-flare. Our caps were turned inside out to display our dayglow patches to the sky so that we could be identified and, as the choppers came roaring in, I said "You are over our position now". The timing could not have been better.

The choppers immediately went into orbit and gooks broke from the houses. In the grey of first light, the new machine gun on the K car looked like something from Star Wars. The first gooks were taken out in seconds. Maj Henson in the K car did a sterling job and we soon linked up with RLI into a sweep line. A few hours later we had collected a number of weapons and other kit and had 11 kills, with a couple of wounded captured. I was very proud of the RAR.

When we arrived back in camp there was great jubilation and excitement from both RAR and RLI. A truck arrived in camp from Col Aust. There were 11 Crates of beer, a crate of beer for each kill! Then the party began. Chappy and I teamed up for the night and reminisced on good friends and times out in Bulawayo. Major Snelgar joined us for a few.

As the beer flowed and inhibitions were lost, RAR entertained the Commando with "Sweet Banana" and various fighting songs like "Ndiyo MAG" etc. and RLI responded with "The Dance of the Flaming Arseholes". Five guys stripped naked and placed toilet paper between the cheeks of their bums and proceeded to dance around the fire with flaming tails, while singing bawdy songs. The RAR soldiers' response was from collapsed hilarity to absolute shock, but as the paper got shorter and posteriors were burnt the guys thought it hilarious. Many friends were made that night.

A few days later we said our goodbyes, but many addresses were exchanged and the soldiers corresponded for months afterwards.

As I was about to climb into my vehicle, Bruce Snelgar pulled me aside. He told me that the K Car chopper pilot, on returning to base had told Col Aust and Major Henson that it was the best talk into contact he had ever had.

Little did I realise that this was the last time I would ever see Maj Snelgar or Chappy again. Salute and Respect.

FRANTAN DROP by Captain Tony Clark

During October 1978 12 Pl, D Coy, 1RAR were on Fire Force based at Rutenga and reacted to a call out of CTs about 10 km away. As Stop One, I was dropped on a huge granite dwala devoid of any vegetation. Whilst this was a great vantage point, it also gave the enemy perfect silhouettes of the four of us. Towards the end of the contact K Car saw one CT crawling along the base of our hill through a shallow swamp filled with reeds. Glen Reed, K Car Comd, indicated as best he could where the foe was, and, like a toss, I stuck my head over the ledge for a better view. This was greeted by a burst of AK fire indicating that the CT knew we were there.

I tried rolling two M962 grenades over the edge but, after they detonated, I was not prepared to risk checking. The Lynx pilot then offered to indicate and started manoeuvring into position. He turned and began his strike flight. I realised that he was to strike right into our faces and called on the radio "Stop, stop, stop." The K car wanted to know the reason for my call and the Lynx pilot interjected that he would be using smoke and there was no reason for concern!

Nevertheless, there were four RAR men whose eyes stuck to the Lynx's wings like glue. To our horror we did not see the plumes from the rocket pods indicating smoke rockets but an ugly cylindrical object release from the left wing. We did not wait to have the result and all of us baled over the other side of the dwala, screaming "Fran!" and many obscenities to the pilot's mother. After what seemed a lifetime, there was no explosion and, resuming my composure, I got back on my radio and told the Lynx pilot what an arsehole he was. After we returned to our FF base the pilot came to me, apologised profusely and offered me a trip in the Lynx which I gladly accepted. After all, we had not been fried!!

AN ALL B COMPANY 1RAR 'PARTY' by Major Tom Fulton

In the middle of 1976, B Company 1RAR took over Fire Force duties at Mtoko from A Company. They had been very successful. The Ground Force Commander, Lt Des Passaportis, had been awarded a well-earned Bronze Cross, had been wounded in the process and frankly needed a break. Regrettably, they had lost Pte Dzingirayi and Major Mike Ainslie in action in the few months I had been there.

I had been involved in my first contact some weeks before when I had deployed with my platoon as the second wave of a Fire Force deployment that was already in contact. Des had virtually taken my hand and led me through it. (He knew I would eventually be taking over from him, and I thank him, to this day, for the patience he showed in guiding me through such things as post contact procedures – these were evolving all the time and difficult to teach at School of Infantry level.)

I was twenty years old and had no misconceptions about what would be demanded of me and, was frankly very nervous about the adequacy of my performance. All the rigorous and lengthy training had culminated in this acid test, and big match nerves were the order of the day. My huge saving grace, however, was the excellence of the troops I would be leading into battle.

The concept of the Fire Force, as it stood at that stage of the Rhodesian War, was to provide rapid response to sightings of the enemy by forces deployed either in an Observation Post (OP) posture, or by specialist pseudo-terrorist operating groups. That was the strategy that was followed by the tactic of vertical, heliborne envelopment. This reaction force comprised a K Car – providing the berth for the airborne commander (Major Wayne Thompson) and providing intimate support with the lethal 20mm canon armament it carried. Able to put down high explosive incendiary rounds at a rate of 350 rounds per minute, it was invaluable to the ground forces in providing intimate, immediate and devastating support.

The three, four man sticks of the first wave were carried by lightly armed G Cars who would deploy the troops at the K Car commander's direction and, would usually be sent back to collect the second wave.

The Lynx was a civilian aircraft manufactured by Cessna with a push-pull propeller configuration. Numerous modifications had produced a formidable ground attack platform, from which an assortment of weapons could be delivered. Their weapons manifest included Sneb rockets, 20-gallon Frantan (napalm) and mini-golf bombs. These weapons were carried in varying connotations and mixes, dependent on the nature of the operations and the critical weights.

Firstly, reliant mainly on Selous Scouts OPs for action, we had been frustrated by a number of lemons. At one stage, we were called out by one of our own B Company OPs, onto a hapless Selous Scouts pseudo group. The frantic waving of a dayglow panel that looked the size of a double-bed blanket from the air, had saved a potential tragedy.

Operating in an area adjacent to the Scouts, our OPs from 6 Platoon (Bill Liversidge) were deployed clandestinely. 5 Platoon took the reins as the Fire Force first wave, and on this particular Saturday afternoon were gathered in small groups in the meagre shade offered by the aircraft on the hard-standing.

I sauntered over to check on my men, noticing that Sergeant Major Africa was lecturing some of the private soldiers in radio Voice Procedure. Seeing my approach, Sergeant Saul brought the platoon to attention and saluted. I returned the compliment and asked to speak with all the stick commanders.

When my command element had assembled, I explained that the OP occupied by Corporal Kambira and his stick had located and, were watching what was very likely to be a live target, at the foot of the hill on which they sat. Up until that time, they had yet to positively identify a weapon, but as soon as they did, the Fire Force would be scrambled.

The stick commanders dispersed to pass on the latest news to their respective sticks. The atmosphere was expectant, as Kambira was a highly respected operator. He was afflicted by a terrible stutter which was greatly exacerbated by excitement, and the company signallers had reported that his conversations, though difficult to follow, were an almost definite indication that he was onto something valuable…he simply wasn't the type to cry wolf.

I was about to return to the Ops Room when the hot stillness was ruptured by the mournful moan of the call-out siren. All the stick commanders followed me in a short sprint to the Ops Room. Ignoring the clerk standing at the door with maps, as these had been handed out hours before, we assembled in front of the wall map with the pilots for the briefing. The Commanding Officer and the Adjutant, Lieutenant Colonel Dave Heppenstall and Captain Martin Wake, confirmed that weapons had been sighted, and we were to react immediately.

We left the Ops Room at a run and my batman Apollo stood before our chopper, holding up my webbing for me to step into. The technicians had already started the engines, and the rotor blades slowly increased in speed at the demand of the pilot. The four helicopters of Amber Section taxied from the hardstanding to the runway, followed by the Lynx, which turned at the end of the apron to make use of the full length of the runway for take-off.

It was a cloudless day in June, and we travelled at treetop level. The K Car leading Amber Section across dry cropless fields, punctuated and demarcated by hedgerows of indigenous trees and shrubs. The occasional water-course, dry at this time of year, was recognisable by the larger trees and the thickness of the vegetation which grew in profusion on the banks. I smiled to myself at the way the fowls in the kraals reacted to the passing helicopters. Perhaps mistaking them for noisy, overgrown raptors, they exploded shrieking from their roosts. They looked a little like ducks, struggling to get airborne from a pond, with their wings flapping vigorously at the dust, shedding feathers all the way.

The pilots had chosen a tactical route, so that the sound of the approaching aircraft would be masked by the hill feature, from which Corporal Kambira was now quaintly stammering through updates on activity in the target area. It sounded as though civilians were transporting food into the suspected camp area.

It was decided that target indication would be achieved by the K Car overflying Kambira's position, in the rough direction of the target. At Kambira's word, a phosphorus grenade would be dropped from the K Car, and corrections given from the copious smoke it would characteristically give off.

Simultaneously, the G Cars would swing right of Kambira's hill feature and enter a left hand orbit around the smoke generated by the indicating phosphorus grenade. The target was on the edge of a river-line that ran roughly north to south, and although the bush was typically thick and riverine, the leaves had mostly fallen at the time of year, and visibility at ground level was comparatively good.

I had recently been subjected to accurate ground fire whilst airborne, resulting in two of my men sustaining gunshot wounds and the technician being killed, so my ears were very finely attuned. I was listening for the tell-tale typewriter-like clatter, that was the hallmark of incoming ground fire, passing uncomfortably close to the aircraft. Thankfully, the target area was ghostly quiet – the enemy probably still a bit incredulous at being located.

The radio sprang to life. Amber lead, this is K Car, over.

Amber lead, acknowledged our pilot.

About 200 metres south of the target, there's a field with two huge Msasa trees – got it?

Affirmative. I have it visual.

Drop Stop One in that clearing, over.

Amber Lead. Roger that.

The K Car pilot was a South African by the name of Trevor Troupe. He was amongst the contingent of South African pilots and techs on loan to us, with their helicopters, from the SADF. He and his tech were blooded in the Namibian and Angolan campaigns. Highly professional and a pleasure to work with. The K Car pilot's job entailed a great deal more than simply flying his aircraft.

I warned my soldiers of the impending deployment, and all eyes remained on the strangely sinister, although deathly quiet, target area. We landed in a moribund mielie field in a cloud of dust and dead mielie leaves. Deplaning, as soon as the craft was down, we hurriedly adopted positions in all round defence.

The chopper lifted again, showering us once more with debris. No sooner was it back into the left-hand orbit, when Amber Two landed in its place and Stop Three with Sgt Saul in command disgorged, and were soon joining my men and me, as we formed a sweep line, facing the target.

K Car's under fire! Sustained automatic fire was being directed at the command helicopter. As a result of my recent traumatic experience, I could empathise with Major Wayne and could imagine him trying to make his massive frame a little smaller! It was a dangerous way to positively identify whether the target was live, but the firing confirmed that we were definitely in business!

I deployed Sgt Saul's stick on my left and we shook out into a sweep line with about 10 yards between each man. Sar'major Africa had been deployed with his Stop Two to the north, and opposite the target, to act as a stop group. His position would be reinforced with troops of the second wave. They would eventually form what amounted to an area ambush, blocking off potential routes of escape.

K Cars Under fire! We heard the sudden burst of fire erupt from the area to our front. The K Car's 20mm canon made a belligerent reply, its clamour making the adrenaline course through everyone's veins, and increasing the urge to close with, and kill the enemy.

Stop One this is 29. This was the Major's personal call-sign.

29 from Stop One, go ahead I replied.

Roger, as you've heard, we're taking a shit-load of fire. I want you to advance on the target immediately. I'm expecting Stop Four to arrive at any minute. I'll drop them with you when they do, over.

Roger that I replied.

The sweep commenced, and Sgt Saul and I maintained visual contact. Saul's two outermost soldiers were exposed in some open ground, so he ordered them to move tactically and cover each other, without getting ahead of the main body.

I heard over the radio that Stop Two under Sar'major Africa had killed one gook who had tried to make good his escape through the area he was policing. The enemy continued to engage the orbiting helicopters and it was an excellent indication to us on the ground, as to exactly where the target lurked. We continued to advance at a reasonably brisk pace. Anxious to get on with the job at hand, but also aware that the aircraft were coming under intense pressure from ground fire, and we needed to get a move on.

Our sweep-line suddenly came under fairly heavy fire – the disadvantage of sweeping towards an enemy, was that we were the first to be seen. I realised by the amount of fire being directed at me personally – that my white skin was attracting a lot of unhealthy attention – although I took diligent pains with my personal camouflage, I knew it was impossible to be mistaken for an African soldier – blue eyes and straight hair…

We started skirmishing towards the source of the fire and were soon into the base camp itself. Shooting was at short-range opportunity targets – the men worked swiftly and with lethal economy. When Private Kwira was shot through the upper arm, I reluctantly called a halt, to deal with him.

After having him casevaced, we resumed the sweep and immediately came under withering fire from our front. So far, we had killed two gooks at the edge of the base, but the job was evidently far from over. Concerned about taking any further unnecessary casualties, I made the decision to call in an air strike by the Lynx who was slowly orbiting at a safe altitude above the contact area.

Delta Four this is Stop One, I called.

Go ahead Tom. Phil Haig was the pilot.

Roger Phil, we've got ourselves into a bit of a spot. I've marked my FLOT (Forward Line of Own Troops) with two maps. Roger?

Roger, I have your FLOT visual. What can I do for you?

I'm using a fireball (a hand held mini-flare fired from a pencil projector) to indicate the target. Tell me when you're ready.

OK, send fireball, over, Phil requested, as he watched the area central to the two maps, for my target indicator.

The luminescent fireball from the mini-flare projector scribed a lazy, hissing arc through the air, and landed in the area the fire was coming from.

My fireball is on target Phil. I'll give you covering fire when you report 'turning in', over.

Stop Four under the command of Corporal Gumbo Owen had joined our sweep by now, and I had put him on my right. I warned him and Saul to standby to give the Lynx some covering fire.

Thanks Tom. I'll be coming in from your right to your left, and I'll be tossing them a fran.

(The Lynx wasn't armed with a front gun (yet?), and this made it very vulnerable when it stooped into a dive to deliver its weapons. So, it was imperative that we keep the gook's heads down while he was in his delivery dive.)

Delta Four, is turning in live declared Flight Lieutenant Phillip Haig.

The Lynx's left wing dipped momentarily, as the pilot lined his aircraft up to zero in on the target, and keeping the direction of his delivery dive, parallel to the FLOT.

The entire wrath of three sticks of 5 Platoon inclusive of 3 squad machine guns peppered the air, in the areas in and around the target. The 20 gallon incendiary bomb was locally made, and had a very impressive 'splash pattern', following the point of impact. Its soapy liquid splashed soapy, flaming liquid that stuck to anything and everything in its path. I reckoned it must be an awful way to die.

With the weapon landing with impressive accuracy, I immediately gave orders for the advance to recommence, and this was done at a loping run, the quicker to 'sort-out' any survivors of the strike, whatever that meant? I had to make the right decisions to suit the moment – even if 101 possible scenarios were galloping through my head. I was eternally indebted to my instructors for the fact that I was completely confident.

At the slow jog, we were into the main target area before I slowed things to a careful walk. Much smoke marred visibility and our advance was at a snail's pace, with spaces between the men now 10 feet, instead of the usual 10 yards. An exploding magazine on one of the AKs went off, and had us all sprawled on to the blackened earth, until we realised what it was, and had us all laughing at our own nerves.

In what was ground zero, five bodies lay sprawled. The 'splash' had done its job, all right. The smoking cadavers lay on their sides, knees drawn up under them. Charred hands held up in silent, pleading supplication, or a macabre, foetal, pugilistic pose. I recognised, what used to once be a woman. The intense heat had melted the lips back from her teeth. Her burst eyeballs viewed me with a sinister, accusing grin. Poor bitch, I thought to myself. Gunned down, or braaied; not a very savoury choice.

I noted, largely from the smouldering remnants of their clothing, there were four men and the woman. We left the four weapons where they were, for the time being – none was worth retrieving now, and we still ran the risk of more exploding, nerve-wracking magazine cook-offs.

It had been a good afternoon's work. Sar'major Africa had captured one completely unscathed, when he brazenly waltzed into the stop group dressed as a woman! (AK secreted under a dress).

We had accounted for all eight of the group, seven dead, one captured. Some women had also been killed in the crossfire. They had been a feeding party, at the time of the envelopment, and considered acceptable collateral casualties.

Morale was understandably high on our return to the Forward Air Field. The ebullience overflowed into song, as we joined in unison, singing a popular Battalion song. I looked into their smiling faces, understanding completely, and myself very much a part of the atmosphere of righteous arrogance.

I gazed out at the dusty Rhodesian Tribal Trust land that was whizzing past beneath us. I said silently to myself as I looked back into their still-smiling faces. I might still be a pup in some of these veteran eyes, but man, am I proud to be included in their number.

CONTACT, CONTACT by Captain Andrew Telfer

Fireforce contacts were different in several ways to those that occurred during patrol operations. Firstly, in Fireforce operations we had the huge advantage of top cover, providing air to ground command and strike capability, whereas in patrol contacts, you were on your own. Secondly, we had more ground support in Fireforce as we were part of a deployed Company; when patrolling, you could be a single stick of just four men. Thirdly, contacts were more predictable when on a Fireforce rotation, as we knew that we would be called out, and each call-out began with a siren and an air flight to contact. On patrols, the contacts came out of nowhere.

Sometimes, however, even Fireforce contacts came out of the blue. One evening we were flying home after a day-long contact, cold beers on our minds, when our G Car suddenly banked, swooped and flared, dropping us on the edge of a long village of classic African huts (small, circular, thatched-roof structures with pole and mud walls). As the chopper lifted off, I was told on the radio that an OP had sighted a group of terrorists hiding in the village and we were to quickly engage them before it got dark. We were only one stick, four men, with the K Car overhead. We grouped together, and I briefed my puzzled soldiers on what I'd been told. Sending two soldiers to run to the far end of the long village to act as a stop group, two of us began entering and clearing the huts.

Hut-clearing is dangerous because the advantage is with the person in the hut, not the one entering it. The inside is dark, so it's very easy to shoot a person silhouetted in the open doorway who cannot see a thing with eyes adjusted to outside light. For the first couple of huts we threw in grenades before we entered but then we had no more, so we just rushed inside one hut after another. In a few minutes the huts were cleared, and the enemy killed. I remember one terrorist making a break for it out one of the last huts, and recall going down on one knee, sighting into the middle of his fleeing back, squeezing the trigger and seeing him pitch forward as if pushed hard from behind… and then we flew home, wondering what had just happened.

Usually, Fireforce involved moving under the direction of the Company Commander in the K Car, searching for and being guided onto terrorists. That did not mean that basic infantry and ground / air tactics did not apply. They did, very much, as illustrated by the following two examples.

The first of these examples involved a pair of terrorists hidden in a rocky kopje. A 'kopje' is a small hill, often a jumbled pile of huge rocks, infilled with stunted trees and thick bush. I have described elsewhere the difficulty of sweeping through thick bush, but the presence of large rocks made the situation even more unfavourable as they provided the enemy with cover from view and from fire. I once had my rifle shot out of my hands at close range by a terrorist hiding between two such rocks. On this occasion, the terrorists waited until we were close and then opened fire. There was a lot of noise but nothing to see and we had no idea where they were firing from, so the OC (Major Bryan McDermott in the K Car) called for an airstrike by the Lynx.

This is a relatively simple procedure involving marking one's own sweep-line with smoke at either end (the FLOT, or 'forward line of own troops'), a brief target indication and the projection of a mini-flare into the target area as the aircraft ran in 'live in the dive'. The pilot struck with frantan (napalm), bringing an explosion of flame and a scorching wind of hot, burning air across our front but, miraculously, the two terrorists continued to fire upon us. The only thing to break the stalemate was to attack from a flank. As other soldiers fired into the target area, two of us hooked around to the right and crept through the big rocks. Moving around the side of one rock, I came upon the flank of a terrorist who rolled around to open fire. The roll spoiled his aim and I was able to kill him.

The other terrorist was spotted by the K Car, slipping away from the side of the kopje, running across an open field and hiding in a drainage ditch. I don't know why the K Car didn't shoot him, perhaps it had a stoppage, but the OC was able to tell me where he was. I asked which way he was facing and was told that he was facing towards my left, so I ran across the field in a wide right-hand arc, arriving at the drainage ditch quite far to his flank. It was quite surreal creeping up on him as he crouched almost still, only his head peeking above the ditch to see where we were. Suddenly, he must have felt my presence and turned. We fired together, and he was killed.

Whereas many sweep lines moved forward in a skirmish line, pepper-potting in bursts, while we did apply the principle of fire and movement, we used flanking attacks as often as possible, another basic infantry tactic. As the firing started, I would break right or left with some soldiers while others fired on the enemy. Then, we'd over-run them from the flank, frequently without them even seeing us coming.

In the next example, we ran into a group of terrorists well-hidden in a rocky kopje. Again, the firing from the outcrop was intense but we couldn't see where it was coming from. RAR soldiers don't tend to take cover, they rather crouch and dart, bobbing and weaving like a boxer, rifle and eyes searching for the enemy. Then, all of us saw one of the terrorists, a dark blue patch under a bush, and all of us fired into him, but we couldn't see the others. Once again, in went the airstrike and off we went in a flanking attack, scrambling around huge boulders, ducking under branches (I recall Private Jera's hat hooked off on one of them), almost falling over each other to get at them. If you go too slowly with RAR soldiers, they'll leave you behind. This time we killed five of them.

What really fascinated me about these contacts (and the point of these last two examples) was how the use of air support and of simple military tactics, all taught at the School of Infantry, completely overwhelmed the terrorists. From then onwards, I greatly favoured quick little flanking attacks in preference to skirmishing.

Parachuting added another dimension to the Rhodesian Fireforce, covered more fully in a later chapter. Curiously, although being a 'paratrooper' seems to attract respectful attention, it was less dangerous than being deployed by helicopter and, therefore of course, more effective. When parachuted from the Dakota, you were part of a sweep-line of 16 soldiers which was a lot by Rhodesian standards. When deployed by chopper, there were initially only four of you, so heli-borne contacts were more exposed, like patrol contacts, until other callsigns joined you.

Nevertheless, parachuting into random drop zones is not a walk in the park, as I found when I parachuted into a Fireforce contact and injured my ankle on landing. I've told that story in *Chibaya Moyo 1*, but I raise it here because a valuable leadership lesson was learned that day. RAR soldiers expected officers to lead from the front and were extraordinarily brave and aggressive if you did so, but they would not have appreciated the departure of their officer from the scene at the start of a contact. My ankle was badly injured and, afterwards, would need encasing in plaster for several weeks, but I am glad to this day that I stayed with them and didn't request a casevac. That moment of choice was an opportunity and our choices mould us.

We had a long and successful contact that day, killing six in the initial contact and two more in a riverbed afterwards. I still remember that riverbed so vividly: hearing a burst of firing after we'd thought the contact was already over, seeing Private Gwangirayi running towards me, eyes wide and mouth open in shock, his partly-severed arm rotating at the elbow like a propeller. I recall feeling vengeful, limping to the edge of the riverbank, sensing that the enemy were under a thick bush-like tree growing out of the side of the bank, turning my change lever to automatic and jumping about two metres down into the shallow water, seeing two terrorists aiming and firing, a flash of pain from my collapsing ankle, falling sideways, then just shooting and shooting at each other until they both folded up, finding the paracord burned through near my rifle's gas port, joined by Corporal Ali, telling him to call soldiers to get the bodies, leaning against the side of the bank, feeling so tired...

Reflecting now, I think that day, with the decision not to be casevaced leading to the firefight in the river, was the high-point of my service as an RAR officer. Pain, in some form or other, is always the price that must be paid for achievement.

I changed my appearance. Gone were the shorts and T-shirt. I wore a camouflaged jumpsuit or a long-sleeved shirt and trousers, lightweight and camouflaged. I dressed like that on every operation, my hands and face blackened, and my hair concealed by a face veil tied like a pirate. It wasn't for show but to conceal the fact that I was white. When a terrorist was confronted by a sweep line, who would want to stand out as the white officer? I moved my pouches so that the antenna of my radio was straight up my back, out of sight from the front. I carried

The Devil's Playground

more grenades and used chest webbing for my magazines. I was starting to think of every little thing physically and become cold inside mentally.

There was great benefit to be had in becoming emotionally detached from what we were doing, in becoming more objective and less involved. I think I reached that point by early-1978. At only 24 years of age, I had become an 'old soldier', by which I mean no longer excited by what I was doing but operating with deliberate objectivity. It was around that time that I left behind the fear that I tried to express in my earlier article, *We Searched*. But, leaving behind emotion doesn't mean that it's replaced with another type of feeling. Sometimes, I read people, somewhere in the world, using the language of 'fist-pumping exultation' to describe feelings after combat and wonder whether they've genuinely experienced the real thing. I just don't think you feel that way. I think you begin scared and evolve to empty.

However, you never become invulnerable. The death of Private Isaac Chirwa during a Fireforce contact was one of the saddest days of my service with the RAR. His death still haunts me because he was such a fine and decent human being. It is described in *Chibaya Moyo 1*, under the title *A Final Contact* and was not only my last contact but also the first one in which I lost a soldier killed. I'd had wounded soldiers, but none killed, and I knew I was considered a lucky officer to be with by our soldiers. Isaac was moving right alongside me when he was shot by a burst from an RPD and, although we did get the terrorist, it was no compensation for his loss of life. Grief is a terrible thing, like a heavy stone pressing upon the lungs.

There were, of course, many more Fireforce contacts but they have mostly blurred into a kaleidoscope of images that I cannot wholly form into events. These carried the stand-out lessons and were thus the most memorable. One was simply so quick and such a surprise that it remains as a vivid and brief 'happening'. Two of them are significant to me because they underscored the importance of doing what we had been taught at the School of Infantry, making intelligent use of air power and basic infantry tactics. And the other two: one was best day, the zenith of my career, while the other was the nadir, my worst day.

COMMENTS ON CONTACTS by Captain Russell Fulton

I am of the firm opinion that contacts were the 'arbiter' of one's life in uniform. Those who served in infantry units and were engaged in contact will agree that, oftentimes, those in one's midst who were perceived to be rough and ready gung-ho types were the least inclined to bare their teeth and lead from the front in contact. I witnessed it many times. Those who paid close attention to their instructors during introductory basic tactics (and beyond) and, applied those principles, were the ones most likely to succeed. Emotions during those times were not unlike the inside of a pressure cooker left carelessly close to a burning wood fire. Without strong, aggressive and decisive leadership, defeat and unadulterated terror within the ranks would be your just reward.

I too had my share of engagements and with those came emotions that percolated deep inside me. I recall my first Fireforce deployment and contact in the RLI like it was yesterday. Before I set eyes upon a dead gook, I saw one of our own killed in action, Rifleman David Barclay, the date was 7 July 1977, Inyazura, Op Thrasher. We did our job that day as if we were on auto-pilot but, that night when the revelry back at Grand Reef was behind us, I lay on my stretcher and reflected upon that afternoon. It was a potent cocktail of mixed emotion; the adrenaline-charged high induced by mortal combat and an overwhelming sense of grief. A million thoughts flickered through my mind and, I confess, I had to wrestle with myself to suppress tears. I was a teenager, and this was a true baptism by fire. The next day, it was business as usual.

There are three very important messages that come through strongly in Andy's piece and these relate to our outstanding instruction in basic tactics; 'do the basics right and the rest will fall into place'. The second was to never allow emotion in the heat of battle to cloud one's better judgement and the third was, by virtue of the role we played and the exigencies of our war, becoming "emotionally detached". Whether a commander or one of the rank and file, we all 'fed-off' one another and one's emotional stability, or lack thereof, would spread infectiously in positive or deleterious fashion. Fear is an important emotion that can either motivate a man to higher levels of success or confine him to the pits of despair. I saw it all during my service and I can say, without hindrance, that fear was my omnipresent companion; it was simply a question of how that fear was 'managed'.

Those who saw action are not boastful but there are others who seek to fan their overtly grandiose opinions of their personal standing by grandstanding about situations they played no part in. Andy Telfer is patently one of the former, who lead his men into contact with a broken foot and against all physical and emotional odds, set an exemplary example to the good men under his command. He writes, almost self-deprecatingly, "I was considered a lucky officer to be with by our soldiers". I say we make our own luck and the observation by his men had nothing to do with luck but everything to do with his inspired leadership.

TOBY by Lieutenant Michael Matthews

During mid-March 1978 and whilst still based at Mtoko, A Company 1RAR received a callout to Bushu TTL which, like Nyajena, was a 'frozen' area and a ZANLA stronghold. A sighting had been made by a pair of Selous Scouts who had been in a clandestine O.P. for a few days, and they estimated a terrorist group of about ten to twelve.

Our Fireforce excursion resulted in seven confirmed terrorist kills and, whilst awaiting extraction by chopper, we were ordered to torch the village from whence the terrorists had come in order to send a clear message to the locals that no affiliation with the enemy would be tolerated by Rhodesian forces. Not unusually, the village was deserted, since its inhabitants understood their involvement with the terrorists hadn't passed unnoticed, and they were well aware that they could expect little sympathy from the army in the circumstances.

We ignited the thatched roofs of all the dwellings in the village and combed the grain bins for arms caches. Whilst we were waiting for the choppers to arrive to uplift us, I saw a tiny form creeping out of one of the fiery huts. It was a little puppy, and it was too much for a 'bunny-hugger' like me to leave it behind, where it was simply too small to stand any chance of survival.

I ran back into the village and scooped the puppy up, carrying it to the choppers, which had just arrived. On arrival back at camp I decided that I would call this little bundle of fur 'Toby', and thus started a wonderful relationship between us which was unfortunately destined to be short-lived. Rwanqa became Batman not only to me, but also to Toby. He was absolutely spoilt and doted upon by all the troops in A Company, and soon enough became the Company's unofficial mascot. Toby quickly came to terms with the sound of helicopters and aircraft and knew that this invariably meant that we would be parting company for a while, although I could always expect a slobbery greeting on my return to camp.

No question, the month of May 1978 constituted easily the most intense period of combat I was to be involved in for my entire two-year stint. It was therefore with much relief that we were all dispatched home for just short of one weeks R&R. I had a relaxing break, frequenting well known institutions, Club Tomorrow (otherwise known as 'Clubbies') and the Oasis Hotel with monotonous regularity, and with such of my mates who were similarly fortunate to have R&R at the same time, or who were locally based.

'A' Company assembled at 1RR in Salisbury toward the end of May 1978 and we made our way by Bedford to the Mtoko airfield in the heart of the Hurricane area for our next Fireforce rotation. The day after our arrival, and since things had been rather quiet in the area during the past few days, we had a 'fun jump' (which many would consider to be an oxymoron) over the airfield to clear the rust out. For the first and only time we jumped at two thousand feet, some four times higher than the five hundred feet we had become accustomed to jumping at. Our old Dak warhorse probably took about half an hour to slowly orbit to achieve the required altitude. But it was well worth the wait. My 3 Platoon jumped in idyllic, windless conditions on 1st June 1978, and I will never forget the wonderful weightless sensation as we all drifted slowly down to earth.

Other than the occasional laugh or scream of exhilaration from most of us during our descent, the wonderful panorama around us and the feeling that we were in suspension, defying gravity, was unforgettable and awe-inspiring. My *Masodja* had taken to jumping like a croc to water and I was very proud of them and their incomparable gung-ho spirit. To cap it all, I achieved a rare 'stand up' landing.

It wasn't long before we received our first call out, an OP sighting in Rushinga TTL. We achieved three kills and were called out often twice a day for the next week. A particularly traumatic day began to unfold for me when we were called out during mid-morning on 5th June to a sighting at nearby Tanda TTL.

Perhaps a portent that things weren't going to go well that day was that despite a frantic, but ultimately unsuccessful attempt to steer clear of some low shrub-like vegetation on descent, I landed bum first in a thorn bush – ouch!

We achieved three kills that day, and during the afternoon our choppers commenced ferrying us back to Mtoko. My stick got back just before dark, and I was surprised to see neither Toby nor Private Rwanqa there to greet me when we arrived as they usually were. In fact, I found most of the Company who had remained at camp that day evasive, and unwilling to engage me in conversation.

Bush Volleyball

As I approached my tent, I saw Rwanqa fleeing in tears, and I knew then and there that something had become of Toby. I confronted our CSM, normally not one to exhibit a great deal of emotion, and he hesitantly broke it to me that Toby had been killed. It transpired that, in his boredom, a land-based Flight Sergeant in the Fireforce camp adjacent to ours had used Toby and a few other dogs at or near the camp for target practice, ostensibly since he said that he had thought that they may be rabies-infested. Everyone knew, however, that Toby was my dog and the Company's official mascot, and that he was in perfectly good health.

I stormed off to the air force Sergeant's Mess and summonsed the perpetrator, who well knew the purpose of my visit, apologising for what he called a mistake. I am not easily moved to violent acts, but I didn't find it difficult to punch the idiot square on the nose and deck him. Nobody likes to lose a beloved pet, but in times where the human/animal relationship was a rare link with normality, and with family far away, Toby's death was a particularly bitter pill to swallow.

Several months later and whilst at camp between routine patrols, it became clear to me the level of 'publicity' that my loss had created. My O.C., Major Getliffe was contacted by none other than the Chief of the Air Force, and advised that another pup had been located, and would I like it. I was touched by the gesture, particularly having come from such lofty heights, but with my two-year stint of National Service coming to an end and with first year varsity in Cape Town just around the corner it just didn't make sense to accept the invitation, and I had to decline.

RIP Toby.

NIGHTMARE IN INYANGA NORTH by Major Tom Fulton

It was a hot, clear July day in Mtoko, and the troops of 5 Platoon, B Company 1RAR were busy helping the technicians to clean the helicopters of Amber Section, the Alouette 111 helicopters responsible for delivering the men onto the targets, when the Fire Force was scrambled.

I sauntered out of the Ops Room with the news that something was brewing, in the northern extremity of the Operation Thrasher area – Elim Mission, in Inyanga North. The brief, as it stood at that time, was that a retired BSAP Sergeant had reported to the local Territorial Army camp, that six gooks had arrived at his kraal that morning. His wives had been painstakingly brewing the much favoured "seven day", and today would be the Saturday, when friends would visit and imbibe in the noxious, potent brew. (It seemed that the gooks weren't going to miss the party.) The reporting Sergeant was still at the army camp.

It was a long way to fly, and local deployments of a framework nature, could conceivably provide us with a more tangible, closer target, at any time. So, we waited.

About an hour later, the stick commanders and I were called to the Ops Room with the pilots. It seemed that the crucial time factor was being discussed amongst our very capable planners, and if we were to go to Inyanga North, we had to go now. If we left immediately, we would have a practical amount of time to deal with the target, and still have time to get home to Mtoko. (This was imperative because of our duties as the Mtoko Fire Force, and also for the night time protection of the precious aircraft.) It was the CO, Lieutenant Colonel Dave Heppenstall who eventually decided we should go, and unlike usual deployments, we sauntered out to the choppers, emplaned and got airborne. As we had taxied past the Special Branch Offices, all the assembled cops gave us the "thumbs up".

They've never done that before I thought to myself. Neither have we ever walked to the choppers? Things were already getting creepy…

The journey would use up most of the fuel, but there was a supply of Avtur for the choppers at the army camp, and some Jet A1 at the local aerodrome for the Lynx. The Alouette 111 was equipped with a self-sealing fuel tank, and was powered by a paraffin (kerosene) engine – greatly reducing the lethal risk of an on-board fire.

I watched absently, as the flight of aircraft, flying almost due east, swallowed up the distance between us and the target area, Elim Mission. We had been on Fire Force for enough time for most of the landscape to be familiar, but as we approached a huge range of hills, the vegetation started to change discernibly – everybody felt the same uneasy discomfiture, which naturally comes with entering an alien, and unfamiliar environment.

We had attended call-outs further south, where the vegetation was typically Inyangan – with massive mountains, and treacherously thick vegetation that ensured that contact with the enemy was an intimate, personal thing. We all hated going there.

Once we had hurdled the mountain range, however, we were confronted to a vista that nobody imagined. This particular part of the country, by some cruel trick of nature, lies in what we learned at school to be "a rain shadow area." Although most areas in Rhodesia were arid at this time of the year, the dryness was in sharp contrast with the country we were used to working in. It had the distinct advantage to a Fire Force, in that visibility from the air to the ground was excellent.

After crossing the range, we had come down in altitude considerably, and the choppers used the drop to accelerate their machines to their maximum. We were greeted by an unhospitable dry moonscape, with sparsely wooded hill features, and infrequent river-lines, that were ungenerously graced with some meagre tree cover. The area was stark and depressing, harsh and foreboding.

We landed en masse in the vehicle park of the camp, exchanging greetings with the various sundry bystanders, I made my way to the Ops Room with my stick commanders. We were introduced to the local officers, and the retired BSAP Sergeant. The greying old retired cop seemed a bit annoyed at our tardiness, and the amount of his beer the gooks had probably already drunk.

After brief discussion, it was decided that the old man would be squeezed into the K Car, so that he would be physically present, to indicate the target. Once that had been achieved, the OC would make a quick assessment, and deploy the Stops accordingly.

With less than five minutes flying to the target, we were overhead before we knew it. The old Sergeant flipped a phosphorus grenade out of the command helicopter and it landed on a small, sparsely wooded ridge, on the outskirts of his kraal.

Before the corrections could be given, the K Car reported being under fire, and the 20mm cannon made a characteristically angry reply – only to have the firing pin sheer!

To us incredulous helicopter borne troops, it was eye-popping to see two gooks run out of the cover, standing brazenly in a cultivated land, as they engaged the passing helicopters - as if they were shooting at ducks in an amusement park! With the K Car now unable to bring its cannon to effectively bear, one of the G Cars' machine guns eventually found the mark, and a gook went down, sprawling in the dust to the cheers of my men.

FOR FUCK SAKES PUT ME DOWN DANNY! I screamed with unnecessary nervous candour, into the mouthpiece of my headset, to Danny Svoboda, who was piloting our machine. No sooner had the words left my mouth when the K Car called.

Amber lead from K Car, go left.

Reacting immediately to the instruction, the pilot began to bank to the left, not realising that the K Car had inadvertently talked us over the original target area on the ridge. By now, I had almost left my seat, the better to see first-hand, what the hell was going on, on the ground!

Passing aloft of the originally targeted hill feature, I clearly saw that a gook had positioned an RPD light machine-gun, bipods splayed, and facing up. I distinctly remember the oddity of the right-to-left feed of the belts, as the barrel released a swarm of green-coloured bees, at our general direction. The thoughts in my mind at the time, was a comfortable assumption that the shooter had led us by too much – my not-inconsiderable experience at shooting wild duck, told me so – but when the salvo reached the same height as the aircraft, it seemed to cruelly curve into the cockpit.

Never was the analogy of the bees more pertinent, than when the volley of rounds passed through the cockpit. I remember pieces of Perspex from the helicopter's canopy hitting everything its path, being splattered by something or other, seeing my machine gunner, Khanye Mazenzo doubling-up in apparent agony.

I remember being conscious of Sergeant Pat Graham, the helicopter technician, lying across the lap of my batman, Private Apollo, who sat next to me. Apollo was bleeding from a wound across the back of his head, and his whole body hung forward

Flt Sgt Pat Graham, 7 Sqn RhAF

in semi-consciousness, covering the visor of Sergeant Graham with his blood. Gingerly, I undid the mouthpiece of the stricken airman, and discovered he had suffered no pain.

My machine gunner, Mazenzo, had been sitting opposite the tech, his hand hanging through the leather strop that assisted emplaning. A bullet had struck him on the point of the elbow, cruelly inflicting permanent and hideous damage on its exit.

The pilot asked me for a situation report, and I replied, "We better head for the mission hospital, Danny. I've got two ouens with oil-leaks here and I'm sorry to say, we lost Pat".

The pilot glanced back and shook his head in disbelief.

I joined Danny as we limped the Alouette back to Mtoko that night. We had left Privates Mazenzo and Apollo under the personal guard of our platoon medic, Corporal Peter Tarsisious, at the mission hospital – they would soon be regrouped with us, in one way or another.

Alone with the pilot, on the dark moonless return to our home base, I operated the powerful spotlight to assist in guiding us over the formidable escarpment down which we had experienced such an exhilarating ride on the way in.

I've never seen Danny Svoboda since that day but predict our reunion will be one of solemn remembrance, and warm camaraderie.

To date, I cannot tell how many gooks were killed at Elim on that dark afternoon; it seems completely irrelevant.

Rest in Peace, Pat.

AFTER ACTION HOSPITALITY by Captain Andy Barrett

Fire Force Deployment

Rutenga, February 1979. As two G-Cars had been withdrawn for Selous Scouts operations, Fire Force Delta at Beit Bridge had been reduced to that of a Lynx, K-Car and a single G-Car. Nevertheless, a message from Sub-JOC Rutenga was received that an OP to their north west had sited ten terrs.

A briefing was undertaken at Rutenga (FAF 9) as we were informed that the number of terrs visual had risen to 25. Flying along the railway line north west from Rutenga to the Sarahuru siding, we suddenly swung due west for about seven minutes. On arriving at the contact zone in the Manyuchi district, the terrain representing that of the rugged Matopos and Mtoko; the OP continually misguiding the K-Car commander.

After twice having attempted to mark the target area with smoke grenades, a frustrated Major Price deployed Stop 1 (Cpl Phil O'Donnell, Sgt Theo Nel, Sgt

Fire Force Success! 1 (Indep) Coy RAR Rutenga 1979. L-R Capt Tom Fulton (1Bde MIO), Sgt Beaver Shaw (7Sqn RhAF), Unknown, Lt Arthur Keagle (1 [Indep] Coy RAR)

Mark Hellam and Capt Andy Barrett) to an area he thought the most likely. The setting was majestic with great slabs of glistening silver-grey rock towering around us, punctuated by puffs of marshmallow cloud. It was not time to admire the surroundings, so I retracted my thoughts to concentrate on the task. It would have been a crying shame if I checked out now. I'd been a bad boy in the past and got away with all of that too. Maybe it was my turn next; fate, karma, Sod's law, Murphy's Law, or just plain old tough shit, call it what you will.

In an extended sweep line, we advanced on a small thickly wooded area, we gingerly chiselled our way forward expecting a burst of AK fire with every step we took. We made eye contact simultaneously only to engage the enemy from approximately 10 metres in a very brief and noisy firefight, fractionally before they did us. All four of us directed our fire with phenomenal ferocity into the thicket, especially Phil who, firing from the hip, virtually emptied an entire magazine, his barrel was smoking.

Although the contact was short lived, the gooks must be credited for their tenacity at such short range. Four gooks dressed in East German rice-fleck camouflage had their lives terminated as the FN and RPD bullets crashed through their bodies and webbing. The remainder of the operation did not prove fruitful as the rest of the gooks had presumably escaped due to the very unnecessary delay in deployment - the organ grinder was not impressed.

We spent the night at FAF 9 (Rutenga) and headed for Beit Bridge the following morning, landing the Fire Force in the cool air on the main Beit Bridge to Salisbury road, opposite the Lion and Elephant Hotel adjacent to the Bubye River. Here the owner and staff very enthusiastically provided us with a most welcome snack of tea and sandwiches. This was Rhodesian hospitality, always most welcoming, free and warm with similar hospitality regularly provided and experienced at the homes of Robin and Paxie Watson of Makado Ranch; John and Marie Barclay, Mazunga section of Liebig's Ranch and many others – all very solid, hospitable, generous and warm Rhodesians; wonderful people.

THE BATTLE by Mrs Judy Dixon

The choppers, whirring, hovering, clattering
Dust devils scurry and cloud.
Our troopies debus steady and ready
Firing through the heat and the haze.

No time to look, only to see
As feet hit the ground with a thud.

The battle is raging, violent and fuming
The soldiers stoop and take cover.
And cover their mates
With their fire.

No time to look, only to see
As tracer streaks the air.

Thick heat wavering, shimmering, billowing
Masking the enemies' faces.
Cloaking their bolt holes
Concealed and deadly, in shadows and places unseen.

No time to look, only to see
Whilst the bush is pulsating with noise.

The battle ground covered, smouldering, quivering
The screams and the shouts clearly heard.
Adrenalin coursing, sweating and cursing
The Brave have made this day.

The Battle is won! Thank God we are clear!

Choppers, clattering, hovering, whirring
Waiting, in the haze and the heat.
Time for the pick-up,
A job well done, a slap on the back!
Home for a smoke and a beer.

With love and gratitude for your sacrifice and service.

THE HOME STRETCH by Lieutenant Michael Matthews

Early in September 1978 A Company 1RAR was reassigned to Fireforce duty, based at Mount Darwin.

Amongst the Dak pilots assigned to Fireforce during the period was Professor Dick Christie, better known amongst his law students at the University of Rhodesia as Prof Christie, the author of the premier work on the South African Law of Contract for many years and to this day. In fact, his work on contract law was and is regularly referenced by me in the legal profession I ultimately pursued. Dick had been a Dakota pilot in the Second World War and was part of the Rhodesian Reserve Air Wing.

We had a few more Fireforce deployments during September, none of which was more memorable (for all the wrong reasons) than a call out we received to an O.P. sighting at the Nyadire River, near Mrewa. This was to be my last Fireforce deployment.

On 18th September 1978, we received news of the sighting, and my platoon was on Dak duty. Our Dak pilot was none other than Dick Christie. We reached a point near our DZ where we began orbiting, awaiting word from Major Getliffe to commence a run in once all the stop groups had been deployed. Eventually the instruction came, and we prepared to jump.

The Home Stretch

As usual, I was first out of the door, and my platoon streamed out after me. What Dick hadn't taken account of, however, was that there was a kopje looming in our deployment line. The result was that my last two or three troops were deployed at a height of no more than three hundred and fifty feet! I watched in horror as the chutes of the few deployed only moments before they landed, and I regard it as a miracle that only one of them sustained a leg fracture.

Shortly before the end of our Mount Darwin tour, one of the Air Force personnel also succeeded in fracturing his leg, but in far more innocuous circumstances – his camp bed, no more than about one foot from the ground, slipped underneath him, with a resultant fracture, and the need for quick and expert medical attention.

I had become quite friendly with Flight Lieutenant "Brick" Bryson, the pilot of the Lynx then assigned to Mount Darwin, and he invited me to accompany him back to Salisbury to deliver the poor unfortunate to hospital. Since an evening in Salisbury was not to be passed up under any circumstances, probably only a countermand from my O.C. would have stopped me from joining him, and once our invalid had been dispatched to hospital, we had a great time in Salisbury in the few hours available to us.

The next morning, however, presented us with very different weather. It was overcast and raining in Salisbury, and there was a thick and low-lying blanket of cloud shrouding the Mount Darwin airfield. Since the Lynx was an integral part of the Air Force's limited arsenal, it was vital that we get back to

Mount Darwin immediately, and so we left at first light the next day, feeling a little the worse for wear.

All was well until we neared Mount Darwin itself. We had been flying above the cloud all the time and now we had to descend blind through thick cloud, the base of which we were told was no more than about three hundred feet high. What followed was one of my most harrowing experiences. Brick's descent would rely on the Mount Darwin air traffic controller's perception of where we were based on sound alone, there being no sophisticated radar or other facility available, and in an area surrounded by mountains.

We began our descent based entirely on the reassurance of the Mount Darwin air traffic controller, and it seemed that we were descending through something like pea soup for hours, whereas it was probably only about two long, inexorable minutes. Both Brick and I had broken into a sweat and still this thick grey blanket confronted us when, after what seemed an eternity, we broke through the cloud. Brick pulled the plane up sharply, and it seemed that we levelled out almost at ground level – what a relief!

Happily, for those of us doing our National Service, the powers that be decided to remove us from the 'firing line', and the remainder of our military commitment was rather sedentary by comparison with what had gone before. During the closing three months of my conscription, I could think of little other than getting 'Down South' to Cape Town so that I could commence my studies.

I returned to Methuen Barracks for the last time and handed in my kit, and I will never forget how I felt walking out of the Battalion's armoury having handed in my rifle. As happy as I was to be returning to civvy life, I felt terribly vulnerable for a long time after I left the army without the comfort of my ever-present companion for almost two years. I said a final goodbye to my faithful *Masodja* one by one but, with the wisdom age and hindsight invariably bring, believe that this then twenty-one-year-old could have made more of the poignant occasion which was about to take us in different directions for good, save that I had the privilege of exercising options which they couldn't.

I look back now, some forty years later, and I think how fortunate I was not to come to grief in those heady days. They were a fantastic adventure and a wonderful growing experience for me which I shall never forget. In fact, as much as I yearned in the latter stages of my National Service for the freedom that civilian life brings, so do I now often think how wonderful it would be to once again sit in solitude with my faithful *Masodja* on one of those kopjes in that most beautiful country, without a care in the world.

CHAPTER FIFTEEN

PARACHUTING

INTRODUCTION: MILITARY PARACHUTING by Captain Andrew Telfer

As we have seen, the Fireforce concept centred, firstly, on the location of the enemy (usually by covert OPs) and, secondly, on the rapid deployment by air of infantry to engage them. Prior to 1977, in Rhodesia, only Special Forces were para-trained, and air transport of infantry soldiers into combat was limited to Alouette III G-Cars, each carrying only four soldiers. As there were usually only three G-Cars allocated to a Fireforce, a mere twelve soldiers could be carried into contact in the first wave. Often, this was insufficient, as the terrorists could not be effectively located and contained. Thus, the decision was made to train RLI and RAR soldiers in static-line parachuting from old but serviceable Dakota transport aircraft, developed from the civilian Douglas DC-3 airliner, as used by the Allies during WW II. This article looks at the concept of deploying infantry by parachute.

The world's first operational military parachute jump occurred during WW I, on 9 August 1918, when Lieutenant Alessandro Tandura of the Italian Army was dropped at night behind Austro-Hungarian lines near Vittorio Veneto on a reconnaissance and sabotage mission. Between the two World Wars, the Italians developed the technique of static line deployment, enabling larger-scale jumps at lower altitude than when rip-cords were used. The Soviets recognised the potential for mass deployment of troops by parachute and practised the tactic in a series of exercises in the mid-1930s. Their paratroopers had to exit Tupolev TB-3 transporters via a hatch in the roof of the fuselage, shuffle out and line up on the wings, and then jump off together. Hardly a quick exit but one that enabled them to drop 1,000 troops in one massed jump, watched by foreign observers including a very thoughtful Hermann Göring.

By 1938, Göring had formed the first of what would be ten Parachute Divisions as part of the Luftwaffe. German paratroopers were known as *Fallschirmjäger* ('parachute hunters') and were commanded throughout World War II by Kurt Student. It is fair to say that the *Fallschirmjäger* were the most successful airborne troops in the War. During the German invasions of Poland and

Norway, they formed an essential component of *Blitzkrieg* ('lightning war'), capturing enemy airfields ahead of the ground forces to prevent their use against the invaders. On the Maginot Line in May 1940, their training and commitment were vividly displayed when 85 members of *Sturmgruppe Granit* ('Assault Group Granite') captured the massive fortification and gun emplacements of Eben Emael, the largest fortification in the world at that time, defended by 1,200 Belgian troops. Nevertheless, military parachute operations were revealed as a high-risk enterprise; in the invasion of Crete in 1941, 22,000 *Fallschirmjäger* successfully captured the island in an airborne assault, but at a loss of 3,250 killed and 3,400 wounded (30 percent casualties).

Military parachuting is not complicated; it is a means of transportation, enabling the deployment of troops from an aircraft without the need to land the plane. However, because it involves overcoming the natural human fear of heights, a mystique has grown up around the image of the double-rugged, steely-eyed, romping-stomping paratrooper (even the term is so much more martial than 'parachutist'). This image, and the soldiers it attracts, has led to the establishment of a kind of second tier in the military hierarchy, between first tier special forces and the earth-bound infantry. The Parachute Regiment of the British Army, the South African Parabats, and the United States 101st and 82nd Airborne Divisions are examples of this. The stature of these units derives, not so much from the act of parachuting, as from the type of people attracted to it and from the relatively tough physical selection processes that they will endure to gain entrance, nurturing esprit de corps and fighting potential.

There is nothing wrong with that, as anything that improves unit pride and fighting spirit has great merit. US General Maxwell Taylor, who commanded the 101st Airborne Division in WW II, captured this concept in his book *Swords and Plowshares*:

Dakota (C47) Jump signal

'A standard question for a new man was why he had volunteered for parachuting and whether he enjoyed it. On one occasion, a bright-eyed recruit startled me by replying to the latter question with a resounding "No, sir." "Why, then, if you don't like jumping did you volunteer to be a parachutist?" I asked. "Sir, I like to be with people who do like to jump," was the reply.'

Returning to the Rhodesian Bush War, the scale of military parachuting in Rhodesia was extraordinary, not in the overall volume of jumps (as it was such a small Army), but in the number of *operational* jumps carried out by *individual* soldiers. While, in other theatres of war, it was unusual for a soldier to carry out even two or three operational jumps in his entire career, in Rhodesia it was common to have jumped into combat twenty or thirty times, and some soldiers had double those figures.

Combined with effective OPs, it was also highly successful. The addition of sixteen soldiers to the first wave of troops entering a Fireforce contact more than doubled those available to the military commander of the operation. In addition, the use of round, practically un-steerable canopies and low altitude (500 feet AGL) drops, kept the troops close together on the DZ, providing the commander with a ready-made sweep line. The use of this sweep line to drive terrorists into heli-borne stop groups, accounted for hundreds of terrorist casualties during the Rhodesian Bush War.

Paratroopers are airborne infantry and the primary role of the infantry is to 'close with and destroy the enemy'. There are three ways for infantry to 'close with' the enemy: by water, by land and by air. While the German *Fallschirmjäger* made the most effective use of parachuting in the history of conventional warfare, the Rhodesian Army made the most effective use of parachuting in the history of counter-insurgency operations.

Chibaya Moyo is fortunate that Squadron Leader Derek de Kock, the exemplary Officer Commanding, the Rhodesian Air Force Parachute Training School at New Sarum, has kindly contributed the following three articles that describe the essential nature of military parachuting in Rhodesia.

THE RHODESIAN AIR FORCE PARACHUTE TRAINING SCHOOL, THE VERY BEST by Squadron Leader Derek de Kock

I have tried to make these ramblings readable to the reader interested in the history of a small central African country which became a world leader in the use of paratroops.

These airborne soldiers were all students of the Rhodesian Air Force Parachute Training School and, after rigorous training, were deployed on Fireforce – a tactic we developed. Before jumping, they were checked and dispatched by a Parachute Jumping Instructor who was responsible for their safe delivery into battle onto a suitable Drop Zone. On occasion the same troops, many mere teenagers, were dispatched up to three times a day into battle. At RAF Abingdon we were told that more than two training parachute descents in day was considered dangerous.

In 1961 six Royal Rhodesian Air Force airmen were sent to The Royal Air Force Parachute Training School at RAF Abingdon – five of us were successful in qualifying for the RAF Parachute Jumping Instructor brevet. We were trained in exactly the same way the RAF trained their PJIs and became skilled in the use of the three 'F' principles of instruction: Firm Fair and Friendly. Initially students were astounded by this form of instruction – they couldn't comprehend how pleasant we instructors were. We were not the usual yelling, snarling type of military teachers. The only time we raised our voices (in theory) was to shout the word "Go!" which was used for every order.

Unlike other military instructors, we also did not differentiate between rank, age, gender or race. Everyone was treated exactly the same, the only acknowledgement of higher rank was to say "Sir" to officers. Being an officer was no excuse for not doing push ups when an error was made either, and it can safely be said that more push ups were carried out in the PTS hangar than any other place in Rhodesia. This calm, respectful, even-handed teaching style was invaluable – it resulted in calm, confident paratroopers who had the utmost faith in the PJIs and would respond to their commands in even the most stressful circumstances.

Whilst we continued to use this RAF teaching style, there were many other things we did improve upon. The biggest problem with the RAF parachute training methods was that nothing had changed, either in the training or the equipment used, since WW II, with the exception of the introduction of the 24ft Reserve parachute. The main parachute was still the 28ft X type which had been used on the 'D' Day Landings in Normandy, on Operation 'Market Garden' of a 'Bridge Too Far' fame, and in 1956 when the Parachute Regiment was dropped at Suez to secure the Canal.

Nearly 20 years after WW II, parachute training in the RAF had also changed very little. The main reason for this was nobody had bothered to ask the soldiers if what they were being taught was relevant. Nobody, for example, had asked the soldiers if the parachutes should be improved, or what could be done to make their weapons more accessible after landing, or if they would be prepared to jump at 500ft, or if it was safe, possibly safer, to jump into trees?

At the time, rifles, machine guns, Bren guns or rocket launchers were always carried in a suspended load and were 15ft away upon landing. In addition, the suspended load was made from heavy duty canvas which took a very long time to pack and an equally long time to unpack. Just to get at the rifle was a major undertaking of undoing straps and unlacing yards of cord. Not ideal if the enemy was shooting at you.

Not that we knew any different at the time of our course at RAF Abingdon. We were just airmen, and nobody was even trying to change things. Because of this attitude we were also stuck with the "good old ways" because we'd been trained by the RAF and, it was expected, if the RAF did it that way we had to follow suit. This was the case until the end of the Federation on 31 Dec 1963. Suddenly there were only 31 SAS Other Ranks in the Army and six PJIs and we were very nearly folded up.

Fortunately, somebody in the higher ranks of the Army and Air Force remembered the 1959 debacle in Fort Hill. So, almost as an after-thought, it was decided to keep the SAS. And, if you had an SAS, you also needed Parachute Jumping Instructors and a Parachute Training School. They anticipated we PJIs would keep quiet, not rock the boat, and just train the SAS when they required training using the familiar old methods. It was also a great way to show visiting dignitaries how advanced we were, just drop a Dakota load of PJI's, or if handy, paratroops, down the runway. Always impressive.

However, once UDI was declared on 11th November 1965 we no longer felt compelled to stick to the old methods we'd inherited. In fact, due to sanctions (which resulted in no information and no supplies,) the nature of our Bush War, and our hot and high conditions, we were frequently forced to improvise and experiment. We were also fortunate to have a number of experienced soldiers join our ranks. They were always willing to give us practical advice from the soldiers' perspective. Combined, these factors led to a great spirit of innovation which saw us develop new parachuting methods and equipment to become world leaders in military parachuting on a very tight budget.

We encouraged our staff to bring us their ideas and every idea was explored. It was either adopted or rejected only after thorough scrutiny. Sometimes these ideas were silly but even so they were still looked at. (Just remember the safety fuse we used to open the parachute on the free fall boxes silly in the modern context, but it worked!)

Innovative we may have been, but safety was always our first concern. Troops needed to land in one piece in order to do their job – our training drills reinforced safety at all stages of the jump and were repeated until the soldiers could perform, under any circumstances, without even thinking. For this reason, our death and injury rate was extremely low – a fact of which we can be justifiably proud.

In the Rhodesian Air Force Parachute Training School we made it our job to always find better ways to drop paratroops into action. We never stopped questioning the old methods. Was there a better and safer way to carry equipment into action? Could the soldier get hold of his weapon if he was stuck up a tree? Was it a good idea to give the paratrooper a pistol to use if he did get caught up in a tree? Was it even sensible to jump into the bloody trees in the first place?

We did not stop asking questions and sometimes sanctions worked in our favour. For example, in the beginning, we had trouble accessing parachutes and were forced to search out alternatives.

The Royal Air Force, with their choice of X type parachute, were still restricted to a flax webbing harness that had to be adjusted to fit the individual with no body band to hold a weapon and they were happy to stay that way. But, we were not and when we received the 35 ft PT10 American parachute with a body band and Capewells, we were able to devise new ways of carrying the weapon, so it was at hand on landing. The body band allowed the soldier to strap the rifle or machine gun to his body, so it was immediately accessible - a fantastic improvement as was the 35ft shaped canopy. No late swings on landing!!! Later we got the South African copy called the SAVIAC which was stronger and easier to repair therefore better.

Once we discovered, through PJI experimentation, that landing in scrubby trees was not only possible, but soft and also had the added benefit of providing instant cover, we asked for parachutes fitted with Capewell canopy release systems, so the soldiers could get out of trees easily.

We always tried to maintain good and open relationships with the men we trained and were especially great friends with the SAS. We listened to them, when they made suggestions about the equipment and the way the personal weapons were carried – after all they were the end- user and there was no point in dropping troops if they were too injured, or too disadvantaged by poor equipment to fight after landing.

We personally trialled our innovations to ensure they were safe and practical. We practised with every parachute type, and every parachute modification before allowing the troops to use them. We parachuted into different DZs; into trees, into mud, onto ploughed fields, into maize fields before we allowed the troops to do these things. Likewise, we experimented with weapon carrying and found the best method was to carry the rifle attached to the body, loaded with a round in the breach with the safety on. The MAG machine gun could be carried in the same way, with a 50-round belt of ammo wrapped around the breach. Much better than scrambling around in the dark, up a tree, trying to find a weapon which, in the old days, could be dangling 15ft below you!

The RAF gave us a fine grounding in the safe way to parachute and the safe way to get troops into a set battle plan – the type of battle which took a long time and many meetings to prepare. I remembered carrying out DZ Recce's before the SAS Operational drops in September 1962. What a farce! We were able to successfully carry out this type of operation too, as described earlier in the blog under Operation Dingo and Operation Gatling where DZ's were chosen from aerial photographs.

However, we broke new ground with our Fireforce techniques. We were never taught how to drop troops at very short notice into a fast-moving battle. Due to the guerrilla-style tactics of our enemy we needed to develop methods to hit back hard and hit back fast. We could not allow bands of terrorists to simply cross the border to safety, so we had to create a way to quickly drop troops, into variable terrain, to ambush the escaping enemy. This was Fireforce – a unique style of attack developed and perfected by the Rhodesian Armed Forces.

Once the enemy was spotted from an observation point, within a very short time we attacked with helicopter borne troops and paratroops dropped in very close proximity – surrounded the bastards and killed them. The first time we saw the DZ was when we were running in for the drop, which was at only 500ft AGL. The wind-speed on the ground was judged by the smoke from a smoke grenade dropped by the helicopter gunship marking the DZ position. I can't imagine the RAF, or for that matter, any other Airborne Forces, carrying out the types of Fireforce operations we did in Rhodesia without first conducting reconnaissance, feasibility studies, health and safety assessments and finally talking themselves out of it altogether. But we found this method was deadly and efficient.

Our Bush War was probably the last time paratroops were used in such large numbers and with such devastating effect. I am very proud to have been a part of The Rhodesian Parachute Training School – we maintained an impressive safety record even in the most trying circumstances, and we developed training and tactics which revolutionised military parachuting. None of this would have been possible without the support of the dedicated PJIs, parachute packers, dispatchers, pilots and of course the troops.

PARACHUTE TRAINING SCHOOL STATISTICS by Squadron Leader Derek de Kock

I am very fortunate to have been a part of the Rhodesian Parachute Training School from its inception in 1961 until February 1979. As Rhodesia became Zimbabwe in 1980, I was with the School for most of its existence as the "Rhodesian Parachute Training School." After I left Frank Hales became the CO and upon his departure in 1980, Kevin Milligan took over after the country changed its name to Zimbabwe and the school became the Zimbabwe Parachute Training School. These men continued the proud tradition and high standards set from the start.

I believe we, the Rhodesians, were the last armed force to use parachuting on a large scale, as an integral part of operations. Although parachuting is still used occasionally the technology of modern warfare has largely superseded the need for paratroopers. Certainly, other countries drop troops as part of specialist missions, but not in the manner, and certainly not with the frequency that we did.

In our Bush War, paratroopers were used extensively. They were routinely used as part of a Fireforce in which troops would be strategically dropped to surround and attack the fleeing enemy. Between 1976 and 1979 hardly a day went by when Fireforce drops did not happen, usually 16 men would be dropped, but sometimes 24 would be crammed in, especially by the RAR. As mentioned in the first chapter, there were often several such operations in a single day, with PTS staff involved grabbing a quick bite between drops. This alone would account for many thousand individual parachute drops.

Less frequently, but just as effectively, paratroops were used as an offensive deployment to attack enemy base camps outside our borders. I described a few of these ops, such as Operation Dingo and Operation Gatling in earlier chapters. These operations resulted in massive devastation to the terrorists, and their equipment, and an extremely low injury and death rate on our side. In these operations we generally dropped between 100 and 300 men, and also performed practise jumps prior.

Smaller sorties into enemy territory were carried out frequently. Because records were destroyed and also information was shared on a strict 'needs to know' basis, I have no idea how many parachute drops took place across our borders into Mozambique or Zambia. However, I personally carried out over 50 HALO sorties into Mozambique, a few less into Zambia and one very far up the side of Malawi. I also dispatched some Selous Scouts into Botswana one night. At one stage I was dropping HALO troops from the SAS to the North and East up to three times a week, and on alternate days I would be dropping Selous Scouts to the South and East. Also, at this time I was trying to keep an eye on the HALO training every morning at PTS. I was a very busy boy.

During my time with the PTS, the injury rate was extremely low - less than 1 injury for every 100 parachute jumps in training and even less than that for operational jumps in the bush. This very low injury rate was due to the extremely high calibre of instruction by the Parachute Jumping Instructors and the SAVIAC static line parachutes we used. In addition, parachute drops into the Rhodesian bushes long grass and savanna type trees helped to cushion the landings.

Added to this, we did preparatory training, including a jump, whenever possible before operations. This was to practise the required formation and to reinforce technique. As we became busier some of our RLI troops were trained in South Africa. However, there is always a problem when other countries train your fighting soldiers and in this case it was in the Dakota Aircraft Drill and the carrying of the personal weapon. The South Africans still used the side cable and strop in the Dakota, whilst we used the overhead cable. The South Africans had the personal weapon in a suspended load, we had it on the body. To overcome this we required all the South African trained RLI to do a 4 jump conversion course into one of our bush DZs before deployment to a Fireforce. Training of this kind is never wasted and the more parachuting these troops could do the better, as they were less likely to suffer parachuting injuries on operations.

We were very safety conscious – sloppy technique was not tolerated, and neither was unnecessary risk taking. Discipline, and absolute adherence to correct drill was expected from all our students, and it is a credit to the young men who went through the School that this was almost always maintained – even in the most stressful or extreme conditions.

We only suffered one death during training whilst I was with the PTS. An RAR soldier was killed on a basic training parachute jump when he made an incorrect exit and the static line of his parachute wrapped around the butt of his MAG (M60 machine gun). The friction caused by this severed the static line. Unfortunately, this soldier failed to pull his reserve soon enough and plunged to his death.

As mentioned earlier in the blog, we also had three deaths during operational jumps. The first fatal operational parachute jump was on our very first HALO operation when Sgt Frank Wilmot failed to pull his ripcord and was killed inside Mozambique. The second and third were caused when a stick of RAR paratroops was dropped too low on a Fireforce deployment and the parachutes did not open properly. On the board of enquiry, it was calculated that the drop took place at 168ft AGL.

The Fireforce PJI was responsible for sending in the manifests of all the troops who jumped into action or who carried out a training jump. This information was then entered into the Master Log of all jumps both operational and training and was held in PTS. Unfortunately, this Master Log, along with much of the other PTS records, was destroyed when Rhodesia became Zimbabwe and the Mugabe regime took control. We did not want any repercussions, and this was a detailed record of all parachute drops, when they had taken place, and who had done them.

However, the majority of the regular Army were trained to parachute and, judging from photographs taken of each course, it is safe to say we trained approximately 2,500 men in static line parachuting. Each static line course consisted of 8 jumps, so again this accounts for many thousands of individual parachute drops.

As well as this, Selous Scouts and SAS were often dropped from high altitude to perform clandestine operations. In order to do this, they were trained as

Free Fall parachutists – the course for this originally consisted of 20 jumps, but this was soon increased to 60, with 20 at night. For most jumps, the student was followed down by an instructor who would provide a critique of technique after landing. Again, these courses alone accounted for several thousand jumps.

The parachute school expanded to such an extent that we were running static line courses of over 100 and freefall courses of eight, and also doing the 4-jump refresher training for the South African-trained troops all at the same time. This meant we would have up to five Dakotas in the circuit for morning parachuting, each doing two or three lifts just to keep the training going. An incredible achievement by #3 Transport Squadron. This added up to over 300 parachute descents per day in training alone. The parachute training school had taken over the entire hangar and we were running courses of over 100 basic static line parachutists every 3 weeks. During my time with the PTS we conducted 100+ static line courses and 30+ Free Fall courses.

Meanwhile, the other three Dakotas were out in the bush, fulfilling the Fireforce role. I am still amazed at how the Safety Equipment Workers managed to keep up. In 1978 alone, over 15,000 operational jumps took place. This meant the parachute packers were working 24hrs per day in 8hr shifts. During my service there was not a single packing failure - an absolutely phenomenal record.

By 1978, the staff of the school had expanded to four officers and approximately 20+ PJIs. We had to utilize junior NCOs from the RLI, National Service Recruits and Number 3 Air Supply Platoon as dispatchers to assist on Fireforce. These dispatchers were trained in PTS and although some were not posted specifically to the school, they became a huge asset to the staff. Somehow, I managed to have a few young men doing their initial call up allocated to PTS to be trained as Dispatchers. All these young men were required to carry out a full parachute course and would then be utilized at the PJIs discretion on the Fireforce. Most if not all these dispatchers were trained by Paul Hogan our Australian PJI and Tony Hughes. By this time Tony had been promoted to Warrant Officer and was regarded by all the PTS staff as one of the very best instructors in the school.

In retrospect the Parachute Training School of the Rhodesian Air Force can be proud of their incredible achievements in the field of military parachuting. We were few, but we did the job. During my years in the Parachute Training School, I was fortunate to associate with some of the most dedicated, safety-conscious people in the world. I was truly privileged to command this small band of highly-motivated, intelligent, and professional men. They came from all walks of life and from all over the world. They showed me absolute loyalty and I can honestly say I was never, ever, let down by any of them. Thanks guys you were the greatest.

A RECORD WE DID NOT WANT – THE LOWEST RECORDED STATIC LINE OPERATIONAL DROP by Squadron Leader Derek de Kock

Despite our excellent safety record and our very low injury rate, jumping from aeroplanes was a dangerous occupation and did, from time to time, result in injury, or even death.

Not all the records we set were deliberate. For example, the lowest drop ever done, using T10/Saviac Type parachutes, was by Rhodesian African Rifles at a shockingly low 168ft AGL. At this height, the parachutes would have opened only moments before landing.

Claims that a static line parachute will fall 250ft before opening are correct, but only if jumped from a balloon, cliff or building without slipstream to help deployment. When jumping from the Dakota, the pilots were told to fly at 95kts or faster, so the slipstream created could help blow the parachutes open. This reduced the actual drop from 250ft to approximately 100ft. It was because of this lucky fact that the casualties were not higher in the following incident.

It was just south of the mining town of Bindura where the lowest parachute drop took place during the terrorist bush war in Rhodesia. A stick of 16 Rhodesian African Rifles soldiers was dropped at 168ft AGL which resulted in two men breaking legs on landing and a number of others sustaining minor injuries. Unfortunately, one of the soldiers who broke his leg died 3 days later after suffering an embolus. A sad day for all at the PTS and #3 Squadron.

In this instance, the second pilot was on his first deployment, and still learning the skills of dropping paratroops onto bush DZs. Through inexperience he made a fatal error when setting QFE on the altimeter. In war times, our training was sometimes conducted on the job, in a dangerous and tense setting. Unfortunately for the second pilot, and for the man who subsequently died, this was one of those occasions.

As always, we were determined to learn from mistakes and Air Force HQ immediately instigated a board of inquiry. Capt Paul Simmons of the SAS and I, were the two officers appointed to investigate, work out what happened and how to avoid similar mistakes in future. After this all PJIs were instructed to look out of the door on all drop runs to visually check the height AGL. Also, as always happens after such a tragedy, all Dakota aircraft operated by 3 Sqn, were fitted with radar altimeters to guarantee accurate drop heights.

Many, from various units in the Rhodesian conflict, stake claim to the lowest drop. However, there is no doubt this incident was it – it was not a record we planned to set, and certainly not one we ever endeavoured to break.

YOU ARE COMING INTO … SEWERAGE by Lieutenant Michael Matthews

From about October 1977 RAR Battalions started to undergo para training for the Fireforce role, and in due course of time A Coy 1RAR and my 3 Platoon got their turn. In March 1978 3 Platoon made the trip in a '45 from our base at Methuen Barracks to New Sarum, the military air base just outside Salisbury. We were provided accommodation at the Rhodesia Regiment at Cranborne Barracks and commuted daily for our para training, a course which lasted about two weeks between March and April 1978.

There had been much said as to whether or not black troops were made of the right stuff to participate in this aspect of COIN warfare, and some of the RLI sceptics on our course believed that black soldiers didn't have the aptitude to jump out of a plane. It became a personal mission of mine to prove them wrong, and I am proud to say that not one of my Platoon flunked the course.

Not surprisingly, there was a significant amount of theory and ground work to get through before we took to the sky, but it wasn't long before we were facing our first 'live' static line jump. At 06h00 on 21st March 1978, we took off in a trusty Dakota from New Sarum runway. I would be lying if I said that I wasn't

You are Coming in to...Sewerage

mortified at the thought of jumping out of a plane, albeit that my static line would cause my parachute to deploy immediately I left the aircraft but, perhaps more than at any time in my relatively brief military career, I felt it imperative to lead by example, and I simply did my best to calm my own troops, and assure them that jumping was a real cake walk!

We jumped at a thousand feet, whereas the operational jumping height is five hundred feet. The call came for us to "stand up and hook up", with which we all stood up and hooked the clasp of our static lines onto a cable strung along the length of the fuselage. I was fourth out when we achieved our altitude, and will always recall our course instructor, Sergeant Chris Pisarro, an American, directing me to "stand in the door!" Next thing I felt an immense rush of wind and I was out of the plane. I recall thinking what an exhilarating feeling it was to be drifting back to earth, and how incredibly quiet and serene it was.

I could see my *Masodja* drifting earthward on either side of me, and I remember thinking how relieved I was that none of them had balked or refused to jump. The landing was a bit unnerving, since although the ground had seemed to be approaching slowly at higher altitude, its approach appeared to gain momentum the closer I got to it. I completed my 'para roll' as best I could, and simply lay on my back, absorbing the huge exhilaration and relief of having completed my first jump.

From that moment on, I and most (although certainly not all) of my *Masodja* couldn't wait to get back into the air. We completed eight jumps in all, the second last of which was required to be a 'night' jump, and this jump constituted the most enduring memory of my para training course. Self-evidently, we were required to perform this jump at night, complete with our rifle and webbing. This time around I was second out of the door and, apart from the understandable uncertainty as to when to execute my para roll on impact, particularly since there was about a quarter moon, I had gained considerably in confidence and was even looking forward to the jump.

We again jumped at a thousand feet, and the now familiar routine wound itself out like clockwork. It was a still autumn evening when we stood in the door and exited the Dak. This time I was not aware as to where any of my men were in relation to me and, to my horror, I saw directly below me what seemed to be the concrete roof of some sort of circular building. I panicked, since I well knew that I would not be able to accurately gauge when to execute my para roll. In short, I truly believed that both of my ankles would break on impact since, despite the considerable size of our parachute canopies, our rate of descent was such that the para roll was in most cases a vital component of a relatively comfortable landing.

I pulled down furiously on my rigging lines in a vain attempt to steer my canopy away from the roof, but to no avail. These canopies were simply not constructed for precision landings, but simply to deliver a person back to mother earth in one piece.

The roof was rushing at me, and I braced myself for what I thought would be a hospital landing, when………sploosh! What had seemed in the stillness of the night to be a concrete roof was nothing more, or more appropriately less, than an open sewage pit. Thankfully, the pit was only about five feet deep, making it possible for me to stand in it and unbuckle myself from the parachute harness. I shudder to think what would have happened if the pit was deeper, since I had had absolutely no training in freeing myself of my parachute and harness in such (shitty) conditions. I believe that I really would have been in the proverbial…

We were taken back to New Sarum, although such was the stench emanating from my person that I was given a very wide berth on our Bedford by my *Masodja*, who could not conceal their mirth at my plight. Their 'Ishe' was also well able to see the funny side of things, and there is no doubt in my mind that the course helped to bring us even closer to each other.

I suppose smelling rank beats the heck out of broken ankles, and there is no question that this was the softest landing I was to have. After a five hundred foot jump the following day, we were all awarded our wings, and returned to Bulawayo to join our Company.

You're landing in … Sewerage

SHIRI YE DENGA by Captain Andrew Telfer

'Shiri ye Denga' translates as 'Bird of the Sky'. I first saw those words written in black permanent marker across the front of the parachute helmet of Private Zuvarinopisa of 10 Platoon, D Company, 2RAR. Our soldiers didn't emblazon their helmets with macho slogans like 'Death from the Sky' as I saw elsewhere. Their take on parachuting was more adventurous than martial. His name also had a lyrical African quality to it: 'Zuvarinopisa' means 'the sun is hot'. This article seeks to capture images of parachuting with the RAR.

While on Fireforce rotation, each morning at first light, we would lay out our webbing ready for when the siren sounded across the airfield, calling us to action. At that time, after nervous wees and last smokes, we put on our equipment and our parachutes, helping one another to kit up. Despatchers, often from the RLI under the watchful eye of an Instructor from the Parachute Training School (PTS), checked us and placed the static line over our left shoulder, and then helped us climb aboard the Dakota. Inside, in two rows along the sides of the aircraft, we sat on steel framed benches with canvas seats. It was hot, stuffy and cramped in our tightly-rigged harnesses. We were glad to take off.

In the air, with the port side door open, the aircraft cooled down and we waited silently and patiently. We knew that the heli-borne sticks would land first and that we would only be deployed if they or the helicopters made contact with the enemy. The Despatchers would hear first, through their headsets, suddenly springing to life, gesturing to us to stand up and shouting the order: "Stand up, hook up, check equipment!"

That sent the adrenaline pumping and our well-practised PTS drills into effect. We stood, hooked the metal snap-hook of the static line onto an overhead steel cable that ran the length of the aircraft, inserted the pin and turned to face the rear. Then we carried out our equipment checks, in the prescribed sequence: top hook and pin, bottom hook and pin, static line clear to the left hand side, helmet, reserve, quick release box, body band. We checked the man in front: top hook and pin, bottom hook and pin, static line clear to the left hand side, stowage of the static line, centre pack tie. Tap him and give thumbs up. On completion we waited for the order "Tell off for equipment check!" to shout in turn that each one of us was OK.

At this point, our left hand was on the static line, just below the snap hook, our right forearm was across the reserve chute, we were facing the rear and tightly packed, with our left foot just in front of our right. Then came the command: "Action Stations!" Immediately, we begin marching, without crossing our feet, stamping and shouting "One! – Two! – One! – Two!" The shouting and rhythmic stamping in unison was all about mustering spirit and it worked.

I always placed myself in the position of being first to exit the aircraft. Tactically, it could be argued that 8th to exit was the best position as it would put the officer in the centre of the line on the ground, but this was irrelevant as we all got mixed up in the air. I did it because that was what was expected of RAR officers. Because of this, I would be the first to be stopped by the Despatchers, just before the door, my left hand releasing the static line and placed firmly above the door frame as I half-turned towards the door. One of my lasting images of my soldiers is in the Dakota, at that stage of the drill, when I always looked back into the aircraft at the row of shining black faces with big eyes under para helmets. All I had to do was smile and give a clenched fist salute and every face lit up with a huge smile, in rows of white teeth.

Looking out at the scene from 500 feet above ground level, it was easily possible to make out people on the ground. It wasn't possible, however, to make any sense of the tactical situation, only the immediate images. In the kaleidoscope of pictures that come back to me now, I see the round thatched roofs of African villages, interspersed with rough fields of cultivation, wooded stream lines and thickly wooded rocky kopjes. Amongst them I see smoke, people laying down, some running, and some turning to fire at the aircraft, curving lines of green tracer, arcing upwards. In the air, I can see Alouette helicopters circling, the K Car tilted to port, firing its cannon, and the fixed-wing Lynx running in on air-to-ground strikes. On one occasion in Mozambique, I recall seeing helicopters, the Lynx and a Canberra, all in one frame as I looked through the door.

Then the lights above the door changed and I was ordered to "Stand in the door!" In a drill movement, my left hand swept down to outside the door frame at waist height, my right forearm remained on the reserve, my chest and face were almost out of the aircraft and my legs bent and poised to spring. The Despatchers held me back from either side; if they released, I would go. Then they saw the light change again and did release my energy, shouting "Go!" and whacking my body, doing the same to each soldier in line, as they followed me into space.

There would be a brief few moments in the slipstream, with the sensation of falling in a very strong wind, and then a big tug as the parachute deployed, opened by the static line. Then silence, before the aircraft and other noises were realised again. We had very little time to carry out our drills in the air because the drop height was so low. We looked up to check the canopy, carried out a quick all-around observation to check for other parachutists, kicked out of any twists in our rigging lines, slipped out of our seat straps and prepared for landing.

Sometimes, we were fired upon as we descended but never hit; I don't know why not. Sometimes, we saw memorable things – for example, on that descent in Mozambique, the Canberra bombed a target about a kilometre in front of me, creating shockwaves that rocked me under my canopy as I looked out over a smoke-filled plain onto a hillside with a huge cross on top – but, mostly, we just went through our drills. Elbows in, chin on chest, feet and knees together, soles of the feet parallel to the ground… THUMP! I did damage my ankle once, and badly, but that was through landing on a stump, not because I didn't know what to do.

Suspended containers were not used in Fireforce operations and not all Rhodesian paratroopers were even taught how to use them (I wasn't on my course in July 1977). Soldiers jumped wearing their webbing, with rifles or MAGs strapped to the body. Even so lightly equipped, there were still vulnerable moments on landing and we took to carrying 9mm pistols attached to a paracord lanyard and tucked under the bungees of the reserve parachute. It was one such pistol that RAR Corporal Ananias Ali SCR famously used to shoot a terrorist just after landing: the terrorist, noticing Ali's rifle was strapped in an unreachable position, smiled and raised his rifle; Ali smiled back, said "Got another one" (in chiShona) and shot him dead.

Drop Zones (DZs), as Squadron Leader de Kock has explained, were subject to none of the reconnaissance undertaken by other Armies. DZs were quickly chosen by the K Car pilot and Army OC for tactical advantage. We were dropped into trees, fields of stumps, across streams with high banks, across fence lines, into towering sugar cane once in Mozambique... virtually anywhere except grass. We knew and accepted the nature of the DZs, and the injury rate was very low. I put that down to the remarkably professional training that we received at the Parachute Training School. Every RAR soldier remembered his PTS instructor by name and spoke of him with great respect and affection.

Once landed, we struggled out of our harnesses, cocked our weapons and, while I called on the radio to the OC in the K Car, my NCOs organised the sweep line on either side of me. The order would come "Sweep towards the K Car now" and off we went. We wouldn't know where the terrorists were, exactly, only that they were there somewhere, or we wouldn't have been dropped. See *We Searched* in the *Fireforce* chapter.

The Dakota initially carried sixteen paratroopers (four multiples of four, to facilitate later uplift by the G-Cars). Later, when it was found that time was being wasted packing parachutes after the contact was over, an additional two soldiers jumped, tasked with remaining on the DZ to pack parachutes during the contact. This enabled more rapid redeployment of the troops to a subsequent sighting. As mentioned in *Chibaya Moyo 1*, the two soldiers who remained on the DZ were given the callsign 'Wanker' by Major Colin Hendrie, OC B Company 2RAR. He did this because they weren't doing any fighting that day and there was only humour, no offence, taken at the use of the term:

"Wanker One, this is 29. Are the chutes packed yet? Over..."

"Ah! This is ah-Wanker One. Affirmaah-tiff... the choots are pack-ed OVAH!"

I hope that I've captured something of the nature of the experience of parachuting with the RAR. In closing, I would just like to add that most African soldiers had only flown in helicopters, if at all, before their parachute course. This meant that the first time they ever embarked on a fixed-wing aircraft, they were required to jump out of it. Nevertheless, RAR soldiers took to parachuting as they took to everything, with a smile and the philosophy: "Ishe, if you lead, I will follow".

RAR PARATROOPER by Private Gift Munana, A Company, 2RAR

I joined A Company on 12 of January 1976. I came from recruits' course at Balla Balla. When I arrived at the company, I was introduced to all the commanders in the company. One of these was Corporal Barbson Pongweni whom I gave the nickname of 'Dzansemomotera' or 'Easy come, easy go' or 'Chief Nhema' because of his funny stories, and Major Dennison whom we called 'K-car' because of the way he grips his rifle and I was also very pleased on the day I was nominated to go for a para course and worked very hard and passed the course.

How funny and lovely to be a paratrooper enjoying yourself diving out of a plane while it is in motion and I call myself a skydiver. I must not forget to mention the 2IC Captain Meiring who usually calls us 'Wankers!' with a nice lovely voice and our CSM Benjamin Makurira who is nicknamed 'Chipembere' [rhino]. I wish you could all have such leaders as Major Dennison and Captain Meiring. Everyone in A Company is happy! We have a company song we call 'Gange mukange Song' and 'Tirivaduku tauyawo'.

NO COMMS by Captain Tony Clark

In late November 1977 my platoon of newly trained paras (12 Pl D Coy 1 RAR) was attached to A Coy who were on Fire Force duty based at Rutenga (I think!). At about 08h00 the siren sounded indicating deployment to a sighting of CTs.

Within minutes all my guys were kitted up and doing buddy checks to the sound of the Alouette 111s and the old Dak warming up. K Car commander was Capt Glenn Reed and the G Car sticks had Lt Chris Clay as their commander.

The sighting was quite close, and we were not airborne for longer than 10 minutes when we sensed the Dak going into a holding pattern whilst the choppers dropped their sticks a commanded by K Car comd. We soon got the order to "stand up, hook up and check equipment". Within seconds I was standing in the door waiting for the green light. The dispatcher managed to shout in my ear "if you don t make it can I have your watch?" before the much anticipated "Go!"

Those op jumps were from approximately 500 feet and you merely had time to do the 4 drills before the ground was rushing at you. I noticed that we were above a village complex and was chuffed that I was heading towards a vegetable garden that had a lot of bamboo trees (soft landing). When I fell through the banana trees, I landed in a narrow stream that was running.

Much to my dismay, my boots sank into clay-like mud whilst my canopy collapsed over me. I struggled to disengage from the mud whilst I removed my chute cape-wells. My radio crackled… K Car wanting to know where the fuck was Sunray 43…me. After what appeared to be hours, I manoeuvred myself out of the mud and, when I explained my situation, all I got was "Move your arse, there is a fuckin war on."

At the end of that action we accounted for several CTs and weapons, none of which was attributed to my soldiering. Moral of this story: soft landings are not always the best.

Bananarama

CHAPTER SIXTEEN

EXTERNAL OPERATIONS

INTRODUCTION: EXTERNAL OPERATIONS by Captain Andrew Telfer

In 2015, I was surprised to read that the Rhodesian African Rifles' entry in Wikipedia stated that the RAR had never been deployed 'outside its borders'. Reading further, I found so many other factual errors that I re-wrote the Wikipedia entry in full. It has been edited since then by others and will of course continue to be so but, at least for one moment in time, it was accurate. The Rhodesian African Rifles has never been a stranger to operations beyond its borders. On the contrary, both the RAR and its predecessor, the Rhodesia Native Regiment, were in originally formed *for that very purpose*.

East Africa Campaign

The RNR was raised to fight in the First World War and did so with distinction in the East African Campaign from 1916 to 1918. During that campaign, the battalion saw action in German East Africa, Nyasaland and Portuguese East Africa. Their story was described earlier in this book and in detail by Professor Timothy J Stapleton in his book *No Insignificant Part: the Rhodesia Native Regiment and the East Africa Campaign of the First World War*.

The RNR was created in 1916 because the small pioneer population of Rhodesia wanted to contribute to the 'war effort' but lacked the manpower to send more young men than they already were. Black Africans, many of whom were from other countries, joined the RNR for a variety of reasons, some because they were former soldiers or policemen, some were migrant labourers wanting to escape the conditions in the mines, and others simply wanted a paid job.

Historian Tim Stapleton (2006) describes what faced them: 'The RNR experienced the harshest conditions that the German East Africa Campaign had to offer. They marched thousands of miles on rough tracks and through thick bush and swamps. Like other units, they suffered terribly from tropical diseases such as malaria, which worsened during the rainy season. Some European officers and

NCOs could not cope with the physical demands of the campaign and had to be sent home. Despite European stereotypes, Africans were not immune to these hardships and often had to make do without boots or medicine. Reliance on supply carriers meant that all ranks of the regiment often had little or no rations for days or even weeks and living off the land was common.'

Operationally, the African soldiers of the RNR proved themselves. Stapleton: 'Throughout the campaign, in which small patrols were often vital in collecting intelligence and denying food resources to the enemy, racial stereotypes about leadership began to break down. The white senior officers of the RNR initially did not trust African corporals and sergeants to perform important tasks that required individual initiative or lead larger patrols that would engage the enemy... [But] increasingly, certain African NCOs such as Tanganyika, Rita, and Salima were regularly called upon as leaders of all types of patrols, including platoon-sized ones with combat missions. They proved to be daring, intelligent and highly skilled. The unit could never have functioned effectively without them.'

One really has to wonder why it took another sixty years before the first African soldiers were commissioned.

Burma

As we have recorded earlier, in May 1940, the first Commanding Officer of the RAR, Major FJ Wane ISO, a former RNR officer, received the following orders in his call-up papers: 'There will be an African regiment; you will command it and the regiment will build its own camp on the Borrowdale road.' While he was busy carrying out this task, in July 1940, he would have received government notice GN 374/1940, telling him that the regiment was charged 'with the defence of the colony, the maintenance of order, and such duties as the minister may define' and, significantly, *'the regiment may be employed outside the colony.'* That final clause would have come as no surprise to him as he knew exactly why the RAR was being formed: to come to the aid of Britain once again, this time in its 'darkest hour'.

More than a million soldiers from the African continent would fight in WW II for the colonial powers, with very little initial understanding of what they were fighting for or against... but, just as in WW I, fight they would. On 17 November 1943, the newly-formed RAR left Salisbury on a journey that would take them to Burma where they joined the 22nd East African Infantry Brigade, part of Field Marshall William Slim's 14th Army, fighting the Japanese in the jungle.

Operating in the Burmese jungle required adaption, firstly to the environment. The following extracts from *We Gave Our Today* by William Fowler (2009), illustrate what they would be up against.

'About the size of France and Belgium combined, the country has two monsoon seasons and is extremely hot and humid from May to November.'

Lieutenant John Hudson, who commanded a company of the Royal Bombay Sappers & Miners, remembered:

'Getting soaked went with jungle life. We were often so wet, night and day, that our whole bodies became white and wrinkled like an old washerwoman's hands. Shirts rotted off soldiers' backs, and the bodies of the dead deteriorated in the heat: they became shiny, translucent black and bloated.'

Lieutenant Sam Horner, of 2 Royal Norfolks, recalled:

'The heat, humidity, altitude and the slope of almost every foot of ground combined to knock the hell out of the stoutest constitution. You gasp for air, which doesn't come, you drag your legs upwards till they seem reduced to the strength of matchsticks, and all the time sweat is pouring off you.'

Secondly, they had to adapt to fighting the Japanese. Fowler:

'The Japanese attacked with a fanatical, brutish courage, even when they appeared to be fatally wounded.

As Peter Young recalled: "They had to be very thoroughly slain."

Never had the Allied soldiers seen such self-belief in an army. The Japanese soldier believed in a spiritual essence which would overcome all obstacles. It was called *seishin* or strength of will, a mystical force which they were convinced would allow them to defeat technologically and numerically superior forces.'

That mentality is reflected in an Order of the Day issued by a Japanese general to his troops:

"Continue in the task till all your ammunition is expended. If your hands are broken, fight with your feet. If your hands and feet are broken, fight with your teeth. If there is no breath left in your body, fight with your spirit. Lack of weapons is no excuse for defeat."

The RAR overcame the challenge of the environment and defeated the Japanese wherever they found them. Read *Letters from Burma*, earlier in this book, for an insight into the impressions Burma made on individual RAR soldiers.

Their operations would continue beyond the formal surrender by Japan in July 1945. They remained to hunt hard-core Japanese 'no-surrender groups' until finally returning to Southern Rhodesia in May 1946.

Egypt

On 28 November 1951, the RAR were called upon to serve in Egypt to assist the British Army in the Suez Canal Zone. There, they were deployed to work with the

Royal Engineers in construction projects and to guard three bases: Longbeach, El Kirsch and Port Said, mostly against the efforts of local Egyptian thieves in their persistent burglary attempts.

Although operating in the bleak wasteland of the Arabian desert, the RAR soldiers brought their bush-craft skills with them. They soon put their tracking ability to good use and earned a reputation for locating culprits by following their spoor. During the time they were there, they killed two thieves, wounded three, captured twenty-five, and liberated eleven getaway bicycles. After just over a year, no doubt to the relief of the surviving thieves, they returned to Southern Rhodesia, arriving at Salisbury Railway Station on 10 December 1952.

Malaya

The RAR were deployed into the Malayan jungle in June 1956 against the Communist Terrorists (CTs) of the Malayan National Liberation Army (MNLA). They were back in the jungles of South East Asia once again but fighting a different kind of war to that which they had fought against the Japanese. This time, it was a counter-insurgency (COIN) war. The ethnic-Chinese MNLA employed classic guerrilla tactics: living in the jungle; carrying out hit and run attacks on installations, rubber plantations, transportation and infrastructure; avoiding contact with the security forces; and depending upon the approximately 500,000 Chinese farmers living on the edge of the jungle for food, information and recruits.

RAR patrols hunted the elusive CTs in thick jungle vegetation, employing fighting patrols, long and short-term ambushes, following tracks when located, and gaining kills in fleeting contacts. Elsewhere in *Chibaya Moyo*, read the story of WO2 Pisayi Muzerecho MM and Corporal Tabuya to see how well they rose to the challenge. The intensive patrolling maintained constant pressure on the enemy and, together with the granting of Malayan Independence in August 1957, led to many CT surrenders and the eventual end of the Emergency. Early in February 1958, the RAR began their journey homewards.

As in East Africa, Burma and Egypt, African soldiers adapted rapidly to the specific challenges posed by the unfamiliar environment, the mission and the enemy's characteristics. They applied their strength of character, physical resilience, tactical nous and bush-craft skills to succeed in their mission and it should perhaps be remembered that the only other Rhodesian unit deployed into the Malayan jungle was that which would become C Squadron, SAS.

Congo Border

In 1961, 1RAR was deployed along the Congolese/Northern Rhodesia border to prevent the Katangese secessionist war spreading over the border into the Federation.

The Rhodesian Bush War

Returning to Southern Rhodesia, the RAR were tasked with supporting the BSAP during outbreaks of civil unrest, often in the form of riot control. In 1963, the Central African Federation broke up, to be replaced by the separate nations of Rhodesia, Zambia and Malawi. The RAR came under sole command of the Rhodesian Army and was mostly deployed along the Zambezi Valley, on border control duties.

On 11 November 1965, Rhodesia unilaterally declared independence from Britain. By that time, the African nationalists had divided along tribal lines. The mainly Shona, Zimbabwe African National Union (ZANU), ultimately led by Robert Mugabe, its military wing the Zimbabwe African Liberation Army (ZANLA), was supported by China and operated from Mozambique and Tanzania.

The Zimbabwe African People's Union (ZAPU) was mainly Ndebele, was led by Joshua Nkomo, supported by Russia, its military wing was the Zimbabwe People's Revolutionary Army (ZIPRA), and it operated from Zambia and Botswana.

Beginning in 1966, terrorist groups began an escalating series of incursions into Rhodesia with the aim of subverting the local population and overthrowing the government. The Rhodesian Security Forces, including the RAR, were deployed against them throughout what would be known as the 'Bush War' to us, and as 'Chimurenga' (Liberation War) to the terrorists. It would last until a Commonwealth-brokered Ceasefire in February 1980.

Throughout this period, Rhodesian security forces carried out operations against the insurgents in neighbouring states ('external operations' or 'externals'). The implication of the term *external operations*, is that there exists a difference between such operations and those within a nation's borders. In conventional warfare, that is accurate as there is a profound difference; uninvited military incursion into a foreign nation is an invasion, whether the intent is to occupy territory or not, and is illegal without a formal declaration of war. In counter-insurgency warfare, however, such thinking (in the operational context) is a mistake, a self-limiting boundary not shared by the insurgents.

Terms applied to the Rhodesian Army, like '*internal security operations,*' '*aid to the civil power*', '*assistance to the civil authority*' and even '*security forces*' relate to the creeping nature of the onset of an insurgency. Without a singular declaration of war to or from a hostile nation, a country does not 'go to war'. Instead, it increasingly finds itself protecting its internal security against the actions of dissident members its own domestic population, seen as troublemakers (initially) and recognised as insurgents (eventually). Even though Mozambique, Zambia and Botswana provided havens and support for our enemy, without a declaration of war, we were politically reluctant to see their territory as simply an extension of our own operational area.

When we did cross the border, we spoke of 'hot pursuit' of fleeing terrorists or sought to establish 'deniability'. Rhodesian Special Forces (SAS and Selous Scouts) operated externally with spectacular success, interdicting enemy forces, attacking bases, destroying infrastructure and impeding terrorist movement into and out of Rhodesia. To enable deniability, they used Eastern bloc weapons and uniforms and, where they could, credited resistance movements like Renamo with their actions. Where they couldn't, they took intense criticism from the international community. The RLI took part in camp attacks against groups far outnumbering themselves, again achieving extraordinary results. The RAR did operate across all three borders (Mozambique, Zambia and Botswana) but not often enough.

I know from first-hand experience (described in *Chibaya Moyo 1*) that the territory just across the border was a very good hunting ground and it felt good to be there with RAR soldiers.

The terrorists 'switched on' when entering Rhodesia, naturally becoming more alert when they crossed the cordon sanitaire. They were less alert before they crossed or after they had returned to the sanctuary of their host country. When we operated across the border, we were able to turn this psychological factor to our advantage and hunt with greater success, something that suited and motivated us. For example, ambushes laid just a few kilometres across the border were so much more successful than those laid inside our own country. It was only about ten kilometres into Mozambique, in August 1977, that WO2 Gwatirera, PWO of 10 Pl, D Coy, 2RAR initiated his successful ambush described in *The Sergeant Major's Ambush*, later in this chapter.

We could have taken this advantage further. We were not there often enough, and the border should never have been perceived as a boundary for any Rhodesian operation. On our JOC maps, the boundaries of the Operational Areas followed the national border, naturally constraining the deployment of infantry accordingly. Significantly, the deployment of Rhodesia's most effective tactical combination, Observation Posts and Fireforce, should have straddled the border. Across it, groups were larger and more likely to move by day, dispersing after crossing into Rhodesia and moving more cautiously, often at night. Thus, the external zone could have been a highly productive territory for that tactical combination, with the added benefit of reducing collateral damage and casualties to Rhodesian villagers.

In conclusion, the RAR had a long and successful history of external warfare. The Germans in East Africa, the Japanese in Burma, the Chinese communist terrorists in Malaya, and even Egyptian thieves, knew full well what they were capable of. In those conflicts, the need for adaption had been a much greater challenge than simply extending current tactics across a border into a neighbouring state. Yet, in the Bush War, our highest commanders failed to take *full* advantage of this proven capability and an opportunity was missed. There were, of course, external operations of such a highly specialised nature that they belonged with the SAS or the Selous Scouts, but normal infantry operations by the RAR should not have recognised the border.

A paradigm that saw the Rhodesian Operational Areas extending into our neighbouring states, even as little as 20 kilometres, would have produced superior outcomes. That we did not do so as a matter of course was, perhaps, born out of the self-limiting belief that we were involved in what was essentially an internal security operation. It wasn't. It was war.

References:

Binda, A 2007, *Masodja*, 30 Degrees South, Pinetown, South Africa.
Fowler, W 2009, *We Gave Our Today*, Weidenfeld and Nicholson, United Kingdom.
Stapleton, T 2006, *No Insignificant Part: The Rhodesia Native Regiment and the East Africa Campaign of the First World War*, Wilfred Laurier University Press, Waterloo, Ontario, Canada.

COMMENTS ON EXTERNAL OPERATIONS by Captain Russell Fulton

I was perhaps fortunate (or not, depending on one's sense of humour) to have been on externals to Zambia, Mozambique and Botswana during my time in uniform and, with hindsight, it is very challenging to reflect upon all of them some forty years after the fact. Many were conducted during my time in the RLI as a troopie and those experiences remain with me to this day.

Commissioned and posted to the RAR after the fact, it was a completely different situation being in command. What I remember with crystal clarity was the feeling of incredible foreboding the very moment that you set foot in, or flew over, the border of international boundaries.

My first external was a ten-day deployment with Anti-Tank Troop, Support Commando, 1RLI to recce a ZANLA camp in ZANLA's Sector 1, Musikavanhu Sector. The moment we crossed the Cordon Sanitaire and cleared the Rhodesian/Mozambican border fence (literally that), everything felt and sounded different...including the birds! It was as unwelcoming as it was inhospitable.

Whilst this comment is not intended to unfairly criticize, it is, by contrast, important to reflect upon the import of preparation for externals including, but not limited to detailed orders and comprehensive rehearsals. Incredibly important lessons were learnt during my time as a troopie as it was the rank and file who were, oftentimes, very critical of their commanders.

Whilst I may be far from a model RAR commander in the eyes of those I once was privileged to command, I took my duty as a platoon commander extremely seriously as many men under my command were raw recruits from Depot RAR who looked to their commander for leadership and their general wellbeing. Flagrant disregard for security, cuffing the preparation and issuing of orders in minute detail and, the biggest cuff of all by some, rehearsals. The very lives of good men were at stake and compromising the basics was never entertained by most of us but, and I hasten to add, I do not speak for all of us. They were the exception but not the rule.

The RAR went on external operations, more often than not, without direct air support and CASEVAC capability. Any RAR officer will tell you that the all-important sub-heading in our Orders Groups was Adm & Log that covered action on casualty/casevac. More often than not we managed without airborne CASEVAC and that is a credit to all who served in the RAR.

Externals were always a challenge to those selected to go on them. No-one wanted to die on foreign soil, but we did what we were ordered to do and, broadly speaking, we executed as expected. There is a well-worn cliché in the military that refers to reconnaissance: "Time spent on Recce is seldom wasted." The same statement can be applied to every aspect of RAR operations.

Success or failure was borne of discipline or a lack thereof. Officers and NCO's were constantly being judged by their subordinates, and rightly so in my very humble opinion. I am reminded of my time in TAC Wing at the School of Infantry writing end of course reports and recommendations: "The cloak of leadership fell lightly upon his shoulders" when I wrote about a 'political wanker' (thanks to Roget's Thesaurus), an oft quipped reference to those candidates who failed to understand and/or neglected the basics. Some slipped through the cracks and were appointed to command positions, but our men were our only true judges and these sorts failed.

The RAR had a few officers whose contribution to our regiment are without parallel where external operations are concerned, and then some! One need only read the citations of Maj Don Price BCR, former OC 1 (Indep) Coy, RAR and Lt Patrick 'Flawless' Lawless SCR, 81mm Mortar Pl, Sp Coy, 1RAR and an account from (then) Lt David Padbury (from *Chibaya Moyo 1*) for examples of beacons of extreme professionalism on external operations.

Many before, and after, came, went and failed and the question is very simply 'Why?' and that is most definitely not a judgemental question. Where lives were concerned, and beyond the reach of expected air support, you are looking at a different breed of humanity. The pressure to execute as ordered, alone and without any form of direct or indirect support is an extraordinary thing. Few will begin to comprehend that level of pressure, particularly those who have not been in that mentally, emotionally and physically charged and demanding situation.

External operations were not for the faint-of-heart but, as history must fairly record, the RAR never failed to execute.

BAPTISM OF FIRE by Major Colin Hendrie

Pte Jewel completed his basic training at the end of March 1974 at Methuen Barracks and was immediately sent to the operational area to join C Company 1 RAR under the command of Major John Templar. The company was positioned at an airfield on the southern banks of the Zambezi River North of Musengedzi Mission in order to carry out some attacks on terrorist bases about 30 kilometres to the North in Mozambique.

On arrival at the Company base Pte Jewel was part of the heliborne assault group and dropped on the ground to sweep the target area. The attack was initiated with air strikes and sadly a Canberra bomber had a malfunction with a bomb detonating on release from the aircraft causing it to crash. The two pilots, Air Sub Lts Airey and Goddard were both killed. Lt Martin Wake and I were tasked with recovering the bodies and also the recovery of parts of the aircraft over the next two days. After the attack troops were returned to the base on the Zambezi River. For a few days after the attack helicopters were still involved in recovery at the crash site and on the second day following the attacks it was noticed that whenever the helicopters crossed the Zambezi River one or two shots of rifle fire were heard. Assuming these may have been terrorists mortar fire was aimed at the area from where the shots had been heard.

It was at this point that the CSM reported to Major Templar that one soldier was missing following the attacks, namely Pte Jewel. It then dawned on us that the shots from across the river may be Pte Jewel signalling his location. We immediately despatched a helicopter to investigate and it was not long before we noticed a soldier waving at us rather desperately. Sure enough it was Pte Jewel who wasted no time in boarding the helicopter with rifle but no back pack. When asked where his backpack was he pointed to it on the ground but showed no enthusiasm in getting out of the helicopter so we obliged.

Once back at base Pte Jewel recounted his experience. When the troops were being evacuated by helicopters following a sweep of the base camp, in the confusion Pte Jewel missed boarding the aircraft and was left behind. After searching the area for any other troops but to no avail he decided to head south to the Zambezi River. After a two day trek where he had to avoid a number of locals, he arrived at a point on the river opposite where he could hear the activity of helicopters. He then fired a shot each time a helicopter passed by but it was one further day before he was recovered. His introduction to operations was an experience he will never forget.

A BAD NIGHT'S SLEEP by Lieutenant Michael Matthews

The whole of A Company 1RAR having now been awarded our wings, our first operational jump was, somewhat disconcertingly, not in the context of Fireforce. We teamed up with B Company at Mount Darwin where we learnt that we would be going on an external operation into Mozambique. There had apparently been a sighting of a large terrorist presence in the Tete Province, and about twenty kilometres from the Mozambican border. The idea was to conduct a large-scale sweep of a particular area to search for and destroy food caches and to close with and confront the enemy if the situation presented itself.

On 7th April 1978 and at about midday we took off in two Dakotas and four G-Cars to the scene of the sighting without our passports. The intention was to sweep for about three hours, and to be extracted piecemeal by helicopter a little later in the day. After about an hour we were overhead the start point for our sweep. As had become my custom for most of our operational jumps, I was the first out of the door. Our drop zone ('DZ') was full of trees, and I remembered seeing very few open patches.

Unfortunately, I was not fortunate enough to land in an open space, and as I came into a large patch of quite dense forest my chute became entangled in some high branches, leaving me dangling helplessly about twenty feet from the ground. I felt somewhat exposed and easy pickings for any passing gook or Frelimo since

I was highly visible and could hear rifle fire going on all around me. It was too high for me to release my harness and jump without doing myself a damage, and I therefore decided to deploy my reserve chute, the canopy of which fell to the ground, allowing me to climb down its rigging lines. Other than perhaps being surprised by gooks whilst answering the call of nature in the bush with your rods around your ankles, I can't imagine any more compromised feeling than dangling helplessly from the boughs of a tree in a hostile situation.

I made radio contact with my O.C., Major Getliffe, who informed me that a few of B Company's troops had still not linked up with their own, with the result that our sweep commenced appreciably later than anticipated. During that afternoon, we combed through several small villages, although any gooks who might have been there had long since legged it. It transpired that the initial fire fight I had heard was conducted at some distance, but the gooks obviously had no intention of engaging us.

A clear recollection for me was the amazingly fertile soil which played host to maize and any number of root vegetables and enormous fat marrows, the like of which I had never before seen, lay swollen and ripe for the picking on the rich dark soil. There was no shortage of sustenance for the enemy here as we set about burning grain bins, mainly with the help of incendiaries.

Fire Force Mount Darwin

It was fast becoming dark when we were contacted by a pilot of one of the G-Cars which were on their way to ferry us out. Since our Alouettes were unable to fly after dark, needing either adequate light or an horizon to fly by, there was precious little time left for them to ferry all of our troops back to camp, and it soon enough became apparent that I and most of my platoon would be facing an uncomfortable and hungry night in hiding in Mozambique. Not for the first time, I think we all felt very alone when we saw the last chopper disappear as a distant speck against the horizon, despite the assurances of the chopper pilots that we would see them at first light the next day, and we resigned ourselves to the prospect of an unwelcome sleep over in "Injun territory". I selected what seemed to be the best position for us to bivouac overnight, even though we had no sleeping bags or food, given that our sortie was intended to be completed within a day.

Our presence in the area had quite obviously been noticed by many, and not just the locals with whom we had come into contact during our sweep. This much became obvious when, at about 20h00, we came under mortar fire. We had seen a Frelimo convoy some distance away shortly before dark, and I assumed that they had teamed up with the gooks who had initially been sighted. They had become aware that not all of us had been withdrawn from Mozambique, and that they had established our approximate position. Although the mortar fire was initially inaccurate, I was concerned that it would only be a matter of time before the mortars found their range, and I ordered a move to a new location about four hundred metres away. The mortar fire continued sporadically until late in the night, treating us to a spectacular, if unwelcome, impromptu fireworks display. Happily, however, no harm was done.

My main concern was sunrise the following day, and whether and to what extent our adversaries would seek to confront us. We were eight in number and would be heavily outgunned, particularly if Frelimo joined the fray as well. The arrangement made with our chopper pilots the previous night was that they would RV with us at the point where they had left us the previous evening, and approximately one hour after sunrise. Shortly after it became light enough to see at least some distance ahead of us, we cautiously made our way back to our pick-up point and waited in hiding for our extraction.

Happily, as it became lighter it seemed that the Frelimo and their allies had disappeared, since there was little movement other than civilians busying themselves in and about their huts and in their fields. It occurred to me that the mortar bombardment of the previous evening may well have been based on their belief that there may well still be Rhodesian troops on the ground, and not on any reliable intelligence.

On cue, we heard the welcome sound of two Alouettes approaching us at low level, and for the first time since they had left the previous evening, I broke radio silence and contacted them.

We returned, without incident, to Mount Darwin and a welcome breakfast.

OF GOOKS, LEMONS AND THE BDF by Captain Russell Fulton

Whilst a young, 'one-pip' subaltern serving in 1RAR and immediately following joint Fireforce operations with elements of 1 (SA) Parachute Battalion out of Gwanda airfield, my OC at the time, Maj Ron Marillier BCR, summoned me to his operations vehicle and informed me that I was being assigned a very sensitive operation that would require stealth, speed and tactical savvy to successfully execute said mission.

The operation, approved by HQ 1Bde, required me to attend a detailed briefing from the 'Bailiff Acorn' (Special Branch) rep who headed up the S.B. (Special Branch) ZIPRA Desk at HQ 1Bde, one 'Grae' Branfield (RIP). To cut a very long story short, this was a 'snatch and grab' operation in to neighbouring Botswana and the target was some 'hot shot' ZIPRA commander.

With the passage of time I have forgotten his name, so I shall simply refer to him as Comrade X. This fellow was responsible for the ZIPRA Southern Front (Region 3) and the exfiltration of ZIPRA 'recruits' out of Rhodesia into Botswana and from Botswana to Zambia and elsewhere for training, including the deployment of ZIPRA into south western and southern Matabeleland.

During the briefing, I was informed that Branfield and two 'turned' ZIPRA cadres would escort me and my small callsign to positively identify Comrade X's kaya and him too. I didn't like the idea one bit as I had never operated with any of the three, had no idea as to their field craft skills or lack thereof nor their preparedness to stand and fight if the shit hit the fan. At my insistence, it was agreed that said ZIPRA cadres would be unarmed despite protestations from the highest level of SB at 1Bde. And so, what was left was for me to prepare my detailed orders but this not before I had conducted a recce of the area, potential crossing points and routes in and out.

Only after this would I go about rehearsals, and plenty of them including, but not limited to: action on meeting locals, action on crossing obstacles, action on being split-up, action on encountering the BDF (Botswana Defence Force), action on contact, and so on and so forth. I was given strict orders to ensure that contact with the BDF was avoided at all costs as it could/would spark an international incident because our two countries were not 'officially' at war. In the event of my call sign taking casualties there could be no CASEVAC on the Botswana side and I would simply have to "make a plan" as the situation on the ground would determine how that would play itself out.

I accompanied Ron Marillier in an unmarked RhAF Cessna 185 'Skywagon' (on loan from the SAAF I believe) for an aerial reconnaissance that we conducted running parallel with the Shashe River (the Rhodesia/Botswana border) and about

5km's inside our side of the 'fence' to minimise suspicion on the Botswana side and risk of compromise. We flew at an altitude of +/-2,000m and the visibility was excellent enabling me to view the planned route in and out with considerable ease. The going would be tough initially, crossing the Shashe River through an area that was dry, but the ground was very broken and wall-to-wall with thick riverine bush; thereafter the going would be easy, and we would be able to make rapid progress through open mopani and acacia woodland and across 'basalt' plains. I could also just make out the village complex where 'our man' was supposed to be; drinking copious quantities of 'Shake-Shake' and scratching his pile-encrusted arse no doubt!

Prior to issuing my orders group I hand-picked the men I thought best to take and for a variety of reasons. I had been given carte blanche by my OC to select any man from within A Coy and that we were at liberty to carry whatever weapon we wished with the principle focus being men who were supremely fit and possessing the very best bush-craft, navigation and soldiering skills. I decided on three men for the 'external' with two sections in reserve on the Rhodesian side armed with more MAG's than were probably necessary but, that's what I wanted.

My first choice was my PWO, Munyika Collins, who was a man of incredible soldiering skill, a bush war veteran and an outstanding 2ic who, I know, would lay down his life for his 'Ishe' and without hesitation.

Corporal 'Steiner', A Coy, 1RAR 1979

Next, I selected a Corporal from 1Platoon ('Steiner' was his preferred nom de guerre taken from the gung-ho lead character of a 1977 war movie entitled "Cross of Iron") and with whom I had operated on Fireforce with 1 (SA) Para Bn. Cpl 'Steiner' had impressed me with his soldiering skills, fitness and raw aggression; short in stature and wiry of build but a man who was always up for a scrap. My final selection was my platoon medic who was 'MA3' qualified and as good an infantry soldier as any of my men. His selection would provide that all important constituent element in any orders group, that being 'maintenance of morale'. In this instance it meant what would happen in the event of casualties being sustained during all stages of the operation including plans for CASEVAC that fell under the orders heading 'Co-ordinating Instructions' (sub and sub-sub paras: Action on Casualties: Out, On Objective and In). Our "Starlight's" primary role would be to tend to any unsolicited oil leaks that may happen themselves upon our 'personage' but he had proven himself a rock-solid and aggressive soldier with a surprising, but pleasing appetite for 'hondo'.

My orders issued, and rehearsals completed to my satisfaction, we boarded the 3 Platoon vehicles and departed for Sun Yet Sen Police Station in the Mbongolo TTL where we were to meet-up with Branfield and his 'tame terrs', and lay-up for the night before I issued my final orders, conducted more rehearsals and departure the following afternoon towards the Rhodesia/Botswana border and execution of the operation. The Member-In-Charge was a man I had heard much about as had most other Rhodesians. It was none other than Section Officer David Smith of Rhodesia and Springbok rugby fame. David was the exact opposite to what I had honestly anticipated from a man of his almost reverential standing as a 'Bok'; a mischievous, completely unassuming and genuinely good bloke who went out of his way to be welcoming, accommodating and keen to assist us in any way.

We received an 'INT' briefing from David and an update from Branfield of ZIPRA operations in the general area. David had been out early on the morning of our arrival and had shot a good size Impala ram that he had had skinned, gutted and it was being turned slowly on a homemade rotisserie above a halved 44-gallon drum containing a bed of glowing Mopani firewood. Well now, we can't all be happy I thought fleetingly.

That night we chatted about anything and everything and laughed frequently at the seemingly endless flow of filthy jokes that David had compartmentalised in that BSAP head of his. We ate heartily and swallowed a few ice cold 'chibulis' before sacking it by 20:00B. We were embussed and on our way by 04:30B arriving at our drop-off point about 5 clicks north of the Shashe River by early afternoon. My men were placed in an all-round defensive position and I took my

PWO with me and went forward to physically recce the river for the best crossing point and made a mental note of the obstacles that lay to our front.

At 10 minutes after last light, around 18:00B, we crossed our 'Start Line', the Shashe River, negotiated the border fences and were in 'Indian Country' within fifteen minutes. It's a funny thing, that 'external' business; you could "feel" that you were no longer on home soil as everything around you seemed different somehow. We had a roughly 50 click (kilometre) round-trip so we had to get moving and my coordinating instructions had planned on executing the snatch and grab by no later than 01:00B provided we didn't encounter locals or bad fellas on the way in. I had allowed for 30 minutes to recce the target, execute the snatch and for us to be on our way back to Rhodesia by 01:30B which would see us close to the border fence by around 07:00B.

The BDF patrolled the border road by vehicle every day and passed our area at around 07:30 each morning. If we weren't completely alert and anti-tracking on the way in/out, we risked compromise and that wasn't on the agenda. I was also not overly inclined to being on the receiving end of a piece of lead, neatly clad in a copper jacket, delivered via a BDF 7.62mm FN rifle either. If we were cut-off by the BDF before we arrived at the river, we had a Plan B and C, but they were not 'plans' I wanted to entertain as they would involve complex escape and evade tactics. The last time I did anything remotely similar was when I was a regular officer cadet during the latter stages of the fabled 'Endurance Exercise' that ended our first phase; the prospect of a real-life 'giddy-up' scenario wasn't part of my current mind-set.

After we had marched about 20km's and were within striking distance of our target, Grae Branfield asked for an unscheduled rest; things were about to go horribly pear-shaped from this point! He had corked his knee when he stepped in a small hole and I was forced in to making a tactical decision that he would take no further direct involvement in the operation; it was a judgement call I had to make, and I still stand by it.

My detailed orders had prepared me for such a contingency and my orders were to leave him where he sat, in a concealed position, whilst we continued to our objective. Graham was left in a small rocky outcrop, but my sub-conscious mind was becoming bothered about what the walk out would be like with one of my 'snatch party' now effectively 'lame'. With his type of injury, as we know, once you 'cool down' you are in for a rude awakening when you need to get 'arse-in-gear' as the joints and muscles start to 'seize'; I just knew that the return march wasn't going to be comfortable for any of us!

We arrived at the target in good time and I found a fold in the ground that afforded me an excellent, slightly elevated position from which to view the lay of the land. I positioned my call sign and went forward with one of the tame terrs whom, earlier, I had cautioned about entertaining any notion of compromising us on fear of his life; it wasn't an idle threat…it was a promise that I fully intended to act upon and courtesy of a razor-sharp Gerber boot knife. That didn't sit well with him, but I didn't rightly care. All's fair in love and war…right? We moved forward with stealth like cold, devilish reptilian-spectres in the night and arrived at Comrade X's hut door that was, surprisingly, ajar!

I could "smell" a 'Lemon' and I didn't much like it! The SB gook entered and whispered Comrade X's name so as not to alarm him nor anyone else in the hut. There was a deafening silence! My night vision sharpened, and it was clear that Comrade X had taken the gap… or, perhaps, he was fraternising with one of the local 'ladies of the night' elsewhere or whatever the hell but he wasn't where we expected him to be and I was almost overcome with a blinding rage!

I entered the hut, and everything seemed reasonably in order and there was no obvious evidence to suggest a hasty exit that would have pointed towards compromise; cold comfort indeed! There was a small table with files tidily stacked in one corner; I took them in case they contained INT (intelligence) that would be beneficial to our cause.

Time was fleeting, and we had to get moving, and pronto! If Comrade X was 'getting lucky' somewhere when we came house-calling, I now hoped that he would return to his kaya with a very hostile and exotic venereal disease that would both incapacitate and torment him for the rest of his days! We took-off in a south-westerly direction and further inland. After a couple of clicks we dog-legged back towards the outcrop where Graham had been whiling the time away, picking his nose or contemplating his navel (or both), and found him alert but in some considerable discomfort. Well now, it wasn't all beers and skittles you know, and I helped him to his feet and forced him to march.

I liked Grae, quite a lot, but I was growing annoyed with his constant whinging. I told 'Starlight' (my medic) to administer a Sosogon shot and to strap his knee 'ikozvino' (immediately) and we were on our way. By now, it was close to 02:30B and we were an hour behind schedule and had a lot of ground to cover before first light. We stopped for five minutes every half hour to ensure that everyone remained alert to the prospects of compromise. As the sun was rising, we were still a few kilometres from the Botswana/Rhodesia border and we moved to within a kilometre of the border road for a short rest and so that I could send a 'Stop Press' to Ron Marillier. A short while later we heard the ominous sound of vehicles approaching from the south east. I suspected that it was the BDF border patrol; they didn't disappoint me!

It wasn't the usual one vehicle this time, but three, and each loaded with BDF troops bristling with all manner of unfriendly weaponry! Bugger me if the last vehicle didn't stop right in front of us and the BDF troops debussed. They formed-up in extended line either side of the road. We had either been compromised overnight and the BDF were responding or this was now part of their border security S.O.P. (Standing Operating Procedure)? Either way, it didn't much matter one iota now did it? We were in a perilous situation and the shit was about to hit the fan.

We lay dead still as the sweep line started moving north-west up the road towards the point, we had entered the previous evening and about 800m distant. Whilst we had made every effort to anti-track, we had done so in darkness and there was the very real prospect that there might be tell-tale signs that an alert 'Sparrow' (tracker) would detect. "Plan B" was executed silently and swiftly and this saw my PWO Munyika Collins take one of the tame gooks, Grae Branfield and our Medic. Cpl Steiner, the second tame gook and I made up the second group. My PWO moved swiftly under cover of the riverine bush and in a south-easterly direction for a few clicks before crossing the road and re-entered Rhodesia.

For my call-sign the day was about to change in both mood and tempo. We had remained in situ observing the BDF patrol and covering PWO Munyika's withdrawal, and we were now within proximity to the area of our earlier entry. We were compromised and there was an audible exchange of chatter amongst the BDF call sign (a section strength of at least nine men). They started casting for spoor and found it and were on it like shit-off-a-shovel.

We remained concealed and watched this unfold with a morbid curiosity and, as I recall, with annoyance, someone who once quipped: "My dear subbie, if you can't take a joke you should never have joined the army!" Crossing the border road with the BDF within sight and well within snap-shooting range wasn't an option so I backtracked in the general direction from whence we had come keeping distance between us and the BDF. The plan was to create time and distance between the parties and then, when I considered it safe, I would dog-leg south-east and cross the fence.

Within the hour I heard the drone of an aircraft and soon had sight of it; it was a BDF Trislander Gunship come to seek us out. That awful song by 'Paul McCartney and Wings' (entitled "Band-On-The Run") now had a peculiar resonance and I disliked it even more.

Evidently, there was comms between the BDF on the ground and this 'wendege' (Trislander) that had clearly spotted us. That deathly 'bush-quiet' we all know was, suddenly, interrupted by the loud chatter of a heavy weight of incoming gunfire from the direction of the BDF ground troops and whilst it was more of a 'harassing' nature, it was 'cracking' close overhead and leaves and shattered sticks rained down all around us. They were clearly trying to draw us in to an engagement, but we did not return the courtesy. We moved at a fast canter towards the border with those BDF types now in very agitated and hot pursuit. The Trislander flew-in directly overhead and wagged its wings; I was sorely tempted to give it a good 'squirt' but knew that nothing good would come of it.

We got through both fences swiftly and heard the BDF troops shouting in our direction. I returned their chorus in a parched and barked retort; "Too late she cried!" ending the tirade in ungentlemanly fashion with the crass retort, "AND F***-OFF TOO!" If they wished to follow us across the fence, I was more than willing to engage them as it would now be them who were on the wrong side of the "fence".

I got on the blower and gave Ron Marillier a SITREP and set about RV'ing with my PWO who would be in the immediate vicinity. Branfield was ashen but safe and everyone was, thankfully, unscathed. I sat with Branfield and we went through the files I had thieved from Comrade X's kaya; there was a veritable treasure that had come out of "Aladdin's Cave". Branfield was delighted; it seemed as though 'Second Prize' had now become first prize. Not quite you understand, but something is always better than nothing?

Another one of those all-too-frequent cross-border trips where nor passports were required.

There was seldom a dull moment back in the day and I truly miss them so. So many good and gallant men filled with effervescent joie de vivre. It was both a pleasure and a great privilege to have rubbed shoulders 'in the thick of it' with far better men than me.

THE SERGEANT MAJOR'S AMBUSH by Captain Andrew Telfer

When, in August 1977, Major Bryan McDermott was appointed Officer Commanding D Company 2RAR, I was one of its three Platoon Commanders, along with Lt Kay Choruma and Lt Tudor Pope. Our first deployment under his command was to the Rhodesian north-eastern border near Mukumbura. Establishing a company base camp, we went to the ops tent for orders. I was fascinated to hear that 10 Platoon was to be deployed across the border into the area of Mozambique known to the terrorists as the Nehanda sector. Our task was to undertake a reconnaissance of the area beyond the border to identify infiltration routes and, in the event of finding one, ambush it.

Major McD was a highly professional officer who understood the importance of proper planning and preparation, and made sure we had time to do it. In addition to our normal battle procedure (orders, rations, ammunition, maps, radios etc.), we carefully rehearsed our immediate action drills and the conduct of a long-term ambush. Conscious that our radio communications may be monitored by Frelimo, he and I prepared duplicate tables, with grid squares annotated A, B, C, D, E etc. across the top and 1, 2, 3, 4, 5 etc. down the side. Then we wrote into the tables all the place names on the map, as well as every likely word that we might need to use in communication (*terrorist, weapon, casevac, kill, water, resupply, go to, helicopter* etc.). As a result, our callsigns would be able to communicate with each other quickly and in code.

On our second night, we were driven near the border, given a place to cross, and then left to our own devices. I had been commissioned just six months earlier and I was excited about the task ahead. It was the type of operation that I'd joined the Army to do and I felt more confident than my experience level deserved. My soldiers moved quietly and carefully through the night as we left the border further and further behind us. With us, and always close to me, was WO2 Alex Gwatirera, my Platoon Warrant Officer. He was a very experienced soldier with a great attitude, who had helped me immeasurably since my arrival. The following story from *Masodja* (Binda 2007, pp. 336-337) illustrates his character well:

'On 8 July 1978, the D Company 2RAR Fireforce, under command Major Bryan McDermott, were uplifted by helicopter from one contact to be flown to another, a second sighting ten kilometres away. The OP directed the K Car onto the target. Its position was marked with smoke by the K Car, which then fired a burst into the thick vegetation where the enemy was believed to be concealed. Heavy fire was immediately returned by the insurgents engaging the K Car whose cannon had a stoppage. This gave the insurgents the opportunity to break cover and, running across open ground, they took refuge in the riverside jesse, unscathed.

Stops were deployed, the para-sticks being helicoptered in from the earlier firefight. The Lynx dropped two Frantans into the riverine vegetation. Almost immediately after being dropped off, callsign C2 saw two insurgents along the river line and engaged them. A fight ensued with both insurgents, like cornered rats, putting up a desperate resistance. Each hurled a stick grenade, one of which damaged the radio while the other wounded the stick commander, WO2 Gwatirera, in the eye and an arm. Despite his wounds, Gwatirera was able to indicate to the K Car that his radio was inoperative and promptly went on to kill both insurgents. Once the other stick joined him, he took over full command and gave the K Car commander a good briefing on the situation. He also briefed the additional stick before allowing himself to be casevaced. He was, deservedly, recommended for an award. Regrettably, the award was never forthcoming.'

Got the idea? A very good man. Now, back to August 1977...

Around midnight, we arrived at a place that we had noticed on the map, where a low, linear topographical feature ran parallel to the border about 10 kilometres inside Mozambique. On the ground, we found it to be quite an obstacle to anyone heading to or from Rhodesia. It was a ridgeline, not very high but thickly wooded with trees overhead, clumps of bushes and many huge rocks and boulders. At night, it would clearly tend to channel people into where we had navigated to, a bottle-neck pass through a saddle. To support that theory, we could see a dirt path in the moonlight, winding its way through the obstacles.

When we stopped, our soldiers automatically went into all round defence. After a brief discussion, WO2 Gwatirera and I decided to site our ambush in this bottleneck. We gathered the stick commanders to us and quickly briefed them in whispers. Warning them to stay off the path, we sent a stick ahead of us and another back the way we'd come, to give an early warning if anyone came while we were working. Then, while the remainder of the platoon protected our perimeter, we laid out the ambush.

We carefully sited the MAGs, checking that their arcs of fire covered the killing ground and its approaches, ensuring that they overlapped. We laid the claymore mines, directional anti-personnel mines that are command-detonated and directional, meaning that they are fired by remote-control and blast metal fragments into the killing ground like a shotgun. We made sure that their arcs also overlapped and that they backed onto large trees or boulders to guard against the back blast. Then we ran their wires back to the site chosen for the command element but didn't insert the detonators.

Telling the stick commanders what we were doing (which way we were exiting and which way we were going to return) we went out of our perimeter to each of our early warning groups. I thought we'd have to site each one but found that they had positioned themselves perfectly. Our rehearsals had paid off and there was nothing to say to them. They would provide two functions from now on, a warning of anyone approaching and a stop group for anyone fleeing after the ambush was sprung. The warning signal was known already: no speaking, simply two depressions of the radio pressel switch which would be heard on our other radios as a low hiss.

Returning to the ambush position, we moved our soldiers out of the perimeter and into two locations: the killer group concealed alongside the killing ground, and the support group in a laying up place about 30 metres to the rear, behind boulders and out of sight, where they could rest. The system, routes and timing of rotation between all the groups had been rehearsed and was understood by everyone. I took first command of the killer group, inserted the detonators into the claymores and connected the 'clacker' (a hand-held device that, when squeezed, would send an electric charge down the wires to the detonators). From now until the end of the ambush, there would be no movement outside the prescribed rotation, no smoking and no cooking. There would also be no speaking; sitreps would be sent once a day only, in brief whispered code and only from the laying up place.

Nothing happened during the remainder of that night, nor the next day. I decided that, during the second night, I would take three men and move further into Mozambique to recce the area beyond the ridgeline while the remainder of the Platoon, under WO2 Gwatirera, remained in ambush on the path. That night, ensuring that everyone knew exactly what we were doing, we four slipped away.

The terrain beyond the ridgeline was undulating and open. Except for areas of ground that had been burnt, which we avoided because we would have left clear spoor, the going was unimpeded. By the following night (night three of the ambush), we four were far away. Then, we heard a distant boom from the direction of the ambush. It was far, but we thought we could also hear firing. We could. WO2 Gwatirera had initiated the ambush and created the event that would become his favourite war story for ever more, the 'Sergeant Major's Ambush'.

This redoubtable soldier never tired of telling how he'd watched a terrorist group walk into his killing ground, talking quite loudly. He heard one of them scold the others to be quiet and another respond, "Why? We are safe now". At this point in his story, he would pause for dramatic effect, look at each of his listeners in turn, and then go on to say, "And, *at that very moment*, I pressed the initiator on my claymores and seven terrorists died".

THE MORNING AFTER by Captain Andrew Telfer

The morning after WO2 Gwatirera's ambush, my recce patrol began to make its way back towards the Sergeant Major's position. On the way, we had a contact that I mentioned in a paragraph in *Chibaya Moyo 1*, but I think the bravery of three African soldiers is worth more than just a paragraph. So, the aim of this article is to place on record the courage of three very young RAR soldiers across the border in Mozambique in August 1977.

With me on that patrol, were Privates Mdhluli, Moyo Morgan (MAG) and Jera (batman). All three were recently-trained soldiers, graduating from the RAR Regimental Depot at Balla Balla during the time that I had been an Officer Cadet the previous year. Therefore, our average military experience was probably around six months to a year. Pte Mdhluli was an Ndebele from the Gwaai district, short and stocky, with a very strong, clear face. He spoke English fluently, was sincere and humorous. Pte Moyo Morgan was a Shona from the Zaka district. He was tall, with the lean, broad-shouldered physique often found in boxers. A quiet man, he was a born soldier, from a military family, with uncles and brothers throughout the RAR.

Pte Jera was a Shona from the Mrewa district who had grown up with a strong terrorist presence in his area. He was hard and wild, had to be constrained and channelled, which was why the PWO had made him the Platoon Commander's batman. For him it was a make or break job that would precipitate maturity or failure. Later, I would want the batman role to go to the next-in-line for Lance

Corporal, so that I could teach him, but at this stage I was too new to be even thinking about those kinds of changes.

During the night, as described in the previous story, we'd heard the explosion of WO2 Gwatirera's claymores and felt that we could also hear firing. At dawn, I tried to contact him on the radio but there was no reply, our signal almost certainly blocked by the ridgeline that had facilitated his ambush position. It was obvious that we should return to his location. Firstly, I felt sure the noise in the night would have compromised us (I would turn out to be wrong about that). Secondly, I had no idea whether the ambush had been successful or not and was concerned for my Platoon. So, we turned back towards the ridgeline and their location.

I'm not exactly sure how far away from the Platoon we were, but I think it was about ten or twelve kilometres. We'd reached a river, the limit of exploitation given by our OC, Major McDermott, during his Orders Group. The ground between it and the ridgeline was smooth, not broken or eroded, but undulating and grassed, with the occasional small tree. The undulations created shallow troughs of dead ground (out-of-sight areas) and low vantage points, rather like sailing through rolling waves. The grass, where it hadn't been burnt, was about chest-height. I didn't like the burned-out areas, because of the clear tracks that we would obviously create and the absence of cover, so we avoided them.

Even in August, the area across the Mozambique border from Mukumbura is hot, but we had filled our water bottles at the river. We moved in extended line (line abreast) with Jera on my left, Moyo my right, and Mdhluli on his right. We weren't moving quickly but cautiously, cresting each rise slowly, peering ahead over the long grass. What was I thinking? Probably something mundane like borrowing Bruce Thompson's curved leather maker's needle to sew together two of my pouches that were rubbing together; we were still sorting out our webbing in those early days. What was I doing? Watching, all the time watching the unfolding terrain... It was nearly midday.

Small birds rose from the grass ahead of us... My soldiers tensed and stopped, alert and leaning forward. I sensed their posture, rather than looked at them for there in front of us, where the ground was rising gently towards the ridgeline, at a range of about 40 metres, a single file of men was emerging from a fold in the ground in our eleven o'clock. Moyo Morgan's MAG spoke first. Standing erect, firing in bursts from the hip, he advanced on them. Mdhluli took off to the right at a full sprint, beginning a diagonal assault towards their right flank. Jera, from my left, flew after him, as did I, doing my best to keep up!

Sometimes, in a movie, the camera moves on a rail, sweeping from the front of an object through ninety degrees to the side. That's how I experienced the sight of the terrorist group. Incredibly, they weren't looking at us. They were completely distracted by Pte Moyo, who was closing on them in an inexorable walk, firing low, lethal bursts, making them dive and scurry for cover. Ptes Mdhluli and Jera, accompanied by their Platoon Commander, rushed the prone terrorists from the side, over-running them. We scampered over their bodies, shooting into them. One, I remember vividly, was lying behind a tree aiming and firing at Moyo. He didn't see me at all, even as I fired into the back of his head at less than a metre. His head seemed to swell with the discharge of energy and I stared at it transfixed for a moment, before my feet took me onwards.

In the ear-ringing silence that followed the assault, we first moved beyond the group, further into the fold in the ground, to see if there were more. Then we moved back to the bodies and then we all started laughing at once. There were ten dead. It was all over before it seemed to have started.

It wasn't long after, that we moved up the side of the ridgeline and regained radio comms with WO2 Gwatirera. We spoke in clear as our code was obviously irrelevant now that our presence had been so openly demonstrated. Our reunion was classic. I can still see my Sergeant Major's beaming smile as he came forward to greet us, then all the RAR double-handshakes and everyone telling war stories at once.

In conclusion, I want to emphasise the independent initiative taken by the three RAR soldiers. I did not command their actions in that contact; I accompanied them... keeping up as best I could!

CHAPTER SEVENTEEN

REGIMENTAL LIFE

INTRODUCTION: REGIMENTAL LIFE by Captain Andrew Telfer

When Rhodesian Army officer cadets approached the end of their cadet course, they were asked for their preference of regiment or corps. Characteristically, the question was phrased along the lines of 'In the unlikely event that you are commissioned, which regiment would you prefer to be inflicted upon?'

Cadets who had already served in a unit may ask to return there. Others would opt to follow a family member, such as an older brother or father. For many without a prior connection, a regiment's reputation and heritage became influential in the choice, especially if they personally identified with it. As cadets, we carried out a COIN exercise with RAR recruits in the Tjolotjo and watched them in training at Balla Balla. I enjoyed their spirit, respected their bush craft skills and was interested in their culture, so my mind was made up.

Becoming an officer is more than being a junior leader of troops in battle. On joining a regiment, one inherits its history and becomes part of its ancestry. Pride in that heritage and a sense of duty to uphold its traditions are placed like a mantle across the shoulders of the subaltern. There is a big difference between those who understand that and those who are oblivious to it.

The best officers are genuinely interested in their regimental history, are knowledgeable about its traditions and heritage, and appreciate their value. This characteristic of honouring the legacy will, much later, distinguish those can command a battalion *inspirationally* from those who will only ever be able to do so *competently*. Why? Because soldiers will rise to a higher level of performance when their sense of duty to history is called into play. The best commanders knew how to 'deploy' the ranks of the dead onto the battlefield.

Regimental identity also provides a sense of belonging, visibly indicated to the world by the wearing of regimental insignia and nurtured by membership of the Mess. Belonging in a group is a deep-seated human need. Factors such as the height of the selection hurdle to join a group; the lasting character of the relationship; the identification of members with its heritage; the shared experiences with others, especially extreme ones; the commonly understood jargon; all of this fosters a sense of community and people are intrinsically tribal.

Membership, however, comes at a price. Adoption of regimental identity calls upon the junior officer to conform to the norms and cultural values of the group and some behaviours must be sacrificed. This begins on cadet course and is developed through immersion, leading to a shedding of pre-cadet identity and the adoption of that of a junior officer within a regiment. In some, the evolution is minor but in others, quite profound. Some become stereotypical officers who, I am sure, salute themselves in the morning, while others have the common sense to retain the individuality that got them selected in the first place.

A book could be written about the traditions, customs, ceremonies, symbols and arrangements that make up regimental identity but, at the core of it all, lies the development of a feeling of pride and mutual loyalty among members of the group: *esprit de corps*.

Finally, all of the above would apply through peacetime as well as in war but, during the latter, another powerful force comes into effect. People who do the fighting are usually very young and warfare is stressful. Regimental life is a supportive environment, somewhere to let off steam among a family of people who understand and care, turning potentially destructive forces into sources of good humour.

THE CHIVAS REGAL EVENING by Mrs Helena Dennison

The bush war took its toll on families as well as the men and women serving 'in the line of fire'. Now we would look on battle fatigue as an expected outcome of the constant separation from normality, but in the 70s PTSD was not a label allocated to the various, rather odd, behaviours that manifested themselves during that brief, exciting 10 day period of R&R. Battle fatigue also affected spouses who had to pack six weeks' worth of unanswered questions and discussions into such a short period before losing their men again for another session. I do not use this as an excuse for the following story, but my subsequent work with ex-servicemen and women with mental and emotional problems has been useful in putting de-stressing behaviours into context.

Out of hand use of drink, drugs and sex are commonplace and broken relationships are encountered in about 95% of cases. One officer told me recently that he doesn't talk about the bush war because it is only in the last year that he has stopped having nightmares every night and they have reduced to once or twice a month. On this sobering note I offer you the following anecdote.

One of the ways my husband (Andre Dennison) rid himself of bush weariness was to drink to oblivion on the first night home. How his liver must have looked I shudder to think. But he wasn't the only one to kill his demons this way, and I have to say he was the most amiable drunk I have ever met - he would simply drop off to sleep and be back to charming, intelligent, articulate and loving by the following day, when we would generally go off to play golf and picnic with children and nanny accompanying. His favourite tipple for effecting this 'cure' was whisky, Black Bushmills if some kind person had brought it from UK but any other brand (apart from the Rhodesian home brew) was acceptable.

AT & HD Post Chivas Night

So, on one trip to South Africa Graham Schrag brought Andre back a bottle of Chivas Regal. With great pride and excitement, he and Andy Telfer, turned up at our house in McGhie Avenue in Fort Victoria with bottle in hand. Andre was on ops at the time. Both of Andre's 'children' were thrilled at the prospect of their Ishe's delight at receiving this present and we sat and chatted and at some stage I offered them dinner. After we had eaten and drunk some of the locally produced red wine (having been brought up by my father who was a wine buff, this was something of a trial, but I forced it down), someone suggested we ought to sample the Chivas Regal, 'in case it wasn't up to standard'.

I have to hold a hand up at this point and admit that nobody had ever explained to me that red wine and whisky don't mix well. Between us we killed a modest half bottle - I would like to think it was less than that, but I need to tell the truth here. The guys disappeared into the night and I went off to bed, 'feeling fine'. I woke next morning, opened my eyes and the ceiling, which was decorated in

Artex swirls, spun in and out much as you see an animal's eyes do in a cartoon when they are hit on the head. I hastily shut my eyes but the swirling continued.

I remembered that someone had once told me that if you were drunk in the morning and put one foot on the floor before getting out of bed, that the dizziness would go away. It is not the case. Gingerly I stood upright, whereupon I felt as though someone had just kicked me in the liver. Doubled over, I crept into the bathroom and reached for the 'greenies' which some of you may remember were large analgesic and vitamin tablets doled out for those who knew they were going to have a hard night of it. You were supposed to take them before going to bed, not after but I thought I'd give it a try anyway.

Our maid, Agnes, was busy sweeping the dining room as I ventured out and cast me a withering look. She had cleared the night's excesses and washed up. I couldn't face the kitchen and decided to take the car round to see Mickey Bentley and cadge a coffee off her. Driving rather carefully down to Mickey's flat, I was surprised to see Andy Telfer walking along the road with one hand in the air supported at the elbow by his other hand and holding his index finger upright. It was an arresting posture that required further investigation, so I stopped the car, wound down the window and asked what he was doing. 'Someone stepped on my finger last night, and I think it's broken,' was his reply. 'I'm going to the hospital'. He couldn't recall who had done this. Bemused, I offered him a ride. We went to Mickey's for coffee and poured out our respective woes. She was surprisingly unsympathetic. And I don't recall Andre's reaction to finding his subalterns' gift somewhat depleted on his next R&R. I have never drunk whisky again.

SLAVERS by Colonel Ian Pullar

During periods of R&R, the younger Officers of 2RAR spent a fair amount of time at the bar of the Zimbabwe Ruins Hotel, and at one period this was made doubly attractive by the fact that the owner, Bob Baxter, had decided to partly finance a film about the slave trade in Nyasaland (now Malawi) in the late 1800's. A replica paddle steamboat had been built and Kyle Dam became the substitute for Lake Nyasa. The film was called Slavers and although I never saw it, it must have had some moderate success because it had a top star cast, all of whom lived at the Zimbabwe Ruins Hotel.

On any evening for a three month period, Trevor Howard could be seen firmly established in the corner of the bar. He had his own spot. Cameron Mitchell, who was a very well-known Western star of High Chaparral fame, was another, and Ken Gampu, a South African, was also in the film. Heading the line-up was Britt Ekland, which of course made the drive from Fort Victoria well worth it.

Although she did spend a great deal of most evenings on the phone speaking to her then boyfriend, Rod Stewart, she was around long enough to make the evenings interesting.

I think one of the attractions of this sort of contact was that it gave the 2RAR Officers an insight into the wider world, and although it was unintentional, the owner of the Zimbabwe Ruins Hotel did a great deal for Officers' morale by investing in this movie.

One day, I recall flying by Police Reserve aircraft from Chiredzi to Fort Victoria. As Lake Kyle appeared beneath us, the pilot descended quite quickly and circled a vessel which had a number of people on it waving frantically. We waved back and carried on to the airfield, not knowing until later that we had ruined a large part of the Slavers shoot for that day, a Piper Apache not being the sort of thing that would have existed in Nyasaland in 1880.

We were not actually being waved to, we were being sworn at.

MY 1RAR ADVENTURES by Captain Mike Munroe

In late 1976 all the army medical officers who had completed their intern year were summoned to Medical Directorate, King George the VI Barracks to be addressed by Col Ainslie, the director of medical services. We were then assigned to the units we were to serve with. I was posted to 1RAR, Bulawayo. I had only been to Bulawayo once in my life!

Arriving at Methuen Barracks in early January 1977 I was shown around after introducing myself and then saw the quartermaster for kitting out. I met the staff at the Methuen camp hospital and had a look around that facility. In one bed was a very well looking young African soldier curled up and groaning loudly and refusing to eat or drink, constantly saying he was going to die. I could find nothing medically amiss with him. The ever reliable and astute nurse, Ethel Myers, told me he was 'tagati' or bewitched and could only be 'cured' by going to see a witch doctor to have the spell reversed. She told me that this was one battle western medicine would not win. She advised me to give him two weeks sick leave and $200.00 from company funds and release him from hospital. I yielded to the advice. The soldier returned two weeks later after seeing a 'nyanga', fit, alert and ready for duty.

Lt Tom Fulton was assigned to take me to the shooting range and give me some time on the FN rifle and MAG, in case I needed to protect myself down the track. I was surprised by the unexpected adrenaline rush I got when firing the MAG. Afterwards I was fully expecting to be invited to join an infantry unit, but it never happened. I suppose the army was very short of medical officers.

In an unrelated story, one of my friends had a wife who was a medical specialist and who went in and out of hospital to see patients at all sorts of hours. A police friend suggested to her that it was time for her to learn to use a hand gun and carry it when travelling. He took her out to the range and she practised with said weapon. After about an hour she asked him how she was going. The response was, "If you ever want to kill your husband, I suggest you use a syringe!"

One of my brothers had emigrated in early 1977 and had a male English pointer dog called Nick that he could not find a home for. Nick was a great character and I could not see him euthanized so I adopted him, and he came to Bulawayo with me. My first staff car was an olive-green VW Beetle. Nick sometimes sat on the front seat next to me with the window down. As we drove past the African soldiers and children going to school, he would look back at them with his head out the window and big black ears flapping in the breeze. There was much pointing and giggling by the children.

Whenever I was away there was never any shortage of people willing to look after Nick. When I was in camp Nick would always slip away at about 12 noon on Sundays and return about two hours later. I followed him one day and found him having a roast lunch with Capt. Trevor Hughes and his wife. When I asked Trevor how often this happened, he said it was whenever I was in camp. I assumed Nick could smell the cooking!

One day Nick followed me to the camp hospital. He was of course not allowed to frequent it. He came strolling down the passage. One my medics, Cpl Patrick Pedzi, pointed him out and asked if I knew him. My brother had taught Nick to smile and shake hands when meeting new people. Corporal. Patrick was a very happy, cheerful and capable person. When Nick shook hands and smiled Patrick nearly collapsed laughing. The African soldiers had never seen an English pointer before but immediately recognized him as a hunting dog. There were many offers to buy him or use him for 'stud' duties, but I declined. Such was the interest in him I was fearful that he might be abducted but that never happened.

Lt Bill Liversidge once told me to feed Nick more than I was because Nick was so skinny. I suggested Bill take Nick for a walk, it would be - educational. Usually Nick would go from horizon to horizon on each walk - backward and forwards. Bill returned about an hour later and said, "OK I get it. I can see why he is so skinny."

On a cold winter's night in 1978 in Wankie town we had a coal fire burning in the fireplace in the 1RAR officer mess. Nick was sound asleep on the carpet in front of the fire. We had all had a few beers and Major John Templar went up to Nick and said, "Talk to me Nick". There was no sign that Nick had heard anything. John went down on all fours next to Nick and repeated, "Talk to me Nick". Nick's upper eye flicked open and he raised his upper paw, placing it over his ear to block out the noise.

One of the HQ African soldiers who was a driver had developed repetitive vomiting with weight loss and came to see me. He had been ill for about six weeks and was very emaciated. My assessment was that he had developed an ulcer at the outlet of his stomach with scarring and subsequent narrowing of the outlet. A very simple operation would fix the problem. He told me that he was sure that he would die. I decided that this was one battle that western medicine was going to win! I referred him to the local hospital who advised him that they could not help him. I did not accept that advice and asked Mr. Frank Grave, one of the Bulawayo surgeons to see him.

Frank agreed with my assessment and planned the operation. The soldier came to see me before the operation and bet me a bottle of wine that he would die. I pointed out that that was a bet I could not lose, and he pointed out that if he died, he could not lose either! The operation went ahead, and he made a rapid, uneventful and full recovery. One afternoon there was a knock on my office door. Opening it, he stood there with a bottle in a brown paper bag. He had come to pay his bet! When I pointed out that it was my job to look after him and his getting better was my reward, he would have none of this. A bet was a bet and honour must be paid and urged that I must accept it. It was a bottle of Portuguese Dao red… very nice.

As the Battalion approached Christmas 1977, companies came in and out of Methuen Barracks at regular intervals. I was attached to HQ Company 1RAR but of course looked after everyone in the Battalion. This had its hazards as I was invited to every company Christmas party if I was in barracks. As we all know the African soldiers did not believe that you had had a good party if you could still stand upright at the end of it. I was surprised to see that most of the older RAR African soldiers had a fondness for Scotch whiskey. Curious, I asked them how this had developed. I was told that they had acquired a taste for it during their service in Malaya in the 1960's. We feasted on roast goat meat and other goodies and as the evening progressed, the African soldiers started to pass around a huge earthenware pot of traditional African beer. I had several swigs from it and ended the evening doing impersonations of a Charlie Chaplin walk.

In April 1978 I was in Wankie Town with 1RAR. Late on a Friday afternoon at about 5 pm a signal came through to say that an Internal Affairs convoy under RDR protection had been ambushed in the Zambezi Valley. The only army officers present at the JOC were myself, (a Captain then) and Lt Chris Clay. There were also six 1RAR base camp African soldiers. After discussion with the Air Force reps, a pilot agreed to fly us in an islander aircraft to a disued air strip about three kilometres from the ambush site. We flew for a few minutes parallel to the Zambesi

River and were tracked from the Zambian side of the river by a Zambian Air Force jet, which eventually banked away and left. We arrived at the airfield at about 18.20 and it was still light. The pilot said that we would do one sweep of the airfield, (the grass was chest high), to check that there were no trees or stumps and if clear, would put us down. As soon as the aircraft stopped, we were to go to each corner of the airfield and protect it and he would fly out immediately.

We landed in a sea of grass with the propellers chopping our way through like a giant mower. Luckily, we did not encounter any tree stumps! Before we landed the pilot told us that he would be going back to Wankie for the night, we would have no radio contact overnight due to the terrain but that he would return at first light to check on us. A dirt road led to the ambush site, but we decided to go cross country through bush to get there. At the ambush position, we found two dead RDR soldiers and two disabled RL trucks, the end result of an RPG rocket attack.

We collected the living and wounded, (none of whom were critical fortunately) and withdrew from the ambush site into the bush. It was warm in the early evening but very cold at 2 am. Corporal Bonanza Chiyengwa pointed out that in my hurry to leave the JOC I had not brought my sleeping 'mpashla' with me. Because there would always be someone on sentry duty, the RAR soldiers would give me one of their sleeping bags and rotate with each other. What gentlemen! At first light I was greeted by Cpl Bonanza with a huge smile, a pannikin of tea and a 'dog biscuit' (one of those huge army ration pack biscuits).

Chris Clay and I checked the road in and found a boobie trap consisting of a hand grenade plus an RPG 7 rocket connected to a trip wire. Further down the road were two anti-vehicle land-mines planted side by side on one track of the dirt road. It had rained during the night and washed around them showing their outlines. Chris and I also counted thirty-five ambush firing positions along the sides of the road. It was a good thing that we had not approached along the road the previous evening.

The Islander aircraft duly arrived overhead just after sunrise to check on our progress overnight. We requested an engineer to deal with the boobie trap and landmines. Two Alouette helicopters arrived a short time after with an engineer and we were subsequently uplifted back to JOC Wankie. We were met by a very relieved CO Lt Col Mike Shute and adjutant Kevin Johnson who had not been able to contact us overnight. Kevin asked me if I had managed to carve any new notches on my stethoscope (like the old gunslingers in the Wild West)!

MEMORIES THAT MADE SERVING MEMORABLE by Major Jim Hill

Pondering the content of Chibaya Moyo 1, and the occasional anecdote that enriches the RAR Facebook page, I wondered why it is that such a short period of life has remained, consistently, at the forefront of my mind. There is not a day in my life without some unbidden memory or other coming to mind at unexpected moments and they are usually not the memories of significant moments. Could it be that the 'little' things, the, supposedly, insignificant moments are actually those that, without doubt or exception, made serving the RAR the best time of my life.

Like most Rhodesian officers, I commenced my officer training at the School of Infantry but then, unlike most, I was selected for training in South Africa and departed the School in Gwelo for the Military Academy in Saldanha Bay and the Infantry School in Oudtshoorn. I returned some 18 months later to a temporary posting at Army HQ where I wandered around 'lonely as a cloud' adorned in my Officer Cadet uniform for about two months awaiting my fate.

Having served some time in RLI I knew, from a Troopie's perspective, about that unit but I had no knowledge at all of the RAR and so it was a bit of a shock to receive a posting to that illustrious unit.

Having received my joining orders I drove down to Bulawayo and approached the Methuen Barracks' front gate with some trepidation. The respect accorded my bright and shiny brand new single pip by the Guard Commander was my first surprise and the second was the, "What on earth are you doing here?" (or irritated military type words to that effect) reception from the Adjutant, Captain Terry Hammond, who was, apparently, having a bad day. I had arrived a day earlier than expected.

Some 20 minutes or so later and now with my first meeting with the CO, Lt Col Bert Barnard, behind me the Adjutant had recovered his humour and introduced me to the life of RAR over an early beer in the Mess – "This is your home now, better you find your way here quickly".

December 1972 and Op Hurricane broke out. B Company 1 RAR was deployed on framework type operations with the aim of determining levels of insurrection in the Matabeleland area. 4 Platoon headed towards the Gwanda area with brand new 2 Lt Hill as its Commander.

Still trying to fathom the personalities of my Platoon, I was utilising various training techniques taught to me in South Africa, techniques that were somewhat strange to my African troops. I had been taken with the concept that much of the training given to soldiers in peacetime training was seldom tested until the troops went into action for the first time. As with myself, this axiom applied to many of my soldiers as well and so I set about 'testing'.

For some peculiar, forgotten reason I had managed to get my hands on a Sterling sub machine gun and a goodly stock of 9mm ammunition for it (I carted that thing around for quite some time). Thinking to test the camp sentries' reactions one afternoon, I advised my PWO that I was going to slip out of camp into some dead ground and fire a few rounds off. He was a) to not advise the sentries beforehand and b) he was to closely observe reactions for future reference. He was horrified!

Just as I reached my hole in the ground, I became aware of another presence behind me but before I could do anything silly, my batman made himself known. A whispered conversation along the lines of, "What are you doing here, you silly person?" enabled him to inform me that the PWO had sent him along so that he could loudly inform the Platoon that they were not actually under attack should the need arise.

Looking back I wonder at the concern of the older African soldier for the impudent youth appointed to command him.

At some point before B Company joined the rest of the Battalion in Sipolilo (Guruve), 4 Platoon was despatched in a hurry to join D Company at Deka. High grade intelligence suggested a gathering of the forces across the mighty Zambezi and a couple of weeks intensive ambushing/observation was enjoyed before the Platoon re-joined the Company strength but remained in the Deka area. Based at a temporarily vacated DC camp we patrolled, interviewed what local presence we could find and generally made our presence known.

One particular morning three patrols had to be uplifted from different areas and vehicle escorts were a bit short so I tagged along on the RL. On the way home, the vehicle broke down with a mysterious fuel problem which we overcame, temporarily, by dribbling petrol directly into the carburettor!

As the driver was a better dribbler than me, I was driving with the driver dribbling when a series of loud bangs on the roof prompted a hasty stop. "Ishe," called the Platoon Sergeant urgently, "do you got that Stelling here?" "I do." "Give it me, quick, quick." Handing the weapon over quick, quick I was urged to proceed a bit slow. Being curious by nature, I proceeded a bit slow with the driver adjusting the dribbling accordingly.

Tap, tap - tap, tap the Sterling rattled over our heads and then the bang, bang, bang to stop. "Ishe, we got good lunch!" Each tap, tap had got a rabbit.

We were deployed in the Chiweshe Tribal Trust Land south of Centenary and 4 Platoon had just finished establishing a base close to an area believed to be on an infiltration route. It was late afternoon and Sections were preparing to deploy for night patrols when there was a loud explosion and, shortly thereafter, a huge cloud of dust not far from our base. It had to be a mine.

Deploying with escorts and trackers I drove some way towards the dust and then ran into the scene from about a kilometre away. We were not aware of any official movement in the area so I was expecting to find a civilian vehicle and therefore casualties.

The sight of the remains of a scotch cart on its side in the road surrounded by broken grain sacks and a small crowd gathered on the sides of the road brought me up short. We approached cautiously to discover three injured males, two of them juveniles and one elderly man who was severely wounded lying a little way from the cart. The two oxen that had been pulling the cart were staggering around, both pouring blood and still tethered together. It was a shocking sight.

We cleared a route to the injured people and removed them from the road after calling for medical assistance but, just we started to give what first aid we could, the old man called for me and with my tracker interpreting pleaded with me to first of all tend to the wounded animals.

When we explained the nature of their injuries, he said that those two animals had helped his family since they were calves and they did not deserve to be injured in that way. Please would I end their suffering quickly?

We were driving in convoy towards an airfield where I was to be uplifted when the lead vehicle swerved off the road and stopped. The driver had seen a disturbance a short way ahead. We scouted cautiously through the grass along the road verge and found where tracks leading to the spot had been covered. 2 + 2 equals mine.

Without Engineer support around, we had to clear the road and I decided it was up to me to do the dirty work. Not having any explosives other than our grenades it became one of those jobs covered in Officer training but never tested. No bayonet to hand, a screwdriver from the vehicle would have to suffice.

Moving the vehicles back (after scouting the road behind us just in case) I approached the disturbed site and then crawled the final very long, very dusty and sweaty ten metres to where I could start probing very, very gently.

Fortunately, the mine was a TM 46 and clear of any booby traps so I was able to clear enough soil from around it to enable our grappling hook to get a good purchase but…. We couldn't pull the damn thing out of the ground, the hole was too tight a fit and jammed the sides of the mine. Physics, levers – back to school time. A forked stick, another hole in the road to secure the base of the stick, rope over the fork and pop out it came.

The bugger who laid it so carefully forgot to arm it so Murphy worked to our advantage that day.

When the Independent Companies rebadged as RAR together with the RAR troops we received an African CSM. In the case of 5 (Indep) the new ACSM had been one of my Training Sergeants from the days when I was Battalion Recruit Training Officer. He had been posted to one of the Rifle companies, promoted to PWO and then onto us as CSM. A tall, lean, unbelievably smart Matabele he was a fine soldier and man in every way.

Working side by side with the ECSM he did great things with the raw soldiers that were posted in to the Unit. He would have done no less had he remained in one of the battalions but in the isolation of the (Indep) Company this was a man on his own.

I had noticed that he was becoming somewhat withdrawn and took advantage one evening of the opportunity to sit with him on a bunker overlooking Mozambique and share a beer. His story reflects the closeness and bonds of the RAR family to its members, and the reliance those members placed on it.

The CSM took great pride in his promotion and considered his position as one of importance considering the rawness of our troops and their isolation from other soldiers of experience. He, however, found himself isolated in an isolated position. There were no other senior African NCOs in the unit. All the NCOs were European National Servicemen and likewise, so were the junior officers. Senior Officers and the ECSM were all married men who lived out of barracks, his wife and family were in Bulawayo.

At 'home', our CSM was, after hours, alone and, for a man from the RAR family, that was terribly, terribly difficult and 5(Indep) spent about 50% of its operational time operating from its barracks in Umtali. In the field the situation was different. There we were all together all the time and the loneliness was non-existent.

The military machine, especially in a wartime situation, is not able to fully care for every single one of its members but the memory of this man, even today, tugs hard on my heart strings and I salute the service of all like him.

War time and sanctions meant that Rhodesia had to utilise every possible means available to generate foreign capital and that included the export of much of the country's prime beef. The civilian population had, therefore, to exist on lesser grades of meat. Fortunately, with the quality of the beef the country produced this wasn't a total disaster. The Army, however, ensured that beef supplied to troops as part of their fresh rations was top quality.

Chipinga airfield was a base occupied, on rotation, by 5 and 6 (Indep) Companies as well as other TA units at times. On one occasion a rather strange message was received from Brigade to the effect that we were to have the services of the one of the country's leading surgeons as MO for a week or two. He would be arriving in one of the relief helicopters, he had some unusual luggage and no comment about his hairstyle would be tolerated.

The chopper arrived and a tall figure sporting a long pony tail emerged somewhat awkwardly. "Goodness me!" said the OC (or words to that effect), look at his hair and then, "He's got a bloody chicken on his arm!" And then the OC, an ex para from the Brit army, departed to cool down so I had to greet our new MO.

The 'chicken' turned out be an African Hawk Eagle, the MO, who was a preeminent surgeon in world terms, was an enthusiastic falconer and he hoped to try hawking by the light of the forthcoming full moon on the airstrip.

Back to beef! Come supper and Sgt Ding Bell served up his usual excellent fare, in the case of this meal, T Bone steak, egg and chips accompanied by salad. The new MO studied his plate for a long moment and launched, loudly, into a medical description of the hazards of the combination of cholesterol, protein and fats that lay before us. In the ensuing silence he downed half his beer in one go and then pronounced, "but F*** me, it makes a f***ing tasty meal!" before setting to with a gusto that would have done a starving Dobermann proud.

Around the same period (we were getting a lot of steak at that time) the meal was served and one of the NS NCOs was heard to, peevishly, declare, "F***, steak AGAIN! I hate it, I'm going to become a vegetarian."

A few minutes later mail was handed out and the same NCO received a letter from home that indicated his mother was probably looking forward to his upcoming R&R more than him. In the letter she stated (more or less), "As you probably know, we're having difficulties getting really good meat as it's all being exported but I was able to talk nicely to the local butcher and he has given me a nice big packet of top quality steak that I'm keeping in the freezer for your return."

4 (INDEP) COY RAR by Major Sean von Stranz

I was posted to 4 (Indep) Coy in 1974 as 2IC. At that time the only real action was taking place in Northern Mashonaland (Op Hurricane). I was therefore disappointed to be sent to the backwater of Wankie. It did not take long for elation to take the place of disappointment. I found Wankie quickly dispelled any doubts that I would be bored!! Brand new barracks, new marriage quarters on Baobab Hill; Sunset Close overlooked the famous coal mining town and when the sun set, the whole horizon turned blood red in the evening. The main attractions were the 'tourist-free' Wankie National Park, Victoria Falls National Park, Zambezi River and Lake Kariba all on our doorstep! The colliery provided all I could ask for in terms of social life, sport and hot, dry weather.

In those days, our deployments included Op Hurricane (a couple of times), 'Surfing and Bezante at Mukumbura', HDF ops in Mt Darwin and one crazy deployment to Mashonaland that ended in Binga a week later. During this time I learnt to admire and respect our young men in National Service. From all walks of life they added new and innovative ideas to soldiering. What they lacked in training, they more than made up for with brains, talent and skills; many had been to university. At this time, Major Peter Gilchrest was OC. He was followed by Major Charlie Piers.

When I took over the Coy in 1976 as OC, one of my first tasks was to tell these young men that National Service had been extended to one year; later extended to eighteen months. Naturally they were appalled but soon settled down to become professional soldiers. This extension of service allowed for the soldiers to gain knowledge and confidence. They rapidly morphed into a serious fighting force with many skills. Sgt Theo Nel became one of our finest examples of professionalism, dedication to duty and fearlessness. He showed an incredible aptitude for tracking and his follow-ups were legendary. After many contacts with the enemy and displaying great courage, he rescued one of his men in a desperate fire fight. We, in 4 (Indep), were very proud when Theo received his Bronze Cross of Rhodesia for these exploits after I had submitted his citation.

I might add that ZIPRA was a force to be reckoned with. They crossed the Zambezi/Lake Kariba in flimsy craft, marched for days in the hot arid bush of Northern Matabeleland and when pursued and cornered, fought hard. They had little contact with the locals and the only sign of their passing was their spoor. With Sgt. Nel and his team we built up a fair idea of their Modus Operandi and routes. 4 (Indep) Coy, during my tenure as OC, was mainly confined to Northern Matabeleland from Tjolotjo in the south to Kazungula in the North including Victoria Falls and Binga, and to the Sengwa River in the East. It was the size of Wales; a lot of ground to cover with one infantry company.

We deployed to Victoria Falls in early 1977 where we had a few successes but also tragedies. 2nd Lt Laurie Watermeyer was shot in the 'arse' in one contact. 2nd Lt Pete Wells had most of his shin shot off, in another. Very sadly 2nd Lt Derek Kingsley-Jones was killed whilst carrying out a daring operation on the Zambezi River between Victoria Falls and Kazungula.

Although we came under HQ 1 Bde we were really independent operationally. From a Commander's point of view this was exhilarating as one had a certain amount of autonomy and decisions could be made on the spot. After this six months stint in Victoria Falls, the Company was deployed to the Binga. As there was a resident TA Coy there for the first week, I decided to base at Milibizi fishing camp. I had known and admired the owner of this delightful fishing camp, near the inlet of Lake Kariba, having based there off and on as a platoon commander of A Coy 1 RAR during border control days. Mike Johnson was one of the most enterprising men I have ever known. He made us most welcome and we based up at the old croc farm.

It didn't take long before we realised that this area was in fact the main crossing point into Rhodesia for ZIPRA, so I decided to continue making Milibizi our base. For the next six months, we established ZIPRA crossing points on the Zambezi and the Lake up to Sebungwe Narrows (itself a crossing point). The intel led us to look at interception techniques and tactics on the lake.

If we could find them on the water, we could eliminate a lot of terrs. Mike Johnson and I loved playing in boats and as a Police Reservist and resident, he knew the lake very well. He and I began to visit the Rhodesian Engineer radar post at Sebungwe Narrows manned by NS. We both became intrigued with the radar's potential to locate enemy boats and dinghies on the lake. We spent every night testing and practising possible contact situations. Mike helped the radar operators to 'zero' their radar using various reference points in the Sebungwe basin. As there was no presence of Op Splinter west of Sebungwe Narrows, Mike and I decided to fill the gap with a borrowed boat (a Bumi) and equipped it with night vision capabilities and mounted a machine gun. The radar could pick us up from the halfway point from Milibizi to Sebungwe Narrows but we weren't sure what an inflatable would look like on their screen.

Our efforts paid off one night when the Sebungwe radar spotted a blip on their screen and directed us towards it. However it was fairly close to shore and as it heard our approach it managed to beach before we could reach it. With the light intensifier, I could see the terrs running up the beach and opened fire. They returned fire from the cover of the trees and the two of us decided to return to camp and organise what few elements of company HQ were available, to investigate the area in the morning. At first light we found one inflatable zodiac dinghy and tracks of about seven leading into the tree line. Unfortunately tracks soon petered out on the very stony ground. However from this episode we learnt a few of their tactics. With an inflatable to play with, we were able to discover more about the efficiency of radar. If we lay low on the floor of the inflatable we were almost invisible to the radar.

From similar incidents happening on the lake east of Sebungwe, Op Splinter decided to base 'the Fletcher' (an old DC's boat) with me in Milibizi, again manned by NS. This was a godsend as it meant extra radar coverage and enabled our Bumi crew to catch up on much needed sleep. Assistance, bloody mindedness and luck paid off. One night after much effort and innovation, plus I admit, much shouting and swearing, we managed to set sail with only one motor running. Suddenly Sebungwe came on the air and announced they had spotted an object five kms west of them in the lake. A few minutes later, we confirmed the sighting on the Fletcher and when we were within a couple of kms of the target, we (Mike, myself and a machine gunner) detached from the Fletcher and sped in the direction of the sighting. It was a pitch black night, no moon or starlight. Sebungwe and Fletcher lost contact with the target but could still see us on their screen (the terrs were presumably lying low in their dinghies, having heard us). They continued to guide us to where they had seen the last sighting and as we neared the target we slowed down and edged closer.

I suddenly saw two smudges on the water with the use of the light intensifier. Mike slowed down and I was able to discern two inflatable zodiac dinghies tied head to toe. The terrs, who by now knew that they had been rumbled, decided to sit up in the dinghies from their prone positions, with their weapons at the ready. As previously practised, we continued circling the terrs in a slow, anticlockwise direction similar to a K Car in Fire Force. When I felt we were not in danger of directing fire towards the Fletcher, I fired off a tracer which resulted in a satisfying thump presumably hitting one of the dinghies. The machine gunner let rip following the line of the tracer. The terrs immediately returned fire. We were still moving in an anticlockwise direction and getting closer all the time. We continued firing with tracer and MG. Their rounds were going high and slightly behind us and eventually their firing slowed to a stop and we got close enough to observe one survivor in the water hanging on to one of the deflated dinghies. We put a spotlight on him and he started to plead with us not to shoot. As we were worried he might have a grenade in his hand, we told him to put his hands up. The farce continued for a while with us telling him to "get your hands up" and him replying "I can't swim" and "if I let go the dinghy I will sink".

Our adrenalin levels were slowly decreasing and I asked Mike to pull up and we dragged him on board. I called the Fletcher in and we recovered the two ripped, deflated zodiacs and put the prisoner on board. I then ordered them to return to Milibizi. Prior to this I had done a quick interrogation of the prisoner who said that there had been nineteen of them in total crossing from Rhodesia to Zambia. He said he felt that all his comrades had either been killed or drowned in the contact. They had been operating in the Insiza and Gokwe areas before attempting to return to Zambia. They had been a group that had attacked a farmer's club and killed a European baby in a pram, among other incidents. Company HQ came back to me and said a fixed wing aircraft was on its way from FAF 1 Wankie, which I had earlier requested, with flares. For the next hour or so, we ranged over that part of the lake looking for any further survivors. There were none. SB Wankie confirmed all the details the prisoner had given us. With that little success, we were given every support we asked for, including an Alouette helicopter, for the next few weeks, but we did not have any more naval successes. Shortly after this, I was posted out of 4 (Indep) back to Bulawayo. I then served with 4 RR and finally had the honour of commanding A Coy 2 RAR.

I have served with regular Gurkhas, as well as European and African soldiers. I found our young NS as good as any of them. The added six months to their total time in service made a big difference to their professionalism and I found it was incredibly satisfying to see young school boys transformed into very capable men in a short period of time. I know that most of them have moved onto successful careers all over the world. I commend them.

CHIBAYA MOYO, MY EXPERIENCES IN 1RAR by Colour Sergeant Jenny Smith

January 1976 - We had just moved to Mtoko and I needed to find work so, Mtoko being the tiny little village that it was, the first port of call was the DC's office. The DC informed me that I needed to go to the JOC (what is a JOC I had to ask), and he would put a call in to the CO and I had to ask for him.

Off I went to the JOC and on driving through the gates, suddenly, strangely felt at home. I went into the Ops Room, was interviewed by Capt Allan Schrag and then asked to sign the papers – it was at this point that I realised I was signing up to join the Army (up until then I had no idea!) It was one of the easiest decisions I have ever made and driving home afterwards, I felt immense pride that I had been 'invited' to enlist.

Next thing I knew, I was en route to Salisbury, kitted out in camo and dress kit, and the training commenced, Intake 18, RWS – rank Private. For a 19 year old girl, this was all new to me but I was so excited to be playing my part. Two of the best aspects of my training which I loved the most, were the firearm training and drill. However having said that, on my second day on the drill square (memories of the drill sergeant in 'Officer and a Gentleman' seeping through), I was singled out, 'eye-balled' and told 'not to be a wimp and do not cry girl'... well once you are eye-balled a few times by a very stern face, sadly the girl in me found tears running down my face. This was enough to set the drill sergeant off, and I was told to leave the parade square!

Thankfully, that was the wake up call to toughen up and that is exactly what I did and from that moment on aimed to march with perfection and not another tear was shed!

On completion of my training, I headed back to JOC Mtoko and was blown away by my own wooden bathroom which had been erected for me in my absence, complete with pink curtains. The memory of that still touches me deeply to this day. I was the only girl at the JOC and I am sure the men must have thought that weird at first, but that bathroom on my first day back, was incredible for me.

There are always initiations although mine was of the sobering kind. I am ashamed to say that the memory of the actual initiation overshadowed the memory of who actually asked me to do this. I think it was (the then Major?) Eric Sobie. He asked me to go with him and we walked to the wire enclosure where the terrs were dropped from the fire force chopper on return from a contact. I was told to walk around the enclosure, looking intently at the bodies lying there, which as you all know, were not ever all in one piece, and to only stop walking when I had absorbed it all.

This was another moment in time when everything stood still. For a 'civvie girl of just 19', this was war in all its rawness. When I stopped by Major Sobie after about four rounds, all he said to me was "Remember, you are now a soldier and this is war." We walked back to the Ops Room in silence. Later that night, I reflected on this, and realised it was the only way to show me that this was real, this was war. It is only once you have seen death in its raw state that you can appreciate the enormity of what it is all about. From that moment on, my respect for every soldier (Officers and NCO's alike) was enormous.

I was welcomed into 1RAR with such warmth, I never felt intimidated or out of place. In hindsight that is incredible as this was a war situation and there were some very stressful times but I was never regarded as 'just a girl' or demeaned in any way. Sometimes respect both ways is just unspoken yet tangible. Col Heppenstall was our CO when I joined, Major Sobie the 2 1/c. Lt Col Mike Shute replaced Col Heppenstall after a couple of months. My little office was in the entrance to the Ops Room and I spent my time between the two rooms, listening and learning.

The rush of the news of a sighting and deployment of the Fire Force... the whirring of the Alouette blades... everyone's adrenaline was palpable... then the waiting. For one who was never deployed to a contact, my memories of those initial moments will be vastly different to the ones who went of course. I remember being tense and waiting for news, of listening to the radio, pacing the floor, waiting, then either exclamations of triumph with a success or the horrified gasp of everyone when something was not right...then the fear for our men, the desperate need for comms. Then the sound of the Alouette returning home, and racing to the air strip to welcome them back, tired weary, brave men.

Due to personal circumstances, I put in a request for a transfer to Methuen Barracks. I left the JOC very sadly and commenced work at Methuen. Again, with 1RAR not having had a female there before, Lt Col Mike Shute still to this day comments that it was because of me that he started buying tissues for his office!

The girl in me at times required a tissue and a listening ear, both of which he always wonderfully, professionally provided.

Methuen was good, although the lure of the JOC and being part of it all was still strong. It was a completely different world of course, being in HQ. I remember the sounds of the Last Post being played on the field when we had lost on of our own, and the grey cloud that hung over us all. Each time I saw the troops coming back from the bush they all looked weary but always upbeat – strong, united men. When they all climbed into the 45s to leave again, I felt my heart going with them. I still hear the sounds of Sweet Banana ringing out. Mike Shute came to my office one day and asked if I would like to work at JOC Fort Vic. Well I doubt he had even drawn a breath yet and I was already up and asking "when do we leave?"

So the next step was to pack up my flat (done in record time), pack and board a .45 for the trip to Fort Vic. Here I found three other RWS who were attached to different units and we were all housed in our own little wooden huts. I learnt so much at Fort Vic, one of which was how difficult it is to lose a good friend in a contact. Lt Jerry Fisher was a very good friend and on that very sad day, they brought his back pack to me to keep at my desk until later when it would be collected. The memory of that still haunts me, and fills me with sadness. Jerry was a lover of Francois Hardie and had lent me many of his LPs, and even now when I hear one of her songs, I remember Jerry. RIP Sir. A new tradition for me was when I was told that we would be having a wake in the Officers Mess for Jerry. I asked how it would be possible to drink and celebrate after a death and I was told that that was the point.. you celebrate the life and show respect by all being together. Another lesson learnt and I have never forgotten that either. This girl was growing up day by day.

One day one of the officers came to my desk and said that he was sure he had not seen me go home for any R&R. I smiled and said I had (although I had not). He confirmed that he was pretty sure I had not been away and that it was standard for everyone to have R&R and that I needed to sort that out. I said I definitely would try, although I felt so at home there and hated the thought that I would miss something if I was away. So I stayed (apologies for disobeying Sir!)

There were many experiences in Fort Vic. Times which were made up of planning, stress, relief, times where moments stood still as we crowded around the radios in the Ops Room. Memories too many to write down, but which are stored firmly in my heart.

It was during my 'supposed to be away on R&R breaks' when I had some afternoons off, and discovered that the Blues had made a make shift basket-ball court. So I joined in from time to time which was good fun and in doing so, mentioned that I would love to learn how to parachute.

So they decided to train me whenever we were all free at the same time. So my learning commenced. They would take me through the landings, the rolls etc (please note it was only basic teaching, and in no way compared to the excellent training any of the parachutists had – I would never have been at any kind of impressive level with the basics I was learning). One evening, I was in the Sergeant's Mess and was called as Mike Shute was outside. I was told to go and pack as we were leaving at first light for Wankie. Imagine my dismay. I told Mike that we could not go tomorrow as I was learning to jump. I will never forget Mike's face as he sternly reproached me "Colour, do you think the war will go on hold while you do a jump?" Well as one would imagine, this Colour immediately went back to her hut to pack! We left for Wankie the next morning at first light.

JOC Wankie. More new experiences. I was housed in a flat in town, luxury after the little hut in Fort Vic (which I actually loved!) and travelled back and forth to the JOC daily in my little .25 which I always thought was so cute especially after driving the .45s in Fort Vic! There seemed to be a few more free hours at Wankie, so there was time when we could actually have some social 'in the world' socialising. I discovered the Booze cruise down the Zambezi – the Baobab hotel, and not least of all, the Greek toga evenings in the Officers Mess with the hooligan juice!

The road from Wankie to Bulawayo was never a care free journey. Somehow I always seemed to be tasked with standing up on the front seat, FN at the ready and head out of the top. Constantly searching.

The tailor at the JOC took pity on me (have no clue why) and called me one day to offer to make me some camo skirts out of old camo shirts as they would be cooler. I willingly accepted and so began my days of a camo shirt and skirt with my vellies. Well the JOC had a mascot who was a hornbill called Harvey. Harvey was the cutest bird and used to go and sit on the wings of the Lynx and wait until they would taxi out to the bottom of the runway when he would hop off as the engines fired for take-off. He was amazing and also used to hear the Lynx returning from miles away and would go down to the bottom of the airstrip and wait for it to land and slow down enough to enable him to jump on. He would then ride on the wing till it parked! When the JOC disbanded, Harvey was sent to Chipangali the animal sanctuary. Anyway, as much as I loved Harvey, he hated me when I wore the skirts. I was fine in camo longs, but heaven help me if I arrived one morning in a skirt. Harvey would go for my ankles and nip them constantly. Those skirts were cool for the hot Wankie weather, but were hardly worn as my ankles took a severe beating!

When we were disbanded from JOC Wankie, I was sent to Army HQ (as a lot of us were), and that is a whole new story and I eventually left the Rhodesian

Army in July 1980 with the rank of Colour Sergeant. However, to sum up my memories of 1RAR in a very small nutshell, I have the fondest, proudest memories of an extra-ordinary Regiment. The Officers were (and still are) outstanding and the soldiers remarkable. I grew up in my years in 1RAR, and I wish to thank each and every one for giving me something to cherish all these years. The bond we have all formed is something that is unique and on meeting up with Officers and NCOs all within the past five years, has sparked so many memories and soul touching moments that I treasure each one. I would like to share a moment I had with one of our Masodja's on their visit to the UK. I was saying farewell to them and one took my hand and said "Miss Jenny, please come back to Zimbabwe with us, we will all look after you". How does one put into words the feeling I had then and still do on reflection? The bond between us all, is strong. I close as I sing our song, "Sweet Banana". Thank you to each one.

A COLONEL TO DIE FOR by Major Butch Zeederberg

It would have been understandable if Mike Shute never wanted to have anything to do with me or any of his other C Company subbies, so it came as some surprise some years later when he asked me to be his adjutant when he took Command of the 1st Battalion.

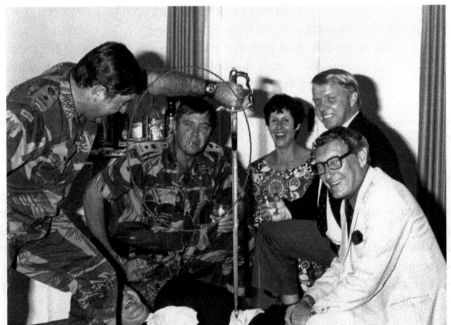

L-R: Lt Col John McVey MLM (CO 2RAR), Lt Col Mike Shute OLM (CO 1RAR), Mrs Hobson, Capt 'Hobo' Hobson, unknown

During one Christmas time deployment we were based at JOC Thrasher (Fort Vic). The Colonel suggested that I take the non-combatant Officers (IO, RSO, Glow Worm etc.) for a relaxing evening at the Ruins hotel.

On the way home in the Seagulls gin palace land rover it was pouring down and the strip road was tortuous. Suffice it to say, that I flipped the vehicle and in so doing the canopy popped off and threw the occupants into the nearby bush.

Unfortunately, I had also offered to give some civilians a lift and they too were scrambling to recover themselves to the road. If memory is correct only Acorn Bill Liversidge was badly injured (dislocated or badly bruised hip).

We radioed for help and soon enough help arrived, but so too did the unmistakeable red caps. Statements were taken, and we were recovered to Fort Vic.

From the resulting summary of evidence (Board of Inquiry?); I was charged with carrying civilians without authority, reckless driving and not compiling the vehicle log book.

In due course I appeared before Acting Brigade Commander Vic Walker at Brady and expected the worse. I felt I had a good defence of the reckless driving charge – the conditions were appalling; the strips were in awful condition and gin palaces notorious for flipping for no good reason. The serious charge related to the carrying of civilians.

Enter soldier's friend and saviour – one Lieutenant Colonel Shute.

The CO had prepared and back dated Unit Part One Orders stating that Unit Officers of the rank of Captain and above should, during the Christmas period, give help and assistance to the civilian population, including lifts in military transport and such like. He presented a copy of the Orders and also attested to the condition of the road and the poor weather.

Which really only left the charge of not completing the log book – which every officer was nearly always guilty of; including I suspect, Colonel Walker. So, I marched out a free man and with a clear conduct sheet.

What a leader, what a General – thanks Boss!

LIFE IN THE RAR: A BIRD'S EYE VIEW by Mrs Bridget Wells-West

When we were planning our wedding, the traditional Guard of Honour was, of course, to be a distinctive feature of the occasion and I delighted in the idea. Events however dictated otherwise. News came that the Battalion was on standby for duty in Malawi (then Nyasaland) and only the two Best Men could be spared. Fortunately the bridegroom was on leave. On the day, however, the situation had eased sufficiently to allow the original plans to go ahead. The Guard of Honour was reinstated, the local bottle store was urgently contacted and our wedding day was perfect.

That was the first and possibly the most important lesson for a wife in the Regiment and over the years such flexibility featured in a wide variety of ways. Having returned from Malindi and settled happily in Llewellin's 'Subaltern Slums', we threw our first dinner party which was really good fun. Our guests, well dined and wined, departed and in due course we went to bed only to be awakened in the early hours by an urgent rapping on the bedroom window. The guests had returned and in response to John's less than polite suggestion that they finish the party elsewhere, insisted that it was 'APPLE' (or something equally unmemorable) upon which John got up and after a rapid conversation in the lounge, returned to say that the Battalion had been called out and would be leaving imminently. "Where to?" I naively enquired and had to accept the reply, "I can't say."!!!! So he stuffed some kit into a large khaki pack and some blank cheques under my pillow and when I asked when he would be back, said he didn't know. A Land Rover came and he went, saying encouragingly, that he'd be in touch - and he was. Lesson Number 2.

Lesson number 3 was a little different and focussed on 'The Yuta Manhunt' between Christmas and New Year in 1959. Alex Binda in his book 'Masodja' tells the story of the Battalion's search for an escaped convict, Yuta, who had attacked and murdered an Inyati farmer, Charles Williamson on Christmas Eve. The burning question for the families was whether the eagerly anticipated New Year party would take place. The only means of communication was the Orderly Sergeant in his Land Rover; phones were not standard fittings. So, as they always did, the wives gathered in groups, with the children, drank tea and chatted and waited.

Then it was supper time and there was still no definite news. Would the party happen?? Should evening dresses be readied? Should baby sitters be organised?? Who knew? Then came a message to say that the party was on. So we made the necessary preparations and after more waiting were more or less ready when at about 9.30 Land Rovers were heard and seen and the parties began, conventionally in the relevant Messes. Breakfast was a moveable feast which morphed into midday drinks and sundowners with people coming and going here and there, attendance and venue seemingly dictated by parental responsibilities and stamina. It was a memorable celebration of determination, resourcefulness and fun.

Perhaps the greatest contribution to the fun was made by the Band. Under the direction and the musicianship first of Tam Lewis, and then, after Tam's retirement, Ken Macdonald, it played an integral part of life in the RAR and was an unfailing source of pride and pleasure to us all. The sight of the bandsmen, immaculately turned out in starched khaki or more formally, and latterly in infantry green, instruments gleaming, marching with vigour and precision made us feel that we were part of something very special - a feeling intensified as the first notes of 'Sweet Banana' sounded, demanding attention and asserting identity.

That was the pride. The pleasure was engendered by the talent, skill and energy of the musicians, playing for an ever-appreciative audience or dancers unable to resist the infectious rhythms of waltzes, quicksteps, rock'n'roll or a conga. Often, as the evening wore on, enthusiastic amateurs might find themselves inspired to offer their contributions and the generous bandsmen would, with smiling tolerance, accommodate the efforts of such volunteers. There were some memorable renditions of the 'Dead March' from 'Saul', 'Mac the Knife' (in Shona to the bandsmen's delight), Tom Jones' greatest hits and many other performances, all bearing testimony to the versatility of the musicians and aspirations of the performers. Whether beating Retreat, accompanying parades, or providing the music for Drumhead Services and Christmas parties for the families, the Band was the beating heart of the Regiment.

For the men and their families, the various Messes were the focal points of most social activity. The Christmas parties for the children were occasions of special jollification and the role of Father Christmas was assigned to the newest subaltern who was ably and sympathetically supported by his brother officers, suitably fortified and refreshed. The children were generally as generous as the bandsmen; one bewhiskered and red-coated Santa, delivered to the assembled brood by donkey cart, greeted the kids with, "Hi!!! How the hell are you?" They cheered enthusiastically as their parents collapsed, overcome with mirth.

Mess occasions could be quite demanding for the wives since the task of decorating and flower arranging fell to them, tasks that were willingly carried out with varying degrees of artistry for the most part. However, with laudable lateral thinking and initiative, one lady, uncertain of what was needful, ordered suitable floral decorations from a Bulawayo florist. There were different conventions too. One, strictly observed, prohibited table flower arrangements, to the dismay of a talented newcomer who had not been informed of that particular idiosyncrasy. Another far more serious breach of Mess etiquette was the wilful and flagrant gate-crashing of an Officers' Dining In Night by a gaggle of behatted and gloved wives under the leadership of the Colonel's Lady. Their reception was muted.

As the years passed and the security situation became ever more demanding, greater stress imposed its hardships on the wives and children of the RAR. Often without the support of husbands and Dads for long weeks, the wives and Mums had to manage on their own. Except of course, they were not wholly and entirely 'on their own' ensconced as they were in a well- developed 'family' tradition.

Friendships flourished and endured, nourished by shared activities and interests. There was a Wives' Club which encouraged skills in sewing, knitting and handcrafts. Tennis and squash were available for those interested. Some people played bridge. The swimming pool was a great attraction especially for the children as was a Saddle Club. The garrison had reasonable library and a theatre for touring shows and occasional films and of course, there were parties: coffee parties, dinner parties, sundowner parties and hen parties, though not quite in today's idiom! Children's birthday parties were naturally the most important of all.

There was no need for DIY since anything like that was quickly and efficiently dealt with and there was always the Orderly Sergeant in his Land Rover, ready to share a problem or report any difficulty to the relevant Regimental authority. The Garrison Shop was our General Store and much else was provided by Mollie Anand in his dimly-lighted but well-stocked treasure house. Ranchod Kika made weekly rounds of the Married Quarters in a specially modified but battered old Ford truck fitted with shelves and racks for fresh fruit and vegetables - and flowers when required.

Kika, who became a great favourite particularly with the children, was a good friend of the community and at Christmas delivered gifts of flowers to the churches for their Christmas services. In time the old Ford gave way to a splendid modern refrigerated van but Kika never seemed to change. Downing's Bakery in Bulawayo supplied us with fresh bread three times a week, and on occasions, when elements of the Battalion were deployed in the Townships as 'Aid to the Civil Power' would deliver letters collected on the driver's rounds in the affected areas to customers in Llewellin.

All in all, the Regiment's wives and families were well cared for in the companiable and compassionate nesting colony of Llewellin. We rejoiced when the Regiment was in Barracks and, for the most part, endured the forced separations. We turned out in our finery for greater and lesser occasions, notably Tanlwe Chaung Day and the annual Regimental Ball and sombrely and sadly mourned the loss, in operations, of irreplaceable family members and friends. Those were unforgettable years in memorable company and will always be cherished with involuntary tears and irrepressible laughter.

REGGIE: MUSENGEZI by Major Gavin Rawstron

In 1974, C Coy 1 RAR where based at the Old Mission Station at Musengezi and were tasked with the evacuation of all the local population into Protective Villages (PV's). To assist us, we had a chopper attached to help move the women, children and elderly. That chopper (D7) was piloted by Fl Lt Ian Harvey.

There was an elderly paraplegic who was airlifted from a village in Mocambique and, unfortunately, a man of his handicap was not looked on favourably by the local masses and had to fend for himself. Whether it was due to superstition, I was not sure. Anyway, he was duly brought across the border and dumped outside the PV. Due to his handicap, he was only able to crawl as his lower limbs were useless. I summoned one of our RAR NCO's to have a chat to him as I thought he was the ideal person to get some intelligence regarding ters activity in the area.

It transpired that he was virtually regarded by the locals as an outcast and was totally reliant on his only companion.... a donkey named Reggie. This man's only means of getting around was on a make-shift sled made out of a fork of a tree that was pulled by Reggie.

Unfortunately, his only form of transport was now in Mocambique. I happened to mention this to Ian Harvey over lunch and never gave it another thought until that mid-afternoon when I was summoned to the ops room by D7 who was now on a return trip to the camp.

"Hello 3, this Delta 7, fetch Sunray Minor over."

"Sunray Minor... go ahead"

"Would you like to take a peak outside for a moment?"

There above the dust was D7 with a cargo sling carrying a donkey who was clearly not very comfortable, but ears pricked up until landing and the dust cleared.

Message was immediately passed to the owner of Reggie who proceeded to make haste in a cloud of dust larger than that put up by the chopper, dragging himself to his long lost friend, with tears streaming down his face. After freeing himself from the cargo net, Reggie ran towards his master, who reached up and grabbed Reggie's neck as if his life depended on it. The joy was evident from both parties.

Ian deplaned with a smirkish grin on his face that would have been the equivalent of the aftermath of a contact where he'd killed 100 CT's. The home-made sled was then offloaded from the chopper and with the help of the AS, Reggie, his master/friend and sled were sent on their way to the PV, a short distance away.

It wasn't a couple of days later that I was summoned by D7 to the Ops room again. Same story, "Gavin, come check this out." I could not believe what I saw once the dust had cleared!

Sitting in the chopper, on the collective, were about six kids, packed up behind them were another ten, and next to the Tech were another three. It took nearly five minutes for them to dismount. A total of 19 excluding Pilot and tech got out of that chopper. A record.... I don't know, but it must have been a bit heavy on the nose.

EARLY BOYHOOD INTRODUCTION TO THE RAR Colonel John
Pritchard

My father, Fred Pritchard, served in the RAR as a warrant officer and, in 1944, was commissioned and continued to serve until being discharged after the war. He made a number of lasting friends, of whom I vividly recall seeing three of them on a number of occasions as I was growing up in Bulawayo. Lt Hedley Sheffield and his family became very close friends of ours, with our respective families visiting and holidaying together on many occasions. Lt John Salt, later to command 1RAR in 1958 and Lt George Pitt MC later to retire as Colonel Pitt frequented our house from time to time. On one their visits to our house in North End (I was maybe 10) George had brought his dress sword. My father called me and instructed me to kiss the basket of his sword (if this was a tradition or merely a show of respect for George, I do not know to this day). However I did what I was told and then left them to talk over several whiskeys.

In my mid to late teens I recall the annual TC nights at Methuen Barracks as told by our mother. Every year my father and 'Uncle' Hedley would make the journey out to the Mess and each time my mother would say "Your father and Uncle Hedley are going to be drunk tonight – they have gone out to the Army". It took me until the 25 April 1967 to understand what my mother used to refer to. That year, as a Second Lieutenant, I had the honour/duty (some of us would have called it a chore as it inhibited our own celebrations to some degree) of acting as waiter to all the guests, including my father, who had been invited out to the Officer's Mess to celebrate TC Day. That night, when I bade farewell to my father and Uncle Hedley as they drove off back to Bulawayo, I recalled my mother's words of years gone by and understood. Hell it was a great evening. Like father like son I think we were both merry having had a most memorable time. Fortunately for them, and the dozens of guests each year, there were no such thing as booze buses on the road back into Bulawayo and to my knowledge, no accidents to speak off. We subalterns only had to negotiate our way back to single quarters.

A SOLDIER'S FRIEND by Captain Russell Fulton

During one's commissioned life in the regiment there were frequent, unsolicited, but expected duties that fell outside the scope of one's normal duties as 'sabre-toothed jousters of our feral communist foe'.

When it came to creativity, none usurped the creative machinations of our respective Adjutant's minds. There was a (seemingly) endless stream of regimental duties that our Seagull (Adjutant) was able to serve-up for us to perform and which we all strived our very best to shy-away from. These included BOI's (Boards-of-Inquiry) and, being a 'Soldiers Friend'. Boards of Inquiry were an annoyance on every conceivable level, but they were important and were, apart from their import, a measure of a subbies preparedness to be thorough. Everything we ever did as subalterns was a measured and considered part of profiling the person behind the rank. As cadets, we had received detailed instruction on BOI's and understood that there was never a tolerance for 'cuffing' them. Attention to detail was the name of the game as it was with all things because it was us, ultimately, who ventured in to the jaws of hell.

Preamble

Less common, but of equal importance, was a requirement for subalterns to represent their men in Courts Martial as, and appropriately quipped, 'A Soldier's Friend'. Those so 'anointed', were expected to act, in a military an officerly fashion, but in a manner not unlike 'Perry Mason'. You were the defender of the 'accused' and it was your duty to represent and defend said 'accused' and plead his innocence, oftentimes, with calculated deviations from the 'truth'.

Courts Martial were a very serious business, chaired by officers' light-years above our pay-grade, and endowed with greater wisdom than we 'mere mortals' were capable of reasonably comprehending.

In short, a "Court Martial is empowered to determine the guilt of members of the armed forces subject to military law, and, if the defendant is found guilty, to decide upon punishment. Most military forces maintain a judicial system that tries defendants for breaches of military discipline." In the Rhodesian Army, our legal system was governed by two neatly presented and respected guides; The Act (Chapter 94) and Defence Forces Discipline Regulations 38. ("Contrary to the prejudice of military order and good discipline, in that.......")

Trial by Default

Private Kananda, Jeffrey: 3 Platoon, A Company 1RAR

Following a night of esprit de corps, drinking in 'no go areas', grievous assault of one very large, imposing and decidedly anti-*Masodja* 'security guard' that involved a fracas with Sunray 13, the following took place:

This was the second occasion that I had, rather foolishly, involved myself in spending some social time with my men in a less-than salubrious establishment, prescribed by 'those-in-the-know', as a 'No Go' area. I remain 'guilty as charged' but it was not my normal modus operandi I assure you. Oftentimes, back in the day (a convenient excuse), one did what one did regardless of the consequences which could well have been grave. Forfeiture of seniority, forfeiture of pay, cashiering and the like were all on the legal table, but this is not about 'Moi' you understand?

I had, previously, engaged in some hostilities with a civilian 'bouncer' and, on not dissimilar grounds, but I did what was required, without hesitation nor consideration of the implications that this could/would have on my career. Never mind that.

On this occasion we had overnighted at Methuen Barracks, home to 1RAR, en route to deployment in southern Matabeleland and had been given a pass until 23:59B and I had taken my platoon for a few pints at an establishment of their choosing in the Bulawayo railway station environs (paints a very nasty picture does it not!).

A Soldier's Friend

It seems, with that wonderful thing called 'hindsight', I had not learnt from previous experience having another impressive fracas with a decidedly large 'hotel Impi'. What happened after the fact, almost like de-ja-vu, was when Private Kananda issued said 'bouncer' a well-directed 'clip' about his enlarged, brainless cranium with a full bottle of Castle Lager (a waste of 'hops' if you ask me) and rendered this fellow both comatose and in need of major suturing. I'd seen far worse, but it was, and nonetheless, all a bit of an untidy mess.

The local BSAP uniformed branch constabulary arrived with sirens blaring and blue lights flashing quite unnecessarily and dramatically escalating the matter before arresting Private Kananda without further ado. He was taken to Bulawayo Central Police station where he was incarcerated for assault and GBH (grievous bodily harm).

It was now a civil matter, but it soon reached the very pronounced 'ears' of the corridors of DLS (Directorate of Legal Services) and soon became the subject of a military Courts Martial. Tup-tup-tup! I was surprised, but somewhat relieved, to hear that I had been summoned by Sunray Minor 1RAR to return promptly to Bulawayo to represent Pte Kananda in his Court Martial.

The gravitas of the offence was related to me in the clearest and most unambiguous terms by our Battalion 2ic, Major Charlie Piers, as was the absolute need to uphold the fine, upstanding reputation of the 1st Battalion: "Kananda MUST be acquitted Russell! That's your responsibility and if you fail, we'll have to have another more serious chat!" It was no longer a frivolous matter but one that could spell an end to Kananda's career in the regular army and a lengthy period in gaol. I swore to myself, and Kananda, that I would do whatever it took to exonerate him, within my very limited knowledge of the bounds of military legalise but, and most certainly, with some embroidery if that's what it took. Everything was contingent upon the demeanour of the personalities of the Board whom I would 'suss-out' (assess) before delivering our defence.

The Court Martial

On the appointed day, date and time, I collected Kananda from gaol and issued him with a freshly laundered and starched set of kit and polish/brushes for his boots. He was divested of his Colours (Stable belt and beret), in strict conformance with Courts Martial protocols and to reinforce the fact that he was in 'shit-street'.

Before us sat the proverbial 'venue of vultures', festooned with various and impressive shoulder rank slides and the seriousness of these proceedings left me with an unpleasant foreboding of what might follow. The charges were read out and Kananda was invited to enter a plea.

"Not Guilty Sir", I plead on Kananda's behalf.

I recounted the night's activities and the circumstances leading up to the 'alleged' assault. I went to some length to expound upon the gallantry in action of Private Kananda and his worth in the good fight we were engaged in, how he might have perceived the assault on his Ishe, and his duty to protect and defend him (me), that he was of normal sober habits and a respectful, professional and very proud member of my platoon. I submitted in to evidence, a citation that I had drafted recommending Kananda for an MFC (Ops) to highlight his gallant contribution to our military cause and a profile of the man he truly was. Kananda was, most certainly, one of those still waters that ran very deep. I tendered his sincere apologies to the defendant (absent) for the harm he had caused explaining that he had acted instinctively and aggressively, as was our wont as infantry soldiers when exposed to danger. I went on, perhaps too laboriously, to remind those gilt shouldered officers to my front, that the job of the infantry was to respond to aggression with a far greater measure of it and with deliberate and deadly intent, and we always did. I also expounded upon the fact that our Company had had a combined total of less than four weeks R&R after nigh on eight months in the bush. That was none of their doing of course, but it weighed heavily, but fairly, in my argument. I rested our case and sat, in nervous trepidation as the Board adjourned to consider their findings. One hoped that a little embroidery never harmed our cause. "Too late she cried".

The case against Kananda was dismissed on the grounds of (aggravated) self-defence with forfeiture of one week's pay. Extremely relieved, I personally made good this fine from my own pay. Kananda had stood up for me and I would never allow him to be penalised for doing so. It was tantamount to me condoning an act 'unbecoming' but, as a young subaltern, these were the only actions that I considered worthy and the welfare of my men was my only consideration. Back in the day, it would be fair to say that I knew my *Masodja* better than I did my own family; that's the simple truth of the matter. If I am to be poorly judged by those who read this, I truly couldn't care less. I will always consider myself privileged to have served in the company of, and commanded, better men than myself.

Conclusion

Consider the plight of A Company 1RAR who, during my service, never once had a six-week bush trip with two weeks R&R. Our shortest deployment was twelve weeks and we only ever had one full week of R&R. Now consider the pent-up adrenalin, angst and aggression that built-up like a pressure cooker without release; the result was inevitable. We all had those in-built switches would 'short-circuit' at some point in time and it was only a question of 'when'. Good luck to anyone who fell afoul of the sodja whose fuse blew because it was what it was. The actions of this good man are revealed in this anecdote to simply highlight the loyalty of our wonderful, loyal men who would compromise everything to ensure the welfare of their Ishe. We lived a privileged life in the company of outstanding men. Tinorwira kukunda! We fight to win!
.... here endeth the lesson.

ANTS! by Major Tom Fulton
(Adapted by the author from *Into the Vortex*)

After having myself crocked by a landmine in 1977, the Battalion found interesting things to keep me busy until I received a posting to Headquarters 1 Brigade, as the Military Intelligence Officer. Despite the misfortune of the injuries, my career seemed to be following a reasonably characteristic path. Postings of this nature, at the time of one's career were quite normal, and I was thankful to be staying reasonably close to my 1RAR home.

It was indeed a relief that the initially foreboding Brigade headquarters was packed to hilt with members of the RAR. The Brigade Commander, Brigadier Mike Shute was my old CO. Major Roy Matkovich, the Brigade Major, although now badged RLI, was as RAR as the regimental goat! (Although thankfully, a lot less cantankerous.) The Station Commander and ASO2 was Major Mike Hickman (the General's brother), Captains Dave Rawlins, Graham Schrag and Tudor Pope were all RAR badged. My partner in crime and opposite number in the Operations portfolio in G Branch, was the inimitable Athol Gillespie, or Guiseppe, as he was better known - fresh from a term as an operator in the Selous Scouts, he was also originally an RAR masodja, and still wore our livery proudly.

Amongst the myriad duties required of an Intelligence Officer, I had been tasked with the assessment of existing intelligence, with a view to the deployment of a Q Car operation. The Q Car concept was by no means a new one, and it involved deploying a civilian type vehicle, suitably modified, armed and manned, into an area where the gooks were habitually carrying out robberies. Need any more be said?

The operation was due to be undertaken by members of Headquarters Special Forces. The contingent was under the command of Captain Mick Hardy OLM, a product of the same Regular Cadet Course as Guiseppe, and the familiar camaraderie between the two was warming. The two had also operated together in the Selous Scouts, so they were evidently completely on the same wave-length operationally.

I briefed Mick and his Sergeant in the Tangent Ops Room and was able to provide the visiting operators with three areas of immediate interest, and the two men left, after exchanging telephone numbers with me.

The contingent had decided to make use of the Motor Racing circuit, slightly out of town, and on the road to Victoria Falls. Through old boy network contacts, we were able to have the telephone there connected immediately, and the comparative remoteness of the chosen base seemed to be perfect for launching an operation of this nature.

At about mid-afternoon on that same day, I received a very garbled phone call on my private line from Mick Hardy's Sergeant. The man, obviously almost catatonic, had been trying to convey something about somebody being shot to me. When I asked in annoyance to speak to Captain Hardy, he replied quite clearly. No Sir, you don't understand. It's Captain Hardy that has been shot!

The long and the short of it was that Mick had had a verbal confrontation with a tame gook he had brought from the Scouts, as a batman. Off-loading Mick's personal belongings, the disgruntled man had shot Mick at point blank range with his own rifle, as he pored over his maps, planning his impending operation. Guiseppe and I were the first to the scene, and found that the gook had turned the rifle on himself, after murdering Mick in such a cowardly manner.

Knock off time meant a couple of beers in the mess, and home for supper and bed – but nothing could possibly be attempted without the beer. Morosely, Guiseppe and I nursed our drinks in the Officer's Mess bar. Most of the habitual daily imbibers had gone home to their families, and only a few single members remained.

Helen and I had invited Mick around for supper tonight. Of course I've told her, but she'd already done a lot of the cooking before it happened – would you like to come round? Guiseppe asked.

Considering my reply, I thought back at how shattered I had been when my own course mate Spider Webber had been KIA. It seemed to me, that my friend Guiseppe was sorely in need of some masculine company on that night.

I'd be honoured, my mate, I replied and immediately sensed his relief.

A delightful surprise, in the form of a female friend of Helen's from Salisbury, greeted us at Guiseppe's door. She was tall, slim and pretty, but was aware of the day's tragedy and showed an astutely measured air of gaiety. It was a beanbag night, so while the girl and I were getting ourselves comfortable on the floor cushions, Guiseppe produced a bottle of single malt whiskey, and said,
I was going to drink this with Hardy tonight – better not lose that thought!

Perhaps out of respect for Mick, we never actually sat at the table to eat. Helen and the girl brought the food through on platters and Guiseppe and I nibbled listlessly. Neither of us had any appetite and the whiskey was slipping down our throats like nectar. I was, at long last starting to feel a bit pissed, and was pleased that my subtle amorous advances to the visiting girl weren't being shunned.

It was when Guiseppe surreptitiously unscrewed the cap to a second bottle, that Helen and the girl said their goodnights and went off for the night. With a bravado that I was fast beginning to drunkenly doubt, I called cheekily to the departing girl.

I always sleep closest to the door – and I don't snore, I added unnecessarily. I received only a girlish titter in reply…

Guiseppe and I drank and talked long, and well into the night. The drinking had slowed down considerably, as we seemed to have reached an uncomfortable level of inebriation. Giving me a set of clean camouflage for work the next day, we parted company for the night.

Using the passage wall in an endeavour to retain a respectable amount of the perpendicular, I edged myself slowly down the passage until I came to the first door. I knew that this was the girl's room, and noticed that it was slightly ajar. Simply far too drunk to feel anything close to Shakespeare's Lothario, I couldn't help but construe this as something of an invitation?

I entered the room and took off my clothes, before sliding into a suspiciously inviting space, which just may have been left for me? I was very conscious of how revolting my breath must have been – the dollop of toothpaste I had purloined in the bathroom on the way, would be overwhelmed by the whiskey fumes in minutes. The response from the girl was both welcoming and understanding – perhaps she never knew how completely safe she was! Also naked, she cuddled into the crook of my arm. It was blissful, I am sure, although I wouldn't say I remember anything after that.

In Rhodesia there exists a tiny black ant which seasonally manifests the nooks and many crannies of urban dwellings. It becomes more common in the colder months, when it enters homes in search of moisture, and to secure strongholds from which to colonise and thrive. I had lost consciousness with my head against the wall.

Coming up the wall with a distinct form of military organisation, the little creatures first sent forward a hesitant, probing and suspicious reconnaissance patrol. Once they had ventured into my hairline, they sent back the all clear to the vanguard and the main body. Very soon, a delicate duplicate of The Ho Chi Minh trail started to evolve, and my entire head was steadily invaded by thousands of these little insects. They sought the moisture in the corners of my eyes and mouth, and by their sheer volume, evidently had no problem waiting their turn. They were up my nose so that I was blowing them out into my hankie for weeks, they reconnoitred my aural cavities in some obvious strength and depth, and they seemed to adhere to the wax in my ears, inquisitive for something new to eat or drink.

When Mrs Helen Gillespie brought in my coffee in the morning, it was all she could do to stop dropping the mug. She hurriedly beckoned Guiseppe and I very piously thank my God to this day that cell phones with cameras never existed!

OF WATCH DEPOSITS AND CHEVY MINES by Second Lieutenant Paul Kuhn

During a deployment to Urungwe with 2 (Indep) Coy RAR, I was called to company headquarters in Karoi by the OC. I took my batman plus one other soldier with me and because we arrived late, decided to spend the night. The two men asked permission to go to the township, and off they went.

Early the next morning, feeling a bit worse for wear after a gruelling night of lie dice at the Twin River with Rufus and Major Theo Williams, I was woken by one of my men (better he remains nameless). He was however the stereotypical RAR soldier, with lots of enthusiasm in the bush, too much energy in camp, very popular with the men in his platoon and a born entertainer.

In his impeccable drill form standing to attention, he asked if he could borrow $2. I asked if it was for last night's bar bill, or something else.

"Well, sah, I was at the bar but I paid for that. Whilst there, however, I met this girl and after some few drinks, she asked if I wanted to go home with her. Ahh, it's been too long since we were in Kariba, so I went. But this morning, when I woke up, she asked for $2. I said to her, "But I thought that was for love?" Now because I had no money left after the bar, she would not let me go, so I left her my watch until I could get $2."

Not only did I give him the $2, but I actually drove him to the girl's house just to be sure he got his watch back!

Around the same time, one of my call signs said they had come across a mine on the Magunje – Binga road. I shot out there, feeling vulnerable in my 2.5 and when I arrived, the area had been cordoned off with branches on either side in good local style. The detonator looked exactly like the TM46s we had been taught about at the School of Infantry, but this had clearly been driven over several times as it was in some seriously hard gravel near the centre of the road.

I figured that this had to be a dud, but Cpl Makore whose stick had found it, said he had seen a mine just like it when he was with 1RAR and we should take no chances. I radioed in to Coy HQ and Engineers were dispatched from Salisbury arriving the next day. Cpl Makore and his men spent the night in the bush nearby until the Engineers arrived. An intrepid Sapper Sergeant did his whole crawl forward and dug for ages with a bayonet around the detonator. Suddenly the whole thing became unearthed and he got a hell of a fright and just lay there for a long while. Finally, he reached over and my TM46 turned out to be nothing more than the centre of an old Chevy steering wheel complete with emblem – the part you push to sound the horn!

If it could fool an experienced engineer, I didn't feel quite so foolish!

PLUGS, SPARK by Major Tom Fulton

It is unfortunately an inescapable fact that there was a period when subalterns who were wounded or injured on operations were relegated to ignominious positions, simply, I had to presume, to get them out of the way. (Not very encouraging for a career officer!) After being injured in early 1977 in a landmine incident, I found myself in just such a position. I was afforded a little relief when Chris McLennan was shot, and found himself alongside me - in the land, as it turned out, of ambiguous appointment titles.

It was the appointment of Kevin Johnson as Adjutant, that saw Chris and I find a new promise in our careers. Kevin decided to use us to relieve himself of some of the considerable pressure an Adjutant is constantly under. As a result, either Chris, or I would be referred to as the Assistant Adjutant and we would alternate between 1RAR (Rear) at Methuen Barracks, or 1RAR (Main) – in Fort Victoria, at the time. (This was indeed a fine stroke of man-management brilliance – so typical of officers like Lt Col Mike Shute and Capt Kevin Johnson).

Spark Plug McLennan

Of course, this new arrangement was not without some minor teething problems, as was later evidenced.

Every personality in the Battalion Headquarters had an Appointment Title that we used as a form of personal identification when using the Battalion radio net. The Adjutant was referred to as Seagull, the RSM Seagull Minor, so when I needed to refer to myself, I simply called myself Assistant Seagull.

One afternoon whilst Kevin and I were in his office at Rear, we overheard a radio conversation between Chris at 1RAR (Main) speaking with someone at the QM store. At the end of the conservation, the stores-person asked Chris to identify himself.

Now, perhaps in Kevin's absence, he may have been excused the assumption, but never the presumption that he could use the Adjutants hallowed Title. I did nothing to stifle my laugh when Kevin exploded, "Who the hell dares to call himself Seagull of callsign zero?"

Poor Stoffel, realising he had overstepped the mark enquired meekly, "Roger, what am I supposed to call myself?.....over". It was by any account, a reasonable reply, and would have been marginally acceptable if he hadn't made it sound so much as if he wanted to say Sir, instead of over!

By now my status had deteriorated into paroxysms of uncontrollable laughter in the chair across the room. Kevin, perhaps a little caught for words said, "S...S...Sparkplug! Yes, Sparkplug is what you will call yourself from this day forth!"

Picturing all the Signallers in the far-flung, deployed Rifle Companies, hurriedly updating their lists in the various ops rooms set me off, howling anew!

Sparkplug...never to be used by another. Chris became a living legend...

MAKOMBI by Major Gavin Rawstron

In 1974, C Coy 1 RAR were based at Musengezi with a Forward Operations Base at Makombi on the Zambezi River in Mocambique. Major Fluff Templar was OC and I was 2i/c at the time. We had 7 Sqn (Chopper) and 4 Sqn (Provost) based at Musengezi at night and they would position themselves at Makombi during the day to assist in troop movement and top cover as required. I would normally hitch a lift on a Prov each day to assist Maj Fluff and return that evening.

We were sitting under the trees at Makombi around lunch time with a couple of 'Blue Jobs' when we heard a shot fired from across the River, followed by another approximately 20 minutes later. This was unusual as the other side was regarded as enemy territory. We also had a section of 81mm Mortars attached to us from Sp Coy 1RAR, so Maj Fluff decided to have them fire a couple of rounds generally in the area to see what the response would be. Absolute silence! We were just about to relax when 20 mins later another shot, then another and another every 20 minutes or so. Each shot met with a couple of rounds from the Mortars.

There seemed to be something wrong with the whole episode, so Maj Fluff called the CSM and asked if all personnel where accounted for. All at Makombi were accounted for, so I then contacted our Rear Base at Musengezi and was advised sometime later by the CQMS that one of the new recruits was missing. Maj Fluff decided to send a chopper over the river to investigate. 30 minutes later, the chopper returned with beaming recruit in-hand, very dirty, smelly and having shed a few kilos. He was told to get fed, cleaned up and then debriefed.

This was his story.

He was part of a new group of recruits that arrived at Musengezi where they were kitted out and allocated to their respective platoons. Within 24 hrs of arriving, the new recruits were broken up into sticks and were told they would join the remainder of the Company in an attack on a CT Base somewhere in Mocambique. They had not yet joined their respective Platoons, so had no idea of where they were going.

The CT Base was upriver between Makombi and Feira, some 30 kms from Makombi and the attack took place four days prior to him being rescued. He found himself in a stick on a chopper, heading for the op area. He remembered crossing a very large River (Zambezi) that was unknown to him. Next he was being dropped in amongst very high grass, dropping his pack and taking cover until the choppers left. He could not find his pack nor any of his stick until he heard shots being fired to his north. Fearing running into his own troops, he decided to stay put until everything died down. It was now sundown so, choosing to hide in amongst the reeds and grass, he waited until the following morning. Just before dawn he collected his pack and kit (which he eventually found) and decided to get out of the area, going along the river in the general area that he remembered from the chopper approach.

Makombi 1974

He continued eastwards every day toward where he noted aircraft activity until he reached opposite from where they were landing. During these three days, he encountered elephant, hippo and crocs, as well as a number of terr patrols which he managed to avoid. Once opposite the camp, he would remove his magazine from his rifle, take a single round and fire it in the air, replace his magazine and run like hell to get away from where he fired that shot. If there were any ters in the area, he was not going to make it easy for them. He still had a full magazine to defend himself.

Only problem.... HIS OWN TROOPS were now firing on him with mortars. Each time he would fire one shot and move until he heard the chopper circling overhead. Running out into open piece of ground, he managed to get the choppers attention and was picked up. So elated was he, that he almost jumped right though

467

from one side of the chopper to the other. The chopper tech's comment was that he had never seen someone so happy and with such a big smile as on that day.

For a new recruit to have used common sense and ingenuity as he did, it was no wonder that he was promoted to L/Cpl within a very short period. I am just sorry that I cannot remember his name.

I REMEMBER…, by Mrs Judy Dixon

A small recollection dedicated to my Dad, Captain Peter Noel Smee.

As a child I remember Methuen Barracks as flat featureless ground, just before the fork in the road, which took you either to Married Quarters (left hand fork) or onwards to Llewellin Barracks. The Married Quarters was a bleak place, 'suburbs' divided according to rank, those old houses (some of them condemned) were built ostensibly to accommodate airmen and their families during the second World War when Llewellin was a flying school. The still-standing hangars proof of the work which went on there. In fact, one particular hangar was reported to house a lone pilot, fully rigged in his flying gear, whose heavy footsteps could be heard on dark and windy nights…

The parade square at Methuen was a vast dusty space surrounded by low office buildings, and the long drive up to the Headquarters was bordered by neat little cottages, some with hedges, some with colourful gardens, always with children running in and out.

My Dad, for a time the Admin Officer, was proud to be counted amongst the number of such a revered battalion. When celebrations such as Tanlwe Chaung Day arrived, he went to great pains to explain the relevance thereof; how the men of the RAR had earned their battle honours with fierce bravery and ultimate sacrifice.

I remember watching rehearsals for the esteemed day, the screeching NCO's, the Regimental goat, which always misbehaved, and the RAR Band marching with precision under the baton of the incomparable Bandy MacDonald.

Rehearsals complete, time for the real thing: the parade, awe-inspiring, the soldiers smart and proud. The music rousing, encouraging the synchronicity of those marching feet, which blared and dimmed depending where the Band was on the parade square. So special the time when my Dad was (for the day) ADC to the General, I swell with pride just remembering. He looked serious and very handsome, his kit in perfect order as he stood behind the podium. My Mum, resplendent in hat and gloves and of course a new outfit made from fabric bought at Molly Anand's dusty old shop. That shop dressed all the wives in camp for all occasions, it was their saving grace.

I remember the mock battles after the parade, where the Masodja showed off their fighting skills. A scene stands out for me: through the dust and the noise of the battle a poor old soldier was dragged unceremoniously away, he was 'an enemy casualty', but we never knew if he was 'killed' or if he was merely injured. If the latter, he would have sustained more than a gunshot wound by the time he reached the 'starlight' on duty! The sound of rifle shots (loaded with blanks of course) and the shouts and cries of the men engaging in skirmishes here and there, marked by coloured smoke bombs was breath-holding excitement for me and my little brother Noel as we watched the action unfold.

Capt Peter Smee-Admin Offr 1RAR

The evening, of course, was saved for the Ball. My Mum was always (for me) the Belle of the Ball with my Father in his Mess kit they made a handsome pair. The next day was family day where we kids were able to partake in the delectable leftovers from the feast, always rather special, always plentiful. We'd sit on the cobra-polished verandah whilst waiters in pristine white would serve copious gin and tonics to the grown-ups and cool-drinks to the kids.

I remember the opening of the outdoor cinema at Methuen. So much excitement surrounded that event. As it was to be ostensibly for the Masodja and their families who lived at Methuen, we were honoured to be invited to attend the opening. Picnic blankets were strewn and low folding chairs (for the grown-ups) were scattered all around.

I recall the Masodjas' children, some in their Sunday best, some barefoot, staring at us shyly for we must have been a strange sight. I can't for the life of me remember the film, but I do remember being bitten by armies of rampaging mosquitoes on every inch of exposed flesh. And as the African dusk turned to instant night the opening credits began to roll... a night to remember indeed.

I remember vividly one evening at the RAR Officers' Mess where families were invited to a performance of Matabele Dancers, they were of course soldiers who kept alive their tradition of storytelling through movement. Arrogantly proud, they were dressed in traditional skins and feathers, holding aloft imposing shields and darting spears. They entertained us with their coordinated dance to the beat of several tribal drums. Africans love to perform, and competition was fierce as they egged each other on, each one vying for the most applause. I remember feeling that primordial beat pulsating through my body, thrilling me.

The bush war started in earnest and one brave and gutsy lady, by the name of Deidre Hickman organised various ladies and teenage girls into 'baking parties'. We were to bake biscuits for our troops. The RAR Officers' Mess kitchen was commandeered whilst the mess cooks beat a hasty retreat and left those mad 'madams' to it. Much fun and laughter ensued and we all thoroughly enjoyed the chance to 'do our bit'. We had an assembly line of ingredients, mixed dough, biscuit presses and baking sheets, then into the ovens. If I can recall our duty was done when the biscuits came out of the ovens. There was another group of ladies who actually packed the treats and sent them on their way. But I do remember that the dedicated Deidre was there every step of the way.

My father's time in the RAR was cut short but I know he was immensely proud to have served in that wonderful Regiment.

God Bless the RAR.

FETCH PRONTO OVER by Brigadier Patrick Lawless

It came to pass that 1 RAR's RSO changed out sometime in 1977 or 1978; Captain Guy Thornton RhSigs was attached to C Coy as a platoon commander, and his place was taken by Lieutenant Giles Chinyenze RhSigs.

Giles was a lovely man who had been commissioned from the Ranks. He was competent, witty and slotted in well with his fellow Subbies. A wise, grey-haired man for whom a beer at the bar was inevitably rewarded with a wise insight or tip either on the vexed problem of comms, or helpful tips on handling our *Masodja*.

I guess business might have been slow on operations; whatever, a plot was hatched at 1RAR (Main) at Wankie to catch Giles at an unguarded moment. Complicit were Officers Zeederberg, (Sunray Sp Coy), Liversidge (Acorn), Clark (Seagull), Munro (Starlight), Jones M R (Sunray c/s 73 and McLennan (Sparkplug) – prize awarded for spotting the spoof appointment title!

To initiate the 'jape' the Bluejobs COMMCEN was infiltrated and a spoof teleprinter message (SECRET) derived … you may remember the indecipherable four-letter blocks? ….. LJHG YGTR BBSB…and all that sort of thing? In brief, 1 BDE (Op Tangent, Bulawayo) was becoming concerned that the propagation of Xenon rays in the Earth's atmosphere was having a detrimental effect on operational communications. RSO 1 RAR had been selected by COMOPS personally, to conduct an urgent sampling exercise at BN HQ and Company locations.

The signal went on to suggest Pronto consult Molar for the provision of clean jam jars with screw-on lids, and to request Playtime help distribute and collect samples. Samples were to be obtained at points 2' distant point at the 12, 3, 6 and 9 o'clock positions at the top of both HF and VHF antenna by sweeping the open jar in a circular motion at the collection points, then screwing the lid firmly back on to trap any Xenon rays in the jar. COMOPS recognised the inherent danger of balancing precariously on top of a ladder adjacent to the mast to obtain samples. Detailed notes and photos were to be maintained from each location and COMOPS hoped Pronto 1 RAR might set a personal example by taking the opportunity to lead the task of collection. COMOPS concluded by saying that the exercise was of huge national strategic significance and had the personal blessing of Dir RhSigs (Bleep).

"....Fetch Pronto, Over...."

Well... for the next week the operational area reverberated to the sounds of clinking jam jars. Those complicit took every opportunity to further wind Giles up. Eventually Giles had assembled some 100 sample jars which were suitably labelled and despatched to the Brigade Signal Officer who would have been surprised to receive them. His subsequent call to Giles apparently made this point especially clear.

I have no idea if Xenon is even a word, much less a dangerous ray in the Earth's atmosphere. And if this prank resulted in any of you 'Dear Readers' shimmying up a pole or ladder clutching a jam jar somewhere in the Bush, sometime in 1977 or 1978, then you have my unreserved apologies.

If Giles could have blushed on learning the truth, then I am sure he would have – but if seemed very funny at the time. He promised to get his own back on us one day, so I remain vigilant just in case he is still alive and retains a stock of jam jars.

MINISTER GOES MISSING by Major Gavin Rawstron

As 1RAR Intelligence Officer, I was detached for a while in 1975 to assist Maj Ian Bait (Tufty) (1RLI) in running the JOC at Bumi Hills. We had a small contingent of SAP choppers attached to us as things were hotting up in the Matusadona area of Kariba.

I was called in by Maj Bait one morning and advised that we were to have a visitor for a couple of days and that I was to look after him. Maj Bait felt uncomfortable having anyone looking over his shoulder and wanted this visitor out of his way.

Later that morning, a Dakota with its passenger arrived and, as obediently as possible, I went to meet and take care of him. I was aware who it was. Alighting from the aircraft in his long shorts, 7th Hussars Stable belt and beret, khaki bush shirt and stockings, was the Minister of Defence, The Hon P.K. Van der Byl, otherwise known as 'PK'. I knew him personally as he and my uncle were neighbours and hunted elephant together. We exchanged greetings and proceeded to the Ops Room where I gave him a run down as to the situation in the area.

PK van dr Bijl

We had not been there long when I received a message from Maj Bait to send a vehicle to a nearby (18 kms) LZ to collect drums of Avtur for the choppers. Unfortunately, we had no escorts and without any hesitation, PK offered to assist by going along... only his personal weapon, an AK, was still in Salisbury.

So, under his instructions, I was to contact his Secretary at Defence HQ and arrange for the Dak to fly back to Salisbury and collect it "Post Haste". A few hours later, the Dak arrives with the AK for PK. With much smiles, Landrover, driver, guard and PK leave in a cloud of dust into the distant yonder.

Tea time in the Ops Room, Maj Bait looks at me, looks around and asks: "Gavin, where's The Minister?"

"He's gone on a vehicle patrol to collect those drums of Avtur you asked for."

Silence....more silence, then suddenly! "He's gone where!!!!!?"

I repeated the answer but with a little apprehension and hesitation.

His red face and hair seemed to take on the appearance of Dayglo as he shouted "WHATTTTT! You've sent him where?????"

PANIC STATIONS as thoughts of 'Minister of Defence the Right Hon P.K. Van der Byl goes missing whilst guarding Fuel drums in the operational area' appear in The Rhodesian Herald.

Mad scramble to get hold of the vehicle, no comms. More panic... two hours go by, he should have been back by now.... still no comms. People running all over the camp. Another hour goes by. Still nothing. Choppers are all out.

More panic.

Just as we were about to resign ourselves to the unthinkable, in comes our Minister on the back of the LR as if he's been on the trip of a lifetime and wondering what all the fuss is about. Typical PK.

All I can say is PHEWWWW!

FLYING by Colonel Ian Pullar

In addition to the Rhodesian Air Force, which was a professional outfit, there were plenty of part-time aviators taking to the air in various guises (goggles, scarves, you name it). Consequently, we flew in a variety of aircraft, many of them serviceable, flown by an even wider variety of pilots, some of them qualified.

On one occasion, Peter Hosking and I were flying to Salisbury in an Air Wing Cherokee, I think it was. Peter was next to the pilot. We had climbed to around 8,000 feet because there had been turbulence below that. Somewhere above Enkeldoorn the engine stopped. The propeller was still turning but not under power. From his apparent frantic checking of knobs and switches, it seemed that the pilot did not know what had caused the problem. The fact that we were descending was obvious without watching the altimeter. Peter turned around and simply raised his eyebrows. Unflappable as always. He then asked the pilot if it could be a fuel blockage. The pilot pulled a handle near the trim wheel, which was presumably to switch to the second tank. The engine started. Just as well we had been up a bit because we came down rather a long way…

When we were at Grand Reef, somebody at a much higher level had decided that an attack should be made on a small town in Mocambique, south of Umtali near the Rhodesian border. I can't remember the name nor the reasons, but it required most of our battalion to be used in this assault. I was to be the OC on the ground. John McVey summoned myself and some other officers from Fort Victoria to Grand Reef to work out plans for this particular operation. We flew in a Dakota which apparently had Reserve Officers as pilots and it was a somewhat scary journey to say the least. Just as we cleared the airfield, the pilot banked to the right, I thought too steeply for the speed and altitude and as the wingtip brushed the top of a large Msasa tree I felt my fears to be justified.

We stayed low level, which was the policy, to avoid missiles, and suddenly we banked again and descended at which time there was a series of loud bangs which started at the front and ran up the middle of the aircraft. I thought a cable of some sort had parted until I saw the holes in the floor and the aircraft took a sharp dip downwards. At this point I assumed the pilots had been hit by ground fire and we were about to crash. We gradually started levelling out pretty close to the ground and started to breathe again. Then we climbed and continued to climb and bugger the low level rule. Eventually we got to Grand Reef where we landed with a flat tail wheel and a bit of a slither. The pilot said that he had seen a number of buses stopped at a road junction and he wanted to have a look. I refrained from suggesting he should take a Trojan next time he felt so inclined. When we got to Grand Reef we were told that the operation had been cancelled.

My assumption of Battalion command coincided with the death of Bruce Thompson on the same day. That was at the end of June 1978. I asked the Air Force for a flight to A Company Headquarters to visit them just after this event and an Air Wing Aircraft was provided. The pilot took off from Fort Victoria and, after about twenty minutes, he started flying towards very heavy towers of dark cumulonimbus clouds and I suggested that we turn around because I did not think that an aircraft of this type would be able to fly through that. He said that it was not a problem and he had flown through such weather on previous occasions. The implication being that I was out of order. We were now flying into heavy rain and the aircraft was being seriously buffeted. I told the pilot to turn around, and after some argument he did so. He made a complaint to the Air Force about me taking over the aircraft and myself and the Air Force Commander at the JOC Victoria had words.

I recall another memorable flight when I was CO. Andre Dennison and I took off from Fort Victoria on a recce of the Nuanetsi area east of the Beit Bridge Road. After we had flown for about half an hour, fairly dense cloud started to build up. Not stormy but the rolling misty type that sometimes affected the SE. It was called "Guti" The pilot climbed through it which, even to me, seemed an unusual thing to do as we would eventually have to go down through it without knowing the ceiling. This we did and very nearly collided with one of the stone monoliths that abound South of Fort Victoria. It also meant that we were seriously off course and too far West. The cloud was not improving and I suggested that we return low level. The pilot refused. Before I responded, Andre, who was in the back and had been attempting to map read our position, more or less insisted in such a manner and half over the front seat, that the pilot was seriously upset. He did return though and, of course, there was another Air Force discussion about who controlled what.

Perhaps Douglas Adams was right when, in The Hitchhiker's Guide to the Galaxy, he wrote: 'There is an art... or rather, a knack to flying. The knack lies in learning how to throw yourself at the ground and miss. Pick a nice day... and try it.'

MUSHONGA by Major Butch Zeederberg

On joining the 1st Battalion in April 1969, I was appointed Platoon Commander of 8 Platoon, C Company. Champion Company competitions had just started in earnest and Major Mike Shute had arranged inter platoon competitions to select the best Company teams.

First up was soccer – a game I had never played in my life. I was alarmed that we went down 0 – 3 to 9 platoon within a matter of 15 minutes and it was clear our goal keeper was either blind or at least sadly lacking in depth perception. Despite having only been in the Unit for a matter of days, I consulted with PWO Paradzai and Sergeant Dovongwani (Mavengere) and insisted the goalie be replaced. Apparently, there was no other candidate and I decided that despite having zero experience that I could hardly do any worse and so, barefooted took to the field.

I do not recall the result of that game, but Mike Shute and CSM Pfupa decided that I was the keeper for the Company, which somehow led to me being selected by the Col. Hep, Cpl Bebo Tavashure and CSgt Miles to represent the Battalion in league and Army Cup knockout competitions. And so, my experiences with the Mushonga rituals began.

Prior to any major game, Cpl Bere the stalwart centre back, was despatched to somewhere near Zaka to consult with a powerful Nganga and establish what was needing to be done in order to secure victory. (Not surprising that Bere is the local name for hyena – that most frightening animal in African superstition.) Of course, transport was provided as well as the necessary 'stipend' from PRI or other secret resources under the command of Col Hep.

That year we had eliminated (amongst others), the powerful RLI and Brady Barracks teams and the final was against Inkomo Barracks - at Inkomo.

We travelled up in the standard 3-ton Bedford RL a couple of days before the game and were met there by Cpl Bere who had detoured via Zaka. One of the strictest rules imposed by the Nganga was that no player should have any contact whatsoever with a member of the opposite sex; and so I was quartered in Officers Mess and had a full time guard to ensure that this was observed – as did the remainder of the team in a barrack room in the lines.

The day before the game we had to give Bere all our kit, which he then kept in a large box with all sorts of herbs and other medicines provided by the Nganga. Then about 2 hours before the game we all met in the barrack room where all the windows had been blanketed out and the doors thoroughly secured and guarded.

Mushonga

We sat in a circle and Bere handed us our kit which had by now taken on an indescribable aroma. In front of each of us was placed a small pyramid of hyena droppings which were then set alight and allowed and allowed to burn out. To say the smell was pungent would be unfair to Hyenas. We then sprinkled the ashes in our boots and were allowed to get dressed.

Prior to leaving for the field, we were each lightly touched on the inside of each elbow by a small wooden phallic symbol and required to rub a concoction of honey and some pungent smelling liquid into our hair.

On the way to the field we passed the many seated spectators, including Mrs. Eunice Walls who was to present the Trophy. Having met here previously she naturally waved and said hello. Stupidly I forgot that any contact with the other sex would leave one weak and drained and the exchange did not go unnoticed by my teammates.

As the game was about to get underway, I went through my own routine which include leaving my face towel and four false teeth next to the right goal post and generally psyching myself up.

Only a few minutes into the game a completely harmless through ball came trickling into the box and in looking for someone to pass it to upon collection I managed to let it roll between my legs for a goal. The ball did not even have enough pace to reach the back of the net!

1 – 0 Inkomo.

And a lot of bewildered team mates; some of whom began associating my greetings to Mrs Walls with my lack of focus. I instead put it down to simple carelessness until I went to retrieve my face flannel to wipe the nervous sweat from my hands and face but low and behold, my teeth were gone!

The Inkomo spectators had decided that the teeth were the Mushonga that we counted on, and the fact that I had conceded such an easy goal seemed to support this.

No amount of protesting at half time brought any return of the teeth and the second half got underway with Inkomo still leading 1 – 0.

But by now I was somewhat angry and put on a second half performance that Peter Shilton or Bruce Grobbelaar would have been proud of and made some important and difficult saves; which got Bebo, Philemon and others out of their reverie and soon set up Cpl Madochi, Sgt Gibby Gibson and other(s) for a memorable 3 – 1 victory.

A toothless goalie collected the trophy from Mrs Walls, with mouth firmly closed and it wasn't until we were leaving through the Barracks gates that an Inkomo Regimental Policeman returned my teeth.

With my own personal Mushonga safely where they should be, we had a joyful return to Methuen.

(C Company also won the Champion Company Competition – what a journey – what a year!)

BEEF WELLINGTON? AGAIN? by Corporal Alan Doyle

My first months at 2RAR in 1978 were spent at JOC Ft Vic, on the side of Ft Vic Airport. Life centred on a grassy quadrangle bordered on one side by the runway, and on two sides by the standard MoW pre-fab buildings familiar to anyone who ever had to deal with Rhodesian officialdom in any of its incarnations. On the fourth edge was a largish wooden shed, the all-ranks mess, out of which jutted the back end of an even more largish steam engine - a relic of a WW2-era camp for Italian POWs who ran a laundry there. There was - still is – a rather lovely chapel nearby built by those POWs. Immediately across the runway was a large corrugated iron shed. The Selous Scouts' "Fort".

The daily Viscount shuttle landed further up near the terminal building on the opposite side of the runway, leaving plenty of space right in front of the JOC for itinerant Fire Forces to spend the night when it was getting too dark for the

Alouettes to fly, or when fuel was running low. The arrival of 3 Cdo RLI one evening led to the all-ranks mess being found in a semi-demolished state the next morning. That's another story, but a sober reminder of the deadly business in which the JOC was involved, however remotely, was the knowledge that Fire Force Charlie, manned by 2RAR companies in rotation, inevitably took off over nearby Masvingo Barracks, and the wives and families of those in the helicopters and Paradak.

Daily briefings on incidents over the previous 24 hours were held in the map room for the Army, Air Force, BSAP and Intaf reps. The walls were covered floor to ceiling with 1:50 000 maps of JOC Repulse, marked-up each morning with sticky-back plastic disks in various colours according to incident, and very prone to falling off mid-briefing. There were two large Bakelite telephones of early Battle of Britain vintage, one of which enabled scrambled conversations to be had with Comops in Salisbury. I never saw it used.

Life was as boring as beans, enlivened extremely rarely. There was an Engineers' Captain – an American with one leg which had been shortened by standing on an anti-personnel mine in Vietnam – who decided that the provision of a swimming pool would improve the JOC no end. Excavations revealed a very large boulder which couldn't be shifted, until he turned up with about five miles of Cortex. He destroyed it without breaking a single window, but I don't think the swimming pool was ever completed. Orders from above, no doubt.

The only time I ever visited Masvingo Barracks was for CO's Orders, on a charge after I arrived a nano-second late for muster parade. The duty Sergeant treated that default as if I been caught trying to murder him in his sleep. Even the presiding officer seemed to agree he had over-reacted - my punishment was one extra. That Sergeant never forgave me, or him. A TF man arrived on six weeks' call-up - a prison officer of Eeyorish-disposition who told ghoulish stories of judicial executions at which he had been an official witness. Too much information.

There was once an outbreak of foot and mouth. A District Vet flew in in his personal Auster, a very small plane of dubious airworthiness, trust in which was not encouraged by the fact that he had to open the cowling and set about some part of the engine with a hammer before the thing would start. His radio was incompatible with those of his men on the ground, so one or other of us had to go with him with an A63 stuck out of the window to convey his orders as to which herd of livestock should be moved where so as to create a cordon sanitaire. I'm ashamed to say we drew straws. Loser flew.

And then an order did arrive from Comops. The regular battalion HQ was to move out into the field to make its presence more keenly felt, and so command of the 2RAR Companies, which till then had run somewhat in parallel with the JOC operational command, was to be detached as a mobile TAC HQ in charge of a battle group. In short order a 4.5 arrived from the MT workshop on the back of which had been fitted an Ops Room, with work surfaces running the length of each side and map display boards rising up from them. A filing cabinet marked "Top Secret" was bolted to the floor up against the cab, and a fold-down steel stair allowed easy access at the rear.

Two full sets of the dozens of maps of JOC Repulse and other areas were collated, and the task began of marking them up with the borders of the Selous Scouts' "Frozen Areas", and various other details which required some precision if future blue-on-blue incidents were to be avoided. The Bakelite telephones were replaced with every radio set imaginable. Together with a 2.5-mounted tele-printer room with a micro-wave aerial on loan from Signals, and the battalion's own signals net run from a small marquee, the TAC HQ could talk to anyone, anywhere.

RSO Lt Taffy Machiridza climbing into the Tac HQ teleprinter room.

RSO Lt Taffy Machiridza was in seventh heaven.

With the addition of CO Lt Col Ian Pullar's personal armoured 2.5 with double-mounted MAGs sticking out all over, plus catering and stores vehicles and the 2.5s of a mortar detachment from Sp Coy, the TAC HQ comprised a most out-of-the ordinary looking convoy, and off we set, like a travelling fairground, but with guns. From then on the 2RAR TAC HQ was almost permanently away from Ft Vic. The TAC HQ was the mobile headquarters for Fire Force Charlie and the 2RAR companies deployed on the standard infantry OP, ambush or patrol duties in JOC Repulse. There weren't many parts of the south-east which we did not visit, and almost all the time one Fire Force or another – some with RhAF crew, some with SAAF men - moved with us. Those months instilled in me a deep regard for the southern African low-veld, dust-dry and unforgiving as it is, which I have never lost.

Occasionally, both RSM Hallamore and RSM Muchinguri would be in camp, which certainly added a certain frisson to the routine. Informality was permitted – shorts, t-shirts, vellies and no headgear (to reduce the incidence of saluting) were de rigueur in summer – but slovenliness was not. Every time camp was made, a flagpole was erected somewhere central on a base made from an old 4.5 wheel rim, and the regimental flag was raised at day-break and lowered at sunset. After dusk and supper, the indistinct conversation of scattered groups of African soldiers was a comforting soundtrack to the dark.

The food was a distinct improvement on the fare at JOC Ft Vic. Gone were the days of feeling permanently hungry on food which seemed to take more energy to consume than it provided. Officers and NCOs maintained separate fridges of soft-drinks and beers. You could time with precision the arrival of a ration resupply, because a few days beforehand one of the subbies would be dispatched to the NCOs to negotiate the price of a "loan" of stock until repayment in kind could be made. The Fire Force pilots and crew had separate accommodation some distance from us. They had their own land-tail, and rumours were rife of the legendary secluded splendours in which they relaxed.

Visitors were frequent. Gen Walls flew in by PRAW one morning – we were at Bolo Ranch down towards the Limpopo – amongst other things to tear a strip off Maj Dennison of A Coy for breaching chain-of-command protocol in a complaint he had made, which had put several Salisbury noses out of joint. None of us were privy to the proceedings, but I somehow doubt Maj Dennison lost much sleep. There was the occasional journalist, domestic or foreign. The other companies were fairly regular visitors, either manning the Fire Force, or passing through on their way to or from deployments in the surrounding area.

If the TF prison officer was Eeyore, then Maj Morgan-Davies, OC Sp Coy, was Tigger. He would bounce down from his 2.5 and before the engine had stopped ticking was ensconced with a beer in the officers' marquee. There were any number of subbies (a simplicity of subalterns, the reference books say. I couldn't possibly comment…) their outward enthusiasm belying the difficult and dangerous job they did daily – sometime several times daily. The other extroverts stand out in my memory: Maj Hammond, Maj Dennison, 2 Lts Telfer and Vincent.

My immediate boss was the Adjutant, Capt Chris Bentley – one of the good guys. He was a stout man with jet black hair - from his part-Burmese ancestry, I think - the forelock of which he would continually twist around an index finger. Ex-British Army, with a low Sandhurst drawl and a mordant sense of humour, he possessed a large black dog of indeterminate parentage which took delight in dragging into camp the smelliest animal remains it could find in the surrounding bush.

On occasion Capt Bentley would spot Banje (after its full name, Chisambanje) as he emerged from the bush with cadaver in tow. Leaping up, he would chase after the dog, yelling "Banje! Banje!" in the same sort of anguished tone as Mick Jagger in "Angie". In vain. The disintegrating corpses inevitably ended up in Capt Bentley's tent on Capt Bentley's bed.

The war was a lot closer than at Ft Vic. Fire Forces would return with exhausted troops, for whom the catering staff somehow managed to provide food and drink. Aircraft were refuelled, re-armed and maintained on the small bush airstrips besides which we habitually made camp, although we were once based on a large granite kopje near Zimbabwe Ruins, where all the Alouettes managed to land, stuck to the curved bald surface like bees on a picnic apple. One day – bored as hell – we scoured the hut remains on that kopje with the Tac HQ mine detector, and came away with a treasure-trove of bangles and beads. Occasionally a body would be solemnly unloaded from one of the helicopters. It didn't happen often, but when it did it brought an immediate stillness to the encampment.

On occasion, even the TAC HQ personnel were deployed, on OPs or elsewhere. It wasn't on anything like the scale of what the line companies faced day after day. If nothing else, it made us feel a little better. But our bread and butter was the endless chain of duty-shifts in the Ops Room, and when there wasn't a night time radio shift, it was guard duty in one of the perimeter trenches.

It was always either stinking hot or brass-monkey cold under the canvas. Long hours of tedium could be relieved by digging into the "Top Secret" cabinet and reading its contents. Standing orders for an advance into Mozambique; Personnel records. Who cared about security clearance. Marking-up the new radio codes when they changed at midnight, keeping the previous day's codes available in case a call sign hadn't noticed the time. Perhaps a paper-back read by the dim light of the small battery-powered lights.

Pack upon pack of Madisons were smoked to the filter in that Ops Room and then stubbed out in capacious ashtrays made of expended rat-pack gas canisters. And then the hiss of the radios would be broken as a call-sign reported a sighting or a contact to his OC. File down, pencil and pad in hand, notes taken and locstats marked on the maps, before a decision was made as to whether to wake the Adjutant or CO. And then it was flat out until the aircraft had left and finally returned several hours later.

On one occasion, a BSAP PATU stick – middle-aged Police Reservists on call-up - radioed in around midnight. They had bumped into a far superior force near a kraal line in the pitch dark. The contact went on until dawn, when the Fire Force arrived to find the stick physically unhurt, and having accounted for a fair number of the enemy. But they were deeply shocked by their experience. The Fire Force was quite often despatched at first light to overnight calls such as this.

During daylight hours, the Ops Room was the central coordinating centre for the Fire Force, as well as the local clearing house for Fire Force requests. These local requests came in all shapes and forms, permission for which had to be cleared with Salisbury. More than once a helicopter was detached for a hot extraction from Mozambique. Comops were the final arbiter.

The main roads in Victoria Province were notorious for ambushes. One of the ranchers from near Ngundu Halt had painted a large heart around the bullet holes in the door of his bakkie. "From Russia, With Love" it said along a long pink Cupid's Arrow. Only a heartless pedant would have pointed out that the bullets in that area – a ZANLA area of operation - most probably came from China.

And then, no sooner had we fully settled down in one place than the order would come to strike camp and move on. Camouflage netting, which routinely got firmly entwined in the branches of the surrounding trees, had to be quickly removed from the tops of the trucks and packed away. Every tiny little thing had to be stowed away securely so it couldn't break or get lost, and then the trucks moved slowly through the bush until they could form up on the nearest road. Moving is almost as traumatic as divorce, they say. Not when you're young, but it was a chore we would happily have done without.

It was on one of these movements from camp to camp that the Ops Room got detached from the rest of the convoy. For some reason now lost to memory, a visit had to be made to the army camp - "Ulcer Gulch" it said on the sign at the entrance – at Rutenga. Once business was completed, the Ops Room, the cab containing Capt Bentley, a driver, and me riding shotgun, set off again in the rapidly disappearing light. It wasn't long before it became apparent that we were not precisely sure down which bush track the rest of the convoy had disappeared.

Capt Bentley pushed himself up through the manhole in the top of the cab and navigated from there, shouting barely-heard instructions down to the driver, with the map he was holding repeatedly blowing up into his face, which in turn brought about some of the most extended strings of expletives I have ever had the pleasure of hearing. Many smirks were exchanged within the cab. After much agonisingly slow driving on the untended sand roads, where, in the dark, the surrounding sparse bush appears to be composed of a solid wall of vegetation of staggering height, we did find everyone else.

One of the upsides in arriving late is that the hard work of raising tents, digging trenches and erecting the rest of the infrastructure is already mostly done. One of the downsides … actually, there are no downsides. Better late. We were in good time for supper, which the enterprising catering Sergeant had been cooking on the back of a 4.5 during the journey. A splendid Sunday evening meal, a real treat, with ice-cream – Ice-Cream! – for dessert. And then Capt Bentley uttered a phrase which I don't think he was ever allowed to forget. As his plate was served in front of him, he cried: "What! Beef Wellington? Again?!!"

THE CO'S NEW STAFF CAR by Captain Tony Clark

In November 1978 we received notification at Bn HQ that we were to receive two new officers posted to 1 RAR: Lt Willard Fleetwood (to A Coy) and Lt Dave Hill (to D Coy) both had served in the United States Forces. They were to arrive on the evening train at Bulawayo station and plans were made that Maj Wayne Thompson (OC Rear) and I (Adjt Rear) would meet them and bring them back to the Officers' Mess for dinner and pack them into their respective beds. Introduction to Methuen Barracks was planned for after breakfast the next day. We had taken delivery of the CO's (Col McKenna's) new staff car, a larny cream-coloured Peugeot 404 the previous day and, as the CO was at Wankie Main, he told us not to send it as he was soon on R&R and would collect the vehicle.

We arrived in good time at the station and Maj T chose to park on a centre parking. We then met the train and introduced ourselves to Willard, Dave and Dave s lovely Vietnamese wife Ky San. Maj T told me to get the vehicle whilst he helped the Yanks with their luggage. I checked the car park but could not see any sign of the Peugeot; after ten minutes of frantic search I located it …downhill from where we parked, with its left front headlight trying to eat a brick wall. I shat myself and firmly believed that it would have been better if it had been stolen. I knew that I would be blamed for the damage as Maj T would have left the vehicle parked and in good order. To make matters even more kuk, the CO was due back in two days!

I joined the team and reported the damage to Maj T who reacted as anticipated asking "What I had hit?"!!

Without further incident we got to the Mess and Maj T immediately phoned Capt Ronny Harrison our MTO.

At 05h00 the next morning the CO's new car was at Harrison's office who immediately whisked it away to a specialist panel beater friend in Bulawayo. The repair and paint job took less than 48 hours and, on his return from the bush, Colonel McKenna took over the keys of his brand new (second hand) Staff Car. We never had the guts to tell him the story and Ronny Harrison was threatened with his life!

THE DAY MY LIFE CHANGED by Major Gavin Rawstron

It was during Mar/April 1979 that B Coy 1 RAR were occupying the abandoned hotel at Birchenough Bridge. I was Company Commander at the time and had just completed giving orders for an operation destined for the following day. I had retreated to my room and was sitting on my stretcher going over some of the issues that we were possibly going to face. There was an uneasy feeling in my stomach which was quite normal prior to an operation, but this time it would not go away. No matter how hard I tried to ignore it, it remained.

I eventually reached for a small Gideon's Bible which I carried in my denims side pocket but never opened. I took a deep breath and opened it randomly on Psalm 27:1 which read:

'The Lord is my light and my salvation; whom shall I fear? The Lord is the strength of my life; of whom shall I be afraid?

'Though an host encamp against me, my heart shall not fear: though war should rise against me, in this will I be confident.

'And now shall mine head be lifted up above mine enemies round about me; therefore will I offer in His Tabernacle sacrifices of joy; I will sing, yea, I will sing praises unto The Lord.'

One must understand that I was not a follower but had always believed and that when Bibles were handed out they were for everyone else, not me.

For the first time ever, The Word became ALIVE and I really believed The Lord was talking to me...and I wept! Not because of my fears, but because The Lord had revealed Himself to me for the first time.

Imagine now, if one of my subbies or fellow soldiers entered my room, they would have second thoughts about the operation the following day. That was enough to snap me out of it. I was suddenly overcome with a sense of joy, lay down and fell into a deep sleep.

From that day on, my life changed. I believe I became a better man. It was never easy as there were major issues in my life that had to be dealt with. I am still "Work in progress" 40 years later with no regrets. The Lord Jesus still my guide.

A MEASURE OF THE MAN by Major Tom Fulton

I returned, on cycle for duty at the Sub JOC in Fort Victoria and, being already familiar with the routines, was quickly immersed in the conduct of the war.

One of the personalities of the Battalion Headquarters was the Regimental Signals Instructor (RSI), who was basically a 2ic to the Regimental Signals Officer. In the case of 1RAR, the appointment took the form of one Staff Sergeant

Bernie Le Roux. Le Roux was a rangy, wiry sort, with a shock of almost-blonde hair and a preposterously thick pair of black-rimmed glasses. Judging by the standard of the signallers at sub unit level, he and the RSO were doing a very fine job indeed.

The RSI was likeable but largely an unknown quantity to me as he went about his signals business and seldom needed to make any personal contact with me. I was therefore more than happy to accept an invitation to drinks at the WOs and Sgts Mess that Friday night.

Excusing myself early from the Officer's Mess Prayer Meeting, I arrived at the WOs and Sgts Mess around 10 'o clock. SSgt Le Roux introduced me to the attendant crowd, who comprised mostly Signals Corps personnel. I recognised Sergeant Major Tom St Dare, who had been one of my instructors on my Cadet Course Signals Course. Staff Sergeant Dickie Munckton was perhaps one of the Rhodesian Army's most colourful characters. He wore the same campaign ribbons as my father from the Second World War and apparently held some sort of record for the number of times he had been reduced in rank. He stood about five six in his shoes, and his reddish-grey handlebar moustache was of Jimmy Edwards's proportions, playing dangerously close to encroaching on military regulations.

Perhaps the most colourful story was of when he was stationed at KGVI Barracks, and at constant odds with the RSM. The RSM was a keen bowler and the Sgts Mess boasted a bowling green that was the constant source of pride to the RSM. Their manicured finish appealed to his military eye, as did anything orderly and in straight lines.

After a particularly venomous exchange with the RSM, which included a substantial addition to the long line of extra duties he was already doing, Dickie decided that enough was enough – he would hit back where it hurt. He took firm hold of the handle of the bowling green's perforator – a roller modified with spikes for the purpose of aerating the turf – and drew it diagonally across the pristine greens. Reaching into his pocket, he drew a fistful of maize seed. Getting on all fours, he dropped a single maize seed in each hole, carefully pressing the mouth of the hole closed with his fingers to disguise its presence (and guaranteeing its germination in the humidity below!).

Of infinitely more interest to me than devastated bowling greens was the presence of a half a dozen ladies from the RWS. The Signals Corps needed Cypher Operators in the forward bases and I had to admit they were a very refreshing diversion from what was normally all-male company. Summing it up in my mind I thought, this is an interesting hormonal mix indeed. The pheromones are buzzing, the testosterone is exposed in the bravado. Can't see the evening following any dreary course!

No sooner had the thought left my head, when Sar'major Tom St Dare declared suddenly and brazenly, "Sir. I'll bet you a crate of beer that I've got a bigger dick than you."

The attendant girls steadied their tittering in anticipation of my reply. My mind was racing as I sought through the archives of my normally acute repartee. My immediate problem was it was imperative that I stand up to the bombast, without departing from the decorum expected of an officer. I admitted to myself that if one considered the confidence of the Sar'major, perhaps his 'tweeds' were the lair of a lurking serpent of leviathan proportions? I simply had to think of a deft side step, but that wasn't easy without being clumsy.

"That's a rather ridiculous thing to say Sar'major, especially since you haven't had the experience of seeing me in the shower. Let's just say that if your dick is as big as you're full of shit, you'll beat me hands down." The audience laughed rather dutifully, but the matter was in a relieving, but temporary abeyance.

The side step had been clumsy, and everybody knew it.

I took the opportunity to chat to the walrus moustachioed Dickie Monckton, and was delighted to hear that he had known my late father, who was also in the Signals Corps. They had served together in the Western desert and Italy during the Second World War, along with RSM Snowy Hubbard, also a signals corpsman. As the conversation was warming, we were interrupted my Sar'major St Dare once more. "Sir, I'll bet you that same crate, that even Staff Le Roux has a bigger dick than you."

I looked over at Staff Le Roux, regarding him carefully with a little masculine arrogance. I then inquired, "Are you into this shit, Staff? Do you REALLY think that you have a bigger dick than me? Or are you, like the Sar'major, and just dying to see MY dick?"

This remark elicited a big laugh again from the attendant girls, but were hushed by a persistent Le Roux, who declared: "It's still one crate of beer Sir. If you still think you've got it."

This time the mirth was at my expense and I reluctantly played my last card. "OK Staff. Let's see what you've got."

It was probable that nobody present expected, for one minute that I would expose myself, but Le Roux's bravado had truly sunk me. Now all that remained was for Le Roux to do the deed. That Le Roux was a showman was left in no doubt when he began to theatrically, and slowly, undo his fly buttons. Completely, if not altogether unnecessarily undoing his entire waistband ensemble, stable belt, and all. Holding down the waistband of his underpants with his left hand, Staff Sergeant Bernie Le Roux delved with his right. With a suspiciously practiced and dexterous flick of his wrist, he produced a venous monster that made everybody in the audiences' jaw drop. I likened it in appearance to a six month old baby's arm holding a Granny Smith apple. I made a mental comparison with my own equipment, and concluded that mine was perhaps little larger than the bulbous, rope-like vein that graced the top of his manhood – that fed and sustained Bernie Le Roux's appendage…a separate, living entity.

OF SUN TAN LOTION AND MINCED MEAT by Captain Andy Barrett

While awaiting a Fire Force call-out, all the Fire Force call-signs would invariably hang out around the self-made swimming pool within the camp – eight 44 gallon Avtur drums placed into a square and then lined by a fuel bladder. This kept morale high as the lads kept wet and cool trying to evade the intense Beit Bridge heat as they chatted, teased each other, smoked their Madison and drank large volumes of jungle juice. The craze was to catch rays to the maximum so that one appeared heavily bronzed by the next R&R. In order to accelerate this process a 1(Indep) sun tan lotion was formulated consisting of equal parts of Olivine cooking oil, vehicle brake fluid and household vinegar. Believe me, as weird and harsh as it may appear, it did the job magnificently.

Minced Meat Night, November 1978: The OC Major Don Price shot an eland and a wildebeest as rations for the camp. There was more than enough meat for the entire camp, plus more, so a large quantity was taken to the SB house of Ed 'Nyoni' Bird and Brian Perkins in Beit Bridge where a few of us firstly cut the meat into cubes followed by manually mincing this mountainous volume of game meat to produce sausage.

Loud music from Boney M's *Rivers of Babylon* (1978), *Brown Girl In The Ring* (1978), *Ma Baker* (1977), *Daddy Cool* (1976) and *Rasputin* (1978); *Buccaneer* (1978) by the McCully Workshop, Pussycat's depressing and mournful *Mississippi* (1976) and *Georgie* (1978), *Barracuda* (1977) by Heart, *Walking On A Love Cloud* (1976) sung by 5000 Volts, plus the likes of Leroy Gomez with Santa Esmeralda's energetic *Don't Let Me Be Misunderstood* (1977), thumped and vibrated furiously through the establishment as the fast rotating overhead fan blades, sounding like those of the Alouette, attempted to cool the intense heat of the Beit Bridge air, simultaneously trying to rid the room of moths, mosquitoes and stick insects.

Extensive lengths of game meat sausage of various flavours, beer, rum, cane spirits, Coca-Cola and vodka, were manufactured only then to be cooked and eaten to sample the final product. After several hours of this practice with bellies on the verge of exploding, not much of the meat had been minced although so it appeared anyway. It was the phenomenal volume available that created that impression.

Subsequently, all and sundry commenced to throw hands-full of raw meat at each other and into the overhead fans, dispersing meat in every conceivable direction, only to strike and splatter across the windows, doors, walls, floor, participants, cupboards and fridge etc. It could well have been a scene taken from Tobe Hooper's 1974 movie production of The Texas Chainsaw Massacre, as the room was in such a bloody, hideous and frightful mess. The establishment was later cleaned, and the dispersed game meat cooked and fed to the pets, both at the SB house and those at camp.

BINGA FISHING CAPERS by Lieutenant Michael Matthews

As we know, army life (outside of R&R) wasn't always all work and no play, and an ultimately aborted fishing sojourn at Binga was no exception...

Late in 1977 as I recall, 3 Platoon, A Coy 1RAR had reason to be in Binga for a day and night, and it was here that I met up with my friend Simon Todd. Simon was on OSBY with me and, being a degreed engineer, it came as no surprise that he was commissioned into the Engineer Corps and was at that stage responsible for seeing to all things mechanical at Binga, especially one or two 'Rhodesian Navy' craft.

Eschewing our FN's for fishing rods, we determined to try our hand at some fishing since there was some down time available to us, and Simon managed to source two rods, some tackle, and a tin of juicy worms which we hoped the resident bream/chessa/nkupe/barbel would find difficult to resist. Simon had the use of a Hyena and, feeling lazy, decided that we should use his transport to make our way down to and along the nearby long, narrow, causeway running out into the Southern reaches of Lake Kariba.

The causeway was little wider than a jeep track, with a sharp drop off into the water on both sides and it soon enough became apparent to Simon, already three quarters of the way along the causeway, that the return journey could be a bit tricky, since there was insufficient room to make a turn at the end. He thus decided that at this late stage we should reverse back to the 'mainland' and I climbed to the back of the Hyena to guide us.

Simon commenced his reversing manoeuvre, and all seemed to be going quite well, when the rear left wheel started to leave the jeep track. Seemingly oblivious to my vain screams, Simon proceeded on his new and ill-advised path with gusto. Inevitably, the Hyena listed over to the left and the sheer weight of the rear pulled this decidedly non-amphibian vehicle into the murky depths.

With roll bars above me I couldn't throw myself clear of a vehicle which was clearly now making its own arrangements, and I held my breath in anticipation of taking an inevitable but unexpected dip. I guess that the water was about 8-10 foot deep, and I quickly enough came up spluttering and looked around for Simon who was nowhere to be seen amongst all the rising bubbles emanating from the now fully submerged Hyena.

Whilst my troops were all laughing their heads off at our misfortune (being the highly empathetic bunch they were!) I personally shat myself, thinking Simon to be trapped behind the wheel and swam toward where I thought he should have surfaced. As I was making ready to dive down to grope around for him in the murky depths, he surfaced. No panic for Simon, just a broad grin as he held a tin aloft and proudly announced, "I saved the worms!" I don't think that I've ever laughed as much as I did then. What a clown!

Our trusty Four-Five was eventually able to extricate the stricken Hyena with the help of my able *Masodja* and, amazingly, the Hyena spluttered back to life after the engine and its components got a good dry off and some sun. The recovery process took quite some time so, regrettably, fish wasn't on the menu that night.

MBAMBO by Lieutenant Peter Baxter

In October/November 1980 A Company 3 RAR was deployed to the Gatooma Hartley area to do road blocks and general patrolling.

1,2 and 3 platoons were all assigned different areas to patrol and to spring surprise roadblocks to curb the newly unrestricted ZIPRA cadres from wending their way willy-nilly up to Salisbury to scout out their ZANLA opposition and to sum up how much of a threat the ZANLA cadres actually were.

My platoon, 2 Platoon got the main stretch of road between Gatooma and Hartley. The weather was miserable, rain, thundershowers, rivers flooding and all the mayhem that goes with that.

One morning in my 75 MAP I noted that we had a new addition to the platoon. It was a tiny blue vervet monkey that Lance Corporal Mbambo, one of my stick leaders, had fished out of one of the flooding rivers that we had camped next to. The new recruit was duly given his rescuer's name, Mbambo, and had a belt added around his waist with a piece of rope that dangled from it so that he could be controlled if need be.

The endless roadblocks and patrols came to an end in mid-November and we returned to Inyanga our Company base.

Mbambo, the new recruit, had in the meantime become an instant hit with the troops and he grew up very quickly in the company of the RAR soldiers. I am sure that he gleaned 99% of his mischievousness from his RAR teachers. He soon learned who to sit with on the back of the 75 whilst it lunged its way perilously down the narrow Rhodesian roads back to Inyanga, who would feed him and with whom he was safe to sleep at night.

When we got back to Inyanga I duly had a leather stable belt made for him onto which his leash was tied. He was a member of the platoon now.

He settled in to base life in the first week but then he started to go AWOL. He would disappear for a few hours and then arrive back for food and TLC from his RAR troopers. This went on for a few days and he endeared himself to the Admin Staff at the offices.

Mbambo was a feature at the base for a few weeks, but, he AWOLLED more and more and became a pest.

His favourite trick was to escape and race down to the Officers' Mess where he would terrorise Shadrack the Barman and Lovemore the Waiter and try to steal the bottles of marmalade and jam off the table in the dining room.

Mbambo's final parting gift before he AWOLLED for good was his final escape from Lance Corporal Mbambo's care and his foray into the Officers' Mess where he wreaked havoc in the extreme. He raced into the Mess to be confronted by Shadrack the barman waving the mop at him to chase him out. Mbambo leapt onto the back display of the bar counter and a few bottles of liqueur and spirts were dislodged as he tried to escape Shadrack's mop. The liqueur and spirits bottles shattered on the floor.

Meanwhile Lovemore in the kitchen had figured out that something was amiss by the sounds of the smashing bottles and he came in to help Shadrack, armed with a broom.

Mbambo (the monkey) meanwhile decided that discretion was the better part of valour and retreated to the trees up the hill away from the Officers' Mess. Shadrack and Lovemore withdrew to the Mess to clean up the mess that Mbambo had made.

About an hour later, Lovemore was arisen from his lunchtime siesta in his chair outside the kitchen by the sound of more breaking glass. He raced into the Mess to find Mbambo under the dining room table. Mbambo had grown tired of trying to get one bottle of marmalade or jam open at a time so he had pulled the whole table cloth with all the bottles of marmalade, strawberry jam, syrup and other condiments on to the floor and he was eating as much of it as fast as he could.

Lovemore aimed a few blows at him with his broom and, after about five tries, connected with a body blow. Mbambo then decided that retreat was the answer on that day and escaped before Shadrack could join in to club him into submission. Mbambo was then gone. He had AWOLLED forever, obviously disgusted at the fact that Lovemore had given him a good klap.

Lovemore and Shadrack cleaned up the mess under the table and, when I arrived back that night from a local deployment, Lovemore, with his incredibly enchanting laugh and illuminating smile told me about the whole event. I was sitting at the bar with him and Shadrack telling me and playing out their roles as to how they had had to deal with the marauder. It was hilarious. Their descriptions, as only Rhodesian Africans mimic and describe things, had me in fits of laughter.

Lovemore was so engaged in his portrayal that his gleaming smile, his big white teeth and the tears of mirth that rolled out of his eyes are a sight that I will not forget to this day. No photograph could portray or do justice to that image of Lovemore and his smile and tears in my mind.

The next day they explained all the goings on to the Camp Commandant WO2 George Moffat and to Sergeant Gretchen the base chef. They too were in hysterics about it.

The final straw was when the Admin clerk asked me if I could sign Mbambo's AWOL discharge document because the little bugger had not come back. "Ishe" he said "Recruit Mbambo has AWOLLED again. This is his last time."

That was the story of Mbambo. He was a lucky little blue vervet monkey that was fished out of a river from an untimely death to become a part of 2 Platoon A Company 3rd Battalion Rhodesian African Rifles folklore.

GOLD BRAID AND PRESSED HAM by Major Tom Fulton
(Adapted by the author from Into the Vortex)

During my time as MIO of 1 Brigade, my opposite number, with the Grade III staff officer portfolio for Operations was Captain Athol Alistair Gillespie (RAR), or Guiseppe as he was universally known. Without peer in the field of practical joking, there was nothing sacred to the man. Whilst his reputation bordered on legendary, it seemed that he was able to get away with things that would have had us mere mortals facing the austere wrath of the unforgiving military discipline system.

Charitably sharing finely sliced biltong with me that he had stolen from the hallowed precincts of the BM's desk, Major Butch Duncan (RAR) was one such prank. Feeding me the delicacy whilst knowing the BM would appear at any time, and then making himself scarce was a typical Guiseppe move. Only weeks later, just as a meeting from Comops was about to break for lunch, Guiseppe, showing the timing of a maestro, had placed the heavily gold-braided hat of the Chief of Staff (Administration) Major General Sandy McLean (RAR) on my head, just as that distinguished gentleman was leaving the Ops Room. Without a trace of a smile, the General had retrieved his heavy, gold encrusted hat and said drily, "Be a long time before you wear one of these, young man," and added unkindly, "If ever." (I couldn't help musing listlessly, what a 20-year Lieutenant's Pay Scale looked like.)

These, and many other lesser events of varying hilarity (thankfully not always involving me!) had earned him a fierce reputation, and if I the truth be told, kept everybody remotely in his sphere of influence, on a constant diligent vigil against any unsolicited surprises.

Intelligence indicated a substantial ZIPRA build up in the area of a place in Zambia called Kabanga Mission. Preparations were made for an attack to be mounted on the camp, and I went about the frenetic preparations for the presentation of the intelligence at hand, when the time came.

I tasked the few men with the necessary Top-Secret clearance, in the RIC Mapping Section to produce an enlarged map for me, and they blew my socks off with the end result. Each grid square of a 1:50 000 map was blow up to the size of a bread plate, and the map covered the exact extent of the roller mounted map in the Tangent Ops Room. Only unchangeable physical features from the UTM map were depicted. Intimate detail from recent aerial photographs provided detail of individual trenches, anti-aircraft emplacements and non-permanent bashas, slap-dash adobe buildings and tents. With my comprehensively rehearsed narrative, and this jaw-dropping aid, I would in turn, blow Comops' socks off!

The seating had been labelled with stencilled cards, and the BM had personally sited these with his better cognisance of the protocols involved. At his insistence, the surrounding Brigade map coverage was covered with linen so that all attention was directed at the central map, mounted on coasters. A group of cleaners added the first coat of polish to the floor since the Matabele Uprising, and a nervously blinking neon light was replaced. The finesse of the School of Infantry training was evident in the overall air of showmanship, and everyone involved, was gripped by the big-match nerves of an opening theatrical performance.

To round it off, the Mapping Section also produced a full-colour handout of the scaled down, but intimately detailed map of the target for each visitor – although these were for local reference during the conference, their security classification making it necessary to retrieve them.

The chronology of the day's presentations was a kick-off introduction by the BM who outlined the ZIPRA problem, went through the programme, before introducing my intelligence briefing. Guiseppe's office was behind the audience and in the stage left, back of the room. A 1m long by ,75m window allowed panoramic vision of the interior of the Ops Room and, was neatly finished with well fitted GS curtains on slick metal runners.

We had heard the BM's spiel before, and I knew when my cue was near. Guiseppe and I had been covertly watching the briefing from a modest crack in the curtains, a fish-eye lens effect, made the entire room visible.

On cue, I entered the Ops Room with my senior clerk, Corporal Plonks van der Horn, and we turned the roller-mounted map board through 180 degrees. It may well have been my imagination, but I thought I heard a gasp – I wasn't in the least bit surprised.

I went on with my presentation, acutely aware that I faced the entire Command and Planning element of Combined Operations Headquarters. Lieutenant General Peter Walls, Air Marshall Frank Mussel, Major General Bertie Barnard (RAR), the Police Commissioner, P. K. Allum, and spy-boss Ken Flower were amongst the audience. I was extremely confident in my subject, so that when the time for questions arose, I felt a bit like the proverbial batsman on 99, but undaunted, I fielded the inquiries as best I could.

It was only then, that my peripheral vision picked up some movement from Guiseppe's window. He had wrenched the curtains open, almost to their full extent. I watched in incredulous, fascinated horror, as Guiseppe began to undo the buttons of his fly. I watched with increasing disbelief as he took hold his manhood at its base, and encompassing his hairy testicles in a broad grip, he pushed the obscene ensemble up against the glass of the window.

The visual effect of the compressed privates, I could liken to a flesh coloured rose, the foreskin forming the petals...no, it was more like a pressed ham. It was all I could do to suppress the laughter that was slowly and uncontrollably welling up from the base of my abdomen. Trying to avert my eyes, I failed dismally, and by the nonchalant expression on his face, seemed as though his lips would purse into a nonplussed whistle of contentment – almost as though he were taking an unhindered pee?

In a quite hopeless endeavour to mask the explosive laugh which lay just below the surface of my very being, I broke into a paroxysm of feigned coughing. The audience included such austere persons as Brian Robinson, the SAS commander and Butch Duncan, neither men particularly famous for their joviality or senses of humour, and I was convinced that my career had gone from a peak to the abyss, in one simple manoeuvre.

With uncontrolled tears streaming down my cheeks, my only saving grace was that my briefing was complete, and I was able to gain enough composure to beg my leave and take my pathetically convulsing body from the room.

Being the next person to address the meeting, Guiseppe and I crossed paths as I was leaving my door. This isn't over, I'm going to get you, you swine, I mumbled as we passed each other.

I went straight into Guiseppe's office, already wracking my brains for a suitable riposte. It was obvious that in order to have anywhere near the required impact, I would have to exceed the set, and already considerable bounds of outrageousness.

With the G Branch clerks away temporarily for tea, the foyer of the Ops Room was deserted. Standing by the closed door to the presentation, I made the preparations to give Guiseppe A Jumbo. A Jumbo involved the dangling of one's penis from the fly, whilst simultaneously pulling out ones trouser pockets, and wiggling ones bum for effect. (This was supposed to emulate an elephant's trunk and ears – it was a very common party trick, at the time).

In the long journey through life, in my case, although not exclusively, I have experienced many instances of absolute grace under pressure. (Des Passaportis used to laugh at other men's discomfiture under heavy enemy fire – as if it was as commonplace as a light drizzle!) Hemingway's characters were all capable of this, but never have I witnessed it to so infinite a point.

Guiseppe's face never altered an iota, as he looked into my face and brazenly enquired simply, but loudly, Yes Tom?

My reaction was puff adder quick as my hand flew up like lightning and pulled the door to. Sometimes one must simply concede defeat...I was no match and would never be.

CHANGING TIMES by Major Jim Hill

Part One: Personal Weapons Handling

As the Rhodesian war rolled on and pressures, both political and military, grew, the need to expand the Regular Army to meet not only the war needs, but to bolster a Territorial Force that was rapidly declining in strength due to emigration, was recognised. Obviously, the only available potential source of manpower lay within the black Rhodesian population and, equally obvious, the most effective way to rapidly create a viable unit was to build on an existing one – the RAR. With two Battalions already in effective action, 3RAR was initiated by utilising the basis of the Independent Companies that had previously been the initial posting for National Service infantrymen in addition to the resources of 1 and 2 RAR.

The Independent Companies were a rather strange concept for an Army but they had served Rhodesia very well and had proved to be effective military units. The strangeness came from the fact that they were stand-alone units and that they operated on their own coming, most of the time, under the direct command of their respective Brigade Headquarters. They were manned, at the beginning of each NS

Intake's service, by completely raw troops commanded by equally raw Platoon Commanders and NCOs. By the time the "Indep" phase of NS was complete the troops were experienced soldiers who had, usually, transformed from boys to men and had become a real asset to the Unit. Then they would be posted out en masse to various units around the country and the Indep company process would begin again with the next intake of NS personnel. It made life for the Regulars in the unit more than a little awkward and so, with each intake's arrival, a period of close scrutiny was entered into.

The arrival of the first intake of integrated troops was anticipated with some trepidation as we had been given very little background concerning these men and rumours were rife. Their training had been reduced, they were conscripts with very poor morale and on and on. Brigade and Army responses to queries were poor and lacked detail indicating to those concerned that senior staff did not really know what was going on. We would have to grin and bear it relying on our own judgement to overcome and prevail.

It was with great relief that we discovered that the worst of the rumours were all unfounded. Arriving with the men was a RAR CSM to provide a Regimental link and discipline to men who had no unit background or sense of belonging. Working hand in hand with the European CSM the ACSM would prove to be a valuable and vital asset in our drive to create an effective fighting force. A detailed debrief of the ACSM gave an insight into the training of this group of new men, who they were and what they were like. It was not a completely inspiring insight and an assessment/training programme was rapidly drawn up.

Drill, weapon handling, basic action drills were all fine and the two CSMs, backed by keen Platoon Commanders and Platoon Sergeants all anxious to, themselves, learn, rapidly polished rough edges. Range work, however, was another story! Shooting could best be described as adequate – in other words, not nearly good enough for combat situations so the local range was booked solid for quite a while. It was probably advantageous to me, as OC of 5 (Indep), to have a solid RAR presence in Brigade Headquarters starting with Brigadier Peter Hoskings as the Brigade Commander, Colonel Eric Sobey as Deputy and Major Terry Leaver commanding 6 (Indep), our sister company who we shared Addams Barracks with. With Brigade support, our requests for extra training ammunition and stores were attended to rapidly and we were able to keep all men not on standby very actively occupied.

Whilst a Platoon Commander in 1 RAR I had trained my men to shoot low and had devised a scoring system for certain types of exercise where only ricochets counted. Lt Theo Williams had recounted to me after his first contact that his men had, generally, fired very high when they were initially fired on and so I tried to ensure that my men would shoot low. Jungle lanes using only Figure 12 targets at ground level or Figure 11s laid on their sides, detect and kill shoots where targets were hidden and troops had to identify and "kill" them.

It was the latter that gave the two CSMs and myself the biggest headaches. These new soldiers did not seem capable of holding their weapons correctly if they were not on a formal range and they certainly did not control their fire. I went to see the Brigade Deputy Commander who took me to see the Commander. He phoned someone he knew in Services at Army and, two days later, we took delivery of 25 No 5 Jungle Carbine Rifles and about 5000 rounds of their 303 ammunition. (My year at Army HQ had some benefits).

The strategy was simple. Each time someone was seen to be firing his FN incorrectly he was given a 303 and 20 rounds to use on the shoot. It usually took about 3 or 4 rounds before he could be seen to be firming his grip up and starting to really look for the targets. He became, literally, painfully aware of the need to hold his weapon correctly and only use one round where appropriate.

The first 'victim' of this remedial action turned to me the next day, when we were back on the range, and I offered him the use, again, of the 303 and asked, "Sir, how did the British fight a whole war with these weapons?" As I remember it now, the strategy was very effective although, unfortunately, the men did not see very much use for their improved weapon handling in action.

Part Two: Support Weapons, Maintaining Awareness and Lack of Coordination

Three Independent Companies operated in the Op Thrasher area in addition to various TA units and, of course, the Grand Reef Fire Force manned by RLI and, from time to time RAR. 3 (Indep) was based at Inyanga and 5 and 6 were based at Addams Barracks in Umtali. The three companies covered the Inyanga, Umtali and Chipinga areas by rotating to cover R&R periods but, in the main, 5 and 6 served Umtali and Chipinga. At times JOC Chipinga would be run by 8RR, I seem to remember, and then, usually, the Indep company would be based somewhere around Melsetter.

5 (Indep) was occupying an abandoned farm house just off the main road between Melsetter and Chipinga near a pass called Skyline Junction. Operations, as usual in that part of the world, seemed to be encompassed by the words of that great song, "Climb every mountain, ford every stream" but the dream was extremely elusive and it was boring, tiring work for the troops. Providing interesting variations to the routine was required to maintain morale and motivation on the part of the men.

We had several 60mm commando mortars on our books but they were usually only to be found strategically placed around our base area where they could be handled by the regular members of the unit experienced in their use. The almost total lack of knowledge about and lack of experience with these weapons amongst our young AS was obviously not ideal and neither was their general lack of awareness in the field. Unlike their brethren in the two RAR battalions, many of these young men had originated in the towns and cities of Rhodesia and they had not lived a life in the bush. A boredom busting informational training session was planned for them and I made a trip to the nearest Engineer squadron.

A morning was given over to demonstrating the construction of booby traps using ready to hand materials and much amusement was derived from the efforts being made to cut bottles with indented bottoms using string and paraffin, dent bully beef tins into shaped charge moulds and the like. Much less amusement but great interest came from creating activation switches from clothes pegs and twigs and a degree of trepidation came with preparing the charges to resemble mini claymores. Various store rooms and tactical sites were set up with booby traps that were activated to engage preplaced targets and the enthusiastic response to each successful explosion was gratifying. A successful training session that had each man thinking before he entered the empty houses/ huts/stores that were abundant throughout the area of operation.

Inter service communication in the field was not always what it should have been and a particularly obtuse BSAP Member-in-Charge who, seemingly, felt cheated of his command 'glory' by having an Army unit based in his territory, led to the local community remaining completely unaware of our activities. As far as we were concerned the area around our base camp, to a radius of approximately five kilometres, was unoccupied by civilians and, to all intents and purposes, no go for them. We were always kept informed by the Forestry companies of their activities and, indeed, we used that information on occasions to determine our own activities. So, it was with confidence that a 60mm mortar informational training session was organised in the area of our base one late afternoon.

The CSMs gave a presentation to remind the men of what they had learned on recruit training and then firing commenced. A mortar bomb detonating 200m from one's position gives a very satisfying burst of smoke, dust and debris without being overly threatening but one landing, as it would when fired defensively in close support, is another story. The cockiest volunteer chosen to fire onto a predetermined target area some 50m outside our perimeter fence was given a smoke bomb (rather than the real life HE) and reminded, just he was about to insert the bomb into the tube, to think about the wind which was blowing towards the base. Cocky volunteer realigned his aim a tad and released the bomb, which, on charge 0, headed skywards slowly enough to be observed by the now exceedingly nervous gallery lurking in their covered positions. Up, up, up went the little projectile before it arced over and plummeted earthwards – seemingly straight towards our base plate position!

"Bloggs (not his real name but see my anecdote on recruit training in CM1), you F*!"%^£**g A%^$&hole, you didn't allow enough for the wind!" (or words to that effect) were the kindest comment from Bloggs', no longer, mates. Anyway, Bloggs had allowed enough windage and his bomb landed smack on the target much to the relief of all his, once again, mates.

A now increasingly confident surge of volunteers raised hands for the next task – to mortar our night standing patrol position about 150m away from the base.

A road led down into the nearby valley and provided an easy, completely covered approach close to our base so we established a night time OP in an outcrop of rocks that covered the road. Each night, after dark, an early warning patrol equipped with night vision equipment would be deployed there. This position was designated a target in our defensive fire plan as it dominated the base and the mortar exercise would allow us to place accurate aiming marks.

Volunteer No 1 placed his HE bomb a little off target so, after a public debrief about the need to keep one's eyes open and not cringe when dropping the bomb down the tube, volunteer No 2 took over. To this day, I do not know why I changed his round to Smoke rather than HE but it was a fortuitous decision.

We had a pair of sentries watching the main road which ran past the base and they warned of an approaching vehicle but that should not have been an issue and, in expectation of that vehicle continuing past us on its way to Chipinga, I gave the order to fire. It was with shock and horror that, as we watched the bomb arcing its way upwards, I realised that the vehicle had turned onto the road we were now mortaring. "Medic! Get going!" and the ambulance was leaving the gate as the bomb turned earthwards – the medic had come to the same conclusion as myself and was moving before I spoke.

A blast of smoke erupted from the perfectly hit target as the vehicle was about 25m away from it and, with the wind blowing as it was, enveloped the vehicle almost immediately and completely obscured it. The medic was the first on the scene and he emerged, bewildered, from the smoke to shout that there was no vehicle! Then, for a minute or two, came the sound of a wildly revving engine from the road below and then silence. A 2.5 despatched with a search party headed down into the valley and returned some two hours later in the dark having failed to find any vehicle.

The obtuse BSAP Member-in-Charge was not amused at being roused from his beer to be told that someone unknown had been placed in a dangerous position by being where he shouldn't have been and was missing. It was never discovered just who the driver was (the sentries confirmed it was a white man driving a pick-up so it was probably a local farmer) and supposition was that he was probably on his way clandestinely to see what was available on a nearby farm that had been abandoned about a month earlier.

Communication and precautions! Both important and both probably neglected more than they should have been in many instances during our war.

SLEEPING WITH THE ENEMY by Corporal Alan Doyle

Everyone knows about the regular RAR battalions: 1RAR, 2RAR, and later on 3RAR. Slightly less well known are the Independent RAR Companies, dating from late 1977 when national servicemen and regular RAR soldiers were integrated into the same units, rebadged from Rhodesia Regiment to Rhodesian African Rifles. (In fact, 3RAR was formed around the nucleus of 3 (Indep), 5 (Indep) and 6 (Indep) along the eastern border of the country.)

Elements of C Coy 6RR leaving Essexvale Battle Camp (image courtesy John Hopkins)

But often forgotten are the RAR soldiers who served full-time in the part-time territorial battalions. At one stage - not long after Frelimo became the government of Mozambique and the whole south-eastern border opened up to ZANLA infiltration - territorials were being called up for indefinite service. A large expansion in the training of regular RAR troops was started to deal with this shortage of manpower in all parts of the army. Regular RAR soldiers, trained at Depot RAR in Balla Balla, joined the eight territorial Rhodesia Regiment battalions in late 1977, shortly before the first RAR soldiers joined the Independent Companies.

It must have been a difficult experience for them.

As the RAR troops joined, the territorials' call-up commitment was reduced to six-weeks-in/six-weeks-out. So the regular RAR were having to get used to one half of the territorial strength of the battalion in one six-week period, and the other half in the next, with ten days R&R and a short battle-camp to get the territorials back up to speed in between. The fact that they were badged RAR while the territorials remained RR could not have helped. By the end of the war, 68 of these RAR soldiers had given their lives while serving with the territorial battalions.

I finished my national service at the end of June 1979. I was given a little more than six week's grace before being called up with C Coy 6RR, and became one half of the very depleted territorial strength that met our RAR comrades at the Essexvale battle-camp. That call-up, in late 1979 was, you might say, hectic. The initial Lancaster House talks leading to the end of the war were in progress, and ZANLA and ZIPRA were manoeuvring for control of the countryside before the elections which all sides knew were probably on the cards. So we found ourselves in the slightly strange situation of ZIPRA and ZANLA attacking each other rather than us, on an axis that ran very roughly from Beitbridge to Victoria Falls.

Accordingly, we travelled in that six weeks from just north of Beitbridge to as far north as Tsholotsho, with stop-offs at Mtshabezi, Diana's Pools and the Matopos along the way, and were kept busy the whole time. In one area, ZIPRA informants were relaying the whereabouts of ZANLA gangs through Special Branch in the hope that the army would sort out their problems for them. On one occasion, precise information was relayed by an elderly gentleman wobbliying towards us on his bicycle. It was strange in a number of other ways - like sitting on top of a kopje in the Gwanda area one night, seeing the bright lights of the Bulawayo Sun hotel on one side and tracer from a distant firefight on the other.

But the strangest had to be our deployment into Tsholotsho. The Company upped sticks from wherever we had been camped, and we found ourselves being taken to Bulawayo Railway Station one evening at dusk. Well away from the normal passenger platforms, we encountered, under gloomy yellow industrial lighting, the train about to travel back to Wankie after disgorging its load of coal for the Bulawayo power station close nearby. And so we clambered aboard the empty coal wagons – much further from the ground than you might think – and waited for the train to begin its journey north.

Not pleasant. A Garratt locomotive steaming up the line produces a lot of sooty smoke, and a lot of red-hot cinders, both of which swirled down in quantity into the uncovered coal trucks filled with troops. And coal trucks don't have passenger-friendly suspension, which lead to a lot of heavily bruised thighs and buttocks.

I'm not sure whether the company commander up on the footplate with the driver had it that much better. Almost three hours of cruel and unusual punishment - hands and necks scarred, caps and uniforms scorched through with little holes, and with an epidemic of desperate coughing and hawking spreading right down the train.

Eventually we passed through Sawmills, and shortly afterwards, in the middle of nowhere, the train slowed to a halt with a short screech and a tired exhalation of steam. De-training, even on a moonlit night, proved to be more difficult than entraining in the Bulawayo marshalling yards. There were a number of turned ankles as the heavily burdened company leaped down onto the slippy slope of granite ballast chips below the rails. Formed up, we set off in extended line and eventually made our way into a large wooded area – as wooded as you could expect in the poor sandy Tsholotsho soil - and bedded ourselves down by section.

And when dawn came, we found we had slept interspersed almost precisely amongst the VERY newly-vacated sleeping positions of our enemy. Or had they become our friends? A ZIPRA group appeared to have used exactly the same laying-up place. We never did catch up with them. Perhaps, again, they were hoping that we'd deal with their real enemies - ZANLA. The rivalry between the two boiled over very seriously after the ceasefire which came a few months after this episode, when groups of both ZIPRA and ZANLA encamped in the Bulawayo township of Entumbane tried very hard - and not for the last time - to exterminate each other.

THE STORY OF NHOWO by Lieutenant Colonel Donald 'Hobo' Hobson

Shortly after being posted from 1RAR to Army Headquarters, I was approached by Lt Col David Heppenstall to produce a Regimental Magazine for the RAR, which had, by this time, expanded from just 1RAR, to include 2 RAR and Depot RAR. Lt Col Heppenstall recalled that the original cyclostyled newsletter called *The Shield,* had been produced for the last 35 years at the whim of the CO of 1RAR, and was irregular in production and content.

With the growth of RAR it was felt that a properly presented Regimental Magazine was needed to meet the interests and history of all the Battalions that now constituted the Regiment. The launch of the first edition of *NhoWO1*n April 1976 reflected the changes that had occurred, and brought the RAR family of Officers, Warrant Officers, NCO's and soldiers and Retired members of the Regiment into closer contact. The name *Nhowo* (Shona for 'shield'), was chosen to avoid confusion with another publication called 'The Shield'.

Two editions of *Nhowo* were produced in 1976, and the 3rd edition in April 1977 featured a new-look contents and editorial layout in which the principal Regimental appointments were identified, including CO's, 2i/c's, Adjutants and RSMs. This edition ran to 72 pages. With each subsequent edition of *Nhowo* the calibre of the articles submitted from all sources improved, and interest in the magazine was overwhelming. The last issue of *Nhowo* was in October 1978 before the formation of 3 RAR. The editor, Captain 'Hobo' Hobson, at the time, was also the editor of *Assegai*, the Rhodesian Army magazine, and *Cheetah*, the Regimental magazine of the Rhodesian Light Infantry. This was over and above his role as SO2 RhAEC. It was felt by the Director Army Education that there were now too many conflicting interests, and Captain Hobson reluctantly gave up the editorship of *Nhowo* and *Cheetah* to concentrate on *Assegai*. There were no further issues of *Nhowo*.

Nhowo still has an important function in acting as a point of contact for all ex-RAR members wherever they are in the world. Now, more than ever, the need to keep in contact is a reality that we must all accept in order that that vital spark, which was such an important part of our lives, remains alive and well. We are all that is left of that band of brothers who fought for a country that no longer exists except in our memories.

THE ORIGIN OF CHIBAYA MOYO by Major Colin Hendrie

Having had the privilege of commanding B Company 2RAR I thought it may be of interest as to the origin of the motto and also company song *Chibaya Moyo*. Major John Pritchard took command of B Company following a short spell by Major John Russell and was very much part of the formation stage of the second battalion and particularly B Company. Early in his tenure as OC he tasked the CSM WO2 Hamandishe with coming up with a company motto and song. After consultation with the men the CSM advised that *Chibaya Moyo* had been selected and explained that translated it meant "stab through the heart-in love and or battle". In my biased opinion I believe the song was the envy of the other companies and regret that I cannot remember the entire lyrics to the song.

CHAPTER EIGHTEEN

CHARACTERS

COLONEL FJ WANE ISO by Detective Inspector Andrew Young

Francis John Wane was born October 1880 in High Wycombe, Buckinghamshire, the son of a prosperous merchant who owned and operated the Red Barn Grain and Feed Merchants in the town. His mother was a music teacher. The UK census of 1890 show that his grandparents managed 'Red Barn' farm which was owned by his grandmothers' father who owned a number of farms in the County. Apparently, Francis father moved into town to set up his Grain and Feed merchants to sell produce from the farms and cut out the 'middle man' in such business transactions. That his family was doing quite well in business is witnessed by the same census which indicates that as well as himself and his parents and one sister living at their home in High Wycombe there was also a housekeeper resident at the property, something only the relatively affluent could afford in those days.

As was common with many in the upper and middle classes of society Francis joined the Royal Buckinghamshire Hussars Yeomanry, what was then a militia (Territorial) Regiment. These militia units were for home defence only and could not be sent overseas. Shortly after the outbreak of the Boer War and a number of British defeats, the British government realized they were going to need more troops than just the regular army, and a Royal Warrant was issued on 24 December 1899, creating the Imperial Yeomanry. The Royal Warrant asked standing Yeomanry regiments to provide service companies of approximately 115 men each for overseas service, these were all volunteer units.

Col FJ Wane ISO

Francis Wane was such a volunteer and as a private soldier joined the 38th (High Wycombe) Company, which was raised from volunteers from the Royal

Buckinghamshire Yeomanry and was made part of the 10th Battalion, Imperial Yeomanry. These volunteers enlisted for one year's service in South Africa.

The 10th Battalion IY arrived in Cape Town in February 1900. Wane was obviously quickly promoted to Corporal and later commissioned. Newspapers of the time shows that Wane served in the Battalion as orderly to the Commanding Officer, Colonel Lawson. The Bucks Herald dated 18th January 1902 notes: "Earl Roberts has given a commission to Corpl. Francis John Wane of High Wycombe, who served with the Company of Imperial Yeomanry, and was orderly to Colonel W.A.W. Lawson." Medal Rolls show Wane being awarded the 1902 clasp to the Queens South Africa Medal, so one can gather he had volunteered to extend his service in South Africa and was still there when he was commissioned.

The medal roll also shows that in 1902 he was serving with the 32nd Battalion IY. Having tracked the campaigns of the 10th IY it is apparent that Wane was entitled to wear five bars on his Queens South Africa Medal, as depicted here. Lieutenant Wane was mentioned in The London Gazette, March 13, 1903, as being transferred to the Reserve of Officers, the entry reads: 'Honorary Lieutenant Francis John Wane, late of the 32nd Battalion Imperial Yeomanry posted to the Reserve as Lieutenant'. I then found Wane listed as a passenger on the steamship SS Johannesburg bound from London to Cape Town departing 11th March 1903. Obviously young Wane took some time to travel to Salisbury where on 12 January 1904, he attested into the BSAP, Regimental Number 593. He left the BSAP on the 6th October 1905, on transfer to the Native Affairs Department where the Rhodesia Civil Rolls show him to have been appointed as a Clerk in the Charter District.

Wane returned to the colours in 1916 and was appointed a Captain (later Major) serving under Lt. Col. Tomlinson in the 1st Rhodesia Native Regiment. Wane obviously distinguished himself whilst serving with the RNR as the Supplement to the London Gazette, 31 August 1917, lists Captain Francis John Wane, Rhodesia Native Regiment, as having been awarded the Italian Medaglia d'Argento al Valore Militare (Silver Medal of Military Valour) which is the Italian equivalent of the British Military Cross. Captain Wane was later wounded in action on the 12th November 1917, at Songea in German East Africa. The following is a summary of the action: "On 11th November von Falkenstein's troops approached Songea whilst one of his patrols successfully ambushed a British re-supply column on the Wiedhafen track. The porters dropped the four-day' supply of rations that they were carrying and ran into Songea. Perhaps due to misinformation from local villagers von Falkenstein had come to believe that the British garrison was weak and ill-trained. But he was also an impatient man and he did not wait for von Grawert but attacked at first light on 12th November with his 180 men and one machine gun. The German attack came in from the south-east just as the Rhodesia Native Regiment "stood to" in an alert position in their trenches. The German machine gun jammed after firing a few bursts and from then on both sides depended upon the weight and accuracy of their rifle fire.

Whilst engaging the withdrawing enemy machine gunners Captain Wane was shot in the shoulder, whilst a drummer in the regimental band, Private Rupea, was shot dead when defending the eastern section of the perimeter. A number of villagers and porters added confusion to the battlefield by getting shot as they ran to jump into the Rhodesian trenches. Around noon von German reinforcements arrived on the scene and with a machine gun firing effectively in support more than 200 men attacked from the north and east. But the Germans could not suppress the Rhodesian rifle fire or the rifle grenades that the defenders fired.

Francis Wane finished the war as a Major in the RNR and in the Supplement to the London Gazette, 7 March 1918. He was Mentioned in Dispatches by General Northey for exemplary conduct in German East Africa. He would therefore have been entitled to wear an oak leaf on the ribbon of the 1914-18 Victory Medal.

Following the end of the war Major Wane returned to the Native Affairs Department until he was once again summonsed to the colours in 1940, and with a cadre of officers from the BSAP and Native Affairs Department and a cadre of men from the BSAP Askari Platoon he was tasked with raising the 1st Battalion of the Rhodesian African Rifles. In the Kings Birthday Honours list of 1941, whilst commanding the regiment Lt. Colonel Wane was made a Companion of the Imperial Service Order. The entry reads: Francis John Wane. For services as a Native Commissioner in Southern Rhodesia. (Now Temporary Lieutenant-Colonel, Rhodesian African Rifles.)'

Lt. Col. Wane successfully raised and trained the battalion which was eventually sent to East Africa in 1943 and then on to Ceylon and Burma.

By the time the battalion deployed for active service Wane was 63 years old and it was decided, quite correctly, that this was not an age that a man should be commanding an infantry battalion on active service, so he handed over command to Lt Col J F MacDonald. On relinquishing command Wane was appointed as Honorary Colonel of the Regiment, a position he held until his death. Francis Wane always took a keen interest in the daily life of the Rhodesian African Rifles and appears in a number of photographs of the era when significant events took place involving the RAR.

THE MAN WHO WOULD BE 'INDUNA' by Brigadier John 'Digger' Essex-Clark

Maj Stan Morris (MiD x2)

The celebration of the 26th April each year as Tanlwe Chaung Day, the RAR Regimental Day, is a direct result of the courageous leadership of one man. Major Stanley Ernest Morris ID, GLM, CMG was born of Pioneer stock, his father, Ernest Morris, having arrived in Mashonaland shortly after the Pioneer Column in 1891, later becoming an early Native Commissioner. Stan Morris was a tall well-built man with a loud commanding voice. He also was an extraordinarily popular officer with the askari, who are most likely to have nicknamed him 'Induna' (isiNdebele for 'Chief').

On 26th April 1945, he led his own, as well as elements of other companies, to defeat the dug-in and concealed Japanese on the two objectives of Tanlwe Chaung, the twin saddle-linked peaks of *Bergner* and *Valerie*. It was his initiative and inspirational leadership that restored the momentum after the evacuation of a wounded platoon commander had temporarily stalled the attack. Morris had a strong hand in capturing both of the RAR's objectives, and his compelling and inspirational leadership was contagious amongst junior leaders and his askari. His personal courage under fire and severe enemy pressure, including MMG, LMG, sniper fire, grenades and mortars, was almost food for his undauntable energy and enthusiasm for combat.

He was awarded a Mention in Despatches for the Tanlwe Chaung effort, which seemed deserving of the Military Cross for which he had been cited. He displayed inspirational and contagious leadership, essential initiative, sheer courage, and achievement of a most difficult and dangerous but vital task. What a splendid but unrecognised Ma'Oto he was, an infantry officer of the first water. Morris Depot, the BSAP training establishment in Salisbury is believed to be named after him.

The citation for the award of the Military Cross, was written 'In the Field' by Lt Col G.H.W. Goode, CO 1RAR. Major Morris was eventually awarded a Mention in Despatches on 18 August 1945, endorsed by General Bill Slim, Commander-in-Chief Allied Land Forces, South East Asia. The citation reads as follows:

'During the attack on a strongly defended enemy position on the Tanlwe Chaung, Arakan, on 26 April 1945, the leading platoon of Major Morris' company were engaged by heavy LMG and MMG fire and his only remaining subaltern officer was wounded. The Company hesitated to go forward, and the attack was losing its momentum. Major Morris immediately came forward and with complete disregard for his own safety personally encouraged his men forward along the narrow precipitous track which was the only approach to the enemy machine gun position. By his own personal example and determination Major Morris restored the situation and led his men into the enemy position where they silenced the machine gun and took the position despite casualties.'

Gerry van Tonder added the following:

Morris held the post of Chief Native Commissioner from 1956 to 1962, in the most difficult period in the history of the department. In his annual report for 1961, Morris was openly critical of the government's Land Apportionment Act, describing it as a government breach of faith that took away Africans equal rights to acquire agricultural land.

In 1962, when the Native Department became the Ministry of Internal Affairs, Morris advocated a non-racial ministry, based on a 68-year history of 'material transformations in the life of an African people not surpassed anywhere else in Africa on such a scale'.

Although his views met with disfavour in many political circles, Morris went on to become Secretary for Internal Affairs, the top position in the ministry.

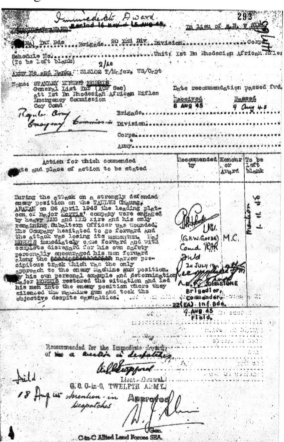

Maj Stan Morris Recommendation for MC

Honours and Awards

On 1 November 1945, Morris was awarded a second Mention in Despatches 'for gallant and distinguished services in Burma'.

On 1 January 1960, in recognition of his services to Southern Rhodesia as Secretary for Native Affairs and Chief Native Commissioner, Morris was appointed a Companion of the Most Distinguished Order of Saint Michael and Saint George (CMG).

On 11 November 1970, he was awarded the Independence Medal (ID) 'for persons who played a notable and significant part in the Unilateral Declaration of Independence in 1965'. At the time he was chairman of the Public Services Board.

On 11 November 1973, he was appointed a Grand Officer of the Legion of Merit (GLM) 'for outstanding service to Rhodesia'.

AN OFFICER AND A GENTELMAN by Captain Russell Fulton

Leadership and man management are as diametrically opposed as is the oft and, misguided impression, that an Officer is also a Gentleman. Each has its own specific meaning but, and more specifically, they are broadly perceived to be intrinsically inter-related qualities and the cornerstone of successful military command. To lead and to manage people requires a basket of vastly different skill sets.

Lt Col MD Shute CO 1RAR

To be an officer was one thing, and commissions were granted to countless hundreds in the Rhodesian military machine during our war (and pre) but, being a commissioned officer did not, in actuality, entitle everyone to the high distinction of being regarded as 'a gentleman'. In my very humble opinion, the latter was borne of one's upbringing and regardless of social standing: "Neither personal wealth, nor titles maketh the man". What does is upholding the sanctity of virtue, chivalry, pride in oneself and honour to one's family, men and regiment, all exercised without conscious thought and as a part of one's day-today persona. To possess all four characteristics, and be recognised by your subordinates, peers and superiors as such, was a distinction that was quite rare and those few who did, require little introduction because, rightly, their reputations precede them.

There is an old but very apt quip that sums this up quite succinctly, yet eruditely: "Rank is something that you wear. Respect is something that you have to earn!"

Major General M.D. Shute OLM:

The following is written from the heart and with the full support of my good Mother who, with me, were the beneficiaries of a level of extraordinary kindness, empathy, concern and support rendered in the true spirit of being a part of the broader 'RAR Family'.

It was early Sunday morning, 9 January 1977 and I had, the evening before, returned from attendance on a Regular Officer Cadet Selection Board at the School of Infantry. For my sins, I had received a 'Failed-Watch' (qualities of leadership displayed but too quiet); that knocked the wind from my misplaced, arrogant, 'billowing' sails. My Mother, uncompromising in her steadfast support of her sons, disbelieved the news. It was what it was. That fateful Sunday morning I awoke early in my Mothers cottage on a smallholding that was a stone-throw from Cement Siding on the outskirts of Bulawayo and no more than 15 minutes' drive from the home of 1RAR, Methuen Barracks.

It was a miserable, grey and overcast morning and I made myself a mug of coffee and was seated in the lounge when I heard an approaching vehicle. I looked between the curtains and saw an olive-green Peugeot 504 staff car pull up. My older brother Tom, a subaltern in 1RAR, had told my Mother and me not to worry about him until, if ever, a staff car pulled up and an Army Chaplain alighted the vehicle. Two officers alighted who were dressed in combat fatigues; Lt Col Mike Shute (CO 1RAR) and Maj Wayne Thompson (OC HQ Coy, 1RAR). I nearly shat myself!

Trying to put on a brave face for my Mother, I knocked on her door with a little too much urgency to alert her to the arrival of these RAR officers. I was freshly out of high school, a pimply, gangly and an altogether unimpressive adolescent but...I was afraid! My Mother emerged from her room, swiftly and immaculately groomed and opened the front door and invited Col Shute and Maj Thompson in to her humble abode. I made a tray of tea and the 'adult' discourse was light-hearted until the pleasantries were exhausted. Col Shute informed us that Tom's lead platoon vehicle had struck a landmine in the early hours of the morning in the northern reaches of Op Tangent (Binga area) and that he had sustained non-life threatening but very serious leg injuries. He had been casevacd to Wankie General Hospital and to know that the RAR would support our family and Tom.

That Monday, 10 January 1977, Col Mike contacted my Mother to tell her that there was a Rhodesian Air Force Britten Norman Islander aircraft that was flying to Wankie from the 1 Brigade aerodrome and that he had arranged for me to fly up to Wankie to see Tom. He had also arranged with 1 (Indep) Coy RAR, based at Wankie under the command of Maj Don Price, to collect me from the Wankie FAF aerodrome, to billet me in their barracks, feed me and to transport me to/from the hospital as required!

When I called on Tom later that afternoon he was in high spirits despite a pair of decidedly shattered 'gumbo' (Tibia and Fibula) and his recovery would be long and painful, even to an ignoramus like me. He was one of those fortunate sods who had the charm, confidence and good looks that appealed to the fairer sex and he lay in his 'pit of iniquity' and revelled in the overtly flirtatious attention he received. A couple of days later, confident he was on the mend, in good care and without the need of further family support, I flew back to Bulawayo.

What's the import of this anecdote you might well ask:

General Mike Shute inspired me, a young adolescent, to greater heights. I had my own views on what an officer and gentleman might mean, what leadership and man management might require, and I witnessed and experienced all four and at first hand.

In July 2015, I was privileged to attend the unveiling and dedication of the RNR-RAR Memorial at the National Memorial Arboretum in Alrewas, Staffordshire. During that time, I chatted to General Shute and I asked him if he recalled Tom's 'incident' and was not disappointed; he very clearly did. When I asked him if he remembered what he had done in arranging for me to visit my brother, he did not. Not one bit of it!

That's the single most important message that I wish to highlight: General Shute (then Lieutenant Colonel and Commanding Officer of 1RAR) had forgotten those humane, personal and desperately important actions to provide comfort to a concerned family. It is a very clear testimonial of the great man that he was and remains to this day: he decided what he thought was best to relieve anxiety from a concerned family and he delivered, above and beyond the call of duty. To any young readers, aspiring to careers in management, let this be a simple yet important message: Actions speak louder than words!

That is the measure of a true Officer, a Gentleman, a Leader and a Manager of Men. General Shute has my and my broader family's complete and enduring gratitude, respect and affection. For my part, years below his pay grade, I have always striven to emulate him. I would like to think, in my own small way, that I have achieved a measure of what he would expect of me, but I will always walk in the shadow of a far greater, much loved and enormously respected man.

In closing, it is both fitting and right to acknowledge, for the public record, that General Mike supported *Chibaya Moyo* from our initial approach to him as the (then) Chairman of the RAR Regimental Association. Not only did he give us his blessing but with that came his unqualified support and excellent anecdotes. Now in his 80's, retired from day-to-day Association duties, he remains passionate in his support of all matters related to our Regiment. Andy and I had only fleetingly considered a follow-up book, but that position changed when we received an email from General Mike encouraging us to do so. It was all the prompting we needed. This second journey has been as gratifying to us both as the first but not without its expected challenges. It is difficult to obtain anecdotes from the military diaspora, especially new material, and we approached General Mike for his assistance. It was received in the form of a personal, signed letter appealing to numerous former RAR officers and that he personally undertook to send. Not only did he do so but he attended to it promptly, cheerfully and with his uncompromising efficiency. Time and again, General Mike has stood up and delivered; that is an enormous credit to him where countless others 10-20 years his junior have failed. Makes you think doesn't it!

Tinotenda chaizvo Ishe.

Salute.

MAJOR MARTIN NKATAZO TUMBARE MLM DSM (ESM) by Captain Russell Fulton

Comments from Martin Tumbare (son):

Martin Nkatazo Tumbare was born in Umvuma on 15 June 1928 being the first-born child of Ndukuzenduba Tumbare, a descendant of the great Rozvi Warrior General Tumbare who led the Rozvi army. He was educated at Daramombe in Chivhu. He joined the Southern Rhodesia army in 1948 at the age of 20 years after working with the veterinarian in the Umvuma area. He married Angeline Tumbare with whom they had nine children: five boys and four girls. He also had two daughters from his previous marriage.

At the creation of Central Estates, he moved from his home in the Gobo area of Umvuma to Silobela.

In 1980 he was posted to Shaw Barracks at Balla Balla (Depot RAR) during the integration of the former Rhodesian Army, ZIPRA and ZANLA into the new

Zimbabwe National Army where he remained until his retirement from the army following 36 years of unbroken service. During his time and as a Captain, at the newly named 1st Infantry Training Depot, he was OC HQ Company and later became 2i/c of the Depot when he was promoted to Major in 1982, a rank he held until his retirement.

Lt Martin Tumbare with Mrs Rule

He bought a 110-acre smallholding in the Greenvale area of Gweru where he settled and practised farming. Throughout his life, he was a committed Anglican parishioner and a sub-deacon. As a father, he taught us to always be humble, that we were no different from other kids in the camps or in the areas we lived and that the rank he wore was his and not ours. His point was that we had to have our own life and work hard for its rewards.

He was a keen tennis player and practiced a lot and influenced the whole family to take up the sport and to follow it.

Comments by Captain Russell Fulton:

As a former 1 and 3RAR officer, I am humbled and extremely proud to be in a position to record, for the sake of our regimental history and posterity, a few words about an exemplary and venerated member of our Regiment.

In June 1977, the first black officers were commissioned at the School of Infantry, Gwelo. At a ceremony at Army HQ, 1RAR A-RSM, WO1 Martin Tumbare MLM, DMM and 2RAR A-RSM, WO1 Wurarayi Mutero BCR, DMM received their commissions separately. Tumbare, a highly respected soldier with

29 years impeccable service, attended a very moving ceremony at Methuen Barracks the previous evening where he had been presented with the gift of a shotgun by the Commanding Officer of 1RAR, Lt Col M.D. Shute. Later, on 25 August 1977, he was presented with the late 'Kim' Rule's sword (Commanding Officer of 1RAR 1950-1955) by his widow, Mrs Rule. It had been Kim Rule's wish that his sword be presented to the first African to be commissioned in the Rhodesian Army. Fittingly, it was a member of the battalion he had once commanded who received the honour.

COMMANDER of Combined Operations Lieut.-General Peter Walls congratulating Lieutenant N. M. Tumbare, of the Rhodesian African Rifles, after last Thursday's investiture at Government House. General Walls was made a Grand Officer of the Order of the Legion of Merit, and Lieutenant Tumbare was made a member of the Order of the Legion of Merit.

Lt Gen Peter Walls GCLM and Lt Martin Tumbare MLM after their investitures

During his long and exemplary service, he was awarded the Member of the Legion of Merit (MLM) and, in so doing, became the first African recipient. His medal grouping was preceded by the Defence Force Medal for Meritorious Service (DMM) and the Exemplary Service Medal (ESM).

When I joined 1RAR in February 1979 following my own commissioning, Martin Tumbare was already a RAR 'brand'. His reputation truly preceded him, justifiably and then some. I doubt that there is a single RAR officer or soldier alive today who has not heard of this good, loyal and upright RAR man's name. He set the bar high for those African senior NCO's who would follow in his and Wurayayi Mutero's footsteps.

That statement is made without equivocation as there were a great many of his subordinates who, through their own hard work and commitment, aspired to Martin Tumbare's commissioned heights and served the Rhodesian Army with honour.

Speaking at their commissioning ceremony, General Peter Walls stated:
"The Army has always been prepared to accept black men on commissioning if they measured up, potentially, to the standard required of leaders. Equally, the Army has always been prepared to train white and black men together as officers, provided the finished product could be accepted into the society of our land as being fully-fledged members of the

Officer Corps with no graduate, irrespective of colour, appearing to be a second-class officer".

The commissioning of Lieutenants Tumbare and Mutero would see a number of highly skilled senior NCO's attend future P.O.C. Courses at the School of Infantry in Gwelo and receive their deserved commissions. These men went on to prove themselves the measure of any of their white counterparts and it is a damn shame that Army HQ did not act sooner in

Lt MN Tumbare receiving his MLM from His Excellency the President JJ Wrathall

commissioning competent African soldiers. Had they, a fourth RAR Battalion could well have been established in Op Hurricane. That's very much in the past of course but, we who served, were proud of our fellow African officers and grateful for what they taught us.

2RAR RSM WO1 Mutero BCR and 1RAR RSM WO1 Tumbare with Maj Gen Derry Macintyre and Army Comd Lt Gen Sandy Maclean pre-commissioning

Major Tumbare passed away at his home in Gweru, Zimbabwe on 27 April 2007 two months before his 80th birthday, having lived a long and distinguished military career in service to his Country. He was a legend in his own lifetime, was respected, envied by many and, in some quarters, revered. He became the unwitting exemplar to aspiring African officers and his service to our proud regiment will never be forgotten.

In an extraordinary and quite unexpected revelation, Martin's son shared with me that his father and Wurayayi Mutero BCR were cousins and both were from the Gobo area. "When my Father and Wurayayi Wurarayai received their commissions, both were posted to Nkomo and 1POU until 1980 and my father was posted to Shaw Barracks and Wurayayi returned to the former home of 2RAR. Wurayayi bought a farm in the Mvuma on retirement where he lived out the rest of his life".

Zororayi Murugare Ishe. Tichazo Sangana.

WO1 (RSM) OBERT VEREMU DMM (ESM) by Captain Russell Fulton

WO1 Obert Veremu DMM attested into the Rhodesian Army on 23rd February 1953, rising from a Private Soldier to Lance Corporal and then Corporal during his service in the Malayan Emergency. In 1957 he was promoted and posted to A Coy, 1RAR as a platoon sergeant and two years later, in 1959, he was promoted again to PWO (Platoon Warrant Officer) and transferred to C Company. During this time, he represented the 1RAR Shooting Team where he proved his worth as a deadly shot in both the MAG and FN events.

In 1969, he was promoted again, this time from PWO to WO2 and CSM of E Company. In 1976 Support Company was formed and WO2 Veremu became the Company's first CSM. One year later, in 1977, WO2

RSM Obert Veremu DMM (ESM) in the UK in 2015

Veremu reached the pinnacle in the 'non-commissioned' ranks when he was promoted to WO1 becoming the Regimental Sergeant Major of the 1st Battalion (A-RSM), a distinction he fully deserved. Two years later, in 1979, with the expansion of the Regiment and the formation of the 3rd Battalion in Op Tangent,

515

he was posted to Addams Barracks in Umtali as their first A-RSM. RSM Veremu held this post until his retirement from the now Zimbabwe National Army in 1985. He died at his home in the Vumba on 11 July 2018.

RSM Veremu served our Regiment, The Rhodesian African Rifles, proudly, faithfully and continuously for a period of 27 years. His last 5 years were in what became 33 Infantry Battalion.

I first met RSM Veremu in early 1979 as a newly commissioned subaltern in the 1st Battalion and whilst my Company was on deployment in Op Hurricane. After reporting to the Adjutant, Battalion 2ic and the Commanding Officer, A-RSM Veremu and the E-RSM TMH Kirrane came and introduced themselves to me and invited me to join them on an orientation tour of Methuen Barracks. During this time, they spoke openly and forthrightly to me offering me some sound (almost paternal) advice. This included, but was not limited to, how to treat the men of the RAR, what their expectations would be of their Platoon Commander and how best to fit in to life in the Regiment.

I was deeply touched by this very kind and welcoming approach towards me, a "wet behind the ears" subaltern and, probably, too full of my own self-importance. I had found during my time in the RLI and at 'Hooters' that WO1's in general, and RSM's in particular, were men you were best advised to stay on the right side of. Being of the 'one-pipped variety' didn't mean a thing and these fine, experienced soldiers demanded respect; it was their due and I gave it freely and respectfully. My older brother Tom had served in B, Support and HQ Companies and he was well known to both RSM's so that held me in better stead than my virginal peers; that's my personal view anyway.

The following day I was summoned to the Adjutant's office and was informed that I was to be 'OC Funeral Party' for the military funeral for Sergeant Mleya, George who would have been my Platoon Sergeant (KOAS). This included rehearsals under the instruction of both RSM's. I spent some time with RSM Veremu and picked his brain further on pointers to observe when I joined my platoon the following week. I never forgot this and remain indebted to this outstanding man. Both RSM's provided me with advice during my time in the 1st Battalion and I feel privileged that they saw fit to afford a young 2nd Lieutenant some of their personal time and guidance. I served with RSM later in the 3rd Battalion and I consider this invaluable in profiling me as a young officer. I salute them and respect them always.

Citation: Defence Medal for Meritorious Service, WO1 Obert Veremu, 11 November 1971

'Warrant Officer Class One Veremu attested in to the Rhodesian Army on 23 February 1952. After completing his basic training, he was posted to the 1st Battalion The Rhodesian African Rifles and was deployed to Malaya where he served his Company with distinction. During this time he rose through the ranks from a Private soldier to Lance Corporal and left Malaya as a Corporal. On his return he remained in 1st Battalion The Rhodesian African Rifles where he was to become the African Regimental Sergeant Major in 1977. Throughout his service, Warrant Officer Class One Veremu has displayed devotion to duty which can only be described as exceptional. This has made him an outstanding example to the non-commissioned officers of the Rhodesia Army. During his period of service with the Rhodesian African Rifles, Warrant Officer Class One Veremu held key appointments including that of Platoon Sergeant, Platoon Warrant Officer and Company Sergeant Major.

In all of his appointments and particularly the latter, Warrant Officer Class One Veremu devoted himself to achieving as great a degree of perfection as was possible, working long, irregular hours and sparing no effort. With characteristic drive and determination, Warrant Officer Class One Veremu set about making a success of the appointment. He quickly succeeded in imposing his personality on the non-commissioned officers and men of the unit. The outstanding example for his juniors has made him an invaluable and highly respected member of the Regiment in the eyes of the officers and other ranks alike. His tireless efforts have contributed significantly to the high standards of discipline, morale and operational efficiency achieved by the 1st Battalion The Rhodesian African Rifles under extremely difficult circumstances which have prevailed since his appointment. Warrant Officer Veremu's loyalty and selfless devotion to duty are an inspiration to those with whom he serves.

A tribute, by Brigadier David Heppenstall MLM:

I was shocked and saddened to hear that Obert had died. He was such a fine soldier. He and I first served together when I was commissioned in 1RAR in August 1955 and I was posted to B Company as OC 4 Platoon where he was my leading scout and tracker. In the Malayan jungle he was magnificent and taught me much. Our paths crossed often over the next twenty years as we both rose in the ranks.

On Op Nickel in 1967 he was badly wounded but due to his perseverance and determination he made a full recovery. In 1971 he was one of the first soldiers to be awarded the Defence Force Medal for Meritorious Service (DMM) on the new Rhodesian Honours and Awards List.

He served with distinction as RSM 1RAR. At the end of Independence in 1980 he was RSM of 3RAR in Umtali. Unlike several of his compatriots he refused a commission in the new Zimbabwe Defence Force and retired shortly afterwards.

LIEUTENANT COLONEL BRYAN MCDERMOTT: 1RAR, 2RAR, SINF/ZMA by Captain Russell Fulton

Opening comments from Bryan's brother Jim:

Bryan was born in Lobatse, Bechuanaland Protectorate (later to become Botswana) on 21st February 1948 and one of two sons.

Bryan attended Primary School for the first two years at a little one roomed school in Serowe that had one teacher teaching about 4 or 5 standards. From there we went to boarding school first at Pietersburg English Medium School (before it became Capricorn) and his last two years at Primary school (1959-1960) were at Rondebosch Boys Preparatory School in Cape Town. His high school years, all five years (from Standard 6 to Matric, 1961–1965 were spent at Rondebosch Boys High School, still of course, as a boarder.

Bryan was an outstanding, all-round sportsman at school. He played 1st XV rugby and 1st XI cricket at a school renowned for excellence in sport. As a cricketer he was selected to represent the Western Province Nuffield (Schools) side at a young age.

As youngsters, we lived in some pretty remote places and spent virtually all of our time in the bush. We got up to a lot of mischief, usually initiated by Bryan, and we were often in trouble. Even then, he was unashamedly fearless. The one thing that stands out for me is that he was just about the most positive person I have ever met. Even when his beloved Springboks were 30-0 down to the All Blacks with 5 minutes to go, Bryan would be saying (and believing) "We can still win this!" It wasn't only sport though, Bryan was positive about virtually everything he tackled.

He had enormous self-confidence but, at the same time, was totally lacking in personal arrogance. These are two personality traits that are often inter-related but not so with Bryan. He was a kind, generous and gregarious man who loved company and who people seemed to gravitate towards when introduced to him.

I believe that it was all these qualities that helped to make him such a respected and admired leader of men during his military career.

In closing, I need to say that he handled his illness uncomplainingly, with fortitude and dignity.

Comments by Capt Andy Telfer SCR (MFC [Ops]), one time subaltern in Bryan's D Company, 2RAR:

When I think of Lt Col Bryan Mc Dermott, I remember a 'high comparison', the type of individual who stands at the top of his profession, who others measure themselves against.

I first met him in February 1977 when he was a Captain. On our first day in 2RAR, Cyrille Fournier, Bruce Thompson and I had just arrived in Fort Victoria and reported to Battalion Headquarters which were temporarily housed in the agricultural show grounds while the new barracks was being built. Somewhere between 'Produce' and 'Dairy', we found the Adjutant's office and, just as we arrived at it, out swung the Adjutant himself, Captain Bryan McDermott.

There aren't many people around who impress you immediately, but he was definitely one. With the athletic build of the top-class fast-bowler he had once been and huge natural confidence and good humour, he walked and talked the part and would have

Lt Bryan McDermott

been an Army officer in any era of history. As brand new subbies, he was less impressed with us of course but, after 13 months on Cadet Course with his kindred spirit George L-P, we were used to that.

In August, he was promoted to Major and took command of D Company, soon proving himself a commander to be proud of: clever, professional and determined.

Just prior to his arrival, we had completed a long period under command of a Territorial unit in the North-East, ambushing just inside our border with Mozambique, with no results to show for it. We had been given a stretch of several kilometres of featureless bush to cover with a platoon, with no natural features to funnel the enemy and no pathways to attract them. The pins looked good on the map but, in reality, we were far too few and far between to have any effect.

MacD saw what we saw: select the right terrain and go over the border, "Let's take it to them", he said. In our first bush trip together, he insisted that we were not deployed until we had good intelligence; that we had time to prepare carefully, including devising a simple placard code to communicate with; and that proper planning, rehearsals and so on (that is, proper battle procedure) took place. One very happy night, I carefully slipped across the border with my platoon and walked 15 km into Mozambique to have some fun. Within a week, D Company had chalked up 17 kills and a new operational standard had been set.

For several months, 2RAR had been manning Fire Force Charlie. All the Company Commanders that I encountered in the role were excellent but there was something about MacD that put him in a league of his own as a Fire Force commander. He read the ground and deployed his troops so quickly and so accurately that, if the terrorists were there, we found them. On the radio, his orders were clear and brief but there was a humour in his voice that kept things calm and light. Quotes from songs seemed to flavour his expressions, "another one bites the dust" being a favourite.

In a Fire Force operation, the quality of the DZ was not a factor; the paras were dropped tactically, as a sweep line. Jumping into a field of small stumps one day, I felt a wrench in my ankle and looked at it as I lay on the ground. My foot was twisted towards the outside, so I tried to push it back. On my radio, Bryan MacD was speaking to me: "Move towards the K Car now, the enemy are right in front of you". There was no way I was going to let him and our soldiers down, such is the effect of a true leader on his subordinates. Many terrorists were killed that day.

Contacts blended into contacts and our soldiers were becoming very used to following Bryan's calm humour into one after another. Sometimes, the humour rubbed off on them too. One afternoon, I was standing just against the mud wall of a hut when a terrorist opened fire on automatic into the wall from inside the hut. He must have heard me talking to Bryan on the radio.

Hearing the noise and seeing the pieces of wall coming off right there next to me, I skipped up and down and just about jumped out of my skin. MacD told me later that, when I cut off our conversation, a Corporal standing nearby had come up on his radio to explain: "The Ishe cannot talk now, he's dancing".

I seemed to have a problem with men with beards. Searching through a kopje of balancing rocks during one operation, I looked to my left into a shoulder-width gap between two huge boulders. There was a bearded terrorist sitting with his rifle between his knees, pointing out of the gap. He'd been waiting and fired as soon as I appeared. The round struck my rifle, knocking it out of my hands and me off my feet. When we returned to the airfield, MacD saw that my hand had been bandaged.

"Has it got a hole in it?" he enquired laconically, out of mildly polite interest. "No sir, it's just sprained but look at this." We examined the rifle together. The round had passed between it and my body, scoring a line along part of the stock, across the magazine and the pistol grip, just above where the thumb goes. He saw the funny side in that...?

Through all of our encounters and many more tests, there wasn't a single man in D Company who ever lost his confidence. We took it from our commander, in the sense that he called us up to a higher level, we enjoyed being up there with him and we tried to live up to it. Bryan McDermott had a profoundly positive effect on me as a young officer and I am deeply grateful to him for it.

Comment by Capt Russell Fulton:

Lt Col Bryan McDermott was posted from D Company, 2RAR following an extremely successful period as a field and K-Car commander of the very highest order, respected and admired by the entire Rhodesian Army Officer Corps. He was selected and appointed from the Army Nominal Roll assuming the prestigious post of Chief Instructor at the School of Infantry in Gwelo. His appointment took place during a particularly challenging time; the training, selection and appointment of former ZIPRA and ZANLA combatants as officers in to the newly integrated Zimbabwe National Army Battalions that included former Rhodesian Army officers, NCO's and men. Of course, and with his pedigree, he rose to the occasion with professional military aplomb.

I, like many, had the privilege of serving under him and attest to this without hesitation. He was uncompromising in his high expectations of the various course officers under his command in terms of course preparation, methods of instruction, personal discipline and the like. To all intents and purposes and despite the changeover to the new order, serving at Hooters was no different to the Rhodesian Army days. That's a testament to his true professionalism.

When (then) Lt Col Trevor Desfountain was promoted to full Colonel and posted out as Commander Midlands District, Bryan was promoted to Lieutenant Colonel and became the Commandant of the Zimbabwe Military Academy, a post he held until his retirement and migration to South Africa.

It is worth noting that (then) Major McDermott wrote Andy Telfer's citations for both the award of his Silver Cross (with input from Maj Colin Hendrie) and his MFC (Operations).

Comment by Brig Pat Lawless SCR, Chairman of the RAR Regtl Assn and RhArmy Assn:

I did not have the privilege of serving under Bryan (though it was not uncommon for elements of 1RAR to serve under tactical command of 2RAR for specific operations, and vice versa). But I did serve at the same time. Bryan's fine reputation as an aggressive, highly professional infantry company commander preceded him. We met at SInf on a number of occasions and I recall several conversations. Laconic, witty, oozing experience, he was generous with his teaching and though I doubt he would ever admit it publicly, he was clearly fiercely proud of his officers and soldiers, who loved him deeply in return - at least that's what I think Officer Telfer told me in one of his more sober and lucid moments! We were blessed with good leaders in the RAR, and Bryan epitomised all that was good of a combat company commander.

In closing, a quote that reinforces much of what Andy has shared in his closing paragraph:

> "The most important thing I learned is that soldiers watch what their leaders do. You can give them classes and lecture them forever, but it is your personal example they will follow."
> General Colin Powell

LIEUTENANT GODFREY JAMES GLANVILLE 'SPIDER' WEBBER by Captain Russell Fulton

2nd Lt Godfrey 'Spider' Webber KIA 7 Feb '77

Godfrey, known to all and sundry as 'Spider', was the son of Yvonne Webber who had a store in the Chipinga region and who had also worked at the local Farmer's Co-op. This meant that after his schooling at Chipinga Primary School from 1962 to 1966 he became a boarder at Umtali Boys High School from 1967 until 1971.

Tall, gangly, and with a terrific sense of humour, he was a natural athlete, especially at long distance and cross country. He was also a good hockey player, playing for the School 1st XI in 1971, where he was considered 'the most penetrative forward.' He was selected to play for the Mashonaland Schools 'B' hockey team that same year. He was also a passionate and competent horse rider. But it was at athletics that Spider shone. His talent was already being seen when he won the school Under-14 Mile (1500m) event in 1968, but his best year was 1971.

He won the Under 17 800 metres, 1500 metres as well as the steeplechase at the school and at the Manicaland Schools Championship came first in the 800 metres and the 1500 metres events. In the Mashonaland Schools Championship's, he won the 800 metres, came second in the 3000 metres and 4th in the 800 metres. In the national champs, he was second to Esau Magwaza in the 1500 and 3000 metre events.

'Spider' Webber at UBHS

Spider joined Internal Affairs in 1972 and was posted to Melsetter. He grew restless and decided to attend an SAS selection course in early 1973 which he passed. During this time Spider completed a basic static line para course from 30 April to 18 May 1973 and is pictured in the group photograph of BSL39 as a member of C Sqn, RhSAS, with whom he did numerous operations until December of 1974. In May of the same year, Spider married his sweetheart Jody Smallman.

Spider attended and passed a Regular Officer Selection Board in January 1975, returned to the School of Infantry and attended regular officer cadet course Inf/25(18) where he was commissioned as a 2nd Lieutenant on 20 February 1976. He was posted to C Company 1RAR where he was respected by his peers and loved by his *Masodja*. Some of his escapades whilst with the RAR are legendary.

On 7 September 1977, whilst on operations in the Gwanda region, Spider and four trackers had, for four days, been following the spoor of a ZIPRA gang who had abducted an RAR soldier. Upon entering a village, they were ambushed by the gang and Spider was tragically killed, a mere six and a half months after his commissioning!

He left his wife Jody, two young daughters, his mother, and numerous friends to mourn his passing. A cremation service was held in Bulawayo and his ashes were returned home to Chipinga where they were interred.

At the going down of the sun, and in the morning, we will remember him. Whilst not diminishing nor detracting from the sombre and respectful tone that this post intends, the following is an anecdote penned for *Chibaya Moyo 1* by a fellow regular officer cadet course mate and great friend of Spider's. Its inclusion is intended only to highlight the lighter side of a subaltern's life during a brief respite from our dangerous and protracted operations.

WOLLENDALE, by Tom Fulton

The scene sees some of the intrepid Subalterns of the First Battalion at Wollendale Rifle Range – it is verbatim so my apologies in advance for the language which I believe rather more authentic, than offensive.

Alice (Bill Liversidge) often 'pulled a rabbit out the hat' when it came to the later long -range practices and considering the lateness of these challenges, fared admirably in the face of his, by then, alcoholically impaired status. He had grown up taking ultra-long shots at springbok in his native South Africa. Tom on the other hand was able to display his hunting experience by excelling in the close range standing shoot and the 2 of them had each won a take-home miniature for their efforts.

Spider Webber C SQN RhSAS 1974

Because they would be featuring in the prizegiving, it was necessary for the now well-oiled contingent to stay for the ceremony. Having received the trophies, the group filed out with a smug drunken dignity and made for the car. They had come out to the range in Spider's Fiat which Tom and Chris hadn't travelled in since they were cadets. It was very much a family car as Jodie his wife had given him a second daughter and it smelled faintly of urine and baby puke; but it was still mechanically sound and reliable and although not much to look at, was always kept in a gleaming state by Spider or someone else who seemed to be keen.

The men placed their rifles in the boot of the car – each rifle fastidiously wrapped in a blanket to avoid the sights being bashed about during travel. Alice got up front with Spider driving and Tom and Chris were in the back. Provision had been made for the arduous 20-minute journey by ensuring that a workable quantity of reserve beer was carried.

The road from the Wollendale Rifle Range club house ran along the side of the range and the firing points and led away from the butts or 'target end' of the range. This range road ended in a T junction where they would turn right to go the short distance to the main Matopos tarred road. The Fiat was going on at a fair clip and there was a car ahead which was travelling at a far more sedate speed – it became evident by Spider's actions that it was his intention to over-take this irritant that was throwing up the red Wollendale dust into the path of his hitherto, bright and shining Fiat.

Spider was normally a very good driver and no stranger to Wollendale and this was why all 3 of the passengers realised too late that they were overtaking at the point of reaching the T junction? Because of the dust thrown up by the vehicle ahead, the junction wasn't visible to them; but they knew it was there and so should Spider have, and they sat transfixed in a moment of stoic resignation to the fact that disaster was about to strike and no amount of fuss would serve to avert it.

With the sway of the car at that precise moment, a turn to the left was not an option and to go straight meant ploughing through a stand of small trees and the surface they would have to negotiate would fairly disembowel the brave little Fiat. Spider made his decision in a split second and simultaneously dropped the engine down a gear and started an intrepid and determined effort to negotiate the 90-degree right hand turn. To begin with the tyres found traction for about the first 45 degrees but the inevitable slide started as the degree of the turn became too demanding on the momentum.

They shot across the road with Spider trying frantically to rectify without over-correction – his driving was out of a textbook, but the natures of physics would not be denied. The two passenger side wheels struck the small sand embankment that the continual passage of vehicles had shored up. The inversion of the Fiat onto its roof and the following short slide in a cloud of red dust would have best been described as inelegant; and Tom was inwardly embarrassed that his first thought was for the status of his beloved rifle in the boot!

"For F**k sakes Webber! That was a 'handy' bit of driving" from McLennan reduced them all into paroxysms of topsy-turvy laughter as they, in turn, crawled from the windows out into the fast dispersing dust.

"Shit are you ouens OK?" was the enquiry from the genuinely concerned driver of the vehicle that they had attempted to overtake and the witness to their insane behaviour. Reassuring him that all was fine, he helped them to roll the vehicle back onto its wheels. After a few tortured cranks, the engine fired and only then did they realise what a wreck the car looked. It was all superficial but expensive stuff to fix and they all commiserated with Spider. It was unanimously agreed that his driving had been perfectly laudable and that they should all buy him a beer at the Holiday Inn on the way home.

That he had the confidence to have even considered the undertaking of something so sensationally impossible was worthy of acclaim. Spider's thoughts on how he was going to explain this to his wife was not a subject that was broached because truly, when all was said and done – he had to stand alone as the one who had 'f**ked it all up'."

CAPTAIN RUSSELL FULTON by Captain Andrew Telfer

Capt Russell Fulton

Readers of *Chibaya Moyo 1* and *2*, together with the RAR Facebook page, will know how much Russell Fulton has contributed to the memory of our Regiment, invariably focussing his efforts in recognition of other people. I think the reader might agree that some of the recognition should be returned to him and, reading below, you'll see ample evidence of the accomplished life he has led.

Russell was born in Fort Victoria on 16 August 1958 to Jack and Patricia Fulton, younger brother to Tom. He attended Baines Primary School in Bulawayo and then returned to Fort Vic as a border at Fort Victoria High School. He was a very good sportsman, playing 1st team water polo while still in Form III, later adding first team swimming, athletics, squash, rugby and cricket (the latter two at provincial schools' level). Even at that age he was a leader, captaining the school's athletic, swimming and water polo teams and was appointed Head Boy of Hostel and Head Boy of School in 1976.

In common with many other young men who would later become good infantry officers, on leaving school he first spent a year in the RLI as a troopie, attending recruit course 157 from February to June 1977 and para course at 1 SA Para Bn. Posted to the anti-tank troop in Support Commando, he carried the MAG for Colour Sergeant Jock MacKelvie SCR and Second Lieutenant Simon Willar. Life as an RLI troopie in 1977 was not a passive career choice and he received his share of oil leaks, most famously (when casevaced to Andrew Fleming Hospital with Simon) persuading the ambulance driver to turn on the siren to impress the nurses. He was recommended to attend an Officer Selection Board and passed in January 1978, joining Regular Cadet Course Inf/25(21).

Russell was commissioned in February 1979 and posted as a Second Lieutenant to 3 Platoon, A Company, 1RAR. The following promotions and postings give insight into how quickly he made his mark. He was selected to be Ensign to the RAR Colour for the first (and only) opening of the Zimbabwe-Rhodesia Parliament on 1 June 1979, the last time that the RAR Colour was carried under the Rhodesian flag.

He received accelerated promotion to Lieutenant in June 1979 after 4 months of commissioned service (it usually took 18 months). He was posted to 3RAR in July 1980 as the Adjutant and then 2ic of B Company, 3RAR under the late Maj Marius Meiring. Promoted to Captain in July 1980 after 17 months of commissioned service, the youngest Captain in the Rhodesian Army at the age of just 20 years, he was posted to ZMA as course officer designate of the next regular cadet course. That is a prestige appointment, reserved for officers who would be role models for their cadets. Unfortunately, cadet courses were discontinued and, instead, he ran Lieutenant to Captain GD courses for the newly integrated ZNA Battalions (Rh Army, ZIPRA and ZANLA) in Platoon Commanders' Wing. Later, he moved to Company Commanders' Wing (formerly Tactical Wing) to run courses for Company and Battalion Commanders before resigning his commission in December 1981.

Like many of us, what followed was a period of learning how to make the change to civilian life. After a period in management roles in South Africa, Russell returned to Zimbabwe and joined Bata as Export Manager. His natural rapport with people and sound business sense soon led to success, winning the Confederation of Zimbabwe Industries, Zimbabwe International Exporter of the Year Award an unprecedented five times. Promoted to National Sales and Marketing Manager and Deputy MD, he negotiated the first (and only) license and distribution agreement with NIKE on the African continent that saw the company export in excess of 1 million pairs of athletic footwear in the first year. He left Zimbabwe in February 2002 and emigrated to Australia with his wife Corralee and children, Liam and Nina, adding Aisla to his family just five years ago.

In spite of wrestling with cancer for nearly four years, Russell co-authored and illustrated *Chibaya Moyo 1* and *2*, and continuously adds to the interest and value of the RAR Facebook page. His posts are invariably positive and uplifting, reflecting the character of this exceptional infantry officer, business leader and all-round, first-class human being.

MY MUJIBA by Captain Russell Fulton

Preamble:

One of the finest, most respected and privileged traditions to be accorded to officers within our proud Regiment, The Rhodesian African Rifles, was for officer's to be assigned a 'Batman' on joining. A 'Batman' was, in very simplistic terms, a personal valet.

One's batman was, ordinarily, a private soldier selected by the Platoon Warrant Officer and he was recently joined the Company from recruit course or a private who had been identified as a soldier who had displayed qualities of leadership. The general idea was that said 'Batman' would receive one-on-one instruction from his "Ishe" in any/all matters of basic soldiery encompassing, but not limited to, map reading & navigation skills, basic signals and voice procedure, ground air control, first aid, issuing of formal orders, preparation of sand models, section and platoon support weapons (characteristics and their employment) and whatever else the officer considered appropriate to profile and prepare 'their' man for future junior leader courses and, ultimately, a promotion from the ranks. It was a position envied by many and scorned by some but, when managed correctly, these men went on to bigger and better things.

This paean is a reflection on a short period in time and space that I shared with a fine young man and it gives me immense pride to share it with those of you who care to read it.

I was commissioned on the 9th February 1979 off regular cadet course Inf/25(21) and posted to 1RAR where I was appointed OC 3 Platoon in 'A' Company.

Pte Emmanuel Thomas Mukonoweshuro

Just as an aside and to lend some perspective, regular cadets who were due to receive their commissions, were interviewed by their course officer a few weeks prior to the big day and we were required to list the three units in order of preference that we wished to serve in following commissioning. I had served in the RLI prior to cadet course and loved the Regiment (and I still do) but I had always wanted to be an RAR officer since I was in high school and I listed 1RAR for each of my three choices. I got shat upon from a dizzy height by my course officer (then) Capt Martin "Wakkers" Wake for being too cocky and presumptuous and I had to do it again. I listed 1RAR, 2RAR and 1RLI. I received my commission, and my wish, and was posted to 1RAR.

On the appointed day, and after an all-too-brief 'R&R' following my 13 month cadet course, I presented myself before the 1RAR Adjutant and was duly informed that my Company was currently on deployment and due home for R&R within a matter of days but, and very sadly, I was required to attend a funeral as 'OC Funeral Party', for a man who was to have been my platoon sergeant, 644704 Sgt Mleya, George Mathias (KOAS. RIP. Salute). What a dreadful precursor to my service in our Regiment and my career in the commissioned ranks! Following exhaustive and very sombre funeral drill rehearsals at Methuen Barracks, we bade our fallen comrade farewell. It was a 'wake-up' call I never wanted but death was simply an incontrovertible fact of life back-in-the-day.

We deployed seven days and my company returned from the bush. I was introduced to my PWO (Platoon Warrant Officer) Munyika, Collins (RIP. Salute) who then fell in my platoon and introduced me to each of my men. I was so very proud....my first command and I was determined to prove myself to all of these fine men and to look out for them in every which way that I could.

We deployed in to Op Hurricane and spent the first night adjacent to the Sinoia Sports Club. At first light we were loaded and on our way in to the operational area. The convoy halted at Chief Chirau's village in the Chirau TTL whereupon our OC, Maj Craig Beechell (a former US Army and Vietnam vet) took his subbies to meet the Chief (Lt Willard Fleetwood [a former US Ranger, 2Lt Iain "Putties Macdonald [same cadet course as me] and yours truly). After this bit of 'winning-the-hearts and-minds' business we were offered and were obliged to drink some (warm) 'Chibuku' with him and his headman. After providing some our rations to his wives, we deployed further in to the TTL. It was midday and we set up our admin base in advance of deployment.

Whilst all of this was being conducted and, unbeknown to me, PWO Munyika was busying himself briefing my batman designate with the protocols, duties and so on that would be expected of him; he fell in my platoon and asked me to accompany him. The platoon was brought to attention and one 662636F Private Mukonweshuro, Emmanuel Thomas was ordered to break ranks and fall-in in front of PWO Munyika and myself. I was introduced to this young man, recently joined from his recruit course training at Depot RAR in Balla Balla. With minimal pomp and ceremony, so began a relationship that was as unlikely as it was unique, but the memories of this association I have held almost sacrosanct for several decades.

Our Journey Commences:

I was a brand-new subaltern in the Regiment and unfamiliar with the finer details of protocol serving with "A.S." troops but I had been briefed fairly comprehensively by Tom, my older brother who was now the GSO3 Int. (Military Intelligence Officer) at 1 Brigade.

I had started getting my "Platoon Bible" squared away and was interviewing every member of my platoon. I learned that the Platoon Bible was supposed to have been passed down from one Platoon Commander to the next (?) as a means of sharing a common journey, lessons learnt, and practical solutions to challenges regarding our men, and so on and so forth. There was no such 'Bible' in existence when I joined so I accepted that for what it was (we weren't employed to be regimental scribes after all) and went about compiling my own.

When I interviewed my Batman, I inquired in annoyingly minute detail about his family, but he had volunteered no father, mother nor any siblings (Many decades later, I found this to be a fallacious but a quite emotional revelation). He claims to have been raised by his uncle (his father's brother) and he had made it, remarkably for that time, as far as the end of Form IV (O Level) and had received four passes. It was a remarkable achievement that had a very deep resonance with me as I, and my brother, had lost our Father at a tender age and fighting for the best results we could had taught me a few early, but very important life lessons.

Fast forward:

I recall a deployment in to the Ndanga TTL, adjacent to that notoriously bad piece of real estate and 'liberated prefecture' we all knew, or had heard about, the Nyajena TTL. This was 'gook central' if ever the nom de guerre applied! 'Mabhunu' (Security Forces) were unwelcome and you could bet your bottom dollar on the fact that a few things were going to happen. The first was that you would almost certainly be compromised if you thought that you would be operating here in clandestine fashion and, secondly, once you were 'seen' by the locals, the bush telegraph system would be operating at +5 signal strengths....a good revving by mortar, RPG and/or small arms fire would certainly be on the cards to spoil the evening quiet. Oh yes, and in addition, once your presence was (certainly) known, you could reasonably anticipate the prospects of hitting a couple of strategically buried LM's (Land Mines of the tank variety) including the quite nasty prospect of an eye-watering ambush when the time to depart said TTL arrived.

Anyway, let's move on shall we.

It was mid-1979 and we were moving under cover of darkness towards Bangala Dam from whose general locale we were to establish several OP's watching specific villages that skirted the dam and to observe the behavioural patterns of the locals that would, in time, provide us with the 'tell-tale' signs of ZANLA presence.

It was not long before we had gained an appreciation of what the daily routine was and changes to these social norms would be viewed with deep suspicion and anticipation. I had been 'on watch' with Mujiba and we had shared and recorded the goings-on for the past three hours. I told 'Mujiba' to stand down and to call the next pair, Corporal Maunganidze, Chipo and a private soldier to take over from us. Mujiba moved quickly and silently away from the OP position that was downhill from of our rest-up position and on a slope facing the dam from the eastern slope. He returned promptly and frantically giving me the silent hand signal for 'enemy presence' (a clenched right fist raised shoulder high). It was one of two things; a gook recce party or, more likely, mujibas sent from one of the villages feeding ZANLA to herd goats into the surrounding hills in search of hidden mabhunu (us).

We could not risk compromise whilst we were in the process of gathering a very clear intelligence picture. I left my webbing and grabbed my FN and moved as stealthily as I could in the direction of where these 'two' had last been sighted. My acting platoon sergeant, Corporal Makhulumo, Victor had seen the signal and he too had moved in the direction of the sighting. We moved within a few meters of the two adolescent mujibas and 'my Mujiba' made his presence known when he directed a sound, bone jarring swot with a dried acacia branch across the back of the head of the tallest of the two that any NY Jets baseballer would have been impressed by.

Cpl Victor jumped the other with hand across his mouth to suppress any appeal for help. This was followed by a single but well aimed and mind-blinding blow to the temple with the butt of my FN. Both captives were 'still' but the cacophony that, hitherto, had been the shrill sound of 'Christmas Beetles' also stilled creating a deathly silence. If there was ever a live 'oxymoron'; this was it! As with all matters of this gravity, my heart sank as I knew compromise was inevitable as the families of these two youngsters non-return before last light would signal the presence of the dreaded 'Mabhunu'.... come to rain-down all manner of pestilence and mayhem on and around them.

We handcuffed our captures with black nylon cable ties that I always carried in my kit.....their only method of escape was to chew their arms off at the shoulder and I hadn't ever seen that level of desire to gap-it! I almost felt pity on them but..... not much! Experiencing what we had in the past, this had somehow, incontrovertibly, dulled many of my inherent qualities of a need to care for anyone remotely hostile. I pride myself upon the fact that I was never cruel to my fellow man (my conscience is clear on that) but I was, and nonetheless, short of emotion when my men's welfare was concerned. I make absolutely no apologies whatsoever for that. Being in a perilous environment and, for months-on-end, instilled an almost 'automated' response that evidenced the switching on and off, of one's emotions and that became an 'uncalibrated' reaction. It was, quite simply and, with the benefit of hindsight, what it was.

We withdrew from our OP soon after last light and moved under cover of darkness until we were a good twenty clicks (kilometres) or so away and based up. We interrogated our captures and then handed them over to a local 'Scouter' team (BSAP Ground Coverage) at first light who whistled them away to do whatever they needed to. I received orders to re-enter the area that night and to resume operations.

What can be certain is that 'My Mujiba' had acted professionally but, and more's the point, he had made his Ishe proud. He had saved us from certain compromise and, in the process, had earned himself a deferred call-up to the rookie ranks of the MLB (Major League Baseball) for his 'swot' on the lanky mujiba! I make light of it all of course but let's not forget that this was a young private soldier whose personal initiative had saved the day. In my book, his actions demonstrated character, initiative and common sense and this young soldier had also proven his mettle.

Sometime later, we deployed in the Chibi TTL and it was bastard cold and wet, of course, and what else!! Without wanting to diminish the quite outstanding job that our colleagues in Special Branch were doing in Op Repulse, and elsewhere, this was one of those inevitable deployments that fell under the poor but accurate nomenclature of 'Lemon'. A 'Lemon', for the uninitiated, was a bush trip or deployment 'sans boxing' (without contacts). It was what you least wanted as it was the precursor to a lot of nonsense that would certainly follow....as sure as darkness follows the light.

Nervous tension and pressure built up day-by-day without the release afforded by contact and when the lid blew off, it was unwise to hold company with those so afflicted. Boys will be boys. Never mind. And so, after several days of patrolling, ambushing, doing OP work and whatever else our OC required of us we would, ultimately, base up on high ground (GTI: Ground of Tactical Importance) and, as the platoon commander, I would do everything that was required to ensure our security and prepare to inflict grievous and suppurating wounds upon anyone who sought to disturb our slumber.

One night it was bitterly cold and, as pre-dawn would reveal to us, it was well and truly sub-zero by several degrees. It had rained the day and night before and our clothing, boots, socks, 'fart sacks' (sleeping bags) and whatever else could absorb water had done so. In the wee-hours it became impossible to sleep as the still, frosty air enveloped us in its 'deathly grip'. Mujiba always slept to my right and he had, wittingly or otherwise, snivelled-up and had moulded his body into my back for warmth. Some may question his actions, and some may even judge them to have been disrespectful. I never did. I smiled quietly to myself wondering if he actually knew what he was doing but I viewed it simply as an innocent act. When he arose, before 'Stand To', he looked at me and whispered 'Mangwanani Ishe'. He slid out of his 'pit' and silently gathered his webbing and rifle and took up his stand-to position.

Later that morning I asked him, matter-of-factly (so as not to embarrass him), if he was aware that he had been like a piece of Velcro with me and if he remembered that I had a serious girlfriend in Bulawayo. My attempt at light humour was lost on him and he recoiled at the suggestion of impropriety and responded: "Ahh, aiwa Ishe. Ndinokumbira ruregerero". (Ahh no Sir. I apologise) I came close to you because I knew you were cold…I wanted to give you some warmth, Seh." I told him that I was grateful to him for his kindness knowing that his innocent desire to care for his Ishe might be frowned upon. I squeezed his arm and told him "Ndatenda Mukono".

This small, almost innocuous act by a junior private soldier spoke volumes of the make-up of the RAR soja. Their earnest desire to look out for their Ishe was front and centre and it was an act so innocent but potent that I remain deeply touched by the thought of it to this very day.

A while later, still deployed in the Mangwende TTL, we were awaiting uplift and redeployment and he asked me what kind of music I liked listening to. Where music is concerned, I have a broad taste and I said that it really depended upon the mood I was in but jazz was completely off the radar…I have always held an intensely passionate dislike for the genre. I asked him what 'twisted his dials' and he said his favourite singer was "Phillip Collins". "Who?" I asked? He repeated "Phillip Collins…from Genesis, Ishe!" I laughed aloud; I'd never heard of him being referred to as Phillip. When I corrected him his simple response was, "Ishe, this man is famous! I cannot call him by his nickname….it is too disrespectful, and I have never met him. "What innocence; it's almost infantile of me that I recall this conversation but whenever I hear anything by Phil Collins these days, it reminds me of this fine young soldier. How blessed and privileged I was to have shared, all too briefly, in this young man's life?

My service in the 1st Battalion was all too short and in mid-1980 I was posted to 3RAR as the Adjutant, a post that I forewent in favour of remaining in one of the rifle companies. I was posted to Chipinga as the 2ic of B Company under the command of a first-class man and later, very personal friend, Major Marius Meiring (RIP). Whilst there, I received correspondence from Mujiba and responded in kind; it was a source of immense personal pride that I had, in some small way, touched this young man and that he had found motivation to remain in comms with his Ishe.

About a year ago, I was going through some storage boxes in our garage, from way back when, mostly containing documents, letters and the like. I came across a tattered and very old powder blue coloured envelope bearing a Rhodesian 20c postage stamp. I almost tossed it into the recycling bin but noticed a familiar bit of penmanship on the envelope. I confess, I started weeping immediately.

I do not have a serviceable scanner but have transcribed the letter absolutely verbatim, the last I ever received from my Mujiba:

'Dear Captain Fulton Ishe,

'This is Emmanuel, your Mujiba Sir, How are you Sir? I am well but I am sad because I am not making your tea and talking shit with you in the gangen Sir. I have been selected to go on Junior Leaders Course and I think you are the very one who put my name forward. Thank you, Sir.

'I am selected to go on parachute course soon but I am afraid because it is too high to jump but I remember you telling me Sir, when you were an RLI sodja you did these things and you also told me you were also a little bit afraid. I remember you Sir because you were always kind to me and you treated me like I was your mukomana Sir. Hah Sir we killed lots of magandanga together and that was nice.

'Sir, I will get married when I will be going on R and R and I will call my son Russell. It is not a name we Africans no but I am like your son Sir, handiti ishe? Please send me your picture so I can show my son and my wife also. Please write to me if you are not in the bush Sir.

'Your batman,

'Emmanuel Thomas Mukonoweshuro. 3 Pl, A Coy, 1 RAR'

That was one of the toughest things I have done in nearly forty years, but I am mostly saddened that I never had this brilliant, innocent but perfectly penned letter to include in 'Chibaya Moyo 1'. I commented on my relationship with this man in that first edition but his letter has, through a deep rooted love for this man (and all men of the RAR), reinforced the sentiments of my fellow officers, who were enormously privileged to serve alongside *Masodja* such as this fine man.

Not everyone received a gallantry decoration; MANY should have. Not everyone was demonstrably gallant in 'that sense' but, my God, these were loyal men and brave men who would follow you to the gates of hell and back without even blinking an eye nor thinking about it.

Dramatic? Kwete! Not at all. The absolute truth!

He passed away, sadly and very tragically, in late 1980. I salute you Emmanuel Thomas Mukonoweshoro, my good, loyal and very young "Mujiba".

God bless you my faithful friend. It is your Ishe who is very proud to have served alongside you. Zororayi murugare. Kurara mukoma wangu muduku, kusvikira tasangana zvakare. (Rest in peace. Sleep my little brother, until we meet again). Salute.

How's this for a strange turn of events:

Of Lumpy Throats and Misty Eyes

A few months ago, in a local Canberra supermarket, I was standing behind a black gentleman and his wife at the checkout. Whilst he was being served I overheard him chatting to his wife and my ears suddenly pricked-up because he was speaking chiShona!

I greeted him, "Kwazisa Shamwari" (Greetings Friend). He turned around to look at me and I nearly collapsed in an untidy heap. This was a face so very familiar to me from over forty years ago! He looked at me and, without speaking, reached out with his hand to shake mine. Only then did he return the greeting with a broad and engaging smile. He completed his purchase and waited for me whilst I paid for my mine and we walked outside the shop chatting animatedly. I invited him for a coffee whilst his wife took their shopping to their car and I asked him: "Unonzi ani? Ini ndini Russell" (What's your name? I am Russell). He spoke perfect English and said, "My name is Elijah Mukonoweshuro". I was wearing my RAR regimental tie and when he noticed it, his eyes widened, and he asked, "Is that an RAR tie Russell?"

My initial sense of having recognised something very special from his appearance was about to be revealed.

I told him that I had once commanded 3 Platoon, A Company, 1RAR and that my "Batman's" name was Emmanuel Thomas Mukonoweshuro. He stood up and came to my side of the table and drew me up by my hand and then embraced me. "That's my (late) older brother, Russell!" His eyes became as 'misty' as mine and we just stood there, holding each other! I had learnt of Emmanuel's tragic demise many years ago and he told me, "I remember you now! You came to our home a few times after giving Emmanuel a lift home. My brother loved you Russell, as only soldiers can love one another. He spoke about you all the time whenever he was on R&R. Do you know that Emmanuel has a son, who still lives in Zimbabwe, whom he named Russell?"

My 'Mujiba' had shared that very special compliment with me in his last letter and whilst I was serving in 3RAR. No greater compliment, no greater tribute and no greater an endearment has been paid to me than that.

Elijah and his wife were passing through Canberra on their way to Sydney. I gave him my contact details and he promised to write to me once he was settled.

How special is this life we live! Who would have thought, even in one's remotest dreams, that a chance encounter of this sort would be possible?

As I write this my eyes are filled with tears and my heart aches at the memory of a fine young soldier who once fought bravely by my side.

These are the finest memories I have of my time in the Regiment.

God is good.

NICK DELLA CASA, AN ENIGMATIC SUBALTERN by Captain Andrew Telfer

By the end of 1979, although it would be a while before we fully realised it, the political dimension had overtaken it all and for us the war was over. A ceasefire had been declared to facilitate national elections, the British Commonwealth were providing a monitoring 'force', the terrorists were being gathered into massive Assembly Points in rural areas and the Security Forces were being confined to barracks in the cities.

As this began, I was sent to the School of Infantry to serve as a Course Officer on National Service Officer Cadet Course Inf/26(167) to take place from 14 January to 6 June 1980. I took a room in the Mess and occupied one of the little rondavel offices in Cadet Wing, meeting my Course Instructor, Colour Sergeant Tony Kruger, 1RLI.

At the start in January, there were four squads: A, B, C and D. Initially, I had C squad but, when Captain Jug Thornton left the Army after the Election, I took over B squad as well. We put everything that we could into training the cadets. We still believed that they would be going into the same kind of action that we had experienced, so we emphasised the tactics that had been most prominent in our period of warfare. The tactical focus was on bush warfare: bush craft, patrol movement, observation posts, ambushing and Fireforce operations. For their final exercise, I requested and received troops from my alma mater, D Company, 2RAR and choppers from 7 Squadron, my old friends and comrades. Feedback from the veteran RAR NCOs greatly influenced my final assessment of the individual cadets.

The cadets were fine young men, committed and keen, which inspired us to give them a very tough time. Although the National Service course was much shorter than our Regular Cadet Course (5 months against 13 months), it can be as selective. Ours was, and any cadet who passed it was good, whatever rank he achieved on completion. If commissioned, he was very good, and I believe would have passed a Regular Cadet Course.

One of those to be commissioned in June 1980 was Nick della Casa, posted to the RAR in Umtali. Some weeks later, he called in at the School of Infantry and told me, over a quiet game of snooker in the Mess, that he had shot up the ZANU (PF) headquarters in Umtali with a pistol while driving past at night. Nick was something of an enigma. Reserved, cultured and polite, he was an Englishman with Argentine connections. He was also a little bit wild. I think he was seeking approval for an act driven by frustration at the war ending before he could be part of it. I was happy to approve the style - it was certainly one up on my thunder

SCHOOL OF INFANTRY
CADET WING
Course Inf/26 (167) B: NS OFFICER CADETS
14 JANUARY 1980 – 6 JUNE 1980

Standing L – R : 2 Lt R.B.D. Holmes; Rfn Midgley A.C.; 2 Lt J.S. Gallagher; 2 Lt M.H. Knight; 2 Lt N.G.C. Della – Casa; Cpl Steele W.K.
Seated L – R : 2 Lt P.M. Suttan; L/Cpl Funnekotter B.H.; L/Cpl Grobbelaar J.A.; Lt A.T. Telfer, SCR (Course Officer); 2 Lt I.H. Harris; 2 Lt D.I Clark; Rfn Magowan G.Y.P

flashes in the pioneer column cannon in Fort Victoria or the ascent of the Bogies Clock tower (of which he had been part) - but cautioned him to cool it as he was very lucky that he hadn't been caught.

After Nick left the Army and country, he became involved in cross-border activities sponsored by the South African government, back into Zimbabwe. In what was clearly a brain-fart by someone in a high place in Pretoria, groups of ex-Rhodesian soldiers were sent to 'destabilise' the new Zimbabwe government in some way. Ill-conceived and insignificant, they came to an end shortly after one of the incursions was ambushed and eliminated by a patrol from 42 Infantry Battalion (the former 2RAR) commanded by Lieutenant (formerly RAR Sergeant) Doro. Nick wasn't in that contact as he was, at that time, involved with Renamo in Mozambique, variously being held captive and filming a documentary on them.

He returned to the UK and became a photo-journalist, marrying Rosanna Curling, the daughter of a consultant pathologist at St Bartholomew's hospital. In March 1991, the young couple crossed on foot into Northern Iraq to make a documentary about the Kurds of Iraq for the BBC, accompanied by one Charlie Maxwell.

On Sunday 23 January 1994, the following article by Julie Flint appeared in the Independent newspaper in Britain, under the headline: 'Who Killed Rosanna?' (slightly edited for length):

'For the past three years, Marigold Curling, a consultant pathologist at St Bartholomew's hospital, has been looking for the person - or persons - who killed her daughter Rosanna in the Kurdish mountains of northern Iraq. She has made seven trips to the region, met everyone her daughter met, and retraced all her steps. She has confronted the man accused of killing her and been in court to see him convicted.

'In the past year, she has also had to bear her husband's death in a car crash and the Government's efforts to close Bart's. That battle has been partially won: sections of Bart's have been reprieved. The other battle also goes on: last week, even while wishing she could close her files and find some peace of mind, Dr Curling wrote to tell the Kurdish justice minister she was convinced that Hashem Ciftci, the smuggler jailed for 26 years for killing Rosanna, her husband, Nick della Casa, and his brother-in-law, Charlie Maxwell, shot the two men but not her daughter.

'After killing Nick and Charlie, Ciftci would have wanted to make sure Rosanna could not testify against him," she admits, "But I believe he didn't do it. The judge said he was convicted because there was no one else in the area. But that surely cannot be taken as proof of murder. And there was someone else in the area" - the Kurdish guerrillas of the PKK, who were holed up in the Iraqi mountains all winter, and Turkish commandos who were hunting them.

'Ciftci has always admitted killing Nick della Casa and Charlie Maxwell, who left England in March 1991 to make a documentary about the Kurds of Iraq for the BBC. But he has consistently denied shooting Rosanna, even when offered his life in exchange for a confession. He seems to feel some admiration for Rosanna, who navigated by the stars and cooked wild grasses when they were all lost in mountains so inhospitable that even the Kurds give them a wide berth.

'Although not a journalist, Rosanna had worked with Nick in Tibet and Afghanistan, and was confident as they set out for Iraq: Nick had not only survived 18 months as a captive of Mozambique's Renamo rebels, but also had the courage after his release to return to make an award-winning documentary about them.

'Charlie, a barrister by training, had spent 12 years as an officer in the Black Watch and planned only to accompany the couple across the border into Iraq before returning to England with the first films.

'Rosanna and Nick were married for less than six months. On 29 March, as Iraqi tanks fought their way back into northern Iraq after the Kurds' short-lived rebellion against Saddam Hussein, Rosanna saw her husband die. They were 30, eight years younger than Charlie Maxwell.

'The three had arrived in south-eastern Turkey a week earlier and were told that their BBC fixer would find them a guide in the town of Yuksekova to take them across the embattled Kurdish region into northern Iraq, 'liberated' from Saddam after his invasion of Kuwait and accessible only illegally. In the right hands, the journey would have been difficult but not impossible. But the trio fell into the wrong hands - those of a young man who offered to guide them to Iraq, at a price. The man was Ciftci.

'Rosanna's diary, found after her death, records that she was initially delighted with Ciftci, a slight, soft-spoken Kurd. But they could not communicate directly with him and Ciftci did not disclose that he was a draft-dodger on the run from the Turkish army and lived by smuggling.

'Siamand Banaa, the Kurdish official who eventually tracked him down, said: "He carried heroin from Iran and pornographic films from Turkey. He did arms, sheep, tobacco - everything you can mention. The three should never have been left in his care. Ciftci led the party towards the border on 23 March, leaving the main road whenever he saw a checkpoint. For more than four days they travelled across icy waters and over jagged peaks, sleeping rough and eating little. Villagers thought they were PKK guerrillas and reported them to police.

'On the fifth day, Ciftci turned west to seek help from a relative in the village of Harki, the last village on the Turkish side of the border. The tired and dispirited travellers could not have been brought to a more useless place: the route across the border from Harki led to a wilderness cut off from the rest of Iraqi Kurdistan by a river swollen by snow and rain. The Iraqi army had destroyed all bridges in the area. Ciftci's friend, Obeidullah, says he told Ciftci: "You are leading them nowhere." To which Ciftci replied: "Mind your own business".

'Obeidullah nevertheless led Ciftci across the border on the following morning - 28 March. The four continued alone and soon found their progress blocked exactly as Obeidullah had warned. They had no choice but to follow the curve of the river and soon found themselves travelling north again - back to Turkey. On 29 March they stopped for lunch at a place called Stouni, another stony outcrop that was once inhabited. It was Good Friday. They had covered 10 miles in 24 hours. The only witness to what happened next is Ciftci, who says there was an argument - conducted in sign language - over money. He decided he had had enough and picked up his gun to leave. Nick grabbed the barrel. Ciftci slipped and, feeling at a disadvantage, fired. 'There was a moment of silence," he told an interrogator later. "I looked at the other man and shot him, too. After the first shot, he was still on his feet. With the second, he fell."

'And Rosanna, whose body was discovered four miles away? Ciftci first said that he "took pity" on her as she hid behind a rock. Then he said he fired at her but missed. Then he claimed that he wanted to kill her, but his gun jammed. But he has always maintained that he returned next morning to shoot her but could not find her. Obeidullah, who went with him, corroborates his story and was acquitted by the court.

'Dr Curling cannot see why Ciftci should admit two murders and deny a third. She believes that Rosanna suffered the cruellest ill-luck - and ran into another killer as she fled. "Rosanna would have gone in the opposite direction to Ciftci after Nick and Charlie were killed," she says. "That would have taken her back to Turkey."

'In England, two months passed without news. And then, in mid-May, a deserter from the PKK walked into a Kurd safe haven carrying Charlie Maxwell's boarding card and a page from his passport. He reported finding two bodies.

'The Royal Marines recovered the remains and the Curlings were informed that one of the victims was a woman. They met the plane that carried the coffins home in the belief that one held Rosanna. A week later, they were told they had been misinformed: both victims were men.

'Dr Curling was deeply distressed, imagining Rosanna alive and in torment. She appealed to Massoud Barzani, Iraq's Kurdish leader. Barzani alerted Siamand Banaa, a veteran of his Kurdistan Democratic Party. Banaa soon found Rosanna's tape recorder and Nick's cigarette lighter in Obeidullah's house and learned that Ciftci had been the party's guide. He learned, too, that Ciftci had taken refuge in Iran.

'Peshmerga guerrillas sent to Iran found Ciftci in a refugee camp 15 miles from the border and brought him back to Iraq. "He looked like a lizard," says Banaa. "There was no emotion. I was very tempted to use unsavoury methods, but the most I did was to leave him without food or water for 24 hours. "We tried everything short of torture. Massoud did something he has never done before. He sat down with a criminal and said: 'Listen, my boy, I am your only chance. If you tell me the truth, I will spare your life.' Everyone knows Massoud. Ciftci would have believed him. But he still insisted he did not kill her."

'Rosanna's fate remained a mystery until November, when a group of peshmergas remembered seeing the body of a tall blonde woman four miles away from Stouni many months before. The woman had been shot and was lying, covered in blood, beside a river. They had rolled the body into the river, thinking it was one of the PKK's female fighters, and forgot about it until Barzani appealed for information.

'Dr Curling accepts that the body was Rosanna's and says it strengthens her belief that Ciftci did not kill her. In spite of Dr Curling's efforts, the truth about her daughter still remains a mystery. Nick della Casa himself was also an enigma, a brave and adventurous young man, yet mysterious and difficult to fully understand. Attracted to Rhodesia by a thirst for action, had he come earlier, he would have found it. Imbued with the *spirit of adventure*, it is a great pity that he, his newly-wed wife and his friend should have met such a tragic end.

Reference:
https://www.independent.co.uk/news/uk/who-killed-rosanna-a-london-pathologist-believes-the-kurdish-smuggler-who-murdered-her-son-in-law-1408878.html

CHAPTER NINETEEN

MASODJA

INTRODUCTION: MASODJA by Captain Andrew Telfer

> 'History teaches us that unity is strength and cautions us to submerge and
> overcome our differences in the quest for common goals, to strive, with all
> our combined strength, for the path to true African brotherhood and unity'
> Haile Selassie

It would be hard to read either volume of *Chibaya Moyo* without noticing the
frequent expression of 'brotherhood' felt among members of the RAR. There
definitely was a special bond among the members of our Regiment, a sense of
fellowship bordering on kinship, comradeship close to fraternalism.

While such a bond is not at all unusual among fighting men, brotherhood
between black and white men could never be said to be characteristic of Africa,
even to this day. Furthermore, the tribal differences between the Shona and the
Ndebele had led to open warfare until only a few generations earlier and would
return to it only three years after Robert Mugabe came to power. It seems as if, for
a short time in Rhodesia, a body of men were united in feelings and behaviours
that transcended superficial differences of race or tribe. The aim of this article is
to explore that phenomenon.

A South African helicopter pilot is recorded as saying that he'd never seen
such happy soldiers as the men of the RAR. Happiness appeared to be their default
state and humour their natural way. Grumbling is such a common trait among
soldiers all over the world that 'selfish grumbling' is almost the expected condition
between periods of 'selfless combat'. In the RAR, it was different; the tension of
combat was invariably relieved with mile-wide smiles. Similarly, any traveller in
modern Africa will have experienced an almost institutional surliness from men in
uniform, but not in the RAR, whose soldiers were naturally friendly. Smile at an
RAR soldier and he can't help smiling back.

African WOs and NCOs led extremely well in the absence of officers but, if
an officer were present, there were clear expectations that he would lead from the

front. As a simple example, I recall a night river crossing. We weren't in contact with the enemy but, as it isn't tactically correct for a commander to cross a river first, I stopped on the bank. No-one moved. I signalled someone to cross and received a nervous smile in return. This was my own platoon and I knew these men to be very courageous. They weren't scared, they were confused. In their order of things, this wasn't how it worked. Fortunately, the penny dropped, so I crossed first, and everyone followed happily behind me. Our soldiers were brave, but they expected leadership of a certain kind from their officers; it was the reciprocal of the respect that they gave us.

The establishment of the RAR was unique in the Infantry organisation, in that it included the position of Platoon Warrant Officer (PWO) between that of Platoon Sergeant and Platoon Commander.

A PWO would typically have about ten years' distinguished service, during which he would have displayed qualities of maturity and wisdom. In any army, all junior officers are unfamiliar with command and need their senior NCOs to guide and support them. In the RAR, there was the added unfamiliarity of living closely with black people. It is one of the great paradoxes of Africa that people of different

Rank of the RAR PWO

races live so near to one another but so separately. In an infantry platoon, that separation would have been disastrous, so the PWO provided a bridge of understanding between a junior officer and the African soldiers, a bridge in both directions. This dynamic encompassed the intrinsic nature or indispensable quality of the RAR, something (however abstract) which determined its character and enabled the success of the RAR platoon as a fighting unit and as a community of men. It was therefore appropriate that the position of second-in-command of a platoon was of Warrant Officer status.

The PWO did not, however, replace the officer or reduce his influence. In fact, RAR soldiers reflected their officer. If you were brave, they were brave. If you were hesitant, they held back. This is a very important point. The parallel is of a father with his sons, and it wasn't unusual for RAR soldiers to use that analogy when referring to a good officer's relationship with them. All the officer's values, norms, models and patterns of behaviour would rub off on his soldiers, just as a father influences his children. The officer was the example, the exemplar that the soldiers would tend to follow. If I heard an officer describe his soldiers in certain terms, I knew that he was unconsciously describing himself.

RAR soldiers were capable of extraordinary levels of courage. In the chapter '*RNR-RAR Gallantry Award Recipients*', you will read again and again of acts of gallantry and aggression in numerous anti-terrorist operations and contacts with the enemy. You will read of their contempt for the terrorists and how they challenged them to come closer and fight.

Cpl Stanley, Sp Coy, 1RAR

Under fire, you'll read how they could exercise exceptional calm and discipline to act in ways that would turn a battle, save the life of a comrade or defeat superior numbers. The tactical skill and aggression of RAR soldiers was an inspiration to all who served with them and was responsible for the deaths of hundreds of terrorists during the Rhodesian Bush War.

RAR officers were assigned a batman, a trained soldier who also acted as a kind of valet. This appointment usually fell to the most junior Private soldier but, in my platoon, I made it the soldier next most likely to be promoted to Lance Corporal. Working so closely with me improved his English and enabled me to train him more fully in minor tactics, voice procedure, navigation and so on.

We were issued with ration packs, each containing food for one day. European and African 'rat' packs were different, catering to differing tastes, so the food that my batman and I ate on patrol was a blend of both. For breakfast and supper, I ate three thick 'dog' biscuits, each with a line of butter and one of jam, squeezed out of the toothpaste tubes in which they came. For lunch, we would have my rice one day and his sadza the next, flavoured with spicy relish. Sadza is a stiff porridge made from maize meal, a staple of the African diet. The relish was a mixture of bully beef and African spices. We drank hot, sweet tea by the half-pint mug. There was harmony in our domestic arrangements, a quiet oasis in the armed conflict around us.

African soldiers made interesting drivers. Once, while being ambushed by terrorists on the main Salisbury to Fort Victoria road during the night, my driver took a 4.5 tonne Unimog, with a trailer attached and a full load of soldiers on the back, airborne over a high culvert and successfully landed it on the far bank (to my relief). In another, less encouraging incident, while driving along a sand road, my driver handed me the steering wheel which had somehow detached itself from the column. God knows what he thought I was going to do with it but the *Ishe*, of course, would have a plan...

Of course, the RAR was not isolated from the political and racial dynamics of the time, but our black soldiers somehow rose above them and Rhodesians of all races recognised and respected them. During World War I, 159 soldiers of the Rhodesia Native Regiment, the predecessor to the RAR, lost their lives. A further 69 RAR soldiers died during World War II and 5 more in the Malayan Emergency. During the Rhodesian Bush War, 191 RAR soldiers of all ranks were killed in action, on active service or murdered in their homes because they chose to fight for us rather than join the Black Nationalists. This commitment and sacrifice, together with the fact that 80% of the Rhodesian security forces were black, calls the lie on repeated political attempts to portray Rhodesia as a 'race war'. When you read later articles in this chapter, you will see how positively our soldiers responded to the appreciation and affection they received from the civilian population.

In contrast, you might like to research the treatment of soldiers of colour in other nations. The United States were among Rhodesia's leading critics and drivers of economic sanctions, yet African Americans who fought in World War I and World War II for the ideals of freedom, justice and democracy, returned home to racial terror and violence, including beatings and even lynching for 'wearing Uncle Sam's uniform' (Stevenson, 2017). Muhammad Ali had a fair point when, after refusing to serve in the US military in Vietnam, he famously said, "Man, I ain't got no quarrel with them Viet Cong. No Viet Cong ever called me nigger."

In a world characterised by segregation, the integration of the RAR, the genuine respect in which it was held by the civilian population, the affection between black and white soldiers, all helped engender a sense of a *unique* brotherhood, of belonging to a special and distinctive cohort.

In conclusion, the brotherhood of which we speak and write is not a superficial, idealistic image of a world viewed through rose-coloured spectacles. Nor was it characteristic of the cultural norms of the world at that time or even

Esprit de Corps

today. It was a spiritual bond born in combat and adversity, forged between young men, and much of it based on humour, as it should be. War gave the black and white soldiers of the Rhodesian African Rifles the opportunity to create something extraordinary and I am pleased that we didn't let that opportunity go to waste. Perhaps the RAR was a living example of the 'true African brotherhood' of which Haile Selassie wrote.

References:
Binda, A 2007, *Masodja*, 30 Degrees South, Pinetown, South Africa.
Stevenson, B 2017, *Lynching in America: Targeting Black Veterans*, Equal Justice Initiative, Montgomery, Alabama, USA.

OF MASODJA, TROOPS CANTEENS AND THE WVS 'LOVELIES' by Captain Russell Fulton

At the conclusion of an interesting and exhaustive first bush trip with A Company, 1RAR and en route from Op Hurricane to Methuen Barracks in Bulawayo for some long-overdue R&R, our Company Commander Maj Craig Beachell, pulled the convoy in to the troop's canteen in Hartley for a quick bite and cup of tea.

Troops canteens were manned by volunteer lady folk (Women's Institute and Women's Voluntary Service) who hailed from the town and district in which they lived, and they were, as far as I recall, not-for-profit establishments. Everything was either heavily discounted or free (where donations were welcomed), and all food was always freshly prepared and cooked. These good women gave freely of their time and I never passed a troops canteen during all my years in uniform when they were not open during normal working hours and on weekends. Come rain, shine, wind or hell-fire…they were always open!

On this particular stop, there were a few remarkable things that happened that completely disarmed and endeared me to this quiet little town and which I have never forgotten to this day. We have all heard that well-worn cliché, 'charity begins at home'; most paid lip service to it. That is until Hartley Troops Canteen raised its flag and showed her true colours. I can think of no finer example of the true meaning of this than what I witnessed on that Friday morning, 15 June 1979.

As our CSM barked the order to embus, the WVS ladies and their daughters hastily scrambled from their stations in the kitchen, clearing tables and from behind the counter and formed a line from their front door towards our parked convoy. I stood with my fellow subbies and OC as we watched, misty-eyes and with lumpy-throats, as these wonderful ladies shook hands and/or hugged every one of our men and thanked them for their service. When everyone was aboard, these lovelies started singing 'Sweet Banana'! Before the first verse had left their lips our troops all stood in the back of our TCV's and sang in their hauntingly beautiful harmonised voices "A, B, C, D, Support, Headquarters, I will buy you a sweet Banana..." They continued singing until we were out of the Hartley business district, many with tears running unashamedly down their cheeks.

What did this show our good RAR *Masodja*?

Rhodesians, regardless of race, gender, religion and ethnicity stood by their own, always and with a blinding devotion. To embrace a person of a different colour, especially one of the opposite sex during the days of Rhodesia defied accepted social norms in what was, a very conservative country. There was nothing racist about it, it just wasn't done. The very public and sincere demonstration of genuine goodwill by the WVS of Hartley dispelled any maligned notion of white superiority in our Company and Regiment.

It was as emotionally uplifting and enlightening for our men as it was for their madzishe. I was so enormously proud and touched by the actions of these wonderful ladyfolk who wore their patriotism not on their sleeves but over their hearts. I really hope that one of them will read this anecdote and know how very deeply their actions affected our men. All Troops canteens were staffed by warm and welcoming ladyfolk, but Hartley went a mile ahead. I never heard of anything quite as moving nor did I witness it again. Mind-blowingly special!

I salute all our good women who gave selflessly of their time in support of the Rhodesian defence machine and may God richly bless them all.

THE RAR MASODJA: THROUGH THE EYES OF ONE WHO SERVED
by Colonel John Pritchard

The RAR was the only regiment in Rhodesia to have platoon warrant officer (PWO) posts in every platoon. These warrant officers were the link between the officer and the troops. They were all very experienced soldiers, some having served over 20 years in the battalion in different theatres of war and they commanded enormous respect from officers and troops alike. I truly believe all RAR officers began their careers with a distinct advantage over their colleagues who served elsewhere.

I had the fortune to serve with the late PWO Obert Veremu, DMM (later RSM of 1RAR and 3RAR). I took over 15 Platoon E Company from Mick McKenna (later CO 1RAR in 1979) in early 1967 at Chete in the Binga operational area. The handover was somewhat daunting as I had enormous 'shoes to fill' and Mick could not stress enough how good my soldiers were and "not to ....it up". After he returned to Binga I had a month on my own to get to know my platoon. To say I was apprehensive would have been an understatement and I believe my NCOs and probably most of my troops sensed that. However it never showed.

Obert was always there to guide and counsel me and no decisions were ever made without his input. Besides being an excellent WO, leader, confidant and marksman he was also the battalion's champion 100 mile walker. I got to know him well and together we ran a great platoon. A fine man. Unfortunately he was badly wounded on Op Nickel and we parted company. A sign of his courage and determination was that he recovered from his wounds and returned to active duty after a period of time.

Our CSM was WO II Muzerecho Pisayi, MM, a Malayan veteran with some 15 years of experience when I joined. Although a man of small stature he commanded our respect and, as we platoon commanders got to know him better, we grew to appreciate his subtle advice and sense of humour. He was always cheerful (unless reprimanding some unfortunate AS who had the misfortune to cross his path) and to a point, mischievous.

Some months after commissioning, I was sent on a Bush Survival and Tracking Course and on a subsequent deployment to Binga I decided to put into practice a little of what I leant. At the time I was the reserve platoon based at Company HQ so one day I went out into the surrounding bush and caught and killed a legavaan. On returning to base the CSM asked what I had been up to. I told him what I had killed and that I wanted it cooked and served up to the OC at dinner that night. Muzerecho saw the funny side of my prank and swore L Cpl Murewu, the cook, and a few inquisitive AS to secrecy. As it transpired the cook was also serving roast chicken, an ideal complement as legavaan and chicken are similar in look and taste once prepared. That night after we had eaten I asked the OC if he had enjoyed the meal. He replied "yes" but on being told what he had also eaten he 'lost it' and tore strips off me. I bet the CSM had been listening as he was in good humour the next day. As for me, my platoon and I were soon banished to Chete for the remainder of our tour.

The Battalion RSMs in 1967 were WOI Matambo (commonly referred to by the subalterns as Sticks Matambo as he had extremely scrawny legs) and WOI Korb. As second lieutenants RSMs were to be avoided at all costs. However that was not always easy as they often sought us out for reasons of their own to politely reprimand the "Sir" for our appearance and or behaviour.

John Pritchard, CSM Pisayi Muzerecho MM, Ron Marillier: Binga 1969

One of our duties when at "home" was Duty Officer. Amongst the many different tasks during the 24 hour duty was to close the African WO and Sergeants'

Mess at 10.30 pm. Invariably, the RSM was present and he would greet the officer, offer him a beer and have a chat. This hospitality sometimes had a dual purpose; to keep the Mess open a little longer for the stayers and or to warn the officer of a problem in his platoon. Woe betide the officer who did not listen and accept the advice or take the necessary action suggested. An even more concerning occasion was when the officer entered the Mess to be greeted by both the RSM and one's CSM. Invariably there was a strong message waiting to be delivered to the officer. Not only was one's PWO and senior NCOs there to guide a new officer but also the RSM who knew everything!! An astute officer was well trained in RAR.

The AS' sense of humour was fantastic. They could always see the funny side in any situation. On one operation, the whole battalion was tasked to clear an island in the Zambezi River. The CO at the time, Lt Col GAD Rawlings, treated this as both a training exercise and an op. We had landing parties, beach heads to establish etc. E Coy had the task of clearing one side of the island which was basically a swamp. I must have sunk knee or hip deep into mud on a few occasions and my AS would squelch past giving me a knowing grin as I struggled to extricate myself. As for the ters, they were never there!!

Highlights of one's deployment to Chete were the weekly resupply by air of our rations. The AS loved it. There was never a problem cutting a DZ and then awaiting the arrival overhead of the Dak. All eyes would be glued to the open door watching our boxes being dispatched by members of 3 Air Supply Unit only to plummet to the ground and burst open scattering our precious fresh and dry rations over the DZ. The fun was collecting it all in under the direction of the Pl Sgt. Personally I always looked forward to fried eggs and bacon on resupply day but frequently had to settle for scrambled eggs if I was lucky to recover any. Over the years RhASC and RRAF perfected the "supply box" which did not shatter on impact. Too late for us in the 60s/early 70s!

My fishing at Chete was not by rod but rather by grenade. We were usually based on high ground overlooking the inlet. Once I got to know the local game ranger I would borrow a fishing net (usually confiscated from the local poachers) string it across the inlet with the help of those soldiers who could swim and then practice my throwing. The troops loved it and then the game was on, jumping into the water to gather up all the fish- enough for the platoon for a day or so.
Simple activities like washing in the lake was always fun. The banter and merriment was a joy to witness.

A Coy 2 RAR was established in late 1975 followed by B Coy in early 1976. I had the privilege of being on the 'ground floor' when we formed. The Unit was a mix of NCOs on promotion from 1 RAR and newly trained soldiers from Depot RAR. Our barracks was the Fort Victoria Showgrounds so we were spread amongst the pavilions, stalls and animal pens. Nothing was ever a problem and the soldiers took training and life in barracks in their stride. Of course weekends and later R&R spent in the township were the best. (B Coy's motto was, as this book is titled, *Chibaya Moyo* which can have two meanings: 'to stab at the heart in war and or in love'. B Coy troops certainly did both). I was fortunate to have WOII Hamandishe as our CSM. What a star and what an excellent right hand man to have both in the formation of the company and later on operations. He was a steady influence throughout my time in B Coy.

Our formation training was due to be three months but due to Op Repulse opening up it was cut short. What happened next was two years of constant deployment with R&R being every six – 10 weeks if we were lucky. Operationally we had numerous successes at platoon, company HQ and fire force (FF) levels. FF for us in the early days consisted of one or two choppers based at Coy HQ for a short time. Until we had our own paras we had to rely on the RLI to provide a full FF

(The need for more para trained troops became obvious in 1975 but there was a reluctance amongst some senior officers at Army HQ to train AS. Once again the AS proved the doubters wrong. Both 1 and 2 RAR battalions underwent para training over the next four years and proved to the world how good they were. RAR FFs had a very high kill rate).

For a new company we gelled extremely well and the soldiers were outstanding. Being African they understood bush craft, village layout and local behaviour and were quick to pick up anything suspicious. Many a call out for FF or HQ support was due to this local knowledge. On one occasion having deployed all three platoons on various tasks I was sitting at HQ when, I think it was, Jon Brand's OP reported a sighting. No FF was available so I mustered up a stick of 'cooks and bottle washers' from our HQ and set off by vehicle as quickly as possible. As luck would have it we arrived in time for Jon to talk me on to a gomo (kopje) where the ters had been sighted. Up my stick went and very quickly made contact killing one, capturing one with the third escaping over the top. Follow up was later called off. That day and in all contacts I never experienced any hesitation from our troops.

On one deployment into Gutu TTL we were based not too far from Hamandishe's village. One day he mentioned his family was being plagued by baboons who lived in an adjacent gomo and could we do something to help his family. There was not much going on operationally at that time so I decided we would put in a company attack on the gomo. Well the soldiers thought this would be fun (not sure about the subbies) and fun it was sweeping across the rough terrain, trying to close with the enemy who on seeing us were gone, up trees and over boulders faster than we could shoot them. The troops' laughter was infectious and echoed among the rocks. The result was one to the enemy but I believe we won the psychological battle in that they stayed away from Hamandishe's village for some considerable time.

My last posting to the Regiment (2RAR) was as Bn 2IC in 1979 under the late Lt Col Terry Hammond with RSMs Lou Hallamore MLM and Muchinguri DMM. What a leadership team I joined. The unit was a 'well-oiled battle machine' from top to bottom. Every company was well commanded and combat efficient.

By this stage most of the Battalion was para trained and we often provided our own FFs. One initiative of the CO was to have a composite FF based at Bn HQ on the Rutenga airfield under command of either the CO or 2IC. Sticks and para troops were drawn from different coys so as not to denude any one coy of too many troops. This was a remarkable example of how quickly the AS adapted to different commanders. This FF had amazing success and again proved how ruthless the AS were in combat. In our first month we accounted for the highest number of ters ever in 2RAR, (44 killed and six captured).

Two members I recall being exceptional were Lt Vince McCabe and Sgt Mqayi (A Coy). There were numerous others who every day in combat performed over and above the call of duty but unfortunately time and age prohibit me from remembering their names and the details of the contacts. One particular call out comes to mind, a 'turkey shoot' as we called it later. We were called out to a sighting of six to eight ters who had moved into a dry river bed for shelter. When we came over head I saw it was almost the perfect contact area. The stretch of river where the ters was relatively straight and not too densely wooded. The surrounding terrain was bare. The ters were trapped. I dropped one stick north and one south of the sighting and we slowly closed in. One terr endeavoured to escape but was soon accounted for by the K Car's 20mm. Resistance from those in the river was given but it was not long before it was all over. We had a 100% kill. The AS again proved how adept they were at fire and movement. Other callouts unfortunately were not that easy and resistance was often much stronger.

Sometime in late 1979 a South African Infantry Battalion joined us at Rutenga and came under command 2RAR. The SA hierarchy initially expressed reluctance to work with our AS but this was soon dispelled as our mixed sticks worked well together both on call outs and socialising back at base. Soldiers throughout the world always get on with one another. It is the senior 'shiny bum' officers who doubt their own troops' ability to work with others.

In early 1980 a cease fire was called and Tac HQ withdrew to a base near the Zim Ruins. Companies were still deployed in the field and were responsible for manning/ guarding Assembly Points (APs) into which ZANLA were supposed to gather. It was amazing the majority of 'ters' were young mujibas with a large number of ters remaining outside to continue their intimidation. Needless to say those platoons who were in the APs carried out their duties extremely well. Being surrounded and outnumbered, often 20 to 1, was daunting but again the RAR soldier proved himself a professional soldier and no serious incidents took place.

Conclusion

Militarily, the RAR masodja have always proved themselves worthy soldiers, adaptable to different theatres of war and against enemy troops of varying nationality, tribe or colour. Before my time they served with distinction in Burma, Egypt, Malaya and the Federation. From my personal experience during the Rhodesian War they were formidable in combat, serious in training, enthusiastic in sport and with a sense of humour second to none. Irrespective of the situation they were in, they were always able to see the funny side of it. They were extremely loyal, capable, flexible and professional. History has shown how reliable the RAR soldier has been. Never defeated, the regiment served the government of the day without hesitation or doubt.

WHY DID THEY FIGHT? by Major Michael P Stewart

Editors' Note:
This article is an *edited* extract from Major Michael Stewart's thesis: '*The Rhodesian African Rifles, The Growth and Adaptation of a Multicultural Regiment through the Rhodesian Bush War, 1965-1980*' (1998).

The Article:

When one studies the RAR's actions in the Rhodesian Bush War, one simple question surfaces along with a complicated answer: why would a black African soldier voluntarily fight to preserve a white-rule government in Africa? Many did. By the end of the war, Rhodesian Security Forces boasted three battalions (nearly 80 percent of the regular army) of predominantly-black RAR, and many more RAR battalions could have been established. In addition, many of the BSAP policemen were black, and national service eventually placed black soldiers in the Rhodesia Regiment.

To the RAR soldier, the regiment was a source of income, stability, and family pride – in many instances, he was doing the same job his father and grandfather had done before him. In the regiment, the RAR soldier was a respected member of a team rich in traditions and proud of its history. He was a part of a unique culture all its own. He was not a second-class citizen, nor was he viewed as inferior or incapable. Leaders in the RAR – black and white – were tough, experienced, capable men who led by example and from the front, as do most good leaders in professional armies. While factors such as income, stability and family pride brought recruits to the RAR, they stayed and fought because of loyalty to the regiment and to their leaders.

Two sides – militant nationalism and incumbent white rule – vied for recruits among the black population. Military-aged black males in Rhodesia were often forced to choose their side. Logically, there should have been little motivation for them to volunteer and fight to sustain the white-rule system. To many Rhodesian blacks, ZAPU and ZANU were not exactly the right answer. They represented hatred, communism and unbridled violence. For many more Rhodesian blacks, their lives in the rural tribal areas – politics aside – were increasingly interrupted by clashes and violence surrounding the issue of majority rule. To protest the atrocities of ZANU and ZAPU and protect their own livelihoods and tribal system, many black Africans voluntarily fought for white Rhodesia, in the RAR and in other elements of Rhodesian Security Forces.

In fact, many more black recruits volunteered than could be accepted for service. One former RAR training officer stated that on recruiting days many more volunteers would stand outside the gates of the depot than required to fill 200 available training slots, from which about 130 trained soldiers would be selected and sent to the regiment after a six month training program.

This availability of volunteers did not substantially diminish throughout the Bush War, even after fighting intensified through the late 1970s and the RAR was constantly deployed to fight increasing numbers of ZANLA and ZIPRA. In an interview with *Illustrated Life Rhodesia* in 1975, Lieutenant Colonel David Heppenstall, commander of 1RAR, stated that the regiment had no shortage of candidates, "often 100 per cent more than we require, and sometimes more than that percentage. I can recall one occasion when we required 100 recruits, and 500 applied."

The RAR soldiers were never forced to fight against their fellow tribesmen in the nationalist organisations. However, they chose to do so in great numbers. The rest of this article will explore the reasons why many black soldiers made this choice.

Income

In 1963, the lowest entry-level African soldier in the RAR was paid about 10 percent of what his 'European,' or white, counterpart made in the RLI. This pay system was inherited from the Federal Army of Rhodesia and Nyasaland, and before that, from the British colonial army. The unequal pay scale improved only very slightly, until major reforms were made in 1977–8 to increase pay and opportunities among black and white soldiers in the Rhodesian army. Even so, the relatively modest pay for an African recruit in the RAR was on par or better than most of his other options and placed the RAR soldier in rather good financial standing among his counterparts in the villages and farms of Rhodesia.

Most other black Rhodesians were unskilled labourers in the commercial farms or mines, or lived in the tribal areas as subsistence farmers. With little education and slim opportunity for advancement outside the army or police, there were few opportunities elsewhere. Within the regiment, however, an RAR soldier could expect a solid starting pay and excellent chance for advancement from private to senior NCO in a merit-based promotion system.

Stability

The RAR provided family housing, meals, education and medical care to its African soldiers and their families. When the soldier was in the field, his family received free meals, and they drew from the support network of other families of soldiers and officers on the military barracks. Unlike their white counterparts, black soldiers did not pay into a pension program, nor were they charged for meals themselves. African terms of enlistment were 7 years, compared to 3 years for white enlistments, which provided a stable employment environment and ample opportunity for the RAR soldier to learn his craft and become proficient. The Rhodesian Army Education Corps ran schools for children and wives, as well as for the soldiers themselves, so there was substantial incentive for an RAR soldier to stay with the regiment once he had a family. This system also allowed children of RAR soldiers to grow up with an appreciation of the familial atmosphere of the regiment, which encouraged them to follow in the footsteps of their fathers.

Family Pride

In selecting candidates for entry into the RAR, one of the easiest criteria to use was a family member's service and recommendation. The RAR recruited from all over Rhodesia, but most heavily from the Karanga, a tribe of the Shona people found predominantly in the Fort Victoria (now Masvingo) area in the central and south-eastern part of the country. By recruiting heavily from one tribe, the regiment facilitated a family tradition among the Karanga, where grandfathers served in the Rhodesia Native Regiment during World War I, fathers served in the RAR in World War II, and sons counted the days until they too could stand the line as a masodja (soldier) like their forebears. By recruiting family members of RAR soldiers, the regiment gained known military skills from a ready pool of willing recruits.

This is not to say the RAR was a Karanga tribal army. The demographics of the regiment were nearly identical to the black demographics of the nation. The RAR was about 85-90 percent Shona (not exclusively Karanga), 10-12 percent Ndebele, and a much smaller percentage of other tribes.

Regimental Traditions

The RAR was originally established as a colonial rifle regiment of the British Army, and was like any other colonial regiment, except in its lack of dependence on the British Army for its leadership. Because of its unique status as a self-governing colony after 1923, Southern Rhodesia recruited its own white officers into the RAR. Even the RAR's sister formations to the immediate north - the Northern Rhodesia Regiment and King's African Rifles - relied mainly on seconded officers and NCOs from the British Army, so the investment of RAR officers in fighting for their own regiment, for their own country, was quite a profound difference between the RAR and most other British colonial regiments.

The badge of the regiment represented the multicultural background of the RAR. This badge, devised within months of the establishment of 1st Battalion in 1940, consisted of the Matabele shield (I-Hawu), in brown and white, upon which was vertically placed a knobkerrie (Nkudu) and crossed assegais. Across the bottom left to top right was the Shona digging spear (Museve) with the narrow sharp blade and an iron pick at the base of the shaft. Crossing from bottom right to top left of the badge was the broad-bladed fighting spear of the Zulu warrior (Umkhonto). The badge was supported by a scroll bearing the inscription Rhodesian African Rifles, with black lettering on a red background. The badge and colours were unique to each regiment – the RLI also had its own badge, as did the BSAP and Rhodesia Regiment – and these were proudly displayed by the soldiers of the regiment on their uniforms and on parade.

Parades were extremely important events for the RAR. The regiment conducted parades for many occasions: trooping the colour, the Queen's birthday, reviews for distinguished visitors, Regimental Week (called Tanlwe Chaung, after the RAR's famous fight in Burma), and countless other occasions. Pride in appearance and smart drill were distinct points of pride for the RAR, and the men took great satisfaction in displaying the highest military standards on parade. This formal tradition was a tremendous source of self-esteem for black Rhodesians, who had few other opportunities to work as peers with their white counterparts.

Uniforms were also a source of pride for the men of the RAR, very much in the British colonial mould. African soldiers had a reputation of paying particular attention to detail and proudly wore their uniforms. Early in the war, the RAR soldiers turned out in immaculately starched khakis complete with puttees around their ankles. The RAR bush hat was another item of uniform item that set the regiment apart.

In the pattern of the British regimental system, once an officer was badged into the RAR as his parent regiment, he stayed on the regimental rolls, and continued wearing his RAR uniform (badge, hat and dress uniform) no matter where he was assigned. This created a sense of belonging and ownership between the individual and his regiment. Very rarely did an officer change his parent regiment, and only then with the expressed approval of the Colonel of the Regiment.

African Traditions and Practices of the RAR

In addition to these British traditions, the RAR had a few traditions and practices of its own. Its mascot, songs, and habit of secretly 'naming' officers were all generated by the men and added to the RAR's culture and esprit de corps. Additionally, Platoon Warrant Officers (PWOs) were a unique duty position within the RAR, created to provide black supernumeraries and role models for the soldiers within the platoons. For example, RAR soldiers killed in action usually had two funerals-one for the regiment and one for their family in the kraal. All of these traditions served to cement the bond of loyalty between the African soldier and his regiment, and these bonds proved strong throughout the war.

The regimental mascot, a goat, came about after some selection. Originally, the regiment had chosen a zebra as its mascot, but in practice found both the zebra and its successor, a donkey, unfit for military life. Finally, in May 1965, Chief Cronje of the Fingo Tribe (a people who had accompanied Rhodes' Pioneer Column) solved the problem by presenting the regiment with a three-month old goat, promptly named 'Induna.' Induna rapidly became a favourite among the troops and was trained to kneel on its forelegs and bow its head to 'present arms.' Induna lived to the age of eight, and on his death, was given a guard of honour,

Last Post and Reveille, and was succeeded as the regimental mascot by another goat, Private Tendai.

The soldiers had a habit of singing songs on route marches, details, at parties and anytime the opportunity presented itself. Accounts of the RAR songs marvel at the sound of the voice of the regiment, lifted in unison in 'Sweet Banana,' (the regimental song), or any other song relating to their experience in the war. It was quite common, particularly after some 'lubrication of the throats' with a liberal dosage of Chibuku (African home-brewed beer), for RAR soldiers to burst into boisterous song, mainly about their regiment and their history. These soldiers were extraordinarily happy, and justly proud of their achievements.

African soldiers had a name for every officer in the regiment. It was a sign of acceptance for a white officer to be given a name by his soldiers, The names were not always particularly flattering or exalting, but the existence of a nickname demonstrated acceptance of an officer among the ranks of his soldiers and were shared with the officers only occasionally by the NCOs of his platoon.

Platoon Warrant Officers (PWOs) were a highly effective group of senior leaders in the RAR. These leaders were absolutely essential to sustaining and perpetuating the regimental culture of the RAR. PWO was a rank between Colour Sergeant and Warrant Officer. The PWO was the primary non-commissioned officer in a platoon. Most PWOs had at least 12-14 years of service, and they were responsible for ensuring that the orders of the platoon commander were carried out, caring for the soldiers, and training the members of the platoon-including the young lieutenant in command. If the platoon ever lost its lieutenant, the PWO was there to lead them in combat. The PWO was the principal instrument of regimental culture in the RAR. He knew, taught, and exemplified the history and values of the regiment. Without exception, every former officer interviewed spoke with special respect and reverence for this class of leaders in the regiment.

The RAR truly fostered a familial environment among its soldiers and officers. When the regiment lost a soldier, for example, 'the war stopped' for his platoon. His fellow soldiers held a funeral service at the regiment's chapel before releasing his body to his family in the kraal, where his relatives would gather for a days-long remembrance, drinking Chibuku and singing. On rare occasions, families invited white officers from the regiment to these events, and the officers were honoured to attend. Those officers who did attend tribal funerals recalled the events with great reverence as a profound experience.

Leadership

The RAR was blessed during the course of its history with some outstanding leaders. Like other British colonial units in Africa, the officers were all white (until 1977, when the first black officers were commissioned), and most of the NCOs and all of the soldiers were black. By its nature, the RAR challenged a leader to adapt to cultural norms among his soldiers. Good officers in the RAR tended to be those who learned the languages and tribal customs of their soldiers, to understand what motivated them and what they feared. Leading and training these soldiers took patience, as many of the problems presented by RAR soldiers-from multiple wives to witchcraft and spirit mediums-were completely foreign to white, 'European' culture.

Officers in the Rhodesian Army were very highly selected. In one typical officer intake in 1977, 650 candidates applied, 178 went to a selection board, and 45 were selected as officer cadets. Of these, 18 actually passed out of training as Second Lieutenants. These 18 were then sent out to the Rhodesian Army based on where they were needed, and where their cadre saw that they fit best.

According to a former officer cadet course instructor, "We paid great attention to the leaders we were going to use." Officers who were to serve in the RAR were selected after completing the 13 month officer cadet course at the School of Infantry in Gwelo, after which, "we knew those guys [officer cadets] as well as their dads did." In selecting which newly commissioned officers were sent to the RAR, the selection committee looked for the more serious, more outgoing officers, who were able to interact with people, and who instinctively led by example.

Leadership by example was among the most important traits of an RAR officer. This was what the soldiers expected of their officers. RAR soldiers did not respond well to being given an order and expected to operate with initiative, as could well be done within the commando structure of the RLI. To function best, the RAR officer had to lead from the front, and they were selected and trained to do just that.

Equally important was the leadership of the black non-commissioned officers and warrant officers. The Regimental Sergeants Major (RSMs), Company Sergeants Major (CSMs), Warrant Officers (WOs) and Platoon Warrant Officers (PWOs) were the epitome of what a black soldier could strive to be, until the first black officers were commissioned in July 1977. These men knew, lived, and taught the history and traditions of the regiment to soldiers and officers alike, and they were among the most capable soldiers in Rhodesia.

Leaders in the RAR understood the importance of morale. Napoleon's famous quote, "morale is to the physical as three is to one" was of utmost importance in training and leading African troops. "The aim was to create a unit with high morale; that is . . . the conquest of fear and the will to victory." To that end, officers of the RAR ensured the basic needs of their soldiers-pay, family, education, pride-were met, and that their soldiers were constantly involved, never bored. In preserving morale over time, RAR leaders ensured the lessons and values of the regiment endured across generations and through the challenging situations the regiment faced.

Conclusion

The reasons black soldiers joined the RAR are best summed up by CSM Obert Veremu, who said in 1975:

"I joined the Army when I was 20 years old, in 1953. My uncle is a soldier, and I knew if I joined the Army, I would be all right. I enjoy the work very much, and also it is very good to have everything free – uniforms, rations (our wives, too, get free rations while we are away on active service); medical attention, and schooling for our children...

"These terrs are bad men. I have seen tribesmen who have been beaten to death by them. I also saw the woman whose lip they tore off with pliers. It is very bad what they are doing to their own people."

In many respects, black Rhodesian soldiers enlisted for the same reasons most soldiers enlist in most armies – income, stability, pride, tradition, leadership. These pieces of regimental culture in the RAR are not virtues or characteristics that cannot be found anywhere else. The RAR is remarkable because these reasons and these bonds stayed true through the end of the war, through incredible pressure on black Rhodesians to succumb to the Black Nationalist groups and cast off a government that was portrayed to them as oppressive, racist and hateful.

The experience of the RAR in the Bush War provides an excellent opportunity to examine why soldiers choose to fight. During the course of the war, the atmosphere in which these soldiers worked was constantly changing and fraught with racial, tribal, and international tension. The world in which the RAR soldier lived was turned upside-down, so that by 1980, his former enemy commander was his commander-in-chief. The enemy he had hunted down for 15 years, who had killed his friends, were integrated as peers into his formation. Militarily, the RAR was never defeated, but in the end, its war was lost. Loyalty for this soldier to anything but his regiment evaporated amidst the tremendous shifts resulting from the emergence of a majority-rule state of Zimbabwe.

Through to the end of the Bush War, and beyond, RAR soldiers remained loyal and steadfast to their regiment, and that must be their legacy. In the end, the values of the government – white-rule or otherwise – were irrelevant. It was the regiment that drew these men in, and their loyalty was more to their comrades and their heritage than to any particular government or cause.

Source:
Stewart, Michael P 1998, '*The Rhodesian African Rifles, The Growth and Adaptation of a Multicultural Regiment through the Rhodesian Bush War, 1965– 1980*', US Army Command and General Staff College, pp. 5–6 & 13–24.

THE CAMOUFLAGE YEARS: FEBRUARY 1978 to FEBRUARY 1980 by Corporal Andrew J. ("I was only following orders") Krajewski

'To those who took part (in It), it was a watershed in their lives. Before It, one's appreciation of values was only half developed. Now- new standards and new touchstones. In my case, at least, things I had previously taken for granted, I can now appraise and value in a truer perspective, diverse things, ranging from human character to water supply, from a cup of tea to food and shelter. I learned how much of what we think to be necessary is superfluous; I learned how few things are essential, and how essential these things really are. I had never known hunger or thirst in the sense that I know them now; nor appreciated the vital differences between day and night, moonlight and starlight.

'I had always before supposed that to be cooped up for a long time with the same people meant to quarrel with them. I had supposed that after a long period of strain one would see people at their worst and at their best, but I never guessed how, when all the layers are stripped off one by one, far more people are basically good than bad. I did not know how closely linked food and morale really are. I did not know what it was to be hunted, nor the marvellous sense of relief of deliverance.

'All these things I now know. I hope I shall never forget them. I have lived in its atmosphere ever since.'

Brigadier Bernard Fergusson, *Beyond the Chindwin*, (1962, p.15).

'In its atmosphere...' wrote the Good Brigadier. What does this mean to me? My Camouflage Years started in late February 1978, at Llewellin Barracks, a shite-hole of note. I passed initial screening for officer selection and presented myself, with the host of other hopefuls, for Course Inf/26(161): alpha squad, at the School of Infantry, Gwelo.

My first encounter with the troops of RAR was through the demonstration squad. Through these immaculately turned out, quiet, skilful and thoughtful young men, we learned the essence of fieldcraft. To this day, I'm mindful of how to search the landscape before me; looking for shape, shadow, silhouette, surface, spacing, and movement.

Life lessons in seeing without being seen.

Having completed the 4 ½ month-long course, given the rank of corporal, I was posted to an area of unsurpassed beauty, wildness, solitude and silence. It was an area along the middle Zambezi River, patrolled by elements of No. 2 (Indep.) COY, RAR. It encompassed the eastern basin and shores of Lake Kariba, the entire length of Kariba Gorge, the so-called Flat Lands, from "A" Camp through Chirundu, and east past the defunct sugar estates, and ever on to Mana Pools. More rarely we patrolled the area along the length of the Chewore River, and its confluence with the Zambezi, and downstream to a point about 15 km further along. This was Garden of Eden stuff then, truly: pristine in a sense long-lost and these days, not understood.

Our RAR regular *masodja* were people to be imitated. From them I learned everything of value I came to rely upon as trade-craft. They quickly, effortlessly, elegantly, and comprehensively showed us, fit as we were, and excellent shots too, the difference between the Hooters "Tally ho the fox!" fitness and long-range, operational fitness, moving impossibly heavy packs at a relentless walking speed, in prostrating heat and humidity, and all the while fully vigilant. The value of placing that all-important first shot, when it counts most. And above all, care of weapons and skill in their use.

These men were proud of their weapons and showed great care in keeping them gleamingly clean and serviceable, no matter the weather. I had three *superb* machine gunners in my time Up There: first Private Tembo, then Pte Dube and finally Pte Makore. The sight of a 4 x 2 patch and the heavy scent of Young's .303 gun oil are to this day hard-wired into my soul, with MAG belts stripped one by one, rounds polished and carefully reinserted, and the mechanism oiled and rubbed to a glimmering polish. Never a stoppage, not a single one. Always an economy of ammunition: two to three rounds per burst, at the base of likely cover within the allotted arc of fire. Not a hole blown through a tree trunk higher than 20 cm from the level of the soil. Effective fire the rule and never the exception.

There was real potency in ammunition. Private Banda, turning his "totem", a palm-polished, glimmering 7.62 x 51 mm NATO cartridge, unrolled from its 4 x 2 shroud, endlessly turning end over end between strong, slender, dextrous fingers, saying in his deep and gentle voice: "Now THEES is a *real* bullet-i!". There was another time, later on, with Banda staring, pickled onion-eyed in disbelief at a tiny 5.56 mm (.223 calibre) round from an M16. "Ah, but you cannot shoot the Gooks with this! This one is for the squirrels only!"

And that "sixth sense": I gained an extra layer of vigilance and sense of awareness. "Coporro! We must move **now**: this is a very bad place!" Spooky. After all, sometimes you count The Meat. Sometimes The Meat counts you.

There was yet another side: from these quiet, curiously gentle men, I learned bush-craft among huge and hairy *nyamazaans*: elephant, rhino, hippo, buffalo, lion and leopard. And crocodiles, never forget those Turbo Geckoes. We learned to patrol together, shaking out without conscious thought into appropriate formations, according to ground and likely threat. And always, graciously shared tricks and wrinkles from these seasoned, experienced and courteous brothers- for so they became to me.

These were some of the finest, unforgettable characters I've ever known, a deeper, fuller appreciation for whom has come to me with advancing years. The magnifying effects of time? Not at all: these were good soldiers, and true men. Has this come too late? I hope and pray not.

Above all, ours was a sharing of the highest highs, the lowest lows.

We endured real thirst and hunger, fatigue and pestilences through spiteful and weaponised Buzzers of every kind. We shared sleeplessness, boredom, vulnerability, poor health, terror and extreme hazard. We shared also moments of priceless hilarity, laughter (seemingly always and everywhere), intricate practical jokes, fascinating conversation (always in quiet, gentle yet animated voices), stories and tradition, and great, swelling pride. I was granted intimate insight into the personal lives of people about whom I knew nothing. And perhaps above all, learned by osmosis a deep love and appreciation of contented silence spent in places of great natural beauty. That this long list was conferred so graciously, in my own language, and so seamlessly is remarkable. Yet also these brave, simple men, both rough and wise, offered physical protection, psychological support, and the honour and privilege of being able to lead them.

We honkey *ouens* shared unforgettable times, many never before experienced, nor ever since repeated, with a remarkable cast of characters, and I'm FAR the richer for this, and for the lessons learned at the sides of these magnificent, ferocious, practical and canny *masodja*. These, all of them, were a man's Men. They embodied all the virtues: raw physical courage, fortitude, resilience, optimism, discretion, patience, courtesy, and always pride of- and skill at arms. "Defend your country!" They did that, and a lot more, with dexterity and distinction. I've ever since tried to live my life in honour of Them, and in Their example.

I cannot forget the priceless sense of wonder we shared in nature; the spicy stickiness of a fresh mopane seed, peeled of its seed-coat, wrinkled in the palm of one's hand. The heavy, sticky musk- sweetness of honey, gently winkled out with a clean grass stem through the tiny nest opening made by mopane bees. The sight of a fat, fussy, bright red velvet mite, trundling across a calloused, pink palm ("Touch heem. You see? He is soft like the velvet!"). The churring rattle of a greater honey-guide, dipping in looping flight, chattering in the leafy branches above us ("Ah, but-i, shoowa! He will show us where the bees have their honey!"). Life skills, all.

I have a head brim-full to overflowing. Hard, sharp, diamond-bright images of those times, places and people, crisp in every detail. Only now have I developed the capacity to appreciate all I took for granted; that which I saw, felt, tasted, touched, smelled, heard and actually achieved.

And the images and memories? In the most important sense *"chibaya moyo"*. A spear to the heart. These I have seared into my memory; branded upon my soul. Unburied treasure.

I'm typing these words blanket-swaddled, and seated on our narrow, shady verandah, within sight, sound and smell of the Great Southern Ocean. I hear the shrieking of pink and grey cockatoos- galahs- and Australian magpies warbling in the *Eucalyptus* trees nearby. I'm watching a family of crested pigeons and a tattered Western Rosella gleaning the hulled oats and millet seed Shirley and I put out for them. Is this what now passes for wisdom and contentment? It'll surely do, until something better comes along.

I cannot forget Them. Theirs was a huge appetite for life: men who well and truly sucked the marrow from the bones of life. Consummate athletes too, they moved with grace and agility around a volleyball court, and to drop a soccer-ball at the feet of my own Pte Dube was to see **true** greatness. They sang in perfect harmony, and danced with that fluid, near boneless grace so lacking in Us Honkey Ouens.

To them I owe this life's debt. "Defend your country!" They did, and lots more besides. I can barely put down on paper the feelings I have. My heart is too full. Diamond-bright sensory detail, embodied in memories. I pray these are Eternal Ones.

There are early mornings, fewer now, when I cannot shake a feeling of panic: I look at my hands and see the cuticles of my nails stained with bright blood. I cannot wash the stickiness away. I see M. propped against the rough bark of a mopane tree, a deceptively tiny hole in his left side. He just cannot seem to be able to breathe. He is smiling; calm. My face is stricken. He is the colour of graphite, and his nails are blue.

"Don't cry" he is saying to me. 'I am not afraid". His one hand is grasping the barrel of his machine gun. It is dawn: ring-necked doves in the tree above us, and far away the call of a fish eagle, punctuated by gunfire. Slow, spaced shots. The final, the deep rolling boom of an FN. It is over. His smile widens.

Not far away, I hear the high-pitched whine of an inbound Alouette III helicopter. In a severe hurry. The A-76 radio handset cradled under my ear crackles into life. There is a blizzard of dust. We lift him. The last thing we see is the blood on the ground where he lay.

Chibaya moyo: a spear to the heart. A spear to my heart. That place, that time, those men. *Masodja*, and my memories of them.

A spear to my heart.

A.J. Krajewski

Emu Point, Western Australia

LONG DROPS AND EIGHT-LEGGED IMPALAS by Major General Mike Shute

Here are two little stories that I often relate when we have old soldier gatherings and go down memory lane. To me they are important little snippets of why my time serving with our *Masodja* in the Regiment was so rewarding.

Back in the early days of Border Control, we often ended up in remote bush areas along the border. For 1 Brigade our border was the banks of the Zambezi and Lake Kariba. Deployed for lengthy periods of four to six weeks, semi-permanent camps were often constructed. Later, many of the former temporary camps became constructed permanent bases. Camped in one such base, with Company HQ and one platoon, for an extended period, the traditional Long Drop toilet was constructed. The wooden Thunder Box had been set in to an old anthill, sited some fifty yards from the Zambezi. A hessian screen inland but the opening faced the river with panoramic views of the beautiful Zambezi and beyond. A perfect place for Ishe to relax and enjoy his morning constitutional.

Early one morning, after stand to, I sat relaxed and enjoying the view, when Sgt Sake marched a fatigue party across my front. Sgt Sake was a colourful character, who loved the parade ground, drill and discipline. Perhaps he was more the Drill Pig than the Bush Soldier.

On seeing me, without thinking, his immediate reaction was to shout the order EYES RIGHT and a dozen or so soldiers duly complied. Fortunately, I had my bush hat on and was able to salute and order "eyes front Sgt Sake". Off they went, with some merriment in the ranks as the soldiers undoubtedly saw the funny side to the event.

Sometime later Sgt Sake transferred to HQ Coy. He joined the Regimental Police and was appointed 1RAR Regimental Provost Sergeant, a job at which he excelled. Sadly, I do not recall where his career led, nor where he ended up, I do not think he remained in 1RAR. Perhaps a transfer to Depot RAR or another Battalion. If any reader has some info on his career I would love to hear from you.

My second story is about Cpl Phillip, my company cook, when I was OC C Coy, again on border control deployment. We were based at Binga, where a permanent base camp had been constructed. This was back in the days when time in barracks enabled the Inter Company Championship Competitions to still be held. Was a sad day when long and lengthy deployments on operations put an end to the hotly and often ferocious inter-company competitions being held.

Capt MD Shute - 2IC HQ Coy 1RAR

Before deployment, we had completed all the Champion Company events and had done exceedingly well. However, a few more companies had to compete back at Methuen, which could possibly affect C Coy being appointed Champion Company. In time, a congratulatory signal duly arrived from the Commanding Officer appointing C Coy as the Champion Company. Great jubilation and a need to celebrate. I grouped the Company together in Binga for one night. We could not have a full-blown party, so (with National Parks authority), we shot an Impala for a good fresh meat supper for the troops. Fortuitously the impala had eight legs.

When the troops had eaten the officers retired to the "Mess" for our evening meal prepared by Cpl Phillip. As only Cpl Phillip could arrange, and unbeknown to us, he had obtained a fair portion of roast leg of impala with all the trimmings for our dinner. The fresh vegetables were apparently courtesy of the BSA Police Member in Charges cook, whose house was next to the camp. Thinking that was it, and a great meal it was, in comes the sweet. An apple pie (presume ingredients from the same next-door cook). To our delight the pastry top was displaying C COY CHAMPIONS.

Later, Cpl Phillip was promoted to sergeant and was an Officers Mess cook at Depot RAR Balla Balla. Following my retirement from the army, Aileen and I were on our little farm in Essexvale. One day we had a visitor, and to our delight it was Sgt Phillip. He had come to see us and specifically to bring a gift for Aileen. His wife had knitted a beautiful white mohair type jacket. Recalling this event, nearly forty years later, still brings tears to my eyes, such wonderful memories never to be forgotten.

AFRICAN SUNSET by Mrs Ros Crone

They (the RAR) arrived that morning in Hartley to begin an anti-terrorist operation in the nearby Tribal Trust Land. They set up their base camp on the football field near the police station in preparation for an early start the next morning. The police house we occupied was adjacent to the field and as we set off for an evening in the police pub, there was much activity from the RAR camp as they prepared their evening meal. The RAR officer was already ensconced in the pub and we all gathered for a pleasant evening of darts. We had visitors arriving for dinner at 7pm and so, when the RAR officer got up to leave at about 6pm, we joined him to walk over to our house in the approaching dusk.

As we neared the field all was quiet from the RAR camp and then suddenly a dark figure jumped on to the tailgate of one of the army vehicles and, standing perfectly silhouetted against the bright red sinking sun, he began to sing, raising his magnificent voice in the most haunting African melody I had ever heard. The others took up the melody in a deep resonant tone that seemed to come from a far distance and then rose in volume and resonance as they all moved towards the truck. We stood, transfixed and the goose flesh rose on my arms, a perfect African sunset and magnificent African voices raised in song.

We stood there for ages, listening to this impromptu concert in the bush with all those wonderful voices harmonising so perfectly. Then, as a finale, they all stood to attention as the sun dipped below the horizon and sang their regimental song – *Sweet Banana*. I was motionless in awe with my arms firmly around the children as the tears poured down my cheeks – completely overwhelmed and so deeply touched by the beauty of this lovely country, its people and the moment. The RAR then finally turned away from the truck and went about their evening chores, totally unaware that they had had a small audience who loved this country as much as they.

The following day they were gone, having slipped quietly away before dawn, to fight once more, but they had left behind a memory, which lasts to this day, of a beautiful African sunset in a country I hold so dear and a brave group of men I shall never forget.

Source: *Outpost*, the magazine of the BSAP, 1975.

WHO COMES FIRST? by Brigadier John 'Digger' Essex-Clark

G'Day,

I'm chuffed to be enticed to contribute to the second edition of *Chibaya Moyo* because I felt that the original had insufficient anecdotes about our askaris' leadership and bravery, including my own bland earlier contributions; and that this personally observed defect would now be remedied. I was also asked for a new biography describing my military career with my reflections.

Early Rhodesia

I enlisted as a soldier primarily because of family tradition. My traceable military forbears reach back to the 44th of foot at the Battle of Waterloo. My grandfather was an 'Old Contemptible' from WW I; my great-grand-uncles had fought in the Frontier operation in NW India (now Afghanistan), and my father was a PoW of the Japanese Army in WW II. I was bored at Varsity in South Africa and the Southern Rhodesia Staff Corps was looking for recruits. I went north and joined to do an assessment course followed by an Infantry Weapons and Drill instructors' course which readied me for training territorial battalions, which I enjoyed doing.

While on the course, we privates all, the tubby, the short and the tall; were melded into a strong team, by our superb course instructor a Canadian-Rhodesian PE 500 motor-cyclist, Sergeant Casey de Montille. I enjoyed the feeling of togetherness and when I told them of the Australian 'Digger' legend and speaking in 'Strine' or 'Strayan' (broad Australian pronunciation of the word 'Australian'), I got my nickname.

"Kanjani" – Rhodesian African Rifles

On commissioning I was posted as a platoon commander in 1 RAR at Heany, where I saw good and poor leadership and I experienced the results of that action. I was fortunate to have an excellent company commander, then-major Bill Godwin, who demanded high standards and was an exemplar of them. His tutorship and style remained within me throughout my career in whichever army I was serving. We were training for Malaya at old RAF Heany, later, Llewellin Barracks.

Leadership in those days was not a word in the OED, so the British Army treated it as 'man management' which was a sort of welfare statement in my then bible: 'The Infantry Platoon in Battle' pamphlet. How misleading that was in understanding or being a real leader. Field Marshal Viscount Slim defined the essential qualities of a military leader in a lecture to RMA, Sandhurst, in 1952: 'leadership is a matter of military tradition, plus the individual qualities of physical and moral courage, will-power, initiative, knowledge and integrity.' Future Chief of the Imperial General Staff, his favourite command had been of a platoon in the Royal Warwickshire Regiment.

Remembering, vividly, my first session with my leader group of my askari platoon: 8 Platoon, C Company, 1RAR. The group was my platoon warrant officer, my platoon sergeant, my three corporals and me. I spoke through Sergeant Major Pisayi, my interpreter and conduit for my leadership. I could speak neither chiShona nor chiNyanja, and the only words in chiNyanja that I knew were 'askari' (soldier/s in chiShona) and 'maliwongo' (enemy in chiNyanja). I addressed them with words to the effect of: "We six of us have to get our askari ready in skill and fitness to find and kill maliwongo in the jungles of Malaya. You only have your rank because you have proved you can lead askari: without askari we have no purpose. The askari are our killers, our askari are number one in our purpose. All the time they are our only number one."

We arrived in Malaya confident in our ability to search for and kill terrorists. We left highly satisfied with our achievements on operations that were such that we were more successful than most other platoons in our battalion and our CO had told us so when he came to thank us for his award of the OBE. He singled out our platoon for special praise as we stood on our tiny parade ground at our base on the Tong Lee Rubber Estate and our principal operational area had been declared 'White' i.e. cleared of any significant CT threat. We in 8 Platoon were chuffed and proud.

We all enjoyed a few 'tchwalas' together after that; then we had our final operation into Rengam again, starting the next morning. We ended that operation singing lustily 'Sweet Banana' and other marching songs (M'futi –

Leader Group 8 Pl C Coy 1RAR

M'peni in chiNyanja) as we marched out of the jungle and through the rubber plantation, then through the Tong Lee Estate village to uplifting clapping and cheering by the villagers and their kids waving small Union Jacks.

Interestingly, though I have written many anecdotes about my askari in both editions of this book, not included are narratives of their courage and tactical nous. This is probably so because an aggressive warrior trait is so expected of African warriors of the past that this inherent trait requires no elaboration to a European audience or readers. However, it does for the RAR where I and others saw so many examples of this warrior/ma'Oto trait that it would need a separate book. Whether in Southern Rhodesia, Malaya, or Nyasaland, there were so many thrilling acts of bravery and tactical nous that, afterwards, were so wrapped in modest smiles, and even unbelievable laughter, that it became the norm and mundane, and thus, unremarkable.

Though I have contributed elsewhere in this and the previous edition, I've not described my platoon Warrant Officer Pisayi Muzericho's extraordinary dedication and bravery in capturing, under enemy fire, two armed Communist Terrorists on his own. The bland citation for his award of the Military Medal does not capture the astounding excitement and thrilling raw courage of his extraordinary example of action of 'leading from the front'. However, his bravery may have gone unrecognised if it hadn't followed an announcement that the capture of a CT for intelligence needs would be instantly decorated. If no CT had been handed in, his brave action may not have been recognised, because bravery or courage, as I mentioned above, was considered the norm in the minds of most Europeans.

I wondered how many other acts of bravery were unrecognised in our battalion in Malaya. In fact, at the demonstration of Pisayi's capture, Brigadier Lord Thurloe (responsible for awards in Malaya Command), told me to put in Pisayi for a DCM; and that my Corporal Tabuya, quietly brave and tactically astute in the same crazy contact, be recommended for an MM, which I did so with sufficient justification for both awards, but the powers that be in our battalion headquarters, reduced Pisayi's DCM to an MM; and scrapped Tabuya's most clever and gallant MM where he shot and killed one CT and wounded two others.

We left for Beira on HMT Dilwarra from the docks at Singapore on which were standing, facing us aboard, the band of the famed Fiji Regiment in their dress uniforms of scarlet jackets and jagged-bottom, white 'sulus' and shined sandals. As our ship was tugged away from the dock, the Fijian band struck up with 'Now is the Hour' which caused our askari to cluster around the portholes on the lower decks to see what was going on. Then with a mighty flourish the bandmaster saluted us and the ship erupted with song as his band played a rousing 'Sweet Banana'.

The ship went silent as we slid between the islands surrounding Singapore and our lads had mixed feelings about leaving the gloomy, often swampy, dank, snake, leech, mosquito and terrorist infected jungle, and a non-racist populated Malaya, for Rhodesia. I felt they had trained and proved themselves as ma'Oto and that they would like, as professional soldiers, to prove themselves again overseas.

Few realised, at that time, that the 'Emergency' was virtually over, nor would have expected that 'ere long they would be fighting their own people. As a few said to me, "Will we return, Ishe?" Most of my askari, as professional ma'Oto, had savoured their warrior tasks. Nevertheless, one could feel the joy as they saw the Pungwe river-muddied ocean near the African coast at Beira. We then travelled to Heany station by train via Umtali and Salisbury, where we were met by old stalwarts of the Regiment at each station.

We returned to our old barracks, much of it purloined by the new Depot Rhodesia Regiment, but 1RAR were soon on internal security operations in Nyasaland where Dr Hastings Banda and his cohorts were making nuisances of themselves. At this stage, my company commander had become 2IC of the battalion and I was temporarily OC C Coy. We had a fracas at Kota Kota where a KAR platoon was dispersing a crowd in an alleyway between two godowns at the harbour that was also being dispersed by our C Coy askari from the other end.

Shots were fired from both our sides, and a few local Nyasas were wounded. I also had a clash at Mount Mulanje village that was sorted out by the local a district Commissioner. It was the first time I had used a butt-stroke with an SMLE No 4 rifle, on a man. It was effective, but legally 'non-U,' as we said in those days.

Both the Kota Kota and Mt Mulanje incidents were written off by Lord Monkton, responsible for the investigations, as vagaries or exigencies of confused internal security situations, so I was 'off the hook' and happy, but my bosses less so. The British Colonial masters finally caved-in to the insurgents' demands so we all went home to our camp at Heany near Bulawayo, having seen the first stage in the collapse of the Federation. I was promoted and was to go to AHQ Salisbury.

We had an athletics meeting and my last moments with the RAR were spent listening to the bugle call of 'Retreat' and the askari singing 'Ishe Komberera Afrika' followed by a loud throaty singing of 'Sweet Banana' with our cracker-jack brass band thumping out the tune. I had changed into uniform for the presentation of prizes. It was a vividly emotional moment for me. I stayed, quivering a salute throughout and, after the last notes and strong baritone voices faded, Sergeant Major Pisayi and Sergeant Gondocondo gently led me away. "Sarayi Svakanaka, Ishe!"

What was reinforced to me in 1RAR was mainly that the closer you got to your soldiers (my askari) the stronger got the bonds between us. After some initial racist feelings from others that irritated me, I soon realised that my platoon of askari were the equivalent of Shakespeare's Henry Vth's 'band of brothers' and they moulded my attitude to all my soldiers thereafter. 1RAR was my leadership nursery, and all my askari left a permanent place in my heart. I still get goose-bumps when I think about them, like right now.

What was reinforced to me in 1RAR was mainly that the closer you got to your soldiers (my askari) the stronger got the bonds between us. After some initial racist feelings from others that irritated me, I soon realised that my platoon of askari were the equivalent of Shakespeare's Henry Vth's 'band of brothers' and they moulded my attitude to all my soldiers thereafter. 1RAR was my leadership nursery, and all my askari left a permanent place in my heart. I still get goose-bumps when I think about them, like right now.

Within 1RAR, I first realised that leadership was an art, and not a technique or process. I felt that it was the emotive art of inspiring and motivating a team to achieve clearly-communicated objectives; whereas management is, properly, the science to provide the material and materiel wherewithal to help leaders achieve those objectives. These days, too many confuse the essence of leadership with the responsibilities of management, though the two are best worked in tandem. Command is no more than writing on a piece of paper giving authority to achieve certain objectives with the resources allocated to do so. The responsibility to do so then becomes the leadership responsibility and ability of the appointed commander. With effective leadership as the driver, anything can be done with minimum fuss, but the power and energy must be motivated by and be the responsibility of the leader, or commander, who should delegate management to his subordinates.

Some say that the best leaders have inherited the quality of naturally drawing people to them and manipulate those so drawn. That may be the case for some, but leadership in the military needs an environment for natural leaders to excel with their persuasive skill to verbally, and by their action, inspire others to exert themselves to achieve their leader's objective. I believe that the very best

PWO Pisayi Muzerecho

leaders develop confidence and trust from those they lead, in their leader's common sense, wisdom and drive. Charisma, allied to an exemplary character and sometimes a rare innate gravitas plus communicative skill, can be developed or improved by anyone with the responsibility to achieve a task with a team; and by

Sgt Gondocondo, 8Pl, C Coy, 1RAR

believing in the reason for their effort. Perhaps the best leaders also have an acute empathy for those they lead and an understanding of how to notice how their subordinates react when they are reaching their point of physical or mental exhaustion as can happen in continuous combat as, once past that stage or trauma, unhappy circumstances can occur.

I resigned from the Rhodesian Army to go home and join the Australian Army in late 1963, while attending the British Army Staff College at Camberley, because I lost confidence in the Rhodesian Government and its military hierarchy, and had experienced, first-hand, from lecturers to the college, and from within the UK media, the deceitful and near-traitorous British decolonization desires that threatened Southern Rhodesia's existence as a colony of the UK and would leave the colony wide-open to the voracious and power-hungry tribal whims of Africa.

Australian Army

Arriving in the Australian Army, I was considered a little strange; most hadn't heard of Southern Rhodesia and some thought it was part of South Africa because its rugby players played for the Springboks. I had reverted to the rank of captain and was the only officer of that rank with the post-nominals 'psc' (passed staff college). I was posted to my second 1RAR (1st Battalion, the Royal Australian Regiment); I was also playing for the battalion 1st XV in my first week there.

The officers in the Mess were a bit distant and I was expected, I believed, to have a new-boy's silent reserve but I didn't, and instead was a robust Rugby Union forward and somewhat brash mess member enjoying my new mess culture. Though I played rugby vigorously and possessed a creditable post nominal 'psc' which meant to my fellow officers, that I had studied military matters deeply and the British Army had approved my worth to be a Brigade Major and, with further experience, command of an Infantry battalion. However, I still had to prove that I was capable of leading Australian 'Diggers' and I relished the opportunity. I had already trained and commanded a company of the RLI on operations along and inside the Congo/Northern Rhodesia border and worked with the 'Rurals' of the RRR and their artillery battery.

I was fortunate in that my OC of B Company 1RAR was to leave immediately for Vietnam; while the company, of which I was the new 2IC, was to leave to go south by train to armoured/infantry cooperation and live fire training with Centurion tanks. So, I was now the 'skipper' of a rifle company of three platoons and knew hardly a soul in the group. On arrival at the tank field firing range area, they put our company into tin huts so we four officers, a CSM, CQMS and three sergeants decided we'd have a combined officers' and sergeants' mess in a room in one of the huts. We ate there when not out training and chatted there. I learnt more about the Australian Army and how it ticks or didn't tick in those two weeks at Puckapunyal than I could have imagined, and those NCOs and I really bonded. They heard me briefing our diggers and explain infantry-tank warfare and tactics every morning. I was lucky to have had spent two weeks at the British Armour centre in the UK and had watched armour/infantry training, so I'd seen it before.

My NCOs accompanied me when I visited and chatted with our corporals, Lance Corporals and diggers. They told me that they were satisfied with the way I was handling our diggers compared with the Pommy (Brit or Pongo) officers that they'd experienced before. I drank with them, played cards with them, and I joked and shared stories with them. They 'behind my back' decided on a nickname for me. And on the train home Sergeant 'Dasher' Wheatley, whose bum I pushed valiantly in our 1st XV scrum, and would soon win a self-sacrificial posthumous VC in Vietnam; told me that my nickname was 'The BIG E', because of my size and also after the monster USN nuclear aircraft carrier 'the Enterprise' that had the nickname 'The big E', which had been in Sydney Harbour recently

That name has stuck and any Australian infantrymen who meets me uses it politely in the old European or Afrikaner manner. He further told me that "The diggers love it, Boss." I was chuffed too, I'd been accepted by those who count: our Diggers. I was too afraid and shy to ask what other nicknames had been considered? That nickname stays with me today, used by my seniors who did not once know me, veteran-infantrymen who did, and young current Diggers. Even our Governor General introduced me by my army nickname at a dinner where I was giving an address.

Dasher also warned me that, from other sergeants, that I was unpopular with my peers and to "Watch out for the Duntrooners, skipper, they just look after themselves and they're just jealous". Alarmed I felt that perhaps I had been too robust and muscular in my settling into the culture of the Australian Army: "Would I need to be more cerebral?" I asked Dasher to the reply "What's cerebral, Skipper? Be yourself."

Vietnam

Ere long, I'd been promoted, and the battalion was being secretly considered for deployment to Vietnam to operate with the Americans. It was very hush-hush because of our twitchy politicians. Then with a rush, but very secretly, I and my select recce group of three (a logistician and intelligence officer, and me) flew in civilian clothes to Singapore, then Kuala Lumpur, then changed into uniform on Air Vietnam to Saigon. Then onwards to Bien Hoa (Ben Hwar) to sniff out how and where our battalion would best fit in with what the Americans were starting to do in late 1965. It was decided that we would be best positioned with the 173rd Airborne Brigade, at Bien Hoa to give them much needed operational balance, a third battalion. My recce team settled down with the Airborne Brigade Headquarters to plan how we would work together under their 'operational command', an unclear phrase. We decided that the term meant 'under command' except we may refuse their direction if we thought the task was not in Australia's national interest; but we could use all their operational hardware and logistic support, including aeromedical casualty evacuation 'Dust-Off' and the MASH at

Bien Hoa. Also, we were cleared to receive all US classified documents relating to US or Free World Nations in South Vietnam.

I selected the area for our permanent base-camp and had to argue with their Commanding General (CG) about the real estate we needed to have a defensible area. His other two battalions were in almost Indian-war era forts, within a wet, gloomy and muddy young rubber plantation metric of mosquito-humming, rubber trees. I chose the open plain of a cleared derelict plantation on a reverse slop to War Zone D, across a river and seething with stroppy Viet Cong (VC). The area consisted of old and cleared rubber, enabling us to have our barbed wire covered by fire from automatic weapons manned by Headquarters Company when the rest of the battalion were on operations. It was airily sunny, unless it was raining, and had good drainage for when we returned. We tied in our flanks with US Army units.

The CG, Brigadier-General 'Butch' Williamson' saw our logic and agreed with the real estate that I requested. This was the first of many squabbles we had to win at the start. Logic and common sense, plus tactical acumen had to win the day, so we were thought of by the CG and his staff, as thorough planners and not just colonial warfare-inexperienced dunces. I spent many hours with our 'gung-ho' CG to explain to him our Counter Revolutionary Warfare (CRW) philosophy of stealth and cunning tactics rather than crash and bash conventional and limited warfare tactics of the US Army. I explained our CRW strategy and tactics of conversion of a population by removing the insurgents, rather than invasion and domination. He didn't like it, and never would.

The US Forces and Government had no cohesive strategy for the war; there seemed to be no exit strategy. Just 'defeat the Viet Cong and PAVN (People's Army of Vietnam from communist North Vietnam)'. Our airborne and conventional warfare allies, including the ARVN (Army of the Republic of Vietnam), which was organised, trained and equipped by the US Army, were more gung-ho and often more callous than the US or South Koreans were. Operating together became extraordinarily complex, discombobulating, and fraught with hidden complications that had to be resolved as they occurred. Operational security in Vietnam was pathetically laughable. The staff organisations were riddled with VC informers and the US Army base camps were open to Vietnamese servants working in their messes and cleaning the maps in their Ops Rooms. We did not allow any Vietnamese into our base area, not even ARVN officers accompanying US Army generals. The US Army and USN Marines, to me, were dangerously over-confident. It was as if they expected North Vietnam to surrender.

I found that the US were over-reactive. One shot from a VC 'trail-watcher' would see a massive reaction from a battalion or brigade. The US companies would bring in artillery, air strikes and helicopter gunships to hammer the area where they thought the VC had fired from. Meanwhile the VC sniper or snipers would have scuttled into their temporary bolt holes and the occasional tunnel systems. The major problem we faced was that most VC lived with their families in nearby villages and should have been the task of the ARVN, the South Vietnamese, but no, they had to do the same as their US trainers; and the initiative was lost. I saw these practices and tactics while still with our recce team. How would we fit in to this shallow and inadequate thinking?

We fought well and successfully in Vietnam, irrespective of serious tactical and strategic differences with those of the US Army and ARVN. Our weakness was being unable to follow up successful contacts because we needed what we had in our Rhodesian A.S. battalions: competent trackers. So, by the time my 9 RAR battalion was ready for action in Vietnam, four years later, we had two tracker dogs and their handlers on our establishment.

Our US Army commanders used the old cliché, 'two fine armies separated by a common language.' They soon accepted us using stealth and cunning, they took many more casualties than we did; and, whatever the circumstances, they never stinted with their support for us in artillery, air support, casualty evacuation or logistics. We had strong mutual loyalties and strong friendships between us. Our only 'faux pas' was the habit of calling our soldiers "G'day Digger" - to an Afro-American it sounded like "Nigger" so that habit soon faded, to be replaced with "Airborne" with the response: "All the Way!" their brigade internal greeting. We had to adjust to the minds of our US masters. We did what they asked of us, but Sinatra-like 'we did it our way!'

As I left Vietnam by Qantas 707 with many of my Diggers, having lost three KIA of my company. I had a strange wave of emotion as I chipped an RAASC transport officer trying to bully my diggers to conform to his demands, by saying to him: "Any orders to my men, through me, captain … please!" I thought that everything we do as leaders and officers must be done to ensure the welfare and lives of our diggers: everything, from words, to the media, to writing staff papers to prepare our men and their support in war. 'Diggers first' must be every officer's mantra whatever your job, or whatever you're doing. I thought that without your care of those of your Diggers entering that plane you have no 'raison d'être'.

Post-Vietnam

After Vietnam I was posted to the Jungle Training Centre (now Land Warfare Centre) where I was responsible for instruction in tactics up to brigade level. I soon found and changed tactical learning from parroting set-piece tactical techniques and ageing principles to proper analytical thinking using the full appreciation process rather than rote learning of principles and precedents. This made it harder to assess a student's tick or flick shallow tactical competence or DS solution gauge but would save the lives of our men in war. The lives of our most precious asset, our men, kept reinforcing my beliefs and leadership attitude and responsibilities.

My definition of tactics was: 'Winning Tactics are to defeat your enemy by the meshed use of force and manoeuvre with more speed and cunning than your enemy commander can intellectually or physically cope'. Such tactics must be based on a superior knowledge of your enemy's habits and resources and the effects of terrain and weather on their use.

I AM NOT A HERO BUT I DID HAVE THE HONOUR OF WALKING BESIDE A FEW

By cunning I mean 'crafty or ingenious.' As Thomas Hobbes wrote in 1651 in his 'Leviathan': 'Force and Fraud in war are the two cardinal virtues.' Whereas, we were stupidly teaching dogma and process without any thought of 'cunning;' because, perhaps, it was a nasty word in a gentleman's vocabulary. The US Army uses the word 'deception'. Gaining and holding the tactical or mental initiative by speed, manoeuvre, cunning, surprise or daring is an essential element of winning tactics.

Terrorism and Asymmetric Warfare

I was tasked to research, study and write the Australian military doctrine and training to respond to likely terrorist incidents within Australia. To do so, I visited Israel, the Netherlands, the UK, Canada, and the USA to examine their preparations to deter and counter terrorists. I learnt many things and techniques about the response that I cannot mention; but the keys are immediate and forceful response to eliminate terrorists in difficult hostage situations, not allow lengthy negotiation except to buy time, never allow the decision makers to negotiate, and use negotiation-procrastination to enable the counter-force to arrive, reconnoitre, plan and then execute their action.

As a humorous aside on this vexed matter, never ask a Philippine announcer, all of whom pronounce a 'p' with an 'f' to broadcast anything about a 'parking area'. That happened at Manila airport during a counter terror demonstration watched by VIPs including President Marcos.

I thoroughly enjoyed the rest of my army career from command of an Infantry Battalion; of The Infantry Centre; of the military and leadership training of cadets at the Royal Military College, Duntroon; of The Australian Army Command and Staff College; and, finally, 'flying a desk' as Director General of Military Education and Training at Defence Headquarters, from where I retired, happily but sentimentally and literally, 'hanging up my sword.'

So Long, Soldiering

My values in life, created through military service that were not inherent in my attitude and personality, are: patience, which made me less impetuous; better understanding of the actions and styles of leadership and management; thinking of consequences instead of just results, especially in relation to my soldiers; and learning to be both precise and concise. I also learnt that every person has a limit to their physical and intellectual endurance and people taken beyond that limit crumble.

Much post-traumatic stress and its syndrome is caused by this breakdown and the solution is to take care of your men, whatever you ask of them. I mentioned this earlier in my discussion above on leadership. Too few realise the importance of ensuring that their men, though seemingly invincible and inexhaustible, remain fit for battle and that all need regular rest. My team and my men first: soldiers first!

During my career and its aftermath in civilian life I proved many of my parental and personal maxims such as: 'Good luck, outside gambling, and especially in the military, was no more than sound preparation meeting fleeting opportunity'; 'Don't take yourself too seriously'; plus using the common sense of the 'Serenity Prayer' when under pressure: 'God give me the serenity to accept those things that I cannot change, the courage to change what I can and should, and the wisdom to know the difference'; 'To be yourself and not an actor'; 'Be loyal both upwards, sideways and downwards'; 'Fibs will frazzle you forever'; 'Be straightforward but prudent'; 'Lead from the Front, and Follow me!'; 'Compete hard, but within the rules'; and 'Be Yourself'.

Above all that, I learnt that, apart from immediate family, our Diggers, Askari, *Masodja*, soldiers and ma'Oto come first.

On the invitation of Melbourne University Press, I wrote my biography which describes my deep respect for all those soldiers with whom I served. My Askari and my Diggers get very warm and special praise for their effectiveness as infantrymen, but top of the list are my Askari of our 8 Platoon, 1RAR, because they were so raw and unique, and much needed me, that they have left an indelible imprint on my soul. I was their proud 'in loco parentis', teacher and leader.

Sarayi Svakanaka.
Farewell,
Brigadier John 'Digger' Essex-Clark, DSM.
(Australian Army, well retired)
Canberra, Australia

GUARDIAN ANGEL by Lieutenant Noel Smith

We were in the Chiweshe TTL where our current orders were to conduct extended foot patrols and cover as much ground as possible during the daylight hours and then find a different night base at the close of each day.

I awoke before dawn one morning and tried to make sense of my uncomfortable and broken night's sleep. I had been strangely disturbed by a recurring dream where voices kept telling me not to move out on patrol the following day, warning me that disaster will befall me and my men. It was so very real and more than a little disconcerting as I had never experienced anything like this before.

Regardless, I urged the troops to pack and be ready to move out. I then noticed several furtive glances from my men and even a hint of general apathy which I found most odd. There were no familiar grinning faces or spring in their step which was the daily norm. Then Patrick, my batman, came over to me saying that he wished to discuss an important matter. He was very solemn and went on to explain that the soldiers had not slept well that night. They had all been disturbed by their ancestral voices telling them not to move today because there were very bad spirits about and if we did not listen to these warnings then we would come to serious harm if we ventured out on patrol!!

I was dumbstruck and certainly had no immediate answer to this situation, other than to stay where we were currently based for the rest of the day. What was it – a warning message from my guardian angel and at the same time African tribal ancestors passing on their warning to the soldiers? To this day I have no doubt it was.

Diary notes:

My father, Derek Smith, compiled a history of the Smith family in Rhodesia and I have copied the following passage directly from his diary which relates to an event during my service with 1 RAR sometime in 1975:

'There was a time when he came into the Salisbury office after a "bush trip" literally stinking to high heaven and unshaven (it was dangerous to wash when in the bush because the scented soap smell could give one's position away), to ask for the keys to the car so that he and his batman (Patrick) could go to the house to clean up and have something to eat. All this in front of Fred Haslett (Managing Director on a visit from the S. A. Eagle - Johannesburg) whose nose I could see was distinctly twitching!

'Anyway, I handed over the keys and off they went. Apparently, when arriving at the house, Noel asked Dorothy if there was anything he could give Patrick to eat to which she told him to look in the fridge – which he did and pulled out a hunk of fillet steak which he said would do.

'Mum was rather taken aback and said that the fillet was for dinner to which Noel responded by saying that he couldn't give Patrick any old thing, so it would have to do! In the meantime, Kenadie (our domestic) and Patrick were getting on like a house on fire, Ken's boasting about Noel and Patrick boasting about Mr. Smith, his Officer and what they had been up to in the bush. It transpired that Patrick had said that if ever Mr. Smith was to transfer out of the Regiment, he would never be batman to somebody else and instead, would return to the ranks as an ordinary trooper.'

APPETITES AND CRAVINGS by Corporal Andrew Krajewski

In our army, tobacco was a key component to a general sense of well-being. As a vehement non-smoker, I was able to see, close-up, men under all sorts of stressful and/or boring conditions brung low by *foja/gwaai*. Specifically, by the stress of trying to get some more. I can't now recall anyone else in my platoon (except Foxy and Frik) who *didn't* smoke. So, I'd like to make, if I may, a few observations.

Every dawn there was the chorus of organised coughing, superimposed on the cooing of cape turtle doves, crowing of Swainson's francolin, snorting and puffing of hippos and occasional *bogôm*-ing of the bobos. These lung-wracking vocalisations continued more or less through the day, what with interminable smoke-breaks at all times and everywhere.

Now here was *exquisite* irony, what with heavily-laden fellows, gasping and breathless with the exertion of covering many miles at express speed and under baking temperatures and relentless humidity. So, what did they do? Immediately upon finding some shade in which to sit, and once packs were eased off, out would come the ciggies, and within moments, everyone would be puffing away, filling their tortured lungs with stinking fumes. Now how's *that* ever fun, I always wondered?

As the bush trip progressed past a week, there would be a palpable, mounting anxiety as supplies ran low, and then, God forbid! ran out. Thereafter, those Unfortunates in thrall to the narcotic effects of nicotine would resort to desperate attempts to cadge ciggies (*"Nceli gwaai!"; "Ndipe foja!"*), whilst those others still with a supply of these satanic herbal products, would harden their hearts and refuse to part with any (*"Voetsek wena! Andina foja!"*).

My God, it was pitiful to watch.

As the frenzy mounted there was a great deal of undignified grovelling to retrieve discarded cigarette butts. The longest of these were relit and smoked to oblivion. Others, consisting of a soggy filter plus several millimetres of uncombusted tobacco, were carefully dissected, the tobacco painstakingly retrieved, and re-rolled in a battered and crinkled sheet of paper.

Most connoisseurs used the ever-present lapsed scant list although I once saw a page from W. Somerset Maugham's "The Moon and Sixpence" put to best use as an *ersatz* cigarillo. These sometimes-miniscule roaches were then relit and smoked to vanishing point, held between two thin twigs (like forceps) and to within dangerous proximity of a pair of puffing *sadza* smackers. Every now and again, however, some desperate fellow would so lustily and recklessly puff on these infernal devices that, ignoring the charring of the two twigs, the glowing wad of tobacco would, with a hateful sizzle of burning flesh and a loud yell of pain by the smoker, spot-weld itself to both upper and lower lip. Sad, really.

Often, however, these Poor Ones were faced by the bleakest of all situations: no tobacco. Not even a stompie. *Nikis. iFokolo.* And various ingenious, desperation-driven substitutions were tried. There were several traditional sources of *ersatz* tobacco. All were rolled within the aforementioned paper wrapper, and usually consisted of either dried tea leaves or dried rhino manure. Sometimes custom-blended.

I once saw dried elephant droppings used, hand-rubbed to a fine texture, but am unable to rate these substitutions for their quality. Given the more or less unlimited supply of these fillers, the desperation-driven users usually rolled large, intimidating roaches, splibs, or zolls but occasionally quite stylish, sporty, short panatelas. Given the pin-prick pupils, palpitations and tinnitus often exhibited by those consuming these devices, I am reminded of an old urban legend concerning the smoking of dried pawpaw leaves. Apparently, also quite an experience.

Now it is said that in every problem lies an opportunity, and so it was that our cynical, self-centred platoon sergeant's entrepreneurial streak became apparent. At the beginning of each extended deployment (some of these lasted four weeks) he would ensure that he packed not one, but two 200-cigarette cartons of "Madison". He packed these in the space normally taken up by the equivalent volume of tins and packets of rations. He also packed enough rations for about a week. After about five days he would announce, usually during a smoke-break, to All Assembled "My store is now open!" However, this was usually greeted by a chorus of "Ah, but-i shoowa!" and "Ah, no! We don't buy from dis shop!!" And rightly so. After all, at the time everyone still had cigarettes.

But within a day or so of the depletion of stocks it was a different story. At the height of the madness, a half-smoked *stompie* fetched two-thirds of a can of bully beef. Yet another shameful example of kicking someone when they are down. Addicts are, after all, addicts, and needs must.

Now it wasn't only tobacco in The Valley, what with accounts from Oldentime concerning the militarily-unsound and therefore long-abandoned practice of sending elements of the Rhodesia Defence Regiment (the notorious RDR, known more generally as "The Goffel Ouens") on extended patrols to, of all places, the Chewore River, up to its confluence with the Zambezi.

Within months, their pozzies could be recognised from two features- their proximity to permanent streams or other perennial surface water; and the lurid presence of luminous green weeds, sporting leaves with suspiciously serrated margins; each tended with great care and attention by various camo-clad, Afroed horticulturists. Arm-fulls of foliage were harvested and dried in their season, and later set ablaze in impressive, blue-smoke-emitting zolls.

Now this reckless and unbridled toking led to gross infractions of military procedure. Before long, their long-suffering Honkey Ouen subaltern pulled into one huge call-sign the entire platoon - that is, all 32 ouens - and patrolled as such: a manoeuvre until then unprecedented. What an interesting sight (a ring of red, glowing "fairy lights" at night); sound (what with all that suspicious coughing); and smell (a once-inhaled, never forgotten, sickly-sweetish aroma) must have greeted The Observer. One subbie, plus MAG gunner, plus radio operator in the middle of an expanded ring perimeter of glowing cigarette ends, but this time, not tobacco-fired!

Eventually, and after several disastrous deployments, the entire mob was pulled out and strictly confined to their bases just outside Makuti or astride the Otto Beit road bridge (constructed 1939) at Chirundu. I can only assume they resumed their keen interest in horticulture in these new locations. A keen interest shared by several of our own fellows based up the road at the old SAP Camp on Chirundu gomo.

So now I'm wondering. Having thought about this a lot since those far-away times. In light of the existence in the upper reaches of the Mazowe River of forests of wild, rough lemon trees, allegedly from discarded fruits carried there by Slavers, what I'd ask is this: What might future ethno-botanists make of the origins of The Lost Ganja Groves of Chewore?

Come to think of it, I'm wondering if I shouldn't pre-empt this and put something together for one of those peer-reviewed journals.

Tempting....very tempting!

LANGUAGE by Brigadier John 'Digger' Essex-Clark

In my time with the RAR in the 1950s everyone, including the Mashona and Matabele, plus the European Officers, WOs, and NCOs tried to speak chiNyanja fluently; most failed to do so, and graduated instead to chi-Regiment a mixture of English, Fanagolo, or Chilapalapa and a smattering of chiNyanja words that rang nicely into our regimental vocabulary. An example was chimbudzi or PK (picaninny khaya – small room) for a bush toilet.

The marching songs we sang were old regimental and a'Bantu tunes, but with new chiNyanja verses competing with the chiShona or isiNdebele. The verses about the officers and characters' in the Regiment were sung in Anglofrikaanoshona or Englishona. One knew how one was, or others were doing in their tasks, by listening very carefully to the morale uplifting songs sung on route marches, with 1RAR, every Saturday. One also learnt all the Bantu nicknames for everyone and they were quite amusing; though could change irregularly: one just had to listen and ask the Askari why they had changed to get some startling and subjective reasons.

The reason for the single chiNyanja language in the four Bantu battalions was that three: 1 and 2KAR and 1NRR, and the central training depot spoke chiNyanja; and 1RAR, by direction, followed suit. To me it was an awkward and negative reasoning.

ECLIPSE OF THE SUN: NYAJENA TTL by Captain Tony Clark

In early February 1978 my platoon was deployed into the Nyajena TTL soon after a Selous Scout convoy had been ambushed after they had retrieved family and furniture belonging to one of their NCOs who had been attacked by ZANLA CTs under command one 'Nylon'.

We had been briefed by our Bn IO, Bill Liversidge, to be extra vigilant as the CTs claimed that the area had been 'liberated' and every local was a mujiba who would inform of our presence if seen or left spoor. We deployed at night being dropped in the unoccupied cattle ranching area south of the Nyajena, my plan being to get into OP positions long before first light.

At about 05h00 I received a call from one of my section leaders Corporal Clement that "There was a problem with the sun this morning" and it appeared to be "rotten". I had no idea what he was talking about and was concerned that he was taking this as a bad omen. As I was on the western side of the high ground, I could not see the sun-up and told him I would move so that I had line of sight. It was an eclipse of the sun by the moon and the bottom of the sun was obscured as the moon moved across it. I told him this was temporary, and all will return to normal. I was only able to explain this phenomenon when I next met up with him with the aid of stones and a torch.

LEARNING TO SWIM: KUDZIDZA KUSHAMBIRA by Captain Russell Fulton

After my first 18-week bush trip with A Company, 1RAR and still very much a 'greenhorn' subaltern in the 1st Battalion, I had taken it upon myself to learn as much as I could about the strengths, weaknesses and general psyche of the men I was privileged to command. I achieved much of the ground-work for this whilst compiling my very detailed 'Platoon Bible'.

Background:

This 'academic' process was not without frustration as our *Masodja* were always wont to bathe themselves as pictures of military splendour and, as they were indeed, but this was not about their gallantry in action. I had learned, without the benefit of an unheard-of-internet back in the day, that twelve good men from HQ Company, 1RAR (members of the RAR Band) had tragically drowned in the Fuller Forest, Matetsi area, west of Wankie whilst on active service when the RL they were travelling in crossed a dam wall and their vehicle rolled into the water. The weight of their webbing with ammo, grenades, filled water bottles and the like had pulled them under water. The good men who lost their lives that fateful day were: P Chapange, S Dudzirayi, T Manduna, J Mangandura, K Muchato, B Murambiwa, T Ndaza, G Ngorovani, M Nyikadzino, C Ranganayi, E Takawira and M Wunganayi, and to whose loving memory I dedicate this anecdote.

During a brief respite from operations in Op Hurricane and operating from a Company TAC HQ within close-proximity to Sinoia, I resolved to do what I could to train my men in the basic skills of surviving when confronted by water. My 'interviews' with each of my men had indicated to me that there was a widespread and genuine fear of water. These good men had never, in their lives, been taught the most basic water skills. It was as sobering as it was a tragic and wholly unnecessary fear.

After breakfast following a lengthy patrol deployment, I told my PWO, Munyika Collins, to have our men fall-in, in PT order and with 'Towels, Bath' and to board our TCV's for a few hours of PT with a twist. I had, stealthily and during a night of revelry and general debauchment, befriended the Chairman of the Sinoia Sports Club and his sub-committee chairman of their swimming pool, and cajoled them in to making said 'pond' available to me/my platoon. They did, and without the slightest hesitation and with much thanks, methinks, to the glowing effects of Bolls Brandewyn & Coke!

Let's not forget that the RAR were much loved in this particular Locstat and had, shortly before my joining the Battalion, been accorded the distinct honour of the 'Freedom of the Town of Sinoia'!

When we stopped in the car park of said club, the atmosphere within all ranks was filled with some understandable trepidation. My troops smartly debussed and formed-up in three ranks, they were marched to the swimming pool where they were ordered to remove vests, hosiery and footwear and to fall-in at the shallow-end of the pool where I awaited them in the pool.

There was a cacophony of protest as they wondered what their Ishe had scheduled for them this very day. I ordered them all to enter the pool whilst standing tall in the shallow-end to show them that the water was only waist deep. Reluctantly, they obeyed their Ishe. When they were all in, I guided them through a number of very simple steps to allay them of their fear of what surrounded them. The second step was to teach them to how to hold their breath and to sit down on the bottom of the pool without panicking. It was a tedious exercise borne by a natural and understandable fear of water. Soon enough, when every single member had done what I had asked them to do, and following my lead, they were revelling in their new-found confidence.

The next step was to teach them how to tread-water. This started with exercises at the pools edge where they were shown how to hold on to the trough, extend their bodies and kick with straightened legs. It was a tough process, but my good men were soon laughing raucously as they went through the drills and delightedly mocking their peers who weren't as confident. I knew then that I had 'won the battle' and it was now only a matter of refinement and instilling self-belief. We the moved away from the wall and I taught them how to lower themselves in to the water and how to kick in slow rotations to keep their heads above the water. After several hours, every one of my Platoon was treading water!

They may not have been future Olympians in the making, but they were capable, at the end of the day, of treading water and, in the main, doing 'doggy-paddle'. Between rest periods and boring instruction from their Ishe, several ran to the pool and leapt in without cajoling and, best of all, without any fear!

During my service with 3 Platoon, A Company, 1 RAR I frequently ventured into the very jaws of hell with these men where we smelt, experienced and saw the true horrors of war together. We fought, patrolled hundreds of kilometres, drank and laughed together and all of that gave me enormous pride and pleasure. I may have been little more than a passing platoon commander to them, and, with respect, that's entirely for them to decide, but I loved them all as only one who served with them can understand.

Conclusion:

I have much to be proud of from my days in uniform but, and upon reflection, I truly hope that I might be remembered as having been an officer who cared for his men? That is for my good men to answer and, be that as it may, it is the only thing that is of importance to me.

Drowning...? Not my men and never under my watch. That was, perhaps, my only legacy?

God Bless 'Simanjemanje' (3Pl, A Coy, 1RAR) and the upstanding, loyal and gallant me in our Regiment.

VICTOR DELTA BLUES by Corporal Andrew Krajewski

"Are ye of the spawn of darkness, a tempting beguiling creature from The Pit, wanton limbs steaming from the fleshpots of Hades, in tortured and lubricious thrall to your stygian masters?"- Witch finder Sergeant Shadwell in 'Good Omens' by Terry Pratchett and Neil Gaiman (1990).

"Whence came such turpitude and misery?" I hear you ask. Well, I put it to the Reader that ruinous seeds were planted on our six-weeks-in-ten-days-out military operations. Ample time for various Pressures and Influences coming to bear, heavy and oppressive, upon our Gallants. I remember one steaming summer when the call-sign 22 Bravo (Known and Feared Throughout the Land) were ordered to observe closely and covertly the north bank of the Zambezi River, in the vicinity of B Camp.

We'd settled into a shady, secluded spot under a towering canopy of Acacia albida, peppered with several huge mopane trees, with an abundance of longish grass and shrubs at ground level. It was an ideal position, providing security, an excellent field of view in all directions, and both cover and camouflage, what with several large fallen tree trunks behind which one could hide at a shot's notice. The great age of these fallen trees was evident by their huge girth. If there was anything harder than mopane heart-wood, we were hard pressed to find it anywhere close. Darn-near bullet-proof.

Now as I'm sure The Reader knows, there are few tasks in the military as demanding yet boring as surveillance and observation. And so it was that after several days of deep cover, spent sitting or lying dead-still and in silence, by day five, and with nothing of significance to report, things started to unravel, as they must. Spunky and I had become aware of an increasing clamour at water's edge on the river bank opposite us, in the Sovereign nation of Zambia. We could hear female voices, raised to great volume as are all such in Africa, as water was drawn, washing was done, and people came and went to bathe. It was this latter activity that led to the incident in question.

One day about noon, our Bravos, Privates Vincent ("I am not a bobo! I am a people!") Ngwenya and J. Dube ("Ah but-i shoowa! If a man he does not do chipompo he can go MAD, shoowa!!"), appeared before us under the deep shade. They asked for the loan of our issued pair of Optik Tirol binos and upon receipt of this superb optical instrument slithered off through the long grass in the direction of the vantage point we'd occupied. Peering over the river into Zambia; seeing without being seen.

Now this was a little suspicious, since there was an unobstructed view of the opposite river bank from where we had bivvied up. However, they insisted that they go forward to conduct more detailed surveillance, for such after all were our orders.

Even so, our suspicions aroused, we carefully and quietly followed them only to discover them both lying face down on the grassy bank at river's edge. On the bank and in the shallow water of a sandbar, about 700 metres opposite, were ten young women, thrashing about in voluptuous nakedness. We were close enough to see the lather from several bars of soap.

Both Observers appeared incensed at this, with much sibilant whispering and frequent scuffling over the pair of binos, passed from beady eye to beady eye. After several moments Spunky and I started sniggering and were discovered. Soon, all was revealed:

"Every day we watch thees women! They are bathing every day at thees time. But-i Coporro! They KNOW we are watching!!! They are washing for a long time and VERY, very hard!!"

And so to the stress of combat, the debilitating heat, hordes of biting insects and the scores of hostile nyamazaans was added another burden: unresolved sexual tension arising from military voyeurism and very hard washing. It was a tactic calculated to undermine the morale of any red-blooded onlooker, since the ladies indeed seemed fully aware of several pairs of blood-suffused eyes watching their every jiggle and gyration. Clearly, Harm Could Come To A Lad like that, and these not inconsiderable effects manifested themselves in much muttering and many a heart-felt "Ah, but-i, if a man he cannot do chipompo, he can go mad, shoowa!!"

The cumulative effect of these ablutions by the maidens of Zambia was, at least for two members of 22 Bravo, to bear bitter fruit. For so it was that weeks later, both Privates Dube and Ngwenya, having endured the ritual humiliation of Doc Mike's 'short-Arm' inspection a few days after we'd all got back to Kariba after R & R, took their places along with the rest of Those Infected with venereal disease (VD or Victor Delta) under the shady tree outside the medic's office.

They were unrepentant to the last. "Ah, but-i Coporro Mike! We don't use the condom! A man he cannot fuck the rrrubberrr!" they said with considerable feeling. Apparently, words to live by!

Victor Delta Blues

Now in those days when a platoon went on R & R it was quite something. It started with a debriefing, then a lecture by Doc Mike on "personal hygiene" and the passing round of ghastly prophylactics to jeering and hooting soldiers. After this, payday followed, and thence the six or so hour drive to Salisbury on two or sometimes three RLs. The lads were then dropped off at the train station, from which they bomb-shelled after handing in their weapons and ammunition to be locked up in some convenient armoury until their redeployment, ten days later.

What with the AS in a high state of exhilaration at the prospects of ten days' worth of debauchery and iniquities that could only be imagined, there was something of a Carnival air aboard the vehicles as we went through Kariba, on past the airport, then first Makuti, past Sinoia, then Karoi and ever closer to Salisbury. All and any maidens along the road verges or in the town streets were whistled at and offered a range of proposals none of which shall be repeated here.

A curious onlooker could easily trace the route followed by the RLs by the trail of inflated Army-issue prophylactics discarded by scornful soldiers and left to bob merrily on the road verges where they were later deflated by sharp-eyed schoolchildren throwing stones.

Typical of the military, the issued prophylactics were robust and rugged, wrapped in well-nigh tear-proof gold foil packaging with the words 'Crêpe de Chine' printed thereon in slightly desperate italics. It is probable that a length of bicycle inner-tubing cut to the appropriate length, tied off with a simple overhand knot at one end and lubricated with a handful of fine sand would have served just the same as these dreadful devices. In any case, our Braves scorned them and rejected their use at all times and everywhere. And suffered accordingly.

By the time we hit the city limits our men would be in thrall to strong emotions. Indeed, by the time we arrived in Down-town Salisbury, a number of verbal contracts had apparently been negotiated whilst on the move and indeed formalised, for our vehicles arrived in the car-park at the Station at the head of what appeared to be a convoy, comprising up to a dozen battered, Datsun 1200 'Rixi Taxi 60-666' taxis piloted by leering drivers and each with up to three mahure aboard, many with blouses opened to the waist and with formidable cleavages on display.

From the very instant that the vehicles halted, a frenzied debus ensued, with the hand-in of weapons (made safe at the city limits) and magazines, before a no-holds- barred exit at the high port with AS shedding clothing inside the taxis as they sped off to parts Unknown and on pleasure bent.

Alas! That the en-route issue of prophylactics (ten per man) by the NCOs, and the ES's and troop medics' final exhortations to 'condomise' were so rudely brushed aside with the standard "Ah, but-i Sir! We don' want thees blarr'fuckensheet condom! A man he cannot fuck the rrrrrubber!"

And as to the issue of but ten condoms per man, well, this was just plain insulting, what with each man maintaining that their partners would insist on at least 7 to 8 rounds per night, failing which they would be suspected of infidelity and summarily poisoned with a preparation of chopped leopard's whiskers, or likewise satanic and lethal decoction. Clearly there was more to this than met the eye!

One could only imagine how our comrades spent their R & Rs: presumably in a Demon Drink-fuelled state of more or less permanent priapism, punctuated by surreptitious feeding of the dogs with samples of prepared foodstuffs and then closely observing the canines for signs of poisoning.

For many years I pondered the occult significance of this Rixi Taxi phone number: especially the '...666' part. Clearly, the Devil had found work for more than idle hands...

Ten days later a very different sight would greet us when we re-boarded the vehicles for the return to our unit. Reporting for duty were dozens of red-eyed, flat-broke and shagged-out servicemen, all clearly nursing fearsome hang-overs with several already looking decidedly 'unwell'. They reclaimed their firearms and magazines, and slowly and carefully mounted their vehicles.

Which in most cases was the only mounting they'd be doing for the next six weeks or so, when the whole Dreadful and Godless cycle repeated itself.

By and by, and back at base camp up on Kariba Heights, however, all too familiar scenes ensued where the Braves vied with each other (and most other carbon-based life-forms) in terms of romantic entanglements, all purely commercial transactions, driven by the demon lust, and involving ladies of negotiable affection. These unholy unions bore a terrible harvest, since time and again, by the end of the 10-day R and R *plus* the three days retraining, there was an ever-lengthening line of 'casualties' from the short-arm inspections.

"OK: next! Right: fork it out!" Doc Mike would say, before leaning forward clutching in one hand a special forked stick cut from one of the handy shrubs by the medic's office, dipped in surgical spirit between 'examinations'.

"Oh my God!" Mike would say. "Go stand over there!" and off the bravo would go, buttoning his flies and heckled by his comrades.

After a while even this phlegmatic and hardened troop medic was starting to look harrowed and pale. To make matters worse, eerie and dreadful wailing noises issued forth from the ablution blocks from lines of troops delaying the awful moment of standing at the urinals and letting fly.

This all came to a head, if you'll pardon the expression, one morning when our C/O Major Deon ('Quarter to midnight') Kriel came hurtling down the hill in his dark bottle-green Peugeot 404 staff car, past the shady tree under which all but ONE of the AS in our platoon were re-buttoning their flies and saying such things as "Ah, but-i shoowa!" and "But Corporal! If a man does not do chipompo he can go mad, shoowa!!)".

Deon asked Doc Mike what was going on, and on being told that all but one of the lads were smitten with *Chindoko*, Deon exploded with rage and military indignation. Before you could say "Happy Holidays in Somabhula" he issued orders that ALL the Afflicted were going on patrol with the rest of us, and that each stick leader was to draw the required kit to treat IN THE FIELD these cases, both many and various, of 'Cupid's measles', 'The French Sickness' and/or 'ma-Drop'.

You could have heard a pin ma-Drop!

Well, let me tell you, these gentlemen suffered pangs of the most awful sort. Imagine trudging about the bundu in 40°C-plus heat, 90%-plus humidity, comforted by masses of biting and over-familiar insects, dog-ball pack ripping one's shoulders backwards. All the while, with a rifle cradled in the crook of both arms whilst both hands were fully occupied by trying to hold the heavy and rough fabric of their camo trousers away from so-called 'sensitive bits', many of which closely resembled severely and gruesomely mangled root vegetables. Faces furrowed with pain, sweating bullets and moaning in agony, these lads had once a day to endure the command "Drop 'em!" and act like a dartboard whilst some sniggering nimarangie threw the syringe dart-like and needle-first into the upper, outer quadrant of the buttock and jova-ed them with 5000 i.u of stinging benzyl penicillin. These sallies were punctuated by cries for mercy and pitiful entreaties: "*Ah*, but shoowa, Corporal! Don't THROW it; just-i to push it eeen!!!"

This is something I most fervently hope I never hear another man say to me again.

Anyway, before long, all the braves begged us to relinquish control of the syringes and needles and took to jova-ing each other whilst the rest of us laughed.

Even then, our reminders to "condomise" and (in the words of the Immortal Doctor Albaan) to "Roll down de Rubber, Mon!" met with nothing but contempt.

"Ah but-i shoowa Corporal. A man he *cannot fuck* the rrrrrubber!!!"

Truly, nothing is permanent but woe, and to live is to suffer.

Next R and R, the little devils were at it again!

MAMBA by Lieutenant Peter Baxter

In December 1980 Major Tom Simpson called me into his office at Inyanga our Company base. I was the only Officer left as Angus MacDonald a Scotsman who had volunteered to do his National Service in the Rhodesian Army had finished his service.

Major Simpson briefed me that we were to deploy to Buhera in the vicinity of Assembly Point Foxtrot. He told me to get a set of Convoy orders done and to brief the Company NCO's. We left the next morning to do the long drive to Buhera. The 250-kilometer drive took the whole day. Major Simpson shot ahead in his Command 25 and went to the Buhera Police Station where we were to base up within close proximity. At around 21h30 the convoy pulled into an area that Major Simpson had deemed fit for our occupation not far from the police station.

We were all called to an order group to be given orders for the next day. The PWO's, CSM Sibanda, the CQMS, the Admin Staff and the Major and I were in attendance. Next minute there was a commotion from the vehicles where the troops were bunched together observing one of the soldier's back packs bouncing around on the ground as if possessed. It was the backpack of my batman, James Ndlovu, nicknamed Lord Soames.

The troops and command element observed this bouncing back pack from a respectful distance for a few minutes all commenting with the usual shrieks and howls of laughter. The lights from the vehicles illuminated the scene for us. The CQMS was the most amused by this and his round jovial face was stretched in amusement. He was bellowing with laughter at the spectacle of the pack. This encouraged the troops to join in the merriment.

Suddenly the back pack stopped moving and a total silence enveloped the crowd, who were fortunately not in a complete circle around the pack. The silence was quite eerie and then suddenly the semi-circle scattered in a tactical withdrawal to the vehicles. It took about 4 or 5 paces for all the troops to be up top aboard the vehicles. One of them had spotted the reason for the 'devil's-possessed' backpack. A mighty howl of "Mai We —Nyoka!" and they were all gone.

A 1.5-meter black Mamba had inadvertently decided that Soames' back pack was to be his Camouflage and Concealment when this hoard of soldiers in their trucks had arrived on his territory. The snake had found itself trapped in Soames' back pack with no avenue to escape the din of all the soldiers as they debussed and therefore the back pack had become 'possessed'.

The CQMS had been the one to observe the Mamba bolting out of the back pack and he had motivated the mass withdrawal to the vehicles. Once the Mamba was observed to have departed into the bush, the troops with much bravado, came bounding off the vehicles to send him on his way with a few insults of Satan-and some more detailed profanities.

Calm descended on the merry band of soldiers once this minor event outside the Buhera Police station had taken place and the men then took up their positions for the night before we moved out the next day. The striking thing was that these brave and fearless RAR soldiers were all really respectful of what was in the back pack. Their chatter as we settled in that night was related to Soames' back pack and the spirit that had invaded it. The next day was business as usual and out we all went on patrols to contain the errant Buhera AP Foxtrot Terrorists.

THE ADVENT OF SHOCK PACKS by Captain Tony Clark

After joining D Coy 1 RAR in early 1976, the Rhodesian Army Medical Corp realised the need for all combat troops to able to administer resuscitation packs to colleagues wounded in the field. This was deemed necessary as it was thought that this would greatly assist the wounded in reducing the traumatic effect of shock. We therefore named the units shock packs. They consisted of a litre of Ringers Lactate with tubes and a bloody huge needle known as the intravenous administration set. One afternoon prior to deployment, 12 Platoon was ordered across to Methuen Barracks hospital to be taught how to use the shock packs.

A corporal medic was our instructor and he had his guinea pig with huge veins that made it relatively easy for the shock pack be set into his left arm. The medic was very pleased with his work and announced that six of us should all choose a buddy, a shock pack and tourniquet on the hospital beds in the ward, and he would supervise the live training. My platoon, to a man, were horrified and mumbled "Fuck this" in Shona!! To save the exercise, I told my PWO Pfigeriyi Matavire that I would be his patient and show the men that there was nothing to fear!

I was wrong.

THE RAR by Glen Ashmead

Those fighting men of the RAR,
Longest serving regiment by far.
Their history spread through many a year,
They fought with pride, showing no fear.
Burma, Egypt, Malaya and Rhodesia,
Marching and singing made it easier.
Shaw Barracks at Balla Balla,
Harsh countryside with very little colour.
It's where they practiced their shooting skills,
Then later with Fireforce scored many kills.
Their regimental mascot a goat called Induna,
Had the respect of every *Masodja*.

They patrolled the Zambezi and valley below,
Their skill in tracking we soon came to know.
Led by officers and NCOs,
Many brave soldiers with medals to show,

Proudly displayed row upon row.
Sweet Banana their song of choice,
Sung by all with such a fine voice.
Heart gripping, tear jerking, harmonizing song,
Still listened to now after the battalion's gone.
We will never forget the role they played,
That supreme sacrifice they all made.

And:

They were so young,
When it all begun.
Fighting men, they become,
Father, brother, Son.
It wasn't done for fun,
This war had to be won.
With bullets flying, they didn't run,
All heroes they were, bar none,
Black and white, as one.

CHAPTER TWENTY

RNR-RAR GALLANTRY AWARD RECIPIENTS

INTRODUCTION: MILITARY MEDALS by Captain Andrew Telfer

'Military glory - that attractive rainbow that rises in showers of blood'
Abraham Lincoln

Rhodesian General Service Medal

Leaders can shape the perceptions and beliefs of others in many ways. Ultimately, these perceptions and beliefs influence the way people behave when faced with serious challenges and dangers. Military medals are awarded for that purpose; they are given to identify, promote and encourage behaviours that the nation wants members of its Armed Forces to emulate. Even though the honour is awarded to an individual, the key purpose of giving medals is the effect of them on others. Medals are messages. Political leadership is pointing to what it wants, what will gain the approval of a grateful nation. They exist to encourage militarily useful behaviours. This article introduces the chapter *RNR-RAR Gallantry Award Recipients* with a discussion on the place of medals among other motivators of conduct 'above and beyond the call of duty'.

Firstly, every soldier who keeps his head in battle and does his job is a hero. Most soldiers, let alone most people, never face combat. Those that do, have experienced something traumatic and if, in the moment, they were able to overcome the flight instinct and stayed to fight, they have done well. Of all the bravery medals earned, very few are awarded. There are many soldiers who served for more than a decade of continuous warfare in the Rhodesian Bush War, killing dozens of terrorists in scores of face-to-face firefights, and they have but one medal (the Rhodesian General Service Medal). That medal should be treated with a lot of respect as, in other armies, those men would have been festooned with them for what they accomplished.

Bravery awards are intended to motivate, to provide an incentive for acting in a courageous way. Napoleon Bonaparte's introduction of the *Légion d'honneur* (Legion of Honour) in 1802, was met with disapproval and he was accused of re-instating 'aristocratic baubles' reminiscent of the deposed monarchy. The French Revolution had already abolished orders of chivalry, and his critics were suggesting he was bringing them back. In response, he famously grasped a handful of medals, held them aloft and declared:

> "You call these baubles, well, it is with baubles that men are led... Do you think that you would be able to make men fight by reasoning? Never. That is good only for the scholar in his study. The soldier needs glory, distinctions, rewards"

Napoleon Bonaparte, 1802

Under the French monarchy, military decorations had been limited to officers, orders of chivalry to Roman Catholics, and only noblemen could become knights. All of the opportunities in Napoleon's life, leading from his humble beginnings in Corsica to Emperor of France, had been outcomes of the Revolution, and he had no intention of re-establishing an order of *nobility;* what he wanted was an order of *merit*. His intent was to reward bravery in order to, as he said, "make men fight".

Being 'decorated' is intended to change the recipient's life and it does. When I received a Military Forces Commendation (Operational), I went along to the Quartermaster Store at 2RAR and stood at the counter. The RQMS happened to be there, an old and bold former-RLI Warrant Officer, looking at me as WOs naturally tend to regard Second Lieutenants: with mild interest. Yet, when I asked him for a silver pick to put on my RhGSM, his demeanour changed instantly. I was greeted warmly and helped by him personally.

Again, and again that happened. A year or so later, some weeks after the Silver Cross of Rhodesia had been pinned on my chest by the Army Commander, I was one of two subalterns entering the Officers' Mess of KGVI Barracks on a Friday evening when it was full of Army HQ staff officers; red gorgets were evident on collars everywhere. We tentatively approached the senior group to make the customary greeting to the most senior officer, a Major General. His group surveyed us with blank eyes until those eyes rested on my medal ribbons. Once again, warmth instantly appeared. And so, the life of the recipient of a medal is changed.

We could leave it there, satisfied that the pleasure associated with being decorated is all there is to it, but there's also a stick associated with the carrot. Human beings will move towards *pleasure* and away from *pain*, if they can, and medals are at the 'pleasure' end of the motivational spectrum in military life. At the other extreme, soldiers know there is a source of pain far more potent than anything physical: the shame visited upon those found wanting of courage.

One of the most famous examples of this was the court martial of Admiral John Byng in 1757. Found guilty of failing to 'do his utmost' to prevent Minorca falling to the French, he was sentenced to death and, after pleas for clemency were denied by the King, was shot dead by a firing squad. Prior to this, he was an accomplished naval officer and it's worth noting that he was not even accused of cowardice, just *failing to do his utmost*. So why the firing squad? Because the public execution of such a senior officer sent a very clear message to everyone else. Eminent Naval historian N.A.M. Rodger asserts that it influenced the behaviour of Royal Navy officers for generations, by helping to inculcate:

> 'A culture of aggressive determination which set British officers apart from their foreign contemporaries, and which in time gave them a steadily mounting psychological ascendancy.'

The Admiralty wanted to send a clear message about the consequences of failure. The court martial and execution were the use of visible and forceful actions – both substantive and symbolic – to inculcate a culture that fostered military competitive advantage. In 1805, less than 50 years after Byng's execution, Admiral Lord Nelson sent a famous signal from his flagship HMS Victory just before the Battle of Trafalgar: "England expects that every man will do his duty". That was a reminder.

For their part, the French observed Byng's execution with Gallic irony, satirised by Voltaire:

> "Dans ce pays-ci, il est bon de tuer de temps en temps un amiral pour encourager les autres."

> "In this country, it is good to kill an admiral from time to time, in order to encourage the others."

In *Julius Caesar*, William Shakespeare wrote: 'Cowards die many times before their deaths; the valiant never taste of death but once.' These words require no elaboration and would be understood by every soldier. The penalty for cowardice in the military is shame and dishonour, discredit and condemnation, vilification and contempt. And so, from decorations to shame, we have the classic motivational reward-punishment system applied to induce a desired behaviour: the actor leans into pleasure and away from pain, towards the carrot and away from the stick. But, is that it or are there even more powerful forces at work that inspire ordinary people to do extraordinary things?

Is it patriotism? Certainly, there are examples of people apparently willing to 'die for King and Country'. Many young men joined up during the First World

War inspired by patriotic fervour, but it didn't take long before the notion was questioned. Wilfred Owen (1918), himself the holder of a Military Cross, in his famous poem *'Dulce et Decorum est'* attacked the readiness of older people who had never experienced the grim reality of warfare, to encourage youngsters to fight and die for their country:

'If in some smothering dreams you too could pace
Behind the wagon that we flung him in,
  And watch the white eyes writhing in his face,
  His hanging face, like a devil's sick of sin;
  If you could hear, at every jolt, the blood
  Come gargling from the froth-corrupted lungs,
  Obscene as cancer, bitter as the cud
  Of vile, incurable sores on innocent tongues,
  My friend, you would not tell with such high zest
  To children ardent for some desperate glory,
  The old Lie; Dulce et Decorum est
  Pro patria mori.'

'Dulce et decorum est pro patria mori' translates as *'It is sweet and proper to die for one's country'*. Lieutenant Wilfred Owen MC, veteran of trench warfare on the Western Front, knew that it is not.

Whether Wilfred Owen is seen as right or wrong, patriotism alone does not satisfactorily explain the personal sacrifice and bravery that soldiers can display. Perhaps, then, the brave ones are special... warriors among men? The *warrior culture* is much beloved by Hollywood, fictional novelists and even among soldiers. The concept of a warrior culture implies that there's a special order of men who are more fiercely warlike than their peers, Vikings of the modern era. Look at this, written 2,500 years ago:

'Out of every one hundred men, ten shouldn't even be there, eighty are just targets, nine are the real fighters, and we are lucky to have them, for they make the battle. Ah, but the one, one is a warrior, and he will bring the others back.'
Heraclitus 535-475 BC

Heraclitus was an aristocratic philosopher, not a soldier. I don't agree with him *at all*, but I understand what he is doing when he writes like that. He is stirring the heart, quickening the blood of ardent young men and he's inspiring them to be that one, the warrior. To be seen and spoken of as a warrior is attractive to young men, but there is no such thing, not in the sense that Heraclitus writes. He is telling them the Old Lie and look at how it has endured through the ages. In fact, most medal recipients are relatively quiet and thoughtful people who are unlikely to pass a screen test for movie-hero. Not one sees himself as anyone special, let alone as a 'warrior'.

There is however a case for psychological readiness. The human being gets used to everything in time, even to the most extreme conditions, and *familiarity with combat* can give the illusion of courage. Speaking from experience, by the time I had reached my 24th birthday, in April 1978, I was sufficiently familiar with being in a firefight that I was able to function calmly and confidently in situations that had previously been disturbing and unnerving. This made it possible for me to apply intense concentration to the task at hand, free of emotional distraction, and be at my most effective in the years 1978 and 1979. My mental state was increasingly tranquil and unmoved as I became more familiar with the sense of exposure, able to be more deeply calm and 'in the moment', even though the risk had not diminished. Consider the mental balance of the modern, solo, free-climber, climbing without a rope on a sheer rock face hundreds of metres above the ground; is he brave or simply so familiar as to be free from debilitating fear? Perhaps this psychological state may support the execution of actions that appear courageous but are actually within the expanded comfort zone of the actor.

Psychological readiness may help explain sustained out-of-the-ordinary behaviour but what drives spontaneous bravery, the sudden explosive action by an individual with the often cited: 'complete disregard for his own safety'? The answer to that lies in the nature of warfare, not as it's seen in a history book or documentary, but how it is actually experienced by those who fight it.

Warfare is what Wilfred Owen experienced, youngsters trying to keep each other alive in extreme circumstances, and soldiers will do the most extraordinary things *for each other* and out of a sense of *duty*.

When you are young, with your whole life ahead of you, are you really going to risk it all for a piece of coloured ribbon, or a warlike reputation, or the old *pro patria* lie? No-one thinks like that in combat. A young person does not risk his life for any of those inconsequential things, but he may do so to protect a comrade or to fulfil his perceived duty to mission.

Firstly, in so many instances of extreme battlefield courage, the person was acting to save a friend. In these cases, the essence of what we call 'courage' is *altruism*. Altruism reduces one's own significance, one's own pain, and increases the value of others. We act for *others*.

Secondly, the trigger may be the cognitive ability to understand and change a negative 'formula'. By that, I mean the ability, under conditions of mortal danger, to recognise and understand what is happening, what will likely happen next and then to see how to intervene to achieve a better outcome. That takes calm reasoning, not simply reactive action. Brave soldiers frequently explain that they were only doing their job. They were, but it took exceptional work to do it. In these cases, *duty* is the driver.

Thus, altruism and duty can be motivators but, for motivation to translate into physical action, there is a requirement for strength of character, for trueness to one's self:

'This above all: to thine own self be true, and it must follow, as the night the day, thou canst not then be false to any man'

Shakespeare

Each of us has his own set of values and will adhere to them to the degree that self-discipline imposes itself over external pressures. This is the ability to control one's feelings and overcome one's weaknesses. To describe a soldier as 'fearless' is inaccurate. It is not the absence of fear and doubt, but that fear and doubt aren't allowed to debilitate. Courage, after all, is the ability to do something that frightens one. Courage does not remove the menace, but its presence means that fear adds to performance rather than destabilises it. Bravery does not allow fear to paralyse action but rather allows access to resources hitherto unrecognised.

Courage is values-based. If you know what you stand for, what you'll stand up for and, if you are prepared to adhere to principle even into pain, then you might be brave. It doesn't always feel brave to be brave because it is not what a brave mind *feels* but what a brave mind *does*.

In conclusion, the awarding of medals is symbolic and politically purposeful. It does change the life of the recipient but is not really about the individual; it is more about encouraging the others.

Medals have a place among other factors related to conduct 'above and beyond the call of duty' in that they give recognition for it *afterwards* but it cannot be argued that they motivate it *at the time*. It is more likely that the catalyst for brave action is altruism, arising out of comradeship, and/or a sense of duty, arising out of situational clarity and a feeling of being personally responsible for the outcome of the mission.

References

Rodger, NAM 2004, *The Command of the Ocean: A Naval History of Britain*, Volume 2, 1649–1815, London, UK.

RNR-RAR GALLANTRY AWARD RECIPIENTS by Captain Russell Fulton

Numerous records of RNR-RAR honours and award rolls have been published and several of these have been drawn upon in the compilation of this important chapter. The import of its inclusion in *Chibaya Moyo 2* is to break the stereotypical medal roll and, more importantly, to introduce the reader not only to a series impressive yet impersonal citations but, where it has been possible, to share a little about the man behind the medal.

These were real people, with real emotions like everyone else but they had something very special that separated them from the rest. These mostly quiet and unassuming men whose acts of servitude and gallantry to regiment and country are deserving of respect and the highest honour; these are the stories of good, decent and humble men whose actions are the foundation of the impressive tapestry that is our distinguished regimental history and I am proud to be able to share some of it with you.

Even with our best efforts, we have not been able to obtain details of every award recipient, much to our regret. Nevertheless, out of respect to them for their gallantry, we record their names as follows:

Rhodesia Native Regiment, East Africa Campaign, 1916-1918:
> Captain Charles Grey MC (MID x 2)
> Corporal Nsuga MM
> Private Mkulunyelwa MM
> Lieutenant William Siddons Baker MM (MID)
> Lieutenant Ronald Northcote MM
> Captain Charles Francis Edwards MM (MID)

Rhodesian African Rifles, The Battle of Entumbane, 1981:
> Lieutenant Colonel Lionel Dyck SCZ
> Major Anthony Husher BCZ
> Lieutenant David Hill BCZ
> WO2 Stephen Ncube BCZ

VICTORIA CROSS (VC)

The Victoria Cross is the highest award for acts of bravery in wartime. It was instituted in 1856 by Queen Victoria and made retrospective to 1854 to cover the period of the Crimean War. It is possible for any serving member of the armed forces to obtain this award.

The Victoria Cross was designed, according to the original warrant for the award, to be in the form of the 'Maltese Cross'. Its shape, however, more closely resembles a cross pattée. In the centre of the medal is a lion guardant standing upon the Royal Crown. The

Victoria Cross

words 'For valour' are inscribed below. The Victoria Cross is suspended from a crimson ribbon. On the reverse of the cross the date of the act of bravery is inscribed, along with the name, rank, and unit of the recipient.

Sergeant Frederick Charles Booth VC DCM

Sgt Frederick Booth VC

No. 1630 Sergeant Frederick Charles Booth ranks as our Regiment's most highly decorated member, a soldier of quite impeccable yet unassuming character and the holder of the Victoria Cross, a rare distinction that he alone holds.

He was decorated during the East Africa Campaign for repeated acts of gallantry and received a Distinguished Conduct Medal and a Mention in Dispatches (MID). He was an extraordinary Senior NCO by any measure and a man whose gallantry was emulated throughout our Regiment's proud history.

Booth was born on 16 March 1890 in Bowes Park, Upper Holloway, London, England and was educated at Cheltenham College. He served in the British South Africa Police in Southern Rhodesia from 1912 to 1927.

He was 26 years old at the time and serving as a Sergeant in the British South Africa Police attached to the Rhodesia Native Regiment during the First World War, when the following deed took place and for which he was awarded the VC.

In September 1918 he was commissioned into the Middlesex Regiment and in 1939 served with the Auxiliary Military Pioneer Corps where he rose to the rank of Captain.

Booth died on 14 September 1960 in St Anne's Red Cross Convalescent Hospital for Officers, Kemptown, Brighton, Sussex, England. He is buried at Bear Road Cemetery, Brighton, in the Red Cross Section, Grave ZKZ 36.

Citation for the award of the Victoria Cross, 8 June 1917, Sergeant Frederick Charles Booth:

Preamble: 'The Victoria Cross is the premier Operational Gallantry award given for 'most conspicuous bravery, or some daring or pre-eminent act of valour or self-sacrifice, or extreme devotion to duty in the presence of the enemy'.

C Issue No. 774: London Gazette Supplement 30122, Page 5704, dated 8 June 1917:

VC Presented: 16 January 1918 by King George V at Buckingham Palace, London, England.

No. 1630 Sergeant Frederick Charles Booth, South African Forces, attached Rhodesia Native Regiment.

'For most conspicuous bravery during an attack, in thick bush, on the enemy position.

'Under very heavy rifle fire, Sergeant Booth went forward alone and brought in a man who was dangerously wounded. Later, he rallied native troops who were badly disorganized, and brought them to the firing line.'This N.C.O. has on many previous occasions displayed the greatest bravery, coolness and resource in action, and has set a splendid example of pluck, endurance and determination'.

Medal Grouping: Sgt Frederick Charles Booth VC, DCM, (MID)

THE DISTINGUISHED CONDUCT MEDAL (DCM)

The DCM was instituted by Royal Warrant on 4 December 1854, during the Crimean War, as an award to Warrant Officers, Non-Commissioned Officers and men for 'distinguished, gallant and good conduct in the field'. For all ranks below commissioned officers, it was the second highest award for gallantry in action after the Victoria Cross, and the other ranks' equivalent of the Distinguished Service Order, which was awarded to commissioned officers for bravery. Prior to the institution of this decoration, there had been no medal

Distinguished Conduct Medal

awarded by the British government in recognition of individual acts of gallantry in the Army.

Awarded for conspicuous gallantry in the field, a distinguished award for bravery for NCOs and soldiers of the British Army. It is the oldest British award for gallantry and was a second level military decoration, ranking below the Victoria Cross, until its discontinuation in 1993 when it was replaced by the Conspicuous Gallantry Cross. The medal was also awarded to non-commissioned military personnel of other Commonwealth Dominions and Colonies.

Booth's citation is unavailable

WO1 Lechanda DCM MM

WO1 Lechanda was the RAR's first RSM. He was awarded the DCM while a CSM with 2/1 King's African Rifles and is buried in the War Graves Plot, Pioneer Cemetery, Harare. He was from Nyasaland and had served with the KAR as a boy bugler in Somaliland in 1909 and in the East Africa Campaign during the First World War when he led several successful assaults against German positions. He earned the Military Medal when, with a hastily gathered group of 12 men, he attacked a German force (including three machine guns) that was about to seize a rations dump. He captured one machine gun and, in a follow up, killed nine Germans.

RSM Lechanda was returning from a route march in Salisbury when he fell out onto the side of the Borrowdale Road and died within minutes, the date was 17 October 1942. He was the most decorated RAR African soldier in our regimental history.

Sergeant Rita DCM (MID)

Rita was part of the original RNR contingent in the East Africa Campaign. There are no detailed records on his personal background, but it is likely he was a Ndebele, since most of the first contingent came from Matabeleland and white officers sometimes spelled his name 'Lita' which is Ndebele. As one of the few literate soldiers in the RNR, he was posted to the intelligence section and quickly promoted to corporal. Rita led countless small reconnaissance patrols and became an expert at collecting information on the enemy.

Just before the siege of Songea, he led a patrol that captured a German sergeant. After the siege of Songea, while on patrol, Rita shot a German askari sergeant and was pursued through the bush by forty enemy soldiers. Stealth, reliability and narrow escapes from the enemy became his trademarks. Rita was eventually posted to a rifle platoon and entrusted with leading twenty-man fighting patrols that would locate and engage the Germans. Winning the Imperial Distinguished Conduct Medal and a Mention in Dispatches, Rita was the most highly decorated African soldier in the RNR.

He died of natural causes at Chipambwe 27 Oct 1917 and his family was paid a death gratuity.

MILITARY CROSS (MC)

Awarded for an act or acts of exemplary gallantry during active operations against the enemy on land, to captains or officers of lower rank up to warrant officers. (NCOs or other ranks instead received the Military Medal). The MC was first promulgated by King George V, 28 December 1914, 'We are desirous of signifying Our appreciation of such services by a mark of Our Royal favour We do by these Presents for Us Our heirs and successors institute and create a Cross to be awarded to Officers whose distinguished and meritorious services have been brought to Our notice.'

Military Cross

Lieutenant George Victor Pitt MC
(Attached Long Range Desert Group)

'In March 1945, Lieutenant Pitt was landed with a small patrol of LRDG on the island of Rab (Croatia), where he remained for six weeks. During all this period he was sending back information on enemy movements and positions which was invaluable to the R.A.F. He carried out many daring and personal reconnaissances of enemy gun positions and the excellence of his reports enabled the R.A.F. to destroy the majority of them. He was frequently chased by enemy patrols, who knew of his presence but, by continuous movement he was able to avoid capture.
'When the partisans landed on Rab, Lieutenant Pitt went with them and successfully guided the attacking force on their targets. He later did the same task for the partisans landing on Cherso and his accurate and quick information was of the utmost value to the R.A.F. Throughout all these and other operations Lieutenant Pitt has shown the greatest courage and enthusiasm and the result of his work has been quite outstanding.'

MILITARY MEDAL (MM)

Awarded to personnel of the British Army and other arms of the armed forces, and to personnel of other Commonwealth countries, below the commissioned rank, for bravery in battle on land.

Military Medal

Sergeant Salima MM (MID)

Judging from his name, Salima was probably from Nyasaland and likely came to Southern Rhodesia as a migrant mine worker. He was one of the first recruits to enlist in the RNR. Salima led important fighting patrols that harassed the enemy when the RNR was besieged at Kitanda in January and February 1917 during the East Africa Campaign.

For his actions he was awarded the Military Medal which was the first gallantry decoration awarded to a black RNR soldier. Along with dozens of others, he was discharged in June 1918 in Salisbury, having completed his two years of service. Sadly, nothing is known of his post war life.

Sergeant Tanganyika MM

As a member of the first five hundred RNR recruits, there are no RNR records of Tanganyika's background. His name would seem to indicate an East African origin and there was another Tanganyika, a private, in the RNR who was recorded as a Chewa from Nyasaland (Malawi). However, Tanganyika is also a phrase in the chiShona language meaning "to make the country."

Sergeant Tanganyika was either a Malawian of Chewa ethnicity or a Southern Rhodesian of Shona ethnicity. Since he was literate, he was promoted to corporal fairly rapidly and became one of the most effective patrol readers in the RNR during the East Africa Campaign. In October 1916, whilst leading a reconnaissance patrol near Songea, Tanganyika's six men fled but he still managed to single-handedly capture two enemy German) Askaris. For his many gallant actions, Tanganyika was awarded the Military Medal. The only blemish on his record seems to have been leading the prisoner escort that was responsible for the escape of Private Kurukuru, a deserter. Tanganyika survived the war but there are no records of his post war life.

Sergeant Charles Mark Craxton MM

During the German attack on Songea, General Von Lettow had ordered two groups of troops to cooperate in re-taking Songea. At Kitanda, Captain Walter von Falkenstein was to advance with the 12th Field Company and former Songea garrison. At Likuyu, Maj Gideon von Grawert was to advance with the 7th Schutzen Company of German reservists and the Penzel's Detachment. Von Grawert was appointed to command the attack on Songea.

On 11th November 1916, von Falkenstein's troops approached Songea whilst one of his patrols successfully ambushed a British re-supply column on the Wiedhaven track. The porters dropped the four days' supply of rations that they were carrying and ran into Songea. Perhaps due to misinformation from local villagers von Falkenstein had come to believe that the British garrison was weak and ill-trained. He was also an impatient man and he did not wait for von Grawert but attacked at first light on 12th November with his 180 men and one machine gun. The German attack came in from the south-east just as the Rhodesia Native Regiment 'stood to' in an alert position in their trenches. The German machine gun jammed after firing a few bursts and from that point both sides depended upon the weight and accuracy of their rifle fire. The advantage lay with the defenders as von Falkenstein had lost the element of surprise

Whilst engaging the withdrawing enemy machine gunners, Captain Wane was shot in the shoulder, whilst a drummer in the regimental band, Private Rupea, was shot dead when defending the eastern section of the perimeter. A number of villagers and porters added confusion to the battlefield by getting shot as they ran to jump into the Rhodesian trenches. A party of German troops entered a hospital building that overlooked the trenches and so Sergeant Craxton ran forward 350 meters to set the roof of the building alight. The enemy hastily evacuated the building. For this gallantry under heavy fire, Craxton later received the Military Medal. He was a Bulawayo man of British parentage.

WO2 Alexander Khumalo MM

Recommendation citation as endorsed by General Charles Keightley, Commander-in-Chief Far East Land Forces:

> 'Platoon Warrant Officer Alexander was leading a patrol in the Labis District of Johore on the 19th of June 1957. At 6pm his leading scout saw some smoke rising from the jungle edge about four hundred yards north of their position. Realising that the ground to be covered offered very little concealment, Platoon Warrant Officer Alexander ordered his patrol to crawl

through the long grass, a distance of two hundred and fifty yards, to a stream where they waited until nightfall.

PWO Alexander Khumalo MM

'He could then see a fire burning about fifty yards into the jungle – and saw three armed Communist Terrorists standing around the fire. Again, he waited, as he noticed the approach of a heavy storm.

'When it was raining heavily, Platoon Warrant Officer Alexander, with one other soldier, then began to stalk the terrorists. With one of the most daring and skilful acts of field craft imaginable, he crawled towards them. During his approach he had to crawl over the branches of a fallen tree and was often not in position to use his weapon, had he been seen by the enemy. With complete disregard for his personal safety he managed to get within five yards of the terrorists and, signalling to his companion, they fired at the two who were holding their weapons, killing them instantly.

'The third terrorist, who was wounded, crawled away in the dark and although he twice fired at Platoon Warrant Officer Alexander, he crawled after him and again managed to wound him. In the morning the third terrorist was found and killed.'

Corporal Lengu MM

Recommendation citation as endorsed by General Charles Keightley, Commander-in-Chief Far East Land Forces:

'Corporal Lengu has shown exceptional keenness, efficiency and offensive spirit in operations against the Communist Terrorists in the period covered by this report (January to May 1957). He has always proved himself to be a courageous and resourceful NCO, always willing to undertake the most hazardous of operations.

'On the 16th May 1957, in the Segamat District of Johore, Corporal Lengu was in charge of a patrol. His leading scout stopped, indicating that he had heard voices ahead. Corporal Lengu ordered the patrol to halt whilst he went forward to reconnoitre. He crept forward silently until he came to a small clearing where he saw four armed Communist Terrorists. These terrorists were obviously suspicious and on the alert with their weapons at the ready. Realising that there was no time to call up the rest of the patrol, and make an organised assault, Corporal Lengu decided to attack them himself. To make his attack he would have to cross the clearing in full view of the terrorists at a range of about ten yards. 'With complete disregard for his own safety and fully realising that he could expect no help from the members of his patrol who were some distance behind, Corporal Lengu charged straight at the Communist Terrorists.

Cpl Lengu MM

'As soon as they heard the sound of his assault two of the terrorists took cover at the jungle edge to cover the retreat of the remaining two who turned to engage Corporal Lengu with rifle fire. 'The suddenness and speed of Corporal Lengu's assault so disrupted the terrorists that they were unable to return his fire and he killed the two in the clearing. The two remaining terrorists, seeing the deaths of their comrades, turned and ran, pursued by Corporal Lengu. He followed them for some distance but lost their tracks and was forced to return to the clearing where he collected the rest of his patrol. This extremely brave, gallant and single-handed action by Corporal Lengu against four armed Communist Terrorists is an example of personal bravery which has inspired the rest of the Battalion.'

SILVER CROSS OF RHODESIA (SCR)

Silver Cross of Rhodesia

The Silver Cross of Rhodesia was instituted in 1970 with the first RAR recipient, a 1RAR Lance Corporal, invested in September 1978. The SCR, awarded for Conspicuous Gallantry in action, ranks in precedence behind the Grand Cross of Valour, Rhodesia's highest gallantry decoration.

Since its inception, a total of eight SCR's were awarded to officers and men of the RAR of which the 1st Battalion received two and six went to members of 2RAR. It is fitting to note that the first and last SCR's awarded to RAR men went to African NCO's; 1RAR and 2RAR respectively. The second and second last recipients were awarded to white officers; 2RAR and 1RAR respectively. One award was made posthumously.

Lance-Corporal Chamunorwa Sarirowona SCR

The true spirit of this extraordinary soldier, a man facing a dishonourable discharge who overcame those odds and excelled as a junior operational commander after being given an opportunity to redeem himself, is captured in an anecdote written for *Chibaya Moyo 1* by this outstanding soldier's former OC, Major Wayne Thompson DMM:

I would like to offer what I consider to be the rather interesting story of Corporal (when I last had contact with him) Chamunorwa Sarirowona, SCR of B Company, 1st Battalion The Rhodesian African Rifles. As one of only two individuals, in 1RAR, and a small number in the Rhodesian Army to have been awarded the Silver Cross of Rhodesia for Conspicuous Gallantry and because of the tenacity and determination of this (then) young African Soldier to make a success of his chosen career, I feel his story, or at least that part of it I am able to relate, should be told, so here goes.

My encounter with the then Pte Chamunorwa began when, as a newly appointed Acting Major, I was posted to 1RAR and assigned, by the CO of the time, Lt Col F.G.D. Heppenstall MLM to command the unit's B Company. I was an absolute stranger to the RAR at the time, having been commissioned into 1 RLI and having had two tours of duty with that unit of roughly five and three years duration respectively, followed by a period on the staff of Army HQ and briefly HQ 3 Bde.

It was, therefore with some trepidation that I headed back to my home-town of Bulawayo, duly arriving at Methuen Barracks and whatever the future had in store for me in 1RAR! As I'm certain, any brand-new entrant to 1RAR, (especially those in the commissioned ranks) and no doubt the 2nd & 3rd Battalions as well, will have experienced, one did not simply slip into a command position in an African battalion without being subjected to something of a trial by the AS.

This was, as far as I have established, in discussions with other former RAR Officers, something of a discreet test, by the very discerning AS, of a newcomer bossman's worthiness to command them in combat and to be given their loyalty, trust and respect. The uninitiated should not regard this trial as being in any way disrespectful or malevolent of purpose at all, nor specific in nature or form, but it was, in my view, evident, as it was in fact during my service with RLI, in perhaps a different form. Nevertheless, one could sense and needed to understand that one was on trial! Whether by design or chance, some AS were more inclined to extend their trial of a newcomer officer, for a longer period than most of their contemporaries. One who tended to prolong this trial, in my view, was a certain Private Chamunorwa Sarirowona, whose brief story I would like to have recorded in this book.

Pte Chamunorwa Sarirowona was a Platoon TCV driver when I first encountered him and one who featured regularly in the Company's Minor Offence Report Book, for the most part, on charges of 'Conduct to the prejudice of good order and military discipline'! He was a short, stocky, young man; round faced but with a firm square jaw and something of an arrogant and determined air about him. This was somewhat irritating during his frequent appearances on OC's orders' where his misdemeanours invariably related to disobedience to instructions given to him by junior NCO's.

His various deviations from the straight and narrow were not of such a serious nature as to warrant him being remanded to CO's Orders but were certainly regular enough to make it clear, he was ill disposed towards NCO's and in particular those in the Lance Corporal and Corporal bracket!

He was, in effect, a rebel and a very irritating one at that, not only to me but also very much so to my excellent CSM, WO2 Chitereka. Efforts had been devoted to counselling and correcting his behaviour, occasionally with the CSM's "pace-stick" as an element of encouragement, but to little or no avail. I found Company Commander's Orders a particularly tedious, tiresome, time consuming and irksome process and duty, which certainly served to adversely influence my attitude towards habitual offenders such as Sarirowona.

That, to the point that one day, after a particularly long and irritating set of Orders, following our return to the bush, after a period of R&R, on which my No 1 problem soldier had again appeared, I decided that enough was enough and that I had sufficient ammo at my disposal to warrant writing a recommendation to the CO for this young misfit be discharged; which threat I had levelled at him on at least two previous occasions, if he failed to mend his ways and come to heel.

Despite my irritation and now exhausted patience with this soldier, I thought it appropriate at that point, prior to sending a letter to the CO recommending his discharge, to make one last attempt at stablishing what was actually 'making him tick' in the way he was? I called him into my extremely warm tent and had a good heart-to-heart talk with him, explaining clearly my planned course of action and giving him one final opportunity to vindicate his ongoing rebellious behaviour, especially towards junior NCO's. His response was essentially, that he saw himself as being equally competent if not more so than most junior NCO's in the sub unit, and certainly worthy of being sent on courses, which if he succeeded on, would qualify him for promotion, but that he was never given the opportunity to prove himself in that regard. I explained that his record of disobedience and generally unacceptable conduct did nothing to suggest that he might be worthy of the time and effort that a Basic Drill and Weapons Course, for example, might do for him in terms of eligibility for promotion. His response was "try me"; I'll prove to you that given the chance, "I'll be the best on any course you send me on"!

I agreed to send him on the next available Basic Drill and Weapons Course at Depot RAR on the proviso, that if he failed the course, my recommendation to the CO for his discharge would be submitted and I was certain, under the circumstances, would be supported and be effected by Army HQ.

'He was duly sent on the next available Basic Drill and Weapons Course on which he achieved Top Student! He returned to the sub-unit a changed man and soon earned the first stripe he so desperately sought. On subsequent courses, he achieved equally exceptional results, eventually being "stolen" from B Company to become an instructor. In that capacity, he was detached to a training task with A Coy 1RAR at Glen Clova, at which point he was, as I recall, left in charge of a "base protection element" which came under serious attack from the "liberators", when the rest of the Company was on a period of R&R. This attack, he was almost totally responsible for repelling. He was awarded the Silver Cross of Rhodesia for his bravery and exceptional efforts in that sustained engagement, which just goes to prove, "Never judge a book by its cover". He was, as I am, a proud member of a Regiment which, in my view, remains' worthy of the undying gratitude, respect and remembrance of all who were Rhodesians and all who have an interest in matters military, to this day.'

Citation for the award of the Silver Cross of Rhodesia, 8 September 1978, Lance Corporal Chamunorwa Sarirowona SCR

'Since February 1976 LCpl Sarirowona of B Company 1RAR has been involved in a number of contacts with terrorists. At all times he has displayed outstanding determination to close with and eliminate terrorists, first as a private soldier and since 1977, as a Lance Corporal.

Cpl Chamunorwa Sarirowona SCR

'He has led by example throughout this period, inspiring those around him with gallant and aggressive acts in the face of the enemy. On 2 April, he was one of a small group of soldiers undergoing specialized training at a base camp in the operational area. The subunit normally resident at this base camp was out on duty. The soldiers were all volunteers under training for special tasks, and in addition, they protected the camp. At approximately 2100 hours the sentry reported possible terrorist movement to the south of the camp. While occupants of the base camp were in the process of moving to stand-to positions, approximately twenty terrorists opened fire on them with mortars and small arms. All the soldiers took cover immediately except for the platoon commander and L/Cpl Sarirowona who ran to firing positions close to and overlooking the terrorist position.

'Armed only with a sub-machine gun and one full magazine of ammunition, L/Cpl Sarirowona closed to within 100 metres of the terrorists. With complete disregard for his own safety he continually exposed himself to enemy fire under very hazardous circumstances in an attempt to direct aimed bursts of fire at the enemy. In this position a terrorist mortar bomb exploded approximately 20 metres behind him and he was wounded in the shoulder and leg with shrapnel. The wounds did not stop him from continuing to return fire at the terrorists until he had expended all his ammunition.

'Throughout the action he shouted abuse at the terrorists and challenged them to come closer. Finally deterred by the fierce reaction of the base camp occupants, the terrorists took flight. Despite his wounds, L/Cpl Sarirowona assisted his officer in re-organising the other soldiers and re-issued ammunition before he sought medical attention. As soon as possible after recovery from these wounds, he returned to the operational area.

'On 27 June 1977, along with other members of his platoon, he was a passenger in a vehicle in the operational area. At approximately 1600 hours the vehicle came under effective fire from an estimated group of forty terrorists who were in a well-sited ambush position. The initial enemy fire wounded nine of the eleven passengers in the vehicle, and having sustained mechanical damage from the terrorist fire, the vehicle came to a halt well within effective range of the terrorists' weapons. L/Cpl Sarirowona was one of the two passengers who escaped injury, and seeing the plight of his wounded comrades attempting to take cover, he took the only machine gun from a wounded man and proceeded to provide effective covering fire for his comrades. He did so from a completely exposed position and kept up his covering fire while the other uninjured passenger assisted the wounded off the vehicle and into cover. Despite their numerical superiority and their superior fire power, the terrorists soon abandoned their efforts and withdrew, which must be attributed to L/Cpl Sarirowona's courageous display of aggressiveness.

'Since this incident, L/Cpl Sarirowona has been engaged in further contacts and wounded again with a gunshot in the leg on 13 January 1978, since when he has made a strenuous effort to become fit enough to return to operations. 'These examples of this NCO's gallantry and leadership coupled with his complete contempt for the enemy and his aggressive determination to eliminate them have been, and continue to be, an example and inspiration to his fellow soldiers.

Lieutenant Bruce Thompson SCR (Post)

Lieutenant Bruce Thompson was an outstanding operational platoon commander, described by his Company Commander, Major Andre Dennison MLM BCR, in his War Diary: '…suffice it to say that there was no finer soldier in the Rhodesian Army, so that means in any Army.'

The following was written by Captain Andy Telfer SCR and is included in *Chibaya Moyo 1*. It is beautifully written with a mixture of respect, pathos, sincerity and deep affection

Lt Bruce Thompson SCR (Post)

for a man who was very close to Andy. I have included Bruce's story as his exploits are the stuff that cinematic box-office hits are made.

'This is a brief life, but in its brevity it offers us some splendid moments, some meaningful adventures.'

Rudyard Kipling, Kim

Lieutenant Bruce Malcolm Thompson had an all too brief life, but it had splendid moments. He was the only member of Regular Officer Cadet Course Inf 25/19 with a university degree (in Fine Arts from Natal). After graduating, he'd spent a year as a stoker on the South African Railways, earning enough money to buy a white Jaguar XJ6 which he brought back to Rhodesia, his pride and joy. Superbly fit, before becoming an officer cadet, he'd been a recruit in the SAS, where he'd broken the Speed March record during Selection (Intake 148).

During the Classical War Exercise of our cadet course, we advanced, attacked, defended and withdrew over half the Selukwe Hills in the middle of winter, digging trenches in ground selected not for tactical importance but for its impermeability to pick and shovel. While we scratched away one night, pitifully hoping to break through below waist-deep, Cadet Thompson, as with all things physical, finished his work in record time, producing a perfect fire-trench of exact dimensions and angles. With nothing to do, he began to get cold and thought, quite logically if not tactically, "I'll make a fire", and so he did, in a little wooded copse to the rear of our position. Needless to say, he paid the price when discovered by the Directing Staff (DS).

Bruce excelled during our bush-craft and tracking course with the Selous Scouts at Kariba. Late one evening, we were dropped off individually along a dirt road, each with our rifle and a raw egg. Our task was to make fire with sticks and cook the egg before uplift at dawn. This was heaven, alone and free in the African bush at twilight and, in the gathering darkness, I was drawn to wander, walking along the track, loving the freedom. Then, suddenly out of the night, I heard a voice from above: "Hokoyo shumba!" ("Beware lion!"). I thought perhaps it was the voice of the Lord, curiously speaking to me in Chilapalapa but no, it was that of future Selous Scout officer Simon Willar, up a tree. Thinking that a good place to be, I put my egg in my shirt top pocket and climbed up to join him on his branch, crushing my egg in the process.

We sat for a while like a pair of baboons, listening to the night sounds and chatting quietly. Then we got bored, so we climbed down and went further along the trail looking for the cadet dropped off before Simon. It wasn't hard to find him in the darkness as it turned out to be Bruce and he had, of course, successfully made a fire. The sight of him crouched behind the small fire with his back to a rock overhang, like a bushman, remains today one of my lasting images of the cadet course. We stayed with him until near first light and then returned to our own locations to await pick up and the inevitable assault course from the Scouts for not cooking the egg.

In order to foster detente, to provide us cadets with an opportunity to look at big things like tanks and artillery, and to enable the DS to stock up on Cadbury's chocolate and Nederberg wine, one happy day we all set off "down south", across the border as guests of our big brother, the South African Army. In George, we visited an extraordinary establishment, a female civil service academy run on military lines. There were hundreds of girls there, all Afrikaans, and not a man to be seen. We attended an Assembly in which we sat in the front row in a hall completely packed with young women while a female Brigadier welcomed us from the stage. Clearly struggling with English, she wanted to tell us that the girls had kit layouts on their beds that they would show us, but what she said was: "Now the girls will take you to their barrack room and show you what they do on their beds". The warning look from our DS was enough. None of our faces even twitched.

Colonel Mick McKenna (then OC Cadet Wing) later recalled: "At that function a young female subaltern was very taken with Thompson. How far it all went, I don't know but I remember saying to him at the time, 'Play this one very carefully. You're a private soldier, she is a lieutenant and the South African Army has fairly rigid rules about this sort of situation'. For his sake I hope he totally disregarded everything I said."

Bruce became a 'legend' Platoon Commander in 2RAR, one of those larger than life characters that the *Masodja* love. His extraordinary operational performance is well-documented in his SCR citation but what isn't well-known is how he spent his R&Rs. While the rest of us headed off to the bright lights of Salisbury like scalded cats, he was such a dedicated soldier that he would draw a thousand rounds from RSM Hallamore and spend his days snap shooting targets on the range. He never drank alcohol; he just trained.

On 27 June 1978, D Company was due to take over Fireforce Charlie at Fort Victoria from A Company. As we arrived on our vehicles, we saw the choppers taking off. We kitted up and waited to join them but the contact was over quickly. Bruce Thompson returned in a body bag. I was told that a single round, fired from an SKS, struck him in the throat and exited through his spine. He would have been dead before he hit the ground.

In the whole war, with everything in it, there was no event that moved me more. He was a vibrant human being who absolutely revelled in the physical joy of being alive and to see that vitality snuffed out was tragic. Bruce's life and death were part of the tapestry of the extraordinary experience that we were having: bright threads colourful and humorous, others black with tragedy. He was posthumously awarded the Silver Cross of Rhodesia.'

distinguishing himself in many fierce actions against the German, Italian and Japanese Navies.

CPO Thomas Telfer DSO & Bar (MID)

Petty Officer Thomas Telfer was awarded a DSM on 20 January 1942, a Bar to his DSM on 5 May 1942, both while on HM Submarine Triumph, and a Mention in Despatches on 18 December 1945. Alan Doyle has kindly researched Admiralty records at Kew and located the following (abbreviated) War Patrol report from HMS Triumph:

'On 19 August 1941, Triumph embarked a team of twelve men of No. 2 Commando under Lieutenant D. Schofield, Royal Fusiliers, together with eight Foldboats, 2015 lbs of T.N.T. plastic explosive, and other demolition stores. The Commando's target was the main Messina-Palermo railway.

'Triumph first attacked the Italian battle-fleet north of Messina, torpedoing the cruiser Bolzano; this was immediately followed by a heavy and accurate depth charge counter attack. The Bolzano was later successfully sunk by a 'human torpedo' attack. The submarine withdrew to carry out the Commando raid.

'The next evening, 29th August, Triumph approached and launched the raiding party in their Folboats at Torrente Furiano. Eight boats were launched, four for the raiding party and another four who would bring the raiding party back. Petty Officer Telfer volunteered to join Lieutenant Schofield and his six Commandos, making the strength of the raiding party eight in total. The four boats of the raiding party were smashed on landing and Schofield abandoned any idea of returning to Triumph. He was determined that the bridge should be blown up at all costs and his men were imbued with the same idea. This is borne out by the fact that he sent the remaining four boats back to the submarine instead of ordering them to lie off outside the surf and ferry the remainder back after the demolition had been completed. 'He sent no message back with these four boats. At 0320 hrs on the 30th August 1941 one and a half spans of the railway bridge were successfully demolished, but the Commando party could not be re-embarked and all, including Telfer, were taken prisoner.

'Subsequent awards to the gallant little team included one D.C.M., four M.M.'s and a Bar for Telfer's D.S.M. Triumph continued with her War Patrols but, on 20 January 1942, she was lost with all hands through unknown causes, but is thought to have run into a recently laid enemy minefield. Petty Officer Telfer, as a result of his captivity, became one of very few survivors who had served aboard this famous Submarine.'

Back in England, his fiancée was first informed by the Admiralty that he was 'missing presumed killed', so she joined the WAAF to help strike back in the only way she could. There, she was commissioned. Then, in October 1941, she received a message from his commanding officer, in a letter to Tom's mother that ended with these words:

'I was Captain of the Triumph all the time Petty Officer Telfer was in the ship, and I had the very highest possible opinion of him. He was most popular with all officers and men, a fine seaman, and a brave and cheerful man. We went through a good many nasty moments together, but he never for a moment lost his fine bearing.

'It was a severe blow to us all to lose him. I hope most sincerely that you may have heard from him by now, and I would very much like to know if you have and can spare the time to let me know. If you have not heard, please accept my deepest sympathy in your anxiety, but I do ask you to be brave and confident, like your son, for I am sure that the chances of his being all right are very strong.

'I believe he was thinking of getting married just before he left England, so would you please tell his fiancée how sorry I am that this should have happened, but not to give up hope.'

Yours very sincerely,

W.J.W. Woods, Commander R.N.

Teresa did not give up hope and, when she finally received the telegram that confirmed he was alive, a prisoner of war, she danced. She is Andy's mother.

Tom contracted meningitis in the POW camp and, on 21 March 1943, was exchanged in a Vatican-brokered swop of prisoners considered too ill to fight again. He did, however, recover and returned to submarines, serving in the Pacific until the surrender of the Japanese. His Mention in Despatches speaks of his conduct during that period:

'For courage, efficiency and devotion to duty whilst serving in H.M. Submarines Solent, Selene, Sea Scout, Sleuth, Stygian, Spark and Supreme in aggressive operations against Japanese shipping, often performed in shallow waters and in the face of serious opposition, over a period from July 1944 to August 1945'.

Evidently, gallantry is something that is an inherent quality in the Telfer family as

Medal Grouping CPO Thomas Telfer DSO (Bar), MID L-R: DSO (Bar), 1939-1945 Star, Atlantic Star (MID), War Medal 1939-1945, Defence Medal

Andy emulated his father's heroics by being decorated twice for acts of gallantry (more on this follows). What an extraordinary family.

Andrew Telfer joined the Rhodesian Army in December 1975 and attended Regular Cadet Course Inf/25(19). On 4 February 1977, he was commissioned as a Second Lieutenant and posted to 2RAR as a platoon commander. He served in D Company under Major Bryan McDermott and Support Company under Major Noel Morgan-Davies.

2 Lt Andrew Thomas Telfer SCR, MFC (Ops)

He was frequently detached to other companies on Fireforce duties, where he served under (then) Major Butch Duncan, Major Colin Hendrie, Major Andre Dennison and Lieutenant Colonel Terry Hammond. When the latter was sent to South Africa with RSM Hallamore to orientate the Parabats to Fireforce operations, he selected Andy to go with them. Throughout his service, Andy commanded his men with great distinction, earning the love and deep respect of his *Masodja*.

On the 27th January 1978, Andy was awarded the Military Forces Commendation (Operational) for quick thinking and aggressive leadership in operations in Mozambique in August 1977, less than six months after his commissioning. On the 14th September 1979, Andy was awarded our country's second highest award for conspicuous gallantry, the Silver Cross of Rhodesia, making him one of our Regiment's most highly decorated men.

When the Ceasefire came, and Andy was posted to the School of Infantry, the Commanding Officer of 2RAR, the highly respected Lieutenant Colonel Hammond wrote:

'Since I have known you, I have always been impressed with your professionalism and officer qualities, notwithstanding your demonstrated personal courage. I know that your conduct has been admired and copied by many of our young subalterns which in itself has been a positive contributor, for which I thank you.'

Citation for the award of the Military Forces Commendation (Operational), Second Lieutenant Andrew Thomas Telfer

Capt Andrew Thomas Telfer SCR, MFC (Ops)

'In August 1977 Second Lieutenant Telfer was commanding a patrol in the operational area when a group of terrorists was sighted. He moved his men into an immediate ambush position and they opened fire killing several terrorists in the initial encounter and several more in the follow up contact. Second Lieutenant Telfer's quick thinking and aggressive leadership during the contact was an inspiration to his patrol.'

Citation for the award of the Silver Cross of Rhodesia, 14 September 1979

'Lieutenant Andrew Thomas Telfer joined the Second Battalion RAR in February 1977 as a platoon commander. Since that date he has been deployed almost continually on counter-insurgency operations. Over the period June 1978 to December 1978, Lieutenant Telfer was involved in numerous contacts with terrorists. Since then, he has again been involved in many contacts, both as a ground-force commander and as an airborne commander. In all engagements he has displayed considerable initiative, outstanding leadership and distinguished personal conduct. Under his direction, more than forty terrorists have been eliminated and his personal bravery has been an inspiration of the highest order.

'On 5 June 1978, Lieutenant Telfer and three men were deployed into a Fireforce action by helicopter. Whilst sweeping through the area, he and his men came under heavy fire from two terrorists lodged in a rocky outcrop. Despite two air strikes, the terrorists continued to direct heavy and accurate fire on Lieutenant Telfer's position. With no regard for his personal safety, Lieutenant Telfer led an attack on the terrorist position and although being fired at from less than ten metres, he personally killed one terrorist. The other fled but was re-located, wounded, in a nearby field. Without hesitation Lieutenant Telfer ran across the open field, and although again being subjected to fire from the terrorist, killed him.

'On 26 October 1978, Lieutenant Telfer parachuted into a Fireforce operation. On landing he badly injured his ankle which was subsequently placed into a plaster cast for several weeks. Despite his injury, Lieutenant Telfer continued to lead his men throughout the three-hour operation and was directly responsible for the deaths of four of the six terrorists killed. During the mopping-up phase Lieutenant Telfer's patrol came under heavy fire from two terrorists hiding in a thickly wooded river line. One of his men was wounded and repeated attempts to dislodge the terrorists failed. Again, with no regard for his personal safety, and in considerable pain from his injured ankle, Lieutenant Telfer jumped into the river bed with one of his men and, although under heavy fire the whole time, personally killed both terrorists.

'On 13 November 1978, he was again deployed into a Fireforce action by helicopter. He was immediately subjected to heavy fire from the terrorist position. With commendable coolness, he directed an air strike on to the terrorists and then led an attack on to their position. All five terrorists were killed.

'At last light on 2 February 1979, returning from a successful Fireforce engagement, Lieutenant Telfer and three men were re-deployed to a sighting of ten terrorists. Shortly after being dropped, he sent two of his three men to cut off any terrorists attempting to escape from the contact area. Lieutenant Telfer and one man then ran into the kraal in which the main terrorist group was situated. In fading light, Lieutenant Telfer killed two terrorists and several recruits.

'Throughout these and numerous other contacts, Lieutenant Telfer's personal courage, exemplary leadership and aggressive attitude have inspired all those with whom he has been in action.'

Medal Grouping Captain AT Telfer SCR, (MFC [Ops])

Footnote: The magnificent, gallant actions of Andy Telfer throughout his operational service are the things of which movies are made but there was another side to this young officer who had also served as the Adjutant in 2RAR, an appointment highly respected and valued by all subalterns.

What naturally followed was a posting-out as an officer instructor at the Zimbabwe Military Academy. Officers posted to the School of Infantry/Military Academy were hand-picked by the Commandant from the Corps of Officers Nominal Roll and were officers who were able to display a mature, sensible and practical approach to what was, unquestionably, a sensitive circumstance.

Captain Telfer ran the first Lt-Capt GD (General Duties) course of integration for candidates who came from the former Rhodesian Army, ZIPRA and ZANLA. Each one of the participants was selected for his operational reputation on the basis that if they could integrate, others would follow. The same criterion applied to the selection of Andy as the Course Officer.

That is the measure of this exemplary RAR officer and consistent with the true spirit in which he served. We, who served with him, hold him in the very highest regard and, dare I say it, with a good measure of deserved reverence.

The watercolour painting

Andy is depicted in full para Fireforce kit with that omni-present and engaging smile of his. The image of Andy's face I have taken from one of his wedding photographs, his proudest day, and I have superimposed it on my depiction of a Rhodesian paratrooper taken from several references to conform to how we looked back in those halcyon days. The reserve parachute has the number '360', included with quite deliberate intent, because this man would have your front, sides and back in a 'punch-up' without ever considering the implications of that decision. That is how I view our friendship; it is nonintrusive, but it is sincerity in its very rawest form. After some 100 hours or so, I am hoping that I have captured Andy's likeness but, and more importantly, the spirit of this fine man that is his most enduring and endearing quality. In the first instance, I leave it to Janette and then to those who served alongside this first class and gallant man to decide.

Lieutenant Graeme Trass SCR

Lt Graeme Trass SCR

I pay tribute to another outstanding member of our proud regiment, a young officer, educated at Rathkeale College in Masterton, New Zealand, who came to Rhodesia in search of 'Chibuku' and Mopani Worms, disliked both and quite understandably, joined the Rhodesian Regular Army as a New Zealand national, attended O.S.B. and was commissioned off Regular Officer Cadet Course Inf/25(20) on the 10th February 1978. Newly commissioned and posted to the Rhodesian Army Corps of Engineers, Graham immediately requested a posting to an infantry unit as it had always been his intention to serve on the front line when he enlisted. Thankfully, common sense prevailed in higher echelons and Graham was posted on attachment to the 2nd Battalion, The Rhodesian African Rifles where he was attached to B Company under the command of Major Colin 'Nyengure' Hendrie. The rest, as the saying goes, is history.

The following profile, once again, per very kind favour of Captain Andy Telfer SCR, a fellow 2RAR Officer:

Graeme Trass joined B Coy, 2RAR in early 1978 as a newly commissioned 2Lt from regular cadet course Inf/25(20). He was a New Zealander and shared with his more famous countryman, Sir Edmund Hillary, the tall and craggy appearance of the classic outdoorsman.

It's usually the case that tall, wide-shouldered people wear a uniform well but Graham somehow managed not to. His shoulders advanced not only far to the sides but also to the front, leaving his chest behind, and his waist was so narrow that his uniform hung like a curtain, cinched in the middle by his belt. On top of this unusual edifice, a lantern jaw and a smile as wide as a letterbox beamed out at a world, he found both amusing and adventurous. I write this with great affection as he is, without a doubt, one of the finest people I've encountered anywhere.

If you said his name to any RAR soldier who knew him, they would smile affectionately and tell you a story about him. Graeme was one of those one-of-a-kind characters that our *Masodja* loved. They knew he was brave (a pre-requisite), cared for them (another tick), and could always be counted on to do something special (the icing on the cake). They loved him. You will note in his citation how he went forward under intense fire to extricate a wounded soldier? That's what I mean.

Graeme had an extraordinary 'B-S Radar'. The Rhodesian Army (fortunately) didn't have too many officers who saluted themselves in the morning and adopted the affected mannerisms of the stereotypical army officer but, if one ever entered our Mess, Graeme was onto him. I'd sit back on my bar stool (or the bar counter, or in the rafters if the evening was well-advanced) and watch with amusement as Graeme studied his target with fascination, then (more to amuse himself than anyone else) began to quietly mimic him, then collapsed in heaps of laughter at his own humour, while his unfortunate subject became increasingly bewildered and uncomfortable.

I know that he's got a huge family and I do hope that they are aware of just how fine a man their dad proved himself to be when, as a young fella, back in the day, he bumbled across a distant land doing brave things and winning the affection of all who knew him.'

The following Citation was written by Major Colin Hendrie, OC B Company, 2RAR:

Citation for the award of the Silver Cross of Rhodesia, 14 September 1979, Lieutenant Graeme Leslie Trass SCR

'Second Lieutenant Graeme Leslie Trass has served as a platoon commander in the Second Battalion, the Rhodesian African Rifles since March 1978. During this time he has been involved in numerous contacts and has been responsible for the elimination of a large number of terrorists.

'On 10 August 1978, Second Lieutenant Trass and a patrol of four men were parachuted into a contact area during a Fireforce action. Immediately after landing, he led a sweep line towards the terrorist position. Contact was made, and all six terrorists were killed. Afterwards a patrol of four men was pinned down in open ground by four terrorists hiding in a rocky outcrop. Second Lieutenant Trass and three men were directed to assist. Without hesitation, he led the patrol across the open ground and skirmished through the terrorists' position, the whole time being subjected to intense terrorist fire. In all, four terrorists were killed. In this engagement, a total of ten terrorists were eliminated, due largely to the coolness and leadership of Second Lieutenant Trass.

'On 28 August 1978, a patrol of four men, commanded by an officer, was fired on by two terrorists at very close range. The officer was wounded, and the patrol forced to withdraw in the face of heavy fire. Repeated air attacks failed to dislodge the terrorists. Second Lieutenant Trass and one man skirmished across open ground under fire, and assaulted the terrorist position, killing both terrorists at close quarters.

'On 7 December 1978, a patrol of four men was fired upon by three terrorists entrenched in a narrow and thickly-wooded re-entrant. The officer was wounded, and the patrol forced to withdraw. Subsequent air attacks failed to eliminate the terrorists. Second Lieutenant Trass, leading seven men, attempted to sweep through the terrorist position. At ten metres' range, the terrorists fired upon his men, seriously wounding the machine gunner, who fell within a few yards of the terrorists. His men were forced to withdraw to cover. In the fading light, and believing that the machine gunner was still alive, Second Lieutenant Trass crawled forward and extricated him, under fire from within a few metres of the terrorist, showing great personal courage in so doing.

'On these and other occasions, Second Lieutenant Trass has shown disregard for his own safety, displaying courage and aggressive leadership of the highest order. His conduct has been an inspiration to all who have served with him.'

Post Scriptum:

We who know Graeme, speak of him in the most respectful and glowing terms; an unassuming man who let his actions do the talking for him. His leadership and repeated acts of gallantry under fire are the true hallmark of every recipient of our Country's second highest gallantry award. His good wife Sharon, and their children, should read this tribute and his Citation and remember that they are in the company of a just, upright and good man. Respected by all in our Regiment and our Army; we are indebted to him for his service to Rhodesia and the RAR and we are very pleased to honour him in this small, important but very symbolic way.

Corporal Ananias Ali SCR

I give tribute to a former 2RAR junior NCO, an operational stick commander of the very highest distinction who, fittingly, received his Silver Cross on the same medals parade as his former Platoon Commander, (then) Lieutenant Andy Telfer SCR.

Corporal Ananias Ali SCR: a profile written by Andy Telfer for *Chibaya Moyo 1*:

'There were some men who epitomised the RAR soldier as a fighter. Corporal Ananias Ali SCR was one of them. I first saw him through binoculars when he was moving towards my position to make an RV. Even at a distance, the aggression was evident. In the next promotion round, I made a bid for him and he joined me as a Section Commander. I'd seen that he moved like a predator and I wanted hunters not farmers.'

His citation was written by his Company Commander (then) Major Bryan McDermott:

Citation for the award of the Silver Cross of Rhodesia, 14 September 1979, Corporal Ananias Ali SCR

Cpl Ananias Ali SCR

'Over the period February 1978 to February 1979, Corporal Ali has been involved in numerous contacts with terrorists. In all of these engagements, Corporal Ali has shown outstanding leadership and his determination to close with and kill the enemy has been an inspiration to all. He has personally killed fifteen terrorists and captured four.

'On 16 July 1978, Corporal Ali approached what he thought was a dead terrorist. The terrorist sprang to life and gripped the barrel of Corporal Ali's rifle, trying to wrest it from him. Although Corporal Ali could have pulled the trigger and killed the terrorist, instead he calmly drew his pistol and ordered the terrorist to surrender, which he did. The captured terrorist proved to be a section commander and much valuable information was gleaned from him, leading to several other contacts.

'On 26 October 1978, during the mopping-up stages of a Fireforce action, two terrorists opened fire on Corporal Ali's group of soldiers, wounding one of them. The terrorists were lodged in a thickly - wooded riverbed with steep banks. Corporal Ali borrowed a machine gun from another soldier and with his platoon commander jumped into the riverbed. One terrorist was quickly killed. Corporal Ali saw the second terrorist about to throw a hand grenade and tried to fire at him. His machine gun, however, did not fire due to a stoppage. Although he was completely exposed to the terrorist, he calmly gave an indication to his platoon commander who was able to kill the terrorist. Undoubtedly, his exceptional calm and discipline saved both his life and that of his platoon commander.

'On 9 February 1979, Corporal Ali was in command of a sweep line moving through dense bush, known to contain terrorists. In a most aggressive manner, he led his men through the bush and into contact with the terrorists, accounting for the whole group. He personally killed one terrorist and captured a further two.

'On 20 February 1979, Corporal Ali, while deploying at night, heard firing. Acting on his own initiative, he re-deployed his patrol towards the firing. At first light the following morning he observed suspicious movement some distance from his position. Arming himself with a pistol and accompanied by one other soldier, he observed a group of seven terrorists. He returned to his original position and called for the Fireforce. While awaiting their arrival, he re-positioned his patrol to cut off the terrorist escape routes. After an exceptionally good talk-on to the Fireforce, he calmly controlled the ground forces throughout the highly successful action.

'Throughout these and other engagements, Corporal Ali has consistently shown complete disregard for his own safety. His tactical skill and high degree of aggression throughout have inspired his men and largely been responsible for his sub-unit's considerable successes.'

Lance Corporal Raymond Hariori SCR

I give tribute to former 2RAR junior NCO, an operational stick commander of the very highest distinction who, fittingly, received his Silver Cross from the Commander of the Rhodesian Army, Lieutenant General A.L.C. "Sandy" Maclean OLM, DCD and on the same medals parade as no fewer than seven of his Battalion's officers and fellow NCO's. 14 September 1979 was the most significant honours and awards parade in our Regimental history; it witnessed the award of 4 Silver Crosses and 4 Bronze Crosses in the same award ceremony to members from the same Battalion and at the home of the 2nd Battalion, Masvingo Barracks in Fort Victoria.

From Captain Andy Telfer SCR:

Lance Corporal Hariori was in B Company, 2RAR. His nickname was 'Harris', from his streetwise, almost urban manner, like a bad guy from an African American gangster movie of that era. He was tall and lean, with the athletic build of a fighter, always smiling, said little and was clearly dangerous. He was an MAG gunner when I first started to be attached to B Company in 1977 for Fireforce, when it was commanded by (then) Major Butch Duncan.

There weren't many para-trained soldiers at that time but, as he was one, he was placed with me and stood out for his aggressiveness. As the years passed, I encountered him whenever I returned to B Company. He remained much the same, a quiet, smiling, deadly soldier.

One more memory. When the firing started, back when he was an MAG gunner, he didn't go into that darting, hunting, forward movement that most RAR soldiers made. He walked slowly forward, firing the MAG in short bursts from the hip.

It was quite distinctive, a deliberate kind of aggression, rather than a rush. I regret I cannot remember details of specific contacts involving him to relate, because there were so many, but I liked him a lot and had full confidence in him.'

LCpl Raymond Hariori SCR

Major Colin Hendrie, his Company Commander, wrote his citation.:

Citation for the award of the Silver Cross of Rhodesia, 14 September 1979, Lance Corporal Raymond Hariori SCR

'For the past three and a half years, Lance Corporal Raymond Hariori has been deployed almost continuously on counter-insurgency operations. He has had numerous contacts with terrorists, most of which have been while he was a member of the Fireforce. In all contacts, Lance Corporal Hariori has displayed outstanding leadership and determination to close with and kill the enemy.

'On 10 August 1978, he was a member of a patrol commanded by an officer. The patrol was called upon to assist another group which was pinned down in open ground by a group of terrorists in a rocky outcrop. Taking a machine gun from another soldier, he and his platoon commander assaulted the terrorist position. Lance Corporal Hariori personally killed two of the terrorists.

'On 28 August 1978, Lance Corporal Hariori was in a sweep line when they came under fire from two terrorists hidden in thick bush. Despite the heavy and accurate fire from the terrorist position, Lance Corporal Hariori and his platoon commander skirmished across open ground and killed both terrorists at very close range.

'On 13 February 1979, during a Fireforce action, Lance Corporal Hariori and his patrol were tasked to clear an area of thick cover, known to contain terrorists. In a swift and aggressive manner, he led his patrol through the cover and eliminated three terrorists. On the same day, and in another Fireforce action, he and his patrol were deployed by helicopter after two terrorists had been seen from the air. In fading light and followed by his men, Lance Corporal Hariori tracked the two terrorists into re-entrant where he personally killed one and captured the other. This was the fourth time that day that he had been deployed into action, having started at dawn.

'On 7 March 1979, Lance Corporal Hariori again led his men in an exceptionally aggressive manner against a terrorist group, eliminating two terrorists.

'Throughout these and many other contacts, Lance Corporal Hariori has shown a total disregard for personal danger. His conspicuous gallantry, fine leadership and personal aggression have earned him great respect among his fellow soldiers.'

Lieutenant Patrick Lawless SCR

There will be few, if any, officers and *Masodja* from our Regiment or our man's army who do not personally know, or know of, Pat Lawless. This is a tribute to a former RAR officer, an operational commander of the very highest distinction and a true gentleman whose impeccable reputation in both the military and public life truly precedes him. I have not asked his permission to write these words nor, with the greatest of respect, will I. He has become a good and loyal friend to me and, as a once-upon-a-time subordinate, I am happy to accept any 'Extras' that he wishes to 'dish out' to me. Some things are what they are...

2 Lt Patrick Lawless SCR

As a young man, Pat demonstrated early qualities of leadership and was appointed the Head of College at St Stephen's College in Balla Balla in 1975 before attending Regular Officer Cadet Course Inf/25(19) at the School of Infantry in Gwelo that ran from 19 January 1976 to 4 February 1977. Not long thereafter, St Stephen's College was to close and become the home of Depot RAR.

Pat distinguished himself on this extremely mentally and physically challenging 13-month course:

1. Awarded the Sword of Honour: The cadet who had demonstrated the most potential and deemed the most likely to succeed,

2. Awarded The Army Commander's Award [Sam Browne belt]: The best overall academic results achieved on the course, and

3. Awarded the newly instituted Tactics Proficiency Trophy: Awarded to the cadet displaying the highest tactical proficiency.

It is worthy of mention that there were very few regular officer cadets who received the School of Infantry's two highest honours as cadets.

Pat was commissioned as a 2Lt and posted to The First Battalion The Rhodesian African Rifles as OC 60mm Mortar Platoon in Support Company 'Chiwororo' where he commanded his platoon with great distinction earning the love and deep respect of his *Masodja*. Tom Fulton, a subaltern in the Battalion at the time and recovering from injuries sustained in a landmine detonation in Binga some months earlier was briefly attached to Sp Coy, then under the command of Maj Butch Zeederberg. Tom was tasked with sitting-in on an O Group (Orders Group) that Pat was issuing his platoon pre-deployment. At the end of this Tom reported back to Butch Zeederberg who inquired, "So how was it?" Tom's response, "They were flawless Sir. The most immaculate set of orders I have ever listened to!" And so, with that, Patrick was to receive the respectful 'pseudonym' 'Flawless'. It was a mantra that sat well with this man whose absolute dedication to his men was as uncompromising as was his attention to the minutest detail in all that he did.

On the 30th June 1980, Pat was awarded our Country's second highest award for conspicuous gallantry, the Silver Cross of Rhodesia. Pat was the last European in our Regiment to receive this award and he was joined, fittingly, by a 2RAR A.S. Lance Corporal Alois Matambo, who was the last SCR recipient in our Regiment's long and proud history.

Pat was appointed as the course officer of last regular cadet course, Inf/25(23), an appointment widely regarded as the precursor to higher rank and appointment. The cadets who benefitted from Pat's professional and expert tuition speak of him, to a man, in the most respectful and glowing terms. A testament to the true professional we have always known him to be.

After 5 years and two months service (January 1976 to February 1981), Pat retired from the Rhodesian Army as a substantive Captain, parachute and combat team trained and immigrated to the United Kingdom where he joined the British Army serving for nineteen years (1981 to 2001).

Pat retired as a Brigadier, a rank he achieved by age 43, having had the roles of Deputy Commander and Chief of Staff of the Joint Helicopter Command and a combat qualified helicopter pilot.

Post military, Patrick continues to excel and has held various CEO, COO, CFO appointments with some of the world's preeminent businesses. Pat is the current Chairman of The RAR Regimental Association (UK) maintaining a life-long passion and commitment to all things RAR.

Citation for the award of the Silver Cross of Rhodesia, 30 June 1980, Lieutenant Patrick Lawless SCR

'Lieutenant Patrick Lawless joined the 1st Battalion, the Rhodesian African Rifles on 4 February 1977 as a platoon commander. Throughout his service he has displayed a fierce determination to seek out and destroy the enemy. He has frequently been exposed to extremely dangerous situations in which his calm planning and aggressive action have been outstanding.

'On 11 August 1978, Lt Lawless was in command of a group of seven men tasked with locating a route which was being used by terrorists to infiltrate Rhodesia. Towards last light Lt Lawless' group located a group of three terrorists moving through the area. By skilful and prompt manoeuvre of his men, he succeeded in wounding and capturing one of these terrorists although darkness had fallen by the time contact was made. The terrorist died of his wounds in spite of Lt Lawless' efforts to keep him alive, but before dying, he yielded valuable information.

'The following morning, a group of terrorists, numbering approximately seventy, carried out a surprise attack on Lt Lawless' group. The terrorists, who enjoyed tactical and numerical superiority, made repeated fierce and determined attacks on the small patrol. Lt Lawless so organized and inspired his men that the terrorists were driven back each time until, desperately short of ammunition; he was forced to conduct a tactical withdrawal. At least eight terrorists were killed and a number of others wounded in this action.

'On another occasion Lt Lawless was a member of a Fireforce which responded to a sighting of thirty terrorists. Following a series of contacts with this group, Lt Lawless was tasked to command a sweep to clear the river line along which the terrorists had taken cover. The sweep line was subjected to heavy small-arms and machine-gun fire. Lt Lawless was ordered by the Fireforce commander to withdraw to facilitate use of air weapons against the terrorists' position. During the regrouping phase, Lt

Lawless realized that one officer was missing. Siting machine guns to cover his movement and undaunted by the heavy enemy fire being directed at him, Lt Lawless skirmished alone to the last reported position of the missing officer. He located the officer who had been mortally wounded approximately eight metres from the terrorists' position. The close proximity to the enemy position prohibited the use of air weapons against the terrorists, so Lt Lawless rapidly assessed the situation and moved his machine gun to a better position. In this assault, three terrorists were killed. The sweep line then continued with its task, successfully eliminating a further seven terrorists in the process.

'On reaching a sharp river bend, the sweep came under heavy and effective fire from six terrorists who had positioned themselves among boulders in the riverbed. Lt Lawless moved his men to a position from which they could provide effective covering fire for an assault group on the other side of the river. The initial assault was successful but resulted in one of the officers being wounded in the head. Lt Lawless, appreciating the demoralising effect that the wounded officer would have on his men unless he was attended to rapidly, moved to his assistance. This entailed crossing a river in full view of the terrorists and under heavy small-arms fire. With complete disregard for his own safety, Lt Lawless successfully reached the wounded officer, rendered first aid, and arranged the necessary casevac. He then resumed command of the sweep line and so manoeuvred his men as to facilitate the elimination by the sweep of a further three terrorists. In this fierce action fifteen terrorists in all were accounted for, and a great deal of credit for the success achieved must go to Lt Lawless whose calm leadership and fearless actions inspired those about him.

'In the aforementioned actions and numerous others in which Lt Lawless has been involved, he has repeatedly committed acts of conspicuous gallantry in his determination to close with the enemy. He has earned the undying respect and admiration of those with whom he serves and his conduct is worthy of the highest praise and recognition.'

Corporal Alois Matambo SCR

I pay tribute to a former 2RAR junior NCO, an operational stick commander of the very highest distinction who, fittingly, received the last Silver Cross of Rhodesia awarded by the Rhodesian Army and on the same medals parade as Maj Graham Wilson (1SAS) GCV, SCR, BCR, Maj Bruce Snelgar (1RLI) SCR (Post), Lt BM

Sudbury (8RR) SCR, Lt Patrick Lawless (1RAR) SCR and Maj Nigel Henson (1RLI) OLM.

Cpl Alois Matambo SCR

Citation for the award of the Silver Cross of Rhodesia, 30 June 1978, Corporal Alois Matambo SCR

'Corporal Alois Matambo joined the Second Battalion, the Rhodesian African Rifles, in August 1976. Since then he has been deployed almost continuously on operations and has been in numerous contacts with terrorists. On all occasions his actions have been by fine leadership and determination to close with and kill the enemy.

'During the night of 30 March 1979, Cpl Matambo led a patrol of four men to investigate a beer drink. Cover was sparse, so he and his men crawled over open ground to within 30 metres of the gathering. Simultaneously, the beer finished, and dispersing locals saw the patrol and ran away, shouting to warn the terrorists who were present. The terrorists opened fire on the exposed patrol. Cpl Matambo immediately led an assault directly at the terrorists. One terrorist was killed and another wounded. Both weapons were recovered.

'On 5 April 1979 Cpl Matambo and his patrol of three men, while occupying an observation post, sighted a group of terrorists based up in very thick bush. As the Fireforce was not available to react, Cpl Matambo led his patrol off the hill in an attempt to contact the terrorists. Seeing that the area around the thick bush in which the terrorists were based was open, Cpl Matambo led a charge across the open ground. On breaking cover his patrol was seen and fired on by the terrorists, who then ran away. Cpl Matambo succeeded in killing the terrorist in command of the group. Others were wounded or escaped. In this action, Cpl Matambo's determination to kill the enemy was particularly praiseworthy as he knew at the outset he was heavily outnumbered.

'On the 10 November 1979, Cpl Matambo and his patrol were ambushed from three separate positions at a range of thirty metres by a group of ten terrorists. The patrol was caught in the open with no cover. Totally disregarding his own safety, Cpl Matambo charged the main terrorist position and personally killed three terrorists. He then controlled the ensuing firefight which resulted in a further two terrorists being killed and two wounded. Among those killed were the platoon commander and platoon security officer. Throughout these and other actions, Cpl Matambo has consistently shown outstanding leadership, personal courage and a high degree of aggression. His actions have earned him the respect and admiration of the members of his unit.'

BRONZE CROSS OF RHODESIA (BCR)

Bronze Cross of Rhodesia

The Bronze Cross of Rhodesia was instituted in 1970 with the first RAR recipients invested in October 1970 and the final award made in June 1980. The BCR, awarded for Gallantry, ranks in precedence behind the Silver Cross, Rhodesia's second highest gallantry decoration. Since its inception, a total of 25 BCR's were awarded to officers and men of the RAR of which the 1st Battalion received fourteen, nine went to members of 2RAR and two to 1 (Independent) Company RAR. One award was made posthumously. The first and last recipients were fittingly and, consistent with the SCR, awarded to African soldiers.

Lieutenant Ian Patrick Wardle BCR

Citation for the award of the Bronze Cross of Rhodesia, 1970, Lieutenant Ian Patrick Wardle BCR

'For gallantry and leadership in action. During anti-terrorist operations, while leading a patrol in pursuit of a gang of terrorists, Lt Wardle and his men found themselves in the centre of a well- concealed terrorist position. Lt Wardle immediately directed a heavy weight of fire at one terrorist position thus killing two terrorists and causing the surrender of a further four. On learning from one surrendered terrorist that other terrorists were concealed nearby, Lt Wardle, with complete disregard for his own safety, immediately positioned himself where he could subject this area to fire and, in the ensuing battle, a further six terrorists were killed and two captured. The success of this action can only be attributed to Lt Wardle's quick, fearless action and remarkable qualities of leadership.'

Second Lieutenant Ron Marillier BCR

Maj Ron Marillier BCR

Ron Marillier was born in Sinoia, Southern Rhodesia on 16 December 1948. He was educated at Que Que High School and was appointed Head Boy of the school in his final year. He was tall, athletic and a member of his school's Cricket 1st XI and Rugby 1st XV in 1966.

Ron attended and passed a regular OSB in January 1967, attended that course in February 1967 and was commissioned in February 1968 and was posted to E Company, 1RAR. In 1970, he attended a C Sqn SAS selection course and passed. He qualified as a static line and free-fall paratrooper and was involved in external operations as a 'Pathfinder'. After a short posting as Adjutant to 1RR in 1974, he was posted to 'Hooters' as a National Service course officer in 1975. In 1976 he was posted to 1 (Indep) Coy RR. In 1977 he was posted to Llewellin Barracks, Depot Rhodesia Regiment as a Company Commander where he remained until mid-1979 when he was posted back to 1RAR as OC A Company, 1RAR. Ron was promoted to Lt Col and posted as CO of 33 Infantry Battalion (formerly 3RAR) in 1981 where he remained until his retirement at the end of that year.

On 17 March 1968, 14 Platoon, E Coy, 1RAR under Second Lieutenant Ron Marillier was on the tracks of a small group of insurgents when it was joined by 13 Troop, 3 Commando, 1RLI led by Second Lieutenant C. J. 'Dumpy' Pearce and a BSAP patrol led by Inspector E. Saul. Lieutenant Pearce was in overall command. On the next day the troops realized that the enemy was aware of their presence when they came upon a well-prepared ambush position recently vacated. At 1300 hours, with 13 Troop in the lead, they crossed the Maura River when the RLI Troop came under heavy fire from close quarters directed by over 50 insurgents who were in a first-class all-round defensive position on high ground, dominating all possible approaches. 13 Troop became pinned down but returned fire and hurled grenades; Pearce then asked Marillier to move his platoon in a right flanking attack on the enemy position while 13 Troop provided covering fire. When Marillier approached the right flank and began to deploy his sections into favourable assault positions, observing that they would have to cross over 200 metres of open ground. Nevertheless, he le68his men forward in an attempt to close with the enemy, 13 Troop providing covering fire.

As the platoon advanced, it came under a terrific hail of fire in which Corporal Erisha was killed and Platoon Warrant Officer Herod and Private Wilson were wounded. Although some of them reached the forward edge of the insurgents' position, momentum was lost and Marillier was forced to order a withdrawal. He then began to crawl about the battlefield, valiantly drawing fire upon himself in his efforts to ensure that his men were clear of the area, particularly the wounded Platoon Warrant Officer Herod. It was now 1430 hours and Pearce, observing Marillier's withdrawal, ordered his troops to do the same, under covering fire from the armed helicopters and Provosts. A heavy air strike was then carried out by two Vampires and two Canberras who's earlier circling had, as the insurgents later admitted, proved so demoralising that many of them deserted. Among them was Moffat Hadebe, their overall commander who had been watching the air strike from a point 600 metres south-west of the camp.

After the air strike, the troops attempted another right flanking attack, with 14 Platoon and half of 13 Troop advancing under covering fire from the BSAP patrol and the rest of 13 Troop, but the attack was again unsuccessful and called off in the approaching darkness. The next morning, 13 Troop was reinforced by 10 and 11 Troops 1RLI, who searched the enemy position which had been abandoned during the night. One dead insurgent and a vast amount of kit, including 28,000 rounds of ammunition was found. Marillier was awarded a Bronze Cross for his inspiring courage under fire.

Citation for the award of the Bronze Cross of Rhodesia, 1970, Second Lieutenant Ronald Marillier BCR

> 'For gallantry and leadership in action. 2nd Lt Marillier, a newly-commissioned officer, in command of inexperienced troops, was ordered to withdraw from an exposed position where he and his men had become pinned down under heavy enemy fire. With complete disregard for his own safety, 2nd Lt Marillier crawled over exposed ground, under heavy enemy fire and succeeded in redeploying his men. Throughout this difficult action, 2nd Lt Marillier displayed great gallantry for so young and inexperienced an officer and his conduct was an inspiration to all those present at the action.'

WO2 Wurayayi Mutero BCR

WO2 Wurarayayi Mutero BCR

This man was to set the bar extremely high for his peers in the Regiment, in fact so high that none deserved the status he did nor did they achieve what he did.

Wurayayi Mutero enlisted into the 1st Battalion the Rhodesian African Rifles and served with various companies, working his way through the ranks becoming the CSM of D Company. The following sets forth his remarkable achievements:

He was one of the first recipients of the Bronze Cross of Rhodesia on 23 October 1970 together with three others from our regiment. By virtue of his seniority at their investiture, he was the first African soldier to receive the award (the other being Private Kenias Tovakare BCR); the same medals parade included Lt Ian Patrick Wardle BCR and 2Lt Ron Marillier BCR).

In 1976, he was promoted to WO1 becoming the first A-RSM of 2RAR, no finer distinction in the non-commissioned ranks and one held in the very highest regard by all ranks within the Rhodesian Army.

In 1977, WO1 Mutero was to set a 'first' again when he received his deserved commission as a Lieutenant together with the former 1RAR RSM, WO1

Martin Tumbare DMM. Jointly, they were the first African servicemen to receive a commission in the Rhodesian Army and Defence Force.

In 1976, he was promoted to WO1 becoming the first A-RSM of 2RAR, no finer distinction in the non-commissioned ranks and one held in the very highest regard by all ranks within the Rhodesian Army.

In 1977, WO1 Mutero was to set a 'first' again when he received his deserved commission as a Lieutenant together with the former 1RAR RSM, WO1 Martin Tumbare DMM. Jointly, they were the first African servicemen to receive a commission in the Rhodesian Army and Defence Force.

Lt Mutero BCR went on to receive promotion to Captain and completed his service as a Major at Depot RAR (according to unconfirmed but credible sources). Reports received some time ago confirm that this fine soldier and officer has since passed away; the precise details of which are sadly unknown.

Maj Mutero's service amply demonstrates the enormous strength of character of one of our own; a shining beacon to all. Nothing is beyond one's reach and he demonstrated that with discipline, commitment and hard-work one is deserving of reward. We, his brethren from the RAR, salute a loyal, gallant and faithful servant of our proud Regiment. Zororayi Murugare. Tichazo Sangana.

Citation for the award of the Bronze Cross of Rhodesia, 23 October 1970, WO2 Wurayayi Mutero BCR

> 'For gallantry and leadership in action. Sergeant Major Wurayayi Mutero has taken part in numerous anti-terrorist operations and has been involved in a number of contacts with the enemy. His performance on all these occasions has been outstanding and his determination, qualities of leadership and complete disregard for his own safety have been an inspiration to the men he commands.'

WO2 Gibson Mugadza BCR

There will be few, if any, officers and *Masodja* from C Company, 1RAR or 4 (Independent) Company RAR who will not be familiar with the aggression and professionalism of WO2 Gibson Mugadza BCR. This fine soldier went on to become the RSM of the Zimbabwe Military Academy; due recognition for a man better suited to the non-commissioned ranks and that is meant with the very greatest respect.

This is a tribute to this former 1RAR senior warrant officer, a man amongst men, a leader and an operational commander of the highest distinction.

WO2 Gibson Mugadza BCR

I first met WO2 Gibson when I was 2ic of B Company, 3RAR based in Chipinga (Op Tangent) and my brother Tom was the OC of 4 (Independent) Company RAR and based in Wankie. WO2 Gibson was the CSM. Tom contacted me and said that he wanted to bring his basketball team to Chipinga to play against our team; I hadn't seen Tom for well over twelve months and was delighted with the prospect of seeing him again and engaging in a bit of sport.

During our game I became acquainted with CSM Gibson, then a tall and muscular man who exuded an aura of raw aggression. I forget the score line but we lost quite convincingly and between Maj Fulton and CSM Gibson we found that basketball (one sport that I never liked and was even poorer at playing) was to be played in an aggressive 'Take No Prisoners' manner. It suited us just fine and there were few from both sides who left the court without bloodied noses, skinned knees and elbows and the odd 'shiner' (black eye). CSM Gibson was on court to win and whoever was in his path either got out of his way or was made to get out of the way. Despite this, and whilst we quaffed a few gallons of 'Charles Glass' I found out that he was deeply respectful and not in the remotest bit familiar. He was the consummate professional soldier and I envied my boet having so fine a man as his CSM.

In 2014, whilst scrolling through RAR Facebook group page and I saw a number of photographs taken at an RAR Regimental Association celebration in the UK that included this good man that touched me but also angered me. In a nutshell, I inquired from our members if anyone knew why RSM Gibson was not wearing his BCR.

I had it confirmed that RSM Gibson had stayed on in the new Zimbabwe National Army (ZNA) and, as the holder of the Bronze Cross of Rhodesia, he was required to surrender his BCR and, on the completion of his service, it would be returned to him. It never happened!

I contacted Major General MD Shute OLM, then the RAR Regtl Assn Chairman and asked him if I he was opposed to me trying to find a replica replacement BCR for him to be re-issued. The request was approved, and I started searching until I found one, brand new, and I personally paid for it.

Citation for the award of the Bronze Cross of Rhodesia, 13 September 1974, WO2 Gibson Mugadza BCR

'For gallantry and leadership. While serving as a platoon warrant officer in anti-terrorist operations in the north-eastern border area, Warrant Officer Gibson has been involved in numerous engagements with the terrorists, in which he has displayed outstanding qualities of courage, determination and leadership.

'In an encounter while occupying a night ambush position and seeing three terrorists he could not effectively engage with fire, he took three of his men and followed up until he was within close range when he engaged with and killed them. In another engagement he was in a stop-line position at night with four men when they were attacked from the rear by approximately ten terrorists who put down heavy fire on his position, killing one soldier.

'With his machine gun out of action and only three weapons firing, Warrant Officer Gibson stood his ground and in spite of being outnumbered and facing greatly superior fire power, repulsed the attack. Warrant Officer Gibson moved to a better position, first removing all equipment from the dead soldier so that it could not fall into enemy hands. Having re-organized his defences and encouraging the other three soldiers, his own bravery and determined leadership enabled the small group to beat off three more vigorous attacks during the night. His personal courage and outstanding qualities of leadership under conditions of extreme danger were an inspiration to his men and prevented his position from being overrun.'

Private Kenias Tovakare BCR

Despite the best efforts of the author, very little about 'the man behind the medal' has been obtained which is both sad and very unfortunate. Despite this, perhaps a consequence of the passage of time, the following is a very brief but important snapshot that has been obtained.

Pte Kenias Tovakare BCR enlisted into the 1st Battalion the Rhodesian African Rifles on 5 June 1962 where he served with distinction, working his way through the ranks becoming the Platoon Sergeant of 6 Platoon, B Company, 1RAR and, later, a WO2 in Support Company. Before his discharge from the Zimbabwe

National Army on 31 July 1989, he had been commissioned and left the army holding the rank of Captain having served in 4.3 Infantry Battalion.

This was the culmination of 27 years' service, the vast majority of it proudly in the colours of his parent Regiment, the 1st Battalion the Rhodesian African Rifles. We, his brethren from the RAR, salute a loyal, gallant and faithful servant of our proud Regiment.

Tinotenda chaizvo shamwari! Fambai Zvakanaka.

Pte Kenias Tovokare BCR

Citation for the award of the Bronze Cross of Rhodesia, 23 October 1970, Private Kenias Tovakare BCR

'For gallantry and devotion to duty in action. As a radio operator in a fierce engagement against terrorists, Pte Tovakare remained with his commander and maintained his duties under extremely hazardous conditions until, because of the danger; his commander took over the radio set from him. Later, when as a result of being severely wounded, his commander was forced to abandon the radio, Pte Tovakare, realizing that communications were essential, retrieved the radio and two weapons at great personal risk. Throughout the engagement Pte Tovakare displayed gallantry and devotion to duty under extremely dangerous conditions.'

Private Phinias Foshore BCR

Citation for the award of the Bronze Cross of Rhodesia, 13 September 1974, Private Phinias Foshore BCR

'For gallantry and determination in action. During anti-terrorist operations in the north eastern border area, the platoon of which Pte Phinias was a member was engaged in a contact with twelve to fourteen terrorists. During the engagement Pte Phinias was shot at point blank range through the upper arm by a terrorist. Realising that he could not handle his weapon, he dropped his rifle and attacked the terrorist with his hands, forcing him to the ground before another shot could be fired. During the struggle, while he was attempting to overcome the terrorist with his bare hands, Pte Phinias was again shot in the back by another terrorist. In spite of his wounds, Pte Phinias continued to grapple with the terrorist, refusing to let go until the terrorist was shot and killed and he was assisted off the body. Pte Phinias, who had only recently completed his recruit training, displayed outstanding determination, courage and aggressive spirit for such a young and inexperienced soldier.'

Pte Phinias Foshore BCR

Sergeant Abedenice Ntulini Mazingane BCR

Citation for the award of the Bronze Cross of Rhodesia, 26 September 1975, Sergeant Abedenice Ntulini Mazingane BCR

'For continuous gallantry and leadership in action with the 1st Battalion, The Rhodesian African Rifles. Sergeant Ntulini has been involved in ten contacts with terrorists over the past two and a half years. In these contacts Sergeant Ntulini showed a great degree of reliability as a leader, particularly under fire. In Sergeant Ntulini his men recognized a man of infinite patience and a sense of purpose. In one contact Sergeant Ntulini was involved with six terrorists. He assisted in killing five of the enemy and was an inspiration to the limited number of troops involved in the contact; he made it his business to be in the thick of the fighting and appeared to lack fear by constantly supporting and encouraging the men around him.

'On another occasion three terrorists were sighted and eight men, commanded by Sergeant Ntulini were despatched to the area. The contact that ensued was a text-book encounter involving excellent use of ground and weapons. The use of grenades was superb and devastating, and the ruthless extermination of the gang was entirely attributable to Sergeant Ntulini's common sense, quick action and bold approach. The senior member of this gang was later identified as a sectorial political commissar who had been in the area for 18months. His death had far-reaching results.

'On a more recent occasion while Sergeant Ntulini was a stick commander, twenty-four well-armed terrorists had laid an ambush on high ground around a re-entrant for the platoon that was following their tracks. As the platoon approached, Ntulini heard talking and immediately informed his platoon commander. Having done this, he moved back to his stick which was on high ground on one side of the re-entrant. The platoon came under very heavy fire. However, thanks to his alertness, Sergeant Ntulini prevented the platoon from being surprised. The firefight continued until the platoon skirmished forward and succeeded in clearing the terrorists from the high ground. The terrorist leader, with two other terrorists, saw the assault group and decided to slip into the re-entrant. This move was spotted by Sergeant Ntulini who moved his men to a favourable position and they then killed all three terrorists. One, if not two, of the terrorists was shot by Sergeant Ntulini himself.

'It was undoubtedly due to the courage, initiative, professional skill and good leadership of Sergeant Ntulini that what could have been a disastrous situation was turned into a successful contact, resulting in three enemy killed, one of whom was a terrorist leader. Successes in these and other engagements were entirely attributable to the outstanding powers of leadership, enthusiasm and determined aggression in action by Sergeant Ntulini which have been a constant inspiration to all.'

WO2 Moses Pongweni BCR

The following concerns a quite brilliant warrant officer whose leadership was (rightly) recognised and he became one of our Regiment's first African warrant officers to receive a commission. I clearly remember this man's name in my final year of high school, such was the grand reputation that preceded him. I, like many, am very proud to have met this fine man and, after I was commissioned, to have served alongside him. A rare privilege an insight in to what being a great infantry officer was all about. This man, like so many of his ilk, made an enormous and lasting impression on me.

Citation for the award of the Bronze Cross of Rhodesia, 15 October 1976, WO2 Moses Pongweni BCR

'Warrant Officer Pongweni has, for the past 18 months, been engaged in continuous anti-terrorist operations, both as a platoon warrant officer and, in recent months, as a platoon commander.

'During this period his platoon has been involved in numerous contacts with terrorists in which several of the enemy have been killed and captured. In all these engagements Warrant Officer Pongweni displayed outstanding aggression and leadership. On one occasion Warrant Officer Pongweni and his platoon were flown into stop positions ahead of a follow-up group. When it became apparent that the terrorists had slipped through the net, Warrant Officer Pongweni and his stick were flown into a contact while the battle was in progress. Under fire from the time they de-planed, Warrant Officer Pongweni demonstrated his leadership and calmness by deploying his men into an excellent cut-off position, thus sealing the fate of the terrorist group. In this contact all seven members of the terrorist group were eliminated, and this success was due in no small measure to Warrant Officer Pongweni's courage and determination.

'On another occasion, Warrant Officer Pongweni and his patrol of six men were operating in a remote area of the Honde Valley. Shortly before last light the patrol was ambushed by 15 to 20 terrorists in well-prepared positions. In the first few seconds of the contact one member of the patrol was killed and another injured. Warrant Officer Pongweni himself was in a totally exposed position but with complete disregard for his own safety and under heavy fire at close range, he immediately engaged the terrorists. Such was his example that he was joined

Lt Moses Pongweni BCR

by his machine gunner and together they put the terrorists to flight. Rallying the survivors, Warrant Officer Pongweni gave chase to the terrorists before returning to tend to his dead and wounded. In this engagement there can be no doubt that Warrant Officer Pongweni's personal courage in the face of heavy fire was instrumental in saving the lives of his patrol in a critical situation.

'More recently, Warrant Officer Pongweni and his platoon were returning to base by vehicle when they were ambushed by between 15 and 20 terrorists firing from across a broad and deep river. Warrant Officer Pongweni's presence of mind and rapid orders to his driver enabled the leading vehicle to clear the killing area without loss. Realizing that he was unable to cross the river to assault the terrorist position, Warrant Officer Pongweni skilfully deployed his troops under fire to an excellent position overlooking the area of thick bush in which the terrorists were hiding. Within seconds he had two machine guns in action and very quickly regained the initiative. Such was the effectiveness of the fire that some of the terrorists broke and fled while the remainder, although unseen in the dense bush, were pinned down and remained so until the arrival of Fire force.

'Throughout the engagement which lasted for two hours, Warrant Officer Pongweni was in complete control of the situation and his personal leadership and example were an inspiration to all. Warrant Officer Pongweni's initiative as a platoon commander and his courage and leadership in battle has earned him the respect and admiration of his men. His constant good humour in adversity and his unswerving allegiance have been an inspiration to all who have served with him.'

WO2 Yangama Kupara BCR

I pay tribute to another member of our proud regiment, a Warrant Officer Class 2 and the Company Sergeant Major of A Company, 1RAR who was short on talking but high in aggression; the epitome of an RAR soldier. WO2 Kupara Yangama BCR was the CSM of A Company when I joined as OC 3 Platoon; I remember our meeting with crystal clear clarity.

Our Company 2ic introduced me to the man in the A Company G10 store, the CSM's domain, and it accurately reflected the persona of a man who took great pride in his work. To state that you could eat off the floor would be to understate the fact; nothing was out of place. He stood up, drove his right boot into the concrete mirror-like floor with a deafening bang and gave me one of the most immaculate salutes I ever received. I returned the compliment and he accepted my outstretched hand before inviting me over to where our rifles were racked against the far wall. He removed an FN from the rack, went through the motions of making it safe before handing it to me. It was brand new and still covered in a light coating of its original packing grease. He looked me square in my eyes and said, "This one is special Ishe, it will serve you well". I signed for it together with all the other platoon commander controlled-stores that would remain with me for the duration of my operational service.

WO2 Yangama Kupara BCR

Two weeks later, whilst on deployment in the Op Hurricane area, CSM Kupara approached the OC and requested permission to go on deployment with 'Sunray 13', yours truly. As a young subaltern I confess to having been a little nervous having this no-nonsense CSM shadowing me and sizing me up. "It was what it was" and I accepted it as simply that; time would tell that this would be a period of rapid learning for me; a baptism by fire if you will. CSM Kupara was a "gook magnet", and it wasn't long before we were engaged in the first of several contacts together. I had suggested that he become a member of my stick and that way I could watch him and vice versa; it was an unlikely association but one that would foment a rock-solid relationship with this quietly spoken man. During our ten-day deployment we had several contacts and accounted for seven kills and two captures. One of these included a duplication of CSM Kupara's earlier antics and for which he was cited in his BCR citation. Whilst following-up on tracks after an encounter action with a group of ZANLA, CSM Kupara fired a rifle grenade at a fleeing 'CT' hitting him between the shoulder blades. I asked him why he had fired a 42Z and he simply winked without smiling and said, "For a big 'torroro' I use a big stick Ishe". It was his way.

At the conclusion of the deployment and following debrief with our OC, CSM Kupara marched to my tent and I invited him in. He towered above me and said in a respectful, measured tone: "I am here to tell you that you have won favour with the *Masodja* of 'Simanjemanje' Ishe. They will follow you anywhere. Makorokoto Sir". With that, he saluted, about turned and that was it. It was a proud day for me for I had 'come of age' in the eyes of one of the finest operators our army had.

Citation for the award of the Bronze Cross of Rhodesia, 19 October 1976, WO2 Yangama Kupara BCR

'Warrant Officer Kupara has been continually involved in counter-insurgency operations since 1967, a total of nine years. During this time, he has progressed from section commander to company sergeant-major and has shown outstanding qualities of leadership and competence. Due to the shortage of junior officers, Warrant Officer Kupara frequently commanded platoons on operations for long periods with exceptional ability. In October 1974, he commanded 2 Platoon of A Company 1RAR when they had two very successful contacts, resulting in the death of three terrorist leaders among eight eliminations. On 7 January 1975, Warrant Officer Kupara was leading a patrol which had a fleeting contact with a number of terrorists. He carried out immediate and aggressive action and killed one terrorist personally by a direct hit with a rifle grenade.

'Since January 1976, A Company has taken part in Fireforce operations at regular intervals and have had notable successes. Several kills and captures were attributable to the courage, calmness, tactical skill and excellent bush craft of Warrant Officer Kupara. During a contact on 3 April 1976, Warrant Officer Kupara and his stick were pinned down by accurate fire by a terrorist using an RPD machine- gun. Warrant Officer Kupara threw a white phosphorus grenade and under its cover, moved around behind the RPD gunner and shot him through the head, killing him. Three other terrorists were also killed in this contact.

'On the night of 6 May 1976, Warrant Officer Kupara was commanding the lead vehicle of two vehicles carrying 2 Platoon and Company Tactical Headquarters of A Company when the rear vehicle was ambushed by eight to ten terrorists using RPG, RPD and small arms. The vehicle was immobilized, and one section commander was killed on the vehicle. Warrant Officer Kupara immediately stopped his vehicle, which was out of the killing zone, and directed rifle-grenade fire on to the terrorist position followed by an immediate clearance of the position. Warrant Officer Kupara showed a calm professional approach and handled his men in an excellent manner throughout.

'His determination and confidence had an excellent effect, especially upon some of the younger soldiers, recently out of recruit training, who must have been somewhat shaken by the ambush and death of the section commander during darkness. Warrant Officer Kupara has a quiet personality but is an experienced and well-respected soldier. His tactical ability and calmness in action are first class at all times. He has displayed continuous bravery and competence on counter-insurgency operations over a long period.'

Second Lieutenant Desmond C. Passaportis BCR

A Salisbury member of the large Passaportis clan who volunteered to attend the Regular Officer cadet course INF/25(17) at the School of infantry in Gwelo. "Passi", as he was known to fellow students, worked hard during the course at all aspects and was especially well known to instructors as the man who could polish his boots - most definitely the best 'boned' boots on parade. Passi was commissioned into A Company, 1RAR where he served with distinction as a platoon commander. A widely respected and liked subaltern who participated actively in Subbies Week and other subaltern activities when on R&R.

Passi was a good leader and soldier on the ground. He was on the ground as part of a fire force action when his company commander, Major Mike Ainslie, was killed in the K-Car. Passi served as Stop 1 almost continuously for over 8 months in the 1RAR fire force based in Mtoko for which his actions under fire were noted and he was awarded a deserved BCR.

Tragically, Passi succumbed to a life-threatening illness several years ago but his mischievous personality and joie de vivre remain a fitting and constant memory of the fine officer and friend he was to many.

Citation for the award of the Bronze Cross of Rhodesia, 29 October 1976, Second Lieutenant Desmond C. Passaportis BCR

'Second Lieutenant Passaportis is a platoon commander in A Company 1RAR. During the period 1 February to 18 May 1976, he deployed on operations with his company. A considerable time was spent on Fireforce duties in which 2nd Lt Passaportis acted as ground force commander on numerous occasions. In all, 2nd Lt Passaportis took part in eight contacts, the majority of which were highly successful, resulting in the elimination of numerous terrorists.

'On 13 May, 2nd Lt Passaportis was dropped with his stick in an area where approximately ten terrorists had been contacted. His stick soon came under very accurate and well-controlled fire from a thickly wooded area near a terrorist camp, which effectively pinned him down. During an attempt to take the terrorist position he was superficially wounded in the hand and his combat cap was shot off. Despite the fact that two further contacts were taking place nearby, he directed supporting fire to within ten metres of his own position and moved to a more favourable position to attempt a third assault.

During this manoeuvre he came under further accurate fire and one of his soldiers was mortally wounded in the chest *[646372 Pte Mukoni, Dzingirayi, 3Pl, A Coy, 1RAR: KIA aged 21 years].* 2nd Lt Passaportis crawled forward under fire into the open and dragged the wounded soldier to cover, where he rendered first aid. Throughout the contact which lasted about five hours, repeated air strikes took place and all the aircraft and ground troops were under accurate fire. During this time, 2nd Lt Passaportis gave calm and accurate target indication orders. These were of great assistance to his company commander as Fireforce commander. His calmness and aggression were an inspiration to the troops under his command.

Lt Desmond Passaportis BCR

'On 18 May, the Fireforce was again deployed to a contact during which a terrorist was flushed from cover and wounded. Appreciating the importance of information, the Fireforce commander dropped 2nd Lt Passaportis' stick close by to affect a capture, as the terrorist had dropped his weapon some distance away. When 2nd Lt Passaportis ordered the wounded terrorist to stand up, the terrorist threw a grenade which he had concealed 2Lt Passaportis and another soldier both received serious injuries and the terrorist was killed by the remainder of the stick. Despite the fact that he had sixty-two shrapnel wounds from the grenade, 2nd Lt Passaportis was back in the operational area in less than five weeks after he had been wounded. During all his contacts, 2nd Lt Passaportis has remained cool, calm, cheerful and most efficient. In addition to his obvious bravery, he has shown a keen and subtle sense of humour which has contributed greatly to a high state of morale in his sub-unit. The soldiers under his command have complete confidence in his abilities and he never expects them to do anything which he is not prepared to do himself.'

A/Corporal James Makuwa BCR (Post)

This is a tragic story about a brave 26-year-old Acting Corporal who served in 1 Platoon, A 'Simba' Company, 1RAR, a gallant man who lost his life serving his Regiment and our Country. Lest we forget.

Citation for the award of the Bronze Cross of Rhodesia, 25 March 1977, A/Corporal James Makuwa BCR (Post)

'Corporal Makuwa was part of fire force that responded to a call on 30 April 1976 that an army sub-unit was in contact with about 20 terrorists, three of whom had been killed. During observation duties, Acting Corporal Makuwa, in charge of one position, sighted thirteen terrorists attempting to escape from the contact area. The position of these terrorists was indicated to the pilot and the gunner of the aircraft by Acting Corporal Makuwa, and a second contact ensued, with a firefight developing between the aircraft and the terrorists.

'Corporal Makuwa's stick was then deployed to take part in the contact and accounted for two terrorists killed. In the ensuing action a further four terrorists were killed. His stick was then instructed to regroup and while moving towards the rendezvous they came under heavy fire from two terrorists. Fire was immediately returned, and the terrorists were wounded and surrendered.

'The success achieved in this action can be attributed to a large degree to Corporal Makuwa's initiative, personal courage and qualities of leadership. It was as a result of this and many previous successful actions that Corporal Makuwa had been recommended for promotion to sergeant but, regrettably, this fine non-commissioned officer died as a result of wounds received after a follow-up on 9 May 1976.'

The RNR-RAR Roll of Honour held in our files confirms the following: 644956 ACpl Makuwa, James BCR: 'Killed in an ambush on his vehicle, when a 60mm mortar exploded next to him, resulting in massive haemorrhaging, Uzumba TTL, Op Hurricane. Died aged 26. Source: Death Notice. His B.C.R. citation states that his success in a fire force action in April 1976 was attributed to his initiative, personal courage and leadership qualities. Prior to his death he had been put forward for promotion to Acting Sergeant, a position he would have assumed on 01 June. After completing his training in 1971, James joined A Company, where this keen athlete proved to be a cheerful and popular member.'

Source: *Masodja* and *Nhowo*.

WO2 Abias Mashona BCR

I have drawn on information recorded in *Chibaya Moyo 1* and an anecdote that I penned for the chapter *'My First Encounter with the RAR'*. This is not about the author of this tribute but a personal and very deeply moving experience that brought me face-to-face with an extraordinary man. Once you have read this, I have doubts that anyone will not be as moved by the events that unfolded as I was some 41 years ago.

My second memorable encounter with the RAR was an altogether different matter. By now (mid-1977) I had grown-up a little and was serving in Anti-Tank Troop, Support Commando, 1RLI as a machine gunner.

WO2 Abias Mashona BCR

On one particular bush trip our Commando was deployed on fire force operations in the Op Repulse area and we were based at the Buffalo Range Aerodrome (almost equidistant between Triangle and Chiredzi).

I had been on para course almost immediately after completing my recruit training course and was, and almost without exception after the fact, deployed on fire force sorties in a para-trooping role. I cannot tell a lie for, to me anyway, it was the farthest thing from what one could reasonably call 'fun'. I envied my 'Chinas' who would climb in to the Alouettes whenever the siren for call-out screamed at the FAF's we were based at. They, all comfortable in their personalised webbing, and us para types contorted in to facsimiles of human bananas with our parachute harnesses tensioned to the point of asphyxiation! It was simply as required and in your own time ...carry on!!

One particularly hot and windy morning the siren screamed, and we instinctively sprinted with our weapons and webbing in hand towards the helicopter revetments and the lone Douglas Dakota DC3 parked on the hard-standing adjacent to the helicopter revetments and waited impatiently to receive briefings from our respective Stick Commanders about what was 'brewing'.

We were called to a confirmed sighting of approximately 20 CTs south east of the small mining town of Shabani and some +-35 minutes flying time. When the fire force were about 7 minutes out from the target area our Dak was placed in an anti-clockwise orbit awaiting further information from the security force OP (Observation Post) on the ground. After what seemed an eternity, the nerves and pent-up adrenalin started to get the better of a few of the ouens and those all too common bouts of cotching (vomiting) commenced with a vengeance. First one and then another and a tother! Ably assisted by the prop-wash flooding the aircraft hold from the door-less aircraft that rank, sour smell took everyone by surprise and this set-off an almost chain reaction of similarly vile behaviour.

We received the command from the Number 1 Dispatcher to Stand-Up, hook-up and tell-off for equipment check. We did the Action Stations bit and soon enough it was (almost) a relief to be out of the door despite loathing the activity with an almost pathological dislike. Below and around us our heli-borne troops were being dropped in well selected Stop Group positions to cut-off any attempt at escape from the target area that we paras were soon to sweep though. Little did I know, until much later that day, the fire force had been called out by a lone member from 1RAR. The engagements were fierce and continuous as we repeatedly came up against an aggressive and determined foe but, and as was often the case, we won the day accounting for 14 confirmed kills.

At this time we were still required to recover the bodies for finger printing, I.D. and so forth by our Special Branch folks (rather them than me). Once this grisly task was done I washed my hands with the remaining dregs from one of my two water bottles as I wondered quietly to myself how and why it was that the stench of 'fresh death' seemed to permeate in to one's skin? I was fatigued and starting to feel a burning sensation in my right leg; I looked down and noticed a gouge of missing flesh mid-way up my right thigh; it looked like a woodworker's gouge had been pushed through the flesh as if carving some crude form from a stubborn piece of wood. The results of landing in high wind and the bipod leg of my machine gun driving in to my uncovered flesh. It was superficial enough but a quite sobering thought as I considered those hapless gooks whose bodies were now suspended in cargo nets below two G-Cars and being carted off to the JOC in Ft Vic. I cast it from my mind without a second thought.

Whilst awaiting uplift the afternoon sun was relentless and I sought the refuge and the comfort of some shade. I found it nearby together with an African soldier sitting alone and in the shade of a small sapling. It was on an unobtrusive elevated fold in the ground and no more than fifteen feet high. As I walked over to the soldier I noticed that the combat cap that he was wearing bore the distinctive RAR woven label; I greeted him in the chiShona vernacular "Masikati Ishe" (Good afternoon Sir) as this was one of only a few basic chiShona greetings that formed the extent of my pretty pathetic vocabulary. The soldier looked up at me and returned the salutation before extending his right hand to me in formal greeting. I took the man's hand in my own and shook it firmly, respectfully but fondly before taking a seat close to him. It was at this point that I noticed on the right sleeve of his faded combat jacket, that the man wore the embroidered badge of rank of a Platoon Warrant Officer, a rank unique to the RAR (between a Colour Sergeant and a Warrant Officer Class 2).

I asked where the rest of his call-sign was, and he smiled at me and said, "I am alone in this place". I introduced myself and so too did the PWO, he was Abias Mashona BCR of Support Company, 1RAR. I told him that I hailed from Bulawayo and had an older brother who was an officer in the Battalion. His mood changed visibly on hearing that I had a connection to the RAR and I was no longer, simply, an inquisitive RLI troopie come to make a nuisance of himself. I asked how it was that he came to be alone in this place and he told me, with a tear welling in one of his eyes, that his whole family had been murdered by terrorists simply because he was a RAR sodja.

He could not win the war alone, but he was determined, and as many men in the same predicament would have been, with wanting to ensure that those responsible for murdering his family would pay for their heinous and cowardly crime and that he would, God willing, be an instrument in their demise. Small closure but this demonstrated, unreservedly, that love one has for one's family and the deep strength of character, courage, sense of duty and that deep resolve that few will exercise to exact deserved justice.

For the benefit of those unfamiliar with the term 'Framework Operations', this refers to typical RAR infantry operational pursuits including, but not limited to, Observation Posts, ambushes and patrols that fell under this broad nomenclature. OP's were routinely sighted on high ground overlooking (or within reasonably close proximity) to the target area but, and as a measure of WO2 Mashona's undisputed professionalism and soldiering skills, he had taken up his OP on what was no more than a fold in the ground. It had a few boulders, bushes and a lone sapling and it was as unobtrusive a piece of ground that you could find. So, lacking in what one would consider a classic OP position, he had cunningly and stealthily escaped compromise for two weeks! It was as close to perfection in soldiering skills and field craft excellence as one could ever hope to find.

Mashona had watched the movement of the group of CTs for several days from a distance of no more than 50 meters; he had been urinated upon by a Mujiba aged herd boy (adolescent aged CT sympathiser/collaborator) standing inches from where he lay concealed and, when he was satisfied that he knew all he could regarding their strength, disposition, weapons and daily routine he radioed the JOC at Ft Vic who, in turn, scrambled the Fire Force at Buffalo Range.

This extraordinary act of selfless gallantry was to prove the catalyst in my ultimate decision to join the RAR. That passionate desire to soldier alongside men of WO2 Mashona's ilk and to draw upon their undoubted skills was something that now burned deeply within me like a smouldering Mopani tree following a lightning strike. I completed the next arduous 13-month regular cadet course (the last one of that duration) and I got my wish, a posting to 1RAR on my commissioning. As the well coined cliché goes, the rest is history, or is it?

My anecdote is validated by the comments included in the body of WO2 Mashona's BCR citation.
Citation for the award of the Bronze Cross of Rhodesia, 13 October, Warrant Officer 2nd Class Abias Mashona BCR

'Warrant Officer 2nd Class Mashona has been continually involved in counter-insurgency operations since 1967. During this time, he has progressed from private to warrant officer class II and has shown outstanding qualities of leadership, courage and professionalism. As a junior soldier he was involved in numerous engagements during which his aggression and courage contributed greatly to the elimination of the enemy.

'Such were his qualities that he was periodically drafted to Special Forces for specific operations. Warrant Officer 2nd Class Mashona has studied the enemy in detail. Utilising this knowledge, he has shown an exceptional ability to locate enemy groups and on one occasion, armed with only a pistol, and with complete disregard for his own safety, Warrant Officer 2nd Class Mashona entered an area known to be occupied by terrorists. Exercising guile and cunning, he located the enemy group and then guided ground - and air-borne forces on to their positions. Fourteen of the enemy was killed and two were captured, together with important documents and quantities of weapons and equipment.

'On two other occasions similar successes were recorded as a result of his perseverance to remain undetected in hostile areas for protracted periods. On all the above occasions, Warrant Officer 2nd Class Mashona received high praise from ground and airborne commanders for his accuracy and the simple and clear-cut manner in which he directed them onto the enemy. As a member of the Fireforce, Warrant Officer 2nd Class Mashona has proved to be courageous and aggressive and has recorded a number of personal kills.

'On two occasions while at home in the Tribal Trust Lands, Warrant Officer 2nd Class Mashona has been sought by the enemy. On one of these occasions, seven terrorists surrounded his house and called for him to surrender. With determined and intelligent actions, he managed to escape. He then gave up his leave, returned to the area in a clandestine manner and was able to locate this enemy group and call in forces to a successful contact. Warrant Officer 2nd Class Mashona has earned the unqualified respect of the officers and men of his unit. His unswerving allegiance, dedication, professional ability and bravery are a constant high example and inspiration to all.'

Private Ernest Rashamire BCR

Pte Ernest Rashamire BCR

The following tribute was written by Brig Pat Lawless SCR who commanded Pte Rashamire in 1977:

'LCpl Rashamire arrived in the 60mm Mortar Platoon of Support Company 1RAR at the same time as I did in early 1977. My 'Platoon Bible' attests to the fact he had done well in Recruit Training – not the top recruit, but pretty close. He was close friends (same village) with another soldier in 2RAR whose name I cannot recall but this soldier had lost family in his village to the gooks, and Ernest Rashamire had been motivated to serve in the Army because of it. He spent about 3 months in my Platoon before returning to Methuen Barracks to train on Mortars– again, my notes reflect a solid 'pass'. On his return to the Platoon he undertook parachute training in Salisbury where his latent leadership skills – and dodgy moustache! - began to manifest themselves, as did his infectious humour.

As with the rest of us, he spent a considerable time on Fire Force as a paratrooper, frequently in my Stick. He was an excellent MAG gunner, although not yet promoted to Lance Corporal. He was married, with one young child born in 1978.

'The citation describes well why he was awarded his BCR. It interests me today to reflect that Rashamire was inevitably 'first choice' for those Officers / Warrant Officers / NCOs looking for an aggressive, highly competent and utterly reliable man in their stick or patrol – he saw a lot of action in a short time and – so far as I am aware – survived in the RAR long after my departure. I hope he is alive today.'

Background:

On 11 August 1978, eight members of Support Company 1RAR, commanded by Lieutenant Pat Lawless, were on an external recce/ambush patrol in the Devil's Gorge area of Zambia. They had been tasked with locating an insurgent infiltration route into Rhodesia. This was in conjunction with an SAS regrouping destined for Mozambique. As dusk fell, the soldiers had a last light contact with three insurgents in which two of the enemy were killed and the third member of the group, fatally wounded, was captured. Lawless rendered what first aid he could, while at the same time interrogating the man.

Before he died, the wounded man identified himself as the logistics officer of an insurgent company of about 100 men consisting of three platoons from Zambia. He and his comrades had been on a recce when they clashed with Lawless' patrol. Lawless laid an ambush for the night— he had two MAGs. He also set up a Claymore mine along the track, but nothing happened. However, at first light, as they began to dismantle the Claymore, preparatory to moving on, they saw some 70 insurgents approaching along the track. Every soldier immediately squirmed back into his position and waited for Lawless to spring the ambush.

As soon as the enemy was in the killing ground, the order was given. Eight insurgents were killed and 15 wounded in this initial attack. A further 20 men, initially unseen, tried to outflank the patrol by sneaking down the hillock behind their position. However, Corporal Ernest Rashamire noted the move and, leaping up, charged them, firing bursts from his MAG, killing three. Fire was returned, and so close was it that Rashamire's webbing was shot through. Undeterred, he continued to fire, ultimately hurling a grenade, which put his adversaries to flight. The main enemy group, meanwhile, continued to engage the small patrol, and was driven back several times. Finally, with ammunition running low and taking stock of their position (they were on a slope), the greatly-outnumbered Lawless was forced to conduct a tactical withdrawal. For this and for many earlier and subsequent actions, Lieutenant Lawless was awarded the Silver Cross of Rhodesia on 5 January 1980. For his part in this action, Lance-Corporal Rashamire was awarded the Bronze Cross.

Citation for the Award of the Bronze Cross of Rhodesia, 9 February 1979, Private Ernest Rashamire, Support Company, 1RAR

'Private Rashamire has served with Support Company, 1st Battalion, the Rhodesian African Rifles, since January 1977 during which time he has been involved in numerous contacts with communist terrorists. In all of these actions he has displayed an outstanding determination to eliminate the enemy.

'On one occasion he was a member of an eight-man section which made contact with a group of approximately seventy (70) terrorists. Several terrorists were killed in the initial firefight, but in an unusual display of tenacity, probably related to their greatly superior numerical strength, the terrorists kept up the attack. Under covering fire from their companions, a group of about 20 terrorists attempted to outflank the small army patrol from an area of high and dominating ground.

'The only member of the Security Force patrol to observe this group's movement was Private Rashamire. Realising the tactical advantage that the terrorists would achieve if they gained the dominating ground, Private Rashamire left his covered position and with complete disregard for his own safety, charged at the group, firing his weapon as he ran. He killed two terrorists outright and successfully changed any persistent intentions on the part of the remainder by throwing a hand grenade into their midst.'Private Rashamire's daring act caused the terrorists to flee, thus denying them the use of tactically important ground from which they would almost certainly have inflicted casualties upon the Security Force patrol. His gallantry and clear thinking under the extremely perilous conditions prevailing at the time were an inspiration to those about him and serve as an example to all.'

Lieutenant Graham Schrag BCR

After growing up in Umtali, and for a very short while in Rustenburg RSA, Graham served in C Sqn SAS, RhSigs, 2RAR (for the majority of his service), SInf and HQ 1Bde. After Rhodesia/ Zimbabwe, Graham was an advisor/consultant/entrepreneur in various places around the world including the Sultanate of Oman (several times and in different capacities), Yemen, Egypt, Sri Lanka, Pakistan, Southern Ireland, Switzerland, Canada, France and the UK. Somewhere along the line he also had homes in Thailand, Andorra and Cyprus.

Capt Graham Schrag BCR

I served with 'Shaggis' at SInf/ZMA in late 1980 and got to know him quite well. He was a 'still water' character who seemed to prefer his own company, but his quiet reserve belied a latent aggression, an inherent characteristic found in most (if not all) of our gallantry award recipients and a consistent trait of SAS operators. Sadly, Graham passed away after a long and brave fight with cancer in Zurich, Switzerland on 12 October 2012.

Here is a little bit about the man during his service as a platoon commander under Maj Andre Dennison MLM, BCR (RIP):

'A Company 2RAR, in the form of Graham Schrag's 2 Platoon, was still in the Gona re Zhou area on 8 April when the platoon's call sign 12A under Sergeant Marufu Muchemwa was ordered to ambush a kraal. This was in response to a report from police ground coverage intelligence to the effect that the village would be visited by insurgents that night. Unfortunately, the kraal head sent a warning to the enemy that security forces were in the area. The insurgents then decided to set an ambush for the incoming troops. At 1830 hours in the gathering darkness, Muchemwa's section was moving along a mealie field to lay its ambush when the men heard a noise from a source about ten metres inside the field. Believing this to be caused by cattle, Muchemwa went to investigate. As he moved forward, he was fired at from close range and wounded in the arm. He fell back. The section returned fire and a brisk exchange ensued which lasted for about five minutes.

'Firing ceased when the seven insurgents fled, but the troops, unaware of this and being unable to attack in the exceptional darkness, adopted all-round defence positions and waited. At first light the enemy tracks were followed for about five kilometres until they were washed out by rain. Unknown to the soldiers at this time was the fact that two of the insurgents had been wounded in the firefight. The enemy group had headed back to its base on the Lundi River near its confluence with the Sabi. Morale was low and being short of food, the men were in a poor state physically. One of the wounded was the group commander who was also the provincial political commissar. To aggravate matters, the insurgents were unable to escape into Mozambique by fording the Sabi because the river was in spate having been swollen by the recent rains.

'On 13 April, two call signs from 1 and 2 Platoons led by PWO Benjamin Makurira and Graham Schrag respectively, acting on information from a 'tame terr' (a turned insurgent) began a long 35-kilometre follow-up to what appeared to be an enemy camp. Moving through it, an AS on the right flank saw movement 200 metres north of the camp. Though tired, both call signs gave chase and the contact began when they were 25 metres from the enemy position. In this firefight the previously wounded enemy commander was killed, two insurgents were captured, and five others appeared to have escaped. Fireforce, consisting of Jean Vos's 1 Platoon, was deployed from Mutandhawe with Dennison in the K-car ahead of the G-cars. Near the river, three insurgents were seen running west. The gunner engaged them, killing one and driving the other two into the riverbed. 1 Platoon was dropped past the streambed to do the sweep while 2 Platoon was placed in a stop line to the west of the stream. Sweeping along, 1 Platoon contacted and killed the two surviving insurgents. This successful follow-up and contact had been made possible by the determined leadership of Schrag and Makurira.'

Citation for the award of the Bronze Cross of Rhodesia, 29 July 1977, Lieutenant Graham John Schrag BCR, 1 Platoon, A Company 'Gangeniukange', 2RAR.

'On 31 October 1976, a platoon led by Lt Schrag was involved in a two-phase, set-piece attack on two enemy camps, each of which included a large group of terrorists. Despite coming under heavy fire from the first camp, Lt Schrag led the assault with great determination, forcing the enemy to break and run. Having secured the first camp, the platoon swept through the second camp, coming under close-range fire from two terrorists who had hidden in a riverbed beyond the camp. The platoon went to ground, but Lt Schrag charged into the riverbed alone and killed both terrorists at a range of less than ten metres. He then led his platoon in a sweep of very thick cover where a further four terrorists were killed. Enemy small arms and mortar fire was intense throughout the engagement.'

WO2 Rashayi Vanhuvaone BCR

CSM Vanhuvaone, nicknamed 'Van', was indeed an exceptional soldier. He was a big, fit man who looked like Muhammed Ali and had the same vitality and charisma. When Bruce Thompson was posted to A Coy on commissioning, Major Andre Dennison swopped two PWOs between their platoons to put Van with Bruce. It was clever man-management because, together, they were formidable. He deeply grieved Bruce's death and spoke to me about the loss of our friend. Van became a CSM when he was promoted and posted to Sp Coy where he had a huge impact on the morale and fighting spirit of the men.

CSM Vanhuvaone Rashayi BCR

Citation for the award of the Bronze Cross of Rhodesia, 7 October 1977, WO2 Rashayi Vanhuvaone BCR

'In March 1976, after a long follow-up, his platoon came under fire from a group of terrorists.

In the opening burst, WO2 Rashayi was hit in the leg. Despite his wound, he returned fire, drove a terrorist from cover and killed him as he turned to run. His stick then killed a second terrorist before the rest of the terrorists fled. All the terrorists were killed. In October 1976, WO2 Rashayi killed a terrorist with a hand grenade. In February 1977, WO2 Rashayi's stick wounded and captured a terrorist from whom valuable intelligence was collected.

'In February 1977, he initiated a contact near a kraal by shooting the enemy section leader through the leg and killing the terrorist next to him. At no time did he allow himself to be deterred and his courageous example and determination to kill the enemy were, at all times, an inspiration to his soldiers.'

Comment: Van's citation does not do justice to the exceptional gallantry of this man.

Major André Dennison MLM BCR (MFC [Ops])

Major Dennison was one of our regiment's most highly decorated members, decorated on three separate occasions. The following was written for 'Chibaya Moyo' by one his subalterns, Lt Christopher Vincent BCR.

Major André Dennison, nicknamed 'K-Car' by his soldiers, was born in Yorkshire on 24 July 1935, and joined the British Army on 24 June 1953. He was commissioned from Sandhurst into the York and Lancaster Regiment in February 1955, and the following year took part in the Suez Crisis. Between 1958 and 1959 he was attached to 2 Para in Cyprus and Jordan. Returning to 1 Y & L in Germany, he was promoted Captain in 1961, and the next year was seconded to 22 SAS on active service with Far East Land Forces in Borneo, his achievements there including penetration of the dense and hitherto unmapped Jungle of the Gap with the legendary Sergeant Eddie Lillico.

In 1965, promoted to Major, he was seconded to the 3rd Battalion, Malaysian Rangers on active service first on the Malaysian border with Thailand and afterwards in Sabah and Sarawak. From 1969 to 1971 he was seconded to the Malawi Rifles and, between 1972 and his resignation from the British Army in

1975, Dennison served as a regular training Major with the 6th Battalion, Ulster Defence Regiment during which time, apparently, he was involved in operations in Northern Ireland very unrelated to training. Dennison joined the newly-raised 2nd Battalion, Rhodesian African Rifles on 1 October 1975, as the commander of A Company. The war against guerrilla incursions by the communist-backed Zimbabwe African National Liberation Army (ZANLA) and the Zimbabwe People's Revolutionary Army (ZIPRA), operating from bases in Mozambique, Zambia, and Botswana, was by then fully underway It was as a Fire Force commander between September 1976 and June 1979 that Dennison was to excel.

Maj Andre Dennison MLM, BCR

The potency of Dennison's Fire Force, which initially consisted of a command helicopter, the K-Car, and three others, G-Cars, carrying sticks of four men each, supported by a fixed wing ground attack aircraft carrying napalm or the dreaded "Golf bomb", was increased after March 1977 with the addition of a Dakota, or "Paradak", carrying sixteen African paratroopers. Many of the Dakotas dated from the Second World War.

Dennison kept a war diary, later published by Professor JRT Wood (Ashanti, 1989). It contains full accounts of the combat actions of A Company, all written in his characteristic style. For example: "Elements of 2 Platoon were dozing happily at the Zona Border Post when they came under heavy fire from about a company's worth of FPLM [Army of Mozambique] some 500 metres over the border. The Fire Force helicopters assisting in the deployment of the stops took Major Dennison to the scene of the shoot-out and the K-Car took out two huts from which RPD [light machine gun] fire was issuing. Just as OC A Company [Dennison] was being dropped at the post, FPLM fired an unidentified missile at the helicopters who promptly lost interest ... salvoes of badly directed 82mm mortar bombs were coming our way and we engaged and probably hit two people who we subsequently decided were probably medics checking the burning huts for survivors. After an hour or so both sides lost interest and went home leaving 2 Platoon in possession of the 'Field of Honour'."

In an A Company deployment of August 1977, Dennison's capture of the terrorist holed-up in a cave resulted in his award of an MLM. A Police Anti-Terrorist Unit patrol reported the presence of mixed group of thirty CTs and civilians near St Killian's Mission. Dennison's Fire Force was deployed and after a series of contacts, four terrorists were killed. One of Dennison's subalterns was shot through the shoulder by a CT who then hid in a hillside cave. That evening the brigade commander asked Dennison to capture the terrorist alive if possible and the next day he returned accompanied by policemen and dogs. The War Diary records:

"One of the dogs which was running loose promptly rushed to the cave-mouth and began sniffing round the body of a half-roasted CT which lay there. As no reaction came ... a search of the area revealed the entrance to another cave some fifteen yards up the hillside. One of the police dogs was sent in and immediately indicated some kind of presence. The handler, Inspector Tudor-Jones, considered that whatever it was it was not alive, so Major Dennison snivelled into the cave (armed with his Smith Wesson.44 Magnum) followed unbidden by Inspector Wilkins from Rusape and the dog handler.

"As the handler reached the entrance he was shot from within through the hand, thigh and arm. Major Dennison decided against killing whoever fired in favour of gassing him out and bent his mind to extracting himself and

Inspector Wilkins with the wholest of possible skins. Some thirty metres across the cave more daylight was visible so the intrepid OC snaked across the floor and shot through yet another opening like a flushing pheasant... Insp. Wilkins was shot at as he exited, but this time the CT missed. A protracted scene with tear-gas followed and eventually a bedraggled but virtually unmarked CT emerged, complete with girlfriend."

Dennison had several narrow escapes during the course of his hundred or so contacts with the enemy. In May 1978 his Rhino armoured personnel carrier was ambushed by sixteen CTs who "attempted to do what numerous Egyptians, Cypriots, Irishmen Indonesians and Angry Husbands had failed to do - i.e. scribble OC A." Two months later his pack was shot through during a firefight. A period of sharp fighting followed.

The company was ordered to Buffalo Range to cover a "road-runner scene". A road-runner was a portable transistor radio which was left lying about in a suitable spot for the terrorists to find. Inside was a homing device which could be picked up by a helicopter's homing equipment. On the 19th, after getting a weak road-runner fix, the Fire Force deployed: "One of the G-Cars saw the CTs, and a series of air-strikes was put in as the gooks lobbed RPG7's at the choppers." "The Golf bomb malfunctioned and went off on the ground directly under the Lynx. The Lynx killed a gook with a spot-on frantan (napalm) strike as the Paras were dropped in the thick stuff to the south. None was hurt, and the final tally was six CTs and one AFA killed and a highly suspect AMA captured unhurt. Today's kills brought us to the 250 mark."

On 9 October Dennison was "severely wounded" in his 78th contact, where his "bravery and dedication" to the task in hand won him the Bronze Cross of Rhodesia. The deployment was the result of a Scouts' report of "ten" CTs on the Lundi River and was proceeded by Hunter strikes. The use of Hunters indicates that the target was considerably greater than the Scouts' records show. The War Diary says the Scouts' call-sign 21 Bravo (Commanded by the excellent Paul Holt) originally reported fifty CTs (correct), and states that on the ground at the end of the day there were "38 bodies and one prisoner".

Dennison recorded:

"It was an excellent contact from all points of view. The initiation worked like clockwork, aircrew and ground call-signs really got stuck in and supported each other and the Vultures [Paras] in particular, showed aggression to the nth degree. There is no doubt that we killed over thirty CTs, and Special Branch Superintendent John Leese of Chiredzi got himself crossed off our Xmas card list for this one... there was a long party at Buffalo Range that night and the mob all wound up round the OC's bed at about 2000 hrs. The bullet had hit the end of the femur but must have been an AP (armour piercing) as it did not make too much mess."

The contact near Lundi Mission on 9th October 1978 was "A" Company's most successful and worth expanding on a little. After Bruce Thompson's death, Alan Thrush's posting to the School of Infantry and Graeme Biffen's NS coming to an end and him departing for civilian life and University I was the only subbie in "A" Coy from the start of this bush trip through until January 1979. As of 1 November 1978, A Company had accounted for 271 terrorists killed; 25 terrorists captured; 16 FLPM killed; 82 ZANLA recruits killed; 54 recruits captured; and 139 civilians "running with" the terrorists; all for the cost of seven of his own men killed and 57 wounded. They also recovered over three hundred weapons originating from the Communist countries in the Far East and from behind the Iron Curtain.

Dennison re-joined A Company in January 1979, having spent part of his convalescence in the UK. Fire Force contacts and ambushes continued apace and, in April, Dennison led A Company back into the field for the last time. Fire Force operations from 30 April to 24 May saw only three contacts, four captures, and Dennison's rifle stopping a bullet which otherwise would have taken out the ankle of his remaining good leg.

During the evening of Sunday 3 June, Dennison and his second in command, Lieutenant Jon Brand, were in the bar of the Zimbabwe Ruins Hotel when a large group of guerrillas launched a well-planned attacked on the Hotel. They rushed outside but, in the darkness, Dennison was mistaken for a terrorist by a police officer and shot, dying almost immediately. He was buried with full military honours at Fort Victoria on 11 June 1979, the service being conducted by the Chaplain-General to the Forces. The men of A Company paid their respects in the newspaper Condolence columns with the notice:

"Dennison M.L.M., B.C.R. Major André. To our father and commander, farewell K-Car. You lived as a soldier and died like one. We shall never forget and will carry on with your memory to guide us. Fambai Zvakanaka, Ishe - from all your children of the Big Red."

Citation for the award of Member of the Legion of Merit (Military Division), 23 September 1977

"Major Andre Dennison has been a company commander in 2RAR since its formation in late 1975. The successes the company has had are due, in no small part, to the tireless efforts of Major Dennison. Displaying absolute dedication to the task, he has developed a first-class operational fighting force.

'On many occasions he has himself led his company, or elements of it, into contacts with terrorists, showing to them all determination required in combating the terrorist menace."

Citation for the award of Military Forces Commendation (Operations), 31 March 1978

"In August 1977, Major Andre Dennison was in command of a unit which killed five terrorists and captured one during a contact. However, one terrorist managed to escape into a cave. Despite several attempts to flush him out of the cave, the terrorist managed to find an excellent position to secure himself and to maintain a barrage of heavy and accurate fire upon the Security Force team. The next day, a number of further attempts were made to dislodge the determined terrorist, all to no avail. Major Dennison and two other men then entered the cave via an inclined shaft. The terrorist was concealed in another part of the cave and opened fire on the three intruders, wounding one of them. Major Dennison dragged the injured man clear with the help of the other soldier. Under heavy fire they managed to get him out of the cave. Eventually the terrorist, who was accompanied by a woman, was smoked out and he surrendered."

Citation for the award of Bronze Cross of Rhodesia, 9 February 1979

"During October 1978, Major Dennison was severely wounded in the initial stages of a contact. With a shattered femur and extensive bleeding from his wounds, he lost consciousness. On regaining consciousness, he refused evacuation and continued to direct the battle in a calm and competent manner. After one hour and fifteen minutes, he was taken out of the area, semi-conscious from loss of blood. The contact was extremely successful owing to Major Dennison's bravery and dedication to his task under circumstances far beyond the normal call of duty.

Within the year, this brave soldier was to pay the ultimate cost."

Lieutenant Alan Thrush BCR

A Bulawayo boy and son of the well-known Rhodesia Front Member of Parliament and RBC TV and Radio presenter James Thrush. Alan attended Rhodesian Army regular officer cadet course Inf/25(17) from January 1974 to 21 February 1975. Alan was a very serious student who initially struggled with the military way of life and he also endured quite a lot of pressure from fellow students teasing him, but he stuck through all these pressures with rock solid determination and had earned huge respect from his fellow students when we he was commissioned.

He was disappointed to be posted to the Rhodesian Army Services Corps but when he did his infantry attachment with 1RAR, he was then determined to switch permanently to Infantry and was successful in securing a posting to A Company, 2RAR under Major Andre Dennison MLM, BCR. He earned the nickname 'Fury' where his aggression and leadership resulted in many successful contacts and his award of the coveted BCR. Alan was one of three cadets from his course to be decorated for gallantry.

Lt Alan Thrush BCR

Citation for the award of the Bronze Cross of Rhodesia, 13 October 1978, Lieutenant Alan Thrush BCR

'Since joining the 2nd Battalion, the Rhodesian African Rifles, in November 1977, Lieutenant Thrush has been involved in no fewer than 25 Fire force contacts which accounted for more than 90 terrorists. In every deployment he has been the first man on the ground and usually the first to make contact. With his coolness under fire and his knack of accurately assessing the situation, he has led his men in exemplary fashion, eliminating a large number of terrorists. On 13 April 1978, four terrorists were trapped in a cave. During attempts to get them to surrender, Lieutenant Thrush, with complete disregard for his safety, entered the mouth of the cave and shot and wounded one terrorist. At this, two other terrorists promptly surrendered and the fourth was killed. On 22 April 1978, a similar situation developed and again Lieutenant Thrush took considerable personal risk in clearing several caves with grenades. All these contacts took place during the rainy season when the cover was extremely thick and most encounters took place at ranges well under ten metres. At no time did he allow himself to be deterred and his courageous example and determination to kill the enemy were at all times and inspiration to his soldiers.'

Sergeant Theodore Owen Nel BCR

Citation for the award of the Bronze Cross of Rhodesia, 10 November 1978, Sergeant Theo Nel BCR

'Temporary Sergeant Theodore Owen Nel is the Tracker Platoon commander operating in support of 1 and 4 (Independent) Companies, Rhodesian African Rifles. On 26 August 1977 Sergeant Nel was in command of a six-man patrol following up a group of terrorists estimated to be between eight and twelve in number when the patrol came under heavy fire from close range. Sergeant Nel immediately engaged the enemy, killing one of the sentries and forcing the terrorists to abandon their positions. Sergeant Nel and his patrol pursued the terrorists for twenty-five minutes before locating a recently vacated resting place where they found thirty-four packs which had been abandoned by the terrorists.

'Whilst recovering these, the patrol again came under heavy fire from the terrorist group, now estimated to be over thirty. A fierce firefight ensued with the terrorists' intent on driving off the numerically smaller patrol. Sergeant Nel and his men refused to be driven from their positions, despite the fact that ammunition was running dangerously low. Because of this Sergeant Nel decided to utilize a terrorist rocket launcher which he had seen among the terrorist packs in the open riverbed. With little regard for his own personal safety he made two forays under heavy automatic fire and recovered both the launcher and ammunition. Sergeant Nel then moved to a position from where he engaged the main enemy concentration with

Sgt Theo Nel BCR

accurate fire. The terrorists broke contact and fled, abandoning a large quantity of material, including eighteen landmines. There is no doubt that Sergeant Nel's brave and calculated actions forced the terrorists to abandon their positions and saved what could have been a dangerous situation for his patrol. This action typifies the courage, determination and skill that Sergeant Nel has consistently displayed throughout his service. His resolute pursuit of the enemy has resulted in his being involved in a large number of successful contacts in the past two years.'

Lance Corporal Henry Mawire BCR

Cpl Henry Mawire BCR

Citation for the award of the Bronze Cross of Rhodesia, 1979, Lance Corporal Henry Mawire BCR

'On 24 and 25 March 1978, during extended contacts with terrorists, he personally killed seven terrorists with his machine gun, the whole time being exposed to retaliatory fire. Again, on the 25 March 1978, he forced a terrorist to surrender by firing his machine gun at his feet and finally shooting the terrorist's rifle out of his hands.

'On 5 September 1978, during a Fire Force action, Lance-Corporal Mawire's patrol, while crossing a dry riverbed, was fired upon from the opposite bank by two terrorists. As the rest of the patrol sought what meagre cover was available, Lance-Corporal Mawire coolly stood in the riverbed, exposed to the terrorists' fire, and killed both terrorists by firing his machine gun from the hip, thereby saving his patrol almost certain casualties.

'On the 19 September 1978, while acting as second-in-command to an officer, the sweep line in which he was a member was held up by the fire of two terrorists. Without orders, and disregarding his own personal safety, Lance-Corporal Mawire moved forward and killed both terrorists.

'Throughout these and other actions, Lance-Corporal Mawire has displayed maturity, a high degree of aggression and a total disregard for his own personal safety. His gallant and efficient conduct is an outstanding example to the rest of his company.'

Amplification of his action on 5 September is as follows:

'On the afternoon of 5 September, call sign 75, Support Company 2RAR, manning an OP in the Chipise Tribal Trust Land saw eight insurgents and a number of civilians washing in the Bubye River. Fire Force Charlie, Andre Dennison's A Company 2RAR, was called up to respond to the sighting. Arriving above the target area, the troops saw the insurgents, clad in black Portuguese militia-style jackets and long trousers, splinter and run west along a densely wooded gully. The K-car, commanded by Captain Jean Vos, gave chase and scored two direct hits on the men in the gully itself. A third man, being pursued by a G-car as he ran south, came into the sights of the K-car, which wounded him, and he fell. The stops, Vultures 1 and 2 (Para troop call signs), together with Charlie 2 and 3 then swept along the gully finding two more of the enemy whom they killed. Charlie 1 was deployed to the river's eastern bank where the K-car was engaging an insurgent and his mujiba (CT sympathiser/collaborator), fatally wounding the latter. As the men of Charlie 1 began crossing the Bubye, they came under heavy fire. Lance-Corporal Mawire again distinguished himself as, standing in the open, he engaged the enemy with his MAG while the rest of the stick completed the crossing and, getting under cover, located and killed their quarry. In this encounter, six members of the eight-strong group had been accounted for. When a re-sweep of the area yielded no further insurgents, it was assumed that the outstanding two men had escaped, and three stops were left in ambush positions overnight in case they were still in the vicinity. (This was the fourth occasion in which Lance-Corporal Mawire had thus distinguished himself. He was recommended for an award).

'As at the date of this Citation, Lance Corporal Mawire is credited with a total of 11 personal kills and one capture; this is an extraordinary feat by a single soldier and a clearer demonstration of his quite incredible gallantry would be difficult to parallel in any regiment. What we obviously do not know is how his personal record increased from this point onwards and leading to the ceasefire. This junior NCO's citation, like his decorated peers, demonstrates that fierce commitment to duty to his fellow RAR brothers, his Regiment and his Country.'

Footnote: As I write these simple but wholly inadequate words, I feel singularly humbled about being in a position to share Lance Corporal Mawire's exemplary record and to publicly acknowledge his soldiering skills. We owe this man, and all of our RAR *Masodja*, a debt of enormous gratitude and accord them the respect that they have all earned and fully deserve. Reading his citation and the detailed account of one of the many contacts he was involved in, one can only sit back in awe.

There were very few gallantry awards for a single action (LCpl Russell Phillips SCR being one that immediately springs to mind and whom I was privileged to serve and fight alongside) and only one recipient of a Bar to the BCR (Corporal David Ndhlovu BCR [Bar]: Selous Scouts) but reading this man's citation epitomises everything good and true about the calibre of the men in the RAR. In my humble opinion there can be no doubting that whatsoever. We can be grateful indeed that men of Henry Mawire's calibre chose to stand and fight alongside us; that is my simple message!

Corporal Calvin Ncube BCR

Cpl Calvin Ncube BCR

Citation for the award of the Bronze Cross of Rhodesia, 1979, Lance Corporal Calvin Ncube BCR

'Corporal Calvin Ncube is a section commander in the Second Battalion, the Rhodesian African Rifles. Over the past 18 months he has been in over fifteen contacts with terrorists which have resulted in a large number being eliminated. Throughout all these engagements, Corporal Ncube has displayed a high degree of personal courage and determination to close with and kill the enemy.

'On 31 March 1978, Corporal Ncube and his men were involved in a Fire force action against a large number of terrorists and recruits. Shortly after making contact the K-car became unserviceable and no air support was available. One terrorist broke cover and attempted to escape. The terrorist break-out was indicated to Corporal Ncube by the helicopter pilot. Corporal Ncube, leading his men, sprinted after the terrorist. After a distance of about six hundred metres Corporal Ncube sighted the terrorist running into thick cover. Despite a heavy and accurate burst of fire from the terrorist, which came very close to hitting him, Corporal Ncube continued to give chase and, having outstripped his men and on the point of exhaustion, closed with and killed the terrorist at close range. Immediately after this action, Corporal Ncube and his men were re-directed to the main terrorist position where six terrorists were killed. Throughout this action Corporal Ncube again displayed a high standard of leadership and aggression.

'On 28 August 1978, during the mopping-up stages of a Fireforce action, Corporal Ncube and three men were directed towards an escaping terrorist. Again, leading his men at the run and outstripping them, he finally forced the terrorist to halt and take cover. Without hesitation and completely disregarding the fire directed at him, Corporal Ncube advanced and killed the terrorist at close range. In these and other engagements, Corporal Ncube has displayed total disregard for his own personal safety and has shown outstanding leadership. His aggressive attitude is held in the highest esteem by all who serve with him.'

Second Lieutenant Christopher James Edward Vincent BCR

2 Lt Christopher Edward James Vincent BCR

Chris attended Guinea Fowl High School and then moved to Ft Vic High where he was a border in Tower House. He was an outstanding athlete excelling at cross-country, and long & middle distance running on the athletics track. In his final year at FVHS, he was a school and hostel prefect and decided, on the completion of his M-Levels in 1976, to attend officer selection at the School of Infantry in Gwelo. He passed and attended regular cadet course Inf/25(20) (January 1977-February 1978) from which he was commissioned and posted to 2RAR.

Chris served in A Company ('Gangenukange') as a platoon commander under the late Maj Andre Dennison MLM, BCR.

Citation for the award of the Bronze Cross of Rhodesia, 1979, Second Lieutenant Christopher James Edward Vincent BCR

'Second Lieutenant Christopher James Edward Vincent joined the Second Battalion, The Rhodesian African Rifles, as a platoon commander in March 1978. Since that time, he has been involved in 30 contacts during which his company eliminated 200 terrorists. In all his contacts Second Lieutenant Vincent has displayed commendable coolness and a high degree of aggression which have contributed directly to the successes of his sub-unit. In his first contact, Second Lieutenant Vincent killed the only terrorist accounted for. Shortly afterwards he was concussed by a terrorist grenade which exploded within one yard of him which permanently damaged his ear-drums. Within 24 hours he was again in action and personally killed three of the seven terrorists killed by his company.

'On 26 April 1978, Second Lieutenant Vincent, through his tactical handling of a difficult situation in very thick bush, was responsible for the killing of four terrorists and the capture of two others. On 9 October 1978, he parachuted into action against a large number of terrorists and terrorist recruits. He injured his neck when landing, but despite the acute pain, remained in control of the ground forces for several hours, during which numerous and intense firefights with terrorists took place. Largely due to his aggression and fine command ability, 20 terrorists and a large number of their recruits were killed in action.

'On 15 October 1978, Second Lieutenant Vincent was leading a patrol of three men when they were fired on by two terrorists at very close range. Both machine-guns jammed, leaving Second Lieutenant Vincent with the only weapon in the patrol. Although in extreme danger, he stood his ground and calmly returned the fire, killing both terrorists and thus saving his own life and those of the other two members of his patrol.

'Throughout his operational service, Second Lieutenant Vincent has shown outstanding leadership and a high degree of tactical skill. His personal courage and aggression have inspired all those who have served with him."

Private George Mponda BCR

On 28 March, two four-man call signs from 'Chamuka Nyama', C Company, 2RAR, were ordered to set up OPs in the Ndanga Tribal Trust Land. However, because only one radio was working, both call signs would have to occupy the same OP. The hill selected for this OP had only one route leading to the top. This route was on the northern side of the kopje and was very thickly wooded without any good positions from which to mount surveillance.

Pte George Mponda BCR

Because this was the only route, a sentry was mounted on it and the remainders of the call signs deployed themselves into positions from which they were able to observe any possible enemy movement to the south, southwest and southeast of them. Shortly afterwards, Lance-Corporal Malota needed to answer a call of nature. Moving to the northern side of the hill, he walked past the sentry, Private Mponda telling him where he was going. He then continued on his way, going down the hillside for about ten metres, when Mponda lost sight of him. Unseen by the call sign, a group of 30 insurgents was climbing the hill, using the same access route.

They saw Lance-Corporal Malota and, as he squatted down to relieve himself, they assumed that, having seen them, he had ducked into cover to avoid being seen himself. One of them fired at him, wounding him in the hand. Malota called out to Mponda who thought that the NCO had accidentally discharged his rifle. A split second later, firing intensified and Malota again called out that he was under attack. Mponda, with his MAG at the ready, ran to the left of Malota's position and found himself confronted by 30 insurgents, advancing on a 20-metre front before him. They appeared to be moving in pairs, using the rocks and trees for cover. One of them was advancing on the hapless Malota with a fixed bayonet. With complete disregard for his own safety, Mponda opened fire with his MAG. He was standing up, legs braced, as he sprayed the area from left to right.

The enemy fire intensified but the young soldier, undaunted, actually began to move forward, firing continuously, the empty cartridges flying all round him and the weight of his fire forcing the enemy back. The rest of the call sign had moved around and were also firing but were unable to see the insurgents because of the steep gradient. Mponda was now in line with Malota, covering him. He had used up his 200-round belt. The enemy had fallen back somewhat but were still firing. Running back, Mponda collected his remaining belts, reloaded and resumed his onslaught, firing away. So intense was his fire that the numerically superior enemy finally broke, and turning tail, fled. Many of them, taking the shortest route, lost their footing and virtually rolled down the hill in their desperation to escape.

Mponda claimed to have scored five or six hits, but no bodies were found, and the rocky terrain precluded any search for tracks. Private Mponda's courage was noted. By his action, he had certainly saved Lance-Corporal Malota's life, and single-handedly put 30 men to flight. In his comments on this action, Hopcroft noted that the enemy was emulating the army tactic of deploying into OPs to observe security force movements. He also noted, somewhat dryly, that a lesson had been learned: "If you go to relieve yourself, do so in pairs." (Source: '*Masodja*')

Citation for the award of the Bronze Cross of Rhodesia, 1980, Private George Mponda BCR

'Private George Mponda has served with the Second Battalion, the Rhodesian African Rifles since 16 August 1978. During this period, he has been involved in numerous contacts with terrorists.

'On 28 March 1979, he was a member of an eight-man patrol occupying an observation post. He was positioned as a sentry on the eastern side of the feature with the other members occupying positions on the south and west sides of the same feature. At 1300 hours, the patrol commander moved forward of Private Mponda's position. Shortly after the patrol commander was out of sight, Private Mponda heard a single shot followed by heavy bursts of fire. Carrying his machine gun, Private Mponda ran down the hill towards the firing. Private Mponda saw his patrol commander lying wounded on the ground. A terrorist, with bayonet fixed to his rifle, was approaching the patrol commander. A further twenty-five terrorists, in extended line, were advancing up the feature. At that time, they were approximately twenty metres forward of his position, which was completely exposed. Without hesitation and with total disregard for his own personal safety, Private Mponda opened fire on the terrorist approaching his patrol commander and then fired at the oncoming terrorist group.

'Simultaneously, the terrorists fired at him, many rounds striking the ground around his feet. Private Mponda remained where he was and continued to fire at the advancing terrorists. In the face of his determined and effective opposition, the terrorists broke off their attack and fled down the hillside. Private Mponda then gave covering fire while two other members of his patrol, who had come to his assistance, removed the patrol commander. Subsequent information confirmed that Private Mponda had wounded two of the terrorists. From the terrorists' actions, it is certain that they were mounting an assault on the observation post. In addition to saving the life of his patrol commander, Private Mponda's lone and determined action was an act of outstanding bravery.'

Lance Corporal M Magara BCR

Background and citation regrettably unavailable.

Private Musiiwa BCR

Background and citation regrettably unavailable.

CHAPTER TWENTY ONE

THE END OF THE RHODESIAN ARMY

INTRODUCTION by Captain Andrew Telfer

It is not the purpose of Chibaya Moyo to provide a political commentary but one of the most commonly asked question by readers of *Chibaya Moyo 1* has been "What happened to the Rhodesian African Rifles?" The answer to that question is inextricably linked to what happened to Rhodesia itself. This closing chapter will briefly describe the politically-driven changes that led from Rhodesia to Zimbabwe and give something of the flavour of that sad period in our nation's history.

During 1979, the Rhodesian government came to an 'Internal Settlement' with leaders of opposition factions led by Ndabaningi Sithole and Abel Muzorewa. Education, property and income qualifications for voter rolls were relaxed, establishing the first ever black-majority electorate.

It is important to understand what this meant. Refer back to the article *The Context*, introducing the Rhodesian Bush War, and you will see that it was always Prime Minister Ian Smith's intention to do this. Rhodesia was not South Africa; it did not have a racially-based Apartheid system. Its franchise had been limited by property and income with the intention of ensuring good governance for *all* the people of Rhodesia. Horrified by what had happened in post-Colonial Africa to the north but accepting that black-majority rule was inevitable, the government of Ian Smith wanted time: 'time for African society to evolve, to learn, to develop the capacity to govern intelligently. His profound hope is that, when the black man is finally in the saddle, the fabric of good government will have been woven and there will be enough educated, wealthy and experienced Africans in the country to keep it from being ripped apart.' (Joyce 1974, p. 29)

A general election was held and Muzorewa was elected as the first black Prime Minister of the newly-named Zimbabwe Rhodesia (1 June 1979). Even though this massive step fulfilled their stated demands (a black-majority electorate and a majority black government) Britain and its Commonwealth nations still refused to recognise the new government. Why not? Because Robert Mugabe and Joshua Nkomo, although invited, had refused to participate. They were holding out, not for peace, but for power. Their rejection of the peace process should have excluded them, but Mugabe was the leader of choice for the Commonwealth political leaders. Consequently, the democratically-elected government of Zimbabwe Rhodesia was denied the international recognition that would have brought peace and stability. Western economic sanctions remained in place, China and Russia continued to arm and train the terrorists, the Bush War intensified and the people of Zimbabwe continued to suffer.

The Rhodesian Security Forces fought on. The quality of its counter-insurgency operations had been recognised by British General Sir Walter Walker, when he visited Rhodesia after retiring as NATO's Commander in Chief Allied Forces Northern Europe. Afterwards, he wrote in a letter to The Times:

'Their army cannot be defeated in the field either by terrorists or even a much more sophisticated enemy. In my professional judgment, based on more than 20 years' experience, from lieutenant to general, of counter-insurgency and guerrilla-type operations, there is no doubt that Rhodesia now have the most professional and battleworthy army in the world today for this particular type of warfare.

After an unrestricted visit to the operational area, General Walker found troop morale to be "sky high", while the terrorists are "terrified of meeting them in pitched battle". "Here is a breed of men the like of which has not been seen for many a long age" he wrote.'

However, wars are not won by military means alone and the economic stranglehold of British-led sanctions tightened its grip on the throat of the small nation. In December 1979, in the Commonwealth-brokered 'Lancaster House Agreement', the constitution of Zimbabwe Rhodesia was dissolved and the colony of Southern Rhodesia re-established, under a British Governor, Lord Soames. The British Parliament then passed the Zimbabwe Act to impose the country's future constitution. On 21 December 1979, a Ceasefire Agreement was signed, ending the Bush War and granting a general amnesty to all who had fought. The Commonwealth Monitoring Force, led by the British Army, arrived in the country and set up sixteen Assembly Points (APs) for the terrorists to gather and hand in their weapons. About 18,000 did but many thousands more remained at large to subvert the coming elections. The Rhodesian Army was confined to barracks and dutifully obeyed.

General elections were held in February 1980. In spite of widespread evidence of intimidation by supporters of Mugabe and Nkomo, the results were accepted by the Commonwealth observers as 'free and fair'. ZANU 'won' 57 of the 100 seats and its leader Robert Mugabe became the first Prime Minister of Zimbabwe. In April 1980, the country officially became independent from Britain in a ceremony presided over by Prince Charles. That was the end of democracy for the people of Zimbabwe and the onset of a regime that has brought economic destruction to the country and brutal oppression to its people ever since.

For the Army, in 1980, it meant the establishment of the Zimbabwe National Army through the integration of the former Rhodesian Army, the Zimbabwe People's Revolutionary Army (ZIPRA) and the Zimbabwe African Liberation Army (ZANLA) under the uncomprehending eyes of the British Military Advisory Training Team (BMATT). Mugabe carefully kept one Brigade outside the integration process, the North Korean-trained Fifth Brigade, comprising only ZANLA terrorists, who he would use two years later to slaughter more than 20,000 civilians in the western part of the country.

All the former regiments were renamed along Soviet numerical lines. 1RAR became 11 Infantry Battalion; 2RAR became 42 Infantry Battalion; 3RAR, 33 Infantry Battalion; 1RLI, 1 Commando Battalion, and so on. In addition, we were ordered to remove our regimental insignia and replace our berets and stable belts with those of the neutral Staff Corps. The Soviet and Chinese military cultures, from whom our new masters had learned, did not place the same value on regimental identity as do the British, from whom we'd originally inherited our culture. The Rhodesian Army and, with it, the Rhodesian African Rifles, ceased to exist.

'Yet from those flames,
No light, but rather darkness visible.'
John Milton, *Paradise Lost*

References:
The Times, 1978, reproduced by The Daily News Bureau, London.
Joyce, Peter 1974, *Anatomy of a Rebel*, pp. 29-31, Graham Publishing, Salisbury, Rhodesia.
Smith, Ian 1997, *The Great Betrayal,* John Blake Publishing, United Kingdom.

SECURITY FORCE AUXILIARIES by Major Gavin Rawstron

In February 1979, B Coy 1 RAR were deployed to Karoi as a result of terr activity in the Urungwe TTL. The two Viscounts had previously been downed and it was determined that ZIPRA Forces operating in the TTL had all but subverted the local population, closed all schools, clinics and all forms of local administration. Roads were made inaccessible and the airspace between Kariba and Salisbury had seriously been affected as a result of ZIPRA forces being in possession of SAM 7

(Strella) anti-aircraft weapons and had shown that they were not afraid to use them on any civilian aircraft.

At the time, Urungwe TTL was undergoing a change. The Locals were being recruited, trained, armed and deployed back into their respective areas under the banner of *Pfumo re Vanhu* (The Spear of the People/Nation). They were otherwise referred to as SFAs (Security Force Auxiliaries).

Best Recruit – SFA – Urungwe 1978

The Urungwe TTL was initially allocated as a 'test ground' for SFAs under the name of IGF (Interim Government Forces) in August 1978. It was launched under the supervision of SB John Padbury and his team, who until Feb 1979, were responsible for the training, deployment, administration, command and control of approximately 200. Most were members of the ZANLA faction of Ndabaningi Sithole, their commanders having been ex ters who had been trained in Algeria. The aim was to select volunteers from the Urungwe TTL, train, arm and send them back into their respective areas to regain the confidence of the local population and ultimately to chase the ZIPRA elements out who had been responsible for the downing of the two Viscounts.

Another objective given to operations in the Urungwe prior to the elections was to mobilise the masses by restoring the infrastructure including schools, clinics, roads etc. in order to get a high percentage vote and to establish an environment where free and fair voting could take place. In order for there to be a certain amount of credibility, SFAs were armed with AKs/ G3s and were given dark brown uniforms.

In Feb 1979, following the downing of the two Viscounts by ZIPRA, B Coy 1RAR were given the task of taking over command, training, deployment and administration of all SFA's in the Urungwe TTL. A total of 200 SFAs were deployed in Central Urungwe, another 200 were to undergo training at Chabwino Farm (just outside Karoi) and a further 50 to be trained at Paradys Farm. A total of 262 recruits were trained between Feb and the elections in April 1979 by B Coy 1 RAR instructors at Paradys Farm and Penstock Farm. In all, 700 SFAs were deployed by the time of the Elections, covering approximately 90 % of the Urungwe TTL.

Prior to the deployment of SFAs, all schools had been closed down as a result of CT action, bus services were no longer operating, all dips were closed and only one clinic remained open. All locals in the Urungwe TTL were considered subverted and anti-Government.

The Zimbabwe – Rhodesian Elections were held and Bishop Abel Muzorewa won, becoming the first black Prime Minister. As the other two factions (ZANLA and ZIPRA) refused to participate in these elections and the elections were not recognised by the International Community, the war continued.

In April 1979, The Padbury House in Karoi was closed down and B Coy 1 RAR Base HQ established at Magunje. Chabwino Training Base closed down and Penstock Training Base continued. John Padbury and the majority of his controllers were withdrawn.

B Coy 1 RAR continued to train and deploy, rebuilding schools and clinics. SFAs were integrated with RAR NCOs and troops and control of 90% of the Urungwe TTL was restored. A total of 18 schools re-opened.

In some cases where schools had been destroyed by CTs, the locals re-built them with the help of Security Forces (SF) and SFAs Pupil attendance far exceeded numbers prior to the schools being re-opened. This was partly due to the politicians promising free education during their electioneering campaign. As there was a shortfall of teachers, it became necessary for them to teach the school children on a rotational basis.

Clinics and buses resumed operating and the local population began changing as they experienced our efforts.

As the combined SF and SFAs were deployed into the new areas, a number of contacts ensued where unknown numbers of CTs were wounded. Documents recovered from these contacts revealed that some died as a result of their injuries and that the ZIPRA hierarchy were extremely concerned at the turn of events.

ZIPRA tactics then changed, whereas, in the early stages, they would move around in small groups of 10 to 20, they then moved in groups of 100 plus. They also started to avoid built-up, populated areas and were forced to move to the western area where there was no SFA presence. A number of contacts and sightings took place between SF and CTs, but because air support was not available due to external operations taking place in other parts of the country, results were not as good as they could have been.

It was also established that CTs also had possession of radios and that they were tuning in to SF communications. This created a number of situations that were detrimental to our forces and counter measures had to be implemented. B Coy 1 RAR lost two very good soldiers killed in ambushes as a result of this.

During the period in which B Coy 1 RAR were deployed in the Urungwe, a total of 36 landmines were recovered that had been laid by the enemy. Only one was driven over by one of our vehicles, but fortunately did not detonate as the detonators had been placed in upside-down. The majority of landmines recovered were as a result of information from the locals, indicating the extent of co-operation and assistance from them. There were a number of SFAs that went AWOL, two with their weapons who joined ZIPRA, and the others because they were dead scared of being killed.

Many meetings were held with the headmen and locals and addressed by myself and some of my senior staff. They were very well-received and fruitful, and showed the amount of support that we had been able to obtain, so much so, that when we were eventually given the orders to move back to Methuen Barracks without replacement, a number of local leaders pleaded with us to remain.

However, there were disadvantages. Integrating the Company with semi-trained SFA's had a distinct disadvantage in that the junior ranks were subject to the temptations of drink and women. These vices were readily available to them through the local SFAs. Apart from sexual diseases, morale and discipline took a very definite turn for the worse. Being 'stood down' from this task could not have happened any later and I was glad to restore what had been temporarily lost.

I feel that the fact that we were not replaced would have had a detrimental effect on the morale of the SFAs and the local population as a whole. A tremendous amount of time and effort had been put into getting them 'on side', only to drop them in the proverbial 'Cart'. This would have had a negative impact on the final Elections prior to independence.

The fact that we were not able to carry out our conventional tasks did affect our kill results, but re-establishing our credibility and gaining the support of the locals was a major achievement.

This would not have been possible without the professional contribution of John Padbury and his team. My thanks go out to the Officers, NCO's and men of B Coy 1 RAR who excelled themselves under difficult and unusual circumstances. There are too many names to mention individually, but special thanks to my 2ic Capt Joe Smith, Lt Percy Chiyanike and 2Lts Rich Cook and Gerry Field. To have turned the local inhabitants against the ters was a major turning point for us. I am led to believe that the Urungwe SFA Exercise was considered a major success.

THE WAR IS OVER NOW…. by Lieutenant Noel Smith

This story is not part of my RAR service but was whilst I was with 1 Rhodesia Regiment. Ironic that my first bush trip with the RAR was to Mt Darwin in 1975 and then my last call up was also to Mt Darwin in 1979/80 – a full circle. However, this story had a rather meaningful and unforgettable conclusion for both me and the country.

In late December 1979 the Bush War finally came to an end and preparations were made for the Ceasefire and subsequent elections for early the following year.

At the same time the annual rainy season descended on North Eastern Rhodesia with a vengeance and we were drenched by the continuous daily deluge. The countryside was soaked, roads were washed away; everything was constantly wet and covered in mud and our clothing and equipment started to go mouldy and rot. I had never seen so much rain in my life and it just seemed to be a never-ending torrent. Life was generally pretty miserable and uncomfortable.

I was again based at Mount Darwin and we were confined to camp at one stage because the tropical rains were so heavy and unrelenting that we could not deploy by vehicle and patrolling the bush was a complete waste of time. Even the terrs had ceased their disruptive activities and they either stayed put in the comfort of the Assembly Points or were hidden up in the local villages We went out on the odd deployment to show the locals that we were still active and in control, but in the main we only left base camp if we had specific intelligence to act on and were able to reach the area in question.

I played endless games of cards and dice to ease away the boredom and read as many books and magazines as possible. With not much else to do, the Mess became a popular meeting place and as a result my bar bill was in serious danger of exceeding my pay rate and my darts game improved from a bad standard to now being considered average.

Returning to basecamp after a rare vehicle patrol, we pulled over to give a drenched and cold African family a lift to their next stop. Huddled up on the back of the truck trying hopelessly to keep warm and dry, I struck up a conversation with them. As I selfishly complained about the weather, the wizened and grey haired old African elder (sekuru) looked me steadily in the eye and gave me a very straightforward explanation for the rain and I have never forgotten his words.

"The war is over now and Mwari (God) has sent the rain to wash away the blood and sorrow".

ZIPRA BRIGADE, GWAAI RIVER MINE 1980 by Major Gavin Rawstron

At the end of March 1980, I was sent by Brigadier Mike Shute (Commander 1 Brigade) to Gwaai River Mine with four African soldiers from my B Coy 1 RAR and a platoon from 6RR consisting of African and European soldiers as Liaison Officer to the ZIPRA Brigade who had recently come across from Zambia. I was to meet them at Mpofu Siding Dett, on the edge of the Wankie Game Reserve. We were to base up at Gwaai River Mine for an undetermined period of time.

The ZIPRA Brigade consisted of five Battalions of approx. 1200 combatants, led by Brigade Commander Mike Reynolds (alias Charles Grey). Four of the Battalions were trained in Odessa Russia in conventional warfare and had minimal combat experience from Rhodesian attacking forces whilst awaiting deployment in Zambia. The remaining 5th Battalion was made up of ZIPRA combatants who were relatively well-experienced in guerrilla warfare within Rhodesian borders.

The disembarking at Mpofu took place over the period 2-3 April 1980 and all personnel were ferried by military vehicles to Gwaai River Mine together with medium and light arms and munitions, troop carrying vehicles and medium anti-aircraft weaponry, whilst all heavy equipment including tanks, BTR APC's, Amphibious Landing Craft and heavy weapons were transported to Essexvale by train. A total of 49 railway trucks were offloaded with arms and munitions and transported to Gwaai River Mine.

This is an extract from my report to Brigadier Shute after arriving at Gwaai River Mine:

1 ZIPRA Brigade: Op Little Sparrow:

The ZIPRA Brigade consisting of five Battalions with support weapons arrived at Gwaai River Mine over a two-day period between 2-3 April 1980. The move of all personnel appeared orderly and well disciplined. Transport availability was limited and several trips were necessary from Mpofu Siding.

Four of the five Battalions were immediately deployed with their support weapons into defensive positions around the Mine Area along high ground on arrival. (I later found out that they were concerned that the Rhodesian Airforce was going to attack them). The remaining Battalion was positioned in the mine compound and had the responsibility of providing guards and admin duties. Their organisation and set up of administration buildings etc. went well.

A visit by Army and Brigade Staff including Dumisa Dabengwa and Lookout Masuku on Tuesday 9 April 80 was well-received and the military display by the Guard of Honour was slick and impressive.

I was not given access to the defensive area around the camp and could only visit the internal defence positions, stores, armouries and admin areas. Communication vehicles were out of bounds. The weaponry including Russian Strella (Sam 7), 14.5mm (4-barrel and 2-barrel) and 12.7mm anti-aircraft weapons, 82mm and 60 mm mortars, 122mm and 75mm Recoilless Launchers, vehicles including Gaz and Zill personnel carriers, Russian Jeeps and radio, medical and other tactical vehicles.

Maj Gavin Rawstron

I found out later that they were expecting attacks by the Rhodesian Airforce which would have made our presence interesting. On the basis of this, I requested that the 6 RR platoon attached for our protection return to Bulawayo earliest, as it would only have become a hindrance. I felt we had a better chance of staying alive with a small number. As it was, the first two nights were pretty hairy as we were surrounded by 5500 combatants whose actions were not known. Brigadier Mike Shute was not happy about this but eventually agreed and they returned to Bulawayo the same day. I never gave my reasons over the network as I was not certain how secure it was.

The following four weeks were interesting and I was able to glean information and intelligence from the various commanders on strengths, weaponry and to a certain extent, deployment positions. Mike Reynolds (Charles Grey) was very cagey and was quite nervous with me around. I found the other commanders more amenable.

After approx. a week, a report came through of 13 dissidents operating along the railway line near Sipepa Area and an element under command Chief of Ops (Tobias Mpala) was deployed to apprehend and return them to Gwaai River Mine. Three days later, I was advised that the Chief of Ops had been shot and that his body was being brought back to the Mine for burial. Reynolds could not give me a satisfactory explanation surrounding his death and I heard rumour later that the Chief of Ops had been summarily executed as a result of his failing in his mission to round up all 13 dissidents. As Liaison Officer, I felt it my duty to attend his funeral which I did.

Following this, there was a further report of a larger group of dissidents operating in the Wankie Game Reserve and Tjolotjo Areas and it was decided to deploy two Bns into that area as soon as possible. For this, we required more vehicles and had to send personnel were sent to Bulawayo for driver training. 35 of them passed and were sent with S&T vehicles to Gwaai Mine.

Of these, one had an accident with cattle, one hit a bowser and four others broke down and had to return to Brady Barracks. Deployment of the two Bns into Wankie National Park took place over period 14/15 April 1980, during which nine vehicles broke down (seven with burnt out clutches and a seized engine, one with burnt out electrics complete written off and one with an air lock). All personnel from these vehicles were transferred to remaining vehicles, causing massive overloading. To see these vehicles being destroyed after we had so carefully attempted to look after them during the war, was frustrating. At one stage, I lost it and reprimanded one of the drivers, only to be respectfully taken aside by one the Bde Officers and warned not to get involved and to remember that I was still regarded as the enemy by rank and file. It took another three days to recover these vehicles. Interesting to note, the three Russian Personnel Carriers were more suitable to the terrain and returned to base without fault.

Three days later, we were instructed to move a smaller HQ to Tjolotjo as a number of dissidents had been apprehended and were being taken there. This move took place via Bulawayo over a two day period, arriving at Tjolotjo on 20 April 1980. Three more vehicles met their fate as a result of drink and bad driving. Personnel were disorderly en route, some urinating from the vehicles whilst in motion, others interfering with other traffic during rest breaks. These were reported to Mike Reynolds, who chose to ignore them.

Camp was set up alongside the airfield at Tjolotjo. Anti-aircraft and mortars positioned strategically positioned around camp. There was only a small contingent in the base camp under Mike Reynolds and it was at this stage that I lost contact with the remainder of the brigade at Gwaai Mine.

On the 22nd April, ten dissidents were brought into the camp, followed by their women. This was of concern to those in the camp but was not resolved to my knowledge. At one stage, one of the dissidents decided to make a break for it by running through the centre of camp. He was quickly dispatched and I believe in the confusion one of the camp guards tried to take me out as bullets were flying around me. I suddenly found myself at the bottom of my shell scrape with Mike Reynold's Batman next to me, only to survive another day.

It was shortly after this that I was relieved by Major Charlie Piers (2ic 1 RAR).

Generally, I found the Brigade Officers very amenable and open, but Mike Reynolds arrogant and with a small man syndrome. The change-over came just in time, as it was only a matter of time before I was going to vent my frustration.... not a good idea!

Much of the information that I received was through my own African soldiers attached. They always held their heads up high and their loyalty was unquestionable.

THE GOOD, THE BAD AND THE UGLY by Lieutenant John Garland

As a newly commissioned 18 year old 2Lt, I was posted to 3 RAR, a Battalion recently formed on the eastern border, with its headquarters in Umtali, and Companies in Chipinga and Inyanga. After a short R&R on completion my Officer Cadet training, Inf /25(23), I made my way down to Umtali in my newly purchased 'trustworthy' Triumph 2000, a vehicle that had never passed a pre-start check and should never have been allowed onto a showroom floor to be sold to anyone who valued their lives, breaking down constantly, rattling and shaking to the point where even the bitumen roads quivered when driven on. I left Salisbury on Sunday morning at 0400 hrs to give myself plenty of time for what was normally a 3 hour drive... my car! I didn't know if it would get there that day.

On Monday morning, I reported to Col Lever, my new CO, who informed me that I was to report to Maj Meiring, OC B Coy, located in Chipinga, another bone rattling journey in my untrusty Triumph. On arrival, and after brief introductions to the senior NCO's by 2Lt Brett Nielsen, who was acting 2IC as Captain Russell Fulton was overseas on a short posting to a British Army unit, Maj Meiring informed me that I was to command 4 Platoon,

The following morning the company was assembled on parade where the Regimental song was sung and the flag raised. I was introduced to the Company, and inspected my Platoon. My Platoon Sergeant (Sgt Chisoro) marched the men to the Platoon HQ where I could sit down and meet each soldier individually. I took as much information and mental notes as possible to fill my Platoon Bible. The floor was then opened for questions, the first one being my age! Here I was, a virgin of war, surrounded by veterans who I was to lead and command in a time of uncertainty and political upheaval.

I was taught by the best instructors in the world at the School of Infantry and it was there that it is imbedded into all cadets that you lead from the front and never ask or instruct a soldier to do what you would not do yourself. Being fresh out of training, I assumed that I was at my physical peak (big mistake), so I took it upon myself to undertake the morning PT sessions and lead the runs, up and down the airstrip, and the pokie drill.

The morning run started off with me in the front, alongside the platoon, at a steady pace set by me but, in time the pace was quickened, not by me, but by the front runners. At first it was not such a big problem but, by the second lap of the airstrip, I was struggling to keep up with my platoon. Towards the end of the run, I was clearly out of my depth and thankfully my Platoon Sergeant came to the rescue and bought the men to a halt for push ups and sit ups. Pokie drill was next and, again, my ability to maintain the strength required to keep up with my soldiers was tested. Note to self: "Don't do this again. Never under estimate the strength, endurance and physical attributes of an RAR soldier".

With the bush war officially over, and ceasefire in place, the ex gooks in the Assembly Points around Rhodesia continued to harass, intimidate and abduct the local population. The Platoon spent many weeks around the Melsetter/Chipinga and Sabi areas patrolling and catching the offenders. Tempers of the ex-gooks were always high, abusive in character and on several occasions violent. The way in which the Masoja handled these situations was always carried out in a professional manner. It was a time of political unrest, which the soldiers put to one side in the interest of the general population and their wellbeing.

It wasn't long before I had my first call out with the Platoon. It happened one Saturday night at the local Beer Hall. A bunch of rowdy ex-gooks from Assembly Point (AP) Foxtrot came into town and caused a drunken brawl, too large for the local police to handle. There had been a stabbing and shooting, and the ex-gooks had taken over the Hall, closing the doors and threating to shoot those still inside. I gave orders and we deployed to the township and surrounded the Hall. I called out to the offenders to lay down their arms and come out. After some threating and aggressive abuse, a couple more shots were fired.

I then instructed Sgt Chisoro to tell the offenders that they were surrounded and that we would storm the building shooting them all if they did not surrender themselves. There was no response. On that we raced up to the doors and broke through, weapons at the ready to fire. They immediately dropped their weapons but, in their drunken aggressive state, abused us as we manhandled them out of the hall into the waiting police vans. After that incident, we undertook numerous roadblocks around Chipinga, arresting many an individual from AP Foxtrot on his way into town.

I was called into Maj Meiring's office one morning and given a warning order to put my Platoon on standby. There had been an accident involving a bus not far from Birchenough Bridge. A high ranking ex-gook from AP Foxtrot had been injured and a rowdy crew from the AP were threating bystanders with their lives if he were to die. I was to take my Platoon to AP Foxtrot and pick up some officials, go to the crash scene and defuse the situation.

The Platoon arrived at the AP, where we were immediately surrounded by hundreds of ex-gooks. Nerves were on edge and weapons were at the ready as we were completely outnumbered by their aggressive, hateful faces. I told the drivers to keep the engines running for a quick exit in the event of things getting out of control. A leader approached me and told us to get out of the vehicles and share the weapons. I refused and said I was ordered to pick up some officials and go to the crash scene. The leader became quite agitated and the mob was closing in on the vehicles, demanding weapons as it was "unfair for us to be armed and not them". Again I refused and a Mexican standoff developed.

The situation was getting out of hand and tempers were flaring. The troops and I were in a very dangerous position as we could so easily be over-run. Tensions were so high, with the finger of every soldier on the trigger that the only option was to get out of there. If a shot had been fired, I don't think there would have been a good outcome for us. The professional attitude and nerve of the men during this standoff was to be admired. I gave the order for the drivers to start moving and not stop, even if it meant driving over someone. Every weapon was now pointing over the side of the vehicles as we slowly made our way out of the camp. I never got down to the crash scene so do not know what the outcome was. I do know that I couldn't have been with a better bunch of men than those RAR soldiers. That was a day where so many things could have gone wrong if a shot had been fired.

Many a Chibuku and Chipinga Coffee were drunk that night. My admiration, trust and respect to the masodja is second to none. Salute.

AP FOXTROT: ZANLA MAIN BASE by Major Gavin Rawstron

It was about 4 months after Zimbabwe gained its Independence and the various factions were starting to integrate into the new National Army. I had recently been transferred to HQ 3 Bde as Brigade Major under Brig Dick Tilley and Col Hank Meyer.

Sometime during September, Brig Tilley called me into his office and briefed me of a possible abduction by Zanla Ters of a white policeman from Bikita and believed he was being held hostage at AP Foxtrot. This was the Zanla HQ where most of their combatants were positioned and were awaiting transfer into the National Army. Zanla Army commander Rex Nhongo was being flown to Bikita from Salisbury and would be going into AP Foxtrot to investigate and report back.

He asked me very politely if I would consider accompanying Rex Nhongo but also made it quite clear that I could object should I so desire. Obviously there were unknown risks involved and the decision to go was left up to me. I agreed immediately and was flown to Bikita where a staff car from Ft Vic was standing by to take us into AP Foxtrot.

ZANLA "gooks" A.P. Foxtrot

We departed from Bikita some 4 hours later with Nhongo and driver in the front of an Army Peugeot and myself with his personal bodyguard in the back seat. All were dressed in gook camo bar myself who was in my HQ Rhodie beret, camo shirt, beige longs and vellies. I was unarmed.

The trip over bush roads took about an hour for which I was very thankful. We arrived eventually at the base of a very big granite rock formation at a make-shift boom gate confronted by an untidy guard whose East German camo uniform hadn't been washed since it left the production line. With his RPD slung over his left shoulder he approached the driver side of the vehicle and barked out an inaudible order in Shona. At this point he noticed a white soldier in uniform in the back seat and all attention shifted to me. He was completely ignorant of his own commander sitting in the front seat. His eyes were bloodshot with a hint of brown probably due to his previous night's visit to the local shebeen. Quite the ugliest chap I'd seen in a long time.

Had his attention not been diverted to Nhongo by the driver, I hesitate to think what he had in mind about me. His demeanour suddenly changed, snapped to attention, blurted out a few apologies and quickly lifted the makeshift boom that almost fell off its supports. I could not help but try and suppress a smile. We continued for another mile or so around the base of the rock mountain until we arrived at the HQ nestled in amongst a clump of trees. The message had obviously got through advising them of the visitors as there was a hive of activity when we approached. A row of dilapidated tents lined the one side whilst on the other was a table made out of Msasa poles tied together with *gusytambo* (a rope like fibre made from bark of the Msasa tree).

After the necessary protocol was completed and introductions made, we sat down around the table on home-made stools. Nhongo addressed his commanders in Shona, briefed them about boundary limitations and then popped the question about the missing white policeman from Bikita. (He, Nhongo, was unaware that I spoke and understood Shona and I never gave them any indication of this).

It was at this time that I felt something cold pressed against my neck. I had a feeling what it was and was not about to risk turning around to confirm it. I continued looking towards Nhongo who was seated opposite me. Without any hesitation, he (Nhongo), looked directly at the culprit and without saying a word, flicked his head to one side. I was aware of a number of ters grabbing this chap and marching him off out of sight. Not long after, I heard a shot but cannot confirm whether it was the elimination of this clown or not. I guessed that it would not have been because he dared to challenge me, but because he dared to do it in the presence of Nhongo without Nhongo's instruction.

The briefing continued as if nothing had happened! All the other commanders indicated that the white policeman was not being held in AP Foxtrot.

We departed shortly afterwards with no further mishap and returned to Umtali via the main Chipinga/Umtali road. There was a further issue that Nhongo had to attend to 20 kms outside Umtali as another group of Zanla ters were rebelling. I was not present at this meeting and continued back to Umtali having had enough of these peace-time war games.

GUILLOTINED BY 3:1 INF BN by Captain Russell Fulton

I had recently returned to B Company, 3RAR from an incredibly enlightening attachment to two professional British Army infantry units as part of an exchange officer programme; The Green Howards based at Catterick Garrison and 3 Parachute Battalion in Colchester. Whilst I thoroughly enjoyed these attachments, I truly missed my own regiment and was well pleased when I returned to Chipinga, the home of B Company, 3RAR.

Following the integration process, unit designations and seniority of the former Rhodesian Army were changed, deliberately, to remove the RAR as the senior battalion in 1st, 3rd and 4th Brigades that should have been, logically, a numerical sequential change. The 3rd Battalion Rhodesian African Rifles should have become 3:1 ("3" being the third Brigade and the senior and first battalion in the new Brigade being "1") was, disrespectfully, designated as 3:3 Infantry Battalion. The newly integrated battalion at the Birchenough-Mutare-Chipinga road junction was designated 3:1 Infantry and a third, in Rusape, 3:2 Infantry Battalion. More salt to the wound! 3:1 and 3:2 Infantry battalions were the consequence of integration of former foe (ZIPRA/ZANLA/Rhodesian Army) and were regarded as 'senior' to 3:3 Infantry Battalion (the former 3RAR).

One Sunday afternoon, nursing various haematoma, grazed knees, thighs and eyes following the annual rugby derby against Umtali Sports Club at Chipinga Country Club, Maj Marius Meiring rattled the door on my A-frame prefabricated quarters: "Sunray Minor" (in all the years that I knew this wonderful human being, he never once addressed me as Russell. 'Sunray Minor' was my call-sign from my arrival in Chipinga until his very sad, tragic and untimely demise many years later), "present yourself in the ops room in figures one zero (10 minutes) and be ready for deployment. Copied?" "Copied Sir".

I got dressed in my No. 4's, recleaned and lightly oiled the working parts of my FN rifle, checked my webbing, water bottles, magazines and all those myriad other important pre-deployment battle procedure checks before taking arse-splitting strides towards the Ops Room. We were in peace time mode and this was completely unexpected, but those well-honed basics were still completely intact.

Marius read an Incident Report signal to me from HQ 3 Brigade informing us that, as the nearest sub-unit to 3:1 Infantry Battalion based at the southern side of the intersection of the main Birchenough Bridge-Umtali Road/Chipinga turn-off, we were required to respond promptly with medical support and to assist ZRP in securing the area and assisting the injured. There had been a vehicle accident, a MAP 7.5 TCV from 3:1 Inf Bn, that had rolled and there were significant military and civilian casualties. One of the regular army's duties was to provide 'Military Assistance to the Civil Authority' and this was one of those occasions.

I gathered elements of Company HQ, CSM WO2 Chimuti (later RSM 3:3 Inf Bn) our medical team and a signaller and gave orders for immediate deployment. The line of sight distance was insignificant and belied actual travel time that was compromised by continuous twists and turns and steep climbs and descents. The full extent of the journey was a mere 60km, but travel time was comfortably closer to two hours in our TCV's. We all knew the road like the back of our hand and departed to the scene of the accident, a mere 400 meters from the turnoff to 3:3 Inf Bn (newly formed and clearly without military order and good discipline).

Within 15 kilometres of the accident site we came across a MAP 7.5 TCV that was loading a shit-house full of assorted and very drunken civilians and members of 3:1 Infantry Battalion from a roadside shebeen. We slowed down to observe this pitiful but shameful sight and I knew, full-well, that the accident we were due to arrive at would include passengers of the self-same inebriated ilk. It angered me immensely because this was not what we RAR soldiers did and it was, consequently, impossible for us to relate to.

As we passed, shots were fired in to the air in an act of insolent and unwarranted bravado that was, methinks, a veiled challenge to our post-independence legitimacy. Their reaction to our presence tripped a switch in my 'hard-drive' that short-circuited my otherwise calm demeanour when threats were involved. Like many, I had become somewhat impervious to the perils of violence but, that erstwhile cocky and aggressive characteristic was now primed and available for a joust in whatever form. I had, some years earlier, lost my innocence to our bush war and was now belligerent, and then some, and these 3:3 types were most definitely not my men!

We negotiated a cambered, left hand bend in the road some 500 meters before the main road intersection that was the Birchenough Bridge to Umtali main road where the road levelled out. There it was, directly ahead of us. It was yet another unfortunate example of alcohol and speed…that deadly, uncompromising and unforgiving cocktail!

During my years in uniform I saw it all; that's not bravado, it's an incontrovertible fact and certainly wasn't unique to me. Collateral damage following air strikes, 'frantan' (napalm) strike, grenade, K-Car, mortar, artillery, land mines, machine gun or rifle fire or whatever other deadly military weapon you can think of paints an awful picture, but we greeted those vagaries of our bush-war without refrain and with some indifference. We hear and/or read about sleepless nights, nightmares about the many things that we witnessed and experienced as young men; today it is called PTSD (Post Traumatic Stress Disorder); the acronym never existed back in the day. No man that I served with on operations has been impervious to its malicious machinations.

This is one of my own.

Death is an unwanted but expected outcome of war but, in uniform at least, one became (somewhat) impervious to all its unpleasantness and its dark, foreboding and sombre omni-presence. Ours was simply a matter of 'kill' or be 'killed' but this was peace time and the 'Grim Reaper' always has his own arrangements. In the middle-distance and to our front lay an upended MAP 7.5

troop carrying vehicle on the northern side of the road. The tarred-road bore testament to the events of this horrific accident; the slightly protruding roll bars above the top-line of the armour plating had dug, fiercely and mercilessly, in to the tarred road and gouged-out repetitive striations, a clear testament to repeated and catastrophic roll-over. All M.A.P 7.5 TCV's had three roll-bars; one behind the driver's cab, one in the centre of the troop compartment and one at the rear of the vehicle by the outward opening pair of armour-plated rear doors. Standing in moving vehicles was a chargeable offence in the Rhodesian Army, in fact, convoy orders specified that troops were to be seated, barrels placed through the gun ports and for lap straps to be securely fastened. The new ZNA displayed a contempt for Rhodesian army regulations and this would be a horrific example of just that.

Allow me to share with you that what lay before us to the left, on the road to our front and to the right of it. It was as if a rotary guillotine had been introduced in transit and its sharpened 'blade' (the top edge of the armour plating) had 'guillotined repetitively as the vehicle rolled and 'executed' without prejudice. Littered across the road, for a good 50 meters and in every direction, were body parts of every description. It was horrific to even the most 'seasoned' eyes.

Guillotine edges on M.A.P. 7.5 T.C.V

I had with me an exemplary NCO, Corporal Tinarwo, Stephen, a MA3 trained medic and the son of a former 1RAR senior NCO, who went about rendering first aid as best as he could. Whilst all of this was going on, I set about establishing road blocks with ZRP Chipinga and securing the area and relaying messages via our Company HQ in Chipinga to the Chipinga Hospital to be prepared for multiple 'inbound' casualties including their mortuary. During this time of complete chaos, radio comms with the C.O., 2ic, and Adjutant of 3:3

Infantry Battalion was futile as they were either clueless to what had happened on their doorstep, completely 'pissed', blasé or disinterested (or all the above?). A group of menacing, heavily armed elements from 3:3 Inf Bn approached us on foot and in decidedly shit-order but bristling with RPD's, AK's and the like. We, B Coy 3RAR (3:1 Inf Bn), were performing our duty as ordered by HQ 3 Bde but this group of 'magandanga' had their own ill-considered arrangements' in mind.

No RAR man ever ran from a joust. Why? Because we were committed, we were disciplined, proud of our heritage, we were very highly respected, and we were part of an honourable body of men however...'yank our chain' in the wrong direction and aggression would be your just reward. These 'magandanga' had presumed too much of their own importance. I walked over to this rabble to order them away from the area and was greeted with a beery response laced with invective and exaggerated aggression.

Without warning or prompt, CSM Chimuti MLM, a man of some fearsome physical stature and deportment, strode over and issued the gook with the biggest mouth a slap that would have made George Foreman proud. His lights were out, and CSM Chimuti ordered the remainder to surrender their weapons and summarily placed them under close arrest. It was a magnificent thing to behold! There was the formal method of sorting out errant soldiers (Orders) and there was the CSM's way. It worked a dream. A short while later, the CO of 3:1 arrived, I briefed him, and he ordered his men be taken to their guardroom. That gave me some comfort.

A Rhodesian Army MAP 7.5 TCV was designed to carry a section strength of infantry (+-13 men) depending on Company ORBAT. On this day, there had been 15 members of 3:1 Inf Bn and 7 AMA and AFA civilians; apart from the driver, all had been standing. Seven survived with serious injuries (3 died later) and the rest were dead at the scene; 'guillotined' by 3:1 Infantry Battalion.

Once again, the RAR stood proud and none more so than our Company Medic, Corporal Tinarwo, who is deserving of honour and respect for his duty that day. I recall it with incredible clarity; perhaps that is my penance? Those horrific sights, the sounds and smells but knowing that the RAR stood tall and delivered, that is my reward.

Just another day with a bit of a twist. It was a hell-of-a life...if you didn't weaken.

MY MILITARY CAREER COMES TO AN END by Major Gavin Rawstron

End of November 1980 saw me doing weekend Duty Officer as Brigade Major 3 Bde Umtali whilst Brigadier Dick Tilley and Deputy Col Hank Meyer spent the weekend on R&R in Salisbury.

On Saturday evening, whilst doing my rounds around Bde HQ before heading off to my room for the night, I heard a commotion from the signals room and, upon investigating, found one of the ZANLA Commanders completely 'out of his tree' with most of the signallers with drinks in hand. (Both ZANLA and ZIPRA had command elements attached to Brigades, who were given the temp rank of Lt. Col but wore the epaulettes of Officer Cadet).

I called him aside and asked him his story, upon which he became physical and aggressive, threatening to kill me as he took out his Tokarev. As the signallers were in no state themselves and how quickly the situation had turned, I told him that he would be charged and walked away, followed by him swearing and shouting abuse and insinuating that I would not see the following day. I fully expected a shot to ring out at any time and thought for a moment "is this how it ends?"

It didn't come but I could hear shouting and screaming for some time after. After trying to contact MP's, RP's and the Police without success, I managed to get hold of ZANLA HQ in Umtali and reported the matter. Within minutes, they were there and apprehended the culprit. I never saw him again.

I briefed Brigadier Tilley on his return the following Monday and advised him that I had charged the individual accordingly. This was reported to Army HQ and Comops.

That evening, Brigadier Tilley received an instruction for me to drop the charges, which we discussed. On principal, we thought that if this was the case, it would open a precedent that was contrary to everything we had stood for in our military careers. Brigadier Tilley was then threatened that unless charges were dropped, he stood the chance of losing his pension and everything else.

Brigadier Tilley said the decision was mine and that he would stand by whatever decision I made. As I was not prepared for him to put his head on the block, I dropped charges!

I realised then, that my and even our careers in the Military as I knew it, were over. For a Brigadier to put everything he stood for on the line and back a subordinate at the risk of losing everything, spoke volumes of the type of commanders we served under. Brigadier Tilley Sir, I will not forget that sacrifice.

My resignation followed, and my military career ended 31 December 1980.

CONNEMARA MUTINY by Captain Andrew Telfer

Parts of this story appeared in *Chibaya Moyo 1* but it is now possible to complete the picture and improve the historical record of the 1981 ZIPRA mutiny at Connemara Barracks. Two encounters have made that possible. The first was with Brigadier Vic Walker at the unveiling of the RAR Memorial in July 2015 and the second was with Lieutenant Colonel Ken Johnstone BCR in 2018 in New Zealand. Both officers had played pivotal roles in the affair, Brigadier Walker as Commander 4 Brigade and the (then) Major Johnstone as his Brigade Major (later promoted to Lieutenant Colonel during his service with the SANDF).

While Adjutant 2RAR in late 1980, a signal arrived to tell me that I was to attend a Combat Team Commanders' Course at the School of Infantry. I didn't know it then but that meant the end of my service with the RAR because, when the course finished, I was told that I was to remain at the School of Infantry to run a course for ex-terrorists. This was one of the first steps in the creation of the new Zimbabwe National Army through the integration of the former Rhodesian Army, ZIPRA and ZANLA.

Janette and I were married in Kariba in January 1981 and had, by then, decided to leave Zimbabwe, as had many white members of the Security Forces. From inside the Army, we could see the nature of the individuals being placed in positions of command and it was obvious that the entire structure was going to collapse. The end of responsible government in responsible hands was happening.

It takes three months to leave the Army and, beforehand, I had a course to run. This was to be the first of its kind ever: ten men would be selected from each of the three former enemy forces, men who had distinguished themselves in the eyes of their comrades during the war. The idea was, that if they could be integrated, others would see it and be more ready to follow suit. From the RAR, they were senior NCOs and WOs. From ZANLA and ZIPRA, they were selected from commanders and commissars of operational terrorist gangs. All were black.

I was the course officer, and my task was to train them to be infantry officers. On completion, the RAR members would return to their battalions while the ZIPRA and ZANLA graduates were to become the junior officers of 41 Infantry Battalion, a new battalion comprising cadres drawn equally from their two factions, to be based at Connemara Barracks, a former mine and prison on the main Gwelo-Salisbury road. Concurrently, Tactical Wing was running a course for those who had held more senior terrorist positions. They would populate the command appointments of the new battalion, with a 50/50 balance of ZANLA and ZIPRA, throughout.

On the first day, I found that the students had pulled their desks apart from one another in the lecture room. There was no love lost even between the two terrorist groups, let alone between them and the ex-RAR soldiers. One, from 1RAR, had had every single member of his extended family murdered by terrorists in an attack on his home village. When I walked in, ten RAR soldiers sat smartly to attention, beaming at me, while the other two groups slouched, regarding me with undisguised hostility.

At the outset, I hated the terrorists and the air they breathed but I was a professional with a job to do and, importantly, I was very conscious that the black former Rhodesian Army soldiers were soon to be left without us. They had nowhere to go and this course at least was an opportunity to place them in the officer corps of the new Zimbabwe National Army.

Human nature is strange and unpredictable. You cannot run a course like that without getting to know each other as individual human beings and, once that happens, the purity of enmity is affected. As the weeks passed, hostility was replaced by a formal command relationship. I taught and exercised them properly, hardly believing myself for training them but doing it to the best of my ability. They responded well and were very soon acting just like any student on any course.

They respected their course officer, wanted to learn and to gain recognition, wanted to emulate. They avoided talking about our war, as did I, but wanted to tell me stories about their training, especially those who had been overseas. It was always edgy though. One showed me a photo of him with his East German girlfriend, muffled against the cold in a street somewhere, her blondness a trophy.

There were one or two unusual moments that would not have occurred on a normal course. On a patrols exercise, we heard firing in the distance. The ex-RAR soldiers were relaxed, knowing this was an exercise, but the others were immediately tense, swinging around to look at me, their faces tight with suspicion. They of course had spent years in the bush, never in an exercise scenario, their lives depending on a quick reaction to warning signs like this. There was also an essay, in which I told them to write about the person they most admired (I wanted to assess English literacy).

To a man and without discussion, the ex-ZANLA terrorists wrote about Josiah Tongogara, their former commander who had died in a 'car crash' just before Independence, making way for Rex Nhongo to take over. The rumour was that he could have challenged Mugabe for power and had been assassinated, and the veneration evident in their essays certainly supported that theory.

When I ran them as a squad, the ex-ZANLA group stamped their feet on every fourth step. It created a good rhythm and we adopted it, as you do.

"Where does it come from?" I asked.

"Libya, ishe. It's their commando march" they replied. Libya! It was amazing how so many countries had lined up to help these terrorists against one small community, isolated by sanctions from the Western bloc and besieged in proxy by half the states of the Eastern and Middle Eastern world.

In the end, the course was pronounced a success and was the model upon which subsequent courses were based. The RAR soldiers returned to their battalions as commissioned officers, with my blessings and friendship. The ZANLA and ZIPRA newly commissioned officers were linked up with the batch of senior officers from the higher-level course and sent to populate the command appointments of 41 Infantry Battalion at Connemara Barracks.

It's worth pausing to think about that. The Army had created a new battalion of about 600 men, much less than an RAR battalion but still a potent force. It was made up equally of ZANLA and ZIPRA, factions loyal to different political leaders, known to be hostile to each other and with different tribal roots. The command positions were given to two groups of recent course graduates who were expected to get on with running an independent military unit.

In February 1981, about two weeks after 41 Battalion was formed, we heard that the ZIPRA faction had manipulated the guard roster so that one dark night they were all on duty together. They seized the armoury and the magazine, and shot up the ZANLA contingent, with the survivors fleeing for their lives into the bush. Our ZIPRA colleagues in the new Zimbabwe National Army were now manning a road block on the main Salisbury road, happily robbing passing motorists.

Brigadier Vic Walker (Commander 4 Brigade) and Major Ken Johnstone BCR, arrived at the School of Infantry, as did 'A' Company of 42 Inf Bn (formerly 2RAR), under the command of its 2ic, newly-promoted Captain Kay Mudzingwa. What happened next was bizarre. I was standing in a circle of officers on the verandah of Tactical Wing listening to the Brigadier describe the new government's anger at the turn of events and its order that the mutiny be put down. I knew Brigadier Walker, as both 2RAR and HQ 4 Brigade were in Fort Victoria. Suddenly, he looked at me and told me that I was to prepare to command the operation. At the time, it came as a complete surprise and I had the impression it wasn't planned.

In 2015, at the braai in Alrewas before the RAR Memorial Unveiling in the UK, I asked Brigadier Walker about it:

He explained that he had requested a company from 42 Inf Bn but, for operational security reasons, had not been able to specify the task and had been disappointed when it turned up under its 2ic, reminding me that Kay Mudzingwa was not an experienced commander. Encountering me at the School of Infantry, a more experienced officer from the same battalion, was a solution to his problem. He also corrected my memory of the role of (then) Major Ken Johnstone, telling me that he was his Brigade Major at that time, not a photographic interpretation officer, as I had recalled him. The Brigadier made a point of telling me that Major Johnstone had done exceptionally well during the Connemara affair.

Returning to the School of Infantry in 1981: Brigadier Walker took me aside and told me that he intended to take Lookout Masuku, the former commander of ZIPRA and now a General, into the camp to order the mutineers to lay down their arms. If they refused, he would leave the camp with Masuku, give me a code word over VHF radio, upon which I should attack the barracks, killing or capturing the ZIPRA mutineers. In addition to 'A' Company, he attached elements of the School of Infantry Demonstration Company, NCOs from a mortar course being conducted by Regimental Wing at the time, and air support from RhAF Thornhill. He closed by telling me that I must not carry out a target recce as Masuku was not being told of the potential attack. There would be air photos delivered to me that night.

Janette and I had temporarily moved into a small duplex in town, our first married home. During that night, there was a knock on the door. I turned on a table lamp in the living area and opened the door to Major Johnstone. He had air photos of Connemara Barracks, north-oriented and marked with ruled lines creating 50 x 50 metre grid squares. He briefed me on the features of the camp and showed how the grid pattern was annotated, enabling each square to be referenced. They were extremely helpful.

The next day, I carried out a map and photo recce, and an appreciation and plan, and went to see the Air Force at Thornhill. They were as happy as I was at the opportunity to have another crack. The basic plan was to put a Hunter 'up on a perch' (circling near a known initiating point, in this case above Gwenora Dam wall) from which the pilot could calculate the flight path to attack another known point (in this case, part of the camp, referenced from the air photo). Having just been addressed by Masuku, the enemy would of course be concentrated in one place and the Hunter would be able to hit that point exactly, delivering its strike before they even heard it coming.

Concurrently, my cordon of RAR troops would close in to stop the break-out and then sweep through the camp. The mortars would be in direct support to hit pockets of resistance that I would indicate using the air photo grid references. The Blues liked it and asked only one question: "Andy, didn't you just train these guys?"

"Unfortunately, yes. If they put in a battle drill, it's because I taught them how to do it." We shook our heads at the craziness but were buzzing with the opportunity to return to our true identity.

Later, when I gave orders to the ground troops, I returned to wearing my RAR colours.

The attack never happened. Very recently, I met up again with (now) Lt Col Ken Johnstone BCR and he explained what had happened:

'Brigadier Walker and I drove from Gwelo to the turn off to Connemara Barracks where we were met with hostilities. They fired shots over the vehicle, so we turned around and returned to Gwelo.

'Over the next 36 hours, a plan was put into motion and, because of my previous experience with Joint Services Photographic Interpretation Section, I ordered air photos from Lieutenant Heather Smith which were delivered by air from Salisbury. The attack plan was developed and, once everything was underway, we returned to Connemara in an armoured personnel carrier, this time with General Lookout Masuku, a signaller, a driver and two escorts for protection.

'We arrived at the turn off to Connemara, again came under fire and the vehicle stopped. A stalemate occurred and I said to the Brigadier that if we didn't talk to these guys, we were never going to get in. There was a deathly silence in the APC. Before Walker could stop me, I took off my webbing, left my weapon, and leapt out of the back of the vehicle. I went around the left-hand side and ran into the middle of the road, opposite a small store.

'I immediately came under fire from the direction of the store on the right-hand side of the road and from the top of a kopje on the left-hand side. The whole road around me erupted in strikes hitting the tarmac. At the top of my voice, I shouted "Stop firing! Can't you see that I'm unarmed? I want to speak to whoever is in charge." Suddenly, everything was silent, deathly quiet, no birds chirping, absolute silence.

'About a minute later, that seemed like an eternity, the leader of the group came out and I spoke to him in the middle of the road. I introduced myself and told him that he was immediately to go back to the barracks and, if he didn't comply, that the aircraft they feared so much during the war (Hunters) would be called in and Connemara would be obliterated. I told him they were minutes away, ready to come.

'Literally ten minutes later, all the people in the immediate vicinity assembled and went back on foot towards the barracks. We then drove into the barracks where the Brigadier and Lookout Masuku spoke to the assembled group (a lot of them appeared to be missing). Everything was calmed down and they returned their weapons to the Armoury (many weapons seemed to have disappeared and possibly cached). We returned to Gwelo and the attack operation was cancelled."

After nearly four decades, this account explained to me why the attack had been called off. Ken Johnstone's brave action had stabilised the situation and made it possible for it to be defused.

Afterwards, I was ordered to go to a school in the TTL to meet up with the ZANLA contingent who had re-grouped there after fleeing the mutiny. I was to tell them to remain there while arrangements were made to feed them and to return them to Gwelo. The main point was to dissuade them from going back to their old ways in the bush. As the ex-course officer of the middle-ranking officers, it was assumed I would have some sway so, in the ongoing madness, my role now changed to diplomat.

I took two 2.5 tonne Unimogs with soldiers from the RAR Demonstration Company and off we went. The school was long since abandoned and the presence of several hundred ex-terrorists hadn't enhanced it much. They gathered around our vehicles and I was pleased to see that they weren't armed – they'd had no chance to be, having fled at haste from ZIPRA's 'night of the long knives'. As I entered the room where the officers were sitting, acting on impulse, I took off the webbing belt that held my pistol and put it on a table behind me, out of my sight and beyond my reach while I was seated. God knows what instinct inspired it but that simple act relaxed the whole room. They were friendly, receptive and grateful to me for coming. They agreed to do what I had been sent to ask them and we parted on good terms.

Ken Johnstone takes up the story:

'About a week later, I was ordered to Army HQ to see General MacLean. When I got there, I went to see him, and he thanked me for arriving so quickly. He said that Generals Masuku and Nhongo had a job for me. I asked him what it was, and he said they would explain what was required. I went into the conference room and three-quarters of an hour later they came and briefed me. I was to go to Gwelo and interview every single member of 41 Bn to determine who should stay and who should be discharged from the Zimbabwe National Army. I asked why I was selected to do that job and they said that all the members of 41 Bn respected what I did and that, because of that, I was the ideal man for the job. I said I cannot do that because it would be a kangaroo court and I didn't want to spend the rest of my life in Zimbabwe looking over my shoulder and I had a young family I needed to protect.

'I left the conference room and met General MacLean in the passage and told him that I wasn't prepared to do the job. He told me that I would do it and that I was to go back and thrash out a plan and sequence of events with Masuku and Nhongo. I went back in and told then I'd do it on condition that

I had a ZIPRA and a ZANLA staff officer (Colonel equivalents) with me who would sign every single document relating to the future employment of the soldiers. They assured me that should anything happen to me or my family in the future, the culprit would be instantaneously dealt with.

'I first returned to Fort Victoria and then went to Gwelo where I established an office at 10RR. There, I interviewed every single member of 41 Bn, asking one question: "Why did you leave your base without permission?" If they could not provide a satisfactory answer, they were dismissed from the ZNA, all documented. Those that had returned their weapons and controlled stores, went back to Connemara, collected their personal belongings, received their final pay and were discharged. Those that couldn't tell me where their weapons were or prove that they had returned them, were marched out into a Police van and were held in Police custody until their weapons were recovered.

'This applied equally to ZIPRA and ZANLA personnel and somewhere between 300 to 400 were discharged. There wasn't a single complaint from either of the ZIPRA or ZANLA staff officers. The only complaint came from the Police Area Commander about me filling up his jail.

'Resulting from this whole thing, about two weeks later, after a morning meeting, I returned to my office at Bde HQ in Fort Victoria and found former-ZANLA senior staff officer (Colonel) Perence Shiri reclined in my chair with his feet on my desk, eyes blood shot from drink and possibly drugs, reading a *Scope* magazine. He deliberately lowered the magazine and said "You are a cheeky white bastard. Who do you think you are, firing my soldiers?" He got up and, from the ground, swung his fist and knocked me out cold. I came to as Colonel Ian Pullar walked past my door and said "Ken, what's the matter?" I told him the story and, between he and Brigadier Walker, put Shiri into room arrest. By mid-afternoon, an aircraft arrived and took him away.'

Perence Shiri was sent on Staff Course to Tanzania and later promoted to Brigadier and appointed Commander 5 Brigade, made up of solely ex-ZANLA troops. He led the Gukurahundi genocide in Matabeleland (1983—1985), during which troops under his command tortured, raped and murdered tens of thousands of black Zimbabwean civilians of Ndebele ethnicity. In 1992 he was appointed Commander of the Zimbabwe Air Force with the rank of Air Marshall, raised to Air Chief Marshall on retirement in 2017, and is now Minister of Lands, Agriculture and Rural Resettlement in the Zimbabwe Cabinet.

In stark contrast to the savagery of Shiri, Ken Johnstone personified the professionalism of the Rhodesian Army, both in the courage that he displayed at

Connemara and the by-the-book administration of the post-event Enquiry he conducted at Gwelo. We had remained professional until the end but for us the war was over.

In March 1981, the time finally came to leave the Army and a Dining Out Night was held at the School of Infantry, now renamed the Zimbabwe Military Academy. Under a single spotlight, a lone RAR bugler played the Last Post, used to signal the end of the day. A thousand emotions welled up inside me. I was still young, only 26 years old and married to a wonderful girl, but I was about to leave the career and the country that I loved. As a soldier of Rhodesia, I had done my best and I regret nothing. I thanked God and asked him to bless this wonderful people, as I still do, wherever they are.

I SIT BESIDE THE FIRE AND THINK by Captain Russell Fulton

I sit beside the fire and think
Of wonders I have seen,
Of river glades and mopani flies
In summers that have been.

I sit beside the fire and think
Of people long ago,
Of people who won't see a world
That only we will know.

I sit beside the fire and think
About the chatter of Commie guns,
Roaring in unfriendly tones,
Raining death on everyone.

I sit beside the fire and think
Of good men brave and true,
Who wore the Green and Black like me
Proud and arrogant, dutiful and free.

I sit beside the fire and think
Of *Masodja* young and old,
And shed a tear in solitude
In stoic rectitude.

I sit beside the fire and think
Of all I've seen and done,
And ask myself the question,
What was it all about,
When all is said and done?

I sit beside the fire and think
About many infectious smiles,
The faces of good and innocent men
I will never see again.

I sit beside the fire and think
How proud and privileged was I,
To share but a single day
In the lives of those who died.

I sit beside the fire and think
What I'll do to honour good men,
Whatever I can my friends
For you were gallant men.

THE ORIGINAL PAINTING by Captain Russell Fulton

This watercolour painting was the original concept for *Chibaya Moyo* that Andy and I co-authored. It was changed to what most of you will have seen and that I also painted.

Every scene in this painting represents one or several anecdotes contained within the first edition. The following explains why it is presented thus. Central are "The Antipodeans", me on the left in scarlet Mess Kit and right is Andy in army Number 1's, our formal parade uniform. Andy is wearing the medals he was awarded, the first being irrelevant, the Zimbabwe Independence Medal. (It is the only medal ever awarded to opposing forces engaged in military conflict, so it is somewhat unique from that perspective).

The middle medal is the Silver Cross of Rhodesia awarded for an act/or acts of conspicuous gallantry in action (Andy's citation reads like a script for an Oliver Stone movie). To the right of the SCR is the RhGSM but of importance is the 'pick device' on the medal ribbon. This is the Military Forces Commendation; the pick device is silver denoting that it was awarded for an act/acts of gallantry on operations.

CHIBAYA MOYO 2

The embellishments on both uniforms are those of the RAR with whom we both proudly served. Andy in 2RAR and me in 1RAR. The only reason our characters assume the central position on the draft cover was because we co-authored the book; at no time was the concept intended to focus attention on ourselves.

Whilst Andy and I contributed a number of anecdotes to the first and second editions there were numerous other contributors whose time and brilliant contributions have made our books what they are and it was for that reason that we dropped it as the cover for the first edition. The painting now hangs in Andy and Janette Telfer's home.

Behind Andy and I are the Queen's and Regimental Colours of the Rhodesian African Rifles; no single artefact in our regiment is more sacrosanct. Behind me is the Queen's Colour and behind Andy the Regimental Colour. I was the last officer in our regimental history to be the Ensign to this Colour under the former name of our great country, Rhodesia. The date was 1 June 1979 when Rhodesia became Zimbabwe-Rhodesia. I have little to be proud of outside of my service to our country, but this was an honour bestowed upon me for which I am enormously grateful and singularly proud. The gold and silver Colour sashes are tied together behind Andy and me, symbolic of the inseparable bond between those who served our regiment proudly and honourably.

Above and between Andy and me is our regimental crest that represents the service of good men in 1, 2, 3 and Depot RAR including the various Independent Companies who wore our Colours with pride.

Top left, centre and right is a typical Rhodesian bush scene with kopjes, a favourite hiding place for 'gooks' in times of contact with our security forces and, of course, Msasa forests in autumn. An Alouette III from 7 Squadron, the Rhodesian Air Force coming in to off-load a call sign of troops to close with and kill the enemy. Two DC3 Douglas Dakota fill top and right with paratroopers deploying. The scene on the right represents a true incident when elements of D Company, 1RAR were dropped well below the prescribed operational jump height of 500ft. There were eight serious injuries and, tragically, two RAR soldiers would succumb to the injuries they sustained.

Bottom right is a group of RAR *Masodja* returned from deployment and enjoying a 'fodya' (cigarette) together.

Left of the shirtless private soldier is the Number 1 formal headdress of our Regiment, the famed RAR 'bush hat' with ox hair hackle. This is included because of what it represents to every RAR officer and soldier and a great anecdote written by Andy within the first edition entitled 'The General and the RAR Bush Hat'.

Below the bush hat is a pair of officer Jodhpur Boots with a pile of goat turd covering the toe cap of the right boot. An anecdote I wrote for *Chibaya Moyo* and the turd following the unsolicited bowel movement of our Regimental Mascot, LCpl Nduna, who is saluting on bowed forequarters in fawned supplication for his 'sins'.

The regimental drums take position centre bottom and central below the regimental crest atop. Symbols of our regimental history and proudly bearing our five (5) Battle Honours, namely; The Great War, East Africa 1916-1918, Burma 1944-1945, Arakan Beaches and Taungup.

To the left are scenes that represent personal accounts of injury and loss of brave men who fought in Rhodesia's name. Both books contain many accounts, some in graphic detail.

Above this is a PWO (Platoon Warrant Officer), a post above a Sergeant and below a WO2 that was unique to the RAR, with the ubiquitous Rhodef 2.5 command vehicle to the rear. A pair of Hawker Hunter fighters of 1 Squadron Rhodesian Air Force, fly in the early morning light towards a target; once again coming to assist their 'Brown Job' mates on terra firma.

Directly below Andy and I and running left to right is a depiction of our Regimental 'Stable Belt', the green and black that we wore with enormous pride. It is superimposed with the Rhodesian Army crest, 1 Brigade crest (Op Tangent) home of 1RAR and Depot RAR, 4 Brigade crest (Op Repulse) home to 2RAR and 3 Brigade crest (Op Thrasher) home to 3RAR.

THE LAST POST by Captain Keith Adams

E Mail to my family following the unveiling of the RNR/RAR Memorial on 19th July 2015.

My Dearest Family,
I have just had the most wonderful week escorting 6 old African soldiers from my old Regiment who were invited to the UK to take part in the unveiling of the RNR/RAR memorial at the National Memorial Arboretum in Staffordshire. Sadly I didn't have any of you with me to experience the event and meet these six special old Gentlemen, you would have loved them.

I also had the privilege of being in the company of Brigadier Pat Lawless, also an ex RAR officer who left Zims just after Independence for the UK, had a highly successful career in the British Army, initially flying helicopters and then commanding the Army Air Corps. Pat and I had the pleasure and honour of escorting these six Veterans for their weeks visit to the UK which proved to be a hectic, exhausting, hilarious and very emotional and rewarding week.

Pat and I met at Heathrow to meet and collect the Masodja who had left Harare the previous day on Ethiopian Airways, they had been seen off by Rob Anderson and the British Military Attache . They took ages to come through the arrivals gate, while we were nervously awaiting their arrival, who should wander out the gate but another ex RAR officer, an American, Joe Columbus Smith. The re-union had started and we quickly co-opted Joe into the meet and greet team just before our 6 Veterans came through the arrival gate. 3 of them had visited the UK before but the others were pretty wide eyed at the expanse of Heathrow and had no idea of who was meeting them. To my joy one of the Masodja, Gibson Nkala had served with me in B Coy, 1 RAR in '73-'74. I was delighted to see him looking so fit and well.

Pat had hired a mini-van and was the designated driver, once we had all boarded and were heading towards Marble Arch and the Victory Services Club one of older members wide-eyed at the volume of traffic and busyness of London and in the true RAR tradition of giving nicknames to their commanders announced that the mini-bus would be called the "Mutambalawless Bus Service". Pat deposited us at the Victory Services Club where we were met by Brigadier David Heppenstall, my 1RAR Commanding Officer and a member of the RAR, Regimental Association involved in organising the week's events. David treated us to a quick lunch issued us with our pocket money (£50) for the week and then the fun started.

David escorted our party, myself and the six Veterans to a Primark clothing outlet a short walk from the club. You have to bear in mind that I had the responsibility of looking after our merry band of octogenarians who varied considerably in their state of mobility, vision and hearing and my duty was not merely to escort them but to consider their welfare, security and entertainment. The fun was about to begin!

Gibby Mugadza, (aka K Car) an ex RSM, recipient of the BCR and footballer of note now has mobility issues and can't walk too far without a break.

Pisayi Muzerecho an ex CSM and recipient of the MM in Malaya, 89 years old, bright as a button but has failing eye sight.

Obert Veremu an ex RSM, quiet with a wealth of military experience but sadly not too agile anymore.

Gibson Nkala retired as a Major, a devout Christian, still as fit as a fiddle and always immaculately turned out as he was when he was an army instructor.

Joseph Nyagumbo, also retired as a Major, a little overcome by the scale of what they were embarking on but with a wealth of military experience and the scars to prove it.

Tobias Mutangadura, also a retired Major, the scholar who spent most of his career as a teacher attached to RAR. He is well travelled having been to the UK a couple of times so I wasn't too worried about losing him.

We were hoping to kit out the Veterans in a semblance of uniform, blazers, shirts, trousers and shoes all matching. After an eventful walk down the street, I nearly lost Gibby N, while waiting for Gibby M, had to haul Pisayi of the road after he nearly walked into a taxi, we eventually we arrived at Primark. David lead the way but Primark was full of barging, pushing and shoving customers and I knew instantly that the shopping spree with my charges was going to be testing or hilarious dependant on what stance I took. It was hilarious and started with Pisayi and his failing eye sight, we were riding the escalator upstairs when his ride came to an abrupt end and he staggered off the escalator and almost collided with a buxom mannequin clad in skimpy underwear, about to apologies profusely to the lady he suddenly realised there was no need and scuttled off to the safety of the men's department much to our amusement. They then started shopping in earnest and again great hilarity, the selection was huge and it was not long before David had to round them all up and in true military fashion stated that they were not on a fashion parade and that purple trousers with a gold fleck and shoes with a buckle and 10 inch point were not becoming of Officers and Gentlemen!! We eventually had everyone kitted out but not with trousers, that was to be another interesting encounter, and all handed over their purchases of Navy blue blazers and 2 white shirts to David who had now relinquished his role of QM to that of Paymaster. Once all was paid for we evacuated the store much to the relief of the floor manager, David departed to the station and we returned to the club for a much deserved break, don't forget these old Masodja had been on the move for over 24 hours with very little if any sleep, however before they departed to their rooms I handed out their recent purchases of blazers and white shirts only to discover there was one extra blazer in the package. I checked the invoice and sure enough seven blazers not six had been purchased, I checked the size and wasn't surprised to see it was Pisayi's blazer. Much amusement and a comment from the ex- footballer, Pisayi 1, Brigadier Heppenstall 0. Old soldiers know all the tricks!!

They had to share rooms and unfortunately they were spread all over the club and on different floors which while it wasn't a huge problem it did split us up a little which wasn't ideal. The rooms were not en-suite either which meant they had to go quite a way to the ablutions again not ideal. I managed to talk the manager into allocating us en-suite rooms when we returned on the following Monday and to get us all on the same floor which they did for a slight increase in cost, but it was worth it.

We all met after a well-deserved rest for drinks and an early supper. Joe Columbus Smith who was also staying at the club joined us and quickly volunteered to help me. While Joe and I didn't serve in the RAR at the same time we both served in B Coy, 1RAR as did Gibson Nkala, amazing that after all these years there were the three of us together in London sharing another experience. The day ended with one final amusing incident bought on once again by our diminutive ex CSM from Mazarabani. Pisayi bade us all goodnight and despite suggestions that he may need help finding his room he made his exit unaided.... 15 minutes later he reappeared to questions of what the problem was only to answer, " No problem I was just doing a clearance patrol to ensure all was safe," upon with much hilarity we all joined him and retired.

Friday morning was to start with us all meeting for breakfast however I realised that I hadn't explained or demonstrated to our Veterans where to find the tea for their early morning cuppa. Gibby M and Obert the ex RSM's were a few doors down from me so I knocked on their door to enquire if they had managed to find the tea. A humbling sight confronted me, there sitting on their beds in their underpants and chatting away were these two old soldiers both with obvious war wounds, Obert with scars on his upper arm and Gibby M with scars on his lower back, both had been wounded in action, both highly respected members of our Regiment. They hadn't found the tea and were grateful to have me make them a quick brew.

Next call breakfast, all appeared to have slept well and were pretty ravenous after their long travels, breakfast was a la carte so leant itself to stocking up for the day. Not surprisingly our diminutive Malayan veteran headed up the queue armed with the largest plate on offer and proceeded to load up his plate, fried bread, fagga, fried eggs two, fagga, tomato ne beans, fagga, chi ?, scrambled egg 1 spoon, hash brown, fagga, bacon two pieces ne sausage two, black pudding, aiwa! It was hilarious virtually every head in the dining room turned to see Pisayi with his over laden plate making his way back to the table and devouring every scrap he had served up. Breakfast understandably took a little longer than anticipated but we had time on our hands before Pat returned with the mini-bus to take us on the next leg of our journey so Joe entertained the two RSM's at the Club while I took a walk with the remaining four to do a bit of site seeing, shopping and a visit to Specsavers to have Pisayi and Josephs eyes tested.

Shame, this was a big let-down for Pisayi he was rather hoping for a quick fix and possibly new glasses but the optician advised him that he had cataracts in both eyes and would require an operation to rectify the problem before new glasses could be prescribed. While feeling let down he accepted that there was not a quick fix solution but I assured him we would pursue getting him medical assistance when he returned to Zimbabwe. Josephs appointment fared a little better and we were soon choosing glasses and much to my and my credit card's relief I managed to convince him that the designer glasses, a bit like the 10inch pointy shoes he was keen on weren't becoming of an officer and gentleman! Sadly his glasses had to be made up and would only be ready for collection after he had returned to Zim. Not to be deterred we managed to hatch a plan to get his glasses to him via the Mutangadura family who were staying over for a little longer much to Joseph's relief.

The visit to Specsavers was another humbling experience for me not only because we were able to assist two of the group but it gave me a little one on one time with them to sit and chat while the appointments were going on. We chatted about the situation in Zim and difficulties facing them and their families but it was the lack of contact with their old comrades that saddened them and the question of who was going to record and tell the stories of their service and exploits to their grandchildren.

We booked out of the Club bade farewell to Joe and welcomed Douglas Veremu, Obert's son who resides in the UK, into our party and immediately gave him the task of piloting Gibby M's wheelchair which Pat had recently acquired to assist in getting Gibby M a little more mobile. This also resulted in another nickname being penned, " K Car" because Gibby M had the habit of sticking his stout walking stick/knobkerrie out the side of the wheelchair resembling a 20mm canon and giving unsuspecting pedestrians and jay walkers a gentle prod to let them know he was about. We boarded the "Mutambalawless" mini-bus en route for a Marks and Spencer outlet in High Wycombe with Pat giving us a guided tour of inner London and an example of his expertise and the similarity of flying an Apache helicopter at low level and navigating the "Mutambalawless" mini-bus.

When we arrived at the M&S outlet, I issued strict instructions that we were on a very tight schedule and the only reason we were stopping here was because we had failed to find suitable trousers at Primark, besides M&S was far more up market and suitable for the attire of Officers and Gentlemen and that they were limited to either grey or charcoal "kabdulas". We were greeted by a rather camp floor manager, reminiscent of the salesman in that comedy series, "Are you being served". I could see it was going to be an interesting visit and had the makings of a brand new comedy series! I explained the urgency of our visit and the need to kit everyone out in similar trousers where upon he ushered us to the racks of charcoal trousers, whipped his tape measure off from around his neck and asked the bulky ex RSM to raise his arms for a waist measurement. I watched with interest and realised that the remainder of the party were also taking a keen interest in proceedings however nothing untoward occurred and the floor manager quickly produced the correct size to be tried on. He had soon carried out all but one of the measurements being that of Pisayi who had wondered off and was once again eyeing out the purple trousers with a gold fleck!

Pisayi was wearing his trench coat and had been wearing it since he left Mazarabani two days previously, don't forget it was the middle of winter in Zim … well when Pisayi was asked to raise his arms for his waist measurement the dear little floor manager nearly expired when exposed to Pisayi's Mazarabani cologne and was last seen with a little perfume canister puffing it over his head. We departed in haste with our purchases and decided it best not to involve the floor manager in any further discussion.

Our next leg was a 2 hour drive down the motorway towards Lichfield where we were to meet up with Malcom Clewer, Chairman of our RAR Regimental Association. The drive was uneventful most catching a quick forty winks however Tobias, the scholar, was up front with Pat and myself chatting away on various subjects when he suddenly announced that he thought the braai we were planning for Saturday night would have to be cancelled! Pat and I were a bit taken back because it was hoped it would be a well-attended and grand occasion and give many the opportunity to meet the visiting Masodja whereupon Tobias stated that his suggestion to cancel was based on the fact that we had been travelling down a motorway for almost two hours and he had not seen a single mombe… you can't have a braai without beef… to which there were mumbles of agreement from the rear of the bus. We assured them all was in hand and sadza was also on the menu.

We arrived in Litchfield a little behind schedule and were enthusiastically welcomed by Malcom and David Heppenstall. The Masodja were all booked into the same hotel as Malcom and David so we settled our charges into their rooms and then all met in the pub for not only a well-earned drink but also the start of what was to be a wonderful few days of reminiscing, renewing friendships and forging new friendships. There was already quite a gathering, Russell Fulton and Andy Telfer both ex RAR Officers from my era now living in Aus and New Zealand and who had co-edited a recently published anthology of short stories of life and experiences in the RAR titled "Chibaya Muyo", Brigadier Digger Essex Clark, also living in Aus served with the RAR in the 50's and was in fact Pisayi's Platoon commander in Malaya, Bill Liversidge who also commanded 6 Platoon, 1 RAR, my old Platoon and also sits on the Committee and of course most importantly the wives who were patiently listening to all the banter and nonsense from many years ago.

We were joined by the Masodja a short while later and the initial quiet and reserved greetings soon gave way to raucous greetings and laughter with much back slapping when Pisayi and Digger met each other. It was a joy to witness and to be able to take a bit of a back seat and watch the interaction between everyone and hear the recounting of tales of days served in the Regiment. A few drinks later, a light supper then we, Pat and I, left our charges in the care of Malcom and David and escorted Digger and his friend John du Bois back to their hotel before making a welcome and fairly weary break for our hotel in the next door town only to be greeted, whilst booking in, by our antipodean mates, Bill, their long suffering wives and Andy's sister and her hubby. More stories, more beer and eventually off to bed only to discover that my room was opposite the local night club and it was a Friday night! Not only that but the street sweepers got active at 6 am to clear the streets of the revellers rubbish!

Saturday morning and meeting for a very sociable and friendly RAR breakfast with our fellow officers and their wives soon got me out of my grumpy old git mode before Pat and I departed for Lichfield to uplift the Masodja and proceed to the next door town Alrewas and the National Memorial Arboretum (NMA). The NMA, in a nutshell, is about 30+ acres in size and is centred around a huge monument to honour and remember all British Servicemen lost in action after the Second World War. The NMA is home to hundreds of monuments representing all sorts of units and organisations both military and civilian to honour those that perished while serving. The RAR Regimental Association applied to the NMA to have a monument erected in Remembrance of those lost in action whilst serving in the RNR (First World War) and RAR (Second World War to 1980) because the original monument in Zimbabwe was destroyed and desecrated. Approval was given by the NMA to build the monument, funds were raised and the Memorial was built in a corner of the Arboretum that has been set aside for Rhodesia and Nyasaland. The grand unveiling ceremony took place on 19th July 2015 and was the reason we and our six RAR veterans from Zimbabwe were all here.

Today's gathering was for a number of reasons, to hold the final committee meeting prior to the unveiling ceremony, to have an informal gathering of ex RAR members, their families and guests and to allow the 6 Veterans to view the Monument and pay their respects without the pressure of the crowds. After yet another raucous and emotional gathering of old soldiers we all then dispersed to take part in our meetings. Andy and Russell took over our charges and took them off to view our recently completed Memorial which by all accounts was an emotionally charged visit. Pat and I joined the committee and a couple of invited participants for the meeting chaired by Malcom Clewer. This was the first sit down meeting that the committee had, all previous meetings were conducted as tele conferences and today we were including Tony Lee our padre and Andy McNeil who through contacts and loop holes only known to him managed to organise 2 Helicopters from the Dutch Airforce to give us a fly-past after the Memorial was dedicated. Our meeting got off to a good start but there appeared to be one or two changes to the agreed programme… it was the only time in our hectic week that I saw Pat get a little agitated and give an impression a hand grenade that was about to explode however with admirable control he calmly reminded all of what had been agreed and minuted and suggested we stick to that! Job done meeting over and we all wondered off to view our Monument for the first time which again was a very emotional experience particularly for General Mike Shute who had chaired the fund raising committee. It had been a long and in the end tight schedule for those involved to get the Monument completed but the end result was certainly testimony to their efforts.

On the move again, Pat and I take over our escort duties once again and return the Veterans to their hotel for a spot of lunch and a break. We do an about turn and head back to Alrewas to meet up with John Hopkins and Mike Jones and family and at the Royal British Legion Club the venue for tonight's braai and reunion. Mike and John both served in 1RAR, John now a highly accomplished artist and Mike a farmer and master organiser of braai's and manufacturer of boerewors. Tobias had nothing to fear the braai was most definitely going to take place the 30 kg's of homemade wors and half a mombe would make sure of that! John and I assisted the Jones's with laying out the tables etc for the evening's festivities and soon realised that being in Officer Jones's company meant we were not only required to stir large pots of marinating nyama but drink several glasses of beer in the process. Pat being the designated driver had to do yet another about turn to collect Brigadier Digger Essex-Clark or Brigadier "Six O'clock" as he was affectionately known by our Veterans and his friend John du Bois returning a good hour and half later and leaving us to continue reminiscing, mixing and drinking beer.

The evening's entertainment was about to start so Pat and I did yet another about turn, changed shirts on the move and returned to Lichfield to collect our well rested Masodja for the braai. What a wonderful and well attended evening it turned out to be so many recognisable faces but names not always coming to mind. All were in good spirits and voice and I was pleased to see my great buddy and house mate from our bachelor days Keith Spence had made it. Keith a helicopter and Canberra pilot spent many hours ferrying RAR troops around in helicopters and he was to be my room-mate once again, we are sharing a hotel room for the next two nights. Fortunately he has now become a responsible SAA Captain and no longer indulges in raucous, beer fuelled outbursts of days gone but he is now far more refined and partial to fine single malt whisky... well sort of!

The braai thanks to the Jones's was a huge success and it was great to see members from all branches of the Rhodesian forces present. It was also our only chance to get to meet the Dutch helicopter pilots and techs and to present them with a John Hopkins painting of RAR troops exiting an Alouette helicopter. There

715

was also a presentation made to Jennifer Upton, a lady who had carried out a huge amount of work for the Association fund raising for both the Memorial and the welfare of soldiers back in Zim. One of the veterans, Gibson Nkala, who resides near Bulawayo, was given a flame lily brooch by a Bulawayo resident who had been assisting Jenny with welfare cases and asked if he could pass it on to her. Gibby N confidently and in typical instructor fashion gave a short speech and made a flawless presentation to a very emotional Jennifer. Presentations over the party slowed down and we departed for our hotel after dropping off the Masodja who had thoroughly enjoyed the braai and were highly complementary of Officer Jones's sadza ne nyama.

It was just midnight when we got to our hotel, the end of another long day… well not quite as we reached our hotel doors my door was flung open to reveal my "blue job" mukker and namesake with a silly grin on his face and holding a bottle of fine 15 year old Glen Barry in one hand and two glasses and a tea cup in the other. The day ended at 1.30 with us having solved innumerable problems around the world particularly in regards how best to deploy heli-born troops into remote areas and while all this was happening poor Cherril who had just driven down all the way from Hastings was next door lamenting at what a long day and how hard her hubby Pat had been working.

Sunday 19th. Busy day ahead quick shower... oops nearly forgot it's Jane's birthday, quick call to Cape Town and when my room-mate came swinging out the shower I asked if would like to wish her happy birthday, which he did and as he reached for the phone I nonchalantly mentioned, "oh by the way you're on Facetime" resulting in much ducking and diving from my "blue job" mate. I wasn't really on Facetime but the reaction was good to watch.

So began Sunday, after a hearty breakfast and everyone looking extremely smart in blazers, Regimental ties, medals and berets Pat and I departed to collect our Masodja for this very special day. They were anxiously awaiting our arrival and they too looked very much the part in their newly acquired outfits complete with medals and berets except Gibby N who being a devout Jehovah Witness sadly wasn't able to wear any form of insignia, medals or badges. Before boarding the bus Pat gave us all a quick chat on the significance of the day's events the role we all had to play in making it memorable and meaningful not only for ourselves but to all those we were honouring. On arrival at the NMA we had one final inspection and were about to make our entrance when I noticed Pisayi was agitated called me aside stating he had no medals. His medals, including his Military Medal awarded for gallantry during the Malayan campaign had been destroyed many years back. Unbeknown to Pisayi, Digger had organised for replica medals to be made up for Pisayi and there was to be a short ceremony before the main event where Digger would present Pisayi with his medals and pin them to his chest. I couldn't let on that this was to be the case so I un-pinned my medals and lent them to Pisayi. Problem solved and Pisayi entered with a little more of a spring in his step.

We all gathered in a well laid out marquee full of RAR memorabilia, books and paintings with the crowd quickly growing to an estimated 350 participants, it was good to see from all the various types of headgear on display that there was an impressive cross section of guests. Coffee was interrupted by Digger's booming voice calling us all to order and announcing that he would like to make a presentation. Digger sadly is no longer too mobile so from the comfort of his mobility scooter he invited Pisayi to join him as he wished to present his old platoon warrant officer and comrade with a few gifts these being items such as reading glasses, a torch and an impressive wrist watch but the icing on the cake was when Digger stood up and presented Pisayi with his replica medals. Pisayi was overcome with emotion and pride and with tears in their eyes Digger pinned Pisayi's medals to his chest.

We then had a short address from Malcom Clewer our Chairman giving us the outline of the day's programme and this was followed by another equally emotional presentation carried out by General Mike Shute and Russell Fulton when they presented Gibson Mugadza aka K Car with a replica of his Bronze Cross. The pride and comradeship between them was a pleasure to witness and Gibby's huge chest was puffed out by a few more inches as we all made our way to our memorial for the unveiling and dedication service.

The service conducted by Tony Lee took place at the Memorial and was a dedication and unveiling ceremony. Tony planned the service to include members from the Regiment in the reading of lessons and exhortations, which was great because it included Tobias Mutangadura, whose grandson was in the congregation, undertaking the one reading, Joseph Nyagumbo lowering the Regimental flag during the sounding of the last post and Pisayi was to receive and fold the Regimental flag when Lord Salisbury, the patron of the RAR, unveiled the dedication plaque on the Monument. Well it was all going according to plan until Lord Salisbury's address… I understood he was going to unveil the plaque at the end of his address so just before he ended his address I guided Pisayi up to and next to Tony and behind Lord Salisbury. Tony gave me a strange look as Lord Salisbury ended his address and returned to his seat without removing the Regimental flag covering the plaque, I stood in panic and Pisayi looked totally confused so I whispered in his ear, "Take the far corner of the flag and donsa. I will fold it" which to the astonishment of those in the know we did while the bulk of the congregation were oblivious to the fact that we were completely out of sequence and in fact Lord Salisbury was due to visit the latter in the programme to unveil the plaque…Oops. Tony in his normal unflappable manner continued the service without a blink or further hitch and retrospectively I believe it wasn't a bad thing that our Memorial was unveiled by CSM Pisayi Muzerecho, MM and not Lord Salisbury, the Marquis of Hatfield.

The service ended with a fly past by two Dutch helicopters which certainly gave a befitting end to the service, the Dutch pilots and Andy McNeil, instrumental in inviting them, did us proud and there were a few tears shed when they clattered overhead at the end of the service. The service over the crowds gathered around the Monument with once again much back slapping and hand shaking of recognition of mates from many years ago and slowly the crowd dissipated with those staying for lunch heading back to the marquee and the others making their way home. Lunch was a grand affair interspersed with addresses by Malcom Clewer and David Heppenstall. The Masodja were temporarily out of our care in that they were now afforded VIP status and were seated with the Lords, Ladies and Generals on the top tables while I joined my mate Keith Spence on a table of riff raff, I had a feeling another fun day was to be had.

Lunch ended all too soon with an auction of paintings and a fine bottle of whisky which my good and generous blue job buddy and room-mate became the coveted owner of. The crowd was starting to disperse when Mike Jones gathered all who had served in the RAR to give an excellent rendition of our Regimental March, Sweet Banana. It was a wonderful finale to all that had taken place on the day with the coming together of hundreds of people from all over the world but especially for the six old Masodja proudly sitting in the front of the crowd singing their hearts. Sadly the day had to come to an end and with the knowledge that we may never see some of our old mates again we departed to our hotels.

After dropping our exhausted and emotional charges we returned to our hotel to be greeted once again by our indefatigable blue job mate not holding his recently purchased bottle of fine single malt but the remnants of what had been consumed during last night's debrief. Fortunately our debrief wasn't too lengthily and we collapsed at the end of what had been a most enjoyable and successful day, we had another busy day ahead of us.

Monday. A fairly leisurely start and after another hearty breakfast dropped off our Blue Job companion laden with suitcase, paintings and well-secreted bottle of whisky, at the station and made our way to our Masodja's hotel to commence our return trip to London. Our return trip was to takes us via Hatfield the home of Lord Salisbury and also home to "The Troopie" a bronze statue in commemoration of all members of the RLI who lost their lives during our bush war. The trip was long and uneventful but well worth it. Lord Salisbury's Hatfield Estate is huge and grand with acres of woodlands and lakes and "The Troopie" stands proudly alone on the edge of a forest overlooking a lake, it really is a wonderfully tranquil and peaceful site and lends itself to quiet times of contemplation and remembrance which was exactly why we were there. We made our way to the Statue and stood in silence remembering and honouring our fallen comrades in arms. On the back of the plinth are the names of the fallen with some of the names and the actions they perished in being recalled by our group. This was one of the very few occasions Pat and I had time alone with the Masodja just to sit and chat and reminisce, Pat had downloaded historical footage of the Malayan campaign and while he sat on a bench with Obert and Pisayi, both of whom were Malayan veterans, viewing this historical footage the remainder of us wondered down to the lake chatting away about days gone by. The lake was well stocked with carp and Joseph`s excitement at seeing a monster cruise past us was hilarious with him relating how a Mills 36 grenade was far better for fishing than a pole and hook and was about to demonstrate with a dombo when all thoughts of fishing were interrupted with the arrival of Digger "Six O` Clock`s" party and the RLI contingent who voluntarily safeguard and maintain The Troopie.

Brothers in Arms

Digger held an impromptu ceremony with us all in front of The Troopie and then came the sad time for us to bid farewell to Digger and the RLI Ouens and be on our way back to London. Pisayi in wishing Digger good-bye had one last request, he stood in front of Digger and politely asked if he could have his cloth cap, Digger agreed so Pisayi leant forward gently removed the cap, placed it on his head and with a smile saluted did an about turn and we departed for our mini-bus.

Pat dropped us off at the Victory Services Club where we were warmly welcomed by the staff, our group had made quite an impression from our first visit and we were pleased to have been allocated rooms all in close proximity to each other and they were all en-suite, this extra luxury was a huge boost to morale. Joe Columbus Smith had not given up on us despite having forgotten to pick him up for the braai on Saturday. He had also booked into the club and would be joining our party for dinner later in the evening. After a short break we all met for a drink and a light supper in the lounge. While I was ordering drinks Joseph joined me insistent that he buy me a drink, Joseph was amongst the first senior RAR NCO`s to be commissioned and he too had been injured in combat and with me having sorted out his spectacles a few days previously and the two of us having had many a long chat over the last few days he now bestowed the nickname of "Goldfinger" on me. Goldfinger is the title given to an Army paymaster and from the outset of their visit I was determined that they wouldn`t pay for anything, the £50 pocket money they were issued at the beginning of the trip they could either take home or do a bit of shopping for themselves and their families. So the nickname stuck and was soon circulated with amusement to the remainder of the party.

While Joseph and I were getting the drinks there was an amusing scene developing at our table. Once again we were attracting attention from the locals not only interested in where we were from and what we were doing here but two old biddy`s who had obviously been sipping on a few gin and tonics became concerned about the comfort of one of our ex RSM`s and sidled over armed with cushions and attempted to manoeuvre Obert into a more comfortable position. Obert was completely oblivious as to their intentions, much to the amusement of his fellow RSM and buddies but was also having great difficulty in trying to decipher their strange East London accents. The biddy`s eventually gave up trying to shift Obert`s bulk and with gracious smiles and confused thanks from Obert they returned to their table but not without a sly comment from one of his mates suggesting he had missed out on an opportunity and "Nyama Nyoro"! Dinner was served much to Obert`s relief and taste, he was tiring of the fairly unappetising pub grub of the last few days and his preference for fish was not on the menu but we had overlooked scampi. When I described it being akin to kapenta he was overjoyed and annoyed that this was their last meal and he had only just discovered kapenta! Our evening ended with good humour and anticipation of the next day being the end of their visit to Britain.

Tuesday. We all gathered for breakfast, Pisayi by this stage had gained a kg or two and there was no need for him to load up his plate as before and following breakfast we had a quick O group outlining the days schedule and I suggested that they may like to leave any items that they thought may be incriminating when they returned to Zimbabwe, such as publications and RAR logo'd shirts. I issued out bags with their names and I would keep those items in my possession until such time as it was safe to return it to them. Once we had all packed they assembled in my room to hand over the items for safekeeping, both RSM's elected to leave their medals with me and Gibby M also left his replica citation. Joseph was not going to be parted with his medals and returned with them as did Pisayi. I then asked them to sign my copies of Masodja and Chibaya Moyo as a memento of the memorable week we had spent together. I also had a few gifts which I handed out, cloth caps, winter gloves and scarves being the most popular. After a few kind words of thanks from everyone and moral support from Joe Columbus Smith we signed out of our rooms, Joe volunteered to take those that wished to do a bit of last minute shopping back to Primark while I shorted out all the admin and booked out of the club.

Our final parade was an early lunch at the club which was planned to allow those members that could make it to bid farewell to the Masodja. Pat had arrived back in our trusty mini-bus accompanied by Russell Fulton and Bill Liversidge and shortly afterwards we were joined by General Mike Shute, Brigadier David Heppenstall, Col Malcom Clewer, Hobo Hobson and of course Joe Columbus Smith. After a fairly sombre lunch we had to say our goodbyes with full knowledge that this could well be the last time some would be meeting each other.

Douglas Veremu who hadn't seen his parents for many, many years was about to be parted from his father again and Tobias Mutangadura was staying over in the UK with his family for another couple of weeks. After emotional farewells we climbed into Mutambalawless and headed for Heathrow to check in on the Ethiopian Airways flight. All was not going to plan while I was trying to book in our Masodja, all but Pisayi's boarding passes were in order. A spelling error was found on Pisayi's ticket the name on the ticket and the name on the passport did not match... the ticketing agent in Harare made a spelling error... and no amount of explaining by me was going to resolve the error. This delay was causing much alarm and despondency among our group and not doing my blood pressure any good when the senior ticket agent suggested that he could issue an amended ticket but it would cost another £60. A quick transaction and to everyone's relief the problem was solved but it had delayed us considerably and we had to rush our farewells at the boarding gate. We had a quick group photo at the boarding gate said a quick and emotional goodbye and watched our agitated Masodja being escorted out of sight through security.

The abrupt departure of our Masodja ended a truly memorable week, not only with those six Old Soldiers but also with the new found friends and comrades of old whom I certainly hope we can maintain contact with. What was most rewarding was how we all got stuck in together; it was such a pleasure feeling part of a team that understood each other and worked together but especially that we could acknowledge the service and loyalty of those Masodja that stuck by us through thick and thin.

We all made a hasty departure from airport I with Andy MacNeil and his sons, they were coming home with me and Pat had Bill and Russell in tow. It`s going to hard getting back to the day job but it was an experience I will never forget.

THE EDITORS

Andrew Telfer

After leaving home to buy a bottle of milk and a Bar One, Andy Telfer found himself, in January 1976, on Regular Officer Cadet Course Inf /25(19). He emerged confused but commissioned (typical infantry officer) on 4 February 1977 and was inflicted upon 2RAR. During his service as a platoon commander, he was decorated twice, receiving the Military Forces Commendation (Operational) and the Silver Cross of Rhodesia. More characteristically, he lost six months seniority for firing the Pioneer Column cannon at the Fort Victoria Police Station.

In 1980, he was posted to the School of Infantry where he conducted a National Service Officer Cadet Course, with whom he was captured by the BSAP at the top of Bogie's Clock Tower in the centre of Gwelo; and the first combined RAR/ZIPRA/ZANLA officers' course, the very same ZIPRA officers who later led the mutiny at Connemara Barracks. Having thus distinguished himself, he left the Army and the country with his newlywed wife Janette in 1981, with all their possessions packed into the glove compartment of a Datsun 120Y.

In South Africa, he founded a contracting company in the domestic, commercial and industrial paving markets. It grew to become the largest paving contractor in the province of KwaZulu Natal, a position it still maintains today.

During 1988-89, he took two years off to build sandcastles in the Arabian Desert where, as a Major, he commanded a squadron of Arab Special Forces soldiers for the Sultan of Oman. In an unconnected coincidence, the 1st Gulf War broke out the following year.

Back in South Africa, by 1994, recognising that his paving company had become solid, stable and respectable, and knowing that he was none of those things, he sold it.

Drawing upon his experiences and starting with two Army-surplus tents, he founded the Spirit of Adventure, an organisation that used the medium of adventure on rock-face, bush and water activities to train young people in leadership. Several hundred thousand people of all ages have attended Spirit of Adventure courses at two residential centres: Shongweni near Durban and in the Magaliesberg near Johannesburg. Both centres continue to flourish today, led by young people who had originally served as instructors under Andy.

In 1996, he was invited to present a paper on the subject of '*The Outdoors as a Learning Medium*' to a conference sponsored by the University of Cambridge and, in 2002, he addressed the South African National Conference of Heads of Independent Schools on '*Training Boys in Leadership*'. He served on the Boards

723

of three schools and, for four years, was Chairman of the Board of Thomas More College, a leading independent school. Education in South Africa has yet to recover.

He has led several adventures (is often lost). In 1997 and 2002 he journeyed by canoe with his young sons the full length of Lake Kariba, eight days of dawn to dusk paddling among the wild game of Zimbabwe. He has climbed Mount Kilimanjaro three times, at 5985 meters the highest peak in Africa, each time with one of his three children, in 1998, 2001 and 2018. In 1996, he competed in a two-man team with Colonel Koos Stadler (author of the autobiography '*Recce*') in the first major multi-sport adventure race held in South Africa, the Africa Raid. In 1999, he captained the South African team which became the first team ever from that country to successfully complete the Discovery Channel Eco-Challenge, a twelve-day international expedition race in the Andes mountains of Patagonia involving glacial mountaineering, long distance trekking, horseback riding, kayaking and white-water rafting. In 2003, he led a team of cyclists on a 2,000-km ride across South Africa to raise funds for the Cancer Association. In 2012, still looking for a bottle of milk and a Bar One, he and Janette walked over 1,600-km and canoed 400-km through France and Spain. They added another 1,000-km walking along the coastlines of Portugal and Spain in 2017, evidence that Janette retains a very good sense of humour.

In 2005, Andy migrated with his family to a small coastal town in the Land of the Long White Cloud. He finally qualified in something, an MBA, just in time to retire. Guided through life by his soul-mate Janette, together they have three wonderfully adventurous children spread across ten time zones: Grant, East Africa Ranger Trainer, based in the Serengeti; Jeff, Senior Geotechnical Engineer with Rio Tinto in Utah; and Jenni, teacher and successful entrepreneur in the health and vitality sector in New Zealand.

Russell Fulton

Attended Fort Victoria High School from 1971-1976 inclusive. Head boy of hostel and Head boy of school in 1976. Played 1st XI Cricket, 1st XV Rugby, 1st team Squash, Captain School Athletics team, Captain 1st team Water Polo, Captain School Swimming Team. In between these boisterous activities I tried my hand at academics too...enough said on that score. Received six strokes with a light cane about my abundant 'gluteus maximus' before breakfast on the final morning of my school life for fraternising with the fairer sex and partaking of alcoholic beverages the night before. Well now, it would have been madness not too....right?

January 1977: Joined 1RLI as a regular trooper (Intake 157) and posted to Anti-tank Troop, Support Commando. Para trained in Bloemfontein in July/August 1977. Had a falling-out with K-Car whilst carrying 'gun' for Officer 'Crispy' Willar and received a few "oil leaks" for getting in the way of nasty air-to-ground projectiles. Attended the last 13 month regular cadet course run by the Rhodesian Army (25 Jan 1978 – 9 Feb 1979). Commissioned and posted to 1RAR as OC 3 Platoon, A Coy. Promoted Lieutenant in August 1979. Posted to 3RAR as Adjutant and then 2IC B Company in Chipinga. Promoted Captain after 17 months commissioned service and aged 20 years and some change; informed by Col Trevor DesFountain that I was the youngest substantive Captain in the former Rhodesian Army. Who cares? Sent on an exchange officer attachment to the British Army for 3 months. Posted to the School of Infantry as Regular Cadet Course Officer. Course cancelled and I took up an internal posting in the old Cadet Wing and later TAC Wing instructing GD Courses for Company and Battalion Commanders for integration in to the new ZNA.

Retired from military service, very annoyed and feeling decidedly "short-changed", in December 1981. The rest, as they say, is history. I have procreated like a good Catholic (although, perhaps sadly, I am not one). Have a very beautiful daughter and two grandsons from my first marriage and who both live in South Africa and, from my second innings, a doting wife, a beast of a son who joined the Australian Army and is currently serving in 3RAR (Darwin), a second stunning daughter who wishes to pursue a career in archaeology. I have been blessed with a small jewel, a surprise gift from God, one Aisla Fae Fulton who is now 5 years old. Heishh, life is lekker ne, and never forget…"You won't get away without an Exide!"

THE CONTRIBUTORS

Introduction

Recognising that the reader may want to know what became of the likes of Corporal Andrew "I was only following orders" Krajewski and the other wonderful characters who contributed to Chibaya Moyo 2, the Editors asked them to describe their journeys in their own words.

Not everyone could remember what they've done, where they've been or, indeed, who they are but those that could replied as follows (in alphabetical order by surname):

Keith Adams

Educated at Plumtree, Gaul House `65-`70 on leaving school had a short spell as a farm assistant on Mr Es Micklem's Whaddon Chase farm in Umvukwes. Called up into Intake 119 to undertake National Service, I volunteered to go on SAS selection course and upon successful completion joined the Regular Army late 1971. January 1972 attended and successfully passed the Officer Selection course for Regular Cadet course Inf 25/15. 19th February 1973 commissioned and posted to 6 Platoon, B Coy, 1 RAR. Following a back injury was posted to Army HQ as a junior staff officer in MID, followed by a posting to HQ 3 Bde as ASO3. 1977 attended an aerial photographic interpreter's course in Pretoria resulting in a posting to JSPIS, New Sarum as a photo interpreter. My final posting was back at 3 Brigade before resigning and leaving the Army in August 1980.

I then embarked on a farming career which started in Middle Sabi in late 1980 and ended in Centenary after many happy years in that vibrant farming community on Chiripiro Farm in 1998. A short venture up to Zambia with a Canadian company hoping to venture into tobacco farming but which sadly failed due to the uncertainty of neighboring Zimbabwe's chaotic land seizures. I returned to Zimbabwe and took on the post of estate manager of a Christon Bank estate and in 2003 with my children having completed their secondary we made the decision to leave Zimbabwe and settle in the UK. I started a small lawn care business which we still own and operate.

I became actively involved with the RAR Regimental Association in 2015 by assisting with escorting 6 RAR Veterans for the duration of their visit to take part in the dedication of the RNR/RAR Memorial on 19 July 2015 and have since become a committee member and currently hold the welfare post.

THE CONTRIBUTORS

Roy Amm

After an altercation with my parents, it was decided that it would be best for me to enlist for national service a little over a year before I would have been conscripted. I reported at the recruiting office on a Saturday morning and was handed a bunch of paperwork which I had to have my parents sign as I was under age. The following Monday, I returned and submitted the completed paperwork and after a short while I was given my call up documents for Intake 159 – 13 July 1977; along with these documents was a train ticket good for one-way passage to Heaney Junction for that same Wednesday evening ... nothing like that fantastic feeling of being wanted.

After four and a half months of first, second and third phase training we were considered deadly/safe (deadly for gooks and safe for our countrymen) and were deployed across the country to perform a myriad of military duties. For my sins I was sent to Kariba, the Holiday Mecca of the land and things were starting to look up.

In all I served for three years, deciding to join the regular forces about nine months into my national service. I initially started out in an infantry platoon which was a great experience. After ab ambush injury, I was transferred to the unit mortar platoon and after completing a mortar instructor's course at the School of Infantry in Gwelo, I was promoted to sergeant and placed in charge of the unit mortar platoon. For the next two years our platoon spent our time based at either Kariba or Chirundu.

In February 1980 I was offered a commission if I agreed to sign an extension to my contract. I decided not to chase the illusive pot of gold on offer and opted to leave when my existing contract expired. There was also that thing about actually serving for what I considered the enemy. Perhaps it's just me.

I loved my military career and have never since been so content with any employment. Had that war not ended I have no doubt that I would have signed up for an additional term.

Isn't it funny how life is after all; as it turned out, this army truly was not half bad, and yes, it was truly the life. If I could turn back the clock, I would do it all again in a heartbeat.

Jo Amos

Born in the UK on a dreary day in 1959, where I lived for 5 years before my parents, God Bless them, made the choice to move to the "Colonies", and we arrived in Rhodesia, via South Africa, in 1967. Educated at Redcliff Primary and

Que Que High School, I was soon part of the Rhodesian way of life. Like most young men who had not followed a career in the Regular Army, I was somehow deemed useful, and called up for National Service. During my first week at Llewellin Barracks, I mistook the queue for the OSB Course, for the queue for mess hall, and for the next few days, I ended up running around like a race horse completing the Grand National, complete with numbered bib. Somehow I was chosen to attend officer Training at Hooters. Whilst we were undertaking our basics we were informed that the then Rhodesia Regiment Companies would be re-badging to RAR. In November 1977 I was posted to 2 Indep Co RAR as a Platoon Sergeant. Based in Kariba and Chirundu. I had the honour of serving with my unit until January 1979. Looking back on those days, there is never a moment that I am not proud and honoured to have served my country, and feel privileged having done it alongside such fine men of a distinguished Regiment.

Andy Barrett

When asked what I do for a living, my general response is deliberately evasive suggesting I have lived a spectacularly idle and unproductive existence. I have toiled in many a distant land; roamed, rambled and stumbled along a path of confusion of being a hell raising and reprobate of a student, a soldier, a surgeon, an ace and prize-winning scallywag, scoundrel and swashbuckler. Nevertheless, I have encountered an amazing kaleidoscope of experiences as I trudged and trod, chiselled and chugged along following some obscure and convoluted byway wading through a quagmire of misadventures seeking my purpose in life.

Born in South Africa, raised in Chiredzi and schooled in Fort Victoria; upon completion of my degree from Pretoria University (South Africa), I commenced my National Service with Intake 159 in July 1977 which I voluntarily extended by an additional eighteen months. Initially posted to the Medical Corp (1 Brigade), my avidity to go operational was compelling, finding my way into 1 (Independent) Company RAR under the command of Major Don Price BCR.

After completion of my thirty-month National Service I practiced in South Africa for several years then returned to University in the UK and also South Africa to read my Master's degree in Maxillofacial and Oral Surgery, (surgery of the mouth, jaws, sinuses, face, neck & skull). Upon graduation in March 1994 I worked in the hospital services in South Africa, however, the restrictive environment and my wanderlust eventually triumphed over the crushing belt-fed surgical work load I toiled under daily. I subsequently took an extended leave of absence from my profession and transited through many unrelated jobs – game farm management in Lion's Den, Safari Guiding in the Gwaai and problem animal control in the Omay Communal Area. Driven by itchy feet and an adventurous spirit, my connection to surgery was overpowered as I rambled along life's dusty roads – travelled 61 countries, canoed vast stretches of the Zambezi River, worked in water research, various factories, on the railways, as a salesman and in harbour construction. I also owned my own game farm in the Lowveld of Zimbabwe; however, my beautiful piece of Africa was appropriated by the Zimbabwe Government under their land appropriation without compensation laws. Back to surgery, in 2004 after a three-year stint at a hospital in Saudi Arabia as a Consultant Maxillofacial Surgeon, I finally threw my surgical towel in permanently and entered the security industry in Iraq and later in Afghanistan working both countries for over a decade as an armed security medic contractor running convoys protecting foreign NGO nationals and others requiring safe passage assistance.

When not working, I reside in the company of great like-minded friends dividing my time between the serenity and beauty of majestic Victoria Falls, its magnificent surrounds, and my beach apartment located in an idyllic fishing village in the North Eastern part of Brazil.

Peter Baxter

I was born in Fort Victoria in 1962 on June the 15th. I went to Blairgowrie Junior School, Borrowdale Junior School, Fort Victoria Junior School and Peterhouse.

I was selected by an Officer Selection Board to attend the last Rhodesian Army Regular Officer Cadet Course Inf/25(23) and was, I believe, the youngest (18 years and 3 months old) Regular Officer commissioned. The course ran from mid Jan 1980 until 26th Sept 1980 when we were commissioned. Lieutenant Patrick Lawless was our course Officer and Colour Sergeant Marcus Austin was our first Instructor followed by Warrant Officer Class 2 Chris Miller. Of the eight cadets commissioned, three were posted to 3 R A R They were Peter Baxter, John Garland and Fabian Cohnen. We met up for a drink in Brisbane Australia in 2013, 32 years after last seeing each other at 3RAR in 1981.

This cadet course was extremely lucky to have the training in classical warfare when Rhodesia had two troops of T55 tanks. The Classical War Exercise near Fort Rixon was some of the best training that we could have received. It stood me in good stead in my later military career at 121 Battalion and 101 Battalion (South African Army) where we ended up fighting tanks out of Casspirs with Ratel 90's in support.

I was posted to A Company 3RAR under the command of Major Tom Simpson in October 1980. This was when the Monkey in the Mess and the AP Foxtrot story at Buhera story took place.

Thereafter I was sent to Addams barracks for a short stint to train newly commissioned African officers in administration. I was then posted to Support Company 3RAR at Grand Reef under Major Jim Flanagan in mid-1981. I was the Company 2ic and also the 81mm Mortar Platoon Commander.

In November 1981, I was posted to Zimbabwe Military Academy (ZMA), the old School of Infantry in Gwelo, as the Course Officer for an Officers Course. In March 1982 I resigned from the Army.

From 1982 April to 1985 July I served with 121 Battalion in South Africa. I served with B Company under Captain Chris Garland and then started and trained C Company at 121 Battalion, the Zulus, at St. Lucia in Zululand. I then worked in Cape Town in restaurants, as a driver and in security from '85 until '87.

In 1987 to 1988 I served at 101 Battalion in South West Africa with the Romeo Mikes (RM) (Reaction Force), 902 Special Service Company (SSC) with RM7 as a Team Commander under the command of Bernie de Waal from May to December 1987 and was also the Company Commander for 903 SSC Romeo Mikes for the first five months of 1988. We operated in Casspirs inside Angola. I fought at Cuito Cuanavale and in South Western and Central Southern Angola.

I and went into the scaffolding industry after finishing at 101 Battalion at the end of May 1988. I have worked in Zambia, Tanzania, India, Australia, China, Egypt, Lesotho, Saudi Arabia, South Africa and the United States, where I now live.

I married Kathy, the love of my life, on 20th February 1988, and we have two sons: Byron, who has a BSc Computer Science, and Kyle, who is a Ranger and Airborne Qualified and is going to US Army Ranger RASP in May 2019.

I served with honour and pride in 3rd Battalion Rhodesian African Rifles at A Company in Inyanga and Support Company at Grand Reef, with B and C Company at 121 Battalion and with the Romeo Mikes at 101 Battalion.

Carl Chabata

I, Carl Chabata, was born on 10th March 1954 at Baragwaneth hospital in South Africa and father was from Zimbabwe while my mother was from Cape Town in South Africa. We moved to the then Rhodesia in 1960 and resided at Matsai TTL. We were three boys, myself being the last born.

I joined the RAR at Methuen Barracks in the year 1973 and commenced training on 01 May 1973 and did my pass out parade on 10 October 1973. After pass out parade I was posted to C Coy 1RAR which was based at Inkomo barracks. Whilst there I was involved in external operations in Mozambique and internally.

Early in 1974 in February, I joined the Selous Scouts and went to Makuti for a gruelling selection course which was divided into three phases as follows: Physical fitness, Endurance and Bravery. Physical and endurance are self-explanatory whilst bravery had some victims in the sense that some of the guys failed on this one.

We were briefed that there was a sighting of a terrorists' base in Zambia and as a matter of urgency we attack it. We were informed that we were to board a boat at Kariba dam on our way to the target area. On arrival at Kariba we got into the boat which had compartments under and we could not see where we were going. After a long and anxious hours we were finally told that we have arrived and be ready for the attack. We got out of the boat and saw some fires around the place but it was quite without any resistance thus we secured the area. After searching the area we noticed some friendly forces empty ration packs and we knew that we were not in Zambia but in Rhodesia. Following this exercise, that is when we were told that we had passed the selection course.

Back at Makuti we went for the dark phase where we were taught terrorists' tactics and how they operated. After completing the dark phase we moved to Harare and subsequently to Bindura, our new tented camp near Trojan mine.

I rose through the ranks up to sergeant in the year August 1977. During this period I was first a trooper then troop sergeant.

The job sometimes was dangerous if one was not good in map reading because some of our members were killed by friendly forces. I was also involved in a near disastrous incident with TFs who were on their way to Brady barracks whilst we were waiting for pickup. We saw some vehicles coming and thought it was ours and came out from our hiding place. What followed was they opened fire on us but luckily there was a railway line from Rutenga to Chikwalakwala so we had good cover from fire. As a result we did not return fire and were shouting "Stop, Stop, friendly forces!" and they ordered us to stand up with hands in the air. Out of everyone I stood up with my A63 radio raised in the air just to save the day.

Lucky enough the company commander was a jacked up man and it ended well with no casualties on our side. The rest of the period under review I was involved in many fire force call outs, operating as gooks and OPs including external operations where I had a similar experience of water not being found in the area when we wanted to attack a terrorists' base and the mission was abandoned across the Mukumbura River.

After the war I was integrated into the Zimbabwe army when the unit's name was changed to 4RAR and then First Zimbabwe Parachute Battalion. Firstly I was appointed a platoon commander then acting battalion intelligence officer fighting in the most horrendous war in Mozambique. We attacked all major known bases including the infamous Gorongosa base twice.

The jets would bomb the base first whilst we were orbiting in Dakotas and Casa aircraft then we get dropped by parachute onto the target simultaneously. The battalion suffered minimal casualties in that war since most of the soldiers were former Rhodesian forces.

I retired from the army on 28 February 1995. After retirement I worked briefly in security companies and got a contract with Site Services which was also contracted by the United Nations in Angola as a radio operator. I was deployed in a Quartering area called Lumege close to the border with DRC and Zambia. My job was to record the number of Unita forces who had surrendered and handed in their weapons to Head Quarters in Luanda. The contract was eventually terminated and I went back to Zimbabwe where I got a job as a chief security officer at Thetford estate

Rob Delaney

I was born in the small asbestos-mining town of Shabani in the then Southern Rhodesia, in 1959, the second eldest of four children.

My father worked for the Rhodesian Railways as a signals technician and, due to his work, our family moved around the country on a regular basis, living in places like Bannockburn, Lochinvar, Salisbury, Wankie and Bulawayo. My schooling started at David Livingstone in Salisbury, then Thomas Coulter in Wankie. Senior schooling was started at Plumtree then on to Northlea in Bulawayo.

After finishing school, like most young guys I was called up for National Service, doing basics at Llewellin Barracks, and then posted to 2 (Indep) Coy RAR at Kariba. This is where I met up with and became great friends with the amazing and talented AK.

After the army I started an electrical apprenticeship which I gave up after the 'Bonding Rule' was imposed upon us by the Mugabe Government. In 1982 I moved to South Africa, finished my apprenticeship and have been working as an electrician since 1985.

I live in a town named Meyerton which is about 40km south of Johannesburg.

Helena Dennison

'Just a housewife' was never a nomenclature that was going to sit easy with Helena Dennison, and in 1970s Rhodesia she played around with pattern cutting for a children's wear manufacturer in Salisbury to get extra petrol coupons, teaching local Fort Victorians, the Mess chefs and the Fort Vic Hotel how to build a menu and cook a la Cordon Bleu, and running an Iyengar yoga class. All this went on hold during the 10 days' R&R when Andre was home.

Working to keep two children alive after being widowed in 1979 made work become more of a reality as well as a necessity. She had little or no experience and stepped onto the UK job ladder in 1980, ignorant, penniless and keen to move out of her parent's house to regain her independence. Asked by an acquaintance if she could design wetsuits, she took on the creation of the first coloured wetsuits to hit the UK windsurfing market, swiftly followed by aerobic dance wear to suit the early 80s trend. Moving into sales and marketing, she set up and ran call centres, having been headhunted by US conglomerate GTE to help them break into the UK market. She set up and ran Directline Telemarketing taking this from business plan to 90 employees in year 1 and into profit after 11 months. Progressing this into writing and delivering training programmes she went solo, and consulted across UK industry from retail to finance at board and management levels, specialising in strategy and planning. In 2002, bored with senior management development she gave it all up to weed people's gardens for a year. Ever the entrepreneur she has recently retired from garden design, landscaping and house renovation (well almost anyway) and now attends to her own garden and allotment, walking a mad Saluki and caring for a neighbour just a few weeks off 100.

Judy Dixon

I was but a newly fledged teenager at the time of these anecdotes, securely entrenched in school, the shenanigans of the school bus, ogling delicious troopies across the camp swimming pool, Saturday movies at the camp cinema and generally being as revolting as teenagers are want to be. Life in camp was different but protected and I was happy with friends who would last a lifetime.

Sadly this idyllic life would end with the death of my Darling Dad and we moved back to Salisbury. After finishing school badly with a mere scraping of 'O' Level, I rushed headlong into parties, a job, parties, marriage to a soldier, camp life again, babies and the 'Groot Trek' down South. Phew!

Now, a few (many) years later I live in Cape Town where my children, grown and with families of their own, reside. I work for my Daughter who is a chiropractor which occupies most of my daylight hours, my Grandchildren the rest, of the hours that is. I write when the muse is upon me and have published two children's books as well as writing many adult short stories and poems; my life is good and I am blessed.

Alan Doyle

Not the world's most natural soldier (he was a member of the Rifle Club at Hamilton High School purely because it was a sport you could pursue lying down) he was called up for Intake 160 in January 1978.

He was posted to 2RAR after training, arriving at JOC Fort Vic one lunch time wearing the wrong beret badge, the wrong stable belt and the wrong colour boots, facts which were pointed out several million times until he managed to find a CQMS to replace them the next morning. What is now called a steep-learning-curve then ensued, including very rapidly mastering the ability to recognise rank badges above Major (and their Air Force, BSAP and INTAF equivalents) – persons of such elevated distinction not being part of your standard NS gopher's usual acquaintance.

Month followed week of head-numbing boredom at the JOC, centred round the all ranks mess and the briefing room, with brief escapes to the throbbing nightlife of the town itself. And then the 2RAR contingent were sent on the road and life got more interesting. Early in 1979 he transferred to 5 (Indep) Coy RAR where he re-acquainted himself with walking everywhere. Intake 160 demobilised at the end of June 1979, but time off was short, as he was called up six weeks later by C Coy 6RR. Within eighteen months of beginning his national service he had risen to the dizzy rank of Corporal.

Before and after his call-up to 6RR, Alan was given a pistol, a Land Rover and a clip board by the Bulawayo City Council Liquor Audit Section, and with a colleague was sent out to stem the wholesale theft of sorghum beer from the Council's brewery and beer halls. More than one tanker driver started work indistinguishable from a beanpole and within hardly any time at all was considerably stouter (no pun intended) and owned a pirate taxi business. Could they catch them? Could they hell. Nevertheless, that time was not wasted: in the process of many mid-morning tasting sessions Alan learned to discern the superior qualities of draught Ingwebu compared to decidedly downmarket shake-shake Chibuku.

For four happy years from 1980 to 1983 he studied Economics and Law at Rhodes University and then worked in banking and fund management in

Johannesburg and London. He and Ali live near the Thames upstream from Hampton Court, and have a son and a daughter.

John Essex-Clark

Brigadier John 'Digger' Essex-Clark DSM, FAIM, FASA (Australian Army, Retd); born in Hong Kong; primary education in Hong Kong. ; secondary education in Australia, UK and South Africa; tertiary education in South Africa, UCT, and Australia, UNE.

Rhodesian Army 1951-63: 1RAR 1954-60, 1RLI 1960-63; Australian Army 1964-85: 1RAR 1964-67 (Vietnam); CO 9RAR 1970-73; Commandant Australian Infantry Centre 1976-8; Director, Training Royal Military College, Duntrron1979-80; Commandant Australian Army Command & Staff College 1981-84; Director General Military Training, Army Headquarters 1984-85 (all punctuated with often nugatory staff appointments). Memberships RLIRA. RAR Regtl Assoc; Rhodesian Army Association, Royal Australian Regiment Association, Life Governor Royal Australian Regiment Foundation, US 173rd Airborne Society, Australian RSL Defence Committee (1989 to present).

Formal Military Training: Assessment Course; Instructors' Course; NCOs' Tactics Course; Airportability Course; Parachute Course 1960; Company Commanders' Course 1961; Student Staff College, Camberley UK, 1963 Tactics Instructor Australian Land Warfare Centre; Student US Army Command and General Staff College, Fort Leavenworth, Kansas, 1980-1971' Senior Officers' Strategy Course, Canberra.1982'

Nicknames: Rhodesian Army: 'Digger', 'Mopane'; Australian Army: 'The Big E', 'The Owl'.

Decorations: Distinguished Service Medal (DSM) for Leadership in Action in Vietnam, US Bronze Star For Meritorious Service and Leadership of his own plus American and Vietnamese troops in Combat in Vietnam.

Formal visits to discuss army training and counter terrorist Governmental processes and action in Israel, The Netherlands, the UK, Canada, Philippines, USA, Colombia and Argentina.

Books: Hassett: Australian Leader, Army History Unit, 2009; autobiography Maverick Soldier - the story of an Infantryman's Story, Melbourne University Press, 1991.

Pamphlets: US Airmobile Operations; joint author of The Infantry Battalion in Battle.

Hobbies: family activities; study of military history, leadership, counter-terrorism, Counter Insurgency operations, combat tactics with modern combat and surveillance equipment and new technology; writing articles for various defence and politics-oriented papers and magazines; sketching, oil-painting, reading novels; and he enjoys rolling, strumming, plunking, plinking and riffing bluegrass on his banjo with family and friends.

Tony Faulkner

I was just an ordinary guy doing his NS at I Indep Co (RAR), keen to get stuck into the gooks. I was lucky enough to have a couple of stripes, which at least gave me partial control of my destiny. We operated in the Vic Falls area (often getting wet), then moved to Beit bridge (getting roasted in the October heat). We spent most of the war on 2 week patrols - walking, walking and more walking, in between OP's and occasional Fire Force stints.

After the war I stayed on in Zim and went to Gwebi Agricultural College. I spent a year travelling/backpacking/working, then returned to Zim. I worked on a couple of Tobacco farms before moving to town and working for Wright Rain designing Irrigation systems. I left Zim in 1989 for a job offer in Malawi. It was always my intention to return, however events since 2000 put a halt to that plan.

Today, I am still living in Malawi, semi-retired, but continuing to design irrigation systems. After 'forgetting' the experiences of the war, they have disconcertedly returned, with mixed feelings.

Ian Findlay

Ian Findlay ICD MLM, having been trained in the Rifle Brigade, commissioned into the Green Howard regiment in England and seconded to the 5th /10th Baluch regiment of the Indian army, joined the Native Affairs Department in Southern Rhodesia in August 1948.

He started his career in Shabani followed by service in Gutu, where he was appointed as an Assistant Native Commissioner and Assistant Magistrate, Nyamdhlovu and Wankie. In February 1963 he transferred to Binga as District Commissioner to continue to resettle the Tribal population who had been moved following the construction of the Kariba dam and the birth of Lake Kariba.

He began his association with counter insurgency warfare when the Rhodesian Security Forces, and the Rhodesia African Rifles in particular, moved into the district with the infiltration of both ZANU and ZAPU terrorists into the Zambesi valley area which covered much of his District.

He saw service with JOC Hurricane as District and Provincial Commissioner in Centenary and Bindura and later the Command JOC in Salisbury.

This was followed by his appointment as a Deputy Secretary in the Ministry of Information, where his duties encompassed daily meetings with the Prime Minister, the briefing of foreign visitors and responsibilities relating to the Lancaster House negotiations.

Tom Fulton

Tom Fulton is a product of the Regular Cadet Course system. Commissioned in February 1976 he received the posting of his choice – The Rhodesian African Rifles. As a Platoon Commander in B Company of the First Battalion, he saw service as a Fire Force ground commander, and conducted every manner of counter insurgency operations, in all the major theatres, until badly injured in a landmine incident in early 1977.

When back on his feet (albeit, with the aid of crutches) he was posted to the Battalion Headquarters as the then Adjutant Kevin Johnson's assistant. Tasked by Lieutenant Colonel Mike Shute with the training and formation of the Assault Pioneer Platoon, he was posted to Support Company where he also took command of the Tracker Platoon.

The next phase of his career had him posted to Headquarters 1 Brigade where he took over as the Military Intelligence Officer. Whilst thoroughly enjoying the fascinating world of Top Secret intelligence and doing his utmost to improve the flow of intelligence within the Brigade. He was able to retain some sanity from the incessant paperwork, by assisting with the 1(Independent) Company RAR Fire Force, where he was unofficially attached to assist in the training of the National Service Platoon Commanders in Fire Force procedure.

Posted to 4(Independent) Company RAR in Victoria Falls as the 2ic, he was later to take over command from the newly promoted Lieutenant Colonel Ron Barker, who went off to command the Grey's Scouts. He completed his service in this post although his command was integrated into the National Army shortly before his discharge. In the period prior his last day of service, he served as the Liaison Officer (ZIPRA) and was active and participated in the Entumbane debacle.

Firstly operating a Hunting Safari Company he formed, he explored a few different avenues in the civilian world, before settling into the world of gold mine management. He has one book published, one at the publisher and another on the way, but continues to be connected to the gold mining industry where he uses his now considerable experience as a Mining Engineering and Financial Consultant.

He lives in Zimbabwe, is married to Bronwyn and his son David (27) is also in gold mine management. www.tomfulton-author.com

John Garland

I was born in Mosaboni, India in 1962. My father was a Cambourne School of Mines engineer graduate and, for the good of the British Empire, spent time in Zambia and India on the mines. The family immigrated to Kitwe, Zambia in 1964. I attended the Kitwe Convent and Kitwe Primary schools before going to Aberlour House boarding school in Scotland. In 1972, the family immigrated to Bulawayo, Rhodesia where I finished my junior education at Kumalo Primary School. I spent a year at Milton High school before the family moved to Salisbury where I completed my schooling at Oriel Boys High and St George's College.

I successfully pasted the Officer Cadet Selection (INF 25/23) in January 1980, and was commissioned in September. I was posted to 'B' Company, 3 RAR under the command of Major Marius Meiring, in Chipinga, as a Platoon Commander of 4 Platoon. In March 1981, a new Company was formed in the Battalion, Major Joe Flanagan as OC, (Support Company) at Grand Reef where I was given the command of the Anti-Tank Platoon. It was during this time that I met my soul mate, Gill, a local born and bred Umtali girl who stole my heart. I remained at Grand Reef until I resigned my commission in March 1982.

We immigrated to the Northern Territory (a huge culture shock!), Australia in 1982, and married in 1984. After several years of moving around Queensland trying to 'find our feet' we finally settled in Townsville, far North Queensland. Over the last 30-odd years I have worked in the construction industry, (rigging/scaffolding and crane operating) all around Australia and spending a short time in New Caledonia as a scaffold/crane coordinator. In 2012 I was employed by Hatch as a construction coordinator for a new coal mine being built in Central Qld. We bought a small Dog Grooming business in 2016 and sold it in 2018, after an unfortunate event where a small pooch had a heart attack in the hydro bath, and I had to preform CPR to revive it. Now in my semi-retirement years, working as one of the local 'Posties'. We have a son (Philip) and a daughter (Jenna). In 2008 my son and I walked the Kokoda Track and in 2012 my daughter and I climbed Mt Kilimanjaro.

In 2020, Gill and I are planning to travel to the UK for the (INF 25/23) 40 year reunion.

David Heppenstall

Brigadier David Heppenstall MLM was born in Lymington, Hampshire in March 1932 and completed his National Service with the Royal Hampshire Regiment. He attested into the Southern Rhodesia Staff Corps in 1952 and was attached for six weeks to 1RAR at Borrowdale Road. After a period as an Instructor at the Drill Hall in Bulawayo, he was posted to 1RAR in 1955 and commissioned 2Lt. He served with 1RAR in Malaya from 1956 – 1958 and was Mentioned in Dispatches. He saw service again in the Nyasaland Emergency as RSO 1RAR in 1959.

After the break-up of the Federation in 1963, he was posted to 1RAR as OC D Company. D Coy were first detached to Inkomo Barracks and then engaged in border control and COIN operations in Matabeleland from 1966 – 1970. He was appointed a Member of the Legion of Merit for company successes in those operations.

After appointments at the School of Infantry and Army HQ, and Staff College in Pretoria, he returned to 1RAR as CO from 1974-1976. He held command appointments as Deputy Commander HQ 1Bde from 1976 – 1977, alternating Commander JOC Repulse/Tangent; Commander HQ Midlands District and JOC Grapple; Colonel G Army HQ and Commander Special Forces. He retired from the Army and returned to the UK in 1980.

David and Anne live in Lymington, Hampshire where they owned Prontaprint (Southampton) for 21 years until they retired again in 2002. He is a Life Member of the Lymington Cricket Club, Honorary Life President of the Rhodesian Army Association and founder committee member of the RAR Regimental Association. He commissioned the Regimental History '*Masodja*' (2007) and the 'RNR/RAR Book of Remembrance' (2015). They have a daughter Claire who is an adjudicator and barrister in one of the leading family law firms in London and a son Nigel who is a colonel in the British Army and has already completed three operational tours in Afghanistan.

Jim Hill

After completing a spell in 1 RLI, Jim Hill commenced his Officer training on Course Inf 25/14 in early 1971. In April of that year he was detached for Officer training in South Africa and, initially, attended the South African Military Academy in Saldanha Bay before moving to the Infantry School in Oudtshoorn.

After 18 months of learning about the South African military machine and the vineyards that sustained many of the Potential Officers learning to man that mighty machine Jim, as an Officer Cadet, spent two months as an oddity at Army Headquarters whilst awaiting his Commission. Posted to 1RAR as Platoon Commander, 4 Platoon Jim retained this position until early 1975 when he became Recruit Training Officer until the year end when he was posted to Army Headquarters G Branch.

At the end of 1976, now Captain Hill was posted to 5 (Independent) Company as Second in Command where he served, both in that role and, later, as Officer Commanding, until April 1980 when he retired from the Army.

A career in Agriculture followed in both Zimbabwe and then Zambia before a move into sustainable Forestry. Jim moved to the UK briefly and then Portugal. Currently unemployed, Jim looks forward to continuing either his Agricultural or Forestry careers somewhere in Africa (which will not leave him in peace).

Hobo Hobson

Born in 1938 at the Lady Rodwell, Bulawayo. I have always said Bulawayo is a great place-pity it's so far out of town! My parents were living in Gwanda (even further out of town) before moving to Gwelo, and finally arriving in Salisbury in 1944. From 1945-1950 I attended David Livingstone Primary and Junior School, before being admitted to Churchill High School, the domain of the Legendary Headmaster Jeeves Hougaard - legendary in every sense, with the meanest swinging arm when duks were administered!

I joined the Army in 1964 and my initial posting was to Inkomo Barracks as an Instructor. We spent two happy years there, and I was then posted to RLI as a Staff Sgt Instructor and bought my first house in Chadcombe. I survived many evenings in the WOs and Sgts Mess and at the end of 1969 was posted to HQ 1 Bde as the Unit Education Officer (UEO) with the rank of WO2. It was great to be back in Bulawayo. Promotion to WO1 and a posting back to RLI meant that I was enjoying the benefits of being a senior WO in a great Regiment.

On commissioning, I was posted to 1RAR as the UEO in 1972 where I served until 1975 in various roles, then Special Forces, Salisbury District. At Army HQ in the RhAEC Directorate my posting was SO3, and finally as Deputy Army Educational Corps Director as a Major. I served until December 1980 when I retired.

As a civvie I was employed as the Principal of the Central African Correspondence College in Harare. I had a Professional and Technical Staff of 150, and a student population of 120,000 from Zimbabwe and surrounding African countries.

In 1984, we moved to South Africa where I was employed as the Regional Training Manager of the Clothing Industry Training Board in Natal. I spent 10 years with the CITB, retiring in 1994. During my CITB service, I enlisted with the South African Defence Force in their equivalent of the Territorials. My final promotion, and a highlight of my military career, was that of CO Natal Mounted

Rifles in 2003. I finally retired from the SANDF in the post of SO2 (Reserve Force) at the SA Army Armoured Corps.

Andrew Krajewski

The course instructors and officers of the School of Infantry were spot on! Accordingly, Himself spent the camouflage years at 2 (Indep) Coy, RAR following his posting to Kariba in mid-1978. It was thought that he could do least harm to the war effort in this sphere of operations. Did he have news for those who thought this! The leader of the call-sign 22 Bravo (Known And Feared Throughout The land) was at once assailed by a cascade of baffling mishaps, which confirmed his place as the Infantry's answer to 'Typhoid Mary'. He was perhaps without equal in being able to get lost at all times and everywhere. Also, he once set fire to his Bergen with an "Icarus" flare (not his fault) and survived acute poisoning (probably by one of the baffling ranges of highly toxic alkaloids found in certain otherwise edible-looking plant structures) following the consumption of a delicious looking root (completely his fault).

But wait, there's more. He also had his chest webbing, which he was wearing at the time, set ablaze following an AD with a mini-flare projector. And for which he was groundlessly blamed. In September 1978, he was driven insane by the synergistic effects of heat, thirst, insect attack, and nyamazaan-induced sleep deprivation. The prognosis for full recovery remains poor. After all, Australia is NOT the place to overcome all the listed issues, even if the nyamazaans are 18 years old and drive Holden Commodore and Ford FalconV8s.

In the post-camouflage years, he built on the solid foundation for life provided by conscription, finding new significance to "in your own time carry on"; "watch your front!" and "cock, hook and look". His military experiences have left their mark, exemplified by his violent start when a car backfires or a bottle of bubbly pops; his truly annoying habit of counting shots fired by firearms in movies; his barking at the full moon like a baboon; and by his bouncing up and down and pant-hooting excitedly whenever he lights the braai fire.

Now, darn-near forty years later (how time flies!), and THE poster-child for decrepitude, he's still trying to pin-ball his way through Life, leaning heavily upon his most wonderful wife, and living these last 18 years in Australia. He holds a doctorate in Agriculture, and literally talks to trees. In the last ten years, his condition has deteriorated, since he now talks also to the seething trillions of life forms found in soil. He has not yet found out how to get paid for doing this, and in his defence, put it to the reader that many of these microbes are no more primitive than some humans of voting age around him.

Midyear 2016 marked a watershed in his corporeal existence. He was struck down by extreme heat stroke and dehydration whilst trudging around the outer rim of the Saharan desert at midday with several other lunatics. There followed two full years of the highest drama, during which he drew on the support of some wonderful friends, his experiences in the army, and some truly fiendish medication. Now, on worse than ever speaking terms with most of his vital organs, he more than ever has the body of a God. Buddha, according to his Beloved and highly perceptive wife. He can now, however, only count on fingers and toes to fifteen. He fully realises just how lucky he is to be around to do so, though!

These days he is catastrophically balded, daft, articulate, wildly eccentric, and the People's Choice for Albany's Virtual Tattie-Bogle. He divides his time between a horticultural consultancy business and various hobbies and pursuits. These include writing, and he unreservedly apologises to the gentle reader for these ongoing literary outrages. He now sleeps with a notebook and pencil by his bed and a pocket notebook and pencil in his shirt pocket. After all, one never knows when a long-forgotten memory, random thought, or insight is going to strike.

He is also an avid if frenzied cook, with a thing for sharp kitchen knives. This is sometimes a worry to bystanders, but that's what comes of his being having to take blood thinning medication.

A passionate nature lover and conservationist and friend to bull-ants, Australian ravens, tiger snakes, sting-rays (and Teddy Bears), he continues to devote more time to work-related pursuits than he does on fishing.

By now, he really ought to know better.

Pat Lawless

Educated at Stephens College, Balla Balla, Pat Lawless was commissioned into 1RAR in February 1977. Parachute and mortar trained, he served on continuous operations in Support Company till 1980 when he was despatched back to the School of Infantry in Gwelo to run Inf 25/23 – the last Regular Officer Cadet Course.

Defying the maxim that "… if God had wanted the Army to fly he would have painted the sky brown..." Pat joined the British Army's Army Air Corps as a helicopter pilot. He commanded at troop, squadron, and battle group level on operations in Northern Ireland, the first Gulf War, Bosnia, Angola – and a few other less salubrious spots in between. He completed an exchange tour in the USA flying an array of attack helicopters. He was both a student and DS at the Army Staff College and attended the Higher Command and Staff College in 1998, after which he was swiftly promoted beyond his own level of incompetence to Brigadier. The green suit was exchanged for the pinstripe version in 2000.

Pat has worked his way to becoming a jobbing COO/ CEO. He is currently CEO of a global oil and gas group, and remains solidly wedded to Cherril with whom he has produced three sons of whom he is inordinately proud. He lists his service in the RAR as the most challenging, rewarding and formative experience in his life from which remain the most enduring and meaningful friendships. In what little is left of his spare time, he Chairs the Rhodesian African Rifles Association and – separately – the Rhodesian Army Association. He is the Zimbabwe Council Member for the Royal Commonwealth Ex Services League.

He is still moved to tears at the sound of 'Sweet Banana'. *Chiwororo*!

Mike Matthews

Mike was born in Bulawayo in 1957 and attended Plumtree School, whereafter he began what was then two years of national service and was commissioned into 1RAR in 1977, serving as platoon commander of 3 Platoon A Company under Major Barry Getliffe. He had a great rapport with his *Masodja*......until he exhausted the battery of the TR46 radio on patrol listening to Rhodesia playing Northern Transvaal in the Currie Cup, thus missing his platoon's imminent pickup and having to return hungry to camp by foot 2 days later. Rhodesia lost, so it was a bad call, but his *Masodja* forgave him.

Highly popular on Sally Donaldson's Forces Requests, Mike received a weekly message – it was from Sally personally, and it went.... "and for those who didn't get a message this week..."

In 1979 Mike commenced studying law at the University of Cape Town. After qualifying the combination of being accepted for articles by a large Cape Town legal firm and meeting his wife, Colleen, conspired against his returning to Zimbabwe, and he has made a nuisance of himself in Cape Town since. He has two married daughters, both currently living in Australia, and three granddaughters.

Mike enjoys water polo, playing for Rhodesia and subsequently Western Province, and has scaled Mt. Kilimanjaro with some accomplices. He has always loved rotary aircraft, a passion driven by having been dropped off too often by 7 Squadron pilots who always had a warm bed to return to after a day's work. Unable to afford a helicopter he invested in a gyrocopter, racking up 230 flying hours. Having inexplicably fallen out of the sky twice, Mike decided that third time wasn't necessarily lucky, and he traded his gyrocopter for the relative safety of a motorhome. When he and Colleen can find the excuse, they're traipsing around the Western Cape fishing and experimenting with their potjie pot.

Commencing a law practice for his own account in 1996, Mike has a legal firm in Cape Town's Southern Suburbs and visiting Zimbo's are always welcome to pop in for a cuppa and to shoot the breeze. He is an avid mountain biker and occasional triathlete, and fancies himself becoming a creative writer at some stage in the future before he becomes too madala.

John Peirson

Lt Col John Peirson served as the Second in Command of C Company 1RAR from June 1968 to December 1970.

He and his identical twin Kenneth were born into a military family in Pretoria in 1939. He served for a year as a Gunner in the Union Defence Force in 1958. In 1959, he and Kenneth migrated to S Rhodesia and joined the Federal Army. Having completed the requisite Drill, Weapons and Tactics courses at Central African Command Training School in Gwelo he was posted to C Company DRRR Llewellin Barracks.

In December 1961, having completed a cadet course, he was posted to C Company (later to become 1 Commando) No1 Training Unit 1RLI. Having conducted several months active service on the Northern Rhodesia border during the Congo debacle, 1RLI moved to its permanent home, Cranborne Barracks in Salisbury.

In 1966, as a Captain, he was posted to Headquarters 2 Brigade as GSO 3 Operations. From June 1968 to December 1970, he served with C Company 1 RAR under Maj Mike Shute. In 1970, he was posted to DRR Llewellin Barracks as OC C Company. During this period he married Susan Veitch, daughter of retired Colonel Jimmy Veitch, the first commander of D RRR

.He was awarded Rhodesian Colours having competed in the XI World Parachuting Championships in Tahlequah USA in 1972.

In 1973, he was posted as OC 1 (Indep) Coy RR in Wankie. During this period the Company became the first NS unit to be deployed on Op Hurricane. In 1974, he was awarded PSC having attended a staff course. In 1976, he was posted as OC 6 (Indep) Coy RR in Umtali. In 1978, he was posted to JOC Grapple as GSO 2 under Brig David Heppenstall and subsequently Brig Colin Castle.

In 1979, he was promoted to Lt Col and was posted to Army Headquarters. As the Director of Medical services had retired prematurely, and no suitably qualified member of the Medical Corps existed, he was posted to the Medical Corps as Assistant Director of Medical services, a non-medical administrative post effectively carrying out the role of Director. During this period he introduced the Medical Corps stable belt and maroon beret, a great morale booster for all medical staff. Previously, medics had worn the belt and headdress of whichever unit they were attached to, and were identifiable only by wearing the Corps badge on their headdress.

Following the 1980 Elections, he left Rhodesia and served as the 2i/c 6 Recce Regt in Durban for 2 years. Subsequently he served in a variety of roles in the security industry including commanding a company of Gurkhas in Sierra Leone during the war in 2005. He retired in 2016 and lives in Woking, Surrey.

John Pritchard

Born and brought up in Bulawayo (and the Matopos as a Boy/Queen Scout) John was commissioned into 1RAR in late 1966. What followed over the next 17 and a half years was a typical command and staff career. In 1RAR he served as a platoon commander in E Coy and later as 2IC A Coy.

In 1971 he was posted to DRR as Adjutant and later onto 3 Bde as GSO3 (Ops & Int). As GSO3 he witnessed the spread of Frelimo and ZANLA down the Eastern border. In 1975 he married Rose and shortly after their honeymoon reported for duty at the newly formed 2RAR in Fort Victoria. He helped establish B Coy and spent the next couple of years on ops. Posted out of the battalion in mid-1977 he attended the short intensive Rhodesian Command and Staff Course and on completion of the course was posted to Army HQ as GSO2 (SD) and later to D Mil S as an instructor. This posting was short lived as the war intensified and officers were needed in the combat units. John returned to 2RAR as Bn 2IC under Lt Col Hammond. What followed was about 18 months of operational service during which the Battalion excelled. John counts his regimental service as the highlights of his career.

The next three years was spent in a number of appointments initially at Joint High Command, and then onto 2 Bde as Deputy Commander where ultimately there were 10 Battalions under command. With the posting of ZANLA & ZIPRA officers into senior positions in 1981 John was posted out to Defence HQ and finally served out his time as Col G at Army HQ. Disillusioned with the new order he retired in May 1983.

After a few months out of the army he was head hunted to take over an import/export company in Harare dealing with the supply of military equipment to the forces. While he found his new position interesting and overseas travel exciting running businesses in Zim at that time was stressful.

In 1988 John, Rose and now with Mark and Lyndsay were accepted into Australia. Two businesses in Harare were closed and they arrived in Perth in January 1989. After several months of job hunting John joined a company specialising in capital fundraising for the not-for- profit sector. Ten years later he was made redundant and as a result opened his own fundraising company – a move he never regretted. Philanthropy is alive and well in Perth and over his career he has raised in excess of $70m for different causes.

Unfortunately his marriage broke down in 1998. Two years later he met Rita and they are still an "item" today. John retired in 2014 and remains active in the local tennis club, parish and RSAWA.

Ian Pullar

Three years in the BSAP, then School of Infantry, with Roland Lever as our Course Officer. He and the Commandant and half the Officer Instructors were all badged 2nd Battalion, Kings African Rifles. So before commissioning as a Second Lieutenant, I was told by Roland to apply for the 2nd Bn which was then based in Lusaka. The 1st was in Zomba and there were three others in East Africa. As I had the distinct impression this was not a negotiable deal, that's where I ended up.

Stephenson Barracks, old and run down. The Officers' Mess had been a nurses hostel, probably during the period covered in the Slavers film, not only because it looked like it, but also because it was the KAR, then known as Central Africa Rifles, that was formed in order to combat the slave trade in Nyasaland.

Wonderful unit, amazing privilege to have served with them. Ended up as the Mortar Platoon Commander and had to attend a course at Gwelo to learn the 81mm. We had 3 inch ones that must have been at Arakan by the look of them. Lots of stories there.

Also did a tour as Dem platoon at Gwelo, which meant I missed out on an exchange to Kenya with the Brits.

Was dug in on the Congo Border when the UN Brigade came to the Kasumbalesa border post to cross into Northern Rhodesia to access what was called the Pedicle Road which looped out of Katanga into Northern Rhodesia then back again. They wanted a short cut, as part of their operation to retrieve Katanga from Moise Tshombe. They had an Irish Battalion, an Indian one and I think Swedish was the third. Plus some supporting Arms. Also SAABs whizzing about. I had a Platoon with a 3.5-inch rocket launcher and a two-inch mortar. We also had four MAGs. Great odds.

All KAR officers, being Nyasaland-based, were offered commissions in the British Army at the end of Federation. I chose Southern Rhodesia. Hmmmm!

After the Brits shafted us on the Federal issue I was transferred to The School of Infantry at Gwelo as Adjutant. Imagine that, 2nd Lt, that's how short we were.

Then the RLI Mortar Platoon in its entirety came down to be trained on the 81mm. I was the only trained officer left in Southern Rhodesia. I was sent to Regimental Wing, much to Andy Rawling's relief, and Al Tourle and I trained them. Afterwards, I was posted to the RLI as Mortar Troop Commander where I remained (apart from a brief spell as 2ic 2 Commando) for three years. It was during this time that we went to Matabeleland on Operation Nickel. Jon Cole was the OC. We were also pretty active at Kariba during the UDI debacle.

I was transferred to HQ I Brigade as GSO3 Ops but, after a year, was sent to the Artillery as their Adjutant because someone, who should have known better, assumed that Medium Mortars and Guns are much the same. This started a six-year spell with the Gunners first as Adjutant then as Training Officer, interspersed with about a year as Training Officer 2RR in Bulawayo.

I also completed a Long Gunnery Course in South Africa, seven months of ballistics, maths and all sorts of other stuff like ammo and explosives. The only Infantry Officer ever to have done that course. Of course the Red Sea Parted for the Israelites… nothing was impossible if I passed that course. Then from the Artillery to Directorate Military Studies which was awful and, to make matters worse, I got posted there as an Instructor on completion.

Rescued by Peter Hosking who asked that I be given to him as 2IC to the about to be formed 2 RAR. Later, CO of 2RAR and then to Army HQ as ASO1 Manpower, followed by a short spell in Army HQ as Director Military Intelligence. Then 4 Brigade 2IC to Vic Walker at Masvingo until I left as a Colonel in July of 1981.

Very fortunate to get appointed as Manager of Goldfields Security, part of the Goldfields Group. We provided Security for Goldfields and all the other Mining Houses that were not Anglo or JCI. It was a very big organisation. Stayed there for 14 years.

I was very active in the Private Security Industry and am a Fellow of the SA Institute of Security as well as a life member of the South African Security Association. I was also a ministerially appointed member of two Security Officers' Boards. That was and is the Statutory Body responsible for the Juristic Control of the SA Security Industry. One appointment was by the National Party Government and the other by the ANC, so I must have done something right. That was a total of six years, the first while still with Goldfields and the second after I had retired between 2000 and 2003.

Came to Australia in 2004 with my wife Anne Mare. Lucky to get in. Aging, unskilled and somewhat dim.

Gavin Rawstron

After having retired/resigned at the end of Dec 1980, I was in the process of setting up a Game Management and Capture Company with an ex Game Department Guy in Bulawayo, when I got a phone call from my very good friend Maj Kevin Johnson in Army Headquarters, to say that my name was on the blacklist and that he suggested I make plans to get out of the country as soon as possible. No reasons were given. As I had no clue where to go, he suggested that I go to his brother in East London. To cut a long story short, that's what I did. I flew my family out and followed by vehicle with dogs, cats and other personals.

My first job was one of repairs and maintenance, building alterations etc. Never having put one brick on top of another and having to learn the hard way, I lasted approximately 9 months before landing myself the Border Wynns Agency which I had for 8 years. This enabled me to buy and pay for the smallholding that I now have just outside East London.

Over the years, I managed to establish myself in the motor trade, buying a garage, property and dealing in vehicles and the like. I also got involved with Estate Agency for a while but found that it was not my preference.

My wife Jenny and I are now retired on the farm with our animals and spend as much time with our two children and grandchildren. We are also very involved in The Lord's work and spend a lot of time in being there for others in need.

Bruce Sand

Maj (Retd) Bruce Sand, (RhE, RAR, RCE)

Maj Sand Joined the Rhodesian Army in January 1971 as a Trooper in the Rhodesian Light Infantry (1RLI). After basic training and active service as a machine gunner in 3 Commando 1RLI, including Op Lobster II in Mozambique, he was selected and trained as an officer cadet, in Gwelo at the Rhodesian Army School of Infantry. In February 1973 he was commissioned into the Rhodesian Corps of Engineers (RhE), completed engineer training and deployed on survivability, mobility and counter mobility tasks (Mine clearance, laying) on Ops Hurricane and Tangent. In April 1974 he was employed as an infantry officer to 4 Platoon, B Company the 1st Battalion Rhodesian African Rifles (1RAR). He served as a platoon commander, company 2i/c and acted as Battle Adjutant to Lt Col Mike Shute who commanded the Battalion then.

In June 1976 he returned to the RhE as a Squadron (Sqn) 2i/c then took command of 7 Minefield Sqn followed by command of 4 Fd Engr Sqn in Fort Victoria (Masvingo). After hostilities ceased in late 1979 Major Sand served in Army HQ, Harare until early retirement in September 1981.

Newly married, he and his wife emigrated to Canada in May1982, where he was commissioned direct entry into the Royal Canadian Engineers as a 2Lt in August 1982. His RCE service included: Instructor duties, regimental duties in a combat engineer regiment (1CER), staff duties at the Canadian Army HQ, Technical Staff training in the British Army, Combat Engineer heavy equipment (wheels and tracks), and staff duties at National Defence HQ Ottawa.

Major Sand moved into the military engineer construction world in 1991, until his retirement again as a Major in September 2010 in Victoria, British Columbia. During this period Major Sand saw active service in the former Yugoslavia, (Sarajevo) September 1997 to April 1998, East Timor September 1999 to May 2000 and Haiti September 2006 to April 2007.

Bruce Sand and his spouse Evelyn Kelly live just north of Victoria on Vancouver Island in the village of Shawnigan Lake, British Columbia.

Daniël J. Scholtz (Dan / Danie) (Also known as 'Schultz' by many)

Born October 1953 in Welkom South Africa (that would make me 66 the end of this year (2019). I did my schooling as well as national service in South Africa and attended Pretoria University doing BVSc (Veterinary Science) – which I did not complete.

After a family disagreement I left university, packed my bags, left South Africa and joined the war in Rhodesia. I did my bush thing from Plumtree to Mtoko and even made a turn at School of Infantry in Gwelo.

JOC decided that Intaf needed self-contained, well equipped and trained infantry units to assist Intaf in areas where the gooks had caused the breakdown of civil administration. These units were to be provincial based and called 'Administration Re-Enforcement Units' – 'ARU'. I was approached to get together and command the ARU for Matabeleland South. All my men were volunteers from Intaf, RAR and other Army units. After selection and strenuous training I ended up as the commander of ARU (Mat South) with a bunch of warriors I would not swop with any other unit available.

I left ARU for the last part of the war and did anti stock theft for Cold Storage Commission. I learnt very soon that stock thieves were just gooks doing affirmative stock collection!

After the war I got married to a Rhodesian girl and we had 2 sons (one is in Australia and the other son is in England as is his mother) and a daughter who is still in South Africa but well on her way to join her mother in England. I am presently living in the bushveld about 60km northeast of Pretoria in South Africa.

I consider that eight years in the bush, fighting the war in Rhodesia - gives me the right to call myself Rhodesian – something I am immensely proud of.

I am very proud and feel very humble that I was given the opportunity to serve with and command men of the calibre that the RAR produced. I salute you all.

Mike Shute

Major General Michael Shute OLM was born in Plymouth, England on 5 June 1937 and educated at Plymouth College, a great school with an outstanding cadet force.

His chosen career from an early age was the Army. In 1956, he applied to join the Rhodesian Army and was interviewed at Rhodesia House in London by Military Attaché Col Bob Prentice. He sailed from Southampton to Cape Town and took a train up to Salisbury where he attested and did basic training in Intake 3 at DRRR with the first C Company.

Following basic training, he underwent Instructors Courses at the Central Africa Command Training School at KGV1 Barracks in Salisbury. In 1957, he was promoted to corporal and posted back to DRRR as instructor. He was promoted to sergeant in 1958 and then, in 1959, passed the Officer Selection Board and began an officer cadet course at the School of Infantry.

Mike received his commission in June and was posted to 1KAR in Lusaka, as a platoon commander in C Company. This was his first time for him to serve with askari, as soldiers were called then. "Really enjoyed it, the Nyasa's were good soldiers, always cheerful".

In 1960, he was promoted to Lieutenant and attached to 2nd Bn Coldstream Guards in Gill Gill Kenya for three months. He married Aileen Talbot Davies in Que Que on 17 December 1960.

In 1962, he was promoted Captain, 2IC C Company and, with the break-up of the Federation in 1963, he selected and was accepted by Southern Rhodesian Army. In 1964, he was posted to 1RRR in Salisbury as Adjutant. In 1965, he was posted to 1RAR as 2IC A Coy. He was appointed Acting OC (as UDI arrived before the OC Taffy Marchant did) and defended Wankie awaiting possible invasion. "Impressed with the soldiers' reaction to such a strange scenario. Also deployed to Binga for some reason, first Company to visit this resort".

He then did spells as 2IC HQ Coy and D Coy before being appointed OC E Coy after Operation Nickel, with promotion to Major. The plan was for him to take E Coy to Inkomo for their year's stint, but Army HQ wanted a Major Norman Orsmond (being groomed for D Sigs) to have a year commanding infantry. The result was that he was given E Coy and Mike took over C Coy and moved them back to Methuen Barracks. Together, they had a "fabulous two years and were Champion Company for both those years". In 1969, he was seriously injured when gored by a buffalo and his life was saved when his batman Pte Joa shot the animal as it attacked him on the ground.

He then held a series of Staff appointments and attended the first Rhodesian Staff Course at KGV1 Salisbury. In 1973, he was posted to the School of Infantry as Chief Instructor and then attended the South African Army College Staff Course from July 1974 to March 1975. Afterwards, he served as BM 2 Bde and, promoted to Lt Col, as QMG.

In 1976, Mike was posted to 1RAR and appointed Commanding Officer for "two incredibly rewarding years of soldiering with great Masodja and Officers".

In 1978, he was promoted to Colonel and posted back to Army HQ as Col AQ. In 1979, promoted to Brigadier, he was appointed Commander 1 Brigade. Mike was appointed an Officer of the Legion of Merit (Military Division) for Distinguished Service in the Rhodesian Army. As Comd 1 Bde, he was able to "witness first-hand the incredible achievements of 1RAR with Supporting Arms and a company of 2RAR, defeat ZPRA and ZANLA in the Battles of Entumbane".

In 1981, he was promoted to Major General and appointed Chief of Staff, Defence Headquarters. Mike takes up his story: "In 1982, I resigned after disagreements with Minister of Defence (Sidney Sekerami) and being completely ignored over many issues I was trying to implement in the newly forming Zimbabwe Army. Not least of which was the role of the former Rhodesian Forces and the treatment of the imprisoned Air Force Officers, who I was not allowed to visit and could not help.

"I retired to my little farm in Essexvale and did a year as Bursar at Falcon College where, with the Headmaster, we had serious disagreements with the Ministry of Education.

"I was asked to serve on the Commission of Inquiry into the 5 Brigade atrocities in Matabeleland. This I did, and evidence of atrocities was forthcoming. Suddenly I was advised by the Chairman (a lawyer named Simplisius) that the Commission was not going to meet 'for a while'.

"Now sadly disillusioned with it all, and with a youth camp being built next to my farm, we decided to leave Zimbabwe and left for South Africa where I worked in Finance with a Building Society and an Insurance Company.

"I took a three-year gap and went to Malawi, and Aileen and I ran the Limbe Country Club. We met some old KAR soldiers and visited the Zomba Barracks. Big sign at entrance '1st Battalion Malawi Rifles (Kings African Rifles).' If only we could have done something similar in Rhodesia. Interestingly my old CO there with 1KAR, Paul Lewis, commanded the Malawi Army for five years.

"I returned to England from RSA in 2006 to full retirement. One son, Richard with wife Ingrid, remains in Natal with one daughter, and we have one son Andrew and wife Karen with two daughters here and our daughter Karin here."

Jenny Smith

My writing for this fine book goes some way to describe my wonderful years in 1RAR so I will not repeat any of that (to save boredom of the reader). After leaving JOC Wankie, I was posted to Army HQ at KGVI. I worked in the admin offices for a period until I moved to the 'top brass' Army Commander section. It was when I was in this position that I was offered the post in Pretoria, in the military attaché department of the Rhodesian Diplomatic Mission. This was a vastly different posting to the bush days but enjoyable and extremely interesting. The first lesson I was taught before departure was that I was joining the military team there but that none of us were ever to mention that we were military personnel. We were 'purely a separate diplomatic section behind locked doors'. We used to joke amongst ourselves that "we were so secret that even we did not know we were there". When we needed to travel back and forth between Pretoria (Waterkloof) and Salisbury, our usual mode of transport was the beloved Dak, always a treat.

I was stationed in Pretoria for well over a year and I resigned on that day in April 1980 after we all huddled around the radio in Pretoria, when it was announced that the new leader of the then Zimbabwe / Rhodesia would be inaugurated in July 1980. I was brought back to HQ for the last three months of my service and sadly said goodbye to army life in the same month, July 1980.

I got married and we moved to South Africa, residing mainly in KZN and raised three children, who are the absolute joy of my life. All extremely wonderful, very successful adults who have made me a very proud Granny as well. Sadly their Dad passed away. After leaving the Army I worked as a school bursar for ten years but the rest of my working life has been, and still is, as a Legal Personal Assistant, working for a large law firm in London.

I can honestly say that in all my working life, nothing has ever compared to my years in the Army, most especially my 1RAR years. I have missed those years tremendously but am extremely grateful that I had that opportunity and have those memories.

Noel Smith

Noel Smith did his National Service with Intake 144 and served as a 2Lt with D Company 1st Battalion RAR in 1975/76 before heading off to study at Rhodes University in South Africa.

Noel continued with his military call ups with the 1st Battalion Rhodesia Regiment, then worked as a Town Planner before doing some time with Plessey Military Communications and finally settled down into a career in the agricultural machinery business based in Harare, Zimbabwe.

Noel now lives in Melbourne, Australia and manages his own business manufacturing and marketing bio chemical products for use in waste water and effluent treatment and odour control. He is married to Dene and they have two sons, a daughter and three grandchildren.

Sean von Stranz

Sean was born on 14th May 1946 in Dublin, Eire and grew up in Tanzania, Southern Rhodesia and the Seychelles. As a child he enjoyed hunting, shooting, fishing and sailing. He attended St Michael's & St George's High School in Iringa, Tanzania where he attained colours in rugby, athletics and cross-country. He also played 1st team hockey and cricket. He made school prefect and Head of Oram House.

He joined the British Army in 1964 and was commissioned in 1965 and served three years with the 2nd Gurkhas including operations in Borneo. He joined the Rhodesian Army in 1968 retaining his commission. Sean served as 2 Pl Commander in A Coy 1 RAR and then went on to serve as a staff officer in HQ 1 Brigade. He was then posted as 2IC to 4 (Indep) Coy in 1974 and became OC of 4 (Indep) Coy in 1976. He was later moved to 4RR and became OC of A Coy 2 RAR in 1978 Fort Victoria. He was later posted to Umtali as Brigade Major, 3 Brigade in 1980. He left the army in 1981.

Sean followed a career in farming that took him and his family to the Mazoe Valley for the next 18 years.

Following the tragic death of his first wife Josie, he married Ruth in 2000 and went farming in Mozambique. Later he become the Admin Manager for the whole of The Wattle Co, Nyanga.

Sean had two daughters, Ceri and Pippa, by his first wife and they live in Dubai. He had three step children with Ruth, the eldest Darren (ex Royal Marine and ex Special Forces Communicator) tragically died, Graham who lives in London and is getting married this year in Florence, and Megan who lives in Bristol.

Sean and Ruth currently live in Taunton, Somerset, UK where they have lived for the last 14 years and they have their own lawn business.

Dave Ward

During the time of this scene I was based up at Makado. I was a 'Two Bar' Senior Patrol Officer and member of a small team of Ground Coverage Special Section operators out of Beitbridge. I had over the years (1975 - 1980) worked my unpredictable way across southern Matabeleland from Rustlers Gorge in the Shashi area north of Tuli through to Chikwarakwara by way of Tshitaurapadsi. Along the way I met and got to know quite a few of the men from 1 (Indep) Coy RAR in the operational area.

At other times we would meet for a beer or three and to borrow from Gump "That is all I can say about that".

Our shared common goal made life for both ZIPRA and ZANLA difficult and short lived whenever possible. This was due to the very effective and professional leadership of the Officers, NCOs and rank and file of 1 (Indep) Coy RAR and Fireforce Delta.

I resigned from the BSAP in April of 1980. Completed a Plumbing and Gas Engineers apprenticeship in South Africa and the United Kingdom, moving to Canada in 1992 where I still work within my trade in the Oil and Gas fields of Alberta.

Bridget Wells-West

Born and bred, schooled and wed in Rhodesia, to a Rhodesian, I started my life as an 'RAR Dependent' in 1959, and apart from a couple of gaps, continued as such until John retired when we went to live in Lalapanzi with our four children, one dog, one cat and one canary, John having joined the Personnel Department of a mining company. Sixteen years later, John retired again and we left mining company, farm and country for another new life in the land of our fathers. We still had four children but no dependents which was a good thing.

Between 1959 and 1988, we lived in about twenty different houses and I gained considerable expertise in packing and unpacking households. Changing plugs on domestic electrical appliances became a speciality. From time to time I resumed my original occupation and taught a wide range of pupils in a wide range of schools, and finally ended as a farmer's wife. Now I am a fully paid-up member of the ObSoc (Obsolescent Society) whose only requirement for membership is to be an octogenarian. Fortune has smiled on us and we had an enviable life. The RAR years were undoubtedly among the most fondly remembered.

Rory Williams

I was born in Umtali and went to Umtali Boys high school. I had a great cricketing career ahead of me until the war came along. I chose war. I volunteered aged 17 and joined intake 157 Llewellin barracks. I transferred to the Rhodesian Air Force and signed up for 10 ten years as a an airframe tech. Weeks after finishing another session of training I became aware that to see any action as a chopper tech would take years so I resigned from my apprenticeship and ask to be forwarded to the action. I was sent to Mtoko where I pretty much lived on my own much of the time and was able to attach myself to any passing unit who needed an MAG gunner. I was lucky to be invited to join many ops. In late 1978 I got medically discharged and had to start a new life. My first choice was to join the Rhodesia Railways as an apprentice coppersmith. I learned to use my hands and eye.

In the early 1980's I moved to North Wales where I did another apprenticeship as an industrial/ mountaineering photographer. I spent many seasons climbing peaks in the Alps solo to provide images for books. By the late 1980's I had 12 staff and many awards as a photographer. I sold the business and went surfing around the world. In 1991 I started an apprenticeship as a surf board shaper. I spent over ten years shaping boards around the world for famous labels and factories. In 2000 I settled down in North Wales and I started my own surfboard factory and had a daughter followed 18 months later by another. I spent four years as a house dad. A very rewarding period of my life.

In 2008 I bought a house in Spain close to the surf and in the mountains. Having trained as an arborist in 2004 work was plentiful in Spain and surf close by. I moved to Spain and have been here ever since. I've never given up my photography and painted my whole life. As injuries have limited my job prospects I have fallen back to my artistic skills and now paint for a living. I use Oil, acrylic and watercolour as well as airbrush.

This is but a short summary of a very exciting and extraordinary journey. The in between bits are the real meat of the story.

Butch Zeederberg

In 1969 the forthcoming war was still far away in most people's minds yet some short sighted Officer in the Recruiting Branch of The Army thought it wise to offer me a permanent commission when my nine months National Service expired in April of that year. With little else to do at the age of 21, I signed up and was posted to 1RAR, where I joined 8 Platoon, C Company (Chawuya Chawuya).

After a successful tour with Charlie Company I was fortunate enough to be selected to attend Mortar Instructors Course and became Mortar Platoon Commander in late 1971. In 1973 I departed to 'Hooters' (School of Infantry) where I spent two very happy years instructing National Service Officer Cadets. The Memory is a bit vague nowadays but I think it was in 1975 that I was recalled to the 1st Battalion to assist Maj. Ben Schlachter in the formation of Support Company. In 1976 my previous experience with the then Maj Mike Shute in C Company when we won Champion Company; was good enough for him to ask me to become his Adjutant, and I couldn't wait to take up the post.

Although I thoroughly enjoyed the Adjutant post, I was equally chuffed to take over as OC Support Company in 1977, which by now had both 81 and 60mm Mortar Platoons, the Tracker Platoon, 106mm Recoilless Rifle Platoon and Assault Pioneer Platoon – though I never quite managed to identify the role of the latter!

In early 1979 my luck ran out and I was posted to complete the compulsory staff training as AQSO2 at Salisbury District HQ where I remained until just after the elections.

In the December 1979 posting list I was transferred to command Support Commando 1RLI but this unfortunately never came about as I was suddenly considered to be more useful trying to unite the three warring factions and was appointed Training Officer DRR, which only served to accelerate my resignation and I became a 'civvy' once again.

I joined the Rhodesian Iron and Steel Company as the assistant export manager and soon became the export manager and travelled the world – the cloak of economic sanctions having been removed. In 1986 I was head hunted by a large international steel trading company and moved to Hong Kong.

All in all Val and I spent nine years in the Far East, including two in Taipei and we then moved with the company to New York for two years, and then finally to London. After nearly fourteen years with the same company, trading and freighting ship loads of steel products, I joined the opposition and stayed with them in London until I took my 'first civvy pension' at the age of 60.

We then moved to Dubai where I worked for several international companies trading and shipping steel-making raw materials and semi-finished products before I formed our own company, also bulk trading and freighting materials and semi-finished steel products.

We called it a day in 2014 and retired to Stanford in the Western Cape, where we spend time kayaking, fishing, playing golf and enjoying the local wines and restaurants.

CONCLUSION

On behalf of Andy Telfer and myself, it is my great privilege and honour to write a few closing, but heartfelt words, about a quite incredible journey shared with good and upstanding men from one of the finest infantry regiments in the history of the Federal, Southern Rhodesia and Rhodesian Army: the 1st, 2nd, 3rd Battalions Rhodesian African Rifles and Depot RAR, our literary journey together and in whose respectful memory the compilation of Chibaya Moyo and Chibaya Moyo 2 are dedicated.

What started out as a series of inconsequential anecdotes posted on the RAR Facebook group page in 2013, and merely intended to maintain an interest in our regimental history, gathered momentum and strong words of encouragement followed for the compilation of a book; an anthology of Rhodesian African Rifles anecdotes. This propelled Andy Telfer and me, inexorably, towards a mutual agreement to do just that and, with the approval of the RAR Regimental Association, we embarked upon our first journey together. We never once discussed, even remotely, the proposition that any profit would accrue to us personally; we were completely in sync that any revenue that accrued from book sales would be for the welfare of our former RAR Masodja.

Equally extraordinary, but entirely true, is that we never once communicated by telephone throughout the compilation of the first edition! From the initial agreement to work together until the publication and delivery of stock by sea freight to the United Kingdom in time for the unveiling and dedication of the RNR-RAR Memorial at the National Memorial and Arboretum in Staffordshire on 19 July 2015, the entire process took less than six months! Neither of us had either written or published a book and we entered this process as a pair of unwitting literary baboons; it just goes to show what good old 'Battle Procedure' and 'selection and maintenance of the aim' achieves some forty-plus years after the fact! The first edition, some 542 pages from fifty different contributors made this exercise worthwhile. Reviews far and wide truly exceeded our very best expectations and we accept them all with humility and on behalf of all our contributors. As far as I am aware, and in the military history genre, no other books like ours exist anywhere.

In mid-2017, Andy and I received a letter from Maj Gen Mike Shute OLM encouraging us to consider compiling a second edition. We discussed this telephonically (a new beginning!) and put the proposal to Brig Pat Lawless SCR, our respected RAR Regimental Association Chairman. Andy and I would co-author the second edition, edit and illustrate the manuscript in conformance with publisher requirements, and hand it over to them on 31 March 2019 and they would publish and market the book as they considered appropriate. The proposal was accepted unanimously and here we are, six months later, with a bigger and far superior second edition. A credit to good men who heeded the call to action and contributed to this final record of our regimental history.

In closing, we thank the many contributors who have supported this endeavour, our wives and families who have been tolerant of our extended absences during the long hours we have committed to this project, to our readers who will have spent their 'hard earned' to purchase a copy of one of our books and supporting our Masodja. Above all these things, and with uncompromising affection, respect and heartfelt gratitude, we dedicate our work to the memory of fine men, better than ourselves, who fought and fell in Rhodesia's name, the Masodja of the RAR and their families who sacrificed so much. Chibaya Moyo is a record about you. To have shared some of my youth with you, to march alongside, to sweat, thirst and hunger together, to patrol with, fight and shed blood with you has been the greatest privilege of my life and I, and all others, will never forget nor forsake you nor the lasting memories we have of you all.

"Tinorwira kukunda ne Hama nokusingaperi!" (We fight to win and Brothers forever). Salute!

Russell Fulton
Canberra, Australia

Lightning Source UK Ltd.
Milton Keynes UK
UKHW021922310520
364131UK00006B/187

Citation for the award of the Silver Cross of Rhodesia, 13 October 1978, Lieutenant Bruce Thompson SCR (Post)

'Lieutenant Thompson joined the Second Battalion RAR in March 1977. He was involved in over thirty-five contacts in which more than 170 terrorists were killed. On twenty-nine occasions he parachuted into the contact area, often in high winds and into hazardous dropping zones.

'On 12 September 1977, Thompson and four patrols were flown by helicopter into a narrow valley from which fire had been directed at the aircraft. Hardly had they been deployed when the aircraft was called away to another incident and Thompson was left in command with no air support. In a series of sweeps through rocky terrain in which there were many natural caves, eight terrorists and twelve terrorist recruits were wiped out. During the action Thompson suspected that a terrorist was hiding in a very narrow crevice in the rock face. Taking off his webbing, he squeezed into the crevice and was engaged with a terrorist at such close range that he actually struck the terrorist's rifle aside as he was firing. As the terrorist tried to escape, Lieutenant Thompson shot him dead as well as three other terrorists.

'On 27 February 1978, Thompson killed three terrorists while charging at the head of his men into thick bush under heavy fire. On 4 March 1978, he eliminated three of the thirteen terrorists killed by his company, once again in thick, rough country with the encounters taking place at point blank range.

'On 6 June 1978, eight terrorists and fifty recruits were contacted in thick bush. Thompson's patrol accounted for most of the enemy group. Once again, he led his men at the double in the face of fire from the terrorists. He advanced so quickly that he almost ran into supporting fire from the air in his determination to close with and destroy the enemy.

'On 27 June 1978, Thompson's patrol was ordered to sweep an area in which at least three terrorists were known to be hiding. Almost immediately they came under heavy close-range fire and the machine gunner was badly wounded. Still under fire, Thompson moved forward and dragged the wounded man to cover. He then led his patrol forward and killed two of the enemy. However, in the ensuing chase, Thompson and one of his men were killed.'

Lieutenant Andrew Telfer SCR

Andrew Telfer was born on the 5th April 1954 in the United Kingdom to Chief Petty Officer Thomas and Mrs Teresa Telfer. Andy's father enlisted in the Royal Navy in 1928 and served throughout World War II as a submariner, repeatedly